LETTERS
OF
COMPOSERS
THROUGH
SIX
CENTURIES

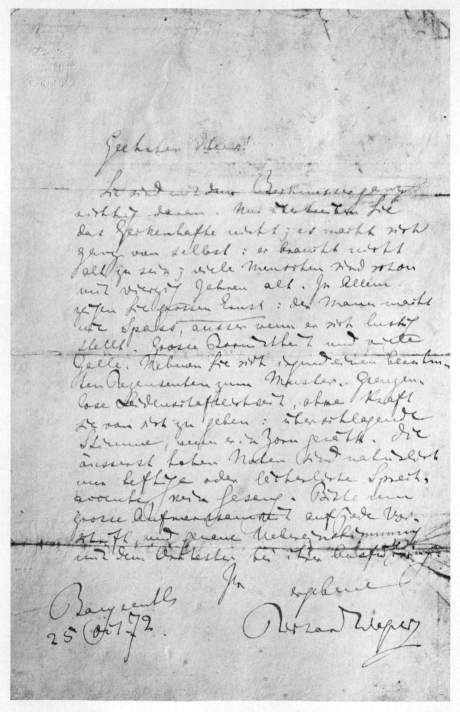

Wagner to Rudolf Freny, 25 Oct. 1872 (Letter 239)

LETTERS
OF
COMPOSERS
THROUGH
SIX
CENTURIES

Compiled and
Edited by

PIERO WEISS

Foreword by
Richard Ellmann

CHILTON BOOK COMPANY   Philadelphia   New York   London

Library of Congress Catalog Card Number 67-28895
Designed by Arnold Levine
Manufactured in the United States of America by
Quinn & Boden Company, Inc., Rahway, N.J.

To my grandmother
FEDERICA SCHMITZ SVEVO

The ancient alliance of music and literature has often been strained, neither art being satisfied with the inferior station. Even though they accompany each other, the two arts disdain equivalence. Yet a relation persists, so that composers and writers of the same epoch seem colleagues even when they are not friends. Today, to take an extreme instance, some composers and some writers find unexpected concord in manipulating silence as an expressive device.

Because musical notes keep their reserve, their linguistic opacity, this collection of composers' letters, so ably edited by Piero Weiss, is especially captivating. It is not that composers, any more than musical critics, can succeed in bringing us verbally to the quick of the creative process, but they hover teasingly near, struggling like a philosopher eager to expound Kant in Twi. They succeed more nearly in rendering experiences having to do with music, as when Mendelssohn tells how Queen Victoria sang D instead of D-sharp, or Prokofiev describes the extraordinary impression he made on his examiner, Rimsky-Korsakov. The key is varied: there is Beethoven's confession of his humiliating deafness, and Bartók's amused impatience at the failure of old Transylvanian peasants to remember for him the songs that old Transylvanian peasants should.

Mr. Weiss brings the talents of a concert pianist, a musicologist, and a linguist to this fresh and original choice of letters. Some of them he has published for the first time, others for the first time in English, still others for the first time in adequate translation. His criterion of selection is to make music his protagonist, rather than any school or group of musicians. Beginning with Guillaume de Machault in the time of Chaucer, he attempts to delineate the continuity of the western musical ambience—the way in which composers, even as they (incommunicably) take each other's music into account, must also take into account each other's existences. Problems of living move side by side with problems of composing, and engross us with a spectrum of human as well as of artistic griefs and pleasures.

RICHARD ELLMANN

Evanston, 1967

vii

The editor wishes to thank the following for permission to reproduce material from the publications specified in each instance:

The editor of *Acta Musicologica* and Professor Thurston Dart; Am-Rus Literary Agency, New York—*The Musorgsky Reader,* ed. and trans. by Jay Leyda and Sergei Bertensson; Cassell and Company Ltd., London—*The Letters and Writings of George Frideric Handel,* ed. by Erich H. Müller; Columbia University Press, New York—*New Letters of Berlioz, 1830–1868,* ed. and trans. by Jacques Barzun; Macmillan & Co. Ltd., London—*Letters from and to Joseph Joachim,* ed. and trans. by Nora Bickley; The Macmillan Company, New York—*Letters of Richard Wagner: The Burrell Collection,* ed. by John N. Burk; the editors of *Music Survey;* W. W. Norton & Co., Inc., New York—*The Bach Reader,* ed. and trans. by Hans T. David and Arthur Mendel, and *Handel: A Documentary Biography* by O. E. Deutsch, New York, 1955, all rights reserved; W. W. Norton & Co., Inc., and J. M. Dent & Sons Ltd., London—*The Schubert Reader,* ed. by O. E. Deutsch, trans. by Eric Blom; Oxford University Press, Inc., New York, and Barrie and Rockliff, London—*The Collected Correspondence and London Notebooks of Joseph Haydn,* ed. and trans. by H. C. Robbins Landon; Theodore Presser Company, Bryn Mawr, and Universal Edition, London—*Die Reihe #2,* copyright 1958 Theodore Presser Company, copyright 1959 Theodore Presser Company; Random House, Inc., New York, and Collins Publishers, London—*A Working Friendship: The Correspondence between Richard Strauss and Hugo von Hofmannsthal,* trans. by Hanns Hammelmann and Ewald Osers; St. Martin's Press, Inc., New York, and Faber and Faber Ltd., London—*Arnold Schoenberg: Letters,* ed. by Erwin Stein, trans. by Eithne Wilkins and Ernst Kaiser; St. Martin's Press, Inc., and Barrie and Rockliff, London—*The Collected Correspondence and Papers of Christoph Willibald Gluck,* ed. by Hedwig and E. H. Mueller von Asow, trans. by Stewart Thomson; G. Schirmer, Inc., New York, and the editors of *The Musical Quarterly.*

Thanks are also due to the following for permitting the translation and inclusion in this book of material from the publications mentioned in each instance:

Bärenreiter-Verlag, Kassel—*Mozart: Briefe und Aufzeichnungen,* ed. by Wilhelm A. Bauer and Otto Erich Deutsch; Durand & Cie, Paris—*Lettres de Debussy à son Editeur,* ed. by Jacques Durand; Garzanti, Milan—*Puccini nelle immagini,* ed. by Leopoldo Marchetti; Éditions Robert Laffont, Paris—*Ravel au miroir de ses lettres,* ed. by René Chalupt; the

ACKNOWLEDGMENTS

editors of *Melos, Zeitschrift für neue Musik;* the editors of *Österreichische Musikzeitschrift* and Dr. Willi Reich; G. Ricordi & C., Milan—*Carteggi pucciniani,* ed. by Eugenio Gara; the editor of *Schweizerische Musikzeitung* and Dr. Willi Reich.

Finally, the editor wishes to express his indebtedness to the individuals who were good enough to permit the publication of the letters listed after their names:

Mr. Victor Bator (the Bartók Archives, New York)—all the Bartók letters; Mrs. Alban Berg—Letters 298, 300, and 315; Mr. Livio Dell'Anna—all the Puccini letters; the late Mrs. Alma Mahler-Werfel—all the Mahler letters; Mr. Lawrence Schoenberg—all the letters of Arnold Schoenberg; Dr. Franz Strauss—Letters 258 and 275; Mr. Igor Stravinsky— Letters 296, 299, and 304; Madame Jeanne Taverne—Letters 299 and 312; and Madame de Tinan—all the letters of Debussy.

x

CONTENTS

Foreword by Richard Ellmann vii
Introduction xxiii
1   Machault to Peronnelle d'Unchair, [1363] 1
2   Machault to the same, 3 Nov. [1363] 2
3   Landini to Franco Sacchetti, [c. 1370] 4
4   John of Aragon to his brother, 4 Jan. 1380 5
5   Squarcialupi to Giovanni de' Medici, 26 Nov. 1450 5
6   Dufay to Piero & Giovanni de' Medici, 22 Feb. 14[54?].... 6
7   Squarcialupi to Guillaume Dufay, 1 May 1467 7
8   Joh. Martini to Isabella d'Este, 2 Sep. 1490 8
9   Gafori to Lodovico Maria Sforza, 22 Apr. 1495 9
10   Hofhaimer to Joachim Vadian, 7 Feb. 1518 10
11   Luther to Ludwig Senfl, 4 Oct. 1530 11
12   Tromboncino to Giovanni del Lago, 2 Apr. 1535 12
13   Gombert to Ferrante Gonzaga, 3 Jun. 1547 13
14   Coclico to Barnim XI of Pomerania-Stettin, 4 Jul. 1547 13
15   Viola to Cosimo I de' Medici, 17 Oct. 1558 15
16   Palestrina to Guglielmo Gonzaga, 2 Feb. 1568 16
17   Palestrina to the same, 3 Mar. 1570 16
18   Lassus to William V of Bavaria, 19 Aug. 1572 17
19   Lassus to the same, 26 Feb. 1574 18
20   Palestrina to Guglielmo Gonzaga, 17 Apr. 1574 19
21   Lassus to William V of Bavaria, [early Jun. 1575] 20
22   Tallis & Byrd to Queen Elizabeth, [before 27 Jun. 1577] ... 21
23   Galilei to Guglielmo Gonzaga, 13 Mar. 1582 22
24   Monte to Charles de l'Écluse, 29 Oct. [1588] 23
25   Cavalieri to Luzzasco Luzzaschi, 31 Oct. 1592 24
26   Monte to Jean Mourentorf, 26 Dec. 1593 26
27   Viadana to Ferdinand I of Tuscany, 7 Jul. 1595 26
28   Dowland to Sir Robert Cecil, 10 Nov. 1595 27
29   Victoria to Francesco Maria II della Rovere, 10 Jun. 1603 ... 31
30   Monteverdi to Vincenzo I Gonzaga, Dec. 1604 32
31   Caccini to Ferdinand I of Tuscany, 19 Feb. 1605 33
32   Monteverdi to Vincenzo I Gonzaga, 9 Jun. 1610 34
33   Bull to the mayor & aldermen of Antwerp, [autumn 1614].. 35
34   Monteverdi to Alessandro Striggio, 9 Dec. 1616 36
35   Schütz to Wilhelm Ludwig Moser, 3 Jul. 1621 39
36   Scheidt to Christian Gueinzius, [2 Apr. 1630] 40
37   Monteverdi to an unnamed correspondent, 2 Feb. 1634 42

xi

38   Monteverdi to the Procurators of St. Mark, [9 Jun. 1637]... 44
39   Henry Lawes to John Milton, [spring 1638] 46
40   Schütz to Johann Georg I of Saxony, 14 Jan. 1651 46
41   Lully to Jean Baptiste Colbert, 3 Jun. 1672 52
42   Lully to the same, [spring 1673] 53
43   Locke to Henry Purcell, 16 Mar. [1677?] 54
44   Thomas Purcell to John Gostling, 8 Feb. 1679 55
45   Corelli to Matteo Zani, 17 Oct. 1685 55
46   Buxtehude to the Elders of the Commercial Guilds, 5 Feb.
        1689 57
47   A. Scarlatti to Prince Ferdinand de' Medici, 30 May 1705... 58
48   J. S. Bach to the St. Blasius parishioners, 25 Jun. 1708 59
49   Bassani to Jacopo Antonio Perti, 28 Jul. 1710 60
50   Marcello to the same, 4 Oct. 1711 61
51   Handel to Johann Mattheson, 24 Feb. 1719 63
52   J. S. Bach to the Leipzig Town Council, 5 May 1723 64
53   Handel to the House of Lords, [before 13 Feb. 1727] 66
54   Rameau to Antoine Houdar de la Motte, [25 Oct. 1727].... 66
55   Telemann to Johann Gottfried Walther, 20 Dec. 1729 69
56   Handel to Francis Colman, 30 Jun. 1730 70
57   J. S. Bach to Georg Erdmann, 28 Oct. 1730 71
58   J. S. Bach to Frederick Augustus II of Saxony, 27 Jul. 1733.. 73
59   J. S. Bach to the Leipzig Town Council, 15 Aug. 1736 74
60   Vivaldi to the Marquis d'Aragona, [16 Nov. 1737] 76
61   Handel to Charles Jennens, 29 Dec. 1741 78
62   Handel to the same, 9 Sep. 1742 79
63   Rameau to M. Mongeot, [1744] 80
64A   Handel to Charles Jennens, 9 Jun. 1744 81
64B   Handel to the same, 19 Jul. 1744 82
64C   Handel to the same, 21 Aug. 1744 82
64D   Handel to the same, 13 Sep. 1744 83
64E   Handel to the same, 2 Oct. 1744 83
65   J. S. Bach to Johann Elias Bach, 6 Oct. 1748 84
66   J. S. Bach to the same, 2 Nov. 1748 85
67   D. Scarlatti to the Duke of Huescar, [spring 1752] 86
68   Rousseau to Toussaint-Pierre Lenieps, 22 Oct. 1752 87
69   Frederick the Great to his sister, 16 [Apr. 1754] 88
70   Rameau to M. Ducharger, 13 Jun. 1754 89
71   Handel to Georg Philipp Telemann, 20 Sep. 1754 89
72   J. C. Bach to Giambattista Martini, 21 May 1757 90
73   Tartini to Maddalena Lombardini, 5 Mar. 1760 91

CONTENTS

74   Boccherini to the Government of Lucca, 28 Aug. 1761   95
75   Haydn to Prince Nicolaus Esterházy, 9 Sep. 1765   96
76   Haydn to an unnamed Austrian monastery, [1768]   98
77   Mozart to his mother & sister, 14 Apr. 1770   100
78   Mozart to his sister, 24 Aug. 1771   101
79   Gluck to the Mercure de France, [Feb. 1773]   102
80   C. P. E. Bach to Johann Nicolaus Forkel, [Dec.? 1774]   104
81   C. P. E. Bach to the same, 13 Jan. 1775   106
82   Mozart to his mother, 14 Jan. 1775   109
83   Rousseau to Prince Alexander Beloselsky, 27 May 1775   110
84   Gluck to the Bailli du Roullet, 2 Dec. 1775   111
85   Haydn to "Mademoiselle Leonore," 6 Jul. 1776   113
86   Gluck to Christoph Martin Wieland, 7 Aug. 1776   115
87   Mozart to his father, 29–30 Sep. 1777   117
88   Mozart to the same, 23–24 Oct. 1777   120
89   Gluck to Baroness Anna von Fries, 16 Nov. 1777   123
90   Mozart to his father, 14 May 1778   125
91   Gluck to Nicolas François Guillard, 17 Jun. 1778   127
92   Mozart to Abbé Joseph Bullinger, 3 Jul. 1778   130
93   Gluck to Abbé François Arnaud, 15 Jul. 1778   131
94   Mozart to his father, 9 May 1781   132
95   Mozart to the same, 26 Sep. 1781   135
96   Gluck to M. Valentin, 17 Apr. 1782   137
97   Mozart to his father, 20 Jul. 1782   139
98   Grétry to Michel Jean Sedaine, 23 Oct. 1784   140
99   C. P. E. Bach to Johann Joachim Eschenburg, 21 Jan. 1786. .   142
100   Mozart to his father, 4 Apr. 1787   143
101   Mozart to Baron Gottfried von Jacquin, [May 1787]   145
102   Beethoven to Joseph Wilhelm von Schaden, 15 Sep. 1787 . . .   145
103   Haydn to Artaria & Co., 7 Oct. 1787   147
104   Haydn to Franz Roth, Dec. 1787   147
105   Haydn to Maria Anna von Genzinger, 9 Feb. 1790   148
106   Mozart to Johann Michael Puchberg, [17? May 1790]   150
107   Mozart to his wife, 30 Sep. 1790   151
108   Haydn to Maria Anna von Genzinger, 8 Jan. 1791   152
109   Mozart to his wife, [4 Jul. 1791]   155
110   Haydn to Johann Michael Puchberg, Jan. 1792   155
111   Grétry to Rouget de Lisle, 4 Nov. 1792   156
112A Haydn to Elector Maximilian Franz of Cologne, 23 Nov. 1793 157
112B Beethoven to the same, 23 Nov. 1793   158
113   Gossec to the Committee of General Security, 19 Mar. 1794. .   159

CONTENTS

114 Dalayrac to a Revolutionary Committee, 4 May 1794 160
115 Beethoven to Nikolaus Simrock, 2 Aug. [1794] 161
116 Haydn to Prince Esterházy's administrator, [1796–97] 162
117 Beethoven to Franz Anton Hoffmeister, 15 Jan. 1801 163
118 Haydn to the Institut National, 14 Apr. 1802 165
119 Paisiello to Napoleon Bonaparte, 18 Jun. 1802 165
120 Beethoven to his brothers, 6–10 Oct. 1802 167
121 Beethoven to Gottfried Christoph Härtel, 26 Aug. 1804 170
122 Haydn to Johann Nepomuk Hummel, 28 Sep. 1804 171
123 Beethoven to Friedrich Sebastian Mayer, [8 Apr. 1806] 172
124 Zelter to Johann Wolfgang von Goethe, 12 Nov. 1808 172
125 Haydn to Prince Nicolaus II Esterházy, 22 Dec. 1808 175
126 Beethoven to Gottfried Christoph Härtel, 6 May [1811] ... 176
127 Hoffmann to Eduard Hitzig, 15 Jul. 1812 177
128 Beethoven to Gottfried Christoph Härtel, 9 Aug. 1812 178
129 Schubert to his brother, 24 Nov. 1812 179
130 Beethoven to Johann Baptist Rupprecht, [c. 22 Dec. 1814].. 180
131 Weber to Friedrich Wieck, 13 Aug. 1815 181
132 Beethoven to Carl Czerny, [12 Feb. 1816] 184
133 Schubert to the Vienna Captaincy of the Civic Guard, [Apr.
      1816] 184
134 Wesley to Vincent Novello, 27 Jul. 1816 185
135 Beethoven to Sigmund Anton Steiner, 23 Jan. 1817 186
136 F. A. Schubert to Gottfried Christoph Härtel, 18 Apr. 1817.. 187
137 Beethoven to Carl Czerny, [1817] 188
138 Berlioz to Ignace Pleyel, 6 Apr. 1819 189
139 Bellini to Filippo Guerrera, 31 Jul. 1819 189
140 Beethoven to Tobias Haslinger, 10 Sep. 1821 190
141 Mendelssohn to Johann Wolfgang von Goethe, 24 May 1822. 192
142 Weber to his wife, 5–6 Oct. 1823 193
143 Schubert to Leopold Kupelwieser, 31 Mar. 1824 195
144 Paër to an unnamed correspondent, 8 Apr. 1824 197
145A Beethoven to Anton Schindler, [Apr. 1824] 198
145B Beethoven to Ignaz Schuppanzigh, [Apr. 1824] 198
145C Beethoven to Count Moritz Lichnowsky, [Apr. 1824] 198
145D Beethoven to Anton Schindler, [Apr. 1824] 198
145E Czerny to Friedrich Wieck, 9 May 1824 199
146 Berlioz to his uncle, [Aug.–Sep. 1824] 202
147 Schubert to Johann Wolfgang von Goethe, [Jun. 1825] 203
148 Schubert to his father & stepmother, 25 Jul. 1825 203
149 Beethoven to Ferdinand Wolanek, [1825] 206

CONTENTS

150   Schubert to Heinrich Albert Probst, 12 Aug. 1826 208
151   Beethoven to B. Schott's Söhne, 19 Aug. 1826 208
152   Beethoven to Ignaz Moscheles, 22 Feb. 1827 209
153   Beethoven to the same, 18 Mar. 1827 210
154   Schubert to Heinrich Albert Probst, 10 May 1828 211
155   Paganini to Luigi Guglielmo Germi, 5 Jul. 1828 212
156A Schumann to Gottlob Wiedebein, 15 Jul. 1828 214
156B Wiedebein to Robert Schumann, 1 Aug. 1828 215
157   Schubert to Heinrich Albert Probst, 2 Oct. 1828 216
158   Schubert to Franz von Schober, [12 Nov. 1828] 217
159   Liszt to Carl Czerny, 23 Dec. 1828 217
160   Berlioz to Johann Wolfgang von Goethe, 10 Apr. 1829 219
161   Chopin to his parents, 12 Aug. 1829 220
162   Schumann to Friedrich Wieck, 6 Nov. 1829 222
163   Schumann to his mother, 30 Jul. 1830 227
164   Wagner to B. Schott's Söhne, 6 Oct. 1830 229
165   Mendelssohn to his family, 24 Jul. 1831 230
166   Schumann to his mother, 8 Aug. 1831 235
167   Paër to C. P. Sotte, 1 Dec. 1831 238
168   Bellini to Giovanni Battista Perucchini, 31 Dec. 1831 239
169   Chopin to Dominik Dziewanowski, [Jan. 1833] 240
170   Liszt, Chopin, & Franchomme to Ferdinand Hiller, 20 Jun.
      1833 242
171   Schumann to Clara Wieck, 13 Jul. 1833 244
172   Schumann to Theodor Töpken, 27 Mar. 1834 245
173   Berlioz to an unnamed correspondent, [22 Nov.(?) 1835] . . 246
174   Cherubini to Jean Auguste Dominique Ingres, 24 Dec. 1835 . . 246
175   Verdi to the mayor of Busseto, 14 Mar. 1836 248
176   Schumann to Heinrich Dorn, 14 Sep. 1836 249
177   Chopin to Juljan Fontana, 3 Dec. 1838 251
178A Paganini to Hector Berlioz, 18 Dec. 1838 252
178B Berlioz to Nicolò Paganini, 18 Dec. 1838 252
179   Schumann to Simonin de Sire, 15 Mar. 1839 253
180   Verdi to Giuseppe Demaldé, 22 Apr. 1839 256
181   Berlioz to Frédéric Chopin, [Apr.–May 1839] 257
182   Chopin to Juljan Fontana, [Oct. 1839] 257
183   Donizetti to the Moniteur Universel, 16 Feb. 1840 258
184A Mendelssohn to his mother, 30 Mar. 1840 259
184B Liszt to Maurice Schlesinger, 14 May 1840 261
185   Schumann to Heinrich Heine, 23 May 1840 262
186   Wagner to Frederick Augustus II of Saxony, 1 Dec. 1840 . . . 263

CONTENTS

187	Wagner to Robert Schumann, 29 Dec. 1840	265
188	Brahms to Otto Cossel, 1 Jan. 1842	266
189	Mendelssohn to his mother, 19 Jul. 1842	266
190	Donizetti to Antonio Vasselli, 4 Jan. 1843	272
191	Berlioz to Felix Mendelssohn Bartholdy, 2 Feb. [1843]	272
192	Chopin to Maurice Schlesinger, 22 Jul. [1843]	273
193	Wagner to Felix Mendelssohn Bartholdy, 10 Jan. 1844	274
194	Donizetti to Giuseppina Appiani, 22 Jan. 1844	274
195	Verdi to Gaetano Donizetti, 18 May 1844	275
196	Berlioz to his father, 19 Aug. 1844	276
197	Schumann to Hans Christian Andersen, 14 Apr. 1845	278
198	Berlioz to George Hainl, 2 Jul. [1845]	279
199	Berlioz to Felix Mendelssohn Bartholdy, 14 Apr. 1846	281
200	Mendelssohn to Ignaz Moscheles, 26 Jun. 1846	282
201	Mendelssohn to César Franck, 22 Dec. 1846	283
202	Verdi to Giovanni Ricordi, 29 Dec. 1846	283
203A	Smetana to Franz Liszt, 23 Mar. 1848	284
203B	Liszt to Bedřich Smetana, 30 Mar. 1848	286
204A	Chopin to Wojciech Grzymała, 11 [May 1848]	287
204B	Chopin to the same, 30 Oct. [1848]	288
205	Wagner to his wife Minna, [14 May 1849]	290
206	Chopin to Marie de Rozières, [14 Aug. 1849]	294
207	Verdi to Carlo Marzari, 14 Dec. 1850	294
208	Verdi to Tito Ricordi, 6 Mar. 1853	296
209A	Schumann to Johann Jacob Brahms, 5 Nov. 1853	296
209B	Brahms to Robert Schumann, [Dec. 1853]	297
210	Rossini to Giuseppe Bellentani, 28 Dec. 1853	297
211	Dietrich to Joseph Joachim, 28 Feb. [1854]	298
212	Wagner to Franz Liszt, [16 (?) Dec. 1854]	300
213A	Brahms to Clara Schumann, 23–24 Feb. 1855	302
213B	Schumann to Johannes Brahms, 11 Mar. 1855	307
214	Wagner to Ernst Benedikt Kietz, [27 Apr. 1855]	308
215	Berlioz to Théodore Ritter, [3 Jul.] 1855	310
216	Berlioz to Richard Wagner, 10 Sep. 1855	311
217A	Brahms to Joseph Joachim, [28 Jul. 1856]	313
217B	Joachim to Gisela von Arnim, [30 Jul. 1856]	313
218	Berlioz to a journalist, 24 Nov. 1857	314
219	Bizet to his mother, 11 Mar. 1858	314
220	Brahms to Joseph Joachim, [28 Jan. 1859]	317
221	Verdi to Vincenzo Jacovacci, 5 Jun. 1859	319
222A	Liszt to Richard Wagner, 22 May [1860]	320

xvi

CONTENTS

222B	Wagner to Franz Liszt, 22 May 1860	320
222C	Berlioz to Richard Wagner, 23 May 1860	323
223	Gounod to Richard Wagner, 18 Mar. 1861	324
224	Wagner to Charles Baudelaire, 15 Apr. 1861	324
225	Verdi to Francesco Maria Piave, 7 Dec. 1861	325
226	Verdi to Count Opprandino Arrivabene, 2 May 1862	325
227	Brahms to Albert Dietrich, [before 8 Sep. 1862]	327
228	Berlioz to Gustave Flaubert, 4 Nov. 1862	328
229	Brahms to his parents, [30 Nov. 1862]	328
230	Berlioz to Edward Jerome Hopkins, 6 Feb. 1863	330
231	Rossini to Ferdinand Hiller, 10 Aug. 1866	331
232	Berlioz to the Grand Duchess Yelena Pavlovna, 4 Jun. 1868	332
233	Verdi to Filippo Filippi, 4 Mar. 1869	333
234	Wagner to an unnamed correspondent, 12 May 1869	334
235	Verdi to Antonio Ghislanzoni, 17 Aug. 1870	336
236	Verdi to Count Opprandino Arrivabene, 13 Sep. 1870	337
237	Mussorgsky to Vladimir Vassilyevich Stasov, 22 Aug. 1871	338
238	Mussorgsky to the same, 25 Jul. 1872	340
239	Wagner to Rudolf Freny, 25 Oct. 1872	345
240	Bizet to Paul Lacombe, [spring 1874]	345
241	Dvořák to the Town Clerk, 15 Jun. 1874	346
242	Mussorgsky to Vladimir Vassilyevich Stasov, Jun. 1874	346
243	Liszt to Henry Wadsworth Longfellow, 22 Nov. 1874	347
244	Bruckner to Moritz von Mayfeld, 12 Jan. 1875	348
245A	Wagner to Johannes Brahms, 6 Jun. 1875	349
245B	Brahms to Richard Wagner, Jun. 1875	350
245C	Wagner to Johannes Brahms, 26 Jun. 1875	351
245D	Brahms to Richard Wagner, Jun. 1875	352
246	Verdi to Count Opprandino Arrivabene, 16 Jul. 1875	353
247	Smetana to Karel Bendl, 24 Jul. 1875	354
248	Mussorgsky to Vladimir Vassilyevich Stasov, 5 Dec. 1875	355
249	Wagner to Theodore Thomas, 8 Feb. 1876	357
250	Verdi to Ferdinand Hiller, 18 Apr. 1877	358
251A	Dvořák to Johannes Brahms, 3 Dec. 1877	359
251B	Brahms to Antonín Dvořák, [Dec. 1877]	360
252	Tchaikovsky to Nadezhda Filaretovna von Meck, 5 Jan. 1878	361
253	Wagner to an unnamed correspondent, [2 Feb. 1878]	366
254	Brahms to Joseph Joachim, [22 Jun. 1879]	367
255	Brahms to Karel Weis, [Dec. 1879]	368
256	Brahms to George Henschel, [Feb. 1880]	368
257	Verdi to Count Opprandino Arrivabene, 18 Oct. 1880	369

CONTENTS

258   R. Strauss to Breitkopf & Härtel, 8 Feb. 1881 370
259   Wagner to Ludwig Strecker, 30 Aug. 1881 371
260   Verdi to Giulio Ricordi, [14 Feb. 1883] 373
261   Brahms to Eduard Hanslick, [May 1884] 373
262   Verdi to Count Opprandino Arrivabene, 10 Jun. 1884 376
263   Mahler to Friedrich Löhr, 1 Jan. 1885 377
264   Debussy to Eugène-Henry Vasnier, [Feb. 1885] 378
265   Brahms to Marie Lipsius, 27 May 1885 380
266   Bruckner to Baron Hans von Wolzogen, 25 Mar. 1886 381
267   Verdi to Franco Faccio, 2 Sep. 1886 382
268A Dvořák to Pyotr Ilyitch Tchaikovsky, 14 Jan. 1889 383
268B Tchaikovsky to Antonín Dvořák, 30 Jan. 1889 384
269   Verdi to Alfredo Soffredini, 11 Dec. 1890 385
270   Verdi to Arrigo Boito, 12 Jun. 1891 385
271A Bülow to Giuseppe Verdi, 7 Apr. 1892 386
271B Verdi to Hans von Bülow, 14 Apr. 1892 387
272   Puccini to *Il Corriere della Sera*, 21 Mar. 1893 388
273   Debussy to Ernest Chausson, [autumn 1893] 389
274   Brahms to Clara Schumann, [Aug. 1894] 390
275   R. Strauss to Giuseppe Verdi, 18 Jan. 1895 391
276   Mahler to Max Marschalk, 26 Mar. 1896 392
277   Wolf to Rosa Mayreder, 16 Jun. 1896 395
278   Brahms to his stepmother, 29 Mar. 1897 396
279   Puccini to Don Pietro Panichelli, Aug. 1898 396
280   Bartók to his mother, 22 Sep. 1899 397
281   Verdi to Arrigo Boito, 20 Oct. 1900 399
282   Ravel to Florent Schmitt, 8 Apr. 1901 400
283   Puccini to Giulio Ricordi, [summer 1902] 401
284   Prokofiev to his father, [22 Sep. 1904] 402
285   Ravel to Maurice Delage, 5 Jul. 1905 406
286   Debussy to Jacques Durand, 11 Sep. 1905 407
287   Bartók to his mother, 11 Apr. 1906 408
288   Bartók to Stefi Geyer, 16 Aug. 1907 410
289   Prokofiev to Reinhold Moritsevich Glière, 5 Mar. 1908 415
290   Ravel to Ida Godebska, 18 Sep. 1908 416
291   Mahler to Bruno Walter, [1909] 417
292A R. Strauss to Hugo von Hofmannsthal, 4 May 1909 419
292B R. Strauss to the same, 9 Jul. 1909 419
293   Schoenberg to Emil Hertzka, 5 Jan. 1910 422
294   Debussy to Georges Jean-Aubry, 25 Mar. 1910 424
295   Webern to Alban Berg, 21 Dec. 1911 425

CONTENTS

296   Debussy to Igor Stravinsky, 13 Apr. 1912 426
297   Puccini to Gabriele D'Annunzio, 16 Jun. 1912 427
298   Berg to Paul Hohenberg, 12 Nov. 1912 428
299   Ravel to Igor Stravinsky, 26 Sep. 1914 429
300   Berg to Paul Hohenberg, 13 Nov. 1915 429
301   Bartók to the directors of the Budapest Philharmonic Society,
          10 Dec. 1915 431
302   Debussy to Jacques Durand, 8 Jun. 1916 432
303   Webern to Alban Berg, 1 Aug. 1919 432
304   Prokofiev to Igor Stravinsky, 10 Dec. 1919 434
305   Schoenberg to the *Deutsche Zeitung Bohemia*, [Nov. 1921] . . 435
306   Puccini to Renato Simoni, 1 May 1922 436
307   Bartók to his mother & aunt, 5 Apr. 1923 437
308   Schoenberg to Josef Matthias Hauer, 1 Dec. 1923 438
309   Bartók to his family, 18 Jan. 1928 441
310A   Ravel to his brother, 20–26 Jan. 1928 442
310B   Ravel to the same, 7 Feb. 1928 443
310C   Ravel to the same, 21 Feb. 1928 443
311A   Schoenberg to Alban Berg, 9 Aug. 1930 444
311B   Berg to Arnold Schoenberg, 13 Aug. 1930 445
312   Ravel to Arturo Toscanini, 9 Sep. 1930 447
313   Schoenberg to Alban Berg, 28 Nov. 1930 448
314   Bartók to his mother & aunt, 13 Jul. 1931 448
315   Berg to Arnold Schoenberg, 28 Aug. 1935 454
316   Bartók to Mrs. Oscar Müller-Widmann, 13 Apr. 1938 456
317   Webern to Willi Reich, 20 Oct. 1939 459
318   Bartók to his sons, 24 Dec. 1940 461
319   Schoenberg to Erwin Stein, 22 Nov. 1943 465
320   Bartók to Joseph Szigeti, 30 Jan. 1944 467
321   Bartók to Mrs. Wilhelmine Creel, 17 Dec. 1944 470
322   Schoenberg to Hans Keller, [10 Jan. 1951] 473
323   Schoenberg to Karl Rankl, 27 Jun. 1951 474
Comments and notes 475
Alphabetical list of the composers and their letters 589
Index 591

Frontispiece

        Wagner to Rudolf Freny, 25 Oct. 1872 (Letter 239)

I/II   Mozart to his wife, 30 Sep. 1790 (Letter 107)

III/IV   Beethoven to Johann Baptist Rupprecht, [c. 22 Dec. 1814]
        (Letter 130)

V/VI   Verdi to Franco Faccio, 2 Sep. 1886 (Letter 267)

VII/VIII   Berg to Paul Hohenberg, 12 Nov. 1912 (Letter 298)

IX/X   Ravel to Arturo Toscanini, 9 Sep. 1930 (Letter 312)

As a rule, composers are not polished writers. Verdi knew this. "Why on earth is it necessary to go digging up a musician's letters?" he wrote to a friend. "Letters that are always written hastily, without taking pains, without importance, since the musician knows he need not live up to a litterateur's reputation. Isn't it enough that he should be hooted at for his notes? No sir! His letters too!" [1] We might rejoin that we do not look for literary recreation in composers' letters. But then why do we read them? Brahms voiced uneasiness on the subject—an uneasiness that Verdi must also have felt, even if he chose not to express it: "I . . . enjoy keeping a letter of Beethoven's as a relic; but I am horrified when I think of all the things such a letter is supposed to mean and to explain!" [2] He sensed that letters are published and read not only for what they were originally meant to convey to their recipients, but for what they unintentionally convey to readers at large. It was the unintentional, unpredictable significance of letters that troubled Brahms and Verdi: the thought that their own correspondence might some day be published posed a threat to their normal wish for privacy; but, much worse, it made them afraid of the interpretations that might be put on the slightest thing they wrote. They were not writers. They did not always mean what they said or succeed in saying what they meant.

We sympathize with their feelings, but we do not need to share them. After all, we do not thirst for damaging revelations any more than we look for finished literary productions, when we read the letters of composers. We read them to discover the truth—not the tabloid-newspaper "truth," but the truth which history, like every other science, attempts to discover so that we may gain a better understanding of ourselves and our world. Boswell, feeling called upon to justify the presence of countless anecdotes and other seemingly irrelevant trivia in his *Life of Samuel Johnson,* declared: "In following so eminent a man from his cradle to his grave, every minute particular, which can throw light on the progress of his mind, is interesting." Boswell was the first modern biographer, and his method was new: not everything he recorded bore directly on an aspect of his subject's life or character; yet every detail contributed imperceptibly to the most lifelike portrayal that had ever been presented to the public. Few writings are more illuminating in this sense than letters. However, we read composers' letters not just to follow the progress of their minds,

---

[1] See Letter 257.
[2] See Letter 265.

but to learn how they lived and made a living, how they felt about their own music and the music of others, how they were affected by their environment and by the cultural and political forces of their times. We read them in order to sense the aura of their times, and we hope to be brought nearer to their music by understanding the spirit in which it was written and received. To paraphrase Boswell, every minute particular, which can throw light on these concerns, is interesting.

This book has a threefold purpose: to provide a more comprehensive selection of composers' letters than has been made available in the past; to offer accurate translations based on reliable texts; and to present the letters in such a way that they may serve to illustrate the history of Western music as well as the lives of its individual composers.

Previous collections have tended to neglect composers earlier than Bach. It was pointed out that very few of their letters have come down to us, and it was assumed (I imagine) that they would in any case be of limited interest to the average music lover. Perhaps so. Nevertheless, I determined to search among the available printed sources (archival research was unhappily out of the question) and to include as many of those early letters as seemed appropriate, on the grounds that public interest in ancient music is growing steadily and that, meanwhile, students and teachers might welcome the convenience of having a number of such texts assembled in one place. The search was not altogether futile. To be sure, it soon became apparent that some of the leading composers of those periods could not be represented in this collection: we have no letters—so far, at any rate—by Vitry, Dunstable, Binchois, Ockeghem, Obrecht, La Rue, Josquin, and many others. Early composers' signatures are occasionally found beneath receipts and legal documents; and with the spread of music printing in the sixteenth century, dedicatory epistles become increasingly common. But neither class of literature can be construed as genuine letters, even though each is of undoubted value to historians.[3] Still, forty-six letters dating from before 1700 seemed of sufficient importance or interest to be included. Most of these appear here for the first time in English.

Another period that stood in need of better representation was the twentieth century. I have tried to supply the deficiency by selecting quite a large number of letters by the principal recent composers, except those who were still alive and a few whose letters were not available for one

---

[3] Dedications and forewords were not always written by the composers themselves, since their high-flown style often required a more expert hand. For some interesting examples, see Strunk (full title on p. 475).

reason or another. Here, too, the reader will find many letters that have not previously been translated, as well as some that have never been published before.[4]

The music that is most familiar to today's concert and opera audiences was written between 1700 and 1900, and the letters of the major composers of that era have been published repeatedly, not only in the original languages but in English. The first extensive translations were made soon after collections of composers' letters began appearing in Germany in the 1860s. They were quite good (one remembers Lady Wallace with the sort of affection one feels for Constance Garnett, the indefatigable translator of Russian classics), but they could not be better than the texts on which they were based, and these were edited according to nineteenth-century standards: at best they were made to conform with current usage, at worst (as, for example, when the editors were members of the composer's family) they were abridged, combined with other letters, and generally transformed to create whatever favorable impression struck the editor's fancy. Today we have some excellent English editions, founded on the best sources available, and I am grateful for permission to make use of them here. On the other hand, I felt obliged to retranslate over a hundred letters by composers whose correspondence existed only in antiquated or otherwise inadequate versions.

In making my translations I have tried to keep in mind the special requirements of letters. As we have seen, they cannot be thought of as literary works; in fact, they obtain much of their interest from the very elements that keep them from being literature—the little mistakes, irregularities, awkward constructions, interrupted thoughts so typical of writings not meant to be made public. We might even say that the more indifferent they are to anything but their immediate business, the more they tell us about the writer. Let us take Beethoven's letters. Not only does he tend to be tortuous and enigmatic, or else so blunt as to be painfully clear, but he makes mincemeat of spelling, punctuation, syntax, and all the other niceties of prose composition in a way that is peculiarly his own and quite unlike that of Mozart, to mention another unorthodox stylist. Yet English translators have never dared to reproduce all these features; instead, they have turned out versions that seem smooth, almost urbane, by comparison with the originals and in so doing have unwittingly given us a falsified image of the composer. Surely translations of letters ought to be as idiomatic or unidiomatic as the original texts themselves. I have attempted, in the two hundred and thirty-two translations I have prepared

---

[4] A list of all the unpublished letters is given below.

for this book, to present the reader with English *equivalents* of the originals, and I have adhered to the same principle in selecting translations from existing publications.

A word about my sources. In the case of letters the best source, when it is extant, is the autograph. I have used autographs and photographic copies of autographs whenever I could. The majority of the texts, however, are based on secondary, published sources, and I have been at some pains to select the best available. If, in rare instances, I have chosen to rely on a patently inferior one rather than discard an unusually interesting letter, I have warned the reader of this fact. Excerpts and abridgments, on the other hand, have been rigorously excluded.[5] Readers interested in this aspect of the book will find precise references to my sources at the foot of each letter.

Though it was not one of my main purposes to discover new material, I have been fortunate enough, in the course of my researches, to come upon a small number of unpublished letters. The following, I think, have not been published before, though a few are known in abridged or distorted versions: Letters 184A, 225, 231, 239, 250, 267, 269, 270, 298, 300, 312, and 317.

The letters have been arranged in chronological order rather than in separate sections devoted to the individual composers. This produces a type of continuity that is usually found in the collected correspondence of one man; but here the only unifying agent is music itself, or better, the history of Western music. Within this broad framework there is great diversity—indeed, the unity may seem illusory at first glance. But if the reader has the time and the patience, he will doubtless begin to notice recurring themes,[6] gradual changes of outlook, passing fashions. He will note the varying impact of wars, pestilences, and revolutions, religious and literary movements, social restrictions and innovations upon virtually all the composers. He will sense subtle shifts of emphasis in their approach to their task, as the great stylistic periods succeed one another. And, most strikingly, he will witness new generations springing up as the old die out and realize, perhaps more vividly than if he were reading a conventional history, that even the most original geniuses must begin where their elders have left off, then slowly find themselves.

In the "Oxen of the Sun" episode of *Ulysses*, James Joyce traced the evolution of English prose by skillfully mimicking its main styles, from

---

[5] The two Haydn fragments (Letters 104 and 110) are surviving remnants of letters that have been lost, rather than excerpts from unpublished letters that still exist.
[6] Some of these are listed in the Index.

the Anglo-Saxon of the chroniclers to twentieth-century journalese and beyond. Had I been another Joyce, I might perhaps have tried to produce the same effect in my translations, to give the reader a sense of the evolution of the original languages as the series of letters unfolds itself. Such a venture was, of course, beyond my powers. Still, I have tried to mirror that evolution (unobtrusively, I hope) by retaining much of the sentence structure found in the original and by avoiding the use of words and expressions that were not yet part of the English language at the time it was written. In substance, however, the language of my translations is modern English.[7]

The chronological arrangement has made it possible to include several letter-exchanges, which would not have found a place in the collection had the material been divided in sections. It has also allowed me to insert letters by minor, even negligible, composers when the contents contributed to various aspects of the book.

Beginning with Monteverdi, perhaps the earliest composer whose correspondence has reached us in some abundance, each major composer is represented by a considerable number of letters. Wherever possible, I have selected these from successive periods of the composers' lives, to mark the main stages of their careers and productivity, and at the same time, of course, have looked for letters that would reflect their musical and social personalities. It would be foolhardy to claim that these and no others were best suited to the purpose. Anyone acquainted with the correspondence of Mozart or Mendelssohn, to take two most prolific and fascinating letter-writers, will realize what an unwelcome task it has been to choose and, even more, to omit.

There is no obligation on the reader to keep to the chronological sequence. Indeed, perhaps only the student of music history will wish to do so. Others may prefer to read one composer's letters at a time and many, no doubt, will simply browse at random. I have tried to accommodate these readers by drawing up an alternative table of contents [8] and by furnishing each letter with sufficient annotations and cross-references to make it intelligible regardless of its position in the sequence. To be sure, the comments and notes have been placed at the end of the book, a location not designed to attract many visitors; but had they been put at the head and foot of each letter, the book itself might have attracted even fewer. Perhaps a brief summary of what is to be found in the annotations will help the

---

[7] But I must be forgiven a few "thee's" and "thou's" in some of my verse translations, as well as an unavoidable "ye" at the beginning of Beethoven's Heiligenstadt Testament (Letter 120).

[8] See pp. 589–90.

reader to decide which ones may interest him. Each letter has a prefatory comment varying in length from a mere cross-reference to a long paragraph. Lesser-known composers, but not the more famous ones, are identified in short biographical sketches, as are the recipients of the letters. Occasionally there is a reference to one of the standard texts in English for further reading. In the main, these prefatory comments are addressed to the musical layman, who will also find most of the technical expressions defined in the numbered notes. As for the latter, they carry the usual information (dates, facts, clarifications) and once in a while something more.

"Mistakes—Mistakes—" wrote Beethoven to his hapless publisher, "you are yourself a singular mistake." [9] These thundering words echo down the corridors of time with a truly Beethovenian intensity. They make one shudder. How many mistakes have crept into this book? How many words have I inadvertently left out, how many illustrious men have I caused to be born too soon or die too late? Not too many, I trust, but I can only hope for the reader's indulgence. I shall be grateful for any corrections he may send me.

I owe special thanks to those who have been kind enough to place autograph letters at my disposal. Mr. Walter Toscanini allowed me to spend some memorable days examining his father's collection and was equally helpful in giving me expert advice, Dr. Rudolf F. Kallir lent me some of his most precious autographs, as did my friend Jacob Lateiner, and Mrs. Suzanne Szekely gave me the opportunity of studying the letters of Alban Berg to her father. Furthermore, Dr. Willi Reich of Zurich and Professor Halsey Stevens of Los Angeles were so good as to send me their own typescripts of autograph letters by Webern and Bartók respectively and to answer many questions in great detail. To all of these I wish to express my gratitude for being so generous with their time and for giving me permission to publish letters in their possession. Similarly, I must thank Mr. Sydney Beck (Head of the Rare Book and Manuscript Collection, Music Division, The New York Public Library), Dr. Dagmar von Busch-Weise (Beethoven-Archiv, Bonn), and Dr. Hedwig Mitringer (Archivist of the Gesellschaft der Musikfreunde, Vienna) for answering queries and supplying me with photographic copies of autographs. I have importuned many eminent experts, and while I cannot allow them to share responsibility for any of this book's shortcomings, I still wish to thank them here. Professor Richard Ellmann (Evanston) read the entire manuscript and made many valuable suggestions which I was happy to follow. Professor Denis Stevens

[9] See Letter 126.

(New York) not only helped me over some difficult passages in the letters of Cavalieri and Monteverdi but was so generous as to put another, quite different accomplishment at my disposal: except for the frontispiece, all the photographs in this book are his handiwork. Mr. Robert Craft (Hollywood), Dr. Leonard Ellinwood (Washington), Mr. David Josephson (New York), Professor Edward A. Lippman (New York), Professor Dragan Plamenac (Urbana), Professor Gilbert Reaney (Los Angeles), and Professor Gustave Reese (New York) were good enough to answer questions and give me helpful advice on certain specific points. Owing to my ignorance of Hungarian and Russian, I had recourse to the abilities of Professor Robert Austerlitz, Chairman of the Department of Linguistics at Columbia University, who translated Bartók's Hungarian letters, and Vera Lateiner (Mrs. Jacob Lateiner), who translated a long Tchaikovsky letter from the Russian. In this connection, I must also thank Mr. Gabriel Banat for many hours of unstinting help. My wife, finally, not only typed out the entire manuscript but put up with three and a half years of talk about its many problems. To her go my best thanks.

P. W.

New York, 1967

La storia è varia e sinuosa e niente di ciò che è essenziale nell'animo umano vi è mai, in ogni sua parte, del tutto assente.*

—Benedetto Croce, *La letteratura italiana del Settecento: note critiche.*

* History is various and sinuous, and no essential part of the human spirit is ever wholly absent from it.

LETTERS
OF
COMPOSERS
THROUGH
SIX
CENTURIES

The letters are numbered consecutively for purposes of cross-reference. Some have been grouped together (e.g., 64A-E) for various reasons that will be apparent in each instance. The names of sender and addressee (with the latter's residence at the time, if known) appear at the head of each letter, followed by an indication, in square brackets, of the language in which the letter was originally written; the following abbreviations have been used:

Eng.	= English	It.	= Italian
Flem.	= Flemish	L.	= Latin
Fr.	= French	Pol.	= Polish
G.	= German	Russ.	= Russian
Hung.	= Hungarian	Sp.	= Spanish

Other languages are spelled out in full. There follows the date, either in the style of the original or (if the original date appears only at the end or is missing altogether) in a standardized form and in square brackets. Indentions, punctuation, etc. adhere to a uniform pattern unless the text is based on a primary source or critical edition, in which case the appearance of the original has been copied as closely as possible. Superior figures refer to the notes at the end of the book, which are arranged, with the comments, beneath the number of the letter in question. Finally, at the foot of each letter, there appears a complete note of its source (or a bracketed cross-reference to such a note, followed by the new page reference). "Tr. by editor," placed *after* this information and separated from it by a dash, indicates that the letter has been translated by the present editor.

[Reims, 1363]

My dearest & most sovereign lady, "he dies reluctantly who never learnt to die," nor can a good heart tell a lie, & "who loves well forgets late." You have, God reward you for it, bestowed on me such pleasance & honor, favor & sweetness, that never did lady bestow so much on her servant & friend, however worthy, as you have on me. And even if there are and have been several [ladies] who gladly offered comfort, they had never the sensibility & the manner which you have. Hence I hold myself to be the happiest man alive. And since I know with certainty that several persons have told you that I am miserable, incapable, & grace-less: however mean I may be, yet by God I have the worthy heart of a friend. And I see well that your noble heart deigns not incline to or hear their words; & you show it well to me by your sweet, pleasant, & most lovely likeness which you have sent me, for which I know not how to thank you as I should: for by my soul, neither my sense nor my understanding is such that I could do my duty in thanking you. For it is the life, the solace, the joy of my soul, & I could not suffer pain or adversity but that seeing or remembering it I should be healed & comforted. And doubtless, never for a single day of my life—either by reason of a thing, or a word said to me—shall I think or believe that you do not wish to be my sovereign lady & that you do not wholeheartedly bestow on me all the good which I receive from you. And, my sovereign lady, a knight must have no calling or science other than: arms, lady, & conscience. Therefore I swear to you & promise that I shall serve you loyally & diligently to the best of my power with all I do & can do, & all to your honor, as Lancelot and Tristram never served their ladies; & have [your likeness] as my earthly deity & as the most precious & glorious relic that ever I did see in any place. And henceforth it shall be my heart, my castle, my treasure, & my comfort against all ills in truth. If it please God, I shall see you before Pentecost; for you & your sweet likeness have brought me to such a point that, the Lord be thanked, you have healed me completely. And I should have left before now; but there is a great company [of soldiers] .VI. & .IIII. leagues from us; therefore riding is most perilous. I send you my book, *Morpheus*, which they call *La Fontaine amoureuse*, in which I have made a song to your order,

1

& it is in the guise of a *rés d'Alemaigne;* [1] & by God it is long since
I have made so good a thing to my satisfaction; & the tenors
are as sweet as unsalted pap. I beg therefore that you deign to hear
it, & know the thing just as it is, without adding or taking
away; & it is to be said in a goodly long measure; & if anyone
play it on the organs, cornemuse, or other instrument, that is
its right nature. I am also sending you a *ballade,* which I made
before receiving your sweet likeness: for I was a little hurt
because of some words which had been said to me; but as soon
as I saw your sweet likeness I was healed & free of melancholy.
My most sovereign lady, I would have brought you my book to
amuse you, wherein are all the things which I have ever made,
but it is in more than .XX. portions, for I had it made for one
of my lords; and so I am having the notes put to it, & that is
why it has to be in portions. [2] And when the notes will have been
put to it, I shall bring it or send it to you, if it please God. My
most sovereign lady, I pray God that he may give you your heart's
desire & such honor as I wish you may have; & God give you
solace & joy, such as I might wish for myself.

Your very loyal friend.

Guillaume de Machaut, *Le Livre du Voir-Dit,* ed. Paulin Paris (Paris: Société
des Bibliophiles François, 1875), 67–70.—Tr. by editor.

2   GUILLAUME DE MACHAULT TO PERONNELLE D'UNCHAIR, DAME D'ARMENTIÈRES [Middle Fr.]

[Reims, 3 November 1363]

My sweetest heart, my sweet sister, & my sweetest love, I have
received your letter from my servant who has told me that you
are well, which pleases me beyond anything in the world. As for
me (if it please you to know), I am in good bodily health as I
write this, Our Lord be thanked who grants it. I did not go to
Saint Quentin, nor to my lord the Duke, [1] because of some enemies
who are in the Beauvaisis. And so I was counseled against it; therefore I remained. My sweetest heart, my sweet sister, & my sweetest

2

love, you have not written me at all concerning my book, nor
passed judgment on my .II. *ballades* which I sent you; ² I made
them for you, even though I ordered that the others be done first.
And it is my opinion that you have written me more briefly than
is your custom. And I do not know whether you have any leisure—
or if you do this in order that I too should write you more briefly.
But it would be a hard thing for me to do, for when I begin I
cannot stop. My sweet heart, my dear sister, & my sweetest love,
I pray that you take good care of my book & that you show it to
as few persons as you can. And if there is any thing which displeases
you, or that may not seem at all good to you, then make a little
sign, & I shall take it away & amend it to my best power. My sweet
heart & my sweetest love, I believe that one of the greatest gifts
& the best fortune which Love & Fortune grant to lovers is that
they may love near to one another; & the greatest misfortune is to
love at a distance, & I know well how to restrain myself & believe
that you do also. For were it not so, I should not wish for anything
in the world other than to live in order to see you at my pleasure
& to serve you. Wherefore I think at such length how we could
put a remedy to this, that it is one of the greatest cares I have. But
I see no way unless it come from you. And, my sweetest heart,
you know how Pyramus & Thisbe, who had been locked in separate
places that they might not see each other, found a way to see each
other; how Leander swam across an arm of the sea to go to his
lady, for otherwise he could not go; & how the Chatelaine of
Vergi ³ sought a way to see her friend, & how Lancelot crossed the
sword-bridge. And they did all this for love of their ladies. And,
my sweetest heart, though I am never as good as they were, there
is nothing in the world my body would not suffer me to undertake
at your command & that I might see you. For your perfect beauty
& your exquisite sweetness, which attract me & my heart as the
magnet attracts iron, would draw me & my heart to them so
sweetly, that nothing could be a burden to me that I might do at
your sweet behest. And you are so wise & therefore know so much,
that "enough asks he who complains"; for I could not offer counsel
unless it came from you. My sweetest heart, I am sending you the
.II. *ballades* which you once saw—and which were made for you—
in writing. And so I humbly beg that you learn them: for I have
made their music in .IIII. parts & have heard them several times
& like them very much. Adieu, my sweet heart, my dear sister, &
my sweetest love. May God give you perfect joy of all that your

3

heart loves, & a good life & a long one; & may he give us time &
a place that we may briefly see each other. Written on the .III.
day of November.

Your loyal friend.

[= Letter 1], 276–78.—Tr. by editor.

---

3   FRANCESCO LANDINI TO FRANCO SACCHETTI [It.]

[c. 1370]

If we can tell from a celestial sign
   That hill and valley soon must have an end,
   Then is the time at hand when we must bend
   Our eyes to demonstration such as thine.
Discord and hunger, strife internecine,
   Pestiferous vapors men cannot forfend
   Be they ne'er so hale—what do they portend?
   Perhaps the day of doom, as you divine.
But if the virtuous are to fall so low,
   As you apprehend, my tears will pour like rain:
   For Vice has gripped the world and brought it woe.
Your song, which moves the heart, I send again
   To you in its new dress, that it may go
   And wander o'er the earth, singing its strain.

Franco Sacchetti, *Il libro delle rime,* ed. A. Chiari (Bari: Gius. Laterza &
Figli, 1936), 284.—Tr. by editor.

4   JOHN OF ARAGON TO HIS BROTHER MARTIN
[Catalan]

[Perpignan, 4 January 1380]

The first-born.

Dear brother: know that on the New Year's holiday just passed, in the presence of some of our singers, we made a *rondell* with notes, with its tenor and contratenor and with its treble, copy of which we are sending you enclosed herewith. We pray, dear brother, that you will sing it and have it sung, and that you will show it or have it shown to all those whom you see fit. And if you or anyone else you know wishes to make a *virolay* or *rondell* or *ballade* in French, send it to us when it is done, for we shall send it [back] to you with notes to new music. Given at Perpignan, under our privy seal, on the .IIII. day of January in the year .MCCCLXXX.   The first-born.

Felipe Pedrell, "Jean I d'Aragon, Compositeur de musique," *Riemann-Festschrift* (Leipzig: Max Hesses Verlag, 1909), 240.—Tr. by editor.

5   ANTONIO SQUARCIALUPI TO GIOVANNI DE' MEDICI, VOLTERRA [It.]

[Siena, 26 November 1450]

My most beloved compeer after due salutations I endlessly commend myself to you.

It is about a month now since I returned from naples as you must know; and it has not ceased raining since, for I was wholly disposed to come to see you. and not only was my coming maimed, but writing [too]; for I was ever in hopes that the weather would take a small vacation from so much rain; god be praised in all things! Were I to tell you of naples, and of the king's majesty and of his court, which are indeed great things to tell and mighty, I should need to hire for at least v days as many writers as are at the court of rome. Which thing I shall pass over in silence for the present, and briefly make known to you how the cardinal of our Sacr. M.^{y} holds his reed-organ very dear, and he is very right,

5

for it is without fail a thing deserving of praise. now I confirm
you that upon yr. return I shall have you hear one, which I
believe without fail will not displease you. which was sent as a
gift to antonio di migliorino, who by reason of his humanity I
am very certain will be glad if I let you see it and hear it. for
the time being I shall weary you no longer, commend me above all
to M[adam] the young countess and to M[y lord] Piero,[1] and so
to all others.

    At Siena this XXVI day of Novembr. 1450 from yr. Compeer
Antonio degli orghani

Giovanni Gaye (ed.), *Carteggio inedito d'artisti dei secoli XIV. XV. XVI.*,
I (Florence: Giuseppe Molini, 1839), 160–61.—Tr. by editor.

6   GUILLAUME DUFAY TO PIERO AND GIOVANNI DE' MEDICI, FLORENCE [Fr.]

[Geneva, 22 February 14(54?)]

Magnificent and noble lords, I begin by commending myself
most humbly. As I well know that you have always taken
pleasure in song, and as I also believe that your inclination has
not changed, I have made bold to send you some songs which
I made but lately, being in France with my lord of Savoy, at the
request of certain gentlemen of the King's household. I have
still others to be sent another time. Item, I have this past year
made iiij. lamentations of constantinople, which are quite good,
iij. of which are for iiij. voices, and the words were sent to me
from naples.[1] I do not know whether you have them there, if
you do not have them, be pleased to let me know and I will send
them to you. Further, I have great praise for master Franchois
Sachet, your steward here, for last year I had occasion to work
at the court of Rome, and he served me most liberally, and
treated me most graciously, for which I thank you as much as
I can. You now have good people in your chapel of saint John
as I have heard, and therefore I will send you my little things
more often than before, if it pleases you. And also for love of
Anthoine [Squarcialupi] your good friend and mine, to whom
be pleased to commend me cordially. Magnificent and noble
lords, if there is anything I may do for your lordships here,

6

acquaint me with it and I will execute it with a good heart. With
our lord's help, may he grant you a good life and long, and
heaven at last. Written at geneva this xxij^d of february.

[L.:]
To the magnificent and noble
lords Peter and John de medicis   Your humble chaplain and petty
his very honorable lords   servant
    In Florence   Guillaume Dufay[2] canon Of
                                   Cambray

Facsimile of the autograph: Heinrich Besseler, "Dufay," *Die Musik in Geschichte
und Gegenwart*, ed. Friedrich Blume, III (Kassel: Bärenreiter-Verlag, 1954),
columns 889–90.—Tr. by editor.

7   ANTONIO SQUARCIALUPI TO GUILLAUME DUFAY, [CAMBRAI?] [L.]

[Florence, 1 May 1467]
My venerable father, most laudable for merit above all others.
   With the greatest delight of my soul did I see and read again
and again your most courteous letter, and I embraced with all
my heart the companions whom you sent—the best cantors of
your church, as you write, and I who have heard them am easily
moved to believe it. For they truly excel in the sweetness of
[their] voices as also in the doctrine and art of singing, and
are worthy of you as [their] teacher. It is impossible to express
what a welcome thing you have done to our Magnificent Piero
de' Medici, who truly loves your reverence greatly and ever
speaks of you most honorably. And he declares that you are the
chief ornament of our age, to which I too assent gladly. Also
Lorenzo de' Medici,[1] Piero's son, honors you marvelously; and
as he takes delight in the other fine arts, because of the excellence
of his divine talent, so does he, ardently, in your accomplished
music. And because of this he admires your art and cherishes
and honors you like a father. He also longs to have for his own
a product of your most excellent gifts. With this letter, therefore,
there will be a song, and he yearns to have it set to music and
adorned with melody by you. Indeed, I earnestly beg you to do

7

it and to send it to him. He is worthy of your kindness because
of his virtue and liberality. You will also do a most welcome
thing to me: and I thank you infinitely. Would that I might see
and hear you, which, as it would seem from your letter, you also
desire. Surely, there is nothing I would set above that pleasure.
I am wholly yours. I commend myself to you. From florence on
the first day of the month of May 1467.

   Antonius de squarcialupis de florentia
   called master Antonio of the organs, the florentine.

Canzona [It.]

 Love, who hast seen each of my heavy thoughts
 And known how true a servitor am I,
 Content me now, or suffer me to die.
 To lead so harsh a life with so much woe,
 To assuage with sighs and tears the soul's distress—
 Surely, my lord, dying were lesser pain.
 If thou, o Love, hast arrows and a bow,
 Why cleav'st thou not a heart so pitiless?
 Mortal lady should not a god restrain,
 Look to thine honor, my desire sustain.
 Allay the martyrdom in which I lie,
 For I draw near unto my utmost sigh.[2]

[= Letter 5], 208–209.—Tr. by editor.

8 JOHANNES MARTINI TO ISABELLA D'ESTE, MANTUA [It.]

[Ferrara, 2 September 1490]

Illustrious and powerful lady—Our most Illustr⁵ L[ord] the
duke [1] has told me and commanded that I come to your
L[adyship] for some days to teach y. L. to sing and I will do it
most willingly and with all my heart, but since time presses me
in part to provide for the needs of my house and in part for
some other necessities, I beg and entreat y. L. to be pleased to
wait for a fortnight so that I may provide for my needs and
then I will come to y. L. immediately and satisfy you as much

8

as I can and more than willingly. I await y. L.'s answer and commend myself to you a thousand times. Farewell. At F[errara] 2 September 1490.

Y. L.'s   Svant Joanes martinus
                           Cantor Mu[sice] *d*[omini] *ducis*
                           H[erculis]

Facsimile of the autograph: Antonio Bertolotti, *Musici alla Corte dei Gonzaga in Mantova dal secolo XV al XVIII* (Milan: G. Ricordi & C., 1890), 14. —Tr. by editor.

9   FRANCHINO GAFORI TO LODOVICO MARIA
SFORZA, DUKE OF MILAN [It.]

[Milan, 22 April 1495]

Most Ill⁸ and Excell^{nt} prince. Since Antonio de Verderio, a priest holding a clerkship worth ten ducats yearly at Sinexio, in the township of Pontirollo in the Duchy of Milan, is gravely burdened with an infirmity, I make bold to appeal to Y[our] most Ill⁸ L[ordship], in whose mercy I have put all my hope, and chiefly that for my continual practice and care, which is to write in music for the utility of our age and of posterity, in perpetual memory and praise of Your most Excell^{nt} L.[1] Wherefore I humbly beseech that, with your accustomed mercy and benignity, you will deign to grant me that clerkship if it falls vacant and write master Jacomo Antiquario, sending him by special letters whatever shall be fitting and necessary thereto. Which thing I will deem a special mercy, binding me forever to Y. prime Excellency. To whom I continually commend myself. Milan 22 April 1495. Your most Clement and Excellent

Lordship's   very devoted servant
                                    and worshipper of God,
                                    presbiter franchinus de
                                    gafuris musice proffes-
                                    sor [*sic*].

Emilio Motta, "Musici alla Corte degli Sforza," *Archivio Storico Lombardo*, XIV (1887), 549.—Tr. by editor.

10   PAUL HOFHAIMER TO JOACHIM VADIAN, VIENNA [G.]

[Augsburg, 7 February 1518]

Honorable, highly learned, gracious, very dear sir. My willing service to you, first and always. I wrote to you before christmas and enclosed that letter in another letter, which I had written to mr. Jacob Fritz of blessed memory, and charged him with delivering the enclosed letter to you himself. Meanwhile he has died and the letter has come home to me again. Now the purport of my writing was but this, that the writings you composed in my praise please me greatly and are made wholly to my liking. And yet, I wish that the epistle and the verse which my disciple sent me from Venice [1] had been included besides, to bear witness that the Italians, who surely are subtle, have also praised me and have also esteemed the music with which god has gifted me; thus the little book would have grown bigger. Indeed, I hope to come to Vienna next summer because of this matter alone, to discuss it with you. I cannot put down everything I mean; yet, if you would be kind enough to order and prepare for the press there what you have written, together with the Venetian epistle and *carmina,* that would please me greatly. And would you first inform me of the expenses this would incur, in case I can order it cheaper here. Let me know your thought and may it not displease you to write me by this messenger. I will, god willing, deserve it of you etc. Ludwig Senffl,[2] by mischance, *id est occasu,*[3] got a bodily wound from a loaded gun which fell to the ground and, falling, caught fire and went off, going through his foot to its mark, so that the next toe to the big one had to be cut off with some bones and little splinters which the ball had mashed up; which may have been written or told to you long ago. Not only I, but many good people are sorry for him. He will hardly be well enough to walk by Easter. No more, for I will await your news; and with this I wish you a happy new year. Given in haste, on the 7th day of February, in the year 18.

Your willing Paul[u]s Hofhaymer.

Hans Joachim Moser, *Paul Hofhaimer, ein Lied- und Orgelmeister des deutschen Humanismus* (Stuttgart: J. G. Cotta'sche Buchhandlung Nachfolger, 1929), 39–40.—Tr. by editor.

11   MARTIN LUTHER TO LUDWIG SENFL, MUNICH [L.]

[Coburg, 4 October 1530]

Grace and peace in Christ. Although my name is so hated that
I must fear the letter I am sending will not be received and read
by you, excellent Ludwig, in sufficient safety: nevertheless
[my] love for music, with which I see you adorned and gifted
by my God, conquers this fear. Which love also awakens the
hope that my letter may not be the bearer of any danger to
you; for who, even in Turkey, would scold, if one should love
art and praise the artificer? Although your Dukes of Bavaria
themselves are extremely ill-disposed toward me, I nevertheless
praise and venerate them mightily above all others, for they
cultivate and honor music in this manner. Nor is there any
doubt that there are many seeds of good virtue in these souls
who like music; indeed, I deem those who do not like it as
the tree-trunks and stones. For we know that music is also
hateful and intolerable to the evil spirits. And I plainly judge,
nor am I ashamed to assert, that there is no art, after theology,
that can match music; for it alone, after theology, lends that
which otherwise only theology lends, to wit, quiet and a contented
mind; a manifest token that the devil, author of baleful cares
and of the restlessness of the multitudes, flies from the voice of
music almost as he flies from the word of theology. Hence it
is that the prophets used no art as they did music, assigning their
theology not to geometry, nor to arithmetic, nor to astronomy
but to music, for they held theology and music in close proximity,
and spoke the truth by means of psalms and canticles. But why
am I now praising music, endeavoring in such a meager letter
to paint, or rather disfigure, so great a thing? But that is how
abundantly and zealously I love it; it has often refreshed me and
freed me from great distress. I return to you, praying that if
you have a copy of this canticle: "In pace in id ipsum"[1] you
will have it transcribed and sent to me. For that tenor has delighted
me from my youth and now much more, since I also understand
the words. I have not seen that antiphon set for several voices.
I do not wish to burden you, however, with the task of setting
[it], but presume you have it from another quarter. I hope
indeed that the end of my life may be near. And the world hates
me, nor can it endure me; I, again, loathe and detest it. And so

11

may the very good and faithful shepherd take my soul. Wherefore
I have already begun to chant this antiphon and desire to hear
it set. Lest you should not have it, or not know it, I herewith
send [it to you], pictured with its notes; if you wish, you can
set it also after I die.[2] The Lord Jesus be with you for ever.
Amen. Forgive my boldness and wordiness. Greet all of your
musical choir with reverence on my behalf. From Coburg, 4
October 1530.

Martinus Luther.

Ernst Ludwig Enders (ed.), *Dr. Martin Luther's Briefwechsel*, VIII (Calw:
Verlag der Vereinsbuchhandlung, 1898), 276–78.—Tr. by editor.

12   BARTOLOMEO TROMBONCINO TO GIOVANNI DEL LAGO, VENICE [It.]

[Vicenza, 2 April 1535]

I could have received no greater pleasure than I did on Thursday evening, hearing from you in yours so precious to me, and I
rejoice indeed at your well-being, most praiseworthy Mr. pre [1]
Joanne. Y. L[ordship] asks me for the rough draft of *Se la mia
morte brami* and so I send it to you very willingly, warning you
that I have made it to be sung to the lute only, that is without
a counter-treble. Wherefore whoever should wish to sing its
counter-treble would be displeased with it. But had I not been in
haste, I should have made one for you that might be sung in 4
parts, one not hindering the other; and upon my return to
Venice, which will be at the beginning of May, I shall, upon
occasion, make one for you in the above-mentioned manner,
giving you to understand that I was and always will be your
inferior; yet grant me this favor: commend me to the magnificent
and very gentle gentleman, lover of virtuosi, Mr. Hyeronimo
Molino, may God keep him in his grace a hundred and a hundred
years. Item, to Mr. pre Bastiano commend me and to madam
Paula, for I have all 4 of you engraved in my heart. Thus, I
shall say no more but ever to commend myself to all.

In Vicenza this 2 April 1535

such as I have said above Tromboncino.

Alfred Einstein, *The Italian Madrigal*, I (Princeton: Princeton University
Press, 1949), 48.—Tr. by editor.

13　NICOLAS GOMBERT TO FERRANTE GONZAGA, VICEROY OF SICILY [Fr.]

[Tournai, 3 June 1547]

My worthy L^d, I commend myself humbly always to your good graces.

My lord, knowing that Yr noble spirit delights in music, I made this motet as a gift for Yr lordship. Being hereabout, I thought you would have an opportunity of coming to tournay. But I hope that for the present you will nevertheless accept it in good part, for I am sending it to you with as good a will and think you will receive it in all benevolence. After which, my l^d, having again commended myself to yr good graces, I pray that our L^d may give you good health and a long life. From tournay, this iij^d of June 1547 from your more than

humble and obedient servant
Nicolas gombert canon
of the above place etc.

Facsimile of the autograph: Liesbeth Weinhold, "Musikerautographen aus fünf Jahrhunderten," *Philobiblon*, XII (Leipzig, 1940), 53.—Tr. by editor.

14　ADRIAEN PETIT COCLICO TO DUKE BARNIM XI OF POMERANIA-STETTIN, STETTIN [G.]

[Stettin, 4 July 1547]

Serene, high-born Prince, gracious Lord, let my willing, submissive service and devout prayers to God be presented to Y[our] P[rincely] G[race] in the beginning.

Gracious Prince and Lord. Since I am forced and driven to go from one land to the other through mishap and misfortune, which has befallen me for the most part because of [my] free profession of the holy word of God, and thus have also now come to Y. P. G.'s principality and land, necessity compels me, as do the laudable repute and laudable name I have heard give Y. P. G., to present to Y. P. G. a humble request and recital of my affairs and the circumstances of my station and my life.

13

I will therefore not hide from Y. P. G., in all humility, that, having been born in *flanders,* and come to acknowledge the holy Gospel, I was put in prison by command of the pope, and lay there for a long time. Yet—for the sake of the art, of *Musica,* in which I had so exercised myself as to gain praise and fame thereby from others—having been freed again by the petition of some great lords, I betook myself afterwards to *Wittenbergk,* to the laudable university, maintained myself there for some time through the princely kindness of the laudable Elector of Saxony [1]—to whom, where he now is, may God grant consolation, mercy, and merciful deliverance—and afterwards betook myself thence to the university in Franckfort [on the Oder]. In both universities I professed and taught *Musica* in such manner as is openly testified in the writings I will submit to Y. P. G. Since, however, I could no longer stay at Franckfort, and mean to go to Prussia, but have also heard that Y. P. G. has *founded a paedagogy* in Y. P. G.'s laudable City of *Stettin,* therefore I proceeded hither; and should a small allowance from Y. P. G. fall to my lot, to the honor and at the pleasure of Your P. G., I should be *eager* to establish that free and laudable art, *Musica,* and the proper way of singing, and *to teach others,* and—should it fall to my lot— would do nothing more gladly. But should it not fall to my lot (for I have a long journey to Prussia [before me], and the means I must live on are scant, but Y. P. G. is renowned as a Prince who is clement toward learned men—as is meet in so laudable a prince, and laudable, and also fitting to your office and to God's command—), I beg Y. P. G. will graciously sustain me on my way with charitable alms and provisions, in princely mercy. This will be richly rewarded by the Almighty and by our savior Jesus Christ, who says: *Inasmuch as ye have done it unto mine own, ye have done it unto me,* [2] and I will ever most willingly repay it with my prayers to God, with willing service, and by declaring and spreading abroad Y. P. G.'s name and fame.

And that I may also—with what God has lent me—honor Y. P. G., I deliver and give to Y. P. G. a song in four parts, put together by me to the text: *Vigilate, quia nescitis qua hora Dominus vester venturus sit.* [3] God give that Y. P. G.—in accordance with this song—and all of Y. P. G.'s land may so await God by truly bettering your lives and by just atonement and prayers to God, that Y. P. G. with all Y. P. G.'s lands and subjects may escape all future and threatening ills; which a kindly and

14

merciful God grant to Y. P. G. and to us all, amen. To whose
gracious and godly protection and shelter I commend Y. P. G.,
and beg Y. P. G. for a comforting and gracious answer.

Given in Y. P. G.'s City of Stettin, on the Monday after *the
visitation of Mary,* in [the year] xlvii.

Y. P. G.'s   submissive w[illing] servant
                                   Adrianus Petit Coclico
                                   flandrus

M. van Crevel, *Adrianus Petit Coclico: Leben und Beziehungen eines nach
Deutschland emigrierten Josquinschülers* (The Hague: Martinus Nijhoff, 1940),
379–81.—Tr. by editor.

15   FRANCESCO VIOLA TO DUKE COSIMO I DE' MEDICI, FLORENCE [It.]

[Ferrara, 17 October 1558]
My ever resp[td], Most Illust[s] and Exc[nt] l[d].

Having caused the music of M[r] Adriano [Willaert], my master,
to be printed, and knowing in what reputation it is held, I could
not omit sending a copy of it to Y. Exc[y], begging you, as I do in
all humility, to deign to favor it by accepting it and liking it,
and at the same time to consider me the very dev[d] servant I
profess myself. Wherewith I most humbly commend myself to
your good graces and pray to the l[d] God for your continued
prosperity and exaltation.

From Ferrara, this XVII of October MDLVIII.

Y. Exc[y]'s
                                   Most humble servant
                                   Francesco Viola

Riccardo Gandolfi, "Lettere inedite scritte da musicisti e letterati, appartenenti
alla seconda metà del secolo XVI, estratte dal R. Archivio di Stato in
Firenze," *Rivista Musicale Italiana,* XX (1913), 545–46.—Tr. by editor.

16   GIOVANNI PIERLUIGI DA PALESTRINA TO DUKE GUGLIELMO GONZAGA, MANTUA [It.]

[Rome, 2 February 1568]

Most Illustr?, Excel.ᵗ and Honorable lord

I am sure that my scant knowledge falls short of the great desire
I entertain of serving yr: Excel.ᶜʸ; nevertheless, I have elected to
show you my insufficiency rather than be ill-mannered through
hiding it, having been commanded by so Excellent a lord and
by the means of so rare a virtuoso as mr. Giacches [de Wert] [1]
to make the Mass enclosed herewith,[2] which I have made after
mr. Aniballe [sic] Cappello's instructions. If on this first occasion
I have not satisfied the mind of yr: Excel.ᶜʸ, may it please you to
command me how you wish this to be, whether short or long, or
so that the words be heard: [3] I will try to serve you according to
my ability, all of which I will ever expend in the service of yr:
Excellency, whose most Illustr? and Excel.ᵗ hands I humbly kiss.
From Rome this 2. of February 1568

Yr: Excellency's

very humble servant il Palestrina

Facsimile of the autograph: Knud Jeppesen, "Pierluigi da Palestrina, Herzog
Guglielmo Gonzaga und die neugefundenen Mantovaner-Messen Palestrina's,"
Acta Musicologica, XXV (1953), 148.—Tr. by editor.

17   GIOVANNI PIERLUIGI DA PALESTRINA TO DUKE GUGLIELMO GONZAGA, MANTUA [It.]

[Rome, 3 March 1570]

Most excellent lord and very honorable Master
Your virtuoso having favored me with an audition of Y.ʳ exc.ʸ's
Motet and Madrigal, he ordered me on your behalf to freely
express my opinion; I say that just as y.ʳ Exc.ʸ surpasses nature
in all your works, so in Music you exceed those who worthily
make it their profession; and the better to contemplate it, I

16

parted [1] the Motet, and having seen the fair, uncommon artistry, and how the words are given a living spirit, in accordance with the meaning, I have marked some places, for it seems to me that if one could do without them, the Harmony would sound better, thus .sixth. and unison, both parts moving; [2] and sixth and fifth ascending and descending; similarly certain Unisons; for fugues [3] drive our parts under compulsion. It also seems to me that because of the close writing in the fugues, the words are hidden from the listener, who cannot enjoy them as in ordinary Music. It is evident that y.^{r} Exc.^{y} knows all these trifles better than I do, but I have said this in order to obey you and so shall I obey you whenever you will favor me by commanding [your] affectionate and most obliged servant; and, praying that our lord may preserve Y.^{r} Exc.^{y}, I close, humbly kissing your hands. From Rome this 3rd of March 1570

> Y. Exc.^{y}'s
> humble and devoted servant Giovanni Petraloysio

[= Letter 16 (printed, not a facsimile)], 156–57.—Tr. by editor.

18 ROLAND DE LASSUS TO DUKE WILLIAM V OF BAVARIA, LANDSHUT [Fr., L., G., It.]

[Munich, 19 August 1572]

[Fr.] Most High, Most Mighty, Flighty: lrd my master Forevermore.

[L.] I have arrived at munich with grace and without privilege,[1] hale, hearty, and lazy. [Fr.] I, who think many a deep thought, have hither the picture brought, [G.] as Y[our] p[rincely] g[race] [L.] has commanded me; [It.] if I can serve you in any other way, you must order and I obey. [Fr.] I pray the Creator may turn and return $\overline{yr}$ Ex^{cy} to bavaria, hale and sound all round, and that he grant my lady's womb a little heir, upon my soul that is my prayer. [It.] To your gentle favor I me commend, and of greetings Two thousand I do send, and eke my boy to you I commend. Adieu till later, though when I

17

can't portend. [Fr.] Forget me not, I pray, [It.] for the rest,
have your own way—

[Fr.] My wife, my little rudolf, and M.ᵣ my own person do
kiss in all humility the hands of y̅r Ex.ᶜʸ and of madam the
princess, while her rump feels no distress. God preserve our
cheerfulness. From munich this .19. day in the month of
august 1572

Y. E.'s

most humble servant

orlando di ♭ ☰ ☲ ²

Adolf Sandberger, *Beiträge zur Geschichte der bayerischen Hofkapelle unter
Orlando di Lasso*, Vol. III, Part I (Leipzig: Breitkopf & Härtel, 1895), 248.—
Tr. by editor.

19   ROLAND DE LASSUS TO DUKE WILLIAM V OF BAVARIA, LANDSHUT [It.]

[Mantua, 26 February 1574]

Most Illustrious and Ex.ⁿᵗ, benign and sweet lord

M.ᵣ Giampietro [di Givarra, master of the horse] and I have
received y̅r Ex.ᶜʸ's letters, and I thank you with all my heart
for the great benevolence you show us; I shall do what y̅r Ex.ᶜʸ
commands me. We arrived at mantua safe and sound by the
grace of god, and y̅r Ex.ᶜʸ's present was presented most gallantly
cum modis et formis.[1] And was benignly received with grateful
words; the rest follows, I shall write y̅r Ex.ᶜʸ at the first
opportunity. [Postmaster Francesco] Brachero has written me
of a fine and well-mannered youth, who plays and sings to the
lute with such Ex.ᶜᵉ, that he has no equal in italy, besides which
he plays many kinds of instruments; and he dwells with the
bishop of Rimini, in Romagna; I shall apply myself in every way
to obtain him. I have written to the said Bracheri on the subject
of M. Andrea Gabriel[i],[2] and hope to get an answer in rome.
As for the cornett-player who dwells with the duke of parma,
he will no longer do, for he is .60. years old and full of the
french disease; I shall inform myself and seek elsewhere. I wrote,
while still at Trent, to M. Antonio della Viola, but he has not
answered yet. As for Venturino, if I should pass through Florence

when I return, I shall do ȳr Ex^{cy}'s bidding; if not, you will
be patient, for I don't yet know what I shall have to do on
my way home; god by his grace guide us and lead us to safety.
I humbly beseech ȳr Ex^{cy} to greet my wife, not having time to
write her now. And with this I kiss ȳr Ex^{cy}'s most honored
hands in haste, for we wish to leave today. From mantua this
.26. february 1574

ȳr Ex^{cy}'s

very humble servant

orlando lasso:—

[= Letter 18], 255–56.—Tr. by editor.

20   GIOVANNI PIERLUIGI DA PALESTRINA TO DUKE GUGLIELMO GONZAGA, MANTUA [It.]

[Rome, 17 April 1574]

Most Illustrious and Excellent lord, my very Honorable master

I believe that m. Don Aniballe is writing y. exc.^{y} why it is the
Mass [1] has been late in returning [to you], which I examined to
obey [you], rather than for any observations it required; and
so I am sending it in partition [2] and where I give my opinion
there are some small crosses. The *pleni* [*sunt caeli*] [3] I have not
touched as I hope that one day, Y. exc.^{y} having some leisure,
you will take pleasure in renovating that terzetto; having no
other desire but to obey and serve Y. exc.^{y} I beg that you will always deign to command me; may our Lord grant you happiness
and fulfill your every desire and I humbly kiss your hands.
From Rome this 17th of April 1574

Y. Illustrious exc.^{y}'s most humble

and devoted Gio: petraloysio

[= Letter 16 (printed, not a facsimile)], 158.—Tr. by editor.

21   ROLAND DE LASSUS TO DUKE WILLIAM V OF BAVARIA, LANDSHUT [L., It., Fr., G.]

[Munich, early June 1575]

[L.] Today, Friday, most Illustrious prince and my great master, there came to me and spoke in secrecy the secretary of $\overline{yr}$ Ex^{cy}; and gave me the magnificent salutation [It.] of my lrd the prince, [Fr.] well-loved by me, who wishes [L.] me to come and visit [Fr.] not the sick, but his Ex^{cy}. [L.] I answer that if the time is convenient for me and your Ex^{cy} [G.] orders "you must do it," [L.] I shall see what I can do. [Fr.] The reason I write thus is that recently (.6. days ago) I took charge of our choristers again and am also teaching them music, so that I cannot stay long from munich; the second reason besides is that carlo tenorista italiano has left for rome, having had leave of our master the lrd duke: and I have sold my horse to him cheap, which $\overline{yr}$ Ex^{cy} had given me, as it appeared to me better suited for giving advice on account of its age than for offering bodily aid, so that for all these reasons I know well how to go but know not how to come back, although I have confidence enough in $\overline{yr}$ Ex^{cy}'s providing me with the means to do so. Further, concerning my money which we discussed: I spoke of it at great length with m^r [Hans Jacob] Fugger,[1] but I see no order in it and should like to use it to buy some landed property; wherefore I leave everything to the goodwill of $\overline{yr}$ Ex^{cy}, whose hands I very humbly kiss and also princess Renée's whose garden I miss, where to drink water or wine I never had the bliss, I'll say no more but end with this. [G.] In great haste, [Fr.] certainly, pray remain covered:

$\overline{yr}$ Ex^{cy}'s very humble servant

orlando lasso:—

[= Letter 18], 273–74.—Tr. by editor.

22   THOMAS TALLIS AND WILLIAM BYRD TO QUEEN ELIZABETH, GREENWICH [Eng.]

[Greenwich, before 27 June 1577]

To the quenes most excellent Matie

Most humblie beseache yor Matie yor poore servñts Thomas
Tallis and William Birde gent of yor highnes chappell. That
whereas the said Thomas Tallys is now verie aged and hath served
yor Matie and yor Royall ancestors these fortie yeres, and hadd
as yet never anie manner of preferment (except onely one lease
w^h yor Matie late deare syster quene Marie gave him, which lease
being now the best ᵱte of his lyvinge is wthin one yere of expiracõn
and the reason thereof by yor Matie graunted on unto another:
And also for that the saide William Birde beinge called to yor
highnes s^{e}rvice from the cathedrall churche of Lincolne where he
was well setled is now through his greate charge of wief and
children come into debt & greate necessitie, by reason that by
his dailie attendaunce in yor Matie saide service he is letted from
reapinge such cõmodytte by teachinge as heretofore he did & still
might have done to the greate releyff of him self and his poore
famylie: And further yor Matie of yor princely goodnes entend-
inge the benefitt of us your said poore s^{e}rv^{e}nts did geve unto us
about ii° years past a lycense for the printinge of musicke. So it
is most gracyous sovereigne that the same hath fallen oute to
oure greate losse and hinderaunce to the value of two hundred
markes at the least. It might therefore please yor Matie of yor
moste aboundant goodnes for the bettar releavings of our poore
estates To graunt unto us wthoute Fyne a lease in revcõn for
the terme of xxj^{te} yeres of the yerely rent of xxx^{li} to the
ten^{e}nte use. So shall we most dutifullie praie unto almightie god
for the prosperous preservacõn of yor Matie longe to Reigne over
us.

[Endorsed:]

At Grenewiche xxvii Junii 1577
It then pleased her Matie to signify her pleasure that thies
peticoners in cõsideracon of their good service don to her highnes
shold have (w^{t}out fine) a lease for xxj^{te} yeres of lande in posses-

21

sion on Reṽsion not exceding the yerely rent of xxx^{li} they
abyding suche order as shold be taken by the L. Thres. or S^r
Walter Mild may Knight for the behoof of the ten^ants in possession
[signed] *Thomas Selford*

Edmund H. Fellowes, *William Byrd* (2nd ed.; London: Oxford University Press, 1948), 9–10.

23   VINCENZO GALILEI TO DUKE GUGLIELMO GONZAGA, MANTUA [It.]

[Florence, 13 March 1582]

Most Ser.^{ne} L.^d

Some days ago I sent Y[our] H[ighness] one of my Dialogues,
on ancient and modern music; [1] and, as I learn, you have looked
on it with great benignity. Which has emboldened me to inform
you that I have but now put an end to setting the Responsories
and the lamentations to music, composed, however, after the
use of the ancient Greeks; for among the other particulars they
observed in it was, as you know, that of letting one person discourse in music alone, and not many all at once as, against all
propriety, they do today. Which music of mine, in the judgment of those who have heard it so far, is not lacking in that
affection to which the Prophet Jeremiah, with praying and
lamenting, sought to induce his listeners. If, therefore, Y[our]
S[erene] H[ighness] should graciously wish to incline your
very purged ears, I should deem it the greatest mercy and favor
to bring it to your hearing with some other things during the
next Holy days (or whenever it may please you). [2] And if, as I
hope, I shall satisfy you, then I would ask [it to be acknowl-
edged] that I have approached the true use of those ancient and
learned musicians; and that at the same time, having matched
my speculations in the above-mentioned Dialogue with the
practical deed, I have attained the desired end. Wherewith,

22

humbly bowing, I kiss your regal hands, and proffer myself to
you with all my heart. May it please God to exalt you with deserved honors. From Florence, this 13 of March 1582.

Y. S. H.'s

most humble servant

Vincentio Galilei

Antonio Bertolotti, "Artisti in relazione coi Gonzaga . . . ," *Atti e Memorie
delle RR. Deputazioni di Storia Patria per le Provincie Modenesi e Parmensi*,
Serie III, Vol. III (1885), 195–96.—Tr. by editor.

24   PHILIPPE DE MONTE TO CHARLES DE L'ÉCLUSE, FRANKFURT [It.]

[Prague, 29 October 1588]

My exc^{nt} most respec^{td} S^{r},

Your letter of the 8th of this month has given me the greatest
pleasure, since I have learnt from it of your safe arrival at
Frankfurt. I dispatched yours to Dr. a Rotis at once, and he
sent me word that he would answer. I'll send for the answer [and]
if he sends it to me it shall go with this. I cannot tell you anything concerning the most serene Maximilian except that the
Poles stand firm.[1] There was talk these past few days of sending
the Duke of Sabioneta, the bishop of Olmutz, and the bishop
of Vesprino [Veszprém], chancellor of Hungary, as commissaries
to Poland, to discuss his deliverance; but the thing has cooled to
such an extent that it is no longer being entertained.

Some days ago $\frac{m}{10}$ Turks [2] with 7 pieces of ordnance appeared
at break of day beneath a castle, whose name I cannot remember, thinking to find it unprepared; but they were much mistaken, for they were greeted with some proper volleys that
kept them at a distance and, seeing their design undone, returned
to the place whence they had come, doing very much harm as
they went, burning and sacking every town they passed through:
our side, hearing of this, gathered 1750 men and went to await
them at a gap through which [the others] had to pass and must
have reached it very late, for night had already fallen when they
came upon them, and they had at them with such fury that

23

they dispersed them and put them to rout, killing about 1500
and taking as many alive. The rest fled to the adjacent mountains and woods; some nevertheless turned back and yielded
themselves to the mercy of their enemies; and they will all have
to do the same, unless they wish to starve to death, there being
no other pass than that where they were put to rout, which is
being watched by our men. Here we sang the Te Deum laudamus,
and in the end there were demonstrations of happiness. With
which I conclude, kissing your hand and praying that God may
give you all contentment. From Prague, this 29th of October.

I am, my exc^{nt} S^r,   Your most affectionate serv^{nt}
Filippe di Monte

Had they captured the castle, they should have been masters
of Hungary's gold mines, and if the encounter had occurred
during the day, I don't know how our men would have succeeded; but the Turks believed them to be equal in number, for
they will not hazard a fight unless they have a great advantage,
and so they lost heart at once; and they were greatly damaged,
too, by being loaded with booty. Dr. a Rotis' answer, I see, is
not here; it will have to await another occasion.[3]

Paul Bergmans, *Quatorze lettres inédites du compositeur Philippe de Monte,*
Tome I, Fasc. II of *Mémoires,* ed. Académie Royale de Belgique, Classe des
Beaux-Arts (Brussels: Maurice Lamertin, 1921), 21–22.—Tr. by editor.

25   EMILIO DE' CAVALIERI TO LUZZASCO LUZZASCHI, FERRARA [It.]

[Florence, 31 October 1592]
Giulio Romano[1] has come to me, as the protector of the music
of the most Ser^{ne} [Grand Duke] of Tuscany, and has given me a
report of the infinite favors he has received, not only from Y[our]
L[ordship] and from all those very Exc^{nt} Ladies,[2] but also from
the most Ser^{ne} [Duke] of Ferrara. And although I had been
burning with an infinite desire to come and receive one day,
through Y. L.'s mediation, the favor of hearing and enjoying the
harmony of those Ladies, I confess that now I am afire to do so.
I requested a description of all the qualities those Ladies possess

24

and, although I had an extensive acquaintance with them, nevertheless I know that, to my belief, such parts have never before been heard together, nor can they be heard anywhere but at Ferrara. I have also seen the gift of Necklaces presented by H. H. and by those Ladies, but the aforesaid Giulio must hold it in yet higher esteem that he was granted the privilege of showing those ladies some of his Airs, for I am quite certain, having been informed of it by Mr. Valeriano Catanei, that those ladies possess every manner of singing, and that any one of them could teach the aforesaid Giulio, though he is a youth who sings very well.

He also told me that he gave Y. L. a report of an Organ I am having built, which will be finished by Christmas, on which not only will it be possible to play harmonically, but the tone will be divided into ten commas.[3] Which [tuning], as he says he told Y. L., I have had sung by a voice to a positive organ in Florence, where it was heard by many. And being a novel and very difficult thing, there are those who will not believe it. Since it is a curious thing for anyone who may take a delight in it, I should deem it a very great favor if, on some occasion, Y. L. could favor Florence with a visit, in order that I might let you hear it, for I should hope, through your mediation and the excellence of those Ladies, to obtain the grace that they might sing a couple of Madrigals in this new manner of dividing the tone into ten parts, and thus I should be rewarded for some past labors.

He has also told me that H. H. was most satisfied with his *Chitarone*[4] [*sic*] and the manner of tuning it, of which H. H. desired to have an abstract; and truly, if Y. L. could hear Antonio Naldi, called Il Bardella, musician to our Highness, who himself invented it and plays it most excellently, I believe it would satisfy Y. L. infinitely, and in particular for singing to. I am taking the present occasion to break my silence of many months, in which I have not written you, assuring you that I desire to serve you as much as any person and begging you to command me, and I kiss your hands.

    From Florence, 31 October 1592.
      Y. Mst Magn^{cnt} L.'s.

                       Most affect^{te} Servant
                       Em. de Cavalieri

Henry Prunières, "Une Lettre inédite d'Emilio del Cavaliere," *La Revue Musicale*, IV, Tome III (June 1923), 131–33.—Tr. by editor.

26   PHILIPPE DE MONTE TO JEAN MOURENTORF, ANTWERP [Fr.]

[Prague, 26 December 1593]

Sir,

I should have answered yours of 29 November two weeks ago and beg you to forgive me for not doing so and to believe that some important affairs have been the cause of it. Now as to my Masses, I have understood the difficulty of printing them at present, Mr. le Mesureur having written me of this before; and I answered him what I thought. This he will have told you, that, since the Low Countries' miseries are so great[1] that scant means can be found of selling them, he should write out the copies at pleasure, or give them to someone or keep them himself if he prefers, or keep them until the occasion presents itself when they can be printed, remitting me for all whenever he likes. And I say this again, as God forbid that printing them should cause you any damage, preferring [as I do] to have an opportunity of doing you service rather than damage. And if it will please you to give me any command, you shall know from the result the desire I have of serving you. Meanwhile I cordially commend myself to your good graces, and pray that God may give you, Sir, all joy and contentment of health and a long life. From Prague, this 26th of December 93.

Your servant and most affectionate and cordial friend
Ph^le de Monte

[= Letter 24], 27–28.—Tr. by editor.

27   LODOVICO VIADANA TO GRAND DUKE FERDINAND I OF TUSCANY, FLORENCE [It.]

[Mantua, 7 July 1595]

Most Serene Lord,

The poor friar Lodovico Viadana of the Observant Minors, unworthy Master of the Chapel at the Cathedral in Mantua and most humble servant of Y[our] S[erene] H[ighness], finds

himself in great straits, being obliged to pay for and support five
nephews of his, who have neither a Father nor a Mother; and
being wards, they cannot even earn their own living. Whence
he has resolved never to abandon them, but to help them and
provide for them, insofar as his meager qualities, and powers too,
will consent. Now, therefore, he has caused some musical works
of his to be printed, to wit, Motets, Masses, Vespers, and Litanies
of Our Lady, and has sent the aforesaid works to some of the Italian
Princes, of whom the very principal is your S. H., and has
elected to send you the aforesaid Litanies of Our Lady, being
particularly devoted to you. But forgive me, most ser^{ne} l^d, if I
send you everything thus, by the ordinary, for I cannot come in
person, being very indisposed; and I entreat you again, in all
affection, to accept them willingly, conjoined with my simplicity.
And if you should condescend (not through any obligation)
but through living charity to help in some manner, he will always
be bound (as he is in any case) to pray to O[ur] L[ord] that He
may bestow all of Heaven's graces upon you; and, favored by a
reply [*sic*], he most humbly bows to you.

From Mantua, 7th July 1595.

Y. S. H.'s

most hum^{ble} serv^{nt}

The aforesaid Friar Lodovico Viadana.

[= Letter 15], 551–52.—Tr. by editor.

28   JOHN DOWLAND TO SIR ROBERT CECIL,
LONDON [Eng.]

[Nuremberg, 10 November 1595]
Right honourable, as I have been most bound unto your honour,
so I must humbly desire your honour to pardon my boldness
and make my choice of your honour to let you understand my
bounden duty and desire of God's preservation of my most dear
Sovereign Queen and country, whom I beseech God ever to bless
and to confound all their enemies what and whomsoever. Fifteen
years since I was in France, servant to Sir Henry Cobham, who
was ambassador for the Queen's Majesty, and lay in Paris, where

I fell acquainted with one Smith, a priest, and one Morgan, sometimes of Her Majesty's chapel, one Verstigan who brake out
of England, being apprehended, and one Moris, a Welshman,
that was our porter, who is at Rome. These men thrust many idle
toys into my head of religion, saying that the Papists' was the
truth and ours in England all false; and, I, being but young, their
fair words over reached me and I believed with them. Within
2 years after I came into England, where I saw men of that faction
condemned and executed, which I thought was great injustice,
taking religion for the only cause, and when my best friends
would persuade me I would not believe them. Then in time passing
one Mr. Johnson died, and I became an humble suitor for his
place (thinking myself most worthiest) wherein I found many
good and honourable friends that spake for me, but I saw that
I was like to go without it, and that any might have preferment
but I. Whereby I began to sound the cause and guessed that my
religion was my hindrance; whereupon, my mind being troubled,
I desired to get beyond the seas, which I durst not attempt
without licence from some of the Privy Council, for fear of being
taken, and so have extreme punishment. And according as I
desired there came a letter to me out of Germany from the Duke
of Brunswick. Whereupon I spake to your honour and to my
lord of Essex, who willingly gave me both your hands (for which
I would be glad if there were any service in me that your
honours could command). When I came to the Duke of Brunswick
he used me kindly and gave me a rich chain of gold, 23*l.* in
money, with velvet and satin and gold lace to make me apparell,
with promise that if I would serve him he would give me as
much as any prince in the world. From thence I went to the
Lantgrave of Hessen, who gave me the greatest welcome that
might be for one of my quality, who sent a ring into England
to my wife, valued at 20*l.* sterling, and gave me a great standing
cup with a cover gilt, full of dollars, with many great offers
for my service. From thence I had great desire to see Italy and
came to Venice and from thence to Florence, where I played [1]
before the Duke and got great favours; and one evening I
was walking upon the *piazzo* in Florence, a gentleman told
me that he espied an English priest, and that his name was Skidmore, and son and heir to Sir John Skidmore of the Court. So,
I being intended to go to Rome to study with a famous musician
named Luca Marenzio,[2] stepped to this Mr. Skidmore, the priest,

28

and asked him if he were an Englishman, and he told me yea,
and whose son he was. And I telling him my name, he was very
glad to see me. So I told him I would go to Rome and desired his
help for my safety; for, said I, if they should mistake me
there my fortune were hard, for I have been thrust off of all
good fortunes, because I am a Catholic, at home; for I heard
that her Majesty, being spoke to for me, said I was a man to
serve any prince in the world, but I was an obstinate papist.
Whereunto he answered, "Mr. Dowlande, if it be not so, make her
words true." So, in further talk, we spake of priests, and I told
him that I did not think it true that any priests (as we said in
England) would kill the Queen, or one go about to touch her
finger, and, said I, "whatsoever my religion be, I will neither meddle
nor make with anything there done, so that they do not anything
against the Queen." Whereunto he answered that I spake as a
good subject to her Majesty. But, said he, in Rome you shall hear
Englishmen, your own countrymen, speak most hardly of her
and wholly seek to overthrow her and all England; and those be
the Jesuits, said he, who are of the Spanish faction. Moreover,
said he, we have many jars with them; and withal wished to God
the Queen were a Catholic. And, said he, to defend my country
against the Spaniards I would come into England and bear a pike
on my shoulders. Among our talk, he told me that he had order
to attach divers English gentlemen, and that he had been three
years England [*sic*]. So I brought him to his lodging door, where
he told me that there was 9 priests come from Rome to go for
England. He came but the day before to Florence; and, I think,
they came all together. He told me that he would stay there in
the town and study in an abbey called *Sancta Maria Novella,*
and that he must keep in for a month, and that he would write
letters of me to Rome, which I should receive very shortly. But
I heard not of him in a month after. And then there came two
friars to my lodgings, the one was an Englishman named Balye,
a Yorkshireman. The next day after my speech with Skidmore,
I dined with my lord Gray and divers other gentlemen, whom I
told of my speech with Skidmor, giving them warning. Whereupon my lord Gray went to Siena and the rest dispersed themselves.
Moreover I told my lord Gray, howsoever I was for religion, if I
did perceive anything in Rome that either touched Her Majesty
or the State of England, I would give notice of it though it
were the loss of my life. Which he liked well, and bade me keep

29

that secret. This Friar Baylie, before named, delivered me a letter
which I have here sent unto your honour, which letter I brake
open before Mr. Josias Bodly, and showed what was written in it
to him, and divers other. After this, this Friar Bayly told me
he had received letters from Rome to hasten me forward, and told
me that my discontentment was known at Rome, and that I should
have a large pension of the Pope, and that his Holiness and all
the Cardinals would make wonderful much of me. Thereupon
I told him of my wife and children, how to get them to me.
Whereunto he told me that I should have acquaintance with such
as should bring them over, if she had any willingness, or else
they would lose their lives; for there came those into England
for such purposes; for, quoth he, Mr. Skidmore brought out of
England, at his last being there, xvij persons, both men and
women, for which the Bishop weeps, when he sees him, for joy.
After my departure I called to mind our conference, and got me
by myself and wept heartily to see my fortune so hard that I
should become servant to the greatest enemy of my prince,
country, wife, children and friends, for want. And to make me
like themselves, God knoweth I never loved treason nor treachery,
nor never knew of any, nor never heard any mass in England,
which I find is great abuse of the people, for, on my soul, I
understand it not. Wherefore I have reformed myself to live
according to her Majesty's laws, as I was born under her Highness,
and that, most humbly, I do crave pardon, protesting if there
were any ability in me I would be most ready to make amends. At
Bolona [3] I met with ij men, the one named Pierce, an Irishman,
the other named Dracot. They are gone, both, to Rome. In Venice
I heard an Italian say that he marvelled that King Philip had
never a good friend in England, that with his dagger would
despatch the Queen's Majesty; "but," said he, "God suffers her
in the end to give her the greater overthrow." Right honourable,
this have I written that her Majesty may know the villany of
these most wicked priests and Jesuits and to beware of them. [4]
I thank God I have both forsaken them and their religion, which
tendeth to nothing but destruction. Thus I beseech God, night
and day, to bless and defend the Queen's Majesty, and to confound
all her enemies, and to preserve your honour and all the rest of
her Majesty's most honourable Privy Council. I think that Skidmore and the other priests are all in England; for he staid not
at Florence, as he said he would to me, and Friar Baylie told me

30

that he was gone into France to study the law. At Venice and all along as I come into Germany say [*sic*] that the King of Spain is making great preparation to come for England this next summer, where, if it pleased your honour to advise me, by my poor wife, I would most willingly lose my life against them. Most humbly beseeching your honour to pardon my ill writing, and worse inditing, and to think that I desire to serve my country and hope to hear of your good opinion of me. Nurnberge, 10 Nov. 1595.

John Doulande

Great Britain, Historical Manuscripts Commission, *Calendar of the Manuscripts of the Most Hon. the Marquis of Salisbury, K. G. &c. &c. &c. preserved at Hatfield House, Hertfordshire,* Part V (London: Eyre and Spottiswoode, 1894), 445–47.

29   TOMAS LUIZ DE VICTORIA TO FRANCESCO MARIA II DELLA ROVERE, DUKE OF URBINO [Sp.]

[Madrid, 10 June 1603]

Most Serene
        Lord

Last year I sent Y. High^{ss} ten little music books with a thousand things [in them] and among others there was a Battle Mass that gave my L[ord] the King much pleasure [1] and since Y. High^{ss} has not had me advised of the Receipt I have determined to send more to Y. High^{ss} and to beg that you will receive them together with my service. And may Y. High^{ss} condescend to give me some largesse to help with the printing, and for whatever will be given I shall be thankful all my life and will pray to our L^{d} for that of Y. High^{ss} and of etc.

Madrid 10 June 1603.

The largesse Y. High^{ss} will give me can be consigned in Rome to Fran[cisc]o de Sotto, Chaplain and Cantor to his Holiness. [2]

Thome de Victoria.
Chaplain to his Majesty.

Felipe Pedrell, "Quelques commentaires à une lettre de l'insigne maître Victoria," *Sammelbände der Internationalen Musikgesellschaft,* XI (1909–10), 469–70. —Tr. by editor.

30   CLAUDIO MONTEVERDI TO DUKE VINCENZO I GONZAGA, MANTUA [It.]

[Cremona, December 1604]

My most Serene L[rd] and most Honble Master

Ten days ago I received from the Courier Y[our] S[erene] H[ighness]'s letter commanding me to make two *entrate,* one for the stars which are to follow the moon and the other for the shepherds who are to follow Endymion, and two *balletti* as well, one for the said stars alone and the other for the stars and shepherds together.[1] Thus, desiring most ardently to obey and attend very promptly upon Y. S. H.'s commands, as I have always done and will always do till I die, I set myself first to making that for the stars. But I did not find in the instructions how many are to dance it: for I wished to make it with refrains [*intercalato*], thinking it would be novel, beautiful, and pleasing; that is, to have a merry and short air played by all the instruments and danced also by all the stars in the beginning; then at once to have the five *viole da brazzo* take up an air different from the first, the other instruments stopping, and only two stars dance to it, the others resting; and at the end of the said *partita a due,* to have the first air taken up again with all the instruments and stars; following that order till all the said stars should have danced two by two. But not having the number, and it being necessary to know this (provided Y. S. H. likes it fashioned with refrains as I have said), I forbore to do it till I should know; and in order to find out, I have written to Mr. Gio[vanni] Batt[ista] the dancer, that he may give me the exact number by means of my brother; and meanwhile have made this for the shepherds and stars, which I now send to Y. S. H. I have indeed made it, my most Serene Lord, with the usual affection and ready willingness to serve you which I have always had and always will have, but not with the consent of my usual powers, pliant to my will, which I have had in the past; for they are still in a weakened state from past labors, and so feeble that not medicine, nor diet, nor the interrupting of studies has restored them to their first vigor, though partly; I hope, nevertheless, to recover them with the help of the Lord. And having them, if it please His Divine Majesty, I shall then entreat Y. S. H. for the

32

love of God not to burden me ever again with so much business at once, or with such shortness of time, for it is certain that my great desire to serve you would draw me unwittingly to my life's abridgment; but if it were to last, it would serve Y. S. H. and benefit my poor children. And so, most Serene Lrd, if Y. S. H. now finds I have not served you, as to beauty or speed, in the way you had perhaps expected and I now and always wished, do not blame my good will nor my intention, for both of these shall ever deem it the highest grace and surest favor that Y. S. H. deigns to command them, to whom I bow most humbly and pray O[ur] L[ord] may grant perfect happiness. From Cremona, this of December 1604.[2]

    Y. most Serene H.'s

Most humble and devoted servant
Claudio Monteverdi

G. Francesco Malipiero, *Claudio Monteverdi* (Milan: Fratelli Treves Editori, 1929), 131–32.—Tr. by editor.

31   GIULIO CACCINI TO GRAND DUKE FERDINAND I OF TUSCANY, FLORENCE [It.]

[Paris, 19 February 1605]

Most Ser.^{ne} Grand Duke,

Since Their Most Christian Majesties [1] have let it be known to me through Mr Concino Concini that they would desire me to leave my daughter Cecchina [2] at their service in France, I answered, while giving thanks to Their Majesties for the great honor and grace which they were conferring me, that being a stipendiary servant of Y[our] S[erene] H[ighness] I wished to give you an account of this, though certain and sure that Y. H. would continue to be greatly pleased that I should serve Their Majesties in all things within my capacity, the more so since on my leaving Florence Y. H. gave me to understand through a letter of Mr Picchena's that whatever I might do in the service of Their Majesties Y. H. would always consider done for your own person. All the abovesaid events took place but now, for when I asked the queen for license to go back to Italy, having in mind to do

the same with the King, she answered me the same morning that
the weather was still too bad; but that on that evening I should
find myself at the Lovero [Louvre] with all my women, which
I did: where, having sung in Italian, Spanish, and French to the
particular and unprecedented delight of the King and of all the
Princes assembled there, this was the reason why they sent me the
abovesaid message the next morning; nay, I perceived it the same
evening, because Monsur lo Grande [Monsieur le Grand?],
approaching my daughter, asked her whether she would willingly
remain in France and serve Their Majesties, and it was in the
evening, and not sooner, that the King said that Cecchina sang
better than anyone in France, and that there was not another
consort equal to ours. I shall then wait for Y. H. to do me the
honor of letting me know your will, as I beg with all my heart
you may do, for I have yet this other [daughter] in the service
of Y. H. who in a very short time will not be inferior to Cecchina
in music, besides the other members of my house; and bowing
to you most humbly, I pray that O. L.ʳᵈ God may give you a full
measure of his greatest happiness.

    From Paris this 19 Febr. 1605   Y. Most Ser.ⁿᵉ H.'s
                       Most humble and most obliged Serv.ᵗ
                         Giulio Caccini di Roma

Angelo Solerti, "Un viaggio in Francia di Giulio Caccini," *Rivista Musicale
Italiana*, X (1903), 709–10.—Tr. by editor.

32   CLAUDIO MONTEVERDI TO DUKE VINCENZO I GONZAGA, MANTUA [It.]

                                 [Mantua, 9 June 1610]
My most Serene Lʳᵈ and most Honᵇˡᵉ master
Mr. Pandolfo charged me on behalf of Y[our] S[erene] H[igh-
ness] with hearing a certain contralto¹ who has come from
Modena wishing to serve Y. S. H. I therefore took him straight-
way to Santo Pietro and had him sing a motet to the organ, and
I heard a fine voice, vigorous and long[-breathed], and singing on
the stage it reached every place very well with no trouble, a thing
Brandini could not do so well. He has a very good *trillo* and an

honest *gorgia* [2] and sings his part in the motets with much
assurance, and I hope Y. S. H. will not be displeased with him.
He has some slight defects; that is to say, at times he chokes
his vowel somewhat, almost after the fashion of Mr. Pandolfo, and
at times he sends it into his nose, and then again he lets it slip
through his teeth, making that word unintelligible; and he does
not strike the *gorgia* well, nor does he soften it at certain other
places. But all these things I am sure would be removed altogether,
as soon as he is instructed. I could not hear him in the madrigals,
for he was on the point of leaving, to place himself at Y. S. H.'s
command; thus I report to Y. S. H. what I have heard him in,
and since you have given me no other command, will end my
letter here, bowing most humbly before Y. S. H. and praying
that O[ur] L[ord] may bountifully keep Y. S. H. in good health
and in His grace. From Mantua, this 9th of June 1610.

    Y.S.H.'s

Most Humble and Obl^d S^{vt}

Claudio Monteverdi

[= Letter 30], 144–45.—Tr. by editor.

33   JOHN BULL TO THE MAYOR AND ALDERMEN OF ANTWERP [Flem.]

[Antwerp, autumn 1614]

Be it humbly known that John Bull, organist, was in the service
of the King of England; [1] and how, in the month of October
in the year 1613, he was forced to take flight thence hither, since
information had been laid against him that he was of the Catholic
faith, and that he would not acknowledge his Majesty as Head
of the Church. Which is a capital offense there. On account of
which Their Highnesses [2] took him into their service, granting him
a salary of 800 guilders a year, as well as exemption from tax,
watch, and other civic charges. But when, some time later, they
learned that this was very displeasing to the aforesaid King of
England, they dismissed him from their service. Wherefore he
left some months ago to come hither into this city, as being the
most famous in Europe for holding all the arts in higher esteem

than elsewhere, and during this time he has given ample evidence to Your Worships and to everyone, in public in the churches, as well as in private houses, of the skill and knowledge of music which the Lord (be it said without boasting) has been pleased to bestow upon him. And since he is resolved to remain in this city, and there to live and die in the Catholic faith; and since he was forced to leave all his goods (with which he was well provided) in England; so he could not fail to offer his humble and willing services to Your Worships and to this city, most humbly craving that you will be pleased to appoint him your organist-pensioner at whatever salary you may think just and reasonable for a person of his quality, granting him in addition exemption from tax, watch, and other civic duties. In return for which he will gladly serve Your Worships not only in whatever church services it shall please you to command, but also to play during banquets and feasts at which the city may desire to uphold its renown by means of music, upon the occasions of visits by lords and princes, without involving you in any additional expense.
Which doing, [he humbly kisses your hands], etc.

[signed] John Bull M. de Zoete [notary]

Thurston Dart, "An unknown letter from Dr. John Bull," *Acta Musicologica,* XXXII (1960), 177. Translated by Professor Dart.

34 CLAUDIO MONTEVERDI TO ALESSANDRO STRIGGIO, MANTUA [It.]

[Venice, 9 December 1616]

Most Illustr^{s} S^{r} and Honble master
I greatly rejoiced at receiving, from Mr Carlo de Torri,[1] your letter and the little book containing the maritime fable of Thetis' wedding; you write, Illustr^{s} S^{r}, that you are sending it to me in order that I may view it diligently and write you my opinion of it afterwards, as it is to be set to music and used at the forthcoming wedding of H[is] S[erene] H[ighness];[2] I, Illustr^{s} S^{r}, having no other desire than to be of some service to H. S. H.,

shall answer first that I am ever ready to attend to anything
H. S. H. will deign to command me and always honored to receive
without demur whatever H. H. will command. So that, should
H. S. H. approve this, it would in consequence be both very
beautiful and much to my liking. But if you bid me speak, I will
obey your orders with all respect and promptness, mindful that
what I say is nothing, being a person of little worth in all things
and a person who honors all virtue, especially [that of] the present
poet whose name I do not know, and the more so as poetry is
not my profession. I would say with all respect, in order to obey
you since so you command, I would say, then, first and generally,
that music wants to be mistress of the air and not only of the
water. I mean by this that all the concerted music described in
this fable is low and close to the ground, much to the detriment
of beautiful harmonies, since the harmonies will be placed amid
the thicker vapors of the air of the stage, made so as to be
heard by all, and played [*concertati*] within the stage; [3] and I
leave this to the judgment of your most refined and intelligent
taste. For through this fault, instead of one *chitarone* [*sic*], [4]
three will be needed; instead of one harp, there would be need
of three and so forth; and instead of a delicate singer's voice,
a vehement one would be needed. Besides, a proper imitation of
the speech ought in my judgment to rest upon wind instruments
rather than delicate stringed instruments, since I should think
that the Tritons' and other sea-gods' harmonies belonged to
trombones and cornetts, and not to citherns or harpsichords and
harps. For this operation, being a maritime one, is in consequence
outside the city; and Plato teaches that *cithara debet esse in
civitate, et thibia in agris;* [5] so that, either the delicate [instru-
ments] will be improper, or the proper ones not delicate. Besides,
I see the interlocutors are to be winds, Cupids, little Zephyrs
and Sirens; and many trebles will be needed in consequence. To
which moreover must be added that the winds are to sing; that
is, the Zephyrs and Boreals. How, dear S^r, shall I be able to imitate
the speech of winds when they don't speak! and how shall I be
able to move the affections by their means! Arianna moved, being
a woman, and also Orfeo moved, being a man and not a wind. [6]
The harmonies imitate their very essence; and not by means
of the discourse and stridulous noise of winds and the bleating
of sheep, the neighing of horses, and so forth; nor do they imitate
the undiscoverable speech of winds. The dances, further, which

are scattered through this fable are not in dancing meter. And
I feel, in my rather deep ignorance, that the whole fable does not
move me a whit; and I hardly understand it either, nor do I feel
that it brings me, by a natural order, to any end that moves
me. Arianna brings me to a just lament and Orfeo to a just prayer;
but this, I know not to what end. And so, Illustrˢ Sʳ, what can
you expect the music to accomplish in it? Nevertheless, I shall
always accept it with all reverence and honor, should H. S. H.
so command and be pleased, for he is my master without exception.
And should H. S. H. command that it be set to music, then,
seeing that in it the gods speak more than others and that I like
to hear such gods sing gracefully, I would say that the three Sisters,
that is Madam Andriana and the others, could sing [their parts]
and also compose them; so could Mʳ Rasco his part, Mʳ D.
Francesco likewise, and so on with the other Gentlemen; thereby
imitating Cardinal Mont'Alto, who wrote a play for which each
person appearing in it composed his own part. For if this were
a thing tending toward a single end, such as Arianna and Orfeo,
it would indeed require a single hand as well, to attend to the
singing speech; and not, as here, to spoken song. And in this
respect also, I hold it is too long-winded in every part, from the
sirens onward, and [there are ?] some other little arguments.
Forgive me, dear Sʳ, if I have said too much; [it was] not to
disparage anything, but out of a desire to obey your commands,
so that, if I am ordered to set it to music, you may take my
thoughts under consideration.⁷ Remember me in all affection, I beg
of you, to His Most Serene Highness, to whom I humbly bow
as the most loyal and humble servᵗ; and I kiss your hands in all
affection, Illustrˢ Sʳ, praying that God may grant you a fullness
of joy. From Venice, this 9th December 1616.
I wish you a happy holiday in all affection and am, Illustrˢ Sʳ,

Your most Humble and Oblᵈ Servᵗ

Claudio Monteverdi

[= Letter 30], 165–67.—Tr. by editor.

35   HEINRICH SCHÜTZ TO WILHELM LUDWIG MOSER, DRESDEN [G.]

[Dresden, 3 July 1621]

My most willing service to begin with, and may high God give you health of body and soul, most Honorable esteemed learned specially gracious and highly respected friend.

I cannot, under the circumstances, refrain from troubling my gracious Secretary of the Treasury with the present writing and from dutifully reporting that some money has been remitted recently to Nürrnberg from the Elect. Treasury here, with which Strings for the Elect. Music were to have been bought of a Wire-drawer there, Jobst Meuler by name, who makes such excellent Steel Instrument-strings that their like cannot be had anywhere else.

Now the said Wiredrawer has informed me in writing that he would Gladly oblige us and produce the strings, but that some others of his fellow masters will not let him make something [that is] unusual and better than they [make]. And if some small Injunction were to go forth to the Council at Nürenbergk from our most Gracious lord, then he would doubtless receive the permission.

Whenas, gracious Mr. Secretary of the Treasury, good strings are no less important to me and my colleagues in our profession than, say, a simple good pistol or other arms to a soldier, pray be not offended if I trouble you with this.

And I dutifully request herewith that you may be pleased to obtain that small Injunction of our most Gracious l[ord]'s to the Council at Nürenberg concerning the said Jobst Meuler, that the latter be asked for as many of the best Instrument-strings as the Elect. Household shall require, and beg you (: since a runner acquainted with these matters will in any case go there in a few days :) to send it to me at the first opportunity.

It is not only in the interest of the whole Music, but of advantage to Our most Gracious Elect. & lord, for we will receive good wares for the money; and I will requite my gracious Mr. Secretary of the Treasury to the best of my Ability upon the

39

next occasion, and herewith commend you assiduously, in closing, to the divine protection. *Datum* at Dresden this 3rd day of July in the Yr. 1621.

My gracious Mr.
Secretary of the Treasury's
wholly dutiful
Heinrich Schütz
Master of the Chapel Mp [1]

Erich H. Müller (ed.), *Heinrich Schütz: Gesammelte Briefe u. Schriften* ("Deutsche Musikbücherei," Vol. XLV; Regensburg: Gustav Bosse Verlag, 1931), 66–68.—Tr. by editor.

36   SAMUEL SCHEIDT TO RECTOR CHRISTIAN GUEINZIUS, HALLE [G.]

[Halle, 2 April 1630]

1. The Rector sent word to me yesterday through Cantor Matthias, saying some distinguished persons had told him that if I have not provided music for these Easter holidays it is the Rector's fault, since he would not let the scholars attend me when I desired them.

2. That if the Chapel were subject to the Rector's authority and not to mine, I should be compelled to apply to him before undertaking any music. It then would be their duty to obey me; and not otherwise. That they came to Halle not for the music's sake but to study and learn somewhat, for they would learn little from me.

Whereupon I ask [*sic!*] the Rector:

If a poor scholar comes to Halle desiring to study and learn somewhat, it is just and proper that he should go to him. But should such a one desire to be of the Chapel and collect bread-doles and alms from the people at the door, then he must go to the Director of Music, to be heard by him and examined whether he can sing, whether he is perfect or imperfect, whether, too, his voice is good and pure, unlike the Chapel's now, whose voices are as the lowing of bullocks, sheep, and calves, their gullets filled with plums besides, so that neither words nor ditty can be understood; yea, they sing so flat that one would rather stop one's ears and flee from the church. Then if the Director finds him sufficient, it is for him to admit him to the Chapel, and not for the Rector, who does not govern the music. And if the Director should appoint a dunce, the mockery would not fall to the Rector but to him who has the direction of the music; and when the Director desires them for some music, they should not first of all be the Rector's boys and apply to him, but if sent for at the Chapel, they must come, for otherwise the cart would be put before the horse. And I know full well that the Rector declares they must not do it, for so he has trained the lads. But, thank God, there are other people in the world besides! I also know full well that they can learn nothing from me, not two words of Latin; but this they can learn, they can learn to sing their semitones and their intervals purely, to distinguish between all sorts of major and minor 6ths, and major and minor Fifths, etc., for which former prefect Tittel was greatly obliged to me. Nb. And is it right that the Rector should weekly desire of their alms, and money too, for his kitchen? It would be far better employed in the maintenance of some good trebles to do service for the glory of God; for it is a grievous injustice. Indeed, it would be lengthy to write about other follies, though we may yet speak of them in the presence of good people. The magistracy shall separate us soon enough! Before submitting to the shame and mockery of his command, I would sooner be a hangman or a jailer. For the honor of my name is dearer to me than silver and gold, and I will not leave to my children a name tainted with this, that a Rector Scholae lorded it over me! *Vale.*

Walter Serauky (ed.), *Samuel Scheidt in seinen Briefen* (Halle: Gebauer-Schwetschke Verlag Nachfolger, 1937), 11–12.—Tr. by editor.

37   CLAUDIO MONTEVERDI TO AN UNNAMED
CORRESPONDENT, ROME [It.]

[Venice, 2 February 1634]

My Illustr.^s and Rev^{nt} S^r and Honble master

I have received two letters from Y. Rev^{nce}: the one before Christmas, while I was wholly occupied in writing the Mass for Christmas Eve, a new Mass by the Master of the Chapel being expected by this city's custom, the other fifteen days ago from the courier, who found me not quite recovered from a catarrhal descent that began to appear over my left eye shortly after Christmas and kept me not only from writing but from reading for many a long day. Nor am I yet whole, for it still afflicts me somewhat; and because of those two real impediments, I beseech Y. Rev^{nce} to forgive the discourtesy of my lateness in writing. I read, not sooner than a fortnight ago, your very gracious and virtuous first letter, from which I extracted most affectionate advice, worthy throughout of my deep consideration; wherefore I thank you infinitely. But the Galilei I have seen before, indeed twenty years ago, where he records that scant practice of the ancients.[1] I valued seeing it at the time, for in that section I saw how the ancients used their practical signs, different from ours. I did not attempt to proceed further in understanding them, being sure that they would prove most obscure ciphers to me or worse, since that ancient practical manner is quite lost. And so I turned my studies another way, founding them upon the best of those philosophers who have investigated nature; and since, from my reading, I see that the affections agree with those reasonings and satisfy nature's requirements when I write practical things with the above observations [in mind], and since I truly feel that the present rules have no connection with those requirements, for these reasons I have given my book the title of *Seconda Pratica;* [2] and hope to make the latter so plainly evident, that the world will not censure it but consider it. In my writing, I keep at a distance that manner of the Greeks, with their words and signs, and employ the terms and characters which we use in our own practice; for it is my intention to show by means of our practice how much I have been able to draw from the minds of those philosophers, for the service of good art and not for the principles of the *prima pratica,* [which was] solely harmonic.

42

Would to God that I might find myself near Y. Rev^nce, [to enjoy] your singular lovingness and singular prudence and advice, for I should tell you everything by word of mouth, entreating you to hear me out, everything, I say, concerning the order as well as the principles and several parts of my book, but this living at a distance prevents me; by reason of the special grace which I received through the supreme goodness of the Most Blessed Virgin during the year of contagion in Venice,[3] I am bounden by a vow to visit the Most Holy House at Loreto; I hope, with the Lord's help, soon to fulfill it, on which occasion I would come to Rome, if it pleased the Lord to let me, and present my service to Y. Rev^nce personally, and delight in the view and most noble sound of your most noble instrument, and receive the honor of your most virtuous discourse.

I have seen [the instrument] drawn upon a piece of paper that you sent me, which far from diminishing my desire has increased it. And since in the said second letter you ordered me to apply to Scapino,[4] that I might send Y. Rev^nce the drawings of the many strange instruments he plays, I was greatly disappointed, for I had entertained a deep desire to take this occasion to serve you and I could not, as he is appearing at Modena and not in Venice; but I have used a little diligence with certain friends, that at least they might describe to me whatever they could remember; and so they have given me the present piece of paper, which I now send to Y. Rev^nce herewith. But I have not failed to write to a friend, [asking] that he charge himself with getting the drawings of those which are most different from the common kind. I have never seen them myself, but from the said slight information which I am sending, it seems to me they are novel as to their shape but not their harmony, as they all fall within the harmonies of the instruments which we use. What I saw thirty years ago at Mantua, played and made by a certain Arab who had just come from Turkey and was lodged at the court of the Lord of Mantua my Master, was a cithern of the same size as ours, stringed with the same strings, and played in like manner, which was different in this, that its cover was half of wood, on the side of the neck, and half of parchment, stretched tightly and glued about the rim of the cithern, on the lower side; whose strings were likewise attached to its lower rim and rested upon a bridge which was placed in the middle of that parchment; and the little finger of this person's hand causing the parchment to quiver as

43

he played the harmonies, those harmonies emerged with a *trem-olo*-motion that had a most pleasing effect, and I have never heard a novel thing more to my liking. I shall be alert, and if I am told of anything which you may like, I will surely send you a little drawing of it at once. I entreat you to keep me in your good graces as your servant, and kiss your hand in all affection and reverence, praying that O[ur] L[ord] may give you a fullness of joy.

From Venice this 2nd Feb^ry 1634.

Y. Most Illustr^s Rev^nce's

Most devoted servant

Claudio Monteverdi

[= Letter 30], 294–97.—Tr. by editor.

38   CLAUDIO MONTEVERDI TO THE PROCURATORS OF ST. MARK, VENICE [It.]

[Venice, 9 June 1637]

Most Illustr^s and Exc^nt L^ds Honble Proc^trs

I Claudio Monteverdi Master of the Chapel at St. Mark's most humble servant of Your Exc^s and of the Most Ser^ne Rep^c come humbly unto your presence in order to make known to you how that Domenico Aldegati cantor at St. Mark's yesterday morning which was the 8 of the present month of June 1637 before the great door of that Church in the hour of the greatest concourse and while the greatest number of Cantors and players were present with whom was also one Benivento Beniventi a musician who was distributing among the Cantors and players certain moneys given him by the Nuns of Santo Daniele for the Vespers which they had celebrated before the processional raising of the Body of Saint John, Duke of Alexandria, whether because he had not received any of the said moneys or because his share had been smaller compared with the other shares, which I do not know as I never meddle in the money-interests of the Cantors, lacking all cause and all justification [and] showing respect neither for the office I hold from the Most Ser^ne Rep^c nor for my own and my priest-hood [1] nor for the honor of my family and of my virtue. But

44

driven by willful rage and with a loud and clamorous voice, after some base ill-usage of my person designed so as to assemble more than fifty people in a semicircle a part of whom were foreigners, among whom were present

Mr. Gio. Batt.a called the Bolognese cantor of the Chapel
Mr. Gasparo Zorino of Brescia who plays the Contrabass
Mr. Alvise Lipomani
Mr. D[on] Anibale Romano cantor of the Chapel
Mr. Gio. Batt.a of Padua who plays the trombone and the said
Mr. Bonivento Boniventi who distributed the said moneys. He said these very words which some of the said witnesses reported to me:

The Master of the Chapel is of a buggerish breed; a thieving . . . cuckold and many other wicked affronts, then he added: and I . . . him and his protectors and so that everyone may understand me I speak of that thieving . . . cuckold of a Claudio Monteverde and I say this to you Bonivento so that you may report it to him on my behalf.

I therefore come to the feet of Your Exc^s not as Claudio Monteverdi the priest for as such I forgive him everything and pray God that He may do likewise, but as Master of the Chapel whose authority derives from the Kingly hand of the Most Ser^{ne} Rep^c begging that you will not consent it to remain thus ill-used and affronted; nor my virtue nor the honor of my family which is protected by the most ser^{ne} hand of this most ser^{ne} Rep^c; but that the other cantors may take the memory of this man as an example, so that they will stay within honorable bounds with regard to him who bears the name of Master of the Chapel; otherwise in order to avoid a second occasion through him or other compeers of his I should be forced to request my discharge so that I might go and take shelter in the freeholds left me by my ancestors [which are] few but enough to support me far from such evils and licentious occasions; hoping in this as a fair cause I bow to the ground before you.

   I Claudio Monteverdi have written this and beg
   that this man's life may not be harmed.

Domenico de' Paoli, *Claudio Monteverdi* (Milan: Ulrico Hoepli, 1945), 302–304.—Tr. by editor.

39   HENRY LAWES TO JOHN MILTON, [HORTON?] [Eng.]

[London, spring 1638]

Sᵣ

I have sent you wᵗʰ this, A letter from my Lord warden of the Cinque-portes under his hand & seale, wᶜʰ wilbe A sufficient warrant, to Justify yoᵣ goinge out of the Kings Dominions. if you intend to wryte yoᵣselfe you canot have a safer Convoy for both, than from Suffolke House, but that I leave to yoᵣ Owne Consideration & remaine

yoᵣ
faithfull frend
& servant
Henry Lawes

Willa McClung Evans, *Henry Lawes: Musician and Friend of Poets* (New York: Modern Language Association, 1941), 150.

40   HEINRICH SCHÜTZ TO THE ELECTOR JOHANN GEORG I OF SAXONY, DRESDEN [G.]

[Dresden, 14 January 1651]
Most Submissive Memorial.
To the
Most Serene Highness the Elec-
tor of Saxony, Burgrave of Magdeburgk,
My most gracious Lord.
Most Serene Highness, High-born Elector
Most Gracious Lord,

With the present most submissive tribute of my little Work,[1] Now brought out under Y. Elect. Highness' exalted Name, I am prompted to touch somewhat upon the rather toilsome Life I have led from Youth until now. I beg with deep Devotion that Y. Elect. Highness will not be wholly undisposed to receive this with favor and to examine it at Your leisure. Viz.: Not long after I had come into this World (: in the Yr. 1585, on St. Burckhard's day [2] :), Indeed already in my thirteenth Year, I came

46

away from my Late Parents' house in Weissenfels and have always lived abroad from that Time forward. At first I served for several years as chorister at the Court Chapel of my Lord the Landgrave Moritz [3] in Cassel, but was kept at School and brought up to learn Latin and other tongues as well as Music.

And as it was never my Late Parents' Wish that I should make Music my Profession then or later, I betook myself to the University of Marpurgk on their advice after I had lost my Treble voice (: together with a Brother of mine, who later became a Doctor of Laws and died in Leibzigk a few Years ago, while serving in Y. Elect. Highness' Supreme Court :), my intention being to pursue, besides Music, those other Studies which I had begun in some measure, pick a definite Profession, and afterwards gain in it an Honorable Station. But this purpose of mine was soon unsettled (: doubtless through the will of God :), for my Lord the Landgrave Moritz came to Marpurgk one day (: he may perhaps have observed, while I was employed as Chorister at His Court, whether Nature had endowed me with any gift for Music :) and let me carry out the following Recommendation: Since, at that Time, a very famous if elderly Musician and Composer [4] was still alive in Italy, I should therefore not miss the opportunity of hearing him and gaining some [knowledge] from Him; and the aforementioned Princ.^ly Highness ordered that a yearly Stipend of 200 thlr. be presented to me for the Accomplishment of that Journey. Then (: being a young Man, and eager to see the World besides :) I quite willingly accepted the Recommendation with submissive Gratitude, whereupon I set out for Venice in the Yr. 1609, against my Parents' Wishes. On my arrival (: and after I had stayed with my master for a while :), I soon observed the Weightiness and Difficulty of the Study which I was undertaking in Composition, and how unfounded and poor a beginning I had made in it so far; and I repented very much, therefore, that I had turned away from those Studies which are common at the German Universities and in which I had already made some progress. Nevertheless, I was forced to dispose myself to patience and to apply myself to what had brought me there. Wherefore I put all my previous Studies out of hand from that Time forward and began to study Music only with all possible diligence, and to try how far I might succeed in it. Then, with God's help, I made such progress in it, in all modesty, that three [sic] years after (: and One Year

47

before I returned from Italy :) I had my First small Musical Work printed there in the Italian tongue,[5] to the particular acclaim of the most distinguished Musicians then at Venice, and sent it thence to my Lord the Landgrave Moritz (: to whom I also Dedicated it in submissive Gratitude :). Having published my aforesaid First small Work, I was exhorted and encouraged not only by my Preceptor Johann Gabriel, But also by the Master of the Chapel [6] and other most distinguished Musicians there to persevere in the Study of Music, for I should comfort myself with excellent successes therein. And as I remained One more year after this (: although at my Parents' expense :) in order to learn somewhat more from these Studies, it Happened that my above-mentioned Preceptor died in Venice, whom I accompanied to his place of Rest. On his deathbed, he had disposed out of special affection that I should receive one of the Rings he left behind as a remembrance of him; which was indeed presented and handed to me after his death by his Father Confessor, an Augustinian Monk (: from the Cloister at which Dr. Luther once sojourned [7] :). The abovesaid grant I had received from my Lord the Landgrave Moritz in Marpurgk was ended, for whoever wished to learn from that supremely gifted Man might not absent himself longer than I.

Now when I left Italy for the first time in the Yr. 1613 and had returned to Germany, I privately resolved to hold back for a few years the good musical foundations I had by then acquired and hide them until I should have Schooled them somewhat further, whereupon I could bring honor upon myself through the publication of a meritorious work. Nor did I then lack for Counsel or inducement from my Parents and kinsfolk whose opinion, briefly, was that I should endeavor to use my Qualities, slight as they were, and seek advancement by other means, and treat Music as a secondary matter. At length I was prevailed upon to heed their repeated, ceaseless Admonitions and was on the point of seeking out the Books I had previously put out of hand; but as God the almighty ordained (: who without doubt had set me apart from birth for the Profession of Music :), I was engaged to come here to Dresden and serve at the forthcoming Princely Baptism of my Lord the Duke August, the Present Administrator of Magdeburgk Archbishopric, in the Yr. 1614 (: I do not know whether at the instance of my Lord Christoff von Loos, then privy Councilor, or of Councilor Wolf-

48

fersdorff, Captain of Weissenfels :). And having come here and
sustained an Examination, I was forthwith most graciously
offered the Direction of your Music in Y. Elect. Highness' name.
Whereupon my Parents and Kinsfolk, and I too, felt the presence
of the unalterable Will of God as to my Person; and so a Goal
was set to my wandering purposes. And I was prompted not to
reject the Honorable condition I had been offered, but to accept
it with most submissive Gratitude and to vow I would take
charge of [the direction] with all the diligence at my disposal.
Y. Elect. Highness will, I hope, recollect in some measure what
my slight, yet not careless, Functions have been since the Yr.
1615 (: in which year I personally assumed the Office here, and
shall therein continue so long as it shall please God and Y. Elect.
Highness :), that is, for over 35 Years until now. And I do
indeed praise the Charity and mercy God has shown me so far
(: over so long a Period :) in that, besides my Private Studies
and the publication of various Musical Works, I have waited
most submissively on Y. Elect. Highness from the beginning of
my Direction at many and sundry Solemnities which have
occurred the while; Such as Imperial, Royal, Electoral, and Princely
Meetings at home and abroad, but more Especially your own
beloved Elect. Children's weddings one and all, no less than their
Christian Baptisms (: saving none, except those of the Present
Lady Landgravine of Darmstadt, and of my Lord the Duke
Johann Georg the Elector Apparent :). I have ever been diligent,
too, in spreading the fame of Y. Elect. Highness' Court Chapel
among other [nations] in Germany as much as possible and have,
I hope, helped to maintain its glory and reputation in some
measure, up to the present hour. Now I most heartily wish that
I could continue having charge over Your Elect. Highness'
Court Chapel in the Manner practised by me until now; but I
cannot by any means trust myself or venture to serve it fittingly
any longer, nor uphold at my present age the rather good name
I gained in younger Years: not only because of the ceaseless Studying, Traveling, writing, and other constant labors in which I
have, in all modesty, been engaged since youth (: which were
absolutely incumbent upon my weighty Profession and Office,
whose difficulties and Hardships only few can really judge of, in
my opinion, not even, indeed, a great part of our scholars, for
such Studies are not pursued at our German Universities :), But
also because old age has now come upon me, and my sight and
49

vital strength have waned. And unless I wish to place my health in imminent danger and, perhaps, sink to the ground, I must henceforth abstain and desist as much as possible, according to the Physicians' Advice, from ceaseless Study, writing, and reflection. For these reasons, therefore, I am inevitably obliged to submit this herewith, in all humbleness, to the gracious consideration of Your Elect. Highness and at the same time to beg with submissive Devotion that you will be Graciously pleased to transfer me henceforth to a somewhat quieter Condition (: not only for the reasons I have Here set forth, But also in view of the fact that Your Elect. Highness' dearest Princely Children are all wedded by now :); and to release me from ordinary service (: so that I may collect and Complete the Musical Works I began in my Youth and have them Printed in my memory :); and at the same time to have me recognized and declared for a Pensioner, to whatever degree it may please Your Elect. Highness. In which case I should even bear it if it graciously pleased Y. Elect. Highness to have my Present salary reduced somewhat. Yet (: insofar as Y. Elect. Highness is unwilling to have me leave your Chapel or to take another Master of the Chapel now, But will be satisfied with the poor services I shall be able to offer with my Strength ebbing daily :) I am both willing and bounden to persevere, to give all possible aid, and to be at pains that I may continue to deserve the Title of [Master of the Chapel] to Y. Elect. Highness and to your exalted house and, I hope, take [that title] with me to the grave in the end; if only Another, qualified Person could henceforth be attached to me to ease the burden of my work, who would busy himself daily with the young people now being brought up in the Electoral Chapel, continue the necessary Exercises, at times also assign the Music and beat the Time in Their midst: especially since all those old Musicians with whom I entered upon my Direction 35 Years ago are all [sic] dead by now, and the very few remaining are no longer particularly suited to further service because of bodily impediments and old age. For it may yet come about, as my strength declines still further (: Y. Elect. Highness will graciously forgive me for mentioning this :), as it did to a not badly qualified Old Cantor living in a Noted place; I knew him well, and he wrote to me for some Time and complained bitterly that his young Town-Councilors were most displeased with the ancient Fashion of his Music and would, therefore, gladly be rid of him; that therefore they had explicitly told him to his face, at the Town Hall, that a Thirty Years' Tailor and a Thirty Years' Cantor were quite useless in this World; [8] for it cannot be but that the young World tends soon to tire of the old customs and Fashions, and to change them. And although I do not expect such a thing from my Lords the Sons of Y. Elect. Highness (: my Gracious, beneficent Masters of long standing :), it may yet happen to me at the hands of others, such as some newly arrived Musicians who, turning their backs on the old, commonly give preference to Their new Fashion, albeit on meager grounds. And since my Lord the Duke Johann Georg the Elector Apparent's Italian Eunuch Andrea Bontempi has often let it be known that He especially devoted himself to Composition since he was young, even more than to Singing, and since of his own accord He has gladly offered to serve in my stead and direct the Music every time I should request it, I have thought well to disclose as much to Y. Elect. Highness at the conclusion of this writing of mine, in order to learn Your gracious opinion on the matter.[9] Namely, whether I might, with your most gracious Consent, employ the abovesaid Andrea Buontempi [sic] and let him direct the Music often in my stead? It is my humble View that Y. Elect. Highness could suffer this to take place (: though not without some dispositions :) the more easily, and at the same time put it on trial by seeing and listening Awhile, since he is seeking No increase in his Salary for such services, nor any Change in his Title; for, with the Maintenance allotted him by his Gracious Lord the Elector Apparent, he is prepared to be content with either Way. And this young man is very well qualified for the Function; I have received enough intelligence, too, from Venice (: where He has sojourned for 8 Years :) to the effect that He has often publicly directed the music in their Churches in the place of the Master of the Chapel, on several celebrated holidays there; which gives even less cause to doubt his good Qualities. And in all his other dealings he has so far appeared to be A discreet, courteous, and tractable fine young man. I now beg to be graciously informed as to Y. Elect. Highness' Will in this Matter, since it would not be proper for me to make constant use of this Person's Services without Y. Elect. Highness' foreknowledge. Whom I loyally commend to the Mighty protection of the Highest for abiding, complete bodily health, long life, blissful Governance and all other good things of the Soul and body which yourself may wish,

51

while [commending] myself most submissively and obediently
to the constant Elect. Clemency. *Datum* at Dresden on the 14th
Day of January. In the Year of Christ Our Only Redeemer and
Saviour, 1651.

>   Y. Elect. Highness'
>   Most submissive most dutiful old servant
>   Heinrich Schütz Master of the Chapel Mp.[10]

[= Letter 35], 207–16.—Tr. by editor.

41   JEAN BAPTISTE LULLY TO JEAN BAPTISTE COLBERT, PARIS [Fr.]

[Paris, 3 June 1672]

My Lord,

Since I had the honor of speaking to you regarding the Académie royale de Musique,[1] I have suffered fresh chicaneries daily
of which I make bold to send you the latest, whence you will
learn, my Lord, that they allege falsehoods throughout, and in
the first place when they say that they obtained the King's letters
patent under Perrin's name; and in the second place by alleging
that I took the King by surprise, when they themselves presented
several petitions to His Majesty and knew his intentions better
than I. You know, my Lord, that I have not followed any course
in this matter other than the one you prescribed for me, and that
in the beginning I believed they were following it also. They,
however, knew better than to submit to your judgment, being
well aware that you would suffer none of the impostures which
they are devising and mean to impose upon the Parliament, and
with which you are better acquainted than anyone in the world.

You have been so gracious as to let me hope for a word in my
favor to M. du Coudray Géniers, my reporter. If I may be so
bold as to beseech you, my Lord, to undeceive him by the same
means concerning all that they allege in their request, you would
show me the greatest benevolence in the world, since, to conclude,
I am utterly afflicted at seeing myself condemned to fight against
falsehoods, while I should be working at what the King has

commanded me and you are so gracious as to honor with your
protection.

I hope, my Lord, that through your kindness the King will
grant me the hall at the Louvre,[2] where, despite the chicaneries
of the trial, I shall immediately set the work going and have
the honor of seeing you with M. Quinault[3] to show you some
projects for the return of the King which, I have no doubt, will
succeed, having your approbation.

I am, my Lord, with all due respect, your most humble and
obedient servant.

Jean Baptiste Lully

From Paris, this 3ᵈ June 1672.

Julien Tiersot, *Lettres de Musiciens écrites en français du XVᵉ au XXᵉ siècle,*
I (Turin: Bocca Frères Éditeurs, 1924), 36–37.—Tr. by editor.

42   JEAN BAPTISTE LULLY TO JEAN BAPTISTE COLBERT, PARIS [Fr.]

[Paris, early spring 1673]

My Lord is most humbly entreated to inform the King that
the Académie royale de Musique requests His Majesty's permission
to elevate the part of the hall in the Palais Royal that is above
the Theater,[1] such elevation being feasible without any prejudice
to the symmetry of the above-named Palais, and without touching
any of the Apartments that are in the said hall.

It also requests that some beams which are broken and on the
point of falling down be changed before the work there is
commenced, because it would be impossible to build any machines
there with safety.[2]

There are, at either side of the Arch of the Theater, two stone
pillars that serve no function, and that on the contrary greatly
obstruct the space for the Decorations: His Majesty is most
humbly entreated to grant permission to remove them and make
use of the stone for the above-named elevation of the Theater's
walls. All this with the stipulation that the Places and works
proposed shall first be visited by the Officers of His Majesty's
buildings, and approved by my Lord Colbert.

The Académie being presently under the necessity of paying Rent for the place it now occupies,[3] of restoring it when moving away, of having the hall [*sic*] and the machines conveyed to the Palais Royal, of paying Rent for the Comédiens Italiens and of making the disbursements necessary for the construction of the new Theater, not including the ordinary wages and maintenance of the Académiciens, all these expenses are so great that It most humbly requests His Majesty to consider that its establishment or its ruin depends entirely on a new Room in the Palais Royal before the winter.

Jean Baptiste Lully

[= Letter 41], 488.—Tr. by editor.

43   MATTHEW LOCKE TO HENRY PURCELL, LONDON [Eng.]

[London, 16 March (1677 or somewhat earlier)]

Dear Harry,

Some of the gentlemen of His Majesties musick will honor my poor lodgings with their company this evening, and I would have you come and join them: bring with thee, Harry, thy last anthem, and also the canon we tried over together at our last meeting. Thine in all kindness,

M. Locke.

Savoy, March 16.

William H. Cummings, *Purcell* (London: Sampson Low, Marston, Searle, & Rivington, 1881), 27.

44   THOMAS PURCELL TO JOHN GOSTLING, CANTERBURY [Eng.]

[London, 8 February 1679]

This ffor Mr. John Gostling, Chaunter of y^e quire of Canterbury Cathedral.   London y^e 8th of ffeb. $\frac{9}{78}$.[1]

Sir, I have re^{ed} y^e favor of yours of y^e 4th with y^e inclosed for my sonne Henry: I am sorry wee are like to be without you soe long as yours mentions: but 'tis very likely you may have a summons to appeare among us sooner than you imagine: for my sonne is composing wherin you will be chiefly concern'd. However, your occasions and tyes where you are must be considered and your conveniences ever complyde withall: in ye meantime assure yourself I shall be carefull of your concern's heir by minding and refreshing our master's memory of his Gratious promis when there is occasion. My wife returns thanks for ye compliment with her servis: and pray ye give both our respects and humble services to Dr. Belk and his Lady, and beleeve ever that I am, Sir, your affectionate and humble servant,

T. Purcell.

Dr. Perce is in toune but I have not seen him since. I have perform'd y^e compliments to Dr. Blow, Will Turner, etc.[2]

F faut: and E lamy [3] are preparing for you.

[= Letter 43], 28.

45   ARCANGELO CORELLI TO MATTEO ZANI, BOLOGNA [It.]

[Rome, 17 October 1685]

I have received, in your very courteous letter, the sheet with the passage from the third sonata, where your Virtuosi are having difficulty, and this does not surprise me at all, while thereby I gain a full understanding of their knowledge, which barely extends beyond the first principles of Composition, and harmonic Modulat.^{n}, since if they had advanced farther in the art, and knew its refinements and profundities, and the essence of

55

Harmony, and in what manner it can delight, and exalt the
human mind, they would not entertain such scruples, which
ordinar.^{ly} are born of ignorance. By strict applicat.^{n} over many
years, and by frequenting the worthiest Music Professors in
Rome, I have made it my study to acquaint myself with their
docum.^{ts}, and their examples, knowing full well that whatever
one does must be governed by reason, or by the example of the
most excellent Professors; nevertheless, to gratify the curiosity
of your V.^{si} and to demonstrate to them that I can answer for
this passage they cannot fathom, as for any other which I have
printed, and that I know fundament.^{ly} why I have it, and wish
it to be so, I will explain myself in part. One may already see
in this passage that I have marked the fifths over the Bass to
show that I, knowing what a fifth is, have not done this by
mistake, but at my own election, to lay bare my intention, for
had I, instead of the quaver rest, put a point to the preceding note,
which would have the same value, the Musical Beginners, who
know nothing beyond the first rules, would find no difficulty
in it whatsoever, but I, wishing the note to be detached and
deadened, as it seemed to me it would sound better, have done
thus. Besides, to cast somewhat more light on my intention for
those who are *in obscuris,* if they will but ponder the beginning
of that little piece of modulation, they will find that it begins
and continues a time-pattern [*tempo*], wherefore it must of
necessity, for those who understand the art, pursue it, if one
wishes to prolong the beauty of the Harmony, according to
the teaching of Euclid, who says = *Tempus est mensura motus
secundum prius, ac posterius.*[1] Therefore, let the beginning,
the middle, and the end of this modulation of mine be pondered,
and my intent.^{n} will be known. Moreover, to satisfy your
Virtuosi, and in order not to rely wholly on my own opinion,
I have shown the above passage to Messrs. Fran.^{co} Foggia,
Antimo Liberati, Matteo Simonelli,[2] and they, all of one mind,
have replied that it is perfectly sound, and that whosoever
has difficulty [with it] does not understand the tie, and that,
should another man write a similar passage in a similar progression,
they would be bound always to defend him. I shall not amplify
farther, as it seems to me that this little notice is sufficient
to gratify the Curiosity of your Virtuosi, and at the same time
to impart some small erudition to their apprenticeship in the
art; I only pray that you will keep me in your affections, and

Command me if I am worthy of Serving you, and I devotedly kiss your hands.

I am, Most Ill.ˢ and Most Rev.ᵗ S.ʳ,

Your very Dev.ᵗ and Obl.ᵈ S.ᵛⁿᵗ

Rome, 17 Oct.ʳ 1685   Arcangelo Corelli

Mr. Bernardo Pasquini and Verdoni send you their affect.ᵗᵉ greetings, as does Paolo Maria, who pays you his cordial respects.[3]

Mario Rinaldi, *Arcangelo Corelli* (Milan: Edizioni Curci, 1953), 429–30. —Tr. by editor.

46   DIETRICH BUXTEHUDE TO THE ELDERS OF THE COMMERCIAL GUILDS, LÜBECK [G.]

[Lübeck, 5 February 1689]

Most Noble, Esteemed, and Eminent Lordships,
very worthy Patrons,

Having, by the grace of God, brought my recently-presented Evening Music of the Prodigal Son[1] to an end after the utmost efforts and unsparing diligence, so that I doubt not, My Highly Honored Lordships and worthy Patrons, but that you will be inclined to be satisfied with me for it; now therefore, in keeping with your well-known kindness, so praiseworthy this past year, for which I owe you the most submissive thanks, condescend to favor me with a further yearly honorarium, that in the future I may have the greater cause to continue this Musical *Ornamentum* and owe that affection for your Most Noble, Esteemed, and Eminent Favors, in the expectation of which I submissively commend you to the generous protection of God, myself, however, to your constant good will.

	And remain
Lübeck	Most submissively obliged
this 5th of February	To Your
A°· 1689.	Most Noble, Esteemed,
	and Eminent Favors
	Dietrich Buxtehude m. p.[2]

A. Hagedorn, "Briefe von Dietrich Buxtehude," *Mittheilungen des Vereins für Lübeckische Geschichte und Alterthumskunde,* III (1887–88), 196.—Tr. by editor.

47   ALESSANDRO SCARLATTI TO PRINCE FERDINAND DE' MEDICI, FLORENCE [It.]

Your Royal Highness   [Rome, 30 May 1705]

My son Domenico [1] humbly places himself and my heart at the feet of Y. Royal H. in token of our debt of deep observance and most humble service. I have severed him by force from Naples, where, though his talent had a place, yet the place was ill-suited to his talent. I am sending him away also from Rome, because Rome offers no roof to Music, which lives here like a beggar. this Son, who is an Eagle that has sprouted Wings, must not stay idly in the nest: nor must I prevent his flight.

Since the Virtuoso Nicolino of Naples is passing through here on his way to Venice, I thought to have him go along; and, furnished with nothing save his ability (much increased since he was able to stay with me, apart from enjoying the honor of person^{ly} serving Y. R^{yl} H., these three years), he goes forth almost a wanderer, to meet whatever opportunities may present themselves to make himself known, which it were useless to await in Rome today. I intend, before he proceeds upon his way to try his fortune, to have him present himself at the feet of Y. R^{yl} H. [and] receive and execute the high and hon^{d} Commands of his and my Greatest mighty Lord, and most clement Master and Benefactor. it is a glory, honor, and advantage to him and me that the World knows us for Y. R^{yl} H.'s most humble servants. this consideration comforts my soul, and gives me occasion to expect the best success for the Pilgrimage of this Son; for, having commended him to Providence and to divine Protection, as to the supreme origin of all good, I next present my most humble plea to the high, most powerful Guardianship of Y. R^{yl} H., to whom I humble myself and do obeisance with the deepest respect and obedience, as for the remainder of my life.

Y. R^{yl} H.'s   Rome 30 May 1705

most humble, devoted, and obliged servant
Alessandro Scarlatti

Facsimile of the autograph: Accademia Musicale Chigiana, *Gli Scarlatti* (Siena: Libreria Editrice Ticci, 1940), 51–52.—Tr. by editor.

48   JOHANN SEBASTIAN BACH TO THE PARISHIONERS
OF ST. BLASIUS'S CHURCH, MÜHLHAUSEN [G.]

[Mühlhausen, 25 June 1708]

Your Magnificence, Honored and Noble Sirs, Honored and
Learned Sirs, Honored and Wise Sirs, Most Gracious Patroni
and Gentlemen! [1]

The manner in which Your Magnificence and my Most Respected
Patrons most graciously engaged my humble self for the post
of organist of the Church of St. Blasius when it became vacant
a year ago, and your graciousness in permitting me to enjoy
a better living, I must ever acknowledge with obedient thanks.
Even though I should always have liked to work toward the
goal, namely, a well-regulated church music, to the Glory of
God and in conformance with your wishes, and would, according
to my small means, have helped out as much as possible with
the church music that is growing up in almost every township,
and often better than the harmony that is fashioned here, and
therefore have acquired from far and wide, not without cost,
a good store of the choicest church compositions, just as I
have also fulfilled my duty in delivering the project for remedying
the faults of the organ and should gladly have discharged
every other duty of my office—yet it has not been possible to
accomplish all this without hindrance, and there are, at present,
hardly any signs that in the future a change may take place
(although it would rejoice the souls belonging to this very
Church); to which I should humbly add that, however simple
my manner of living, I can live but poorly, considering the
house rent and other most necessary expenses.

Now, God has brought it to pass that an unexpected change
should offer itself to me, in which I see the possibility of a more
adequate living and the achievement of my goal of a well-
regulated church music without further vexation, since I have
received the gracious admission of His Serene Highness of
Saxe-Weimar into his Court Chapel and Chamber Music.

Accordingly, I have felt I must bring my intention in this
matter, with obedient respect, to the notice of my Most
Gracious Patrons, and at the same time beg them to content
themselves for the time being with the modest services I have

59

rendered to the Church and to furnish me at the earliest moment with a gracious dismissal. If I can contribute anything further to the service of Your Honors' Church I will do so more in deed than in words, remaining forever,

Honored Sir, Most Gracious Patrons and Gentlemen, Your Honors' most obedient servant

Joh. Seb. Bach

Mühlhausen, June 25, Anno 1708

Hans T. David and Arthur Mendel (eds.), *The Bach Reader: A Life of Johann Sebastian Bach in Letters and Documents* (New York: W. W. Norton & Company, Inc., 1945), 60–61.

49   GIOVANNI BATTISTA BASSANI TO JACOPO ANTONIO PERTI, BOLOGNA [It.]

[Ferrara, 28 July 1710]

Most Illustr.ª Sʳ, My Particˡʳ Masᵗʳ

In order to serve this Cathedral, where I am Master of the Chapel, I find myself engaged in composing many compositions, viz. the Introits to the Principal Solemnities, such as Epiphany, Easter, Ascension, Pentecost, Corpus Dñi, St. Peter, and all the other similar solemnities, nor do I write the Introits alone, but also the Gradual after the Epistle, and the Offertory after the Gospel, as well as the Post-communion after the Agnus Dei, and write the sequences too, for those solemnities that have them, like Easter, Pentecost and Corpus Dõni. now these compositions are for four concerted voices, with their support [*Ripieni*], and Violins—those who ordered them of me are already paying for the paper and the copying, so that the only trouble left to me is that of composing: I have produced, and continue incessantly to compose, a great number of the above-mentioned compositions, and the said compositions must remain at the above-mentioned Cathedral, viz. in the Choir, in perpetuity, to be used yearly on the above-mentioned solemnities. I know that one composer of music may ask for a higher or lower price than another, but I am perplexed in this; meanwhile, he whose office it is to satisfy me keeps telling me to consider how many compositions I am to write, this is true, but there is also much toil in it, but as for that I shall do whatever can be done. I beg a favor of your kindness and it is this, if you were engaged to write the above-mentioned compositions for your chapel of San Petronio what would you ask, viz. for the introit, Gradual, Sequence, Offertory, Post-communion, but this is the favor, viz. each item separately, thus

Introit, —— Scudi,[1]
Gradual, —— Scudi,
Sequence, —— Scudi,
Offertory, —— Scudi,
Post Communion, —— Scudi.

If you will grant my request, and this so that I may be guided, be advised not to write Lire, for they are not used in Ferrara, but scudi and baiocchi, and forgive my boldness, and be assured that I will remain most obliged to you and, greeting you, remain,

Sir,
Your Very Devoted Obl[d] Serv[nt]
Gio: Battā Bassani.

Ferrara, 28 July 1710

Francesco Pasini, "Notes sur la Vie de Giovanni Battista Bassani," *Sammelbände der Internationalen Musikgesellschaft,* VII (1906), 589.—Tr. by editor.

50   BENEDETTO MARCELLO TO JACOPO ANTONIO PERTI, BOLOGNA [It.]

[Venice, 4 October 1711]

Most Illustr[s] and Hon[d] S[r].
As the time for the reunion of the Signori Accademici Filar-
monici draws near, I renew my application to you so
that I may be admitted by them to their glorious Assembly.
To that end, the Rev. Angelo Pradesi will hand you a Mass
à Capella [sic], lately composed by me for His Holiness
Clement XI, which I beg you will have those Virtuosi
Maestri and Accademici hear and indulgently receive as a
present, should they accept me as their unworthy fellow.

I must, however, justify myself before you regarding certain
things in the said Mass, and first

That in some places I have made use of modulations (though
in this style [1] one always strictly adheres to the Tone),
only to lend more gracefulness to the melody now and
then or more expression to the words: to which, further,
the themes impelled me and several Cannons [*sic*] that
are in it. I do not think, therefore, that I shall be gravely
censured for doing this purely for the sake of gracefulness,
which is usually effected by certain departures, so long as
it is well-ordered; and this I have observed in other
Authors. Secondly

I know that, in Cannons, the final note of the Part which
enters last should form the Cannon's end; but I have
neglected this observance in certain places in order to make
the cadences more harmonious, for otherwise they would
be very dry; and I have noticed that severity in many
grave authors, but only in perpetual Cannons which return
to their beginning; but in my case, having to proceed
with the words, I have sometimes been obliged to reach
the cadences by means of some filling-in, as your talent
will easily discern from the signs $\cdot\,{}^{\cdot\,S\,\cdot}_{\cdot\,S\,\cdot}$

In addition, I have sometimes made use of diminishing
black notes, as it seemed to me that in this grave style
some diminution would not be a defect, if it was but
melodious and to the point.

I have said all this for my own peace of mind, and
intend that it should be wholly subject to the meditation
of the Signori Accademici who, as I hope, will lovingly
correct me: Certain it is that I have followed a path
which has sweated other brows than mine, and I have
attempted to combine some good taste with the natural
sterility [2] of the Composition, mindful that

     Omne tulit punctum qui miscuit utile dulci [3]
and this my dear M.r Giacomo Perti will recognize if he
will be pleased to have it performed under his able
direction.

I therefore commend it to you with all my heart, for it is a
specially arduous product of my feeble invention, and I
make bold to ask you, for the love of God, to give me

your esteemed opinion and that of anyone who should be pleased to correct me. Meanwhile I pray that Heaven may grant you a full share of its blessings and me the occasion of hearing from you; and am most cordially,

Illustr^s S^r,

Venice, 4 Oct. 1711

Your Affect^e Obl^d Ser^t
Bened? Marcello.

Facsimile of the autograph: Andrea D'Angeli, *Benedetto Marcello: la vita—le opere* (Milan: Fratelli Bocca, 1946), between pp. 16 and 17.—Tr. by editor.

51　GEORGE FRIDERIC HANDEL TO JOHANN MATTHESON, HAMBURG [Fr.]

London,
Febr. 24, 1719.¹

Sir,

From the Letter which I have just received from you, dated the 21st inst., I find myself so far obliged to satisfy you more particularly than I have done in my preceding letters on the two points in question ² that I cannot but declare that my opinion generally concurs with what you have so well deduced & proved in your book ³ with regard to Solmization & the Greek Modes. The question seems to me to reduce itself to this: whether one should prefer an easy & most perfect Method to another that is accompanied by great difficulties capable not only of disgusting pupils with Music, but also of making them waste much precious time that could better be employed in plunging deeper into this art & in the cultivation of one's genius? It is not that I would put it forward that one cannot draw any use from Solmization: but since one can acquire the same knowledge in less time by the method presently employed with so much success, I do not see why one should not choose the path that leads more easily & in a shorter time to the desired end? As to the Greek Modes, I find, Sir, that you have said all there is to say on the subject. Knowledge of them is no

63

doubt necessary to those who would practise & execute ancient Music, which was composed according to these Modes; but since we have freed ourselves from the narrow bounds of ancient Music, I do not see of what use the Greek Modes can be for modern Music. Those are, Sir, my sentiments, and you would oblige me by letting me know whether they answer what you desired of me.

As for the second point, you can judge for yourself that it requires a great deal of concentration, which I cannot at present give to it because of the pressing business I have before me. As soon as I have freed myself from it somewhat, I will review the principal Epochs I have had in the course of my Profession, to show you the esteem & particular consideration with which I have the honor to be

Sir

your very humble & very
obedient servant
G. F. Handel.

Translation in: Erich H. Müller (ed.), *The Letters and Writings of George Frideric Handel* (London: Cassell and Company, Ltd., 1935), 80–81, revised by present editor in accordance with original text printed in Deutsch [= Letter 53], 86–87.

52   JOHANN SEBASTIAN BACH TO THE LEIPZIG TOWN COUNCIL [G.]

[Leipzig, 5 May 1723]

Whereas the Honorable and Most Wise Council of this Town of Leipzig have engaged me as Cantor of the Thomas-Schule and have desired an undertaking from me in respect to the following points, to wit:

(1) That I shall set the boys a shining example of an honest, retiring manner of life, serve the School industriously, and instruct the boys conscientiously;

(2) Bring the music in both the principal Churches of this town into good estate, to the best of my ability;

(3) Show to the Honorable and Most Wise Council all

proper respect and obedience, and protect and further everywhere as best I may its honor and reputation; likewise if a gentleman of the Council desires the boys for a musical occasion unhesitatingly provide him with the same, but otherwise never permit them to go out of the town to funerals or weddings without the previous knowledge and consent of the Burgomaster and Honorable Directors of the School currently in office;

(4) Give due obedience to the Honorable Inspectors and Directors of the School in each and every instruction which the same shall issue in the name of the Honorable and Most Wise Council;

(5) Not take any boys into the School who have not already laid a foundation in music, or are not at least suited to being instructed therein, nor do the same without the previous knowledge and consent of the Honorable Inspectors and Directors;

(6) So that the Churches may not have to be put to unnecessary expense, faithfully instruct the boys not only in vocal but also in instrumental music;

(7) In order to preserve the good order in the Churches, so arrange the music that it shall not last too long, and shall be of such a nature as not to make an operatic impression, but rather incite the listeners to devotion;

(8) Provide the New Church with good scholars;

(9) Treat the boys in a friendly manner and with caution, but, in case they do not wish to obey, chastise them with moderation or report them to the proper place;

(10) Faithfully attend to the instruction in the School and whatever else it befits me to do;

(11) And if I cannot undertake this myself, arrange that it be done by some other capable person without expense to the Honorable and Most Wise Council or to the School;

(12) Not go out of the town without the permission of the Honorable Burgomaster currently in office;

(13) Always so far as possible walk with the boys at funerals, as is customary;

(14) And shall not accept or wish to accept any office in the University without the consent of the Honorable and Learned Council;

Now therefore I do hereby undertake and bind myself faithfully to observe all of the said requirements, and on pain

65

of losing my post not to act contrary to them, in witness
whereof I have set my hand and seal to this agreement.

[signed] Johann Sebastian Bach

Done in Leipzig, 5 May 1723

[= Letter 48], 91–92.

53   GEORGE FRIDERIC HANDEL TO THE HOUSE
OF LORDS [Eng.]

[London, before 13 February 1727]

To the Right Honourable The Lords Spiritual and Temporal
in Parliament assembled,

The Humble Petition of George Frideric Handel

Sheweth,—

That your petitioner was born at Hall in Saxony, out of His
Majestie's Allegiance, but hath constantly professed the Protestant
Religion, and hath given Testimony of his Loyalty and Fidelity
to His Majesty and the good of this Kingdom,

Therefore the Petitioner humbly prays, That he may be added
to the Bill now pending, entituled 'An Act for Naturalisating
LOUIS SECHEHAYE' [1]

And your petitioner will ever pray, &c.,

George Frideric Handel.

Otto Erich Deutsch, *Handel: A Documentary Biography* (New York: W. W.
Norton & Company, Inc., [1954]), 202.

54   JEAN-PHILIPPE RAMEAU TO ANTOINE HOUDAR
DE LA MOTTE, [PARIS?] [Fr.]

[Paris, 25 October 1727]

Whatever reasons you may have, Sir, for not expecting from
my dramatic music a success as favorable as from that of an
author seemingly more experienced in that type of music, allow

me to oppose them and at the same time to justify the prejudice
I hold in my own favor, without pretending to derive further
advantages from my science than those you will perceive, as I
do, to be legitimate.

By "learned musician," one commonly means a man who
never misses the different ways of combining notes; but one
thinks of him as being so absorbed in these combinations that
he sacrifices all—common sense, feelings, wit, and reason. Now,
that is but a school-musician; of a school where only notes
matter, and nothing else: so that one is right in preferring to
him a musician who piques himself less upon science than upon
taste. Nevertheless, the latter, whose taste is formed merely by
comparisons within the reach of his sensations, can at best excel
only in certain kinds of music [genres], I mean in kinds
related to his temperament. Is he naturally tender? He expresses
tenderness. Is his character lively, playful, waggish, etc.? his
music answers accordingly. But draw him out of these characters
that are natural to him, and you will no longer recognize him.
Besides, since he derives everything from his imagination,
without any help from art in its connection with the expressions,
he exhausts himself at last. In his first ardor, he was quite
brilliant; but his fire wastes away in proportion as he wishes to
rekindle it, and one no longer finds in him anything but
tautologies and platitudes.

It would therefore be desirable that the theater have a musician
who should study nature before painting it and who, by means
of his science, should know how to choose those colors and
shades whose connection with the necessary expressions his wit
and taste should have made evident to him.

I am very far from believing that I am that musician, but,
at least, I have the advantage over the others of being
acquainted with the colors and shades of which they only have
a glimmering and which they employ suitably only by accident.
They have taste and imagination, but wholly limited to the
reservoir of their sensations, where the different objects are
gathered in a small portion of colors, beyond which they perceive
nothing more. Nature has not altogether deprived me of her
gifts, nor have I so delivered myself over to the combining of notes
as to forget their intimate tie with natural beauty, which alone
can afford pleasure, but which cannot easily be found in a soil
that lacks seeds and, above all, has yielded its last.

Inform yourself of the opinion that is held of two cantatas which were taken from me some twelve years ago and copies of which are so widely disseminated in France that I thought it best not to have them engraved, since I might lose their price unless I added to them some others, which I cannot do for lack of words. One of them is entitled *The Rape of Orithyia*: [1]   it has some recitative and some characterized airs; the other is entitled *Thetis,* in which you will notice the degree of anger I give to Neptune and Jupiter, according to whether it is proper to give more indifference or more passion to the one or the other, and according to whether it is proper for the orders of the one or the other to be obeyed.[2] It depends wholly on you whether you will come to hear how I have characterized the singing and dancing of the Savages who appeared at the Théâtre-Italien one or two years ago, and how I have rendered these titles: *The Sighs, The Tender Plaints, The Cyclopes, The Whirls* (that is to say the whirls of dust stirred up by strong winds), *The Conversation of the Muses,* a *Musette,* a *Tambourin,* etc.[3] You shall see, then, that I am no novice in art and that above all it does not appear I make great use of my science in my productions, in which I attempt to conceal art by means of art itself; for they are meant only for persons of taste and not at all for scholars, since there exist many of the former and almost none of the latter. I could let you hear some motets with great choruses, where you would recognize whether or not I feel what I wish to express. In short, here is enough matter to make you ponder.[4]

I am, with all possible esteem, Sir, your very humble and very obedient servant.

Rameau.

Louis Laloy, *Rameau* (Paris: Librairie Félix Alcan, 1919), 29–31.—Tr. by editor.

55   GEORG PHILIPP TELEMANN TO JOHANN GOTTFRIED WALTHER, [WEIMAR?] [G.]

[Hamburg, 20 December 1729]

Most noble, most especially honorable Sir,

That I have not, most noble Sir, answered yrs. esteemed before now is the fault of my many occupations; the writing from Lübeck [?], however, was delivered to me already several weeks ago.

Your relative in Auerstadt cannot have understood me aright, for my speech concerning the late Lippoldt was quite different from the account of it you give me; may he nevertheless rest in peace, and I will forget the whole affair.

Of your *Musica historica* I have [only] the letter A, because no more of it can be obtained here; [1] I find its arrangement quite different from what I had imagined it to be, wherefore I now dismiss some scruples I had entertained in its regard.

I wish you may derive much advantage from it and, for the rest, remain, with the highest regard,

Most noble Sir,

my most especially honorable Master's
very devoted servant
Georg Philip Telemann.

Hamburg, 20th Dec.
1729.

I was born at Magdeburg, of Henricus, a minister at the Church of the Holy Spirit, in the yr. 1681.

My schools were: the Alt-Stadt at Magdeburg, afterwards the Cathedral School, then that at Zellerfeld in the Harz, and finally the *Gymnasium* at Hildesheim.

The university was Leipzig, where I spent 4 years.

I pursued music early and completed an opera (which was also performed at Magdeburg) already at the age of 11 or 12, not to mention the church pieces and the motets for choir, of which I had already made a considerable number before, while at the same time I set several airs for the latter, poetically; no less did I learn the recorder and violin, and the clavier too, on which last I also applied myself to thorough bass. In all this, nature alone was my teacher, without the slightest instruction

69

[*sic*], unless it be that in the beginning I was taught on the clavier for a fortnight.

Regarding my duties, I directed the music already at Hildesheim, at St. Gothard's Church, by the authority of Lutheran Superintendent Riemer of that place.

In Leipzig I became *Direct*[*or*] *Mus*[*ices*] and organist at the new church; thereupon

Capellmeister to Count von Promnitz; further,

Concert- and soon after *Capell-Meister* as well as *Secretarius* at Eisenach; from which place I went, as

Capellmeister, to Frankfurth-am-Mayn, where, at the same time, I was entrusted with the management of the Imper[ial] *Palais* of the Frauenstein [Society], which had an account of more than 100000 fl. attached to it, and where I again received from Eisenach the post of *Capell-Meister, in absentia* [*von Haus*=*aus*], with a salary; finally, I am now

Director Mus: in Hamburg, still, as before, in the Eisenach service, and Correspondent too; here, 4 years ago, I also became *Capell-Meister in absentia* to Bayreuth, with a salary which, however, was dropped under the present Government.

What I have done in the Styles of music is well-known. At first it was the Polish, then followed the French, Church, Chamber, and Opera styles, and that which is called the Italian, which now engages me most of all.

La Mara [Marie Lipsius], *Musikerbriefe aus fünf Jahrhunderten* (Leipzig: Breitkopf & Härtel, [1886]), I, 148–51.—Tr. by editor.

56   GEORGE FRIDERIC HANDEL TO FRANCIS COLMAN, FLORENCE [Fr.]

London $\frac{19}{30}$ June,[1] 1730.

Sir,

Since I had the honor of writing to you, ways have been found of engaging Sig[ra] Merighi once more,[2] and as hers is a Contr'Alto voice it would suit us at present that the Woman to be engaged in Italy should be a Soprano. I am also writing to this effect to Mr. Swinny [3] by the same ordinary, recommending at the same time that any Woman he can suggest to you should be able to play men's Roles as well as Women's. There is reason to believe you have not yet engaged a Female Contr'Alto, but should this have been done, one ought to abide by it. I take the Liberty of asking you again that there should be no mention in the Contracts as to first, second, or third Roles, for that embarrasses us in the choice of Drama and causes great inconvenience besides. Thus, with your assistance, we hope to have a man and a Woman for the coming Season, which begins in the month of October of this Current year and ends in the month of July 1731, and we expect news of this with impatience in order to inform the Court of it.

It only remains for me to reiterate my assurances of the particular obligation under which I shall be for your Goodness towards me in this matter, and I have the honor to be with respectful affection

Sir

Your

very humble and obedient

Servant

George Frideric Handel.

Translation in Müller [= Letter 51], 84–85, revised by present editor in accordance with original text printed in Deutsch [= Letter 53], 256.

57   JOHANN SEBASTIAN BACH TO GEORG ERDMANN, DANZIG [G.]

[Leipzig, 28 October 1730]

Most Honored Sir,

Your Honor will have the goodness to excuse an old and faithful servant for taking the liberty of disturbing you with the present letter. It must be nearly four years since Your Honor favored me with a kind answer to the letter I sent you; I remember that at that time you graciously asked me to give you some news of what had happened to me, and I humbly take this opportunity of providing you with the same. You know the course of my life from my youth up until the change in my fortunes that took me to Cöthen as Capellmeister. There I had a gracious Prince, who both loved and knew music, and in his service I intended to spend the rest of my life. It must happen, however, that the said *Serenissimus* should marry a Princess of Berenburg, and that then the impression should arise that the musical interests of the said Prince had become somewhat lukewarm, especially as the new Princess seemed to be unmusical; and it pleased God that I should be called hither to be *Director Musices* and Cantor at the Thomas-Schule. Though at first, indeed, it did not seem at all proper to me to change my position of Capellmeister for that of Cantor. Wherefore, then, I postponed my decision for a quarter of a year; but this post was described to me in such favorable terms that finally (particularly since my sons seemed inclined toward [university] studies) I cast my lot, in the name of the Lord, and made the journey to Leipzig, took my examination, and then made the change of position. Here, by God's will, I am still in service. But since (1) I find that the post is by no means so lucrative as it had been described to me; (2) I have failed to obtain many of the fees pertaining to the office; (3) the place is very expensive; and (4) the authorities are odd and little interested in music, so that I must live amid almost continual vexation, envy, and persecution; accordingly I shall be forced, with God's help, to seek my fortune elsewhere. Should Your Honor know or find a suitable post in your city for an old and faithful servant, I beg you most humbly to put in a most gracious word of recommendation for me—I shall not fail to do my best to give satisfaction and justify your most gracious intercession in my behalf. My present post amounts to about 700 thaler, and when there are rather more funerals than usual, the fees rise in proportion; but when a healthy wind blows, they fall accordingly, as for example last year, when I lost fees that would ordinarily come in from funerals to an amount of more than 100 thaler. In Thuringia I could get along better on 400 thaler than here with twice that many, because of the excessively high cost of living.

Now I must add a little about my domestic situation. I am married for the second time, my late first wife having died in Cöthen. From the first marriage I have three sons and one daughter living, whom Your Honor will graciously remember having seen in Weimar. From the second marriage I have one son and two daughters living.[1] My eldest son is a *Studiosus Juris*, and of the other two [from the first marriage], one is in the *prima* class and the other in the *secunda*,[2] and the eldest daughter is also still unmarried. The children of my second marriage are still small, the eldest, a boy, being six years old. But they are all born musicians, and I can assure you that I can already form an ensemble both *vocaliter* and *instrumentaliter* within my family, particularly since my present wife sings a good, clear soprano, and my eldest daughter, too, joins in not badly. I shall almost transgress the bounds of courtesy if I burden Your Honor any further, and I therefore hasten to close, remaining with most devoted respect my whole life long

Your Honor's most obedient and devoted servant
Joh. Sebast. Bach

Leipzig, 28 October 1730

[= Letter 48], 125–26.

58   JOHANN SEBASTIAN BACH TO THE ELECTOR
FREDERICK AUGUSTUS II OF SAXONY, DRESDEN [G.]

[Dresden, 27 July 1733]

My Most Gracious Lord, Most Serene Elector, Most Gracious Lord!
    To Your Royal Highness I submit in deepest devotion the present slight labor of that knowledge which I have achieved in *musique*,[1] with the most wholly submissive prayer that Your Highness will look upon it with Most Gracious Eyes, according to Your Highness's World-Famous Clemency and not according to the poor *composition;* and thus deign to take me under Your Most Mighty Protection. For some years and up to the present moment I have had the *Directorium* of the Music in the two principal churches in Leipzig, but have innocently had to suffer one injury or another, and on occasion also a diminution of the fees accruing to me in this office; but these injuries would disappear altogether if Your Royal Highness would grant me the favor of conferring upon me a title of Your Highness's Court *Capelle,* and would let Your High Command for the issuing of such a document go forth to the proper place.[2] Such a most gracious fulfillment of my most humble prayer will bind me to unending devotion, and I offer myself in most indebted obedience to show

73

at all times, upon Your Royal Highness's Most Gracious Desire,
my untiring zeal in the composition of music for the church as
well as for the orchestra, and to devote my entire forces to the
service of Your Highness, remaining in unceasing fidelity
     Your Royal Highness's most humble and most obedient slave
                                          Johann Sebastian Bach
Dressden [sic], 27 July 1733

[= Letter 48], 128–29.

59   JOHANN SEBASTIAN BACH TO THE LEIPZIG
TOWN COUNCIL [G.]

[Leipzig, 15 August 1736]
     Memorandum

The full and true account concerning the student Krause, whom
the Rector wishes to force upon me as First Prefect, is as follows:
     The said Krause last year had already earned such a bad
reputation for his disorderly living and for the debts into which
it had brought him that a meeting was held about him, at which
he was expressly told that although he had fully deserved to be
turned out of school for his profligate way of living, he would,
in view of his needy situation (since he had himself confessed
having contracted debts of over 20 thaler) and on his promise
to mend his ways, be given three months' grace, and then,
depending on whether he had changed his way of living, he
would be given further notification as to whether he would be
suffered to remain or actually expelled. Now, the Rector has
always shown a particular liking for the said Krause and accordingly asked me in conversation to let him have a post of Prefect,
but I remonstrated, saying that he was not at all suited to such a
post. Yet the Rector replied that I should do it anyway, so that
the said Krause might get out of debt, and that thus a disgrace
to the School might be avoided, particularly as his time would
soon be up and thus one would be rid of him with good grace.
Accordingly, I wished to do the Rector a favor and gave Krause
the post of Prefect in the New Church (where the students have
nothing to sing but motets and chorales, and have nothing to do
74

with other *Concert Musique,* since the latter is taken care of by the organist), having in mind the fact that the years of his agreement were all gone but one, and it need not be feared that he would ever come to conduct the Second Choir, much less the First. But when later the Prefect of the First Choir, named Nagel, from Nürnberg, at the time of the singing for last New Year's, complained that because of a weak constitution he would not be able to hold out, it was necessary to make a change in the Prefects before the regular time, to put the Prefect of the Second Choir into the First, and, of necessity, the much-discussed Krause into the Second. But since he made various mistakes in the time, as the Co-Rector (who inspects the Second Choir) told me, for when the said mistakes were investigated the blame for them was placed by the other students solely and entirely on the Prefect, on account of his beating the time incorrectly; and since, in addition, I myself recently made a test of his time, in singing-class, which he failed so badly that he could not accurately give the beat in the two principal kinds of time, namely even, or four-quarter, and uneven, or three-quarter, but now made an even measure of three-quarter, and *vice versa* (as all the students can testify); and since I am accordingly fully convinced of his incompetence; therefore it was impossible for me to entrust the post of Prefect of the First Choir to him, especially since the concerted pieces that are performed by the First Choir, which are mostly of my own composition, are incomparably harder and more intricate than those that are sung by the Second Choir (and this only on Feast Days), so that I must be chiefly guided, in the choice of the same, by the *capacitè* of those who are to perform them. Thus, and although various other reasons could be given to prove even more strongly the *incapacite* of the said Krause, I consider that the *raisons* already given are sufficient to show that the complaint I have lodged with Your Most Noble and Most Wise Council is justified, and requires a prompt and speedy remedy.

Leipzig, 15 August 1736   Joh. Seb. Bach

[= Letter 48], 140–41.

60   ANTONIO VIVALDI TO MARQUIS GUIDO BENTIVOGLIO D'ARAGONA, FERRARA [It.]

[Venice, 16 November 1737]

Excellency,

After so much trafficking and so many labors, here is the opera for Ferrara come to nought. Today our monsignor the Apostolic Nuncio called for me and commanded me, in the name of His Emin^{ce} Ruffo, not to come to Ferrara to produce the opera, and this because I am a religious who does not say Mass, and because of my friendship with Mrs. Girò, the singer.[1] Y. E. can imagine my state at such a blow.

I have on my shoulders the weight of six thousand ducats in engagements signed for this opera, and by now I have disbursed more than one hundred sequins. To produce the opera without Mrs. Girò is impossible, because such a prima donna cannot be found again. I cannot produce the opera without myself, because I do not wish to entrust so great a sum to another's care. On the other hand, I am bound by the engagements, and so here is a sea of misfortunes. What afflicts me most of all is that His Emin^{ce} Ruffo is casting upon these good ladies a taint the world never imputed to them. For fourteen years we have been going together to a good many cities in Europe, and everywhere their virtue has been admired, and Ferrara can vouch it sufficiently. They say their devotions every week, as can be inferred from the affidavits sworn to and authenticated.

I have not been saying Mass for the last twenty-five years, nor shall I ever say it again, not because of any prohibition or command, as His Eminence can ascertain, but at my own election, and this because of an illness I have been suffering *a nativitate,* which keeps me oppressed.[2]

As soon as I was ordained a priest, I said Mass for a year or something over, and then gave it up, having three times been obliged to leave the altar because of that same illness of mine. Wherefore I nearly always live at home, and do not go out except in a gondola or in a carriage, since I cannot walk because of my chest-ache or chest constriction. There is no gentleman who calls me to his home, not even our Prince himself, while everyone knows of my deficiency. Directly after dinner I usually can go, but never on foot. That is the reason why I never celebrate Mass. I have been at three carnivals in Rome to produce operas, and, Y. E. knows it, I never said Mass, and I played at the theater, and it is known that even His Holiness wished to hear me play and what thanks I received. I have been called to Vienna, and never said Mass. In Mantua, I was for three years at the service of the most pious prince [of] Darmstadt, together with these ladies who were ever looked upon with the greatest benevolence by H[is] S[erene] H[ighness], and I never said Mass. My travels always cost me a great deal, because I always went with four or five people to assist me. Whatever good I may accomplish, I do it at home and at my desk. This is why I have the honor to be received at the courts of nine Princely Highnesses, and my letters circulate throughout Europe. This is why I have written to Mr. Muzzuchi that if he will not put his house at my disposal I cannot come to Ferrara. In short, it all arises from this illness of mine, and these ladies are a great help to me, because they are acquainted with all my deficiencies. These truths are known to nearly all of Europe; therefore, I have recourse to Y. E.'s benevolence, that he may be pleased to inform also H. Emin.^{ce} Ruffo of them, while this command is my total ruin. I repeat to Y. E. that, without me, the opera cannot be produced at Ferrara, and you see for how many reasons.

If it is not produced, I must either take it to another place, which I cannot now find, or pay all those engaged, so that should His Eminence not be moved, I would entreat Y. E. at least to obtain the opera's cancelation from H. E. the Legate, that I may be exempted from paying those engaged. I also send Y. E. His Emin^{ce} Albani's letters, which I myself should present.

I have been master of the Pietà for thirty years,[3] and without scandal. I commend myself to the most benevolent patronage of Y. E. and humbly declare myself [Y. E.'s

Most dev^{d} and obl^{d} Servant

Antonio Vivaldi]

Olga Rudge (ed.), *Lettere e dediche di Antonio Vivaldi* ("Quaderni dell'Accademia Chigiana"; Siena: Ticci Editore Libraio, 1942), 23–25.—Tr. by editor.

61   GEORGE FRIDERIC HANDEL TO CHARLES JENNENS,
LONDON [Eng.]

Dublin Decem[br] 29. 1741.

S[r]

   it was with the greatest Pleasure I saw the Continuation of
Your Kindness by the Lines You was pleased to send me, in
Order to be prefix'd to Your Oratorio Messiah, which I set to
Musick before I left England.[1] I am emboldned, Sir, by the
generous Concern You please to take in relation to my affairs,
to give You an Account to the Success I have met here. The
Nobility did me the Hoñour to make amongst themselves a Subscription for 6 Nights, which did fill a Room of 600 Persons,
so that I needed not sell one single Ticket at the Door. and without
Vanity the Performance was received with a general Approbation.
Sig[ra] Avolio, which I brought with me from London pleases
extraordinary, I have form'd an other Tenor Voice which gives
great Satisfaction, the Basses and Counter Tenors are very good,
and the rest of the Chorus Singers (by my Direction) do
exceeding well, as for the Instruments they are really excellent,
M[r] Dubourgh [2] beeng at the Head of them, and the Musick
sounds delightfully in this charming Room, which puts me in
such Spirits (and my Health being so good) that I exert my self
on my Organ with more than usual Success. I opened with the
Allegro, Penseroso, & Moderato and I assure you that the Words
of the Moderato are vastly admired. The Audience being composed
(besides the Flower of Ladyes of Distinction and other People
of the greatest Quality) of so many Bishops, Deans, Heads of
the Colledge,[3] the most eminents People in the Law as the
Chancellor, Auditor General, &tc. all which are very much
taken with the Poetry. So that I am desired to perform it again
the next time. I cannot sufficiently express the kind treatment I
receive here, but the Politeness of this generous Nation can not
be unknown to You, so I let You judge of the satisfaction I
enjoy, passing my time with Honnour, profit and pleasure. They
propose already to have some more Performances, when the 6
Nights of the Subscription are over, and My Lord Duc the Lord
Lieutenant (who is allways present with all His Family on
those Nights) will easily obtain a longer Permission for me by
His Majesty, so that I shall be obliged to make my stay

here longer than I thought. One request I must make to
You, which is that You would insinuate my most devoted
Respects to My Lord and My Lady Shaftesbury, You know how
much Their kind Protection is precious to me. Sir Windham
Knatchbull will find here my respectfull Compliments. You will
encrease my obligations if by occasion You will present my
humble Service to some other Patrons and friends of mine. I
expect with Impatience the Favour of Your News, concerning
Your Health and wellfare, of which I take a real share, as for
the News of Your Opera's,[4] I need not trouble you for all this
Town is full of their ill success, by a number of Letters from
Your quarters to the People of Quality here, and I can't help
saying but that it furnishes great Diversion and laughter. The
first Opera I heard my Self before I left London, and it made
me very merry all along my journey, and of the second Opera,
call'd Penelope, a certain noble man writes very jocosly, il faut
que je dise avec Harlequin, nôtre Penelôpe n'est qu'une Sallôpe.[5]
but I think I have trespassed too much on Your Patience. I beg
You to be persuaded of the sincere Veneration and Esteem with
which I have the Honnour to be

                    S^r
              Your
                    most obliged and most humble Servant
                          George Frideric Handel

[= Letter 53], 530–31.

62   GEORGE FRIDERIC HANDEL TO CHARLES JENNENS,
GOPSALL, LEICESTERSHIRE [Eng.]

                                   London Septr 9th 1742.
    Dear S^r
      It was indeed Your humble Servant which intended You a visit
in my way from Ireland to London, for I certainly could have
given You a better account by word of mouth, as by writing,
how well Your Messiah was received in that Country, yet as a
Noble Lord, and no less then the Bishop of Elphim (a Nobleman
very learned in Musick) has given his Observation in writing
79

of this Oratorio, I send you here annexed the Contents of it in
his own words.—I shall send the printed Book of the Messiah to
Mʳ Sted for You. As for my Success in General in that generous
and polite Nation, I reserve the account of it till I have the
Hoñour to see you in London. The report that the Direction of
the Opera next winter is com̃itted to my Care, is groundless.
The gentlemen who have undertaken to middle with Harmony
can not agree, and are quite in a Confusion. Whether I shall
do some thing in the Oratorio way (as several of my friends
desire) I can not determine as yet. Certain it is that this time 12
month I shall continue my Oratorio's in Ireland, where they are
a going to make a large Subscription allready for that Purpose.[1]

If I had know'n that My Lord Guernsey was so near when I
pass'd Coventry, You may easily imagine, Sir, that I should not
have neglected of paying my Respects to him, since You know
the particular Esteem I have for His Lordship. I think it a very
long time to the month of November next when I can have
some hopes of seeing You here in Town. Pray let me hear
meanwhile of Your Health and Wellfare, of which I take a real
Share beeng with uncommon Sincerity and Respect

Sʳ

Your most obliged humble Servant

George Frideric Handel.

[= Letter 53], 554–55.

63   JEAN-PHILIPPE RAMEAU TO MONSIEUR MONGEOT [Fr.]

[Paris, 1744]

I am very sensible, Sir, of the honor you do me, and at the
same time very mortified that I can only help you in a feeble
way, both because my business does not permit me to set it aside
and because what you request demands much greater detail than
you perhaps imagine. One must be acquainted with the theater,
have studied nature for a long time, to depict it as truthfully as
possible; have all the characters present, be sensible to the dance,
to its movements, not to speak of all the accessories; know the

80

voice, the actors, etc. The Ballet would suit you better than the Tragedy for a beginning. Besides, I believe Mr. Panard is more capable in the one than in the other; he has some merit, but he has not yet given us anything lyrical.[1] It would be necessary, before undertaking so great a work, to have written small ones, cantatas, *divertissements,* and a thousand trifles of the kind that nourish the spirit, fire its imagination, and make one imperceptibly capable of greater things. I have followed the theater since the age of twelve; I did not work for the Opéra before I was fifty years old, even then doubting my capacity to do so; I ventured, I had luck, I continued. I am, with all possible esteem, Sir, your very humble and very obedient servant.

Rameau.

[= Letter 54], 34–35.—Tr. by editor.

64A–E GEORGE FRIDERIC HANDEL TO CHARLES JENNENS, GOPSALL, LEICESTERSHIRE [Eng.]

A

London Juin 9th 1744.

Dear Sir,

It gave me great Pleasure to hear Your safe arrival in the Country, and that Your Health was much improved. I hope it is by this time firmly establichd, and I wish You with all my Heart the Continuation of it, and all the Prosperity.

As You do me the Honour to encourage my Musicall Undertakings, and even to promote them with a particular Kindness, I take the Liberty to trouble you with an account of what Engagement I have hitherto concluded. I have taken the Opera House in the Haymarketh. engaged, as Singers, Sig^{ra} Francesina, Miss Robinson, Beard, Reinhold, Mr Gates with his Boyes's and several of the best Chorus Singers from the Choirs, and I have some hopes that Mrs Cibber will sing for me.[1] She sent me word from Bath (where she is now) that she would perform for me next winter with great pleasure if it did not interfere with her playing, but I think I can obtain Mr Riches's permission (with whom she is engaged to play in Covent Garden House) since so obligingly he gave Leave to Mr Beard and Mr Reinhold.

Now I should be extreamly glad to receive the first Act, or what is ready of the new Oratorio with which you intend to favour me, that I might employ all my attention and time, in order to answer in some measure the great obligation I lay under. this new favour will greatly increase my Obligations. I remain with all possible Gratitude and Respect

S^r

Your

most obliged and most humble
Servant
George Frideric Handel

B

[London,] July 19. 1744

Dear Sir

At my arrival in London, which was Yesterday, I immediately perused the Act of the Oratorio with which you favour'd me, and, the little time only I had it, gives me great Pleasure. Your reasons for the Length of the first act are intirely Satisfactory to me, and it is likewise my Opinion to have the following Acts short. I shall be very glad and much obliged to you, if you will soon favour me with the remaining Acts. Be pleased to point out these passages in the Messiah which You think require altering.—

I desire my humble Respects and thanks to My Lord Guernsey for his many Civility's to me—and believe me to be with the greatest Respect

Sr

Your

Most obedient and most humble
Servant
George Frideric Handel

C

[London, 21 August 1744]

Dear Sir

The Second Act of the Oratorio I have received Safe, and own my self highly obliged to You for it. I am greatly pleased with

82

it, and shall use my best endeavours to do it Justice. I can only
Say that I impatiently wait for the third Act and desire to
believe me to be with great Respect

Sr

Your

London	most obliged and most humble
Agost y 21.	Servant
1744.	George Frideric Handel.

D

[London, 13 September 1744]

Dear Sr

Your most excellent Oratorio has given me great Delight in
setting it to Musick and still engages me warmly. It is indeed a
Noble Piece, very grand and uncommon; it has furnished me
with Expressions, and has given me Opportunity to some very
particular Ideas, besides so many great Choru's. I intreat you
heartily to favour me Soon with the last Act, which I expect
with anxiety, that I may regulate my Self the better as to the
Length of it. I profess my Self highly obliged to You, for so
generous a Present, and desire You to believe me to be with great
Esteem and Respect

Sr

Your

London	Most obliged and most humble
Sept^br 13.	Servant
1744	George Frideric Handel

E

[London, 2 October 1744]

Dear S^r

I received the 3^d Act, with a great deal of pleasure, as you can
imagine, and you may believe that I think it a very fine and
sublime Oratorio, only it is realy to long, if I should extend the
Musick, it would last 4 Hours and more.

I retrench'd already a great deal of the Musick, that I might
preserve the Poetry as much as I could, yet still it may be shortned.
The Anthems come in very proprely. but would not the Words
(tell it out among the Heathen that the Lord is King) [be]

83

Sufficient for one Chorus? The Anthem (I will magnify thee O
God my King, and I will praise thy name for ever and ever,
vers). the Lord preserveth all them that love him, but scattreth
abroad all the ungodly. (vers and chorus) my mouth shall speak
the Praise of the Lord and let all flesh give thanks unto His holy
name for ever and ever Amen.) concludes well the Oratorio. I
hope you will make a visit to London next Winter. I have a
good Set of Singers. S. Francesina performs Nitocris, Miss
Robinson Cyrus, Mrs. Cibber Daniel, Mr. Beard (who is
recovered) Belshazzar, Mr Reinhold Gobrias, and a good Number
of Choir Singers for the Chorus's.[1] I propose 24 Nights to
perform this Season, on Saturdays, but in Lent on Wednesday's
or Fryday's.[2] I shall open on 3^d of Novemb^r [next with] Deborah.[3]
I wish You heartily the Continuation of Your health, and
professing [my?] grateful acknowledgments for your generous
favours, and am with great Esteem and Respect

Sr

London   Your
Octo^{br} 2   most obliged and most humble Servant
1744   George Frideric Handel

[= Letter 53], 590–96.

65   JOHANN SEBASTIAN BACH TO JOHANN ELIAS
BACH, SCHWEINFURT [G.]

Leipzig, 6 October 1748

Honored and Most Noble, Most Esteemed Cousin,
    As time is short I will say much in a few words, by invoking
God's grace and support for a blessed vintage [1] as well as for the
blessed event soon to be expected. I cannot oblige you at present
with the desired copy of the Prussian Fugue,[2] the edition having
been exhausted just today, since I had only 100 printed, most of
which were distributed *gratis* to good friends. But between now
and the New Year's Fair I shall have some more printed, and if
then my honored Cousin is still of a mind to have a copy, he
need only give me notice upon occasion, sending me a thaler at

the same time, and his wish shall be fulfilled. In conclusion, with best greetings again from us all, I remain

Your Honor's devoted
J. S. Bach

P.S. My son in Berlin already has two male heirs: the first was born just about the time we had (alas!) the Prussian Invasion and the second is about two weeks old.[3]

[= Letter 48], 182.

66   JOHANN SEBASTIAN BACH TO JOHANN ELIAS BACH, SCHWEINFURT [G.]

Leipzig, 2 November 1748

Most Noble and Most Esteemed Cousin,

I am assured that you and your dear wife are still well by the agreeable note I received from you yesterday together with the excellent little cask of must you sent me, for which I herewith send you the thanks I owe you. It is, however, greatly to be regretted that the little cask was damaged, either by being shaken up in the wagon or in some other way, for when it was opened for the usual customs inspection here it was almost two-thirds empty, and according to the inspector's report contained no more than six quarts [*Kannen*]; and it is a pity that even the least drop of this noble gift of God should have been spilled. But, while I heartily congratulate my honored Cousin on the rich vintage he has garnered, I must acknowledge my inability, *pro nunc*, not [*sic*] to be in a position to make an appropriate return. But *quod differtur non auffertur*,[1] and I hope to have occasion to acquit my debt in some way. It is indeed to be regretted that the distance between our two cities does not permit us to pay personal visits to each other. Otherwise I should take the liberty of humbly inviting my honored Cousin to the marriage of my daughter Liessgen which will take place in the coming month of January, 1749, to the new organist in Naumburg, Mr. Altnickol.[2] But since owing to the remoteness I have mentioned and the unfavorable season it will presumably not be possible for our honored Cousin to be with us personally, I will at least ask

85

him the favor of assisting them with a Christian wish; whereupon I send best regards to my honored Cousin and remain, with best greetings to you from us all,

Your Honor's wholly devoted and faithful cousin and most willing servant

Joh. Seb. Bach

P.S. Magister Birnbaum was buried, as much as 6 weeks ago.[3]
P[ro]. M[emoria]. Although my honored Cousin kindly offers to oblige with more of the *liqueur,* I must decline his offer on account of the excessive expenses here. For since the carriage charges cost 16 groschen, the delivery man 2 groschen, the customs inspector 2 groschen, the inland duty 5 groschen, 3 pfennig, and the general duty 3 groschen, my honored Cousin can judge for himself that each quart costs me almost 5 groschen, which for a present is really too expensive.

[= Letter 48], 183.

67   DOMENICO SCARLATTI TO THE DUKE OF
HUESCAR, MADRID [It.]

[Madrid, spring 1752]
Most Exc^nt S^r

I thought well to await your happy return in order to pay you the debt of my obedience, not only with these pages [1] which I enclose, but in any other thing Y. E. will deign command me. Unraveling the words, which are in Latin but written in the Gothic abbreviated fashion, has caused more labor than anything else.
Y. E. should preserve the ancient separate parts, as well as the score I have extracted from them, not only to sing the praises of such worthiness, but in order that many modern theatrical composers may observe and profit (if, however, they are so minded) from the true manner and true laws of writing counterpoint; this I see in few today, and yet I hear them praised. If I cannot leave my house, Y. E. is great and strong and Magnanimous and full of health, why then do you not come and comfort me with your sight? perhaps because I am not worthy?

it is true. but where have the virtues their seat, if not in the heart of the great?

I'll say no more. I pray that God may assist and bless you as much as you and I desire. amen

Scarlatti

Facsimile of the autograph: Ralph Kirkpatrick, *Domenico Scarlatti* (Princeton: Princeton University Press, 1953), Fig. 39.—Tr. by editor.

68   JEAN-JACQUES ROUSSEAU TO TOUSSAINT-PIERRE LENIEPS, LYONS [Fr.]

Paris, 22 8^{ber} 1752.

I have not yet recovered, my dear friend, from the agitation which your last letter caused me. The afflictions you have suffered, the dangers to which you have been exposed, are painted there with a vividness that made me palpitate. Now, thank Heaven, you are secure; and if your personal fortunes do not come up to the hopes which you had reason to entertain, your Daughter's situation allows you to have no fears for your own: an assurance that fills me with joy. Nothing remains but to see you in Paris again, living with your friends and enjoying the tranquillity which you have so rightly earned.

I am still pretty much the same as when you left me; same languor, same profession, same hatred of the world, same fancy for my friends, same laziness in writing to them, same need for their indulgence, and ever counting on yours.

The little Opera which I was finishing when you left is now being shown at Court.[1] Its success is marvelous and astonishes even me. I was at Fontainebleau for its first performance. They wanted to present me to the King the next day, and [instead] I came back and copied.[2] I like my obscurity too well to make up my mind to leave it, even if I were rid of the infirmities which make it necessary to me.

Some Italian *Intermèdes* are now being shown at the Opéra, which attract a crowd it needed. I have taken it into my head, on the advice of my friends, to have the finest of these

intermèdes, entitled *la Serva padrona,* engraved; and I hope the
work will be finished toward the middle of next month.[3] If you
know any musical Amateurs at Lyons, you would oblige me by
procuring me the sale of some copies. I cannot fix their exact
price yet: but, by guess, I should estimate that it will be between
six and nine francs.

   Goodbye, my good and dear friend: rely on my endless
attachment.

J. J. Rousseau

Théophile Dufour (ed.), *Correspondance générale de J.-J. Rousseau* (20 vols.;
Paris: Librairie Armand Colin, 1924–34), II, 30–31.—Tr. by editor.

69   FREDERICK THE GREAT TO HIS SISTER
WILHELMINE, MARGRAVIN OF BAYREUTH [Fr.]

[Potsdam (?),] 16th [April 1754]

My dearest sister,

   I take the liberty of placing at your feet a Mexican who is
not yet quite clean.[1] I have taught him to speak French; now he
must learn Italian. But, before putting him to that trouble, I
entreat you to tell me naturally your feeling, and whether you
believe he deserves that one should take such pains. The greater
part of the airs are made not to be repeated;[2] there are only two
of the Emperor's airs and two of Eupaforice's that are meant to
be so. I do not know how you will find it altogether, the linking
of the scenes, the dialogue, and the interest I should like to see
dominant in it; but as there is no need for hurry, I shall easily
be able to change whatever you may find to criticize. It would
even be easy to judge of the effect the spectacle can produce.
You have an admirable company of French players; one would
only need to have them play it in your chamber, even if each
were but to read his part.

   I make a thousand wishes that you may continue in good
health. If the land of Naples resembles the description made
of it to you, I know very well that I shall not go there to seek
my happiness, and I believe your traveler must feel he is most
fortunate to be at your feet. I hope to enjoy the same satisfaction

88

this year, and to assure you *viva voce* that nothing matches the
sentiments of tenderness and high esteem with which I will
be, unto my life's last breath, my dearest sister,

[Your humble servant

Frederick]

Œuvres de Frédéric le Grand, Tome XXVII, Part 1 (Berlin: Imprimerie
Royale [R. Decker], 1856), 273–74.—Tr. by editor.

70   JEAN-PHILIPPE RAMEAU TO MONSIEUR DUCHARGER, ST. MALO [Fr.]

[Paris, 13 June 1754]
Sir,

The book in question is now printed: it is entitled: *Observations on Our Instinct for Music.* I lack the time for writing,
and the health for thinking, for reflecting; excuse me, Sir, I am
old, you are young, and I am your very humble and very
obedient servant.

Rameau.

Paris, 13th June 1754.

[= Letter 54], 69.—Tr. by editor.

71   GEORGE FRIDERIC HANDEL TO GEORG PHILIPP TELEMANN, HAMBURG [Fr.]

[London, 20 September 1754]
Sir

It is some time ago that I had a supply of exotic plants
prepared to send to you, when Jean Carsten the Captain (to
whom I sent, to let you have them) had me informed that he
had learnt you were deceased; you may be sure the report
afflicted me extremely. You can Imagine my Joy therefore on
hearing that you are in perfect Health. The same Captain Jean
Carsten who has just returned here from your parts sends me

this good news through a friend, and that you have Consigned him a List of exotic plants to be procured for you, I have embraced this opportunity with great pleasure, and I have been at Pains to have these plants found, and you shall have almost all of them; Since Captain Ca[r]sten need not leave here till the coming month of December, he has kindly Offered to send them by the first vessel leaving from here, and on the enclosed Note you will find the name of the Captain and the vessel. I hope this little present which I dare offer you will be agreeable to you; I beg you to give me news of your Health, which I hope is perfect, and [I wish you] all Sorts of prosperity, and am with immutable esteem,

          Sir

               your very humble and very obedient servant

                                        G: F: Händel

London, 20 Sep^r.
     1754.

Translation in Müller [= Letter 51], 91–92, revised by present editor in accordance with original text printed in Deutsch [= Letter 53], 754–55.

72   JOHANN CHRISTIAN BACH TO GIAMBATTISTA MARTINI, BOLOGNA [It.]

                                   [Milan, 21 May 1757]

Very Revnd P^{dre}, Very Honble Sir.

I received with deep reverence yours most Esteemed, and from it I see the great kindness with which you continue to favor me. You wish to know [of] my reception here in Milan and I can assure you that I have been received by these very Excell^{nt} Gentlemen [with] all consideration, surpassing my merits in every way, and the latter continue to accord me their good Graces, especially the Cavaliere,[1] who in his Goodness watches on my behalf, that he may do everything to make me successful. He is now trying to find me a fixed Post *for life* here in Milan, and I hope he will shortly succeed.[2] With Mr. Balbi I enjoy all conceivable friendship, and that letter you will have received from him was caused by nothing more than a
90

small question regarding a passage you have already judged and decided upon. The question was only, that I maintained this passage should be called a License, as you too have called it in yours most est^md. Mr. Balbi maintained the contrary, and I did not wish further to warm the Soup, especially as Mr. Balbi seemed somewhat vexed that I should wish to discuss Music with him, and this shall serve me as a guide in the future not to meddle ever again in such discussions, which I would never have entered upon with anyone other than a friend of mine like Mr. Balbi. I have deemed this explanation of the case to be necessary, so Y. R. might be informed of [my] true success, lest you should think of me that I wish to play the Doctor without cause. I shall avail myself of all the generous offers Y. R. makes me and in case of any advice, or I should say any correction, I shall not fail to trouble you with some composition to be purified. At the moment I am working on that office,[3] and have already finished the Invitatory and the Dies irae. Meanwhile, begging Y. R. [to convey] my Greetings to all the Reverend P^dri my Masters and to all the School, I profess myself ever and invariably,

Sir, Y. R.'s and very Honble P^re's most humble and devoted Servant.

Giov. Christiano Bach.

Milan, 21 May
　　1757.

Max Schwarz, "Johann Christian Bach (1735–1782)," *Sammelbände der Internationalen Musikgesellschaft*, II (1900–1901), 440.—Tr. by editor.

73　　GIUSEPPE TARTINI TO MADDALENA LOMBARDINI, VENICE [It.]

Padua, 5 March 1760.

My very much esteemed Signora Maddalena,

At last, God willing, I have disengaged myself from that weighty business which prevented me until now from keeping my promise to you, although it was even too close to my heart, since, in fact, the want of time afflicted me. Let us, then, begin

by letter with the name of God, and if you should not
sufficiently understand what I here set forth, write to me, and
ask for an explanation of everything you do not understand.

Your principal practice and study must be the bow generally,
in order to make yourself absolute mistress of it for whatever
purpose, whether passages or melodies [o sonabile o cantabile].

[Your] first study must be the placing of the bow upon the
string, so lightly that the very beginning of the tone extracted
is like a breath, and not like a percussion upon the string. It
consists of lightness in the wrist and of continuing the stroke
of the bow immediately after it has been placed, pressing at
will, for after it has been lightly placed there is no longer any
danger of harshness and crudity. You must master this light
manner of placing the bow in any of its situations, both at
the middle and at the extremities, and you must master this
on the up-bow and on the down-bow. To accomplish all these
labors at once, one begins with a swell [messa di voce] upon
an open string, for example the second, which is the A-la-mi-re.[1]
One begins pianissimo, growing by slow degrees till one
reaches fortissimo; and this study should be made equally with
the down-bow and with the up-bow.

You should begin this study immediately and spend at least
an hour every day at it, but broken up: a little in the morning,
a little in the evening; and have constantly in mind that this
is the most important and most difficult study of all.

When you have mastered this, you will find it easy to execute
a swell that begins pianissimo, goes to fortissimo, and returns to
pianissimo all in the same stroke of the bow; the best manner
of placing the bow upon the string will be easy and secure
for you, and you will be able to do whatever you please with
your bow.

After this, to acquire that lightness of the wrist from which
the bow's velocity arises, it will be best for you to play, every
day, some flights [2] by Corelli wholly made up of semiquavers,
and there are three such flights in the fifth Opus for violin
alone, indeed the first one is in the first sonata, in D-la-sol-re.
You must gradually play them faster and faster, till you succeed
in playing them as fast as you possibly can. But two precautions
are necessary: the first is, that you play them with a detached
bow, that is, distinctly, and with a little space between one note
and the next. They are written in the following manner:

92

etc., but should be played as if they were written thus:

etc. The second is, that you play them with the point of the bow, when you begin this study; but afterwards, when you have fully mastered them with the point of the bow, then begin doing them, no longer with the point, but with that part of the bow which is between the point and the middle of the bow; and when you are likewise mistress of this part of the bow, then study them in the same way at the middle of the bow; and above all, remember in these studies to begin the flights sometimes with an up-bow, sometimes with a down-bow; and beware of always beginning downwards. To acquire this lightness in the bow, it is extremely useful to skip over a string and to study flights of semiquavers of this kind:

etc.; of such you may at will invent as many as you please, and in any key, and, truly, they are useful and necessary.

With regard to the finger-board hand, I recommend that you study only one thing, which will suffice for all, and it is this.

Take any part for the Violin, either the first or the second, whether from a concerto, or from some Mass or Psalm, anything will serve the purpose. Do not put your hand in its usual place, but upon the half-shift, that is, with the first finger on the *G-sol-re-ut* of the first string; and, constantly keeping the hand in this position, play all of that Violin part, never shifting the hand from that position except to reach the *A-la-mi-re* on the fourth string or the *D-la-sol-re* on the first; but then return your hand to the earlier position, and never to its natural place. Study this till you are quite sure you can play any Violin part (not intended as a solo) at sight. Then advance the hand on the finger board, with the first finger on *A-la-mi-re* on the first string, and in this second position, study exactly as you did in the first. When certain of this too, go on to the third position, with the first finger on *B-mi*

93

on the first string, and make sure of it in the same manner. Being sure, go on to the fourth, with the first [finger] on the C-*sol-fa-ut* of the first string; in sum, this is a Scale of positions, and when you have mastered them you can call yourself mistress of the finger board. This study is necessary, and I recommend it to you.

I pass to the third, which is the shake. I would have it slow, moderate, and fast from you; that is, the two notes succeeding each other slowly, moderately, and fast; and in practice one really needs these different shakes, for it is not true that a shake that will serve for a *grave* should be the same as a shake that will serve for an *allegro*.

To study both at once with the same trouble, begin a sustained stroke of the bow, as for a swell, on an open string, either the second or the first, for it is all the same, and begin the shake very, very slowly, gradually increasing it by insensible degrees to a *presto,* as you see here in the example:

etc. But do not adhere rigorously to this example, in which, given the semiquavers, one immediately goes on to the demi-semiquavers and from these to the next, which are worth half as much, etc. No, this would be a skip, not a gradation; but you must imagine that between the semiquavers and the demisemiquavers there are other notes, worth less than the semiquavers and more than the demisemiquavers, but that, leaving the semiquavers, their value is close to that of the semiquavers, and, according as they advance, they increasingly approach the value of the demisemiquavers, till they become true demisemiquavers; and the same, proportionately, between the demisemiquavers and the next, which are worth half as much. Study this assiduously and attentively, and be sure to begin it on an open string, for if you are once able to do it well on an open string, you will do it much better with the second and third fingers, and also with the fourth, which one must exercise in a particular manner, as it is the smallest among its brethren. I shall, at present, propose no other studies to you; but this is more than enough, if you will speak in earnest, for your part, as I have spoken to you for my part. Answer me whether you have properly understood what I have here proposed to you; meanwhile, presenting you my respects, as I beg you to do on my behalf to Mme. the Prioress and Mmes. Teresa and Chiara, all of them my Patronesses, I affirm myself to be, increasingly,

Y[our] Most Illustrious L[adyship's]

Most Devoted, Affec^te^ Servant

Giuseppe Tartini

Giuseppe Tartini, *Traité des Agréments de la Musique* . . . , ed. Erwin R. Jacobi (Celle: Edition Moeck, 1961), 132–38.—Tr. by editor.

74   LUIGI BOCCHERINI TO THE GOVERNMENT OF LUCCA [It.]

[Lucca, 28 August 1761]

Most Exc.^nt^ L.^ds^, Most Exc.^nt^ Council.

Luigi Boccherini, the very humble serv.^nt^ and subject of Y. Excell.^s^ and of the Most Exc.^nt^ Council, bows humbly [before you] with all due reverence and begs to make known: how that, having finished his studies in Rome and having twice been summoned to Vienna, he later visited all the remaining Electoral Courts of the Empire, where he won universal sympathy for his playing upon the violoncello: which instrument not being practised by anyone in this city, it is necessary to seek a stranger for each service: since, therefore, he wishes to establish himself in his Fatherland at last and flatters himself that he can use his skill, though it be modest, in the service of his most rev.^d^ Prince, he makes bold to present himself before Y. Excell.^s^, Magnif.^nt^ Citizens, and before the Most Exc.^nt^ Council, begging the latter to grant him some relief for his honest maintenance by admitting him among the Musicians of Their Excell.^s'^ Chapel; and hoping in the munificence of his Prince and of the Most Exc.^nt^ Council, he commends himself to it with all possible confidence [1]

from whose grace, &c.

28 Agt. 1761.

Facsimile of the autograph: Arnaldo Bonaventura, *Boccherini* (Milan: Treves, 1931), opposite p. 33.—Tr. by editor.

95

75   JOSEPH HAYDN TO PRINCE NICOLAUS ESTERHÁZY, [SÜTTÖR?¹] [G.]

[Eisenstadt, 9 September 1765]

SERENE HIGHNESS AND NOBLE PRINCE OF THE HOLY ROMAN EMPIRE, GRACIOUS AND DREAD LORD!

I have received with every submissive and dutiful respect YOUR ILLUSTRIOUS AND SERENE HIGHNESS' letter of the 8th inst. addressed to me, and I see from it that Your Highness has taken it very amiss that I protested against the detention of the *flauto traverso* player Frantz Sigl to Herr von Rahier,² whose commands I am now admonished to follow, in order that I may behave better in the future, on penalty of the dread displeasure of my SERENE HIGHNESS. MOST SERENE HIGHNESS! GRACIOUS LORD! On behalf of the above-named *flauto traverso* player, because of whom the fire started, I went with the whole band to Herr von Rahier, and it was not on account of the detention, but only on account of the rude detention and the hard treatment of the subject that I protested, but with all proper respect, to Herr von Rahier. But we could not get anywhere with the administrator, and I even had to put up with his slamming the door in my face, he pushed all the others out, and threatened everyone with detention. Similarly, this very day Friberth fled excitedly from the administrator (on account of not doffing his hat, which must have been an oversight), and does not dare to come home, because this same administrator pretends that the first-mentioned Friberth was rude to him, and that therefore he will mete out his own punishment.³ But I testify, as do all the other musicians, that Friberth did nothing else except that, when the administrator threatened all of us with detention—and without any reason—he said he had no other master but HIS SERENE HIGHNESS, PRINCE ESTERHÁZY. I myself told the administrator to complain to YOUR SERENE AND ILLUSTRIOUS HIGHNESS if he felt his own person to have been insulted, but I was given the answer that the administrator is his own judge and will mete out the punishment himself. Everyone is very upset on this account, they find this treatment very unfair and hope that YOUR SERENE AND GRACIOUS HIGHNESS' intentions certainly do not extend this far, and that for this reason you will graciously put a stop to such a procedure [*Potere*] whereby anyone can be his own judge without differentiating between guilty or not guilty.

The orders of the oft-mentioned administrator (as YOUR SERENE AND GRACIOUS HIGHNESS knows anyway) have been correctly carried out at all times, and as often as I receive through him an order of YOUR SERENE AND GRACIOUS HIGHNESS, I shall always execute it to the best of my ability; if therefore the administrator has complained in this regard, it must be the result of his angry pen. But moreover YOUR SERENE AND ILLUSTRIOUS HIGHNESS must yourself remember, in your graciousness, that I cannot serve two masters, and cannot accept the commands of, and subordinate myself to, the administrator, for YOUR SERENE AND ILLUSTRIOUS HIGHNESS once said to me: COME FIRST TO ME, BECAUSE I AM HIS MASTER.

I am therefore confident that YOUR SERENE AND ILLUSTRIOUS HIGHNESS will not receive ungraciously this my most submissive and obedient letter, but will regard me and the whole band with gracious eyes, and, since everyone is desirous of this grace, that you will watch over us in fatherly protection. I hope for further marks of favor and grace from YOUR HIGHNESS and I remain ever, with every mark of profound respect,

YOUR SERENE AND GRACIOUS HIGHNESS'
most humble and obedient
Josephus Haydn.

Eisenstadt, 9th September 1765

H. C. Robbins Landon (ed. and trans.), *The Collected Correspondence and London Notebooks of Joseph Haydn* (London: Barrie and Rockliff, 1959), 3–4.

76   JOSEPH HAYDN TO AN UNNAMED AUSTRIAN MONASTERY [G.]

[Eisenstadt, 1768]

Since I cannot be present myself at this *Applaus*,[1] I have found it necessary to provide one or two explanations concerning its execution, *viz.*:

First, I would ask you to observe strictly the tempi of all the arias and recitatives, and since the whole text applauds, I would rather have the allegros taken a bit more quickly than usual, especially in the very first ritornello and in one or two of the recitatives; but no less in the two bass arias.

Secondly: for the overture all you need to play is an allegro and an andante, for the opening ritornello takes the place of the final allegro. If I knew the day of the performance, I might perhaps send you a new overture by that time.

Thirdly: in the accompanied recitatives, you must observe that the accompaniment should not enter until the singer has quite finished his text, even though the score often shows the contrary. For instance, at the beginning where the word "metamorphosis" is repeated, and the orchestra comes in at "-phosis," you must nevertheless wait until the last syllable is finished and then enter quickly; for it would be ridiculous if you were to fiddle away the word from the singer's mouth, and understand only the words "quae metamo . . . ." But I leave this to the harpsichord player, and all the others must follow him. N.B.: our scholars in Eisenstadt—and there are very few—disputed a great deal over the word "metamorphosis"; one wanted the penultimate syllable short, the other long; and despite the fact that in Italian one says "metamōrfosi," I have always heard it pronounced "metamorphōsis" in Latin; should I have made a mistake, the error can be easily corrected.[2]

Fourthly: that the fortes and pianos are written correctly throughout, and should be observed exactly; for there is a very great difference between *piano* and *pianissimo*, *forte* and *fortiss*[*imo*], between *crescendo* and *forzando*, and so forth. It should be noted, too, when in the score the one or the other *forte* or *piano* is not marked throughout all the parts,

that the copyist should rectify this when preparing the performance material.

Fifthly: I have often been annoyed at certain violinists in
various concerts, who absolutely ruined the so-called ties—
which are among the most beautiful things in music—in that
they bounced the bows off the tied note, which should have
been joined to the preceding note. And so I would point out
to the first violinist that it would be silly to play the following
(as found in bar 47)

—in which the first two notes are to be taken on one bow—
in such a disagreeable and mistaken way as

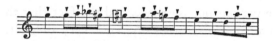

all staccato, and as if there were no ties present.

Sixthly: I would ask you to use two players on the viola
part throughout, for the inner parts sometimes need to be heard
more than the upper parts, and you will find in all my
compositions that the viola rarely doubles the bass.

Seventhly: if you have to copy two sets of violin parts, the
copyist should see that they do not turn their pages at the
same time, because this takes away a great deal of strength
from an orchestra with only a few musicians. The copyist should
also see that the *da capo* signs SS are written in one of the
violin parts as in the score, but in the other he can put the
da capo a couple of bars after the sign SS, and then write the
sign in its proper place.

Eighthly: I suggest that the two boys [soloists] in particular
have a clear pronunciation, singing slowly in recitatives so
that one can understand every syllable; and likewise they
should follow the method of singing the recitation whereby,

for example  must be sung

The penultimate note "g" drops out entirely, and this applies to all similar cases. I rely on the skill of the tenor, who will explain such things to the boys.

Ninthly: I hope for at least three or four rehearsals for the entire work.

Tenthly: in the soprano aria the bassoon can be omitted if absolutely necessary, but I would rather have it present, at least when the bass is *obbligato* throughout. And I prefer a band with 3 bass instruments—'cello, bassoon and double bass—to one with 6 double basses and 3 'celli, because certain passages stand out better that way.

Finally I ask everyone, and especially the musicians, for the sake of my reputation as well as their own, to be as diligent as possible; if I have perhaps not guessed the taste of these gentlemen, I am not to be blamed for it, for I know neither the persons nor the place, and the fact that they were concealed from me really made my work very difficult. For the rest, I hope that this *Applausus* will please the poet, the worthy musicians, and the honorable reverend *Auditorio,* all of whom I greet with profound respect, and for whom I remain

> Your most obedient servant,
> Giuseppe Haydn.
> *Maestro di Cap: di Sua Alt:*
> *Sere: Prencipe d'Estorhazy.*

[= Letter 75], 9–11.

77　WOLFGANG AMADEUS MOZART TO HIS MOTHER AND SISTER, SALZBURG [G.]

[Rome, 14 April 1770]

I am, god be praised and thanked, in good health and so is my miserable pen, and I kiss mama and nanerl[1] a thousand or 1000 times. nb: I only wish my sister were in Rome, for she would surely like this city well, since st: peter's church is Regular and many other things in Rome are Regular. Such lovely flowers they are taking past, papa told me so this very instant. I am a fool, that's well known, oh I am in distress, there is only one bed in our quarters, mama can easily imagine

100

that I find no rest next to papa, I happily look forward to
our new quarters. I have Just sketched st: peter with the keys
st: paul with the sword and st: luke with my sister ec: ec: I have
had the honor to kiss st: peter's foot at saint pietro's, and as I
have the misfortune of being so small, therefore the same old
lout

Wolfgang Mozart
had to be lifted up

Wilhelm A. Bauer and Otto Erich Deutsch (eds.), *Mozart: Briefe und
Aufzeichnungen. Gesamtausgabe herausgegeben von der Internationalen Stiftung
Mozarteum, Salzburg* (4 vols.; Kassel: Bärenreiter, 1962–63), I, 336.—
Tr. by editor.

78   WOLFGANG AMADEUS MOZART TO HIS SISTER, SALZBURG [G.]

[Milan, 24 August 1771]

Dearest sister!
We suffered very much from the heat during the Journey,
and the dust bothered us impertinently all the time, so that
we should certainly have suffocated and languished, had we not
been cleverer. it hasn't rained here for a whole month (: say
the Milanese :), today it began to drip a little, but now the
sun is shining again, and it's very warm again. be sure, I beg
you, to keep what you promised me (: you know well enough
what I mean . . . . oh you darling you! :), I will certainly
be obliged to you.[1] the princess recently suffered from the
busy little discharge or = = shifting; except for that I know
of no news. Write me some news yourself. My Compliments
to all good friends and lady-friends and a handkiss to Mama.
It's so hot now, I'm Just panting! now I'll tear open my jerkin.
Addio. farewell:

Wolfgang

above us there is a violinist, below us another, next to us a
singing master who gives lessons, in the last Room opposite us
an hautboyist. that makes it fun to Compose! gives one many
ideas.

[⇌ Letter 77], 432.—Tr. by editor.

79　　CHRISTOPH WILLIBALD GLUCK TO THE EDITOR
OF THE *MERCURE DE FRANCE*, PARIS [Fr.]

[Vienna, February 1773]

Sir

I would lay myself open to just reproach, and I would reproach myself most severely, if, after having read the letter written from here to one of the directors of the Académie Royale de Musique, which you published in the *Mercure* of October last and the subject of which is the opera *Iphigénie* [1]—if, I say, after having expressed to the author of this letter my appreciation of the praises he was pleased to heap upon me, I did not hasten to point out that his friendship and too strong a prejudice in my favor have undoubtedly carried him away, and that I am very far from flattering myself that I deserve the praise he accords me. I would reproach myself even more, if I consented to accept the credit for having invented the new form of Italian opera, the success of which has fully justified the experiment; it is to M. de Calzabigi [2] that the chief merit belongs; and if my music has met with some approbation, I feel bound to admit that it is to him I am indebted for this, since it is he who made it possible for me to develop the resources of my art. This author, full of genius and talent, has in his poems *Orphée*, *Alceste* and *Paris* pursued a course that is virtually unknown to the Italians. [3] These works are full of happy situations, of those elements of terror and pathos which give a composer the opportunity to express great passion and to create forceful and moving music. Whatever talent the composer may have, he will never create more than mediocre music, if the poet does not arouse in him that enthusiasm without which all artistic productions are weak and spiritless; to imitate nature is the acknowledged aim they must all set themselves. This is the aim I seek to attain: always as simple and natural as possible, my music merely strives to achieve the fullest expression and to reinforce the poetic declamation. That is the reason why I do not employ the trills, passages, or cadenzas in which the Italians revel. Their language, which lends itself to these so easily, therefore has no advantage for me in this respect, though it has doubtless many others; but, born in Germany, any study I may have made of the Italian language, as also of the French language, is not, I believe, sufficient to enable me to appreciate the delicate

102

nuances that may render one preferable to the other, and I think that all foreigners should abstain from judging their respective merits; but what I think is permissible for me to say is that the language that will always appeal to me most is that in which the poet provides me with the most varied opportunities to express the emotions; this is the advantage I believe I have found in the text of the opera *Iphigénie*, in which the poetry seemed to me to have all the vigor required to inspire good music. Although I have never been in the position of offering my works to any theater, I cannot hold it against the writer of the letter to one of the Directors that he proposed my *Iphigénie* to your Académie de Musique. I confess that I would have been pleased to produce it in Paris, because, by its effect and with the help of the famous M. Rousseau of Geneva whom I intended to consult,[4] we might together, in seeking a noble, moving, and natural melody with a declamation in keeping with the prosody of each language and the character of each people, have succeeded in finding the means I have in mind for producing a type of music suited to all nations and in eliminating the absurd distinctions between national forms of music. The study I have made of this great man's works on music, among others the letter in which he analyzes the monologue of Lully's *Armide*,[5] prove the depth of his knowledge and his sureness of taste and have filled me with admiration. I was left with the profound conviction that if he had chosen to devote himself to the application of this art, he would have been able to achieve the prodigious effects which the ancients attributed to music.[6] I am delighted to have this opportunity of paying him publicly this tribute which I believe he deserves.

I beg you, Sir, to have the goodness to publish this letter in your next *Mercure*.

I have the honor to be, etc.
Chevalier Gluck.

Hedwig and E. H. Mueller von Asow (eds.), *The Collected Correspondence and Papers of Christoph Willibald Gluck,* trans. Stewart Thomson (London: Barrie and Rockliff, 1962), 30–31.

80   CARL PHILIPP EMANUEL BACH TO JOHANN
NICOLAUS FORKEL, GÖTTINGEN [G.]

[Hamburg, December (?) 1774]
A little inflammatory fever and a funeral music have prevented
me from sending you before this the enclosed 6 Solos and 4
Concertos of mine. More later. My first Essay is also enclosed.[1]
It costs only 3 rt. Give me the pleasure of your visit here soon,
and then we shall straighten it out. The account of my father's
life in Mizler is, by my help, the most complete.[2] The list of
clavier pieces he wrote as given therein omits: 15 two-part
Inventions and 15 three-part *Sinfonie,* also 6 short Preludes. As
to the church works of the deceased, it may be mentioned that
he worked devoutly, governing himself by the content of the
text, without any strange misplacing of the words, and without
elaborating on individual words at the expense of the sense of the
whole, such as sometimes arouse the admiration of people who
claim to be connoisseurs and are not. No one has ever tried out
organs so severely and yet at the same time so honestly as he.
He understood the whole building of organs in the highest degree.
When an organ builder had worked conscientiously, and incurred
losses by his work, he would persuade the employers to make
amends. No one understood registration at the organ so well as
he. Organists were terrified when he sat down to play on their
organs and drew the stops in his own manner, for they thought
that the effect could not be good as he was planning it; but
then they heard an effect that astounded them. [Marginal note:]
(These sciences perished with him.) The first thing he would do
in trying an organ was this: he would say, in jest, "Above all I
must know whether the organ has good lungs," and, to find out, he
would draw out every speaking stop, and play in the fullest and
richest possible texture. At this the organ builders would often
grow quite pale with fright. The exact tuning of his instruments
as well as of the whole orchestra had his greatest attention. No
one could tune and quill his instruments to please him. He did
everything himself. The placing of an orchestra he understood
perfectly. He made good use of any space. He grasped the sound
properties of any place at the first glance. A remarkable illustration
of that fact is the following: He came to Berlin to visit me; I
showed him the new opera house. He perceived at once its virtues

104

and defects (that is, as regards the sound of music in it). I showed him the great dining hall; we went up to the gallery that goes around the upper part of that hall. He looked at the ceiling, and without further investigation made the statement that the architect had here accomplished a remarkable feat, without intending to do so, and without anyone's knowing about it: namely, that if someone went to one corner of the oblong-shaped hall and whispered a few words very softly upwards against the wall, a person standing in the corner diagonally opposite, with his face to the wall, would hear quite distinctly what was said, while between them, and in the other parts of the room, no one would hear a sound. A feat of architecture hitherto very rare and much admired! This effect was brought about by the arches in the vaulted ceiling, which he saw at once. He heard the slightest wrong note even in the largest combinations. As the greatest expert and judge of harmony, he liked best to play the viola, with appropriate loudness and softness.

In his youth, and until the approach of old age, he played the violin cleanly and penetratingly, and thus kept the orchestra in better order than he could have done with the harpsichord. He understood to perfection the possibilities of all stringed instruments. This is evidenced by his solos for the violin and for the violoncello without [accompanying] bass. One of the greatest violinists told me once that he had seen nothing more perfect for learning to be a good violinist, and could suggest nothing better to anyone eager to learn, than the said violin solos without bass. Thanks to his greatness in harmony, he accompanied trios on more than one occasion on the spur of the moment and, being in a good humor and knowing that the composer would not take it amiss, and on the basis of a sparsely figured continuo part just set before him, converted them into complete quartets, astounding the composer of the trios. When he listened to a rich and many-voiced fugue, he could soon say, after the first entries of the subjects, what contrapuntal devices it would be possible to apply, and which of them the composer by rights ought to apply, and on such occasions, when I was standing next to him, and he had voiced his surmises to me, he would joyfully nudge me when his expectations were fulfilled. He had a good penetrating voice of wide range and a good manner of singing. In counterpoints and fugues no one was as happy as he in all kinds of taste and figuration, and variety of ideas in general.

105

There are many adventurous stories about him. A few of them
may be true, and concern youthful pranks. The deceased never
liked to hear them mentioned, so pray omit these humorous things.
The family tree must be copied, and the description pertains to
it.[3] If you come here soon, this can be done in your presence, or if
you cannot, and are pressed for time, then I will attend to it
soon. In addition to the enclosed Concerto in F, I have made
two Sonatinas for two keyboard instruments [*Flügel*]. The latter,
as well as the other Sonatinas, I have for the time being not
made public. For your kind attempt to help deliver my poor
Israelites from the desert, I thank you devotedly in advance.[4]
I have scribbled out the above *Specialia Patris* without ornament,
just as they occurred to me. Use them as you please, and put them
into better order. To M. and Mme. Heyne my most obedient
respects.

Pray continue to love

Your

Bach.

I am afraid the post may already
have left. Excuse me.

[= Letter 48], 275–78, collated with facsimile of the autograph in:
Veröffentlichungen der Neuen Bachgesellschaft, XVII, No. 3.

81   CARL PHILIPP EMANUEL BACH TO JOHANN
NICOLAUS FORKEL, GÖTTINGEN [G.]

Hamburg, 13 January [17]75

The account of my late father's life in Mitzler,[1] dearest friend,
was thrown together by the late Agricola[2] and me in Berlin, and
Mitzler added only that part from the words "He joined the
Society" to the end. It is not worth much. The departed, like
myself or any true musician, was no lover of dry, mathematical
stuff.

ad 1mum:[3] The instruction received by the departed in Ohrdruf
may well have been designed for an organist and nothing more.

ad 2dum: Besides Froberger, Kerl, and Pachhelbel, he heard and
studied the works of Frescobaldi, the Baden Capellmeister Fischer,

Strunck, some old and good Frenchmen, Buxdehude, Reincken, Bruhns, and [crossed out: his teacher Böhm] the Lüneburg organist Böhm.[4]

ad 3um: I do not know what took him from Lüneburg to Weimar.

ad 4tum: The departed formed his taste by adding his own efforts.

ad 5tum: Through his own study and reflection alone he became even in his youth a pure and strong fugue writer. The above-named favorites were all strong fugue writers.

ad 6tum: As a result of frequent large-scale performances of music in churches, at court, and often in the open air, in strange and inconvenient places, he learnt the placing of the orchestra, without any systematic study of acoustics [*Phonurgie*]. He knew how to make good use of this experience, together with his native understanding of building design so far as it concerns sound; and these were supplemented in turn by his special insight into the proper design of an organ, the disposition of stops, and the placing of the same.

ad 7mum: If I exclude some (but, *nota bene,* not all) of his clavier pieces, particularly those for which he took the material from improvisations on the clavier, he composed everything else without instrument, but later tried it out on one.

ad 8um: Prince Leopold in Cöthen, Duke Ernst August in Weimar, and Duke Christian in Weissenfels particularly loved him, and rewarded him appropriately. In addition, he was particularly honored in Berlin and Dresden. But in general he did not have the most brilliant good fortune, because he did not do what it requires, namely, roam the world over. Yet by connoisseurs and lovers of the art he was sufficiently honored.

ad 9um: Since he himself had composed the most instructive pieces for the clavier, he brought up his pupils on them. In composition he started his pupils at once with what was practical, and omitted all the *dry species* of counterpoint that are given in Fux[5] and others. His pupils had to begin their studies by learning pure four-part thorough bass. From this he went to chorales; first he added the basses to them himself, and they had to invent the alto and tenor. Then he taught them to devise the basses themselves. He particularly insisted on the writing out of the thorough bass in [four real] parts [*Aussetzen der Stimmen im Generalbasse*]. In teaching fugues, he began with two-part ones, and so on. The realization of a thorough bass and the introduction to chorales

107

are without doubt the best method of studying composition, so far as harmony is concerned. As for the invention of ideas, he required this from the very beginning, and anyone who had none he advised to stay away from composition altogether. With his children as well as with other pupils he did not begin the study of composition until he had seen work of theirs in which he detected talent.

ad 10mum: Apart from his sons, the following pupils come to my mind: the organist Schubert, the organist Vogler, Goldberg of Count Brühl's household, the organist Altnicol (my late brother-in-law), the organist Krebs, Agricola, Kirnberger, Müthel in Riga, Voigt in Anspach.[6]

ad 11mum: In his last years he esteemed highly: Fux, Caldara, Händel, Kayser, Hasse, both Grauns, Telemann, Zelenka, Benda, and in general everything that was worthy of esteem in Berlin and Dresden.[7] Except for the first four, he knew the rest personally. In his younger days he saw a good deal of Telemann, who also stood godfather to me. [crossed out: He esteemed him, particularly in his instrumental things, very highly.] In his judgment of works he was, as regards harmony, very severe, but otherwise he valued everything that was really good, and gave it his acclaim even if it contained human weaknesses. With his many activities he hardly had time for the most necessary correspondence, and accordingly would not indulge in lengthy written exchanges. But he had the more opportunity to talk personally to good people as his house was like a beehive, and just as full of life. Association with him was pleasant for everyone, and often very edifying. Since he never wrote down anything about his life, the gaps are unavoidable. I cannot write any more. Farewell, and continue to love your true fr[iend] Bach.

[In the margin:] Which portrait do you wish to have for a frontispiece? The one you have is faulty. I have a beautiful original pastel, a good likeness. The cost of the family tree amounts to 2½ thalers. The present generation, where music is concerned, is degenerate.

I can oblige you with a few things by J. Xstoph,[8] if you wish.

[= Letter 48], 278–80, collated with facsimile of the autograph in *Veröffentlichungen* . . . (cf. Letter 80).

82   WOLFGANG AMADEUS MOZART TO HIS MOTHER, SALZBURG [G.]

Munich 14th january
1775

Thank goodness! My opera went in scena [1] yesterday the 13th; and turned out so well, that I cannot possibly describe the noise to Mama. First of all, the whole theater was so crammed that many people had to turn back again. After each and every Aria there was a constant frightful din of clapping, and shouts of viva Maestro. H: Highness the Electress, and the dowager, (: who were sitting vis à vis to me :) also said bravo to me. when the opera was over, during the time when people keep still until the ballet begins, there was nothing but clapping and shouts of bravo; it would stop, start again, and so forth. After this I went with my papa to a certain Chamber through which the Elector [2] and the whole court Must pass and I kissed the hands of t[heir] h[ighnesses] the Elector and Electress and the [other] highnesses, who were all very gracious. very early today H: princely grace the bishop of Chiemsee [3] sent word and congratulated me over the opera's unique and widespread success. as for our journey back, that won't occur so soon, and Mama should not wish for it either, for Mama well knows how wholesome it is to breathe [freely] [4] – – – – we will come – – soon enough. One right and necessary cause is that the opera will be repeated next friday, and I am very necessary to its Production – – or it would not be recognized again – – – – for it's quite curious here. I kiss Mama's hands 1000 times. My Reg[ards] to all good friends and lady-friends. my Compliments to Mr: Andretter, I beg him to forgive me for not having answered [him] yet, but I had no time at all, I'll do it soon. Addieu. *1000 little kisses* to bimberl.[5]

[= Letter 77], 516–17.—Tr. by editor.

83   JEAN-JACQUES ROUSSEAU TO PRINCE ALEXANDER BELOSELSKY, GENEVA [Fr.]

Paris, 27 May 1775

I am indeed glad, Your Highness, to have your esteem and your confidence. Upright hearts sense and respond to one another; and as I read your letter from Geneva once more, I said: Few men can inspire me with as much again.

You pity my former countrymen for not having risen to my defense when their statesmen were assassinating, so to speak, my soul. The cowards! I forgive them their injustice; it will be for posterity, perhaps, to avenge me.

By now, I am more to be pitied than they: they have lost, you say, a citizen who was their glory; but what is the loss of that brilliant phantasm compared with [the loss] they compelled me to suffer? I weep when I reflect that I no longer have any relations or friends, or a free and flourishing fatherland.

O lake on whose shores I spent the halcyon days of my childhood, delightful landscapes where for the first time I saw the majestic and touching sunrise, where I felt my heart's first emotions, the first transports of a genius that has since become too imperious and too famous—alas! I shall see you no more.

Burn this letter, I beg you; my sentiments might again be misinterpreted.

You ask whether I still copy music.[1] And why not? Is it shameful, perhaps, to work for a living? You wish me to resume writing; no, I will do it no more. I have told mankind some truths; they have taken them amiss; I will say no more.

You must be jesting when you ask for news from Paris. I go out only to walk, and [then] always in the same neighborhood. Some persons of wit do me too great an honor by sending me their books: I have stopped reading. I was brought a new comic opera the other day: the music is by Grétry,[2] whom you like so much, and the words are assuredly by a man of wit. But they have put noblemen on the lyric stage again. I beg your pardon, Your Highness, but those people have no expression, and what you need is honest peasants.[3]

My wife is honored by your remembrance. My misfortunes affect her heart as much as mine, but my head grows feebler.

There is only enough life left in me to suffer, and not even enough to be as sensible to your kindness as I should be. Therefore do not write to me again, Your Highness: I should be unable to answer you a second time. When you return to Paris, come to see me, and we shall talk.

I beg Your Highness to accept my respectful compliments.

J. J. Rousseau

[= Letter 68], XX, 312–14.—Tr. by editor.

84   CHRISTOPH WILLIBALD GLUCK TO THE BAILLI DU ROULLET, PARIS [Fr.]

Vienna 2nd December 1775

I am much obliged to you for the news you give me, which greatly amuses me, in particular that I will prevent you from producing *Iphigénie* if Mr l'Arrivé [1] does not play in it. When will you abandon your scruples concerning *Alceste?* Would you become pale and thin as at the time when we gave *Iphigénie?* I will certainly not tolerate it and I am resolved to cure you for ever on this point. Firstly, you write for the lyrical theater and not a tragedy for the comedians. This changes infinitely one's manner of approach. Though excellent masters in the making of tragedies, neither Racine nor Voltaire has ever been able to make an opera, and no one has measured up to this task as well as you. It is sometimes necessary to laugh at rules and to make one's own rules in order to produce good effects. The old Greeks were men like us with a nose and a pair of eyes. One must not always be *servile pecus* [2] and submit to their rules but, on the contrary, one must break with their habits, sever the chains with which they wish to bind us, and try to become original in our own right. Those persons who wept and who found the dénouement bad, when you read them your work, are sensitive, have a sound instinct, judge with their souls, that I agree, but are they infallible? My wife and I also wept when you read us your work, and, with all that, when I grasped the thing in its entirety, I found many

111

places which were not in keeping with the musical effect, but you mock me when you say that the third act belongs to me; you must think me very foolish or very vain. Do you believe that if one gave fifty pictures to a man, arranged according to one's taste, he could, by arranging them a little differently, imagine that he had painted them? The injustice you do to yourself makes me angry and I will make you angry in your turn by praising my dénouement and criticizing yours. According to your dénouement, the opera with the chorus who, *nota bene*, are actors and very interesting in the piece with the other characters—so it begins with pomp and some grandeur—your chorus are always active and the piece revolves very much around them in the first two acts, for they do not wish to lose so perfect a King and a Queen; now to the third act, where the chorus who took so much interest in preserving their sovereigns are seen no more and are quite forgotten. I say that the piece cannot finish before these poor people have been consoled. It is useless to tell me that Apollo brings them back; this seems to me an *hors d'oeuvre* [3] and one that is dragged in by the hair. Moreover, Apollo must play the sorcerer, for, when he changes the scene in the wood into a magnificent setting, another magic word is needed to transport the people there, who suddenly sing their chorus without being prepared gradually for their happiness. In my dénouement everything is prepared naturally, without any need to have recourse to miracles, and the piece finishes with the same pomp and grandeur but without the help of any alien spirit or artistry, as it had begun. It is not on account of the music that I hold to this, for the music here is of little consequence and very short, but because, in reading and re-reading the opera, I have never succeeded in persuading myself that it progresses naturally and that it can produce any effect. If all this still does not reassure you, I will convince you or you will convince me otherwise when I arrive in Paris. I beg you to continue writing to me on many things even if I do not reply, for I must work at present if I am to send you the first and second acts by the courier who leaves on the first of January next. You write that Mlle Rosalie [Levasseur] wishes to leave, in another letter Mlle la Guerre also. With whom is one to present operas? I foresee that *Alceste* will be the last opera I will be able to give, for without troops one cannot fight battles. My

wife, the little one⁴ and I send our compliments to Madame
la Ménardière, to you, and to Mr l'Abbé.⁵ Adieu, my admirable
friend, I embrace you with all my heart.

[= Letter 79], 75–77.

85 JOSEPH HAYDN TO "MADEMOISELLE LEONORE" [G.]

              Estoras, 6th July 1776.
Mademoiselle!
  You will not take it amiss if I hand you a hotchpotch of all
sorts of things as an answer to your request: to describe such
things properly takes time, and that I don't have; for this
reason, I do not dare write to Mons. Zoller personally, and
therefore ask forgiveness.

  I send you only a rough draft, for neither pride, nor fame,
but solely the great kindness and marked satisfaction that so
learned a national institution has shown towards my previous
compositions, have induced me to comply with their demand.

  I was born on the last day of March 1733,¹ in the market
town of Rohrau, Lower Austria, near Prugg on the Leythä.²
My late father was a wheelwright by profession, and served
Count Harrach, a great lover of music by nature. He [my
father] played the harp without knowing a note of music,
and as a boy of 5, I correctly sang all his simple little pieces:
this induced my father to entrust me to the care of my relative,
the schoolmaster in Haimburg, in order that I might learn the
rudiments of music and the other juvenile acquirements.
Almighty God (to Whom alone I owe the most profound
gratitude) endowed me, especially in music, with such pro-
ficiency that even in my 6th year I was able to sing some
Masses in the choir-loft, and to play a little on the harpsichord
and violin.

  When I was 7, the late *Capellmeister* von Reutter passed
through Haimburg and quite accidentally heard my weak but
pleasant voice. He forthwith took me to the choir house [of
St. Stephen's Cathedral in Vienna] where, apart from my
studies, I learnt the art of singing, the harpsichord, and the

113

violin, from very good masters. Until my 18th year I sang
soprano with great success, not only at St. Stephen's but also
at the Court. Finally I lost my voice, and then had to eke out
a wretched existence for eight whole years, by teaching young
pupils (many geniuses are ruined by having to earn their daily
bread, because they have no time to study): I experienced
this, too, and would never have learnt what little I did, had
I not, in my zeal for composition, composed well into the night;
I wrote diligently, but not quite correctly, until at last I had
the good fortune to learn the true fundamentals of composition
from the celebrated Herr Porpora (who was at that time in
Vienna): [3] finally, by the recommendation of the late Herr
von Fürnberg (from whom I received many marks of favor),
I was engaged as *Directeur* at Herr Count von Morzin's, and
from there as *Capellmeister* of His Highness the Prince
[Esterházy], in whose service I wish to live and die.

   Inter alia the following compositions of mine have received
the most approbation:

The operas
- *Le Pescatrici* [1769: perf. 1770]
- *L'incontro improvizo* [*sic*] [1775]
- *L'infedeltà delusa,* performed in the presence of Her Imperial and Royal Majesty [Maria Theresa, in 1773].

The oratorio *Il Ritorno di Tobia,* performed in Vienna [in 1775]

The *Stabat Mater* [1767], about which I received (through a good friend) a testimonial of our great composer Hasse,[4] containing quite undeserved eulogiums. I shall treasure this testimonial all my life, as if it were gold; not for its contents, but for the sake of so admirable a man.

   In the chamber-music style I have been fortunate enough to
please almost all nations except the Berliners; this is shown by
the public newspapers and letters addressed to me. I only wonder
that the Berlin gentlemen, who are otherwise so reasonable,
preserve no medium in their criticism of my music, for in one
weekly paper they praise me to the skies, whilst in another they

114

dash me sixty fathoms deep into the earth, and this without
explaining why; I know very well why: because they are
incapable of performing some of my works, and are too conceited
to take the trouble to understand them properly, and for other
reasons which, with God's help, I will answer in good time. *Herr
Capellmeister* von Dittersdorf,[5] in Silesia, wrote to me recently
and asked me to defend myself against their hard words, but I
answered that one swallow doesn't make the summer; and that
perhaps one of these days some unprejudiced person would stop
their tongues, as happened to them once before when they accused
me of monotony. Despite this, they try very hard to get all my
works, as Herr Baron von Sviten, the Imperial and Royal
Ambassador at Berlin, told me only last winter, when he was
in Vienna: [6] but enough of this.

Dear *Mademoiselle* Leonore: You will be good enough to give
this present letter, and my compliments, to Mons. Zoller for his
consideration: my highest ambition is only that all the world
regard me as the honest man I am.

I offer all my praises to Almighty God, for I owe them to Him
alone: my sole wish is to offend neither my neighbor, nor my
gracious Prince, nor above all our merciful God.

Meanwhile I remain, *Mademoiselle*, with high esteem,

Your most sincere friend and servant

Josephus Haydn [m.p.] ria [7]

[= Letter 75], 18–20.

86   CHRISTOPH WILLIBALD GLUCK TO CHRISTOPH
MARTIN WIELAND, WEIMAR [G.]

Vienna, 7th August 1776

Most highly esteemed Sir and friend,

Your letter of the 13th July was to me a gift which was all
the more agreeable because I had awaited it with great impatience.
Although time has lessened my pain, as it is wont to subdue all
human passions, even joy, yet your letter did not come too late
to fill the void left by the loss of my child. The friendship of
a Wieland, Klopstock,[1] and other such men is sufficient to

115

compensate and console anyone with feeling for all the sorrows
of this world. You give me hope that I may gain in Herr Goethe
a new friend of this kind, and my joy is now complete. While I
cannot expect either from you or from Herr Goethe a poem on
the good, snow-white, departed soul of my little one, however
much I might wish it, your Muse, dearest Wieland, will never be
unfaithful to you, unless you yourself wished it so; and Goethe,
whose writings, like yours, I have read and devoured, Goethe,
of whom Klopstock said to me, "This is the great man," can surely
not be prevented by any official duties from becoming inspired
and from laying one of his roses upon a grave that merits roses.
Is anything impossible for you and Goethe? Give my respects to
this excellent man and tell him that I would have prepared the
songs from his *Erwin* [2] for the theater here, if the people had not
been lacking to execute the same.

Instead of forgetting your *Antonius* and his *Cleopatra,* rather
forget the thought that this excess of love would shock people
in Vienna, where, in any case, there is now no German opera. [3]
I would gladly work with and for you, if you were willing to
send me your poetry; in Weimar, under such a Prince, in such
good company with Goethe and others, you cannot possibly lack
encouragement. All I would ask is that, instead of the usual
confidants, choruses should be introduced, of Romans on Antony's
side and of Egyptian women on Cleopatra's, for confidants or
other secondary characters make the play dull, because they are
too uninteresting; a further reason is that it is seldom easy to
find more than one good soprano singer. Choruses, however,
produce life and, if they fill the scenes, particularly at the end, they
make a splendid effect.

It may be that my relations with Vienna and Paris will permit
me to make a pleasure trip through Germany. Then Weimar
will be one of the first places I shall visit in order to see there
one of the finest collections of great men and draw fresh inspiration from the source.

I beg you to hand the enclosed to His Serene Highness and
to say as much concerning it on my behalf as you think fit, in
order to keep me in the favor of this illustrious Prince.

Farewell, and may you enjoy all the blessings of life which you
so richly deserve!

                                                Gluck.

[= Letter 79], 87-88.
116

87   WOLFGANG AMADEUS MOZART TO HIS FATHER, SALZBURG [G.]

[Munich, 29–30 September 1777]
that is true! [1] a great many good friends: but unfortunately, most of them can do little or nothing. yesterday at half past 10 I was at count Seau's [2] but found him much more serious and not so natural as the first time. yet it was only outward show. then today I was at Prince Zeil's [3] and he spoke to me very politely as follows. "I believe we shall not accomplish very much here. I talked with the Elector privately at table in Nümphenburg. [4] he said to me. it is still too early now. let him go, [let him] travel to italy, become famous. I am not turning him down. but it is still too early now." there we have it. most of the great nobles have such a frightful Italianate-Paroxysm. still he advised me to go to the Elector and to present my case as usual. today at table I had a confidential talk with Mr: wotschicka; [5] and he gave me an appointment for tomorrow at 9 o'clock, when he will surely arrange an audience for me. we are good friends now. he wished to know absolument who the Person is, [6] but I told him: rest assured that I am and will remain your friend, I too am quite convinced of your friendship; and let that suffice you. Now to resume my shistory [*schistori*]. the bishop of Chiemsee [8] has also talked all alone to the Electress; she shrugged her shoulders, and said: she will do the best she can. only she has great doubts. Now as for count Seau; count Seau asked prince Zeil, (: after the latter had told him everything :): Do you happen to know whether Mozart receives enough from home to allow him to stay here on a small subsidy. I should like to keep him. The bishop answered. I don't know. but I doubt it very much; yet you only need to talk to him about it; and that was the reason why he was so thoughtful on the following day. I like being here; and I am of the Opinion, like many of my good friends, that if I stayed here for only a year or two, I could earn a living and a reputation through my work, and consequently be sought after at court rather than be seeking. Mr: Albert [7] has had a Project in his head ever since my arrival, and its execution seems not impossible to me. that is he would like to assemble 10 good friends, each of whom would only need to spend 1 Ducat a month, that makes 10 Ducats, [or] 50 gulden, a month,
117

[or] 600 gulden a year; if then I received only 200 gulden a
year from count Seau, that would make 800 gulden – – how
does Papa like this idea? – – is it not friendly? – – should it not
be accepted, if by chance it came true? – – I am thoroughly
satisfied with it; I should be close to Salzburg; and were you,
My very dearest Papa, ever to feel like leaving Salzburg (: which
indeed I wish for with all my heart :) and spending your life
in Munich, it would be a very jolly and easy thing to arrange.
For having had 504 gulden to live on in Salzburg, then we could
surely live on 600 or 800 gulden in Munich? – – –
I have 100000 Compliments for you from countess larosè. That
is indeed a most gracious lady! and a very good friend to us.
Mr: von Dufresne told me recently that they both have often
wrangled with the *Praesidentin* [8] in our behalf. Papa stands very
high in countess larosé's favor. she says she has not often seen so
rational a Man!—and he has it written all over his face!—I go
to her every day. her brother is not here. [9]

today the 30^(th) I went to court with M:^(r) Wotschicka at 9
o'clock as had been arranged. everyone there was in hunting
dress. Baron kern was the chamberlain on duty. I would have
gone there yesterday evening, only I could not hurt Mr:
wotschicka's feelings, as he had taken it upon himself to have me
speak to the Elector. at 10 o'clock he led me into a narrow little
Chamber, through which H[is] El[ectoral] Highness would
have to walk to hear Mass before the hunt. count Seau came
past and greeted me in a very friendly manner: your servant,
dearest Mozart. when the Elector walked towards me, I said:
Your Elect[oral] Highness, permit me to fall most humbly at
your feet, and to proffer my services. What, away from
Salzburg altogether? Away altogether, yes Your Elec: Highness.
But why! got into a scrape, have you? – – Oh indeed not, Your
Highn:, I only asked for leave to go on a Journey, he [10] denied
it to me, and so I was obliged to take this step; though I had long
intended to go away: for Salzboug [*sic*] is no place for me, no
indeed. Heyday the young Fellow! but surely your father is
still in Salzboug?—yes, Your Elec: Highn, He falls most humbly
Ect. [*sic*] I have already been to italy Three times, have written
3 operas, am a member of the academy at Bologna, [where I] had
to sustain an Examination that has caused many a maestro to
labor and to sweat for 4 or 5 hours, and I finished it in an hour:
118

may this be a Token that I am capable of serving at any court.
My only desire, however, is to serve Your Elect: Highn: who
yourself are a great = = But my dear boy, there's no vacancy
here. so sorry. if only there was a vacancy. I assure Your Highn:
I would surely Do Honor to Munich. Well well, that is no help
at all, there's no vacancy here. this he said walking away. I now
commended myself to his good graces. Mr: wotschicka advised
me to show myself at the Elector's [court] often. this Afternoon
I went to see count Salern. The countess his daughter is a lady
in waiting now. she attended the hunt. I and Ravani were in
the street when the whole Procession returned. the Elect: and
the Electress greeted me in a very friendly way. countess Salern
recognized me at once. she waved me very many Compliments.
Baron Rumling whom I had seen earlier in the Ante Chamber
was never so *civil* to me before: I will write soon concerning
Salern. it went very well. very civil. and straightforward. now
I beg you to look after your health properly, I kiss Papa's hands
100000 times and am and remain.

[his] most obedient son
Wolfgang Amadé Mozart

P:S: Ma trés chere sœur,
I'll soon write you a special
letter all for yourself.
my Regards to A:B:C:M:R: and more
of the same letters. Addio.
a man built a house here and wrote on it:
To build a house is a great pleasure,
though I knew not it would cost a treasure.   During the night
someone wrote underneath:
and you'd have known you would be bled,
had you not been such a chucklehead:

[= Letter 77], II, 21–24.—Tr. by editor.

88   WOLFGANG AMADEUS MOZART TO HIS FATHER,
SALZBURG [G.]

<hr>

[Augsburg, 23–24 October 1777]

Mon trés cher Pére!

yesterday Wednesday the 22nd my concert went *in scena.*[1]
count wolfeck[2] attended diligently, and brought a few canonesses
along with him. I had already been to his logement to wait on
him during the very first days, but he wasn't here. he came back
some days ago, and when he learnt that I was here, he didn't
wait for me to call on him, but, just as I was picking up hat and
sword to pay him my visit, in he came at the door. now I must
give a description of the preceding days, before I come to the
Concert. last saturday I went to St: ulrich's, as I wrote [to you]
already. several days earlier, my Uncle[3] took me to the Abbot
of hl: kreüz [Heiligkreuz], who is a proper, fine, Honest old
Man. on the saturday before my visit to St: ulrich's, I returned
to the hl: kreüz monastery with my cousin,[4] because the Dean
and the Procurator had not been there the first time, and
because my cousin told me the Procurator was such a jolly man.
[Mozart's mother continues:]
today the 23 Wolfgang dines at hl: Creuz agane, I too was
invited, but as I have a belly ache from all the Cold weather, I
stayd at home. is it so cold at Salzburg too as it is here where
everything is frozen to gether like in the midle of winter, the
day after tomorrow Saturday (if nothing comes between :) we
have it in Mind to leave for wallerstein, the Consert here terned
out superbly, the newspapper will tell more, Mr. stein[5] took
great pains, and showed us mutch kindness, you can thank him
in writeing. I hope you and nanerl[6] are in good health, I am
already quite dejected because we got no letter this week, could
something be the matter with you. do write me soon so I can
stop being anxious. I am very astonished schuster's Duets have
not yet – –
[Mozart continues:]
pshaw! of course he's received them, – – *Mama:* Mercy, he has
been writing that he does not yet have them – – *wolf:* I cannot
endure an argument, he has them sure, and there's an end to it.
Mama: You are mistaken. *wolf:* No, I'm not mistaken, I will
show it to my Mama in writing. *Mama:* indeed, and where?
120

wolf: Here, read. now Mama is just reading it – – – last Sunday
I attended Mass at hl: kreüz. but at 10 o'clock I went to Mr:
stein's. that was the 19:ᵗʰ we Rehearsed a couple of Symphonies
for the Concert. afterwards I dined with my uncle at hl: kreüz:
we had Musique during the meal. badly as they fiddle, I still
prefer the Musique at the monastery to the orchestra at Augspurg.
I performed a symphony, and played vanhall's⁷ Concerto in B
flat on the violin, to the general applauso. The Dean is a fine,
jolly Man, he's a cousin of Eberlin's, his name is *Zeschinger,* he
knows Papa quite well. in the Evening during soupée I played
the strasbourg = Concerto.⁸ it flowed like oil. everybody praised
the lovely, clean Tone. after that they brought in a small
Clavichord. I Preluded, and played a sonata, and the fischer
Variations.⁹ then the others whispered in the Dean's ear that he
only should hear me play in organ style; I asked him to give me
a theme, he declined, but one of the religious gave me one. I
took it walking, and in the middle, (: the fugue was in g minor :)
I began [playing in the] major [mode], quite a witty thing, but
in the same tempo, then at last the theme once more, but
arsewise; it finally occurred to me, could I not use the witty
part along with the fugue theme too? – – I wasted no time
asking, but did it at once, and it went as accurately as if Daser¹⁰
had done the fitting. the Dean was quite beside himself. I give
up, there's no use, he said, I can't believe my ears, you are a
splendid Fellow. It's true my Abbot told me that in all his days
he'd never heard anyone play the organ so convincingly and so
earnestly. (: for he had heard me a few days earlier, but the
Dean wasn't there. :) in the end someone brought in a sonata
written in fugue style. I was to play it. but I said, gentlemen,
this is too much; I must confess it, I shan't be able to play *this*
sonata straight off. I should think not, said the Dean with much
Fervor, for he was wholly on my side. this is too much, no man
alive could do it. However, said I, I'll Attempt it anyhow.
Behind me I kept hearing the Dean: O You Archrascal. o you
rogue; o you you! – – I played till 11 o'clock. I was Bombarded
and as it were besieged with nothing but fugue themes. The
other day at *stein*'s he brought me a Sonata by Becché¹¹ – – I
believe I've written [you] this already. apropos of his little
Girl.¹² whoever can see and hear her play without laughing must
be made of *stone* [*stein*] like her father. She will sit at the very
top opposite the Treble [keys], never in the middle, the better to
121

move about and make grimaces. She will roll her *eyes*. she will smirk. if anything comes twice, she'll play it slower the 2:nd time. if it comes 3 times, slower again. She'll hold her Arm as high as can be when she plays a Passage, and when she lays stress on a Passage, she will do so with her arm, not her fingers, and that with studied heaviness and clumsiness. but best of all, when she plays a Passage (which ought to run as smooth as oil :) in which it is necessary to change fingers, she will not trouble herself very much, but when the time comes, she will leave off, lift her hand, and resume quite Cozily. that way, too, there's more likelihood of catching a wrong note, and that often has a Curious Effect. I am only writing this to give my Papa a notion of Clavier playing and instruction, so that Papa in Turn may derive some Benefit from it. Mr: stein is wholly infatuated with his daughter. she is 8 and a half years old, she learns absolutely everything by heart. she might amount to something: she has genius. but nothing will come of her this way. she will never acquire much speed, because she is at great pains to make her hand heavy. she will never acquire the most necessary and most difficult and the principal thing in Musique, namely *tempo*, because from childhood she has been at great pains never to play in time. Mr: *stein* and I discussed this Point for 2 hours at least. but I have already converted him Somewhat. he now asks for my advice on all matters. he had been wholly infatuated with Becché. now he sees and hears that I play more than Becché; that I make no grimaces and yet play with such expression that nobody, to his knowledge, has ever been able to handle his Piano fortes so well before. that I always play accurately in time. this makes them all wonder. That the left hand should remain quite unaffected by the Tempo rubato in an Adagio, this is inconceivable to them. with them, the left hand always yields. count Wolfeck and several others, who are quite Devoted to Beché, said publicly at the Concert the other day that I make mincemeat of Becché. count wolfeck kept running about in the hall saying, I've never heard the like of it in all my days. to me he said, I must tell you that I've never heard you play as you did today; I'll tell this to your Father too, just as soon as I reach salzbourg. what does Papa think was the first piece after the Symphony? – – The Concerto for 3 *Claviers:* [13] Mr: *Demler* played the First, I: the second, and Mr: *stein* the third. then I played alone, the last Sonata in D, [the one written] for Dürnitz: then my Concerto
122

in B flat.[14] then, alone again, a fugue in c minor quite in the
organ style, and suddenly a Splendid sonata in C major quite out
of my head, with a Rondeau at the end [of it]. there was a perfect
Uproar and din. Mr: stein was so full of admiration, he could
only make faces and grimaces. Mr: *Demler* couldn't stop
laughing. he is such a Curious Fellow that whenever he is very
pleased by anything, he has the most dreadful laughing fits.
this time he even began to swear. addio. I kiss Papa's hands, and
I embrace my sister with all my heart I am your most obedient
son

24 oct: 1777 augusta vindelicorum   Wolfgang Amadé Mozart [15]

[= Letter 77], II, 81–84.—Tr. by editor.

89   CHRISTOPH WILLIBALD GLUCK TO BARONESS
ANNA VON FRIES, VIENNA [Fr.]

                                      [Paris, 16 November 1777]
Madame,
    I have been so plagued over music and I am so disgusted with
it, that at present I would not write a single note for a louis.
So you can imagine the extent of my devotion to you, Madame,
since I could resolve to arrange for the harp the two songs which
I have the honor to send you. Never was a more terrible and
more hotly-disputed battle fought than that over my opera
Armide. The cabals against *Iphigénie*, *Orphée*, and *Alceste* were
by comparison mere petty encounters with minor forces.[1] The
Ambassador of Naples, in order to insure that Piccinni's opera
should be a great success, has been intriguing indefatigably
against me both at Court and amongst the nobility.[2] He has won
over Marmontel, La Harpe, and several academicians to write
against my musical system and my way of composing.[3] M. l'Abbé
Arnaud, M. Suard,[4] and a few others have rallied to my defense
and the quarrel became so heated that insults would have led to
deeds, if mutual friends had not restored order amongst them.
The *Journal de Paris*, which is sold daily, is full of it. This
dispute is making the Editor a fortune, for he already has more

than 2,500 subscribers in Paris. There, then, you have the revolution in French music carried out with the most blatant pomp. The enthusiasts tell me: Monsieur, you are fortunate to enjoy the honors of persecution; all great geniuses have experienced this. I would gladly send them to the devil with their fine speeches. The fact is that the opera which was said to have failed produced in seven performances 37,200 livres without reckoning the boxes rented for the year and the subscribers. Yesterday the eighth performance brought in 5,767 livres. Never has such a terrible crush nor such a sustained silence been known before. The pit was so crowded that one man, who had his hat on and was told by the attendant to remove it, replied: "Come and remove it yourself, for I cannot use my arms." That raised a laugh. I saw people coming out with their hair dishevelled and their clothes wringing wet, as if they had fallen into a river. Only a Frenchman would pay such a price for his pleasure. There are six points in the opera at which the public are forced to lose countenance and are carried away. Come, Madame, and see this tumult; it will amuse you as much as the opera itself. I am in despair that I cannot leave yet on account of the bad road: my wife is too frightened. I beg you to pay my compliments to the Baron and to Monsieur Gontard. I remain with the most perfect esteem,

Madame,

Your very humble and very obedient servant,

Le Chevalier Gluck.

PS. My wife sends you a thousand tender regards.
    Paris, 16 November 1777.

[= Letter 79], 124–25.

90   WOLFGANG AMADEUS MOZART TO HIS FATHER, SALZBURG [G.]

[Paris, 14 May 1778]

I am so busy now, how then will it be during the winter?—I believe I already wrote you in my last letter that the Duc de guines, whose Daughter is my Pupil in Composition, plays the flute surpassingly well, and she the Harp magnifique; [1] she has a great deal of Talent, and genius, [and] in particular an incomparable memory, for she plays all her pieces by heart, and really knows 200 of them. but she seriously doubts whether she also has any genius for Composition—especially with regard to thoughts—ideas;—but her father (who, between ourselves, is a little too much in love with her) says she most certainly has ideas; that it's just bashfulness—that she just lacks self-confidence. Well, we shall see. if she gets no ideas or thoughts (for at the moment she hasn't any at all), then it is all to no avail, for— goodness knows I cannot give her any. it is not the intention of the father to make a great Composer of her, she need not write, *he said*, any operas, any arias, any Concertos, any Symphonies, but merely grand Sonatas for her instrument and for mine. I gave her her 4:th Lesson today, and I'm tolerably pleased with her where the Rules of Composition and part writing are concerned—she set me a pretty good Bass part under the First Minuet I wrote down for her. now she's already beginning to write in 3 parts. it is going quite well; but she is soon Bored; but I cannot help her; I can't possibly move on. it's too early, even if the genius were really there, but unfortunately it is not—it will all have to be done by art. she has no ideas at all. nothing will come. I have Tried all kinds of things with her; among others, it also occurred to me to write down quite a simple Minuet and see whether she might not be able to make a variation on it?—well, that was of no use—Now then, thought I, she just doesn't know how to go about it—and so I began a variation only on the first bar and told her to continue in the same vein and to stick to the idea—this, at last, went pretty well. when it was finished, I asked her to be so good as to begin something herself—Just the top part, a Melody—well, she brooded for a whole quarter of an hour—and nothing came. so then I wrote down 4 bars of a Minuet and said—just see what

125

an Ass I am; here I've begun a Minuet, and can't even finish
the First section—do be so Kind as to complete it; this she
believed to be impossible; Finally with much effort—something
was brought forth; I was glad indeed that for once something
had come. Then she had to finish the whole Minuet—that is,
Only the Top part. but as *homework* I only asked her to vary
my 4 bars, and to write something of her own—to invent another
beginning—even to the same Harmony, so long as the Melody
was different. Well, tomorrow I'll see how it is going.—I believe
I shall soon get the Poem for my opera en deux acts [*sic*].[2] then
I must still present it to the Director, M:[r] de huime,[3] and see
whether he'll accept it. but there is no doubt of that; for
Noverre[4] announced it; and de huime owes his position to
Noverre. Noverre will also soon produce a new Ballet, and I
shall write the Musique for it.[5] Rudolph (the French horn
player) is in the king's service here, and my very good friend.
he has a thorough understanding of Composition and writes
very nicely. he has offered me the organist's post at Versailles,
if I wish to take it. it brings 2000 liv:[res] a year; but I should have
to live at versailles for 6 months. the other 6 in Paris, or wherever
I pleased. but I don't believe I'll take it. I must hear the advice
of some good friends on the subject. 2000 liv:[res] is really not such
a great deal of money. perhaps in german Coin, but not here.
it comes of course to 83 louisd'or and 8 liv:[res] a year, that is, in
our currency, 915 gulden and 45 kreutzer, (that would be a
great deal, of course) but here only 333 thaller and 2 liv:[res]—
that is not much. it's frightening how soon a thaller is gone.
it hardly astonishes me that the louisd'or is so disparaged here,
for it is [worth] very little. 4 such thallers, or one Louis, which
is the same, are gone straight away. Well Adieu. farewell. I kiss
your hands 1000 times and embrace my sister with all my heart
and am your most obedient son

Wolfgang Amadè Mozart

my Regards to all good friends and lady-friends,
especially to Mr: bullinger.[6]

[= Letter 77], II, 356–58.—Tr. by editor.

91   CHRISTOPH WILLIBALD GLUCK TO NICOLAS
FRANÇOIS GUILLARD, PARIS [Fr.]

Vienna, 17th June 1778

Your letters reach me very late, my friend. I received your latest
yesterday; it took sixteen days. I thought that you were ill.

Do you wish me to reply as to the essential points? Gladly. In
the first place, I will say that the changes you have made in
your fourth act are to no purpose, because I have already finished
the duet between Orestes and Pylades and the final air of the
act—"Divinité des grandes âmes!"—and I do not wish to alter
anything in them. In what you call the fifth act, you must cut
down the third strophe of the hymn, or else write a more interesting
one; people would not understand the words, "le spectre fier et
sauvage," which, besides, scarcely make the situation any more
moving. Your verses also must be of the same style, quatre à
quatre; [1] I myself have arranged the second strophe thus:

> Dans les cieux et sur la terre
> Tout est soumis à ta loi;
> Tout ce que l'Erebe enserre
> A ton nom pâlit d'effroi!

If then you wish to write a third strophe, it must go like the
second; and an important thing that must not be forgotten is
that the ceremony takes place while they are singing, and that the
same air must suit the ceremony. I also want Thoas, the high
priest, to enter in a fury, in the fourth scene, singing an air of
invective; and every verse must be written without recitative,
so as to be sung right up to the catastrophe. By this means the
dénouement would be richer by a decisive emotion and warmth,
which would penetrate the actors and chorus with an irresistible
effect. So, as far as you approve my idea, hasten to send me your
words; if not, I will keep to the words already written.

Now we come to the great air that ends the act during the
sacrifices. Here I want an air in which the words explain the
music at the same time as the situation. The sense must terminate
at the end of each verse, and not be repeated either at the
beginning or in the middle of the following verses. This is an
essential condition for the verses; though it may be disregarded

in the recitative, and so much the more happily as this mode of division is a certain means for distinguishing the lyric portion from the recitative, and for relieving the melody.

At the same time, for the words I ask of you, I want a verse of ten syllables, taking care to put a long and sonorous syllable wherever I indicate it:

> se mai senti spirarti sul volto
> lieve fiato que lento s'aggiri
> di, son questi gli estremi sospiri
> del mio fido che muore per me.[2]

I would like the third verse to be cut by a monosyllable as in Italian, for example, "vois nos peines, entends nos cris perçants." Your last verse must be somber and solemn, if you wish it to be congruous with my music.

After these four verses—or eight, if you wish, provided they are all in the same meter—will come the chorus, *Contemplez ces tristes apprêts!* and this appears to me to suit the situation very well. I want the air here to have pretty nearly the same sense. After the chorus, the air will be resumed *da capo,* or else there will simply be the four verses you have written. I explain myself rather confusedly, for my head is excited with music; if you do not understand me, we will leave the thing till my arrival, and then it will be soon done; the rest, I think, we will leave as it is, cutting down the recitatives here and there, wherever they seem to be too long and mere repetitions. This will not damage the work, which ought, I think, to have an astonishing effect.

On the question of my establishment I will await your first letter with the proposals, before I give you my opinion.[3] Meanwhile, arrange it so that the Queen only asks for me for an indefinite period, for a few years, to get me out of here in comfort. But let her do this without losing time, because I can no longer travel in winter. I would leave at the beginning of September. I must know a couple of months in advance so that I can sell my effects and arrange my affairs. Farewell, my very dear friend. I embrace you with all my heart, as also our acquaintances.

PS. I cannot find the Prologo. In any case, the Abbé Pezzona could have it sent from Parma. Mention it to our dear Abbé.[4]

This is how I would like the piece to be divided into four acts:

Scene 1

Orestes and Pylades in chains; the whole scene rests upon and ends with the aria: *unis de la plus tendre enfance.*

Scene 2

Orestes, Pylades, the Minister, the five verses remain cut, for they are superfluous.

Scene 3

Orestes alone

Scene 4

Orestes, the Eumenides

Scene 5

Iphigenia alone with Orestes, without bringing Pylades back. This scene can become interesting in dialogue and the word "Agamemnon," which Orestes repeats three times, is interesting. This will form a kind of duet between the two leading actors. The greater part of what they have to say can remain. That will give added variety to the piece, for Orestes and Pylades are too often together as it is and everything that he [Pylades] says in this scene is unimportant and forced. Orestes by himself is in a good position; Iphigenia almost tears the words from him by force. So it is not necessary for him to be held back by Pylades. Do this scene as quickly as possible; I would like the opera to be finished by the end of July.[5]

Scene 6

The sacrifice scene, then the end of the act. So the opera can remain in four acts. But dividing it into five, the end of the second act is, in my view, bad, because the Eumenides appear to Orestes only in a dream and in his imagination. This destroys the idea that, on seeing Iphigenia, he thinks he sees his mother. He must still be immersed in his dream when he speaks the words: "Ma mère! Ciel!" otherwise they would lose their effect. The act will be a little longer, but no matter. Everything in it is warmer.

[= Letter 79], 130–33.

92   WOLFGANG AMADEUS MOZART TO ABBÉ JOSEPH BULLINGER, SALZBURG [G.]

Dearest friend!   Paris ce 3 julliet
  for you alone.   1778

Mourn with me, my friend!—this was the Saddest Day of my
life—I write this at 2 o'clock in the morning—yet I must tell
it to you, my Mother, My dear Mother is no more!—god has
called her to himself—he wanted to have her, that I saw clearly—
therefore I resigned myself to god's will—He had given her to
me, he could also take her away from me. only imagine all the
disquiet, fears and anxieties I have endured these 14 days—she
died without regaining consciousness—like a light going out.
she was confessed 3 days earlier, and received Communion and
the extreme unction – – but during the past three days her mind
wandered continuously, but today at 21 minutes past 5 o'clock
her Death struggle began, at the same moment she lost all feeling
and all consciousness—I pressed her hand, spoke to her—but
she did not see me, did not hear me, and felt nothing—thus she
lay until she passed away, that is 5 hours later at 21 minutes
past 10 o'clock in the evening—no one was there but myself, a
good friend of ours (whom my father knows) Mr: Haina, and
the nurse—I cannot possibly describe to you the whole [course
of her] illness today—I am of the Opinion that she had to die—
god willed it so. meanwhile I ask you for nothing but an act of
friendship, that you prepare my father very gently for this sad
news—I have written him by the same Post—but only that she
is gravely ill—shall only wait for an answer—so that I may
govern myself accordingly. god give him strength and courage!—
my friend!—I was comforted not now, but long since!—I have
endured all with steadfastness and composure through god's
exceptional mercy. when it became so dangerous, I prayed god
for only 2 things, namely for a happy hour of death for my
Mother, and then for strength and courage for me—and the
good lord has heard me, and given me the 2 blessings in fullest
measure. I beg you therefore, dearest friend, sustain my father
for me, encourage him lest he take it too heavily and cruelly to
heart, when he really hears the worst. I also entrust my sister
to you with all my heart—go out to them at once, I beg you—
do not tell them yet that she is dead, but just prepare **them** for

it—Do what you like,—use every means—only proceed so that I may rest easy—and that I need not look for yet another calamity.—Sustain my dear father for me, and my dear sister. answer me at once, I beg you.—Adieu, I am your

as a precaution.
Rue du gros chenet
vis à vis celle du croissant
à l'hôtel des quatre   most obedient most thankful servant
fils aimont.   Wolfgang Amadè Mozart.

[= Letter 77], II, 390–91.—Tr. by editor.

93   CHRISTOPH WILLIBALD GLUCK TO ABBÉ FRANÇOIS ARNAUD, PARIS [Fr.]

Vienna, 15th July 1778

You are quite right, Monsieur, I will not be able to finish my two operas [1] in Vienna. I must get nearer to the poets, for we do not understand each other well from a distance. I reckon to leave here in the month of September, if Monsieur de Vismes [2] can obtain the Empress's permission for me to go to Paris. Without it I could not leave. M. le Bailly [3] will tell you the reasons. So I will probably have need once more of your redoubtable arm to strike down my enemies this next winter; without you I have not the courage to risk another battle. Meanwhile muster your troops, cajole our allies, particularly Madame de Vaines, [4] to whom I beg you to present my respects as also to all her [*sic*] illustrious society. Has she still that beautiful Circassian head? I often see her in my mind's eye, when I am working and do not feel sufficiently inspired; she must contribute greatly to the success of my operas.

The opera at Bologna was very well patronized. [5] The Duke and Duchess of Parma and the Archduke and Archduchess of Milan went to see it. In general the Italians have called it the great Opera of Bologna. One of my friends who had seen it presented in Vienna wrote to me that de Amici, who played the part of Alceste, was in the nude, that the actor who played Admetos was too old and that the ballets were all topsy-turvy;

131

they danced right into the chorus, "Pleure o patrie, o Thessalie!"
so you can imagine what happened afterwards. My friend
quotes an Italian proverb to compare the opera *Alceste* with the
world: "Il mondo va da se, e non casca, perchè non ha dove
cascare."[6] I will add that the other day, when I was with the
Prince von Kaunitz,[7] the envoy from Naples begged me to have
sent to him all the operas which I have made in France; they are
being asked of him in Naples, where people wish to have all that
I have done. That is an anecdote which will not greatly please
Monsieur l'Ambassadeur, God bless him. My wife pays you a
thousand compliments and I remain, with the greatest admiration
for your genius,

> Monsieur,
> Your very humble and very obedient servant
> Gluck.

[= Letter 79], 135–36.

94   WOLFGANG AMADEUS MOZART TO HIS FATHER, SALZBURG [G.]

Vienne ce 9 de maj

Mon trés cher Pére!   1781:

I am raging still!—and you, my excellent, dearest father, must
do so with me.—they have tried my Patience for so long—but
at last it has foundered. I am no longer so unfortunate as to
be in the service of Salzburg—today was my happy day;
listen:—
twice already that—I don't even know how I should call him[1]—
has said the most stupid and impertinent things to my face,
which I decided not to write you in order to spare you; and
only—because I always had you, my excellent father, before my
eyes, did I not revenge myself on the spot.—he called me a
⟨boy⟩, a ⟨wretched scoundrel⟩—told me to go on—and I—
suffered all—felt that not my Honor alone but also yours was
being impeached thereby—but—you wished it to be so—I
remained silent;—But hear this;—8 days ago the footman came
upstairs unexpectedly and said that I had to be off that Instant;

all the others had been notified of the Day, but not I;—and so
I hastily packed everything into my trunk, and—old Mad:^{me}
Weber [2] was good enough to offer me her home—here I have my
own pretty Room; live with obliging people, who lend me a
helping hand with all those things one often needs quickly and
cannot obtain (: when one is alone :).

I fixed on Wednesday (: that is today the 9:th :) for my Journey
[home] by the stage—but I could not collect the Moneys still
due to me in the time [that remained], therefore I postponed
my Journey till saturday—when I showed myself there today,
the valets told me that the Archbishop wished to give me a
Parcel to take along—I asked whether it was Pressing; and they
said Yes, that it was of great Moment—then I regret I cannot
have the Honor to serve H[is] P[rincely] Grace, since (: for the
above=mentioned reason :) I cannot leave before Saturday;—I
am [residing] outside the household, [and] must live at my
own expense—and so it is quite Natural that I cannot leave until
I am in a position to do so—for no one could wish me to be
ruined.—kleinmayer, Moll, Benecke, and the 2 personal valets
agreed with me entirely.—when I went in to him;—*NB:* first
I must tell you that ⟨schlaucher⟩ suggested I seize the ⟨pretext⟩
that the ⟨stage⟩ was already ⟨full⟩—it would be a stronger
argument with him;—well, when I went in to him, the first
thing was;—*Arch:* Well, when are you going, ⟨Boy⟩? *I:* I
meant to leave Tonight, but the Place was already taken. Then
all in one breath it poured out;—I was ⟨the most wretched
scoundrel he knew—no man⟩ served him so badly as I—he
advised me to leave still today, or he would write home that
the ⟨wages⟩ were to be withdrawn—it was impossible to put in
a word, he raged on like a fire—I listened to everything coolly—
he lied to my face that I receive 500 gulden in wages [3]—called
me a ⟨ne'er-do-well, rascal⟩, a ⟨fool⟩—oh I will not write you
all—At last as my blood began to boil, I said—then Yo[ur]
P[rincely] grace is not satisfied with me?—what, [said he,] do
you threaten me, you ⟨fool⟩ you?—there is the door, look you,
I will have no more to do with such a ⟨miserable boy⟩—
finally I said—nor I with you—then get out—*and I:* as I was
leaving—then it's settled; tomorrow you shall receive it in
writing.—tell me then dearest father whether I did not say this
too late rather than too soon? − − Hear me now;—I hold my
Honor above all else, and I know that so do you.—

133

do not be at all anxious about me;—I am so sure of myself here [in Vienna] that I would have resigned without the least cause—but as now I have had cause to do so, and that 3 times—I no longer deserve any credit for it; O Contraire I was twice used like a dog—the third time I just could not tolerate it;—so long as ⟨the archbishop⟩ remains here, I shall not give any ⟨concerts—that you think⟩ I shall place myself in a false ⟨Position⟩ with ⟨the Nobility⟩ and ⟨the emperor himself⟩, is quite wrong—⟨the archbishop⟩ is hated here, and by the ⟨emperor most of all⟩—this is precisely his grievance, that the emperor has not invited him to laxenburg [4] —I shall send you some Money by the next mail, to prove to you that I am not starving here.

for the rest I beg you to be merry—for my luck is now beginning, and I hope my luck will also be yours.—write me ⟨secretly⟩ that you are pleased with this, and well may you be indeed—⟨officially⟩ however ⟨scold me roundly for it⟩, so that ⟨no blame can be fastened on you—should⟩ however ⟨the archbishop⟩ subject you to the slightest ⟨impertinence⟩, then come ⟨to me in Vienna with my sister⟩ at once—⟨all 3 of us can live⟩ [here], I assure you upon my Honor— yet I should prefer it if you could ⟨hold out⟩ for another Year —write me no more letters to the teutsche haus, or by Packet—I will have no more to do with Salzburg—I hate the Archbishop to the point of madness. Adieu—I kiss your hands 1000 times, and I embrace my dear sister with all my heart and am Ever your obed: Son
just write
to be delivered auf dem

Peter im Aug＝gottes [5]
on the 2nd floor.
⟨give me soon to understand
that you are pleased, for that
is all I lack to make my   W: A: Mozart
present happiness complete.⟩ *Adieu.*

[= Letter 77], III, 110–12.—Tr. by editor.

95   WOLFGANG AMADEUS MOZART TO HIS FATHER,
SALZBURG [G.]

———————————————————————————————————

                                        Vienne ce 26 de *Septembre*
          Mon trés cher Pére!   *1781*
Forgive me for making you pay more Postage recently!—but
I just had no essential news—and thought to please you by
giving you some small Idea of the opera.[1] the opera had begun
with a Monologue, and I asked Mr: Stephani[2] to make a little
arietta out of it—and that, instead of having those two
chattering away after osmin's[3] little song, this be made into
a Duet.—As we have Mr: fischer in mind for the Role of
osmin, and he certainly has a remarkable Bass voice (: notwithstanding the Archbishop's[4] saying to me that he sings
too low for a Bass, but I assured him he'd sing higher the next
time— :) one ought to make Use of such a Man, particularly
as he has the local Public all on his side.—but in the original
libretto this osmin has only that one little song, and nothing
else to sing, except the Terzetto and finale. And so he has
been given an aria in the First Act, and shall have another
in the 2:nd too.—It was I who provided that whole aria to Mr:
Stephani;—and the greater part of the Music for it was already
completed before Stephani had heard a Word about the
matter.—all you have of it is its beginning and the End,
which ought to be very Effective—osmin's rage is made comical
because it is accompanied by turkish Music.—in working out
the aria, I have allowed his beautiful low notes (: spite of the
Salzburg Midas :) to sparkle.—the [passage], *drum beym
Barte des Propheten* etc: is in the same tempo to be sure, but
with fast Notes—and since his rage keeps growing, the allegro
assai—in a quite different meter and in another Key—
[occurring at a point] when one believes the aria has come
to an End—ought to have the very best Effect; for a Man who
finds himself so violently enraged, oversteps all [the bounds
of] order, Moderation and Resolve, he forgets himself—and
so the Music must forget itself too—but since the passions,
violent or otherwise, ought never to be expressed so far as to
excite Disgust, and Music, even in the most frightful situation,
must never offend the Ear, but please it even then, that is,
Must always remain Music, therefore I chose not a key foreign

135

to the f (: the aria's key :), but a neighboring one—not the
nearest, D minor, but the next, A minor.—Now for Bellmont's
aria in A Major, *O wie ängstlich, o wie feurig:* you know
how that is expressed—the throbbing of a heart in love is
also evident—the 2 violins in octaves.—this is the favorite aria
of all those who have heard it—mine too.—and was written
entirely for Adamberger's voice. one can see the trembling
—the wavering—one can see how the breast heaves—which
is expressed by means of a crescendo—one can hear the
murmuring and sighing—which is conveyed by the first violins
with Mutes and a flute in unison with them.—
The Janissaries' Chorus is all one can demand of a Janissaries'
Chorus.—short and merry;—and quite written for the Viennese.
—Konstanze's aria I sacrificed somewhat to Mad:^{selle} Cavallieri's
voluble gullet.—*Trennung war mein banges loos und nun
schwimmt mein aug in Thränen* is what I tried to express, as
much as an italian *aria di bravura* will permit.—I changed that
hui into *schnell,*[5] thus: *doch wie schnell schwand meine freude*
etc: I don't know what our german poets can be thinking of;—
if they cannot understand the theater, where opera is concerned
—at least they ought not to let their characters speak as if
they were confronted with pigs.—*hui Sau;*—
Now for the Terzetto, that is, the conclusion of the first Act.
—Pedrillo has given out that his Master is an Architect, that
he may have an opportunity of meeting his konstanze in the
garden. Bassa [Selim] has taken him into his service;—osmin,
the keeper, who knows nothing of this and is a rude lout and
an Archenemy of all strangers, is impertinent and will not let
them into the garden. the first thing [I] indicated [for you]
is very short—and since the Text permitted it, I set it pretty
well for 3 parts. but then the [section in] major suddenly
begins, pianissimo—it must go very quickly—and the end will
make a good deal of noise—which, anyhow, is all that's
wanted at the end of an Act—The more noise, The better;—
The shorter, The better—so that the people won't cool off before
the applause.—
Of the overture you only have 14 Bars.—it's quite short—
alternates constantly between forte and piano; and the turkish
Music always sets in at the forte.—keeps modulating through
the keys—and I don't think one could go to sleep over it,
even after a quite sleepless Night.—Now I am sitting upon
136

thorns—the First Act was finished over 3 weeks ago—an aria in the 2:nd Act, and the Drunk Duet (: per li Sig:^{ri} vienesi^6 :) which consists of nothing but *my* turkish Tattoo, are already completed;—but I can do no more—for now the whole story is being turned topsy=turvy—and that at my request.—at the beginning of the third Act there's a charming quintet, or rather finale—but I would rather have this at the end of the 2:nd Act. to achieve this, a great change, Indeed a whole New plot must be got up—and Stephani is up to his eyes in work and so a little patience is needed.—everybody grumbles over Stephani—perhaps with me, too, he's only being friendly to my face—but he *is* arranging my libretto—and in fact just as I wish to have it—to a nicety—and more I do not require of him, goodness knows!—Well now that was a long babble about the opera; but it had to be.—please send me the March I mentioned recently.—gylofsky says Daubrawaick is coming soon.—Fräulein von Auerhammer and I are anxiously awaiting the 2 Double Concertos.^{7}—I hope we shall not have to await them as fruitlessly as the Jews the Messiah.—Now Adieu—a hearty farewell, I kiss your hands 1000 times and embrace my dear sister with all my heart (: I hope her health has improved :) and am Ever your most obedient son W: A: Mozart.

[= Letter 77], III, 161–64.—Tr. by editor.

96   CHRISTOPH WILLIBALD GLUCK TO MONSIEUR VALENTIN, AIGUILLON [Fr.]

From Vienna, 17th April 1782

Monsieur,

Your obliging letter gave me great pleasure and I must thank you for it.

It is very flattering to me and I see in it the imprint of an ardent genius, eager to learn, as well as the essential qualities of a good heart and an excellent character, which do you much honor.

If the state of my health permitted it and if I could still

undertake something relating to dramatic art, I could think of nothing more pressing than to accept the offer you have just made me, and I am convinced that we should be both well pleased.

I have been ill for several months following an apoplectic stroke, which came upon me last year. My head is weakened and my right arm is paralyzed. I am incapable of doing the least work which is continuous; I am not allowed, and still less am I able, to apply myself in any way. So you see, Monsieur, that I cannot lend myself to your request, which does you so much credit and me so much honor. It is against my wishes but it is impossible to do otherwise.

You are young, Monsieur, and you are full of goodwill; work, and I have no doubt you will make progress, gain advancement and achieve success.

Determination and courage in your studies, reflection and a sense of unity in a work as a whole, and above all the seeking of truth in expression: all these, allied to the rules of art, will take you far. The simplicity of nature and the force of emotion must be your guides more than all else. He who departs from them invariably slips into absurd incongruities which condemn him to mediocrity.

These are my masters; they must be yours. In this school and with the natural and acquired qualities which are necessary, one finds the right road.

Several stray from it by failing to observe these rules of conduct while following an everyday routine.

Sound them, these masters, consult them, question them. They are gentle with those who seek them. They listen to you; they will reply; they will lead you.

Adieu, Monsieur.

Pray accept these few pieces of advice given to you by an invalid, who is no longer good for anything else, and rest assured of the feeling of esteem which you deserve, which you have inspired in me, and with which I have the honor, Monsieur, to be

Your very humble and very obedient servant
Le Chevalier Gluck.

[= Letter 79], 195–96.

97   WOLFGANG AMADEUS MOZART TO HIS FATHER,
SALZBURG [G.]

vienne ce 20 de Jullet
1782.

Mon trés cher Père!

I hope you safely received my last letter in which I Informed
you of my opera's good reception.[1]—It was given for the
2:nd Time yesterday;—can you imagine that there was an
even Stronger Cabal yesterday than on the first evening?—
the whole First act was hissed at.—still, they could not prevent
loud cheers of *Bravo* during the arias.—and so I placed all my
hopes in the closing trio—but there misfortune caused fischer
to fail—this made Dauer (: Pedrillo :) fail too—and Adamberger alone could hardly repair all the damage—consequently
the whole Effect was lost, and so this time—*it was not encored*.
—I was in such a Rage I did not know myself, Adamberger
too—and said at once—that I would not let the opera be given
[again] without first holding a small Rehearsal (: for the
Singers :).—in the 2:d act both Duets were encored as at the
First performance, and so was Belmont's Rondeau *wenn der
freude thränen fliessen.*—the theater was perhaps even fuller
than the first time.—on the previous day no reserved seats were
to be had either in the Noble parterre or in the 3:rd Tier; no
more loges either. the Opera has brought in 1200 gulden in
2 days.—
with this I send you the original [score] and 2 Libretti.—
You will find much in it that has been crossed out; this is
because I knew that here [in Vienna] the Score would be
Copied out at once—therefore I gave free rein to my thoughts
—and Only before giving it out to be copied did I make my
alterations and abridgments here and there.—and just as you
receive it, so was it performed.—here and there the trumpets
and Kettledrums, flutes, Clarinet, turkish Music are missing—
because I could not get any Paper with so many staves.—
they are written out on Extra sheets—the Copyist has probably
lost them, for he could not find them.—The First Act (: while
I was having it delivered I can't remember where :) unfortunately fell in the muck; that is why it is so dirty.—
My task now is not a trifling one.—by Sunday week my Opera
must be set for wind band—or someone else will do it first—

and have the Profit of it instead of me; and now I am to write a New Symphony besides! [2]—how will that be possible!—you cannot imagine how difficult it is to set such a thing for wind band—so that it will suit the wind instruments, and yet lose none of the Effect in the process.—Ah well, I'll have to spend the Nights at it, there's no other way—and let it be for your sake, my dearest father.—you shall certainly receive something every Posting day—and I will work as fast as I can—and, so far as Haste will permit me—write well.— count Zitchi sends word this very moment, asking me to drive out to laxenburg with him, so he can produce me before prince kaunitz.[3]—Therefore I must close in order to dress— for when I don't mean to go out, I always remain in my Negligèe.
the rest of the Parts have arrived from the Copyist's this very moment.
adieu. I kiss your hands 1000 times, and I embrace my dear sister with all my heart and am Ever your

P:S: My dear konstanze sends her   most obedient Son
     respects to both.[4]   W: A: Mozart

[= Letter 77], III, 212–13.—Tr. by editor.

98   ANDRÉ ERNEST MODESTE GRÉTRY TO MICHEL JEAN SEDAINE, PARIS [Fr.]

[Paris, 23 October 1784]
My friend, all of Paris is busy making up a dénouement for *Richard* [1]; they are pronouncing it no less a success than *Figaro*,[2] provided the king is delivered in a triumphal manner and by a *coup de théâtre* that will astonish the spectators. I, therefore, have also been thinking about it for my own part, and here is what I would propose to you, and a very easy thing to do, so long as Philippe is hoarse. To begin with, during the scene between Marguerite and Blondel in the third act, it would be necessary for Blondel to say to that princess: *Let us*

employ every argument, Madam, to persuade him that his master is a traitor. If Florestan cannot be persuaded, I will leave you and will go fetch the King at the head of your numerous retinue, or die. The Governor will enter, have his scene with Laurette, then Williams, then the Countess hers. During the chorus: *Restore to me the hero I love,* we shall have Florestan say some short phrases two or three times, as, for example: "How unhappy am I . . . I would fulfill your wishes . . . but my duty, my honor . . ." Thereupon Blondel departs, and this exit, I believe, is alarming for the spectator; then we could give Laurette a little song of lively reproach toward her lover. Two or three cannon shots or a drum roll will be heard behind the scenes, even though gunpowder might, perhaps, not have been invented at that time. The scenery at the back will rise, as in your *Déserteur,* and Blondel will be seen, sword in hand, bringing Richard and the garrison arrested by the knights of the countess' retinue. This scene must be designed by an artist: Robert will answer our purpose. The countess will try to fly into Richard's arms, [but] will feel faint as she is about to rush forth; Richard throws himself at her feet; William and Laurette restrain the knight—and the last chorus just as it is.

You can see, my friend, that it is only a matter of a quarter of an hour's work for us to make these changes which, I believe, will have the greatest effect.

I embrace you with all my heart.

Grétry.

Paris, 23 October 1784.

[= Letter 41], 103–104.—Tr. by editor.

99   CARL PHILIPP EMANUEL BACH TO JOHANN
JOACHIM ESCHENBURG, BRUNSWICK [G.]

Hamburg, 21 Jan. [17]86.

I am most obliged to you, my dear Professor, for your Händel.

I am dissatisfied with Mr. Burney['s book] in several places. The same thing happens to Händel that befalls others, when people want to deify them, they generally suffer. Comparisons are hard and indeed there is no need for them. Kayser here in Händel's day greatly surpassed him in Melody and Händel besides would never have become a Hasse, Graun &c in *this*, even had he lived in their recent times.[1] But it was not necessary; he was, particularly in his Oratorios, great enough. But to write concerning organ-playing: *that he surpassed* &c *my father;* this no man can say who lives in England where there are unimportant organs NB all without pedals,[2] who consequently has no insight in the most distinctive part of organ-playing, who perhaps has never seen or heard any organ pieces, who finally is certainly unacquainted with my father's clavier works, particularly those for organ, and in these with the consistent obligato use of the pedals which are given now the main melody, now the alto, now the tenor, at all times in fugues where *a voice is never dropped* and the hardest passages occur, besides which the feet are kept active with the greatest fire and brilliance, en fin countless things of which Burney knows nothing &c [3]

Hasse, Faustina, Quanz [4] and others, who knew Händel well and heard him, said in the yr. 1728 or 1729, when my father played in public at Dressden [sic]: Bach has brought organ-playing to its highest point. *see Quantz's Anweisung.* Seriously, the difference here could not be greater. Did Händel ever write Trios for two manuals and pedals? Certainly not. Consequently, there can be no comparison in this; the disparity is too great. One need but inspect the clavier and organ works of the two men.

Forgive my chatter and scrawl! The drollest thing of all is the gracious precaution of the King, whereby Händel's juvenilia are being preserved with the utmost care.[5]

I do not at all compare myself with Händel, yet I recently

burned more than a ream of my old works and I rejoice that
they are no more. Let this not prevent you from continuing
to love

                                        Your devoted
I believe Mr. Schwanberg [6]   Bach.
is of my opinion.

[1st p., left margin:] A merchant from these parts, Mr.
Michael Theodor Völckers is going to your fair on 25 inst.,
stays there at the Rose on the Kohlmarkt with Mr. Nicolai
and returns again on 4 Febr., he'll gladly bring me the things
that you will give him.

AUTOGRAPH, Rudolf F. Kallir Collection, New York: 1 sheet, 315 ×
195 mm., folded to form 4 pp.; last p. blank; watermark: GR surmounted by
crown.—Tr. by editor.

100   WOLFGANG AMADEUS MOZART TO HIS FATHER, SALZBURG [G.]

                                        [Vienna, 4 April 1787]
    Mon tres cher Père!—
    I find it most annoying that because of storace's [1] Stupidity My
Letter has not reached you;—in it I wrote among other
things that I hoped you had received my last Communication—
but since you make no Mention of that Communication (: it
was my 2nd letter from Prague [2] :) I don't know what to
think; it is quite possible that some Servant of count Thun's
thought good to pocket the Postage;—I would much sooner
indeed pay double the Postage than know my letters have got
into the wrong Hands,—Ramm and *2 Fischers*—the Bass
singer and the Oboist from London—arrived here this Lent. [3]
—if the latter played no better when we knew him in Holland
than he plays now, then he surely doesn't deserve the Renomeè
he enjoys.—*Nevertheless, between ourselves.*—I was then at
an Age when I was incapable of passing judgment—I only
remember that I liked him immensely, as did the whole World;
—this will be thought quite natural, if one remembers that
the taste has changed immensely.—perhaps his Playing is old-
143

fashioned.—but No!—in a Word, he Plays like a Wretched scholar—Young *André* who studied with fiala plays a thousand times better—and then his Concertos!—of his own Composition —Each Ritornello lasts a Quarter of an hour—then in comes the Hero—lifts one leaden foot after the other—and then Plumps them on the Ground by turns—his Tone is quite Nasal —and his sustained notes are like a tremulant on the Organ. would you ever have imagined such a Picture?—and yet it is nothing but the Truth—but a Truth I tell only to *you.*— This very moment I have heard News that greatly dejects me— the more so as from your last [letter] I had Supposed that thank goodness you were in good health;—But now I hear that you really are unwell! I need hardly tell you how ardently I look forward to a Reassuring Word from you personally; and to be sure I hope for it—though I have accustomed myself always to imagine the worst on all Occasions. Since Death (: rightly understood :) is the true Goal of our lives, I have these last Few Years made myself so familiar with that true, best friend of Man, that its Image not only has ceased being an object of terror to me, but on the contrary has become a source of much calm and consolation! and I thank my God for the blessing he bestowed on me by giving me the opportunity (: you understand me [4] :) of recognizing it as the *key* to our true Happiness.—I never lie down on my bed without reflecting that perhaps (: Young as I am :) I may have ceased to exist by the next Day—and yet none of my acquaintances can possibly say that I am morose or sad in their Company—and for this happiness I thank my Creator every Day and wish it for All my fellow Men with my whole Heart.—In the letter (: which storace packed [in her luggage] :) I already exposed my Views on this Point to you (: on the occasion of the tragic Death of My dearest most beloved Friend count von Hatzfeld [5] :)—he was just 31 years old; like myself. I do not pity *him*—but myself, with all my heart, and all those who knew him as well as I did.—I hope and trust you are feeling better even as I write this; but should you against all expectations not feel better, then I beg you by . . . . . . not to conceal it from me, but to write or have someone write me the plain Truth, so that I may fly to your Arms as quickly as is humanly possible; I implore you by all that—is holy to us.—I hope nonetheless to receive a Reassuring

letter from you soon, and in that pleasant Expectation I kiss
your hands 1000 times, as do my Wife and Carl,[6] and am Ever
                              your most obedient Son
                                    W. A. Mozart.[7]

Vienna the 4th of April *1787*

[= Letter 77], IV, 40–42.—Tr. by editor.

101   WOLFGANG AMADEUS MOZART TO BARON
GOTTFRIED VON JACQUIN, VIENNA [G.]

                                   [Vienna, end of May 1787]
Dearest friend!—Please ask Mr: Exner to come at 9 o'clock
tomorrow to Bleed my wife.—With this I send you your
Amynt[1] and the Church song—Be so Good as to give the
Sonata[2] to your Sister with my Regards;—but she ought to
apply herself to it at once, for it is rather difficult.—adieu.—
                                   your true friend
                                 Mozart $\frac{m}{p}$[3]
I inform you that today when I came home I received the
sad News of my beloved Father's Death.[4]—You can imagine
my State!—

[= Letter 77], IV, 48.—Tr. by editor.

102   LUDWIG VAN BEETHOVEN TO JOSEPH WILHELM
VON SCHADEN, AUGSBURG [G.]

15th September   Bonn 1787.

          Most nobly born
     especially valued friend!
what you think of me, I can easily conclude; that you have
justifiable causes to think unfavorably of me I cannot deny;
145

yet I shall not excuse myself before indicating the reasons which lead me to hope that my apologies will be accepted. I must admit to you: that since I left augspurg, my joy and with it my health began to cease; the nearer I came to my Native city, the more letters I received from my father, [urging me] to travel faster than usual, as my mother was not in a propitious state of health, I therefore hurried as much as I could, as I myself began to be unwell: the desire to see my sick mother one more time removed all Obstacles for me and helped me to overcome the greatest hardships. I still chanced to see my mother, but in the most wretched state of health; she was suffering from consumption and finally died approximately seven weeks ago, having endured much pain and suffering. she was such a good kind mother to me, my best friend; o! who was happier than I, when I could still pronounce the sweet name mother, and it was heard, and to whom can I say it now? to the mute likenesses of her, which my imagination pieces together for me? since I have been here, I have enjoyed few pleasurable hours; I have been afflicted with asthma all the time, and I am afraid that a consumption may arise from it perhaps; to this is added melancholy, which is almost as great an evil to me as my illness itself. now put yourself in my place, and I hope to be forgiven for my long silence. the extraordinary kindness and friendliness you showed me in lending me three Krlin [1] at augspurg, I must ask you to still bear with me awhile; my journey cost me a great deal, and here I may not hope for replenishment, not even the slightest; my destiny here in bonn is not favorable.

you will forgive me for detaining you so long with my chatting, it was all necessary for my apology. I beg you not to let your honorable friendship fail me, I have no greater wish than to make myself worthy of your friendship in any way.

I am with all respect
your most obedient servant and friend
l. v. beethoven.
kurf = kölnischer hoforganist. [2]

Facsimile of the autograph: Ludwig Schiedermair, *Der junge Beethoven* (Leipzig: Quelle & Meyer, 1925), between pp. 184–85.—Tr. by editor.

103   JOSEPH HAYDN TO ARTARIA & CO., VIENNA [G.]

Estoras, 7th October 1787.

Mon tres cher amy,

I shall send you the Quartets,[1] at the very first opportunity, and I shall be playing through them today; I cannot send them in the mail bag. I was astonished at your penultimate letter concerning the theft of the Quartets. I assure you on my honor that they were not copied by my copyist, who is a most honest fellow, whereas your copyist is a rascal, for he offered mine 8 gold ducats this winter if he would give him the *Seven Words*.[2] I am sorry not to be in Vienna myself so as to have him arrested: my plan would be to make Herr Lausch appear before Herr von Augusti, the mayor, and make him confess from whom he received the Quartets. Herr von Augusti is an old friend of mine and will certainly help you in this matter, as he did once before in just such an affair. Although you have everything copied on your own premises, you may be swindled all the same, because the rascals put a piece of paper *a parte* under the music, and thus by degrees they secretly copy the part they have in front of them. I am sorry that this misfortune happened to you. In future I shall take the precaution of sending my own copyist up to you. I am, most respectfully,

Your wholly obedient servant,
Haydn.

[= Letter 75], 70–71.

104   JOSEPH HAYDN TO FRANZ ROTH, PRAGUE [G.]

[Estoras,] December 1787.

. . . . You ask me for an *opera buffa*. Most willingly, if you want to have one of my vocal compositions for yourself alone. But if you intend to produce it on the stage at Prague, in that case I cannot comply with your wish, because all my operas are far too closely connected with our personal circle

(Esterház, in Hungary), and moreover they would not produce the proper effect, which I calculated in accordance with the locality. It would be quite another matter if I were to have the great good fortune to compose a brand new libretto for your theater. But even then I should be risking a good deal, for scarcely any man can brook comparison with the great Mozart.

If I could only impress on the soul of every friend of music, and on high personages in particular, how inimitable are Mozart's works, how profound, how musically intelligent, how extraordinarily sensitive! (for this is how I understand them, how I feel them)—why then the nations would vie with each other to possess such a jewel within their frontiers. Prague should hold him fast—but should reward him, too; for without this, the history of great geniuses is sad indeed, and gives but little encouragement to posterity to further exertions; and unfortunately this is why so many promising intellects fall by the wayside. It enrages me to think that this incomparable Mozart is not yet engaged by some imperial or royal court! Forgive me if I lose my head: but I love the man so dearly. I am, &c.

Joseph Hayden [sic].

P.S. My respectful compliments to the Prague Orchestra and all the virtuosi there.

[= Letter 75], 73–74.

105　　JOSEPH HAYDN TO MARIA ANNA VON GENZINGER, VIENNA [G.]

[Estoras, 9 February 1790]

Nobly born,
Most highly respected and kindest Frau von Gennzinger,
    Well, here I sit in my wilderness—forsaken—like a poor waif—almost without any human society—melancholy—full of the memories of past glorious days—yes! past alas!—and who knows when these days will return again? Those wonderful parties? Where the whole circle is one heart, one soul—all

those beautiful musical evenings—which can only be remembered, and not described—where are all those enthusiastic moments?—all gone—and gone for a long time.[1] Your Grace musn't be surprised that I haven't written up to now to thank you. I found everything at home in confusion, and for 3 days I didn't know if I was *Capell*-master or *Capell*-servant. Nothing could console me, my whole house was in confusion, my pianoforte which I usually love so much was perverse and disobedient, it irritated rather than calmed me, I could only sleep very little, even my dreams persecuted me; and then, just when I was happily dreaming that I was listening to the opera *Le nozze di Figaro,* that horrible north wind woke me and almost blew my nightcap off my head; I lost 20 lbs. in weight in 3 days, for the good Viennese food I had in me disappeared on the journey; alas! alas! I thought to myself as I was eating in the mess here, instead of that delicious slice of beef, a chunk of a cow 50 years old; instead of a ragout with little dumplings, an old sheep with carrots; instead of a Bohemian pheasant, a leathery joint; instead of those fine and delicate oranges, a *Dschabl* or so-called *gross Sallat* [*sic*]; instead of pastry, dry apple-fritters and hazelnuts—and that's what I have to eat. Alas! alas! I thought to myself, if I could only have a little bit of what I couldn't eat up in Vienna.—Here in Estoras no one asks me: Would you like some chocolate, with milk or without? Will you take some coffee, black, or with cream? What may I offer you, my dear Haydn? Would you like a vanilla or a pine-apple ice? If only I had a good piece of Parmesan cheese, especially in Lent, so that I could more easily swallow those black dumplings and noodles; just today I told our porter here to send me a couple of pounds.

Forgive me, kindest and most gracious lady, for filling the very first letter with such stupid nonsense, and for killing time with such a wretched scrawl, but you must forgive a man whom the Viennese spoiled terribly. I am gradually getting used to country life, however, and yesterday I studied for the first time, and quite Haydnishly, too. Your Grace will certainly have been more industrious than I. The pleasing Adagio from the Quartet has, I hope, by now received its true expression from your fair fingers. My good friend *Fräulein* Peperl will (I hope) be reminded of her teacher by singing the Cantata frequently;[2] she should remember to have a distinct articulation

149

and a correct vocal production, for it would be a crime if so
beautiful a voice were to remain hidden in her breast; so
therefore I ask her to smile frequently, lest I be disappointed
in her. Likewise I advise *Mons*. Francois [3] to cultivate his
musical talents; even when he sings in his dressing-gown, he
does very nicely. I shall often send him some new things to
encourage him. Meanwhile I again kiss your hands for all your
kind favors, and am, as always, most respectfully,

Your Grace's

most sincere and wholly obedient
servant,

Josephus Haydn.

Estoras, 9th February 1790.

P.S. Please present my respectful compliments to Your Grace's
husband, and also my compliments to *Mons*. Hofmeister Junior,
to *Fräulein* Nanette and the whole Hacker family.

[= Letter 75], 96–98.

106   WOLFGANG AMADEUS MOZART TO JOHANN
MICHAEL PUCHBERG, VIENNA [G.]

[Vienna, on or before 17 May 1790]

Dearest Friend & O.B.[1]

You have doubtless learnt from your People that I was at
your house yesterday, and (: having had your Permission :)
meant to eat there uninvited—You know my Circumstances;
in short—as I can find no true friend, I am obliged to borrow
Money from Usurers; but as it takes Time to seek out and
to find amongst that unchristian Class of Persons those who
at least are the most Christian, I am presently so destitute that
I must beg you dearest Friend by All that is precious to assist
me with whatever you can spare—If as I trust I can get the
Money in 1 or 2 Weeks, then I will at once repay you what
you lend me now—as for the sum I have owed you for so long,
I must unhappily beg you still to be Patient—If only you
knew what Grief and Anxiety all of this causes me—it has
kept me all this Time from finishing my Quartets.[2]—I now

150

have very great Hopes at Court, for I know from a reliable quarter that the E . . . . .[3] has not rejected my Petition with kind or damning words, as he did the others, but has kept it.— That is a good Sign.[4]—Next Saturday I propose to perform my Quartets at my house, to which I cordially invite you and your Lady. Dearest, best Friend & Br[other]—do not, because of my Importunity, withdraw your Friendship from me, and assist me, I depend wholly on you and am

Ever

your most grateful

Mozart $\frac{m}{p}$ [5]

P.S. I now have 2 Scholars. I should like to bring it up to 8 Scholars—endeavor to spread it abroad that I am willing to give Lessons.

[In Puchberg's hand:]
sent 150 gulden on 17 May.

[= Letter 77], IV, 108.—Tr. by editor.

107   WOLFGANG AMADEUS MOZART TO HIS WIFE, VIENNA [G.]

[Frankfurt, 30 September 1790]

Dearest little Wife of my heart!——

If only I'd got a Letter from you, all would be well with me. —I trust you have received my lines from Efferding, and those from Frankfurt.—I wrote you in my last that you are to Speak to Gooseberry=Face; [1]—I should very much appreciate it if, to be on the safe side, I could get 2000 gulden on H . . .'s [2] endorsement;—but you must allege another Reason, namely that I have my Mind on a Speculation of which you have no knowledge;—My love! to be sure, I'll doubtless make something here—but it will certainly not be as much as you and several friends imagine.—I am well enough known and respected here, that is sure.—Well—we shall see.— but I prefer in any case to Play it safe, that is why I should

like to do that stroke of Business with H . . . . , since that
way I'll receive money and will not need to spend any, but
simply work, and that I am glad to do for my little Wife's
sake.—when you write to me, you must always put down
Poste restante.—where do you think I am residing—at Böhm's,
in the selfsame House;—Hofer too.³—we pay 30 gulden a
Month, and that is still remarkably cheap.—we also have our
Meals there. whom do you think I came across here?—the Girl
who so often played at Hide and Seek with us at the aug=gottes ⁴—
Buchner I believe her name was.—now it's Mad^me Porsch, and
she has been married for the second time.—She has asked me to
convey all her best wishes to you.—
since I don't know whether you are in Vienna or in Baaden I
am again addressing this Letter to Hofer's wife.—I rejoice like
a Child at [the thought of] being with you again— —if people
could see into my heart, I should have to feel almost ashamed.—
I find everything cold—ice cold—Now, if you were here with
me, then perhaps I might derive more Pleasure from the people's
gracious Behavior toward me;—instead it is all so empty—
adieu—dear—I am Ever

Frankfurt am Main.
the 30: Sept. 790

yours with all my heart and soul
Mozart

AUTOGRAPH (see Plates I/II), Arturo Toscanini Collection, New York:
1 sheet, 227 × 182 mm., written on both sides.—Tr. by editor.

108   JOSEPH HAYDN TO MARIA ANNA VON
GENZINGER, VIENNA [G.]

London, 8th January 1791.

Nobly born,
Gracious Lady!
   I hope that you will have received my last letter from Calais.
I should have written you immediately after my arrival in
London, but I wanted to wait a few days so as to be able to write
about several things at once. So I can tell you that on the 1st inst.,
New Year's Day, after attending early Mass, I boarded the ship

at 7:30 a.m. and at 5 in the afternoon I arrived, thank God!
safe and sound in Dower [*sic*]. At the beginning, for the first
4 whole hours, we had almost no wind, and the ship went so
slowly that in these 4 hours we went no further than one single
English mile, and there are 24 between Calais and Dower. Our
ship's captain, in an evil temper, said that if the wind did not
change, we should have to spend the whole night at sea.
Fortunately, however, towards 11:30 o'clock a wind arose and
blew so favorably that by 4 o'clock we covered 22 miles. Since
the tide, which had just begun to ebb, prevented our large
vessel from reaching the pier, 2 smaller ships came out to meet
us as we were still fairly far out at sea, and into these we and
our luggage were transferred, and thus at last, though exposed
to a middling gale, we landed safely. The large vessel stood out
to sea five hours longer, till the tide turned and it could finally
dock. Some of the passengers were afraid to board the little
boats and stayed on board, but I followed the example of the
greater number. I remained on deck during the whole passage,
so as to gaze my fill at that mighty monster, the ocean. So long
as it was calm, I wasn't afraid at all, but towards the end, when
the wind grew stronger and stronger, and I saw the monstrous
high waves rushing at us, I became a little frightened, and a
little indisposed, too. But I overcame it all and arrived safely,
without vomiting, on shore. Most of the passengers were ill, and
looked like ghosts, but since I went on to London, I didn't feel
the effects of the journey at once; but then I needed 2 days to
recover. Now, however, I am fresh and well again, and busy
looking at this endlessly huge city of London, whose various
beauties and marvels quite astonished me. I immediately paid the
necessary calls, such as to the Neapolitan Ambassador and to our
own; both called on me in return 2 days later, and 4 days ago
I luncheoned with the former—N.B. at 6 o'clock in the evening, as is the custom here.

My arrival caused a great sensation throughout the whole
city, and I went the round of all the newspapers for 3 successive
days. Everyone wants to know me. I had to dine out 6 times
up to now, and if I wished, I could dine out every day; but
first I must consider my health, and 2nd my work. Except for
the nobility, I admit no callers till 2 o'clock in the afternoon,
and at 4 o'clock I dine at home with *Mon*. Salomon.[1] I have

nice and comfortable, but expensive, lodgings. My landlord is
Italian, and also a cook, and serves me 4 very respectable
meals; we each pay 1 fl. 30 kr. a day excluding wine and beer,
but everything is terribly expensive here. Yesterday I was invited
to a grand amateur concert, but I arrived a bit late, and when
I showed my ticket they wouldn't let me in but led me to an
antechamber, where I had to wait till the piece which was then
being played in the hall was over. Then they opened the door, and
I was conducted, on the arm of the *entrepreneur*, up the center
of the hall to the front of the orchestra, amid universal applause,
and there I was stared at and greeted by a great number of
English compliments. I was assured that such honors had not
been conferred on anyone for 50 years. After the concert I was
taken to a handsome adjoining room, where a table for 200
persons, with many places set, was prepared for all the amateurs;
I was supposed to be seated at the head of the table, but since
I had dined out on that day and had eaten more than usual,
I declined this honor, with the excuse that I was not feeling very
well, but despite this I had to drink the harmonious health, in
Burgundy, of all the gentlemen present; they all returned the
toast, and then allowed me to be taken home. All this, my
gracious lady, was very flattering to me, and yet I wished I
could fly for a time to Vienna, to have more quiet in which to
work, for the noise that the common people make as they sell
their wares in the street is intolerable. At present I am working
on symphonies, because the libretto of the opera is not yet
decided on,[2] but in order to have more quiet I shall have to rent
a room far from the center of town. I would gladly write you
in more detail, but I am afraid of missing the mail-coach.
Meanwhile I am, with kindest regards to your husband, *Fräulein*
Pepi, and all the others, most respectfully,
Your Grace's
most sincere and obedient servant,
Joseph Haydn.
Now I have a request to make of Your Grace. I don't know
whether I left the Symphony in E flat,[3] which Your Grace
returned to me, in my apartments at home, or whether it has
been stolen from me *en route*. I missed it yesterday and need it
urgently, and so I beg you to get it from my kind friend, Herr
von Kees, and to copy it in your own home on small-sized paper
for mailing, and send it here in the mail as soon as possible.

Should Herr von Kees hesitate about this, which I don't think likely, Your Grace can always send him this letter. My address is as follows:

À Mo[ns]:
Mon: Haydn
Nʳᵒ 18 great Pulteney Street

[= Letter 75], 111–13.

109 WOLFGANG AMADEUS MOZART TO HIS WIFE, BADEN (AUSTRIA) [G.]

[Vienna, 4 July 1791]

Dearest little Wife!—

Must be brief—it is half past one, I have not yet dined—I wish I could send you more. Here meanwhile are 3 Gulden, Tomorrow at Noon you shall have more,—be jolly, cheerful—all will yet be well—I kiss you a 1000 times—I'm too faint with Hunger [1]— adjeu ––

ever Yours
Mozart.

I waited until now because I had hoped to be able to send you more Money!—

[= Letter 77], IV, 146.—Tr. by editor.

110 JOSEPH HAYDN TO JOHANN MICHAEL PUCHBERG, VIENNA [G.]

London, January 1792.

. . . . For some time I was beside myself about his [Mozart's] death, and I could not believe that Providence would so soon claim the life of such an indispensable man. I only regret that before his death he could not convince the English, who walk in darkness in this respect, of his greatness—a subject about which I have been preaching to them every single day. . . . You will be good enough, my kind friend, to send me a catalogue of those

155

pieces to promote such works for the widow's benefit; I wrote
the poor woman three weeks ago, and told her that when her
favorite son reaches the necessary age, I shall give him composition
lessons to the very best of my ability, and at no cost, so that he
can, to some extent, fill his father's position. . . .

[= Letter 75], 125.

111 ANDRÉ ERNEST MODESTE GRÉTRY TO CLAUDE JOSEPH ROUGET DE LISLE, HEADQUARTERS OF THE ARMY OF THE ARDENNES [Fr.]

[Paris, 4 November 1792]

I will [gladly] receive your trunk, my dear friend, and I will
return it to *you,* not to your heirs; we have rid our work of
much prolixity (two of *Solier*'s airs, two duets that killed the
action), and on all saints' day it enjoyed a great success, with
receipts of nearly 4000 livres. Now the work will remain and
be given often. the marseillais [1] in the pit had often said and
shouted: *let them give us* the Gallant sans culotte or the two
convents; that is why (if you read the newspapers) the play-
bills announce *monkish despotism uncovered by a gallant sans
culottes* [sic] *or the two convents.*

deprez is at le havre; I have just written to him. I made the
cuts with [the help of] the players, and for my part I am
pleased with the sacrifices I have made. your marseillais couplets
allons enfans de la patrie are sung at all the public spectacles
and in every corner of Paris; the tune is very well grasped by
all, since it is heard every day, sung by good singers. You have
not told me the name of the composer; is it edelman? [2] goodbye
my Gallant, return to your affectionate friend, cover yourself
with glory; one of these days my Country of liège will be
french; I am delighted and filled with pride at the prospect.

Farewell my friend,

Grétry.

Paris, 4 9ber 1792

Georges de Froidcourt (ed.), *La Correspondance générale de Grétry*
(Brussels: Brepols, 1962), 161.—Tr. by editor.

112A   JOSEPH HAYDN TO ELECTOR MAXIMILIAN FRANZ OF COLOGNE, BONN [G.]

[Vienna, 23 November 1793]

Serene Electoral Highness!

I humbly take the liberty of sending Your Serene Electoral Highness some musical works, *viz.*, a Quintet, an eight-part Parthie, an oboe Concerto, Variations for the fortepiano, and a Fugue, compositions of my dear pupil Beethoven, with whose care I have been graciously entrusted.[1] I flatter myself that these pieces, which I may recommend as evidence of his assiduity over and above his actual studies, may be graciously accepted by Your Serene Electoral Highness. Connoisseurs and non-connoisseurs must candidly admit, from these present pieces, that Beethoven will in time fill the position of one of Europe's greatest composers, and I shall be proud to be able to speak of myself as his teacher; I only wish that he might remain with me a little longer.

While we are on the subject of Beethoven, Your Serene Electoral Highness will perhaps permit me to say a few words concerning the state of his finances. 100 #[2] were allotted to him during the past year. Your Serene Electoral Highness is no doubt yourself convinced that this sum was insufficient, and not even enough to live on; undoubtedly Your Highness also had your own reasons for choosing to send him into the great world with such a paltry sum. Under these circumstances, and to prevent him from falling into the hands of usurers, I have in part gone bail for him and in part lent him money myself, with the result that he owes me 500 fl., of which not a Kreutzer was spent unnecessarily; which sum I would ask you to send to him here. And since the interest on borrowed money grows continually, and is in any case very troublesome for an artist like Beethoven, I think that if Your Serene Electoral Highness were to send him 1000 fl. for the coming year, Your Highness would earn his eternal gratitude, and at the same time relieve him of all his distress: for the teachers who are absolutely essential to him, and the display that is necessary if he is to gain admission to numerous salons, reduce this sum to such an extent that only the bare minimum remains. As for the extravagance one fears will tempt any young man who goes into the great world, I think I can answer for that to Your Serene Electoral Highness: for a

157

hundred circumstances have confirmed me in my opinion that he is capable of sacrificing everything quite unconstrainedly for his art. In view of the many tempting occasions, this is most remarkable, and gives every security to Your Serene Electoral Highness—in view of the gracious kindness that we hope for— that Your Highness will not be wasting any part of your goodwill on usurers, where Beethoven is concerned. In the hope that Your Serene Electoral Highness will continue your further patronage of my dear pupil by graciously acceding to this my request, I am, with profound respect,

Your Serene Electoral Highness'
most humble and obedient
Joseph Haydn
Capell Meister to Prince Nicolaus Esterházy

Vienna, 23rd November 1793.

[= Letter 75], 141–42.

112B   LUDWIG VAN BEETHOVEN TO ELECTOR MAXIMILIAN FRANZ OF COLOGNE, BONN [G.]

[Vienna, 23 November 1793]

Most highly worthy, most serene, most gracious Elector and Lord Lord! [3]

My only aspiration is to make myself wholly worthy of the high favor of Your Serene Electoral Highness. With that intention, I have this year applied all my spiritual powers wholly to the art of music, so that in the coming year I might be in a position to send Your Serene Electoral Highness something better suited to your generosity toward me and to your nobility in general than that which is being sent to Your Serene Electoral Highness by Mr. Heiden. Confident that Your Serene Electoral Highness will not deprive me of the goodwill once granted by you, I am, with the deepest reverence, Your Serene Electoral Highness' most submissive, most obedient

Ludwig van Beethoven [4]

Vienna, 23rd November 1793.

Fritz von Rheinöhl, "Neues zu Beethovens Lehrjahr bei Haydn," *Neues Beethoven-Jahrbuch*, VI (1935), 46.—Tr. by editor.

113   FRANÇOIS JOSEPH GOSSEC TO THE COMMITTEE
OF GENERAL SECURITY, PARIS [Fr.]

[Paris, 19 March 1794]

Equity, justice, and truth compel me to attest that Citizen
Gardel, m^{tre} des Balets [sic] of the Opéra National of Paris,
evidenced the utmost zeal in arranging and producing the ceremony of the *Offrande à la Liberté* when I gave him the program
for it in August 1792 (old style). This fact cannot be called
in question, since that ceremony is still given on the stage of the
Opéra today, since it is still directed by citizen Gardel, and
since, finally, the opuscule's success is due more to him than to
myself.

I further declare that this same artist evidenced no less
eagerness in composing two *divertissemens,* the Evolutions, and
the Marches for the *Triomphe de la République* or *Camp de
Grand-pré,* words by citizen *Chenier,*[1] music of my own
composition, performed on 27 January 1793 (old style). I also
certify that citizen Gardel evidenced all the zeal of a good
Republican in composing and directing the ceremony which
took place on   [2] last in front of the
Opéra for the Apotheosis of the two martyrs of Liberty,
Lepelletier and Marat,[3] for which I had composed part of the
music.

Gossec.

This 29 ventose in the 2nd year of the French Republic one
and indivisible, 2nd [year] since the death of the last of our
tyrants.

[= Letter 41], 215.—Tr. by editor.

114   NICOLAS DALAYRAC TO THE REVOLUTIONARY COMMITTEE OF THE SECTION LEPELLETIER, PARIS [Fr.]

[Paris, 4 May 1794]

Citizens,

Approximately three weeks have passed since (following the example of citizen Grétry, musician) I, Dalayrac, musician also, deposited with citizen Potier of Lille, printer, some pewter plates that belong to me and constitute the scores of twelve operas and their separate parts;

These operas have been performed at the théâtre Favart and their music is known to be of my composition.

The object of this deposit was to print off copies whenever I should need them, which is the practice of every musician, in view of the difficulty of transportation, which is very considerable.

Although such deposits are ordinarily made in confidence between the musician and the printer, citizen Pottier had promised me a receipt once the plates were verified, which was to be done the first day but could not be carried out.

The unforeseen arrest of citizen Pottier of Lille prompts me, citizens, to write you the present declaration and to beg you to make a note of it and of its date in the register, so that it will be valid when needed.

Welfare and fraternity.

Dalayrac
mus^n

15 floréal in the 2^d year of the Republic
one and indivisible.

[= Letter 41], 258–59.—Tr. by editor.

115   LUDWIG VAN BEETHOVEN TO NIKOLAUS SIMROCK, BONN [G.]

Vienna, 2 August [1794]

Dear Simrock!

I may deserve a bit of a scolding from you because I have kept your V[ariations] [1] from you for so long, but I am truly not lying when I tell you that I was prevented from correcting [them] so soon by an overload of business. You yourself will discover what is wrong in them; besides I must wish you luck with regard to your engraving, which is beautiful, clear and legible, in truth, if you continue in this way, you will become the chief of stabbing [im Stechen], I mean of course—of music engraving [im Notenstechen].

I promised you in my last letter that I should send you something of mine, and you have interpreted this as being courtier-talk, how then have I deserved that predicate?—fie, who can still use such language in our democratic times; so that I may be rid of the *predicate* you gave me, you'll receive something, as soon as I have undertaken the grand review of my works, which will take place soon, something you'll surely engrave.— As for an agent, I have looked about and found a really excellent, clever man for it. His name is *Traeg,* now all you have to do is to write him or me what conditions you'll accept.[2] He wants you to give him one-third discount. The Devil may understand such trafficking—It's very hot here; the Viennese are anxious, they will soon not have any *ices* left, since the winter was so warm, ice is rare. They have arrested several persons *of consequence* here, they say a revolution was about to break out—but I believe, so long as the Austrian still has *porter* and *sausages,* he won't revolt. It is said the gates to the suburbs are to be closed at 10 o'clock in the night. The soldiers have loaded with ball. You mustn't talk too loud here, or the police will confine you to your quarters.

If your daughters have grown up, train me one as a bride, for if I live in Bonn unmarried, I'll surely not remain there long; [3]—You must also be living in fear now!—[4]

How is dear *Ries,*[5] I'll write to him soon, he can only have

161

unfavorable thoughts about me, but this accursed writing, and I can't reform in this.—*Have you performed my Partita*⁶ *yet.* Write me from time to time.

Your Beethoven.

If you'd only send me a few c[opies] of the first Variations too.⁷

Alfred C. Kalischer (ed.), *Beethovens Sämtliche Briefe* (5 vols.; Berlin: Schuster & Loeffler, 1906–1908), I, 17–18.—Tr. by editor.

116 JOSEPH HAYDN TO PRINCE ESTERHÁZY'S ADMINISTRATOR [G.]

[End of 1796 or beginning of 1797]

Nobly born,
Highly respected Administrator!

From the letter addressed to me and the enclosure of the worthy Privy Economic Administration of His Serene Highness Prince Esterházy, I saw that I am more or less CONDEMNED to pay the debt of Luegmayer,¹ who because of INSOLVENCY is not able to do so. Why? Because I am thought to possess the necessary MEANS: I wish to God it were so! But I SWEAR by the Kyrie eleison which I am at this moment supposed to compose for my FOURTH Prince, that since the death of my SECOND Prince— God rest his soul!—I have fallen into the SAME STATE OF INSOLVENCY as that of Luegmayer, but with the difference that he has fallen from his horse to the back of an ass, whilst I have managed to remain on the horse, but without saddle or harness.

I therefore beg the worthy Privy Economic Administration of His Highness to wait at LEAST till I have finished the Dona nobis pacem, and until the Prince's house-master Luegmayer shall begin to receive the salary rightly due to him from his most gracious Prince, instead of drawing it, as he has hitherto done, from the SMALL salary of *Capellmeister* Haydn (who has been 36 years in the Princely service). For nothing is sadder or more dissonant than one SERVANT paying another SERVANT, in this case the *Capellmeister* having to pay the house-master. If I should, perhaps today or tomorrow, be placed in a BETTER

position, either as a result of my own merits or by the voluntary
impulse of my most gracious Prince (FOR FLATTER AND BEG
I WILL NOT), of course I shall not fail to comply with the above
demand.

    I am, Sir, with every respect,

Your most obliging servant,

Fran[z] J: Haydn

Doctor of Oxford and Princely Esterházy

Capellmeister.

[= Letter 75], 149.

117   LUDWIG VAN BEETHOVEN TO FRANZ ANTON HOFFMEISTER, LEIPZIG [G.]

        Vienna, 15th (or something of the sort january) 1801.
    I read your letter, my dearest Brother and Friend, with much
pleasure, I thank you for the good opinion you have conceived
of me and my works and wish I may deserve it properly; please
render my dutiful thanks to Mr. K[ühnel] [1] too, for his civil
and friendly expressions in my regard.—
    your endeavors please me too, and if works of art can produce
a profit, I wish it may fall to the share of genuine, true artists
rather than mere shopkeepers. ———— that you are planning
the publication of *Sebastian Bach's works* is a thing that gives
much pleasure to my heart, which beats wholly for the lofty,
great art of that forefather of Harmony, and I wish I may
soon see [it] in full career, I hope, as soon as we hear golden
peace proclaimed, to contribute a good deal to it here myself,
when you open a subscription for it. [2] ———— now as for
our own affairs, since you so wish it, may this be of service to
you, I offer you for the moment the following things: Septet
(about which I have already written you, it could also be
arranged for the pianoforte for greater Distribution and gain)
20# [ducats], Symphony 20#, Concerto 10#, Grand Solo
Sonata (allegro, adagio, Minuetto, Rondo) 20#. [3] This Sonata
is capital, dearest Brother! [4] now for the explanation: you will
perhaps wonder that I make no distinction here between
163

Sonata, Septet, Symphony, since I find that a septet or symphony won't sell as easily as a sonata, therefore I do this, even though a symphony ought to be worth more, indisputably. (nb. the Septet consists of a short introductory adagio, then Allegro, Adagio, Minuetto, Andante with Variations, Minuetto, again a short introductory adagio and then presto). —— I am valuing the Concerto at only 10#, because, as I have already written, I am not giving it out as one of my best. ——— I don't believe this will seem exaggerated to you when taken as a whole, I have at least made an effort to make the prices as low as possible for you—as for the draft, since you give me the choice, [you] can have it sent to geimüller or Schüller.—the whole sum then would be of 70# for all 4 works, I understand no money other than Viennese #, how many thaler or gldn. [gulden] that may make in your country, all that is no concern of mine, since I am really a bad negotiator and reckoner. ————

now the sour business is finished, I call it Such because I wish that things were different in the world. there ought only to be a *Storehouse of Art* in the world, where the artist would only have to deliver his works of art in order to take what he needed, as it is, one has to be half a merchant as well, and how is one supposed to find one's self in it all—good Lord—I call it *sour* indeed ——————— As for the Leipzig R [? reviewers], one must let them talk away, they will surely not make anyone immortal with their Chatter, just as they will not take Immortality away from anyone to whom Apollo has allotted it. ——————— Now Heaven protect you *and your confederate*, I haven't been well for some time and so it is getting a little hard for me to write even notes, much less [*sic*] characters, I hope we shall often have the opportunity to assure one another how very much you are my friends and how very much I am

your

Brother and Friend

L. v. Beethoven.

Till you answer soon—adieu

[= Letter 115], 60–62.—Tr. by editor.

118   JOSEPH HAYDN TO THE INSTITUT NATIONAL, PARIS [Fr.]

Vienna, 14th April 1802.

Joseph Haydn to Citizen Vincent, President, and to Citizens La Porte du Theil, and Villat, Secretaries of the *Institut National des Sciences et des Arts*, Paris.

Citizens,

The signal honor which the *Institut National des Sciences et des Arts* has shown me by electing me a NON-RESIDENT MEMBER of the section "Literature and Fine Arts" is a reward so great that the value of my works—even considering the approbation the public has seen fit to bestow on them—can never, in my opinion, be such as to deserve it.

I am keenly aware how flattering it is to have been admitted to a group which is so universally revered, and which has been so justly celebrated for so long a time. My future efforts will have no other goal than to justify this honor, and thus I wish to proffer to the Society, who has admitted me to its illustrious ranks, the emotions of respect and gratitude with which my heart is filled.

I beg you, Citizens, to convey my respects to our colleagues, and to accept yourselves the assurance of my most profound esteem and most sincere regard.

Joseph Haydn [m.p] ria.[1]

[= Letter 75], 204.

119   GIOVANNI PAISIELLO TO NAPOLEON BONAPARTE, [PARIS?] [Fr.]

[Paris, 18 June 1802]

It is with the greatest regret that Paisiello finds himself obliged to interrupt the First Consul for a moment over a small personal matter.[1] But it is by his authority alone that he can be extricated from the extremely embarrassing situation in which he finds himself.

165

When the question arose of obtaining an apartment for
Paisiello, General Duroc [2] was good enough to leave its choice
to him and to inform him, by his letter enclosed herewith, that
he had authorized the government's upholsterer to get him
the necessary furniture, for which he was authorized to give
10,000 francs. Whereupon the furniture was supplied and
Paisiello took possession of his apartment. He had, therefore,
every reason to believe he would enjoy it in peace, but what was
his surprise when he was presented with a summons enjoining
him to appear the next day before the judge in the matter of
the furnishing of his quarters. The First Consul will easily
conceive of the embarrassment of Paisiello's position: a stranger,
ignorant of the country's ways, absolutely unacquainted with
pettifoggery, how could he present himself before a tribunal?
He appealed to State Councilor de Roederer [3] in the hope that he
might extricate him from this embarrassment: but he did him
the honor of answering, by his letter herewith enclosed, that he
should appeal directly to the First Consul. He makes bold,
therefore, to beseech his protection, that he may deign to give
orders to that effect, and in this hope he makes bold to give him
the papers relating to this unhappy affair.

He entreats him to consider that it was to prevent such
altercations in a foreign Country that, when Ambassador Alquier
did him the honor of asking him upon what terms he would
come to Paris, he answered that he confined himself to asking
for lodging, an equipage, and board, that for the rest he felt
amply rewarded by the honor of obeying the First Consul.
Indeed, these discussions are too foreign to his character and
to his mode of life; and if he had to busy himself with them, it
could not but do infinite harm to the labors with which the
First Consul has deigned to charge him, and which demand his
undivided attention. It is for their sake that he makes bold
earnestly to entreat the First Consul to deign to decide his fate
in a positive way, to the end that he need no longer think of
anything but the honor of serving him.

Paisiello

Paris, 29 prairial, year 10.

[= Letter 41], 296–97.—Tr. by editor.

120   LUDWIG VAN BEETHOVEN TO HIS BROTHERS [G.]

[Heiligenstadt, 6–10 October 1802]
For my brothers Carl and [Johann] [1] Beethoven.
O ye men who think or declare that I am hostile stubborn or
Misanthropic, how you wrong me you do not know the secret
motive of what seems thus to you, from Childhood my Heart
and my Mind were inclined to the Gentle Feeling of goodwill,
indeed I was ever disposed To accomplish great Feats, but only
reflect that for the last 6 years an incurable condition has seized
me, worsened by senseless physicians, cheated from year to year
in the Hope of improvement, finally compelled to the prospect
of a *lasting Ailment* (whose Curing may perhaps last for years
or indeed be impossible) born with a fiery Lively Temperament
susceptible even to the Diversions of Society, I soon had to keep
to myself, pass my life in solitude, if I attempted from time to
time to place myself beyond all this, o how harshly then was I
repulsed by the doubly sad Experience of my bad Hearing, and
yet I could not say to People: speak louder, shout, for I am
deaf, alas how could I possibly then admit the Weakness of *a
Faculty* which should exist in me to a more perfect degree than
in others, a Faculty I once possessed to the highest Perfection,
to such a Perfection as few of my Calling surely have or have had
—o I cannot do it, therefore forgive me, if you see me shrinking
back when I should gladly join you my misfortune afflicts me
doubly, since it causes me to be misunderstood, Diversion in
Human Society, civilized Conversation, mutual Effusions cannot
take place for me, all but alone I may enter into society no more
than the greatest Necessity requires, I must live like a Banished
man, if I approach a company, a hot anxiety invades me, as I
am afraid of being put in Danger of letting my Condition be
noticed—and thus has it been this half-year too, which I have
spent in the country, my wise Physician having ordered me to
spare my Hearing as much as possible, he nearly met my present
Disposition, even though I have sometimes let myself be led
astray by an Urge for Society, but what a Mortification if
someone stood next to me and heard a flute from afar and *I*
heard *nothing;* or someone *heard a Shepherd Singing,* and I heard
nothing, such Happenings brought me close to Despair, I was
not far from ending my own life—only Art, only art held me
167

back, ah it seemed impossible to me that I should leave the world before I had produced all that I felt I might, and so I spared this wretched life—truly wretched; a body so susceptible that a somewhat rapid change can remove me from the Best Condition to the worst—*Patience*—so now I must choose Her for my guide, I have done so—I hope that my decision to persevere may be permanent, until it please the inexorable Parcae to break the Thread, perhaps I'll get better, perhaps not, I am resigned—to be forced in my 28th year already to become a Philosopher, that is not easy, for an Artist harder than for anyone else—deity thou lookest down into my innermost being; thou knowest it, thou seest that charity and benevolence dwell within,—o Men, when some day you read this, think then that you have wronged me, and the unhappy one, let him console himself by finding another like himself who, despite all Nature's Impediments, yet did whatever was in his Power to be admitted to the Ranks of worthy Artists and Men—you my Brothers Carl and [Johann], as soon as I am dead, and professor schmid [2] still lives, ask him in my Name to describe my Illness, and append this Sheet of writing to this History of my illness, so that at least after my Death the world may make its peace with me as much as possible—At the same time I here declare you two as the Heirs of the small Riches (if one may call them such) belonging to me, share them fairly, and tolerate and help one another, you know what you have done against me, it has long been forgiven, you Brother Carl I thank again especially for the Attachment you have shown me in these more recent later days, My wish is that you may have a better more untroubled Life than I, commend *Virtue* to your Children, it alone can bring happiness, not Money, I speak from Experience, it was Virtue raised me in my Distress, I have it to thank besides my Art if I did not put an end to my Life through suicide—farewell and love each other,—I thank all Friends, particularly *Prince Lichnowski* [3] and *Professor Schmidt*.—I wish that Prince L.'s Instruments may be preserved by one of you, yet let there arise no Strife between you on that account, but as soon as they can serve you for a more useful purpose, you may sell them if you like, how happy am I, if I can still be of use to you even in my Grave— And so it's done—I hasten with joy towards my Death—should it come before I have had an Opportunity to disclose all my Artistic Capacities, then it shall have come still too soon in spite of my Hard Destiny, and I should indeed wish it later—yet even then am I content, does it not free me from an endless Suffering State?—come, *when* you will, I'll meet you bravely— farewell and do not entirely forget me in Death, I have deserved it of you, since in Life I have often thought of you, to make you happy, so may you be—

Heiglnstadt   Ludwig van Beethoven
6th october
1 8 0 2

[SEAL]

Heiglnstadt 10th October 1802 and so I bid you farewell—and sadly too—yes the cherished Hope—which I brought here with me, that I might be cured at least up to a certain Point—it must abandon me completely now, as Autumn Leaves fall away, wither; so has—it too wilted for me, I go from here— nearly as I came—even the High Courage—which often inspired me during the Lovely Summer Days—has vanished—o Provi- dence—grant me one pure day of *Joy*—the inner reverberation of true Joy has so long been a stranger to me—o when—o when o Deity—may I feel it once more in the Temple of Nature and Mankind,—Never?— — no — o it would be too hard.

[Left margin:] For my brothers Carl and [Johann] to be read and executed after my death—

Facsimile of the autograph: Hedwig M. von Asow (ed.), *Ludwig van Beethoven: Heiligenstädter Testament* (Vienna: Ludwig Doblinger [B. Herzmansky] K.G., 1957), enclosure.—Tr. by editor.

121　LUDWIG VAN BEETHOVEN TO GOTTFRIED CHRISTOPH HÄRTEL, LEIPZIG [G.]

Vienna 26th August
1804

Several reasons induce me, my dear Mr. Härtel, to write to you ————— it may possibly have reached your ears too as though [*sic*] I had sealed a contract for all my works (to the exclusion of all other publishers) with a firm situated in Vienna, being asked about this by several foreign publishers I tell you, even without being invited to do so, that this is not so ————— for you will know yourself that I could not entertain such a request on your part either — at least not yet ————— another thing that weighs on me is that several publishers tarry so frightfully long with my compositions before they see the light of day, each one blames this or that motive as the cause of it ————— I remember very well that you are in a position to produce a prodigious quantity of copies in a few weeks ————— I now have several works, and my wish to have them see the light of day soon may perhaps be fufilled so much the earlier, since I am resolved to let you have all of these ————— therefore I shall only tell you briefly what I can give you: My oratorio; — a *new grand Symphony;* ————— a Concertante for violin, violoncello, and piano-forte with the entire orchestra ————— three new Solo Sonatas, if you wish to have one with an accompaniment, I should engage myself for that too [1] ———— Now if you are disposed to take these things, then you must be good enough to let me know exactly how much time you would require to produce them; since it is my greatest wish that at least the first three works be published as soon as possible, we should establish the time in writing or by means of a contract (according to your preference), to which I should then of course, I tell it to you openly, strictly bind myself. ———— The Oratorio has not been published so far, because I have added an entirely new chorus to it and changed some things, as I wrote the whole oratorio in just a few weeks and afterwards some things did not quite suit me ————— that is why I held it back until now, these changes date from a period subsequent to the time when my brother wrote to you about it ————— The Symphony is actually entitled Bonaparte,

170

apart from all the usual customary instruments there are in it also 3 obbligato horns [2] ———— I think it will interest the musical public —— I should wish that you would publish it in *score,* instead of engraved parts —— I have nothing to add about the other things, although a Concertante with three such solo parts is also indeed a novelty. ———— now if you wish to accept the *proposed* conditions for the publication of these things, I should let you have them against an honorarium of 2000 (two thousand) fl. ———— I assure you upon my honor that I lose with regard to certain works, as for ex. Sonatas, since I am [usually] given close to 60# [ducats] for a single sonata, do not think I am blustering ———— may such a thing be far from me — only, to bring about a quicker publication of my works, I'll gladly lose something ————

but now I beg you to give me an answer to this promptly ——— I hope Mr. Wiems has received my letter, I had taken the liberty of addressing it to you. in the expectation of an early answer I am

yours
Devotedly
Ludwig van Beethoven

[= Letter 115], 139–41.—Tr. by editor.

122   JOSEPH HAYDN TO JOHANN NEPOMUK HUMMEL, EISENSTADT [G.]

Vienna, 28th September 1804.

Dearest Hummel,

I regret terribly that I cannot have the pleasure of conducting my little work [1] for the last time, but on the other hand I am convinced that everyone (WITHOUT EXCEPTION) will do everything in their power to support their old Papa, especially since the worthy Hummel will be their guide.

Yours most sincerely
Joseph Haydn [m.p] ria.[2]

P.S. My compliments to everyone.

[= Letter 75], 233.

123   LUDWIG VAN BEETHOVEN TO FRIEDRICH SEBASTIAN MAYER, VIENNA [G.]

[8 April 1806]

Dear Mayer!

please ask Mr. v. Seyfried [1] to conduct my opera today, I want to see and hear it myself today at a distance, at least that way my patience won't be tested quite so much by hearing my music mangled at such close quarters! I cannot but think it is being done to me on purpose. I will not speak of the wind instruments but —— that all pp.s crescendos, all decresc[endos] and all fortes ff.s should have been struck out of my opera; they are simply not being done at all. All desire to write anything else disappears, if I must hear it in *such* a way! I'll fetch you for dinner tomorrow or the day after tomorrow. Today I am out of sorts once more.

Your Friend
Beethoven

P.S. If the opera is to be performed
again the day after tomorrow, then *tomorrow* —— there must be another rehearsal in the room, — or it will go worse every day!

[= Letter 115], 161.—Tr. by editor.

124   CARL FRIEDRICH ZELTER TO JOHANN WOLFGANG VON GOETHE, WEIMAR [G.]

[Berlin, 12 November 1808]

When the Emperor Napoleon appeared before the gates of this capital with his army, [1] the local municipal council went to meet him, as I believe is the custom, and at that audience received its dismissal, the Emperor declaring: that he wished only to deal with burghers of the city, not with authorities of the former government, if they were not burghers. To that end, the old municipal council had to convoke 2000 burghers in a church. These 2000 had to elect 60, from whom

172

the chargés d'affaires were to be drawn. The 60 had to proceed
to the sacristy, the [other] 1940 were dismissed. It was then
explained to the 60 that they were to elect seven burghers of
their number, who were to constitute a Comité Administratif
and represent the city's highest civilian authority. Now,
among these seven burghers, namely four merchants, one
manufacturer, and two handicraftsmen, am I.[2] This Committee
of Seven was now summoned to the town hall to elect its
representative; also this election devolved on me, but I declined
it and proposed Delagarde, the book dealer, instead, since I
don't have a perfect command of the French language. The
Committee was now sworn in at the palace, along with the
former ministry and all the royal courts of justice. The oath
consisted in the injunction: to provision the French army in a
fitting manner and not to exchange any letters with the
enemies of the French monarchy.

The business of the Committee consists in this: to confiscate
from the townspeople and to hand over anything the French
government may exact for the part of the army that has
occupied the Middle Mark.[3]

And so, my friend, I have presented you with a general
view of what you wished to know. What you surely must
know—that I have no knowledge of finances and of other
business pertaining to the conduct of public affairs—I need
not mention. Had this way of life lasted only for a few weeks
or months, then the honorable confidence on the part of over
a hundred thousand inhabitants of an important capital would
at any rate have been encouraging, especially for me, since I
had not actually considered myself as one of the citizenry,
except insofar as I gained my livelihood from it; while the
perennial pressure on one point [4] made me hate, mistrust,
and roundly curse just those who are nearest to and, in the
end, directly responsible for the former, the present, and future
high authorities. The first eight months (until the Peace of
Tilsit) could have been forgotten; but it is since that peace
that our city has felt the war.[5]—However, don't be anxious
about your friend: he hopes to emerge from the situation, if
not soon and with thanks, then at least cleanly; and his greatest
solace consists in this, that he will always have your confidence
and your love.

Eberwein [6] left here on October 16th, and I received a letter

from him on the 7th instant. He must concentrate a great
deal if he is to succeed. The technical elements of an art
ought actually to be thoroughly mastered in one's early years.
When the spirit moves from within, all concern over the
externals of presentation must be laid aside; and any man who
knows good craftsmanship will admit that it helps the creative
process, as it were, for it nourishes the imagination and sets
the impulses free.

What you say in your letter with regard to the specific
determination of shape, form, and character is perhaps even
truer of music (at least, it is far more difficult to attain there)
than it is of the imitative arts.[7] For each of the poetic souls
you mention I could name you a musical counterpart to
corroborate your judgment: with awe and terror one sees
will-o'-the-wisps and streaks of blood upon Parnassus' horizon.
Talents of the highest magnitude like Cherubini, Beethoven,
and others make use of Hercules' club—to swat flies; at first
it is impossible not to be amazed, but then immediately one
must shrug one's shoulders at this expenditure of talent for
the magnification of trifles and the belittlement of exalted
means. Indeed, it drives me to despair to think that the new
music *must* sink into oblivion if music is ever to become an art.

No art can have a beneficent influence that roams about
so impudently and shapelessly in endless space as does the newer
music, which lays bare its most secret, most lofty delights,
out of context, to the public gaze of the common rabble,
like a cabinet of anatomy or an unpublished collection of love-
secrets, to glut the general curiosity. Let the composers of earlier
centuries be criticized at will (for who is perfect?)—yet they
never threw art away, never sacrificed the inner sanctum;
had *their* ground been built upon further, we should now
have an art and be quite different people from what we must
deem ourselves to be.[8]

I hope my parcel of absolutely authentic Teltow [9] beets
reached you *before the frost;* enjoy them as best you can and
consider that I couldn't have sent you anything better from
here even before the invasion. Had we had and kept in store more
of such authentic stuff, they could not have taken so much
away from us; at least we should not be so poor now.

One of my friends, who also seeks to be worthy of you,
has been collecting manuscripts of important writers for

several years and begs me to obtain something in your handwriting. I won't give anything away; but don't you, perhaps,
have among your papers a poem in your handwriting or
something else I might pass on to him, and would you give
it to me for him? I should think something of the sort might
be found.[10]

Send back your Eberwein just as soon as you please. I'll
teach him nothing but my best.

Z.

12th November 1808.

Friedrich Wilhelm Riemer (ed.), *Briefwechsel zwischen Goethe und Zelter
in den Jahren 1796 bis 1832* (6 vols.; Berlin: Duncker und Humblot, 1833–34),
I, 344–48.—Tr. by editor.

125   JOSEPH HAYDN TO PRINCE NICOLAUS II ESTERHÁZY [G.]

[Vienna, 22 December 1808]

Most Serene Highness,
Gracious Prince and Lord!

I humbly place myself at Your Serene Highness' feet for
the gracious approval of my request, whereby with the utmost
kindness you take over my yearly expenditures for the doctor
and apothecary. By this new act of generosity, Your Serene
Highness has freed me from a most pressing anxiety, and thus
enabled me to await the end of my earthly existence in peace
and serenity. May Heaven grant my zealous wish that Your
Serene Highness live in everlasting well-being and Your
Gracious Highness' illustrious family in ever increasing
prosperity! I remain ever your most devoted and

Your Serene Highness'
humble servant,
Joseph Haydn [m.p] ria.[1]

Vienna, 22nd December 1808.

[= Letter 75], 248.

126   LUDWIG VAN BEETHOVEN TO GOTTFRIED CHRISTOPH HÄRTEL, LEIPZIG [G.]

Vienna, 6th May [1811]

P[raemissis] P[raemittendis] [1]

Mistakes—Mistakes—you are yourself a singular mistake—I must then send my own copyist over, I must go there myself, if I want my works—to appear otherwise than as sheer mistakes—the musical tribunal in L[eipzig] does not apparently produce a single proper proofreader, meanwhile you send off the works before you have even received the c[orrections]— one ought at least to count off the measures in larger works with different parts—but one need only look at the Fantasy [2] etc. to see what is happening—see, in the piano reduction of the Egmont overture a whole measure is missing.

Herewith the catalogue—of mistakes [3]

My warmest thanks for stirring me up so very much over such an interesting thing. = Farewell, I hope for an improvement—the Fantasy is already on its way, the Sonata [4] too is leaving here tomorrow. Make as many mistakes as you like, have as many mistakes made as you like—I esteem you highly nevertheless, this after all is the way of men, that one esteems them because they have not made still greater mistakes.

Your most devoted

Servant

Beethoven

NB. Note that in my corrections of the concerto [5] in the 1st violin part of the 1st All[egr]° page 5 line 7, 1st measure

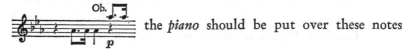 the *piano* should be put over these notes

but not the other way under the violin's notes—

[= Letter 115], II, 11.—Tr. by editor.

127   ERNST THEODOR AMADEUS HOFFMANN TO EDUARD HITZIG, BERLIN [G.]

Bamberg, 15th July 1812

My dear, most cherished friend,

Enclosed herewith you will, as you requested, receive an essay on the local performances of Calderón's plays; its whole tendency is to show under what circumstances those plays still cannot miss having their great effect, even when the stage disposes of no great forces in the matter of eminent actors or costly scenery. Perhaps it will serve for the general diffusion of those heavenly plays, in which case much would be gained.[1] Holbein [2] is in Würzburg at present, and our theater is once again being reorganized; if it is set up in a tolerable way, I'll certainly obtain performances for some Shakespearean plays that have not yet been given (principally his comedies). I am acquainted with Goethe's adaptation of *Romeo and Juliet* [3] only from the news of it imparted by the public prints, and already from these—I must freely confess—I dislike it. The magnificent ending (the families' reconciliation after their loveliest offshoots have fallen a sacrifice to their hatred, Friar Laurence's touching speech), I hear, is omitted altogether—I should really like to put on the original version quite faithfully.—If you should, some day, turn over the pages of the 13th [*recte*: 12th] volume of the [*Allgemeine*] *Musik*[*alische*] *Zeit*[*ung*], you would come across my essay, "The Musical Sufferings of Kapellmeister Johannes Kreisler"; just as in the current volume, shortly: "Kapellmeister Johannes Kreisler's Reflections on the High Value of Music"; both essays are mine, and you will, as I have reason to suppose, laugh quite heartily.[4] But now I come up with an urgent request, which my dear cherished friend must not deny me!— You know I am not at all fluent in versifying and how difficult, therefore, it would be for me to turn *Undine* into an opera.[5] And so, is there not, among your amiable poetical friends, one who might be persuaded to undertake the adaptation of *Undine* for me?—I should communicate my ideas in writing, *in extenso,* without troubling the poet in the least, but I ought not to be kept waiting too long for the text; the fulfillment of my request would be a most agreeable

177

event for me. Be so kind and so friendly as to write to me very soon on the subject.—Has Werner's[6] *Kunegunde,* a scene of which appears in the *Deutsches Museum,* already been published, or is it still in the press, and in whose? That would be a play for Bamberg, where, as is known, the pious Henry lived with his Kunegunde and the Ploughshare Trial took place.[7] The door which the devil once slammed in the pious Empress' face and which, by a mere touch of the finger, she opened again still exists today.—You see what a theater-speculator I have become.—In my thoughts, I am composing nothing but *Undine*—that powerful, wonderful, admonishing Uncle, Kühleborn, makes no mean bass part, and the old Fisherman, in the exposition, speaks out too, in a most genial Romance—you know me, and how strongly an idea can seize and inspire me!—Adio [*sic*] mio carissimo amico!

Wholly yours,
Hoffm

A thousand greetings to your family from myself and my wife, who sends you her best regards!

Walther Harich (ed.), *E. T. A. Hoffmann: Dichtungen und Schriften, sowie Briefe und Tagebücher,* XIV (Weimar: Erich Lichtenstein, 1924), 371–73. —Tr. by editor.

128   LUDWIG VAN BEETHOVEN TO GOTTFRIED CHRISTOPH HÄRTEL, LEIPZIG [G.]

Frantzens Brunn[1]
near Eger 9th aug.
1812   +

Only the most essential: you don't have the title for the Mass,[2] and I have too much of several things, of baths, of doing nothing and etc. I am tired of other unavoidable in- and ac-cidents [*Zu und Auffälligkeiten*]—here now you see me and think of me, My physician is driving me from one

---

+ The climate here is such that one could write 9th November

178

place to the next in order to catch hold of my health in the
end, from Teplitz to Karlsbad, from there hence, at K[arlsbad]
I performed something for the saxons and Prussians as a
benefit for the city of Baden which was burnt down;[3] it
was so to speak a *poor concert* for the *Poor*—Signore polledrone [4]
helped me with it, and after he had worn himself out with
anxiousness as usual, he played well—"To His Excellency the
High-born Prince Kynsky," [5] the title might contain something
of the kind—and now I must refrain from writing any
further, instead I must splash about in the water again, no
sooner have I been forced to saturate my insides with a proper
quantity of it than I must go and have my outside rinsed all
over _____ I'll answer the rest of your letter very
soon—the court atmosphere suits Göthe much More than is
fitting for a Poet, One cannot say much about the laughable
behavior of Virtuosos if Poets, who ought to be regarded as
the prime teachers of the nation, can forget everything else
for that glitter [6] _____

your
Beethoven

[on a separate piece of paper attached to the letter:]

I have just written for Prince Kynsky's full title, therefore
you'll receive it soon enough, as I imagine that you are not
publishing the Mass before autumn _____

[= Letter 115], II, 93–94.—Tr. by editor.

129   FRANZ SCHUBERT TO HIS BROTHER [FERDINAND(?)], VIENNA [G.]

[Vienna,] 24 November 1812

Straight out with what troubles me, and so I shall come
to my purpose the sooner, and you will not be detained by
any precious beating about the bush. I have long been thinking
about my situation and found that, although it is satisfactory
on the whole, it is not beyond some improvement here and
there.[1] You know from experience that we all like to eat a
roll or a few apples sometimes, the more so if after a middling

lunch one may not look for a miserable evening meal for eight and a half hours. This wish, which has often become insistent, is now becoming more and more frequent, and I had willy-nilly to make a change. The few groats I receive from Father go to the deuce the very first days, and what am I to do for the rest of the time? "Whosoever believeth on Him shall not be put to shame." Matthew, iii. 4.[2] I thought so too.—How if you were to let me have a few Kreuzer a month? You would not so much as know it, while I in my cell should think myself lucky, and be content. I repeat, I lean upon the words of the Apostle Matthew, where he says: "He that hath two coats, let him give one to the poor," &c. Meanwhile I hope that you will give ear to the voice that calls unceasingly to you to remember

Your

loving, poor, hopeful

and again poor brother

Franz.

Otto Erich Deutsch, *The Schubert Reader: A Life of Franz Schubert in Letters and Documents,* trans. Eric Blom (New York: W. W. Norton & Company, Inc., 1947), 28.

130   LUDWIG VAN BEETHOVEN TO JOHANN BAPTIST RUPPRECHT, VIENNA [G.]

[Vienna, before 22 December 1814]

With the greatest pleasure my esteemed R[upprecht] will I set your poem to music, and also bring it over to you soon myself ———— whether [it will turn out to be] Heavenly I do not know, as I deem myself earthly, yet I will employ all [my capacities] to come as near as possible to your exaggerated prepossession in my regard.

Your friend

and servant

Beethoven

AUTOGRAPH (see Plates III/IV), Arturo Toscanini Collection, New York: 1 sheet, 183 × 236 mm., folded to form 4 pp.   P. 3 blank; p. 4 has address ("Für Seine / wohlgebohren / Hr: von Ruprecht") & Beethoven's seal.—Tr. by editor.

131   CARL MARIA VON WEBER TO FRIEDRICH WIECK, LEIPZIG [G.]

[Munich, 13 August 1815]

Dear Sir,

Let me first of all thank you most cordially for your inspired songs,[1] which I had the pleasure to receive in Prague on 18 May; and kindly forgive me for not telling you earlier how very much they delighted me. I received them during the great whirl of business attendant on my vacation tour, on which I embarked at the beginning of May. As my plans then stood, I had hoped to visit Leipzig myself, so that I could thank you in person and be better and more thoroughly able to satisfy the wishes expressed in your letter.

Various circumstances deprive me of the pleasure of meeting you personally this year, and so for the present I must content myself with a mere written assurance of my warmest interest in your endeavors.

I believe I cannot give you better proof of my consideration and esteem than by taking the liberty of giving you my open and candid opinion concerning your songs. Indeed, I feel expressly called upon to do so by your trust.

Your melodies are delicately and sensitively conceived and generally interpret the poet most happily. You aspire to avoid the common song-form, and all attempts to attain the Beautiful and the Good are praiseworthy.

But the creation of a new form must be caused by the poem one is setting.

In [composing] my songs, my efforts to render the poets in a wholly genuine way, and with correct declamation, have led me to many a new melodic form. Your voice parts are rather unsingable on occasion, and your harmony is often impure, where purity and naturalness would have been close at hand; and it appears to me as if you had seized upon these imperfections, which at the time you naturally did not recognize as such, merely for the sake of novelty. Your modulations are often diffuse, and rarely is the feeling for the principal key well founded.

Modulation is a sacrosanct thing, and is only appropriate

when it furthers and elevates the expression; otherwise it can just as easily be *disturbing*.

Your declamation is very careless at times and often tears the meaning apart.

You will find proof of all this in the analysis of single instances:

No. I is nicely thought out and felt. In measure 5, I should have chosen *a* instead of *g*; the *g* moves from A major too suddenly;—"true love trails the sorrowing senses with it"— belongs together; you have,—true love trails the sorrowing,— which is caused not only by the printed notes of the voice-part, but even more by the closing harmonic progression.

It might be helped in this way:

Just as wrong is the separation of the words at "Be glad to be rid of sorrow—ye hearts, forever";—very good, but now comes—"throw off Love's" etc.—Why did you not handle the whole second stanza in like manner, since the return of the first tune in the third [stanza] would then have been quite right, as it would have expressed related sentiments, namely that his suffering of life's real sorrow is at the same time his delight. Let me simply mention to you that in measures 30–36 the bass parallels the upper part at the octave.[2]

No. II. You caught the gently rocking, serene character very aptly. But to my mind the harmonic development at measures 7–10 is incorrect, according to the rules of the harmonic modes [*nach den Gesetzen der harmonischen Mode*]. Measure 7 establishes the feeling for A major, instead of leading us back again to D major, which then occurs rather violently in measure 9. Indeed, this would have been much easier, had the singing part come to a cadence in measure 6 (in accordance with the point of repose in the poem).

No. III. Should you not have set the first words here— "truth rests on dismal ground"—in such a way as to give the whole a different meaning than that which is here apparent?

For the tear is the *refreshing* companion of dumb sorrow, which it dissolves gently and consolingly. Indeed, it shares in the happiness too, and is therefore not *melancholy,* but rather *tender* and *heartfelt.* The declamation is wrong at— "If it speak to thee through thy heart"—The first, second and third stanzas required a different declamation in the last verse.

In No. IV the senseless separation of words is at its worst. The time is well chosen, but you move timidly and unnaturally within it.—

E.g., measures 8–9. You gave the last stanza a different ending, why not the others?

No. V. "My Love." Full of beautiful touches of imagination and uncommonly warm and sensitive.

Even though I might have ventured some remarks here too, e.g., that I should like C minor better than D major in measure 10 etc., yet it would really be unfair to allow criticism to predominate in the presence of such fine work. "Words do but profane thee"—is particularly good with relation to— "My maiden's heart is mine"—and excellent also is—"help me to implore" etc. Allow me to congratulate you for this remarkably successful piece.

It is a pity that, after the beautiful first 4 measures of No. VI, you interrupt the quiet flow with that harsh modulation which returns so fast to A major.

No. VII very delicate, sweet, and one of my favorites. The parallel octaves and mistakes in the last 3 measures I should wish to see removed.

No. VIII. Nicely felt and thought out.

You yourself will have noticed a certain number of printer's mistakes, and all I have left to say is that I thank you again most cordially, and beg you to see in my criticisms (which might appear too stern) only the wish to be truly of service to you and to justify the flattering gratitude you have thought good to show me.

Give me further occasions to prove this and believe me to be

Your sincere friend
Carl Maria v. Weber.

Munich, 13 Aug. 1815

A. von Meichsner, *Friedrich Wieck und seine beiden Töchter Clara Schumann, geb. Wieck, u. Marie Wieck* (Leipzig: Verlag von Heinrich Matthes, 1875), 15–21.—Tr. by editor.

132 LUDWIG VAN BEETHOVEN TO CARL CZERNY, VIENNA [G.]

[Vienna, 12 February 1816]

Dear Z,[1]

I can't see you today, tomorrow I myself shall visit you, in order to speak to you. I burst forth yesterday in such a way that I was sorry after it had happened. However, you must forgive this to an Author who would have preferred hearing his work as it was written, no matter how beautifully you played besides [2] —— But I'll make *loud* amends for it at the [performance of the] Violoncello Sonata.[3]

Be assured that as an artist I entertain the greatest goodwill towards you and shall always take pains to manifest [it].

Your true friend
Beethoven

[= Letter 115], III, 31.—Tr. by editor.

133 FRANZ SCHUBERT TO THE VIENNA CAPTAINCY OF THE CIVIC GUARD [G.]

[Vienna, April 1816]

Right Hon. I[mperial] & R[oyal] Captaincy of the Civic Guard,

The undersigned most submissively begs that the vacant post of Musical Director at Laibach may be graciously assigned to him.[1]

He supports this request with the following reasons:

1. He is a pupil of the I. & R. Seminary, ex-choir-boy of the I. & R. Court Chapel and composition scholar of Herr von Salieri,[2] first I. & R. Court Musical Director, on whose benevolent advice he desires to obtain the said post.

184

2. He has gained such knowledge and skill in all branches of composition, in performance on the organ and violin, and in singing that he is declared to be the most suitable among all the applicants for this post, according to the enclosed testimonials.

3. He promises to use his qualifications in the best possible way to do the fullest justice to a gracious consent to his petition.

Franz Schubert
at present assistant teacher at his
Father's school in
Vienna, 10 Himmelpfortgrund.

[= Letter 129], 53–54.

134 SAMUEL WESLEY TO VINCENT NOVELLO, LONDON [Eng.]

[London, 27 July 1816]

A Dialogue which happened on Saturday, July 27th, 1816 in Chappell's Music Shop, between Mr. Jones, the Welsh Harper and Antiquarian, Mr. Ayrton, the Philharmonic Orator and Legislator and S.W.[1]

Jones.—Mr. Wesley, how came you not to be at White's last Musical Auction, where several of Sebastian Bach's Works were sold, and some of them which I think you know nothing of?

S.W.—I saw the Catalogue previous to the Sale, and found no Pieces of Bach with which I was not before acquainted. —I am at present in Possession (as a Loan) of six curious and grand Preludes and Fugues, with an additional Base Line entirely for the Pedals.[2]

Ayrton.—I think these were sold at Salomon's[3] Auction.

S.W.—I am inclined to believe the contrary. I know them to be very scarce in this Country—I doubt whether there be another Copy here.

185

Ayrton.—I'm *sure* 'tis no such thing, there were several Manuscripts of Bach in Salomon's Library which I did think worth bringing forward, and I rather think this Work was among them.

S.W.—I wonder at this Omission of yours as every Note of this Author is valuable.

Ayrton— (with a Sneer). To *you* they may be so, but very few are of your Opinion.

S.W.—All those are of my Opinion who deserve the Name of either Musicians or Judges of Music.—Bach's works are the finest Study possible for *all* our musical Doctors in this Country. —Were he living he would stare not a little to find *how they had ever acquired their title.**

(Exit S.W., Jones and Ayrton staring mutually at each other and at an humble untitled *Mister's* Hardihood, which of Course they dubbed to be Impudence.—N'importe—I came away in high good Humour with myself, and you are not much out of Humour with me for *sarving* it out handsomely to these Vermin.)

W. Barclay Squire, "Some Novello Correspondence," *The Musical Quarterly,* III (1917), 229.

135   LUDWIG VAN BEETHOVEN TO SIGMUND ANTON STEINER, VIENNA [G.]

[Vienna, 23 January 1817]
Publicandum.

Having ourselves conducted an investigation and having held a hearing of our council, we have established and decided that henceforward *Hammerclavier* shall be placed instead of Pianoforte on all our works having a German title page, in accordance with which our excellent L[ieutenan]t G[enera]l and Adjutant as well as all others concerned must immediately conform, and bring this into effect.[1]

---

* N.B. Ayrton's Father was a Doctor of Music, and one of the most egregious Blockheads under the Sun.

Hammerclavier instead of Pianoforte,—
wherewith its origin is hereby established once and for all.
Given etc. etc.
This 23 January 1817   By the
                                                   G[eneralissimu]s
                                                   — — m.p.[2]

Max Unger, *Ludwig van Beethoven und seine Verleger S. A. Steiner und Tobias Haslinger in Wien, Ad. Mart. Schlesinger in Berlin* (Berlin: Schlesingersche Buch- & Musikhandlung, 1921), 58.—Tr. by editor.

136   FRANZ ANTON SCHUBERT TO GOTTFRIED CHRISTOPH HÄRTEL, LEIPZIG [G.]

Dresden 18th April
1817.

Esteemed friend ====

Since Mr. Poledro[1] is traveling to Leipzig, I take this occasion to commend him to your valued friendship and br[otherly][2] love == and beg you to be of assistance to him in his impending concerts. I must also tell you that some 10 days ago I received a valued letter from you, with which you sent me a manuscript supposedly by me, *the Erlkönig by Göthe;*[3] with the greatest astonishment, I signify that this cantata was never composed by me; I shall keep the same in my possession in order perchance to learn who sent you such a clumsy piece of work so uncivilly and also to discover this cavalier who thus misuses my name.[4] In any case, I am much obliged to you for your kind communication and remain with the most perfect consideration

Your

most obliged friend
and brthr ! ! !
Franz Schubert
Royl: Church Composer

Facsimile of the autograph: *Der Bär: Jahrbuch von Breitkopf & Härtel auf das Jahr 1928,* between pp. 8–9.—Tr. by editor.

137   LUDWIG VAN BEETHOVEN TO CARL CZERNY, VIENNA [G.]

[Vienna, 1817]

My dear Czerny!

Please handle Karl [1] with as much patience as possible, even
if matters are not yet progressing as you & I should wish, or
he will accomplish even less, for (this he must not be told)
he is overtaxed because of the bad apportionment of his lesson
hours, unfortunately this cannot readily be changed, therefore
treat him with as much love as possible but *earnestly,* then
success will be more likely under these circumstances, which
are really unfavorable to K. _____ with regard to his playing
for you, let me ask you, once he takes the proper fingering
and then keeps time correctly and plays the notes pretty much
without mistakes, only then to urge him on with regard to
the expression [*Vortrag*], & once you are *so* far, not to stop
him because of little mistakes, & to point these out to him only
at the end of the piece; though I have taught little, yet I
have always followed this method, it soon forms *Musicians,*
which, after all, is one of the prime purposes of art, & is less
fatiguing to both Master & pupil;—in certain passages such as

♪ etc. I should wish that all the fingers

be employed now and then, as also in such things as

♪ etc. ♪ etc. so that one may be able to slur

them, of course they sound as the saying goes "pearly |: when
played with few fingers :| or like a pearl" but sometimes
one wishes for other trinkets too [2] ___ more another time _____
I wish you may receive all this with the same love with which I
have intended it to be said & thought, for the rest I am & shall
ever remain in your debt _____ may my candor in any case serve
you as much as possible as a pledge of the future repayment of
the same. _____   your true
                                          friend
                                          Beethoven.

Microfilm of the autograph, kindly supplied by the Gesellschaft der Musikfreunde, Vienna, its present owners.—Tr. by editor.

138   HECTOR BERLIOZ TO IGNACE PLEYEL, PARIS [Fr.]

La Côte St André, 6 April 1819

Sir   [in another hand:] *Answered on 10th Do.*

Since I am planning to have several musical works of my own
Composition engraved I address myself to you in the hope
that you can realize my objective; I should like you to be
Responsible for the Publication of a pot-pourri Concertant
made up of selected pieces, and concerted for flutte [*sic*],
Horn, two violins, viola and Bass; [1] See if you can do it, and
how many copies you will give me; Answer me as soon as
possible I pray if that is convenient how long it will take
you to engrave it and whether it is necessary to stamp the
Parcel; I have the honor to be your most respectful and obedient
servant
Hector Berlioz.

My address is: to Mr Hector Berlioz.
at la Côte St André Dept of the Isère.

Facsimile of the autograph: Julius Kapp, *Hector Berlioz: eine Biographie*
(Berlin: Schuster & Loeffler, 1917), Anhang.—Tr. by editor.

139   VINCENZO BELLINI TO FILIPPO GUERRERA, MESSINA [It.]

Naples, 31 July 1819

Dearest uncle,

My wishes are wholly satisfied. You tell me that your family
is enjoying perfect health again. I thank God that this terrible
disease has passed, for I was very much afraid of its bad
influence upon the physique. I regret but one thing, that
D[onna] Cristina [1] has given up music. She has the pianoforte,
and it sleeps, while I should wish to have one here to raise
my spirits. I meant to buy a cembalo with hammers,[2] but was
not able to find even one. They make the pianofortes small,
and ask blood for them. And that cousin of mine sets no
store by that fine instrument. God sends bread to those who
have no mouth. Regarding those samples of French muslin,

tell my aunt that I did not get them, because one does not yet know which will be fashionable. All the ladies here wear white during the summer. In the autumn they'll wear colors, and so then I shall see which are most in fashion. In case this should reach you before Y. Worship has sent me the draft for d. 10,³ I must warn you to write as follows on the envelope:

A S. S. Ill. Sig. Don Vincenzo Ferlito Bellini

Napoli.

Not only this time but every time you wish me at your service. The reason is that there is here a certain official whose name is Vincenzo Bellino, and I am therefore afraid that he might take a letter, especially one in which there might be any draft. I kiss your hands and those of my dear Aunt Donna Anna, and Uncle D. Giovanni, and send a thousand greetings to lady cousins D. Ciccia, and D. Cristina and D. Lella, and embrace signor D. Salvatore, Michelino, and Concettella, remaining now and ever:

Your nephew, who loves you
Vincenzo.

Luisa Cambi (ed.), *Vincenzo Bellini: Epistolario* ([Milan:] A. Mondadori, 1943), 20–21.—Tr. by editor.

140   LUDWIG VAN BEETHOVEN TO TOBIAS HASLINGER, VIENNA [G.]

Baden

Most Excellent [friend]!   10th *Septemb*
1821

Yesterday, as I sat in the Carriage on my way to Vienna, I was overcome by sleep, the more so as I had almost never (because of the Early Rising here) slept properly,—now while I slumbered I dreamt I was traveling very far, no less than to Syria, no less than to india, back again no less than to arabia, finally I even reached jerusalem, the Holy city prompted thoughts of the Holy Books, small wonder that the Man Tobias should also have occurred to me then, and how natural that our Tobiasserl and pertobiassing should also have entered my Mind at the same time, now the following canon occurred to me during my Dream = voyage:

190

but the moment I woke
up, gone was the
canon & no part of it
would come back to me again, still, the next Day, as I was
returning here in the same Vehicle (that of a poor austrian
Minstrel) & continuing, now awake, the Dream voyage of the
day before, lo and behold, in conformity with the law of the
association of ideas the same canon occurred to me again, now
being awake I held it fast, just as Menelaus once [held] Proteus,[1]
& allowed it only to transform itself into 3 Voices:

Farewell   very soon
I'll Send something
on Steiner too,
to demonstrate that his
Heart is not Stony.[2]

191

Farewell most Excellent [friend], we desire at all times that you should never be true to the Name of *verleger* ["misplacer"] & never be in *Verlegenheit* ["Difficulties"], but on the contrary [that you be] a *Verleger* ["Publisher"] who is never *Verlegen* ["Confused"], whether in Receiving or remitting ———— sing the Epistles of St. Paul every Day, go every Sunday to father Werner,[3] who will show you the little Book by means of which you will get to Heaven that very Hour,[4] you see how much I care for the Salvation of your Souls, & I remain at all times with the greatest Satisfaction

from Eternity unto Eternity

Your most loyal
Debtor
Beethoven

Microfilm of the autograph, kindly supplied by the Beethovenhaus, Bonn, its present owners.—Tr. by editor.

141   FELIX MENDELSSOHN BARTHOLDY TO JOHANN WOLFGANG VON GOETHE, WEIMAR [G.]

Berlin, 24th May, 1822.

You will herewith receive, Mr. Privy Councilor, a little box of compotes which my parents are sending you, for Professor Zelter has told them that you enjoy eating this kind of preserves. There are various sorts: lemon and bamboo.

Professor Zelter has left us for a while. He is traveling on business. His trip takes him through Frankfurt on the Oder, Celle [Kloster Neuzelle], Herrnhut, Dresden, and Magdeburg. When he is away, the Academy [1] loses its spirit and its liveliness, for it is *he* that elevates everything, also when he is not conducting, the mere sight of him fires everyone. How very much I miss him!

I hope I shall enjoy the pleasure of seeing my dear Weimar again before too long. Father wants to go to Switzerland, and so we must of course pass through Weimar.[2]

Have you moved yet into your country house at Jena? Professor Zelter said that this usually takes place very early, and this time the magnificent spring contributes to it, for there is a summer-like heat here, and the chestnut trees stopped blooming long ago, the grain is bending down. The astronomers are asserting that the earth's position with respect to the sun has shifted, and indeed it is as though we were a month later than we are. The country folk do not know where to put the rich boon. It is even rumored that the cherries are already ripe.

Please be so good as to pay my most devoted respects to Mr. Councilor [3] and his lady.

I remain with the deepest respect, Mr. Privy Councilor,

Your devoted

F. Mendelssohn.

P.S. My parents have just received a long letter from the violin-player Boucher.[4] He was not received in Vienna as well as he could have wished, and his letter is rather ill-humored. He went to see Beethoven, and here are his own words, describing how Beethoven received him: [Fr.] The reception which Beethoven accorded me astonished not only his two friends who led me to him, but the entire musical world here. He fell upon my neck (against his custom), saying: "Goethe has written me about you, he loves you, esteems you, I have no need to hear you in order to appreciate you" etc. etc.

Max Friedländer, "Musikerbriefe," *Goethe-Jahrbuch*, XII (1891), 78–80.— Tr. by editor.

142   CARL MARIA VON WEBER TO HIS WIFE, DRESDEN [G.]

Vienna, 5th October 1823.

The best of good mornings, my dearest life. I'll still chat with you for a few moments, before Hasslinger [1] [sic] fetches me away to Baden. Yesterday, after the first rehearsal of "Euryanthe," which began at 12 o'clock, I sent off my letter from the eating house, where I still hastily scratched down the last words, as it had become quite late by then. Indeed, my own Midge, you cannot imagine the eagerness with which the singers seized upon their parts.—

The 6th, in the morning.

Thus far yesterday, when Hasslinger fetched me. Having
given you and dear Mäzze,[2] who is still asleep, some hearty
morning kisses, I'll take up yesterday's broken thread again,
concerning the day *before* yesterday's "Euryanthe" rehearsal.—
Since the choruses and everyone were assembled and it is not
possible to hold a reading rehearsal of this opera, I seized upon
the expedient of reading it aloud to them. The attention and
interest it evoked were very great. Stage manager Gottdank
asked me whether I wanted an engagement at the theater.—
Then I dismissed the choruses and began to rehearse with the
solo singers. I should have liked to skip Haitzinger's first romance,
but the others would not allow it; he had to sing it; and so it
went, with an ardor that made one oblivious of everything,
until Mrs. Grünbaum, who was sitting by idly during the finale
of the second act, observed that her children must be hungry.
At this, everyone flew upon her, [saying] it was surely quite
early yet; I looked at my watch: *half past three*. Then, of
course, we all ran off to the feeding establishment, and afterwards
I went to the Leopoldstadt, to see "Aline." [3] My dear Midge,
how I laughed there! The thing is excellent, and played?
Capitally. Mr. Raimund, Mmes. Huber and Schuster are great
artists. Then they still gave "Ludlam" till 12 o'clock, in honor
of the Emperor. I was really dog-tired and had to go out again
at 6 o'clock yesterday, because the party for Baden had been
fixed for half past 6. And indeed it took place, with Hasslinger,
Piringer, and Benedikt; [4] but unfortunately in the most
abominable rain. The main object was to see Beethoven. The
latter received me with an affection that was touching; he
embraced me in the heartiest way at least 6–7 times and finally
exclaimed with great enthusiasm: "Ah, you're a devil of a
fellow, an excellent fellow!" We dined together, very cheerfully
and pleasurably. This crude, repelling man really paid me court,
served me at table as attentively as if I had been his lady, etc.,
in short, this day will always be a highly remarkable one for me,
as for all those who were present. It quite elated me to see myself
being overwhelmed with such affectionate attentions by this
great spirit. How depressing is his deafness; one has to write
everything down for him. We viewed the baths and drank from
the Spa. After 5 o'clock, we returned to Vienna, where I still
saw a fairy-ballet that was truly new, surprising, *fairy-like* in

the delicacy of its invention and splendor of its decorations:
"Ismann's Grab." Thereupon I went straight to bed, as the day
had fatigued me very much. Now I have made a faithful
report; now I ask how you are, dearest wife, and Max; I dream
myself by your side. The silly boy costs me a good deal of
money. Whenever I see a child, I can't help giving him something,
and all the children like me. The other day, on the street, I
happened upon a handsome young lad of Max's age; he gave
me his paw straight off, and as I walked away he stretched out
his little hands after me and kept crying "Papa"; that touched
me so, that I came close to blubbering and had to remove myself
from the scene. Here comes the tea. And now adieu. I have a
rehearsal again at 10 o'clock. Adieu, adieu, adieu!

My sweetheart, you would certainly shed tears over many a
passage, so beautifully did these people sing at the second
rehearsal today; I only find it difficult to restrain them, lest
their enthusiasm overcome them too much and exhaust me.
These are wonderful moments for all that, when one sees that
one has touched and affected the human heart. I hope for a
good success; at least it will certainly not depend on the singers.
And now farewell, dearest life, it is past 2 o'clock. This evening
I'll set about the overture. May God give it His blessing too,
just as now I bless both of you from the bottom of my heart;
continue to be well and *good*, and keep in your affections

Your old Hamster-King
Carl.

Alfred Orel (ed.), *Wiener Musikerbriefe aus zwei Jahrhunderten* (Vienna:
A. Hartleben, [1925?]), 39–41.—Tr. by editor.

143   FRANZ SCHUBERT TO LEOPOLD KUPELWIESER, ROME [G.]

[Vienna,] 31 March 1824.

Dear Kupelwieser,

For a long time I have felt the urge to write to you, but I
never knew where to turn. Now, however, Smirsch offers me an
opportunity, and at last I can once again wholly pour out my

soul to someone. For you are so good and honest, you will be
sure to forgive many things which others might take in very
bad part from me.—In a word, I feel myself to be the most
unhappy and wretched creature in the world. Imagine a man
whose health will never be right again, and who in sheer despair
over this ever makes things worse and worse, instead of better;
imagine a man, I say, whose most brilliant hopes have perished,
to whom the felicity of love and friendship has nothing to
offer but pain, at best, whom enthusiasm (at least of the stimulating
kind) for all things beautiful threatens to forsake, and I ask you,
is he not a miserable, unhappy being?—"My peace is gone, my
heart is sore, I shall find it never and nevermore," [1] I may well
sing every day now, for each night, on retiring to bed, I hope I
may not wake again, and each morning but recalls yesterday's
grief.[2] Thus, joyless and friendless, I should pass my days, did
not Schwind [3] visit me now and again and turn on me a ray of
those sweet days of the past.—Our society (reading circle), as
you probably know already, has done itself to death owing to a
reinforcement of that rough chorus of beer-drinkers and
sausage-eaters, for its dissolution is due in a couple of days,
though I had hardly visited it myself since your departure.
Leidesdorf,[4] with whom I have become quite well acquainted,
is in fact a truly thoughtful and good fellow, but so hugely
melancholy that I am almost afraid I owe him more than enough
in that respect; besides, my affairs and his do badly, so that we
never have any money. The opera by your brother (who did
not do any too well in leaving the theater) has been declared
unusable, and thus no claim has been made on my music.[5]
Castelli's opera, *The Conspirators* [*Die Verschworenen*], has
been set in Berlin by a local composer and received with
acclamation.[6] In this way I seem once again to have composed
two operas for nothing. Of songs I have not written many
new ones, but I have tried my hand at several instrumental
works, for I wrote two Quartets for violins, viola, and violoncello
and an Octet, and I want to write another quartet, in fact I
intend to pave my way towards grand symphony in that
manner.[7]—The latest in Vienna is that Beethoven is to give a
concert at which he is to produce his new Symphony, three
movements from the new Mass, and a new Overture.[8]—God
willing, I too am thinking of giving a similar concert next
year. I will close now, so as not to use too much paper, and
196

kiss you 1,000 times. If you were to write to me about your present enthusiastic mood and about your life in general, nothing could more greatly please

In that case my address would be:
    c/o the Art Establishment of
      Sauer & Leidesdorf,
as I go to Hungary with Esterházy [9]
    at the beginning of May.

Your
    faithful Friend
      Frz. Schubert.

Fare well!
Very well!!

[= Letter 129], 338–40.

144   FERDINANDO PAËR TO AN UNNAMED CORRESPONDENT [FR.]

[Paris, 8 April 1824]

Sir,

    I am only too happy if my poor scribble can find a tiny place in the collection of different handwritings you propose to assemble.

    I have found two letters among my papers: one from Rossini (who is enjoying a great vogue) and the other from young Liszt, a Hungarian who at the moment is studying composition with me, who amazes by his performance on the piano and by his lively and precocious imagination.

    If, later on, I can obtain any more for you, I shall do so with the greatest pleasure; your amiability and character will always excite my eagerness to serve you, as you cannot doubt: I wish for opportunities of proving to you, Sir, that I am, and shall constantly remain,

    Sir,

      Your very Devoted

Paris, 8 April 1824

    Servant

      F. Paër

[= Letter 41], 428.—Tr. by editor.

145A LUDWIG VAN BEETHOVEN TO ANTON SCHINDLER, VIENNA [G.]

[Vienna, April 1824]

After six weeks of talking back and forth I am stewed, boiled and roasted, what is to become of the much-discussed concert in the end, if the prices are not raised? What will be left over for me after so many expenses, since just the copying is costing so much already?—

145B LUDWIG VAN BEETHOVEN TO IGNAZ SCHUPPANZIGH, VIENNA [G.]

[Vienna, end of April 1824]

Don't visit me any more. I am giving no concert.

B———vn

145C LUDWIG VAN BEETHOVEN TO COUNT MORITZ LICHNOWSKY, VIENNA [G.]

[Vienna, end of April 1824]

I despise falseness.—Don't visit me any more. Concert shan't take place.—

B———vn

145D LUDWIG VAN BEETHOVEN TO ANTON SCHINDLER, VIENNA [G.]

[Vienna, end of April 1824]

I request you not to come any more till I have you called for.

B———n

Concert shan't take place.

[= Letter 115], V, pp. 12, 11, 11, 12 respectively.—Tr. by editor.

145E CARL CZERNY TO FRIEDRICH WIECK, LEIPZIG [G.]

[Vienna, 9 May 1824]

Most worthy Herr von Wieck!

My silence was due not only to want of time, but also to my resolve not to write you, my honored friend, until *Beethoven*'s long-awaited concert should have taken place. The day before yesterday, at last, after a pause of more than ten years, the praiseworthy Master let us hear a portion of his newest compositions at the *Kärnthner Theater*. His friends had previously fought and overcome a mass of difficulties, real in part, in part imaginary and even fabricated; and a letter, signed by many important friends of the arts, had even been addressed to *him,* indeed made *public:* its aims can only be termed honorable and laudable, but according to the common voice, it did not, perhaps, sufficiently avoid rousing the ghost of a long-dead Rivalry.[1] An Overture, which indeed is said to have been performed before at the inauguration of a suburban theater,[2] but which was quite new to me, opened the program; and although it lays less claim to our admiration, perhaps, than any other of *Beethoven*'s works as concerns originality, nevertheless the splendid elaboration [*Durchführung*] (which is almost entirely in fugal style and makes it a companion piece, as it were, to Mozart's Magic Flute Overture) met with universal approval and is proof that even now the sublime Artist is ever striving to make new discoveries in the profundities of Counterpoint. Next came the Kyrie from his new Mass in D major (which has already received such heartening recognition abroad[3]), and its effect was indescribable; it is perhaps the most successful work of art made to that text!—

In the *Credo* which followed there is a superb fugue, the mere hearing of which almost took my breath away, 3/2 time and very difficult: [it is] the culminating point, and places the great Author by the side of *Handel* and *Sebastian Bach,* without robbing him of his unequaled originality.

The 3rd piece he gave from the Mass (Agnus Dei) appeared less satisfactory, and the discreet listener must defer his judgment of it to future hearings. Now, in conclusion, came his *newest symphony* and perhaps also his greatest (D minor). Here, after a first hearing, any description becomes impossible. The first

199

piece dazzles the ear, just as too bold a look at the sun dazzles the eye. The *Scherzo* (incontestably the greatest thing of its kind in existence) so overwhelmed the entire house that it broke in with thunderous, spontaneous applause, which was repeated at the heavenly Adagio and would have reached its peak even if the Finale had merely consisted of an instrumental piece. However, the idea of having the choir come in with Schiller's Hymn to Joy, while very handsomely conceived and just as handsomely developed (though at some length), would be far better suited to an *independent* Fantasy.

Beethoven is so great and unique as an instrumental composer, that the human voice sooner ties him down than lifts him up. The numerous, select audience manifested an indescribable, yet properly respectful enthusiasm and showed that it can feel and understand great works of art to a higher degree than any other in the world; which is proof that its taste is not so pampered as certain ill-humored persons would have it who, as it seems to me, scold at Rossini-ism for much the same reason that prompts wig makers to bear a grudge against the tousled hair style [*Titusköpfe*]. The large orchestra covered itself with glory and sweat, and *Umlauf* conducted at *Beethoven*'s side with enough fire and dedication to earn himself respect both as man and artist. Next Friday, the entire program is to be repeated at the Redoutensaal.[4]

You have doubtless heard of the impression *Moscheles* and *Kalkbrenner* made on us last autumn.[5] Both have pleased and entertained our public, without moving it to such an extent as to make it impossible to discover the limitations which Nature has imposed on their talents. The two new concertos by *Moscheles* are very proper and answer their purpose. His playing is much more solid than formerly, and on its way to being as consummate as Hummel's [6] when his individuality allows it. *Imagination* is his weak side.

Kalkbrenner's playing is a perfect, even classical mechanism, his D minor concerto pleased, but did not astound. To hear his remarks, one would never believe that he can imitate *Hummel* to the extent he does in the *Rondo brillant* and in the *Effusio Musica*, which last is really far too closely modeled after *Hummel*'s splendid Fantasy in E flat, and does not come up to it.

Beg the musical world's forgiveness for me, dearest friend, for producing such a quantity of small things and so few great ones until now. As a man of my word, I'll endeavor to make up for it. If you have an opportunity, tell Mr. Peters [7] that now I'll soon address myself in earnest to the fulfillment of that business. Excessive occupations have made me incapable of any serious reflection until now, and if he were to give me a few more weeks, the matter would certainly advance. It would please me very much to see my sonata and *Leggerezza* [published] soon.

During the course of the summer, I hope to be able to supply him with some new manuscripts, which will be of some value to him in every respect.—It is apparently not my destiny to leave Vienna yet.

But who knows what slumbers in the dark mists of the Future.

A thousand adieus to you and your worthy family, and to all those who are kind enough to feel an interest in me; and gladden soon again, with a few lines,

Your

devoted friend
Carl Czerny.

Vienna, 9th May 1824.

P.S. That Moscheles played on a *Leschen* seems only consistent to me, as that was also the only piano he sponsored formerly.

He also once improvised on the ruins of the English pianoforte which belongs to *Beethoven,* because *Graf* wouldn't let him have one of his. The player reaped greater honors on that occasion than did the instrument.[8] Haven't you too been scandalized by the shocking eulogies my little rascal and pupil, *Liszt,* is getting in *Paris?* [9] His father's letters are even more interesting upon this subject than the public prints. He is being overwhelmed with favors and honors and makes me the most brilliant offers, if I too will go there. Heaven grant that his little head may not be turned by all this!—

He'll not *learn* much there, he'll unlearn; still, who knows!—

Kalkbrenner played on a *Graf* piano. Of the 100 million tones he produced, not one went astray; yet no one was moved to tears. *Moscheles* is more economical in his playing. It seems to me that the player ought to bring the piano to life, not the piano the player. The majority of piano makers would be in a state of despair if they had to live up to all these piano-heroes' expectations!

[= Letter 131], 27–34.—Tr. by editor.

146   HECTOR BERLIOZ TO HIS UNCLE, ST. ÉTIENNE
DE ST. GEOIRE [Fr.]

Paris, Friday [August–September 1824]

My dear uncle

Neither negligence nor remissness are to blame for my long delay in writing you. The real reason is that I dared not, knowing that you were irritated with me; I did not know how to justify my departure, even though, to be sure, papa later gave you the reasons why it was cloaked in secrecy.[1] It cost me a great deal to leave you without telling you of the new decision I had obtained from his affection; it cost me even more to devote myself to a career of which you disapproved and which was to cause so much sadness in my family, but what could I do? my ominous fate had me in tow despite myself, and any other pursuit would have made me the unhappiest of men. It seems to me, besides, that with the arts one can pay society the tribute it expects of us; this part of our knowledge, and especially music, elevates the soul by giving it greater sensibility, and this attribute being the source of those of the heart, the cultivation of the fine arts cannot deprave a man. As for the greater or lesser renown one might gain thereby, I hope that with the help and support of my Great teacher [2] I may one day distinguish myself in it. I don't believe you share my opinions on the subject, but I dare hope I have not lost your affection, and that you do not doubt that of your respectful and loving nephew

Hector Berlioz.

Please present my respects to my aunt and to Madame Dauriac. The Prudhomme family desire me to convey all good wishes to these ladies.

J.-G. Prod'homme, "Unpublished Berlioziana," *The Musical Quarterly*, V (1919), 399–400.—Tr. by editor.

147   FRANZ SCHUBERT TO JOHANN WOLFGANG VON GOETHE, WEIMAR [G.]

[Vienna, early June 1825]

Your Excellency.

If I should succeed in giving evidence of my unbounded veneration of Your Excellency by the dedication of these compositions of your poems,[1] and possibly in gaining some recognition of my insignificant self, I should regard the favorable fulfillment of this wish as the fairest event of my career.

With the greatest respect, I am,

Your most devoted servant,

Franz Schubert.

[= Letter 129], 420.

148   FRANZ SCHUBERT TO HIS FATHER AND STEPMOTHER, VIENNA [G.]

Steyr, 25 July 1825.

Dear Parents,

I justly deserve the reproach which you made me concerning my long illness; but as I do not like writing empty words and our present time offers little of interest, you will forgive me for only giving you news of me in reply to your affectionate letter. I was very glad to hear that everybody is well, and I may say the same of myself, thanks to the Almighty. I am back at Steyr again, but have been at Gmunden for six weeks, the environs of which are truly heavenly and deeply moved and benefited me, as did its inhabitants, particularly the excellent Traweger. I lived at Traweger's, very free and easy. Later, when Councilor von Schiller was there, who is the monarch of the whole Salzkammergut, we (Vogl and I) dined daily at his house and had music there, as we also often did at Traweger's house.[1] My new songs from Walter Scott's "Lady of the Lake" especially had much success. They also wondered greatly at my piety,

203

which I expressed in a hymn to the Holy Virgin [2] and which, it appears, grips every soul and turns it to devotion. I think this is due to the fact that I have never forced devotion in myself and never compose hymns or prayers of that kind unless it overcomes me unawares; but then it is usually the right and true devotion. From Gmunden we went by way of Puschberg, where we met some acquaintances and stayed a few days, to Linz, where we remained a week, which we spent by turns at Linz itself and at Steyregg. At Linz I took up my quarters at the Spauns' house, where they still greatly lament the removal of Spaun (the one you know) to Lemberg.[3] I read a few letters from him, written at Lemberg, which sound very dejected and betray unmistakable homesickness. I wrote to him to Lemberg and rated him soundly over his womanish demeanor, but should probably feel even more lamentable in his place than he does. In Steyregg we called on Countess Weissenwolf, who is a great admirer of my littleness, possesses all my things and sings many of them quite nicely. The Walter Scott songs made such an excessively good impression on her that she even let it be guessed that the dedication of them would be anything but disagreeable to her.[4] But I intend to use a very different procedure with the publication of these songs from the usual one, which yields so very little, since they bear the celebrated name of Scott at their head and may in that way arouse greater curiosity, and might also make me better known in England by the addition of the English words.[5] If only some decency might be expected of those ——— of art dealers! But the wise and benevolent dispensations of the State have well and truly seen to it that an artist shall ever remain the slave of every wretched huckster.

As regards Mme. Milder's letter, the favorable reception of "Suleika" gave me great pleasure, although I wish I could have had a sight of the criticisms myself, in order to see if something could not be learnt from them; [6] for however favorable a verdict may be, it may at the same time be equally laughable if the critic lacks the required understanding, which is not altogether rarely the case.

In Upper Austria I find my compositions everywhere, especially at the monasteries of Florian and Kremsmünster, where with the aid of a gallant pianoforte player I produced my four-handed Variations and marches with notable success. What pleased especially were the variations in my new Sonata for two hands, which I performed alone and not without merit, since several people assured me that the keys become singing voices under my hands, which, if true, pleases me greatly, since I cannot endure the accursed chopping in which even distinguished pianoforte players indulge and which delights neither the ear nor the mind.[7] I am at the moment at Steyr again, and if you intend to make me happy with a letter soon, it will still find me here, as we shall stay only 10 to 14 days, whereafter we shall leave for Gastein, one of the most famous watering places, about 3 days distant from Steyr. To this journey I look forward with extraordinary pleasure, since I shall thus get to know the finest country, and we shall visit Salzburg on our return, which is so famous for its glorious situation and surroundings. As we shall not return from this journey until the middle of September, and have promised to go to Gmunden, Steyregg and Florian again then, I am hardly likely to arrive in Vienna before the end of October. By the way, please rent my quarters near the Karlskirche for me and kindly deposit the 28 gulden, V.C.,[8] which I shall gratefully refund you on my return, seeing that I had promised it, and it is possible after all that I may arrive sooner than I think. The weather here was very unsettled all through June and half of July, then very hot for 14 days, so that I positively grew thin from sheer perspiration, and now it has been raining for 4 days almost without stopping. Kindest remembrances to Ferdinand [9] and his wife and children. I suppose he still crawls to the "Cross" and cannot get rid of Dornbach; also, he has doubtless been ill 77 times again, and has thought 9 times that he was going to die, as though dying were the worst that can happen to a man! If only he could once see these heavenly mountains and lakes, the sight of which threatens to crush or engulf us, he would not be so attached to puny human life, nor regard it as otherwise than good fortune to be confided to earth's indescribable power of creating new life. What is Karl [10] doing? Is he going to travel or not? He must be busy now, for a married artist's duty is to supply works of nature as well as art, and if he succeeds in both kinds, he will be very praiseworthy, for that is no small matter. I renounce it myself. Ignaz is presumably at Hollpein's just now; [11] for as he is there only in the mornings, afternoons, and evenings, he will hardly be at home. I cannot cease to admire his perseverance, only it is difficult to tell whether it is really a merit or not and whether he deserves more of heaven or of hell thereby. I wish he would enlighten me about it. Schneider and his Schneideress [12] are to look out for the coming little Schneider or little Schneideress, so that the Schneiders may become as numerous as sand by the sea, only let them see to it that there is no superfluity of liars [*Aufschneider*], cutters [*Zuschneider*], slanderers [*Ehrab-schneider*] or cut-throats [*Gurgelabschneider*]. And now I must end this chatter at last, though I felt that I must substitute a long letter for a long silence. Marie, Pepi and little Probstl Andre [13] I kiss 1,000 times. Besides, please remember me most kindly to all who are rememberable. In expectation of a speedy reply, I remain, with all my love,

Your

most faithful son
Franz.

[= Letter 129], 434–37.

149 LUDWIG VAN BEETHOVEN TO FERDINAND WOLANEK, VIENNA [G.]

[Vienna, 1825]

To Mr. Ludwig v Beethoven!

Since I cannot finish putting the Finale into score by Easter, and you can no longer make use of the same at that time, I am sending all the parts, together with those that were begun, at your disposal.

I remain thankfully indebted for the honor you have done me in employing me; as regards the disagreeable conduct towards me I can smilingly look upon the same as only an assumed ebullition of temper. so many dissonances reign in the ideal world of tones why should they not also in the real?

My only consolation is the firm conviction that Mozart & Haydn, those celebrated artists, would, in the capacity of copyists, have met at your hands with a fate similar to mine;

I only request not to be confused with those common Copying Creatures who, even when treated as slaves, consider themselves happy to be able to exist.

For the rest, accept the assurance that I have no cause, not even
a jot, to have to blush before you on account of
> my conduct

> with high esteem
>> obediently
>>> Ferd. Wolanek

[The above crossed out from corner to corner. Scrawled across
it:]

S T U P I D

C O N C E I T E D

A S I N I N E

F E L L O W

[And underneath:]

Is one to exchange compliments with such a ragamuffin, who
steals one's money, instead one pulls him by his donkey's ears

[Verso:]
> DIRTY DAUBER!
> STUPID FELLOW!

CORRECT YOUR MISTAKES MADE THROUGH IGNORANCE,
ARROGANCE, CONCEIT & STUPIDITY, THAT IS MORE SEEMLY THAN
TRYING TO TEACH ME FOR THAT IS EXACTLY AS THOUGH A
SOW WISHED TO TEACH MINERVA.

> Beethoven

[Left-hand margin:]

It was decided already yesterday and even earlier *not* to have
you write for me *any more*:

[Right-hand margin:]

Do you do Mozart & Haidn *the honor* not to mention *them*.

The Musical Times, XXXIII (15 Dec. 1892), 18–19.—Translation revised
by present editor in accordance with facsimile of the autograph inserted *ibid*.

150   FRANZ SCHUBERT TO HEINRICH ALBERT PROBST, LEIPZIG [G.]

Vienna, 12 August 1826.

Sir,

In the hope that my name may not be wholly unknown to you, I most politely inquire whether you would not be disinclined to acquire some of my compositions at reasonable terms, being very desirous of becoming as well known as possible in Germany. You may take your choice among songs with pianoforte accompaniment, string quartets, pianoforte sonatas, 4-handed pieces, &c. &c. I have also written an Octet for two violins, viola, violoncello, double bass, clarinet, bassoon and horn. Esteeming it an honor in any case to have entered into correspondence with you, I remain, in the hope of a speedy reply,[1] with all respect,

Your devoted
Franz Schubert.

My address: On the Wieden,
No. 100, next to the Karlskirche,
5th staircase, 2nd floor.

[= Letter 129], 546–47.

151   LUDWIG VAN BEETHOVEN TO B. SCHOTT'S SÖHNE, MAINZ [G.]

Saturday
19th aug.
1 8 2 6

Gentlemen!

I am only informing you that the quartet was handed over to Frank [1] 7 days ago, you wrote that it ought indeed to be an original quartet, this irritated me, therefore as a joke I wrote next to the title that it was compiled, but it is brand *new*—the metronome indications (the Devil take all machinery) follow

———— follow—follow ———— a great misfortune has befallen me, but with God's help it may yet take a turn for the better perhaps ————

In friendship

The one who has
written you letters several
times, my beloved adopted
son almost lost his life by his own
hand, it is still possible to save him.[2]

yours
faithfully
Beethoven

Facsimile of the autograph: O. G. Sonneck, *Beethoven Letters in America* (New York: The Beethoven Association, 1927), between pp. 144–45.— Tr. by editor.

152   LUDWIG VAN BEETHOVEN TO IGNAZ MOSCHELES, LONDON [G.]

Vienna 22 Febr. 827

My dear Moscheles!

I am convinced you will not take it amiss if I trouble you as well as Sir [George] Smart,[1] for whom a letter is here enclosed, with a petition. The matter shortly told is this. Some years ago already the Philharmonic Society in London made me the handsome offer of arranging a concert for my benefit. At that time, thank God, I was not in such a position as to be obliged to make use of their noble offer. But it is quite another matter now that I have been laid low for nearly 3 months by an extremely wearisome illness. It is dropsy.—Schindler will tell you more about it in the enclosed. You have long been acquainted with my [mode of] life, you also know how and by what means I live. Writing [music] will be out of the question for a long time, and so I may unhappily be placed in a position to be obliged to suffer want. —You have not only a wide circle of acquaintances in London, but also important influence with the Philhar. Society. I beg you, therefore, to use this as far as you can, that the Philhar. Society may adopt once again this noble resolve, and carry it out soon. The enclosed letter to Sir Smart is to the same effect, just as [*sic*] I have sent one already to Mr. Stumpff.[2] I only beg you to

hand the letter to Sir Smart and to unite with him and all my
friends in London for the furtherance of this object.

I am so weak, that even dictating is becoming difficult for
me. Remember me to your amiable wife, and be assured that I
shall always be

Your

Friend

[Beethoven] [3]

Answer me soon, so that I
may hear whether I am to have any hope. [4]

Charlotte Moscheles, *Recent Music and Musicians As Described in the Diaries
and Correspondence of Ignatz Moscheles,* trans. A. D. Coleridge (New York:
Henry Holt and Company, 1873), 95–96. Collated with Stephan Ley,
Beethoven als Freund der Familie Wegeler-v. Breuning (Bonn: Friedrich
Cohen, 1927), 225, & extensively revised by present editor.

153   LUDWIG VAN BEETHOVEN TO IGNAZ MOSCHELES, LONDON [G.]

Vienna, 18 March 827.

My dear good Moscheles!

The feelings with which I read your letter of the 1st of March
I cannot describe in words. The magnanimity of the Philharmonic
Society, which all but anticipated my request, moved me to the
depths of my soul.—I entreat you therefore dear Moscheles to
be the agency through which I may deliver my deepest,
warmest thanks to the Philh. Society for its exceptional sympathy
and support.

I was compelled at once to call in the entire sum of 1000 fl
Conv. Mze, [1] as I was just in the unpleasant position of having
to borrow money, which would have brought me new difficulties.

With regard to the concert which the Philharm. Society has
determined to give for my benefit, I beg the Society not to
abandon this noble project, and to deduct from the receipts of
this conc. the 1000 fl Conv. Mze, which it has remitted me in
advance already now. And should the Society kindly allow me
the surplus, I undertake to render my thanks to the Society
by promising to write for it either a new symphony, which lies

210

already sketched in my desk,[2] or a new overture or something else the Society wants.

May Heaven only give me my health soon again, and I will prove to the noble-hearted English that I know how to appreciate their sympathy with my sad fate.

I shall never forget your noble conduct, just as I shall yet add my thanks to Sir Smart and Mr. Stumpf, in particular.[3]

Farewell! With sentiments of truest friendship I remain
Your

My hearty greeting
to your wife.
I have to thank you
and the Philh. Society
for a new friend in Mr. Rau.
Pray give to the Philharm. Society the metronome indications
for the symphony. They
are here enclosed.[4]

friend who esteems you highly
Ludwig van
Beethoven

C. Moscheles [= Letter 152], 103–104, collated with Ley, *ibid.*, 232–34, & extensively revised by present editor.

154   FRANZ SCHUBERT TO HEINRICH ALBERT PROBST, LEIPZIG [G.]

Vienna, 10 May 1828.

Sir,

Herewith I am sending you the desired Trio,[1] although a song or pianoforte book was understood for the price of 60 gulden, A.C.,[2] and not a trio, for which six times as much work is required. In order, however, to make a beginning at last, I would only ask for the speediest possible publication, and for the dispatch of 6 copies. The cuts indicated in the last movement are to be most scrupulously observed. Be sure to have it performed for the first time by capable people, and most particularly see to a continual uniformity of tempo at the changes of the time-signature in the last movement. The minuet at a moderate pace and *piano* throughout, the trio, on the other hand, vigorous except where *p* and *pp* are marked. In expectation of the earliest publication,[3]

I remain,

respectfully,

your devoted

Frz. Schubert.

[= Letter 129], 774.

155   NICOLÒ PAGANINI TO LUIGI GUGLIELMO GERMI, GENOA [It.]

[Vienna, 5 July 1828]

Dearest friend,

I am infinitely obliged to you for your tokens of friendship and for your continuous concern in my affairs. Since Mr. Bolognesi, Lawyer, made no mention in his latest of 10 June ult. of the half-year ended on 1 April of last year, I have now written to him for an explanation, notifying him that henceforward he is to conduct himself according to the instructions which you, as my Attorney-general, shall send him. That you may be the better informed when you write to him, I enclose an exact copy of his above-mentioned of 10 June ult. of this year. I also annex a copy of the last letter written to me by the late Lawyer Degli Antonj regarding the business agreed upon at Bologna; with all this, you will be able to hasten the necessary arrangements. Here is the copy of Mr. Bolognesi's [letter].

I should have given my fourteenth Recital[1] if I were not in poor health; but I'll give it, if not in the coming week, then in the next following, to comply with the most obliging wishes of H. M. Mme. the Archduchess [Marie] Louise,[2] whom I shall have to inform of my recovery.

The desire to hear me again will always persist. How many Paganinis do you think there are on this earth? . . . I don't believe it would be to my *advantage* or to my glory to give Recitals in small towns; and so in August I shall go on to

212

Munich, Prague, Dresden, Berlin, Frankfurt, Stuttgart, Strasbourg, Châlons, Paris, and, by April of next year, London. Meanwhile, I am preparing some pieces of dramatic music to be performed on the G string alone, with the accompaniment of a grand orchestra, and the following *Suonata drammatica*, called *La tempesta*, is nearly finished: 1. Whirlwind prelude, 2. beginning of storm, 3. maritime alarm, 4. prayer, 5. grave storm, 6. greatest alarm, 7. calm, 8. brilliant finale; and I'll give this composition, together with my third grand concerto, never before performed, in a last Recital of farewell to the Viennese.

The other evening I gave my 13th concert, at the I[mperial] R[oyal] Theater by the Italian gate.[3]

[Antonia] Bianchi has been separated from me for a long time, because she is an evil beast, and never again will I be able to hear her spoken of; but I'll tell you the rest at greater leisure.[4]

If friend Rebizzo wishes to be my inseparable companion, let him say so by return of post, that I may make my arrangements and plans. Love me.

I have delivered to the Austrian bank of Eskeles another 15 thousand Austrian lire, the [previous] 60 thousand to become due on 1 December and the 15 thousand on 1 January 1829. Let this be for your information, as I may decide to withdraw them later, in order to invest them in Genoa.

Farewell. My greetings to all. Your
Paganini
Vienna, 5 July 1828.

Arturo Codignola, *Paganini intimo* (Genoa: Municipio di Genova, 1935), 268–71.—Tr. by editor.

156A ROBERT SCHUMANN TO GOTTLOB WIEDEBEIN, BRUNSWICK [G.]

Leipzig, 15th July 1828.

Your Honor

will, I hope, excuse the forwardness of an eighteen-year-old youth who, enraptured with your peerless book of songs, has himself dared to infringe upon the holy world of sound with his feeble tones.

Your songs have given me many happy moments, and through them I have learnt to understand and decipher Jean Paul's veiled words.[1] Jean Paul's shadowy spirit-tones have only now become lucid and clear to me, through the magic reconditeness of your tonal creations—much as two negatives make an affirmative—and the whole heaven of tones, those tears of joy of the soul, has descended, as if transfigured, upon all my feelings.

Be indulgent with a youth who, uninitiated in the mysteries of tones, has been impelled with an unsure hand toward creations of his own and places these first attempts [2] before you for a benign, yet absolutely impartial judgment.

Kerner's poems (which, having that secret, super-terrestrial power one often finds in the poems of Goethe and Jean Paul, attracted me the most) first prompted me to try my feeble powers, since each word in them is a tone of the spheres that only needs to be fixed by a note.[3] At the same time, I herewith make a most humble request, if indeed it is for me to make any request of a master of tones, and beg, in the name of all who know your songs and fervently look forward to a second book,[4] that you may soon gladden us with settings of Kerner's lyrics, to which only your gentle, soft, melancholy chords can supply the finest text and profoundest meaning. I further beg that, provided your manifold occupations grant you the time, you will at your leisure send the enclosed songs back to me with an answer.

No matter how very much the general praise of strangers may reward you, only the tone-heaven of rapture and delight in which you live can offer you the finest reward and garland.

Let not the standard of your songs be that of mine, and

may each tone gently remind you of a distant, unknown heart to which you have given all. Accept the assurance of my deepest love and profoundest veneration. I remain

Your Honor's

most humble

Robert Schumann

Stud. jur.⁵ residing at the Brühl, No. 454, 1st floor.

156B GOTTLOB WIEDEBEIN TO ROBERT SCHUMANN, LEIPZIG [G.]

Brunswick, 1 Aug. 1828.

Dear sir,

I was gratified by your obliging trust; well, here is candor in exchange for trust.

Your songs have many, at times very many shortcomings; yet I should not call them spiritual so much as natural or youthful sins, and these can indeed be excused and forgiven if a pure poetic feeling, a truthful spirit occasionally sparkles through. And it is this which has pleased me so much.

If, by mentioning those natural and youthful sins, I have tried to hint at a manifest uncertainty regarding the intrinsic elements as well as the higher study of the art, I nevertheless have the liveliest wish to impart a more unequivocal opinion to you some years from now. In the meantime, I hope you will not take amiss or misinterpret some further observations.

We ought wholly to surrender ourselves to the fine rapture of moments of exalted dedication; after which, however, calm, inquiring reason must also assert its rights and intervene with its bear's paw, mercilessly scratching out whatever human failing may have got smuggled in. Wild things grow wildly; nobler fruits demand cultivation. Wine, however, requires not only the most assiduous cultivation, but also the knife; and if both were present in lovely Italy, her heaven-sent gifts would not turn sour with the passage of years.

Above all, look to truth. Truth of melody, of harmony, and of expression—in a word, poetic truth. Wherever you do not find it, or merely see it threatened, there must you tear away, even if it is your dearest creation.

First, examine—each thing singly—the declamation, the
melody, the harmony, and then the expression and spirit that
are to consecrate the whole—then harmonize every part
together; and if you have a sensation akin to that produced
by two strings so tuned as to melt into a single tone: then do
not give the world any thought, for you shall have lifted the
veil. But if any doubts, no matter of what kind, are present,
then, again, believe me: sin has crept in.— —

Much, very much has been granted to you by nature; use
it, and the esteem of the world shall not elude you. But believe
me, our Patriarch is right again, in this as in everything, when
he says: "Even the happiest genius cannot succeed, etc." [6]

I am, with sincerest regards,   Yours

G. Wiedebein.[7]

F. Gustav Jansen, *Die Davidsbündler: Aus Robert Schumann's Sturm- und
Drangperiode* (Leipzig: Breitkopf und Härtel, 1883), 118–19, 119–20.
—Tr. by editor.

157   FRANZ SCHUBERT TO HEINRICH ALBERT PROBST, LEIPZIG [G.]

Vienna, 2 October 1828.

Sir,

I beg to inquire when the Trio is to appear at last. Can it
be that you do not know the opus number yet? It is Op. 100.
I await its appearance with longing.[1] I have composed, among
other things, 3 Sonatas for pianoforte solo, which I should like
to dedicate to Hummel. Moreover, I have set several songs
by Heine of Hamburg, which pleased extraordinarily here,
and finally turned out a Quintet for 2 violins, 1 viola and 2
violoncellos.[2] The Sonatas I have played with much success
in several places, but the Quintet will be tried out only during
the coming days. If perchance any of these compositions would
suit you, let me know.

With much respect,
I subscribe myself,
Frz. Schubert.

My address is: Neue Wieden,
No. 694, at the "City of Ronsperg,"
2nd floor, right.

[= Letter 129], 810–11.

216

158   FRANZ SCHUBERT TO FRANZ VON SCHOBER, VIENNA [G.]

[Vienna, 12 November 1828]

Dear Schober,

I am ill. I have eaten nothing for eleven days and drunk nothing, and I totter feebly and shakily from my chair to bed and back again. Rinna is treating me. If ever I take anything, I bring it up again at once.

Be so kind, then, as to assist me in this desperate situation by means of literature. Of Cooper's I have read "The Last of the Mohicans," "The Spy," "The Pilot," and "The Pioneers." If by any chance you have anything else of his, I implore you to deposit it with Frau von Bogner at the coffee-house for me. My brother, who is conscientiousness itself, will most faithfully pass it on to me. Or anything else.

Your friend

Schubert.

[= Letter 129], 819–20.

159   FRANZ LISZT TO CARL CZERNY, VIENNA [Fr.]

[Paris, 23 December 1828]

My very dear Master,

When I think of all the immense obligations under which I am placed towards you, and at the same time consider how long I have left you without a sign of remembrance, I am perfectly ashamed and miserable, and in despair of ever being forgiven by you! "Yes," I said to myself with a deep feeling of bitterness, "I am an ungrateful fellow; I have forgotten my benefactor, I have forgotten that good master to whom I owe both my talent and my success." . . . At these words a tear starts to my eyes, and I assure you that no repentant tear was ever more sincere! Receive it as an expiation, and pardon me, for I cannot any longer bear the idea that you have any ill-feeling towards me. You will pardon me, my dear Master,

217

won't you? Embrace me then . . . good! Now my heart is light.

You have doubtless heard that I have been playing your admirable works here with the greatest success, and all the glory ought to be given to you. I meant to play your variations on the *Pirate*[1] the day after tomorrow at a very brilliant concert that I was to have given at the theater of H.R.H. Madame, who was to have been present as well as the Duchess of Orleans; but man proposes and God disposes. I have suddenly caught the measles, and have been obliged to say farewell to the concert; but it is not given up because it is put off, and I hope, as soon as ever I am well again, to have the pleasure of making these beautiful variations known to a large public.

Pixis[2] and several other people have spoken much to me of four concertos that you have lately finished, and the reputation of which is already making a stir in Paris. I should be very much pleased, my dear Master, if you would commission me to get them sold. This would be quite easy for me to do, and I should also have the pleasure of playing them *from first hand*, either at the opera or at some big concerts. If my proposition pleases you, send them to me by the Austrian Embassy, marking the price that you would like to have for them. As regards any passages to be altered, if there are any, you need only mark them with a red pencil, according to your plan which I know so well, and I will point them out to the editor with the utmost care. Give me at the same time some news about music and pianists in Vienna; and finally tell me, dear Master, which of your compositions you think would make the best effect in society.

I close by sending you my heartfelt greetings, and begging you once more to pardon the shameful silence I have kept towards you: be assured that it has given me as much pain as yourself!

Your very affectionate and grateful pupil,

F. Liszt

23rd December 1828.

P.S.—Please answer me as soon as possible, for I am longing for a letter from you; and please embrace your excellent parents from me. I add my address (Rue Montholon, No. 7[bis]).

La Mara [Marie Lipsius] (ed.), *Letters of Franz Liszt*, trans. Constance Bache (New York: Charles Scribner's Sons, 1894), I, 3–5.

160   HECTOR BERLIOZ TO JOHANN WOLFGANG VON GOETHE, WEIMAR [Fr.]

[Paris, 10 April 1829]

Monseigneur [1]

For some years *Faust* has been my habitual reading; by dint of pondering on this amazing work (though I can see it only through the mists of translation), it has at length cast a sort of spell over my intellect; musical thoughts grouped themselves in my mind around your poetic thoughts, and although I was firmly resolved never to unite my feeble harmonies with your sublime accents, little by little the enticement became so strong, the spell so violent, that the music to several scenes was made nearly unbeknown to me. [2]

I have just published my score and, however unworthy it may be of being shown to you, I take the liberty today of presenting you with it. I am quite convinced that you have already received a very great number of compositions of all kinds inspired by the marvelous poem; hence I have every reason to fear that, coming after so many others, I shall only be importuning you. But if, in the atmosphere of glory in which you live, obscure tributes cannot move you, I hope at least that you will forgive a young composer, whose heart was filled and imagination fired by your genius, for being unable to suppress a cry of admiration. [3]

I have the honor, Monseigneur, of being with the deepest respect

your very humble and very obedient servant
Hector Berlioz
Rue de Richelieu No. 96 Paris
10 April 1829

[= Letter 141], 99–100.—Tr. by editor.

161   FRÉDÉRIC CHOPIN TO HIS PARENTS, WARSAW [Pol.]

[Vienna,] Wednesday, 12 August 1829

You know from my last letter, dearest parents, that I was persuaded to give a concert. So yesterday, that is, Tuesday evening at 7, in the Imperial and Royal Opera House,[1] I made my entry into the world!

Here they call such an appearance in the theater *"eine musikalische Akademie."*[2] As I was to get nothing for it, and didn't try to get anything, Count Gallenberg[3] anticipated the concert, arranging the program as follows:

A Beethoven *Overture*
My *Variations*
Singing (Miss Veltheim)
My *Rondo.*[4]

Then more singing, then a short ballet to finish the evening.

At rehearsal the orchestra accompanied so badly that I substituted a *freie Phantasie*[5] for the *Rondo.* As soon as I appeared on the stage, the bravos began; after each variation the applause was so loud that I couldn't even hear the orchestra's *tutti.* When I finished, they clapped so much that I had to come out a second time and bow. The *freie Phantasie,* though it did not go quite so well, was even more successful, and I had to come out again. I pulled through because the Germans are appreciative. The whole project had been suggested only on Saturday, and Würfel[6] carried it out by Tuesday; I owe him a great deal.

On Saturday I met Gyrowetz, Lachner, Kreutzer, and Seyfried; I had a long talk with Mayseder.[7] I was standing in front of the theater, when I saw Count Gallenberg. He came up to me and proposed that I should play on Tuesday; so I consented, and I was not hissed! When I come home, I'll tell you all, better than I can write it down. You need have no anxiety for me and my fame.

The journalists have taken a fancy to me; perhaps they will cuff me a bit, but that's necessary to underline the praise. Gallenberg likes my compositions. The stage manager of the theater, Mr. Demar, is very kind and amiable with me. He was so encouraging with his assurances before I went on the stage, and kept my thoughts off it so well, that by the time I presented myself before the public I was not too nervous, especially as the hall wasn't full. My friends and colleagues had spread out over the hall to listen to opinions and criticisms. Celinski can tell you how little fault-finding there was. The worst was what Hube overheard: [8] some lady said, "*Schade um den Jungen, dass er so wenig Tournüre hat.*" [9] If that is all the fault they found (and all my friends assure me they heard only praise and swear they never started the applause themselves) there's no need to worry.

I improvised on a theme from the *Dame blanche*.[10] After the concert the stage manager, who had liked my *Rondo* so much at rehearsal, squeezed my hand and said, "*Ja, das Rondo muss hier gespielt werden,*" [11] and asked me to play a variation on a Polish theme. I chose *Chmiel*.[12] The tune electrified the public, which never has an opportunity of hearing such songs. My spies in the pit assure me that people started up in their seats at it.

Wertheim, who happened to arrive yesterday from Carlsbad with his wife, had gone straight to the theater, not knowing that I was playing there; he called on me today to congratulate me. He saw Hummel [13] in Carlsbad and mentioned me to him. He is writing to him today about my concert.

Haslinger [14] is printing the *Variations*. The poster for the concert will be preserved.

General opinion has it that I played too softly, or rather, too delicately for people used to the piano-pounding of the artists here. I expect to find this reproach in the paper, especially as the daughter of one of the editors thumps frightfully. No matter, there must always be a *but* somewhere, and I prefer this to being told I play too loud. Yesterday Count Dietrichstein,[15] one of the emperor's intimates, came to see me on the stage; we talked at some length, in French. He complimented me and advised me to prolong my stay in Vienna. The orchestra had cursed at my badly-written notes; they sulked up to the improvisation, after which they mingled their applause with the public's bravos and shouts. Now they are mine. As for the other artists, I am not yet sure of their sentiments; they ought not to be hostile, since they know I didn't play for material gain.

And so, my Viennese début was as fortunate as it was

unexpected. Hube says nothing is ever attained by ordinary
means and by attempts to realize prearranged plans patiently.
One must, says he, leave something up to fate. Thus, without
retreating in the face of risk, I let myself be persuaded to
give the concert. If the papers should so demolish me that I
dare not show myself again, I shall become a house painter.
The brush glides delightfully over the wallpaper, and one is
still a son of Apollo!

I wonder what Mr. Elsner [16] will say to all this; perhaps he
won't like it that I played. But they made such a dead set at
me that I could not refuse, and after all I think it did no harm.
Nidecki [17] in particular showed me great friendliness yesterday;
he looked through and corrected the orchestral parts and was
genuinely pleased at the success.

I played on a Graf instrument. [18]

Today I feel wiser and more experienced by at least 4 years.
Ah! You must have been surprised to see my last letter sealed
with "Madeira." But I was so distracted that I took the seal
nearest to hand, which was the waiter's, and applied it to my
letter in a hurry.

Henryk Opieński (ed.), *Chopin's Letters*, trans. E. L. Voynich (New York:
Alfred A. Knopf, 1931), 52–55. [19]

162   ROBERT SCHUMANN TO FRIEDRICH WIECK, LEIPZIG [G.]

Heidelberg, 6 November 1829

I just put the [Hummel] A minor Concerto aside, my
honored master, and quickly rolled down the blinds, lit a cigar,
pulled the table closer to the stool, pressed my forehead
firmly in my hand, and in a flash I was standing at the corner
of the Reichsstrasse, with music under my arm, about to go
to my pianoforte lesson. Ah! why did I leave your Leipzig,
where the whole Olympus of music was so splendidly revealed
to me, and where you stood as my priest and softly and
powerfully removed the veil from the eyes of the dazzled
novice! It has turned out just as I had expected—on the

whole, there is much love for music here but little talent, now and then an antiquated art critic, but little active originality.— You know that I can hardly tolerate pure *theory,* and so I have been living quietly withdrawn, improvising a great deal and playing but little out of music books, beginning many a *symphony* and finishing nothing, inserting from time to time, between *Roman Statute Laws and the Pandects,* a Schubert waltz, often humming the Trio [1] to myself in my dreams, and occasionally thinking of the heavenly lesson at your home which first acquainted me with it—and so I believe I have neither lost much ground nor made much progress, which might of course be thought of as a standstill—yet I feel that my touch has become much richer in the fortes, and in the pianos much more *free* and alive, but I may have lost some dexterity and precision. Without overestimating myself in the least, I am perfectly, if modestly, conscious of my superiority over all the Heidelberg pianoforte players—you have no idea of the slovenly and rough manner of performing and of the poking, twanging, and rumbling, and the whole atrocious feebleness of their playing; touch and tone and melodiousness are out of the question, and they have never in all their lives heard of practicing: finger exercises and scales, etc. Recently someone played me the A minor Concerto; he performed it faithfully, without mistakes, and precisely, in an old-fashioned way, and in a conscientiously rhythmical march time, so much so that I praised him, and he deserved it; but when I played it for him afterwards, he said that he played it as correctly as I did, but that with me everything *sounded* so differently, and where did the *violin-tone* come from etc. I looked smilingly into his eyes, fetched Herz's [2] finger exercises, and told him to play finger exercises for an hour every day and come back after a week and play me the concerto—this he did, and returned some time later, delighted and enthusiastic, and called me his "good genius," it had helped him so much—then he played the concerto ten times better, really.—

I am now learning the last movement of Hummel's F-sharp minor Sonata, a truly great, epic, titanic work and the *picture* of an enormous, fighting, resigned spirit. Let this be the only thing I will play for you at Easter time, and at the same time a yardstick for your criticism of my development.—An opposition party is forming against Thibaut,[3] in which also

I am participating; you would not believe what splendid, pure, noble lessons I had with him and how very much his narrow-mindedness and truly pedantic views on music *hurt*, next to his boundless versatility in jurisprudence and his animating, kindling, *pulverizing* spirit.—

A fortnight ago, I returned from a tour of Switzerland and Italy, poorer by a few napoleons but the richer in knowledge of the world, and with my inmost heart full of high, sacred memories. You have, by God! no notion of Italian music, which should be heard only under the sky that called it forth —under the Italian sky. How often did I think of you at the Scala Theater in Milan, and how charmed I was by—Rossini, or better, by *Pasta*,[4] to whom I'll attach no *epithet*, out of respect and almost out of veneration. In the Leipzig concert hall I have sometimes shuddered, as it were, for delight and have feared the Genius of Music—but in Italy I also learnt to love it, and there has been only one evening in my life during which I have felt as though God were standing before me and were letting me look openly and quietly upon his countenance for a few moments—and that was in Milan, when I heard Pasta and — — Rossini. Do not smile, honored Sir,—it is true.—But this was also the only musical pleasure I heard in Italy; otherwise music in Italy is hardly to be listened to, and you have no idea of the slovenliness and at the same time the fire with which everything is fiddled away.—I'll not speak of other events of the journey, however interesting and new to me many were, and shall save the report for another time, when I can speak and smile with you in person.—

Schubert is still my "one and only Schubert," particularly because he has everything in common with my "one and only Jean Paul";[5] when I play Sch. I feel as if I were reading a novel of Jean Paul's set to music. I recently played his Rondo Op. 107 for four hands, which I count among his best compositions or show me something that will compare with the quiet sultriness and the colossal, hushed, *compressed*, *lyrical* insanity, and the total, profound, soft, ethereal melancholy which hovers over this whole *truthful entity*. I see Schubert walking earnestly to and fro in his chamber, wringing his hands as though in desperation, and in his mind there

constantly sounds: etc.

and he cannot rid himself of the idea and he *puts down* this
great, great melody once more, loud and exalted and *consoled*
in the end, and then the whole thing breathes softly once
more and dies away. I can remember having played this Rondeau
for the first time at an evening party at Mr. Probst's,[6] where
in the end the players and listeners looked long at one another
and didn't know what they wanted or what Schubert wanted.
You too, so far as I know, have never spoken of it; please
look it up again and give me your opinion of it. There is no
music besides Schubert's that is so *psychologically* remarkable
in the *sequence of ideas* [*Ideengang*] and their connection and
in the *apparent* logic of the sudden transitions, and how few
have been able to *stamp* a single individuality as he did upon
one so various a *mass of tone-pictures,* and fewer yet have
written so *for themselves* and for their own heart. What a diary
is to others, in which they *put down* their momentary feelings
etc., a sheet of music paper was to Schubert, to which he
confided his every mood, and his thoroughly musical soul
wrote notes where others use words—in my foolish opinion.—
Years ago already, I started an Aesthetics of Music which
had progressed pretty far, but then I felt quite clearly that
I lacked personal judgment and even more objectivity, with
the result that I would find things here and there where
others missed them and the other way around.—But if you
only knew what urges and impulses are in me, and how I
might already have reached Op. 100 in my *symphonies, had I*
written them down, and how perfectly at home I feel with
the full orchestra, *and [how I] could stand up to enemies,
even, and drive and subdue them, hem them in and repulse
them.* I am not very proud, more through circumstances than
principle (for I affect [pride] in front of some persons who
deserve it)—but sometimes I am so full of sheer music and
so completely overfilled with nothing but tones, that it is
simply impossible for me to write anything down, and that I
could be so rash, while in that mood, as to laugh openly in
the face of an art critic who should say to me: "I don't want
to write, for I *accomplish* nothing," and tell him he didn't
know a thing about it. Excuse my candor, though it *isn't,*
really.—Now requests and nothing but requests! The first
and most deeply-felt one is: "answer me," and the second
and even more deeply-felt one: "and very soon." By God!
225

Your letters are here for me what the Leipzig concerts were, which I must miss.—You have had Paganini in Leipzig, and what's more you have heard him *four times!* no! that *four times, four times* could drive me to despair. Please, write me something about your whole life and activity during the past semester, also about your present pupils, your Klara and your other two children with their big, musical eyes.[7] Do you think you could send me the [*Allgemeine*] *musikalische Zeitung*, from April–September, just for a fortnight; here not a soul reads it, and perhaps you don't need it any longer.

Less important requests: that you send me, *strictly to my account,*

All the Schubert [+)] Waltzes (I believe there are 10–12 books),

Moscheles G minor Concerto ⎤
Hummel's B minor Concerto ⎦ *without* the parts

and *loosely* to my account, i.e. on condition that I may return what I don't like:

all of Schubert's compositions (which have been published since Op. 100); please, don't forget the *Quintet* [8] especially, as I should very much like to become acquainted with it, then: All the piano compositions of interest which have appeared since I left Leipzig and which you think I may like, since you know my taste: something *new* by *Herz* and *Czerny* may also be included, since here I am being introduced to—families. Thibaut must be pushed aside with his Handelian opera arias.

I'm not nearly finished; yet I'll close. Remember me to your esteemed wife, to Dr. Karus, to whom I have written but not yet received an answer, to Mr. Probst who is justly angry with me and whom I *highly* respect in all earnest, and to Madem[oiselle] Reichold, who, I trust, is engaged to be married.[9] Accept, honored master of my *inner being*, the assurance of my

deepest respect

R. Schumann.

Clara Schumann (ed.), *Jugendbriefe von Robert Schumann* (4th ed.; Leipzig: Breitkopf und Härtel, 1910), 78–85.—Tr. by editor.

+) Only those for two hands. I have built up a great deal of Schubert*ianism* here, where his name is hardly known; I also have two lovely, hopeful, blooming —— pupils, English girls, who are delighted with the finger exercises and scales.

Heidelberg, 30 July 1830.
5 o'clock.

Good morning, Mama!

How can I possibly describe to you my bliss at this moment!
—The spirit is burning and sputtering under the coffee
machine and the sky is so pure and golden that I could kiss
it—and the whole soul of the morning is abroad, fresh and
clear.—What's more, your letter lies before me, in which a
whole treasure-house of feeling, understanding, and virtue is
revealed—the cigar, too, tastes fine —— in short, the world
is splendid at times, that is, man, if only he would always rise
early.

There's sunshine and blue sky enough in my life here; but
I miss my Cicerone, and that was Rosen.[1] Two of my closest
acquaintances also, the v. H[eydens] from Pomerania, two
brothers, went away to Italy a week ago, and so I am often
quite alone, that is, quite blissful and quite unhappy by turns,
at random. Every young man gets on better without a
sweetheart than without a friend. Furthermore, I sometimes
feel very hot when I think of myself. My *whole life* has been
a *twenty years' conflict* between poetry and prose, or call it
music and law. I had just as high an ideal before me in
practical life as in art.—The ideal was, in effect, practical
activity and the hope that I should have to struggle in a wide
sphere of action—but what prospects are there, particularly
in *Saxony*, for a commoner who has no great connections and
fortune and no real love for juristic beggarliness and penny-
lawsuits! In Leipzig I lived from day to day with no thought
of planning my life, dreaming and dawdling, and at bottom
not accomplishing anything worthwhile; *here* I have done
more work, but there as here I've become more and more
deeply attached to art. Now I stand at the crossroads and am
frightened by the question: Where to?—If I obey my genius,
it directs me towards art and, as I believe, to the right path.
But actually—don't hold it against me, and I am only saying
this to you lovingly and softly—I have always felt as though
you were barring my way to it; you had your good, motherly

227

reasons which I also understood very well and which you and I called the "uncertain future and precarious bread." But what now? There can be no greater misery for a man than an unhappy, dead, and insipid future for which he himself has prepared the ground. It is also not easy to choose a course of life quite opposite to one's earlier upbringing and vocation, and it requires patience, confidence, and rapid training. My imagination is yet in its prime, and art can still nourish and ennoble it; and I have arrived at the certainty that, with diligence and patience and with a good teacher, I can, within six years, compete against any pianoforte player, since pianoforte playing is nothing but pure mechanics and dexterity; now and then I have imagination too, and perhaps a natural tendency towards independent creativity — — now the question: One or the Other; for only *One* thing can be great and right in one's life;—and I can only give this answer: resolve to do the right and proper thing and, with calm and perseverance, you shall succeed and the goal be attained. I am now more ardent in this fight than ever, my good mother, at times rashly brave and confident of my powers and my will, at other times anxious, when I think of the long path which I might have traversed by now and which I still must traverse.—As for Thibaut,[2] he directed me towards art long ago; a letter from you to him would give me great pleasure, and Thibaut would enjoy it too; but he left for Rome some time ago, so that I shall no longer be speaking to him.

If I decided for the law, I should have to stay here irreversably for another winter, in order to hear Thibaut on the Pandects, which every law student must hear from him. If I decided for music, I should have to leave here beyond any question and return to Leipzig. *Wieck* in L[eipzig], in whom I gladly confide, who knows me and can judge of my capacity, would then have to continue teaching me; later I should have to go to Vienna for a year and, if at all possible, to Moscheles.[3] And now a favor, my good mother, which perhaps you will grant me gladly. *Write to Wieck in Leipzig yourself, and ask him plainly what he thinks of me and my plans for the future.* Ask him for a prompt answer and decision, so that I may hasten my departure from Heidelberg, however difficult it may be for me to go from here, where I'll be leaving behind so many good people, splendid dreams, and a real paradise of nature. If you like, *enclose this*

228

letter with that to Wieck. The question must *in any case* be decided *by Michaelmas,* and then I'll pursue my goal with fresh vigor and without tears.

You can see that this is the most important letter I've ever written or shall ever write, and for this reason grant me the favor without reluctance and answer me soon. No *time* is to be lost.

Farewell, my dear mother, and don't be anxious. Here heaven can only help if man helps too.

Your son, who loves you deeply,
Robert Schumann.

[= Letter 162], 116–19.—Tr. by editor.

164   RICHARD WAGNER TO B. SCHOTT'S SÖHNE, MAINZ [G.]

Leipzig, 6 October 1830.

Dear Sir,

For a long time I have made *Beethoven's* magnificent last symphony the object of my deepest study, and the more I grew familiar with the great value of the work, the more it grieved me that it is so greatly misunderstood, so greatly neglected by the greater part of the public. Now it appeared to me that the way to make this masterpiece more accessible was through a serviceable arrangement for the piano, which, to my great sorrow, I had not yet come across (for that duet arrangement by *Czerny* will never do). With great enthusiasm, therefore, I myself have ventured an attempt to arrange this symphony for *two hands,* and have succeeded thus far in arranging the first and perhaps most difficult movement with all possible clarity and fullness. I therefore address myself now to your resp'd publishing house with the question, whether you might be disposed to accept such an arrangement? (for of course I should not wish to continue so strenuous a task without this certainty). As soon as I have that assurance, I shall promptly

229

set to work and finish what I have begun. I therefore beg you most humbly for an immediate answer,[1] and you may, Sir, count on the greatest zeal on my part.

I am, Sir, your humble servant
Richard Wagner

My address:

Leipzig, Pichhof before the Halle Gate, 1st floor.

Julius Kapp and Emerich Kastner (eds.), *Richard Wagners Gesammelte Briefe* (2 vols.; Leipzig: Hesse & Becker Verlag, 1914), I, 3.—Tr. by editor.

165 FELIX MENDELSSOHN BARTHOLDY TO HIS FAMILY, BERLIN [G.]

On the Isola Bella, 24th July 31

Now you will immediately be smelling the scent of oranges, seeing a blue heaven, a lovely sun, a calm lake, when you only read the date. But no, the weather is atrocious, it's raining furiously, from time to time it thunders too, the mountains have a frightfully desolate aspect, as if the world had been nailed shut with clouds, the lake is gray, the sky dirty, I smell no oranges, and so it might just as well be called the Isola Brutta.[1] It has been like this for the past 3 days already, my poor coat!—

But before I go on with my tale, I must beg forgiveness for not having written in such a long time; here in the mountains it is not possible to consign a letter safely, and so I have already been traveling about for a week with this blank sheet inside my sketch book [2] and haven't found an opportunity of filling it up and sending it away; the post wasn't running, I should have had to send a messenger south, then the letter would first have gone to Milan; that made me angry, and so forgive me; when I write to you, I like to be undisturbed and comfortable, and that is how I feel here, in spite of the senseless weather.

I am notoriously the spirit that always denies [3] (cf. Mother), and as it is now the fashion throughout the world to find the Borromean Islands "not so beautiful" and "rather stiff," and as, besides, the weather seems to have resolved to spoil them for me, therefore out of spite I find them particularly splendid; I

230

was quite taken with the approach to this island, during which one sees the green terraces with those jolly statues over them, many antiquated decorations amid fresh foliage, and southern plants all crowded together—there was even something touching, serious about it. For what I saw last year in abundance and wild profusion everywhere (and I had actually grown used to it) is now transplanted here once more by human hands and wishes to say farewell.⁴ There are lemon groves and orange coppices, jagged, spiky aloes grow out of the walls—I feel as though the beginning of the piece were coming back once more at the end, and I am very fond of that, as you know.

On the steamer there was the first peasant woman in Swiss garb, and people spoke in a bad, Frenchified Italian: this is the last letter from Italy. But believe me, the Italian lakes are not the least thing in the land; *anzi*.⁵ I have never seen anything lovelier; they had tried to persuade me that the colossal forms that loomed up before me as the Swiss Alps of my childhood had expanded in my imagination, and that a snow-capped mountain is not really as immense as I fancied it to be. I was almost afraid of being disappointed, but then, when at Lake Como I saw the first foothills of the Alps wrapped in their clouds (bright snow and sharp black pinnacles peeping out here and there) and dropping sheer to the lake—covered with trees and hamlets at first, then with moss, then barren and desolate and full of snow-crevices, I felt again for the first time as I had in those days and saw that I had not exaggerated at all. In the Alps everything is much freer, keener, coarser if you will, but I feel even better and healthier there. I wish I could describe how fresh I felt when, for the first time since [our] Swiss journey,⁶ I again saw that amazing company of glaciers and peaks: it makes one feel very tiny. And I still have the Valley of Chamouny ahead of me and have been telling myself now and then, since yesterday: A week from today you'll be in the Valley of Chamouny again.

I am making good use of my science of the Refinement of Pleasures, here in the mountains. And even if I have become outwardly coarse, inwardly I am lacquered. True, you would more probably take me for a tramp than for your son, brother, brother-in-law, and uncle if you saw me now, but a man can't equip himself with new things before Geneva, and the old things are falling to pieces—what is one supposed to do, then?

231

A propos, dear mother, all my shirt-collars and cuffs have become
fuzzy, I believe they call it *torn*. Should I have new ones put on,
or buy new shirts altogether, or can one patch them up? Please
write to me regarding this weighty matter; I don't trust foreign
washerwomen. Yesterday I even had to take a walk in my
slippers at Lago Maggiore, because I had worked up a quantity
of blisters under my feet at Lake Como; people said *Poverino,
è zoppo;* [7] my blue cap fell in the water the other day and has
been shrunk ever since, my English greatcoat is consumptive,
for its fiber has wasted away, [8] my beard has grown long—let me
draw the curtain over this picture. Disgraceful weather outside;
it has been thundering for 6 hours with scarcely an interruption,
as if the clouds had taken to vomiting; but it is all of no
importance.—I've just come back from the garden of the castle,
which I visited in the rain. I wished to imitate Albano and called
for a barber, that he might bleed me; [9] but he misunderstood
and shaved me; the misunderstanding was very agreeable.
Gondolas are landing at the island from every side, because they
are celebrating the morrow of yesterday's great feast, for which
father Boromeo [? *sic*] ordered singers and musicians from
Milan, who performed for the islanders. The gardener asked me
whether I knew what a wind instrument was? I said yes with a
good conscience, and then he said I should try to imagine 30
such instruments together, and fiddles and basses besides, or
rather I couldn't imagine it, for such a thing had to be heard to
be believed, it sounded as if it came straight from Heaven, and
the origin of it all was the Philharmonic. I don't know what
precisely he had in mind, but it had made a greater impression
on him than the best orchestra on many a musical connoisseur.
Somebody has just begun playing the organ for the service in
the church across the way; in the following manner:

The bass, with full organ, 16′ Bourdon, and reed pipes, sounds
enchanting. This fellow has also come specially from Milan to
spread confusion in the local church. I will go over there a
while, and so farewell for the moment.—

This evening I shall remain here instead of going across the
lake; I enjoy the little island so very much. True, I have not
slept properly these past two nights, the first because of countless thunderclaps, the other because of countless fleas, and I shall
probably have to deal with both tonight; but since I'll already
be speaking French the day after tomorrow, and shall have left
Italy and crossed the Simplon, I wish to wander about in true
Italian style for the last time today and tomorrow. I'll carry
this letter myself (tomorrow morning on the steamer) to Arona,
site of the great [statue of] St. [Charles] Borromeo. Now I
must add a historical account of how I came here. In Milan
the Ertmanns [10] still called on me at my chamber at the last moment,
and we took a warmer leave than I can remember taking of
anyone in a long time. I was obliged to promise them that I
would send you many greetings, though you do not know them,
and that I would let them hear from me from time to time.
Another very dear acquaintance I made there was that of Mr.
Mozart,[11] who is a clerk there, but actually a musician in his
heart and soul; he must bear the greatest resemblance to his
father, particularly his nature, for one hears him say a quantity
of those things that are so moving in his father's letters because
of their naïveté and openness, and one can't help being fond of
him immediately. I find it wonderfully charming, for ex., that
he should be so jealous of his father's good name and reputation,
as though the latter were a rising young musician, and one
evening at the Ertmanns', when a great deal of Beethoven's
music was being performed, the Baroness whispered to me and
asked me to be so kind now as to play something by Mozart
too, since the son would otherwise not be so happy as usual; and
after I had played the overture to D. Juan, he really began to
thaw and requested the one to the Zauberflöte by "his father"
too and enjoyed it like a child, so that one had to like him. He
gave me letters to acquaintances at Lake Como, and so I also got
an opportunity of peeking into the provincial life of a small
Italian town and spent a couple of days quite tolerably with
the physician, the chemist, the judge, and other local folk.
Some particularly lively discussions took place on the topic of
Sand,[12] and many were disposed to admire him greatly; I found
this peculiar, as it is a rather ancient story and one scarcely
squabbles over it any more. They also talked about Shakespeare's
plays, which are now being translated into Italian; the physician
233

said the tragedies were good, but that there were certain plays dealing with magic that were *too* silly and childish, especially one: *Il Sogno d'una notte di mezza state*.[13] In it the hackneyed device turned up of having a play rehearsed on the stage, and it was teeming with anachronisms and childish ideas. Thereupon everybody agreed that it was very foolish and that I ought not to read it on any account. I meekly kept my peace and made no defense.

Then, I bathed often in the lake, sketched, wore out my feet, crossed the Lake of Lugano, yesterday (its waterfalls and clouded mountains gave it an ominous look), then over the mountains to Luvino; there, as I said before, I went walking in my slippers, and arrived here today by steam. I expect to start for the Simplon tomorrow, after I have handed this letter to St. Borromeo. The steamers are splendid; one flies and yet has time to inspect everything, one may disembark anywhere at pleasure and is never hurried—they go and fetch you every day, wherever you like—in short (forgive me, dear Hensel [14]) they are good creatures after all. *Evening.* I have just returned from the Isola Madre; it was quite marvelous there: it is broad and full of terraces, lemon groves, evergreen coppices—the weather has become human at last, and so the great white house there, with the ruins next to it and the terraces in front of it, had a quite enchanting appearance. It is really a unique country, and I wish I could send a mouthful of air to you in Berlin, just as it was in the boat; there's nothing like it over there, and I would rather you breathed it than all the people who live on it here.

In the boat with me there was a very mustachioed German; he looked at the beauties of nature as if he had to buy them and found them too expensive. Then I came upon a Jean-Paulish story, literally. For as we were walking amid the island's greenery, an Italian who was of the company said: Here one really ought to go walking together with one's beloved and enjoy nature. Ah yes, I sighed gently.

In fact, that is why I separated from my wife 10 years ago and set her up in a small tobacco shop in Venice, he continued, and now I live as I please. You ought to do the same yourself some day.—

The old boatman told of how he had taken General Bonaparte out onto the lake, and he had many stories regarding him and

234

Murat.[15] Quite an odd man, Murat, he said; whenever he took him out, he'd sing aloud to himself without stopping, and once, on a trip, he'd given him his brandy-bottle, saying he would buy himself another one in Milan. I don't know why those little anecdotes, and especially the singing, brought the whole man to my mind better than a history book often does.

The Walpurgisnacht [16] is finished and polished up, the overture will also be up to the mark pretty soon; the only person who knows it so far is Mozart, and he enjoyed it so much that even I took a renewed fancy for the familiar things; he insisted that I have it printed immediately. But first I must perform it at my subscription concerts in Berlin.[17] I received your dear double letter, from Paul and Klingemann, in Milan; [18] England seems to be impressing him with its serene dignity just as it impresses me. I hope I shall have the pleasure of seeing him again there. But first some mule-back excursions must be taken in the mountains and some music played in Paris. Oh dear, forgive me for this free and easy letter; you can surely see from it that I haven't been wearing a neckcloth for a week. But I did wish to write to you how cheerful and healthy I have been feeling in the mountains these days and how very much I look forward to the days ahead. Therein lie gratitude and remembrance.

Your Felix MB

Felix Mendelssohn Bartholdy, *Briefe einer Reise durch Deutschland, Italien und die Schweiz*, ed. Peter Sutermeister (Zurich: Max Niehans Verlag, 1958), 178–85.—Tr. by editor.

166   ROBERT SCHUMANN TO HIS MOTHER, ZWICKAU [G.]

Leipzig, 8 August 1831.

"Do not quite forget me" were your last words at our last parting, my good mother! Eight weeks have gone by since then, and you have indeed cause to interpret your last words in a sense which might make me blush. If I told you that I hardly knew how to manage my time because of all my work and industry, you would hardly believe it—and yet it is so—but if I say to you: do not take it amiss—I am at fault—then perhaps you'll squeeze my hand again as lovingly as you did in former days, when I came [to you] and had been at fault.

But today the sky is so wonderfully blue, that I really wish I had somebody to whom I could say how happy and summer-like I feel, how my inner, quiet artistic life drives back all passions, how my thoughts often turn for minutes on end to an ideal for the future, in a word, how I sometimes really feel the present moment. But to whom could I say it in this way except to you, who always valued me rightly, sometimes almost too highly, overlooking or averting my faults, and trusting in my heart when my head insisted on going astray?—It's a fine thing to be a young poet and perfect to be a young composer. You can hardly believe what sort of a feeling it is when one can say: This work is *wholly* your own, no man will take this property away from you, nor can he take it, for it is wholly your own; oh, if only you could feel that "wholly"! Since the occasion for such a feeling comes but seldom, for genius is but the thing of a moment, it bursts forth in all its splendor and engenders a kind of soothing self-confidence which need fear no criticism. During the entire period of my silence towards you, this [feeling] often stole over me like a dream from which I did not wish to awaken; but then everything around me was quite exalted, and the world rich and resplendent. When one is finally at peace with one's self and inwardly quiet, then conceptions of fame, praise, immortality, etc., of which one likes to dream without doing anything towards their fulfillment, resolve themselves into gentle rules which one must listen for and gather from time, life, and experience. To bring to light something great and calmly beautiful, one must rob Time of sand-grains only; completeness, perfection do not come all at once: still less do they come raining down from heaven. And if occasionally there are moments when one thinks one is regressing, whereas often this is only a more or less hesitant going forward, that is in the nature of things. One need only allow such moments to go by and then set to quickly and bravely once more, and one resumes afresh.

This, my beloved mother, is in brief my life story of the past eight weeks, during which you perhaps gave me up for lost, while I often thought of you silently and at all hours of the day and rejoiced over your future happiness.

My private life too has taken on a different shape; now and

then my talent is recognized, expectations are being awakened, and whoever knows me appears to enjoy my company. I cannot hide altogether a certain timidity before the world; and it would not do much harm if I were less civil at times.

Seeing Wieck [1] more often has brought out a change for the better in me; he seems so sympathetic to me now, which I never believed he could be; he gives in or, if he thinks it necessary, scolds—and always cheers and encourages me. I would value your thanking him with a few lines for his present attentiveness. He recently said to Lühe [2] that he was *astonished* that my family, who after all had to some extent entrusted me to him, had never yet asked how I was actually getting on, whether I was going backward or forward, etc.; the family could not be very interested in me—he just didn't understand it, etc. While it isn't meant as a reproach to you or my brothers, I think that in this he is right. Therefore do me that favor.

Although I am healthy and cheerful, I am still afraid of the cholera, [3] not so much as a disease, but rather because of its consequences. As a precaution, I have drawn up my will, but as amusingly as possible, for I simply can't imagine that I might ever die.

I could tell you many more things, but shall save them all till you reply. Therefore I'll whisper Jean Paul's [4] golden rule to you: that the best way to answer a letter is to do so after reading it through for the first time (in my case, it should be "spelling it out" [5]).

And so farewell, good, excellent mother! Have faith in my industry and in my good genius, may it always be with me.

Your
son, who reveres you deeply,

Robert.

Last night I dreamt of you, but always in a most dreadful way.—Do you like the watch for Rudel? [6] If the cholera comes nearer, perhaps I'll come to Zwickau or Schneeberg.

[= Letter 162], 145–48.—Tr. by editor.

167   FERDINANDO PAËR TO C. P. SOTTE, PARIS [Fr.]

[Paris, 1 December 1831]

Sir,

Mr. Chopin, pianist, who has arrived from Vienna, wishes me to recommend him to you. As this young man has been warmly recommended to me by several persons in Vienna (Austria), notably by Mr. Malfatti,[1] physician to the Emperor, I gladly accede to his wishes, and I beg you to extend him your protection. He is Polish; having left at the time of the Warsaw revolution, he stayed in Vienna, loved and esteemed by the press [and by] Society.[2] He is full of talent and has received an excellent education; thus he deserves your protection. Years have passed since I have had the pleasure of seeing you; it is quite natural, you have your work, and I mine; I esteem and love you nonetheless: I hope for an opportunity to show it to you. Meanwhile, pray accept the affectionate and respectful regards with which I have the honor to be:

Sir

Your very devoted Servant
and friend

Paris, 1st December 1831   Paër
Direct. of the King's Concerts

[Memorandum by Sotte, at the top of the page:]
Mr. Chopin was born in Warsaw of a French father. He asks to be permitted to remain in Paris, in order to practise his art here. He is recommended to me by M. Paër, director of the King's music. I have the hon^r to beg monsieur the Prefect to be so kind as to inform me of his intentions.

C.P. Sotte.

[Marginal note by the prefect:]
Grant the permit, with provision for repeal.
[Illegible signature]

Bronislas Édouard Sydow (ed.), *Correspondance de Frédéric Chopin* (3 vols.; Paris: Richard-Masse, [1953–60]), II, 18–19.—Tr. by editor.

168   VINCENZO BELLINI TO GIOVANNI BATTISTA
PERUCCHINI, VENICE [It.]

Milan 31 December 1831

My dear Perucchini,

It seems impossible that even after 26 December [1] you should
not have written me a line. It is true that you could make the
same reproach to me, because it was I who should have given
you news of the spectacle, but my poor Norma has been persecuted
so cruelly, that they tried to annihilate her at birth as you can
see, for all the papers are shouting *fiasco fiaschissimo;* a party
that is formidable because it is supported by big money, which
that madwoman spends . . .[2] do I make myself clear? But, my
dear Perucchini, money and the most diabolical intrigues cannot
veil the truth for long, but in the end it will shine forth in its
true light, and this light, by my good fortune, was disclosed
almost entirely at the first performance, and quite fully at the
second and third presentation; the proof of this is the great
crowd in the theater, which is always chock-full, and the silence,
especially during the second act, which is the same as that which
reigned in Venice during the last scene of I Capuleti; [3] that is
how I have failed.

Those pieces which will always make an effect, a question
settled after three performances, are: the *introduction* which
consists of a chorus, the first part of Donzelli's *cavatina* (neither
I nor the public like the second), the whole of Pasta's scene and
opening number, then comes a duet between Grisi and Donzelli
which we can rank with the conclusion [*stretta*] of Donzelli's
Cavatina; [4] the first act closes with a terzetto which begins
with a duet between the two women, and this piece remained
warm throughout the duet on the first evening, and when they
commenced the terzetto, the singers were so tired that they were
unable to intone or proffer a single note, and that is why the
first act ended coldly at the first performance, but at the second
and third presentation, the public began to take a liking to it,
as it was better executed, and it brought me a curtain-call. I
will not speak of the second act which caused a decided and
general furore from the very first evening; it is made up of a
delicate duet between the two women, a warriors' chorus, a war
hymn, a duet between Pasta and Donzelli, and a finale made up

239

of a concerted piece and a conclusion, and these last two pieces are of such a novel kind and so effective that they silenced as many enemies as I could have, and I myself assure you that I consider them the best pieces I have yet written.

The papers will be obliged to give themselves the lie, especially the Gazzetta, and the public is so indignant that the Lord knows how many paragraphs they'll have inserted in order to unmask it; enough, I am very satisfied with the success, and especially for having annihilated so many wicked and heartless persons.

If any pieces from this opera should reach you, you will recognize how zealously I have written it, and at the same time you will understand my assertions. Do not let anybody read this, have regard for my modesty. I will leave Milan this week.

I am going to Naples where I shall await your news. I'll return here in April perhaps, and I wonder whether we shall see each other next year. Meanwhile accept sincere wishes, from a friend who loves you, for the beginning of the new year. Remember me to your dear old parents and to all our friends, and continue to love your: most affect. Bellini.

[= Letter 139], 296–97.—Tr. by editor.

169   FRÉDÉRIC CHOPIN TO DOMINIK DZIEWANOWSKI, BERLIN [Pol.]

[Paris, mid-January 1833]

Dear Domus!

If I had a friend with a big crooked nose—for I mean him and none other; if I had a friend with whom I pleasantly lounged away the time at Szafarnia some years ago and who, I trust, loved me sincerely and showed grateful affection for my father and aunt; and if that friend, having gone abroad, left me quite without news, I should have the worst opinion of him. And if, one day, he came crying for forgiveness, I should remain aloof to all his begging. Yet I, Fryc, after all this silence, am brazen enough to defend my negligence and dare show signs of life, like an insect popping its head out of the water when

240

nobody asks it to do so. But I shall not attempt to explain my conduct and prefer admitting my guilt, which, however, seems greater at a distance than when viewed close at hand, for I am just torn a dozen ways at once.

I have got into high society, amidst ambassadors, princes, ministers; by what miracle I do not know, since I have done nothing to force my way in. But, they say, it is essential for me to appear there, for that is where good taste is supposed to emanate from. Suddenly you are very talented, if you have been heard at the English or Austrian Embassy. You play better if Princess de Vaudemont, the last of the Montmorencys, protected you. I cannot say "protects you," because the old lady died a week ago. She was the local equivalent of the late Mme. Zielonkowa and the châtelaine Polaniecka. The court used to visit her. She did a great deal of good. During the first revolution she hid many aristocrats, and she was the first of the ladies to present herself at Louis Philippe's court after the July days.[1] She had a multitude of little black and white dogs, canaries, parrots, and also the most amusing monkey in the whole wide world, which at evening receptions would bite the . . .[2] of the countesses.

I enjoy the friendship and respect of the artists here. I would not say this if, only a year after making my acquaintance, celebrated masters had not dedicated their compositions to me before I had ever dedicated any of mine to them. Yet this is the case with the latest *Variations*, to a military band accompaniment, by Pixis.[3] Also, some of my phrases have been taken as themes for variations, and Kalkbrenner has used a mazurka of mine in this way. The pupils of the Conservatoire, those of Moscheles,[4] Herz,[5] and Kalkbrenner, in a word, accomplished virtuosos, wish to take lessons with me and couple my name with that of Field.[6] In short, if I were even sillier than I am, I might think myself at the summit of my career. But I know how far I am from perfection; I see it the more clearly since I live in the constant society of the greatest artists and know their weaknesses. But I am ashamed of having written all this nonsense. I have been boasting like a child, or like a man with a guilty conscience who hastens to defend himself before he has even been accused. I would scratch it out if I had the time to write another page. Anyhow, perhaps you have not forgotten my true character. The man you remember is much the same today as he was yesterday, but with this difference, that he has only one side whisker on his face, the other one refusing to grow.

I must give five lessons today; do you think I am making a fortune? Undeceive yourself: the carriage and white gloves cost more than I can earn, but without them I would not be *de bon ton.*

I love the Carlists; I can't endure the Philippists; [7] myself, I am a revolutionist and so care nothing for money. I value friendship alone, for which I beg and pray you.

Fryderyk.

[= Letter 161], 168–69.

170   FRANZ LISZT, FRÉDÉRIC CHOPIN, AND AUGUSTE-JOSEPH FRANCHOMME TO FERDINAND HILLER, FRANKFURT [Fr.]

[Paris, 20 June 1833]

[*Liszt:*] This is the twentieth time, at least, that we have tried to meet, first at my house, then here,[1] with the intention of writing to you, and always some visit, or some other unforeseen hindrance, has occurred. I don't know whether Chopin will be strong enough to make excuses to you; for my part, it seems to me that we have been so unmannerly and impertinent that no excuses are now permissible or possible.

We sympathized most deeply in your bereavement,[2] and more deeply did we wish that we could be with you in order to soften, as far as possible, the grief of your heart.

[*Chopin:*] He has said it all so well that I have nothing to add to excuse me specially for my negligence or idleness, or whim or distraction, or—or—or—— You know that I can explain myself better in person, and, this autumn, when I take you home late by the boulevards to your mother, I shall try to obtain your pardon. I am writing to you without knowing what my pen is scribbling, as Liszt is at this moment playing my Etudes [3] and transporting me away from all suitable ideas. I wish I could steal his manner of rendering my own Etudes. With regard to your friends who are still in Paris, I have often seen, during this winter and spring, the Léo family, *and all that follows.*[4] There

242

have been evenings at certain Ambassadresses' houses, and there was not a single one at which somebody living in Frankfurt was not mentioned. Madame Eichthal sends you many kind greetings—Plater, the whole family were very sorry for your departure, and begged me to give you their condolences. [*Liszt:*] Madame d'Apponyi was very much vexed with me for not having taken you there before your departure; she hopes that when you come back you will be sure to remember the promise you made me. I will say as much of a certain Lady who is not an ambassadress.

Do you know Chopin's wonderful Etudes? — — They are admirable! [*Chopin:*] and moreover they will last only until yours appear [*Liszt:*] = an Author's little piece of modesty!!! [*Chopin:*] A little piece of rudeness on the part of the regent, for—to explain the matter fully—he is correcting my spelling [*Franchomme:*] according to the method of Monsieur Marlet.

[*Chopin:*] You will come back in the month of September, isn't it? [*Franchomme:*] try to let us know the day; we have determined to give you a serenade (or Charivari). The company of the most distinguished artists of the capital = M. Franchomme (present), Madame Petzold, and the Abbé Bardin, the leaders of the Rue d'Amboise (and my neighbors), Maurice Schlesinger,[5] uncles, aunts, nephews, nieces, brothers-in-law, sisters-in-law, etc., etc. [*Chopin:*] *en plan du troisième, etc.*

The publishers
F. Liszt

F. Chopin   Aug. Franchomme

[*Chopin:*] By-the-bye, I met Heine yesterday, who begged me to *grüssen* you *herzlich und herzlich.—*

By-the-bye, again, forgive all the *"vous"* [6]—I beg you to excuse them. If you have a moment to spare, give us news of yourself, which would be most welcome. Paris, Rue de la Chaussée d'Antin, No. 5. At present I am occupying Franck's lodging—he is gone to London and Berlin. I am most happy in the rooms which were so often our meeting place. Berlioz sends greetings.

As to *père* Baillot,[7] he is in Switzerland, at Geneva. So now you can guess that I can't send you the Bach concerto.

20th June 1833

[= Letter 159], 10–13.

171   ROBERT SCHUMANN TO CLARA WIECK, LEIPZIG [G.]

[Leipzig, 13 July 1833]

Dear and good Clara,

I want to know whether and in what manner you are living—
there's nothing else in the letter. I hardly wish that you may
still remember me, for I'm wasting away visibly more and more
every day and am growing into a withered, leafless bean-stalk.
The doctor has even forbidden me to yearn excessively, for
you that is, as it's too fatiguing. But today I tore all the bandages
off my wounds and laughed straight in the doctor's face when
he tried to keep me from writing, yes! I threatened to attack
him with my fever and infect him, unless he quietly complied.
He did so.—[1]

It was not my intention, however, to tell you all this, but
something altogether different—namely, a request which you
must grant me. Since now no chain of sparks whatever draws us
together and reminds us of one another, I have formed a
sympathetic proposal—this: tomorrow [night] at 11 sharp
I'll play the Adagio from Chopin's Variations [2] and will think
very hard of you, in fact of you exclusively. Now please do the
same, so that we may see each other and meet in spirit. The place
where our doubles will meet is probably above the Thomaspfört-
chen. If there's a full moon, I recommend it as a letter-mirror.
I hope very much for an answer. If you won't do it and a string
snaps tomorrow at the twelfth hour, it is I. And it is I with all
my heart.

                                        Robert Schumann

13 July 33.

[= Letter 162], 214–15.—Tr. by editor.

172   ROBERT SCHUMANN TO THEODOR TÖPKEN, BREMEN [G.]

Leipzig 27/3. 34.

My dear Töpken,

Why no news of you at all? You know how very much I share your joys and sorrows.—As I'm not sure whether this letter will reach you in Bremen, I shall be brief today, not as Friend, but as Editor of a musical newspaper, in battle dress and Reichstag style. The prospectus tells you everything.[1] The co-editors are Kapellmeister Stegmayer, Wieck, and Ludwig Schunke.[2] If you are still the man you used to be, i.e. who gladly supports all that is noble in art, then we believe you will not turn us down when, by appointing you correspondent for the free Imperial city of Bremen, we kindly invite you to report from time to time on all matters of musical interest. Your situation in life permits you to make strict and determined appraisals, and indeed such are the people we want and like. And so, hand in hand—discuss and hold forth!

I hear that Franz Otto,[3] a remarkable composer of songs, has been engaged at your theater. Would you forward the enclosed letter? If you don't find him, destroy the letter. If you do find him, take an interest in him. He is highly gifted, but coarse and uncouth on the surface.

Do you have my Intermezzi and the Impromptus? A Toccata and a grand Allegro have just appeared, three Sonatas [will appear] shortly.[4] More of all this later, as soon as I have definite news of you.

Answer soon, dear, excellent man!—Would you enjoy sending in an article "on all the musical activity in your native city during the past winter"? That would be splendid! Address everything to the editorial office of the *Neue Leipz[iger] Zeitschrift für Musik* via the bookseller Hartmann. Don't pay the postage on any of your contributions. I'm very dictatorial in letters. Well, you know me.

Many greetings to your dear wife.[5]

Your   Schumann.

F. Gustav Jansen (ed.), *Robert Schumanns Briefe: Neue Folge* (2nd ed.; Leipzig: Breitkopf und Härtel, 1904), 47–48.—Tr. by editor.

173   HECTOR BERLIOZ TO AN UNNAMED CORRESPONDENT, PARIS [Fr.]

[Paris, 22 November (?) 1835]

Dear Sir

I was able to obtain the enclosed pair of tickets only today. I am very glad to be able to offer them to you with my thanks for the fine verses you sent me. My muse is not jealous and you accuse her unjustly, yours being in any case so well-endowed as to have nothing to fear from the pretensions of her sister. Only, mine is very whimsical, and to give you an example, during my stay in Rome the *Fifth of May* [1] which you will hear tonight was constantly in my mind; but having sought in vain for two months the music for the refrain "Poor soldier . . ." I finally gave up. One day, walking along the Tiber my foot slipped and I fell into the water and was stuck in the mud up to my knees. After I had pulled myself out I started to sing the long-sought phrase and so the piece was done. And that is why I dare not promise poets that I shall set their verses, however much I may wish to.

My kindest regards.

Faithfully yours,

H. Berlioz

Jacques Barzun (ed. and trans.), *New Letters of Berlioz, 1830–1868* (New York: Columbia University Press, 1954), 19–21.

174   LUIGI CHERUBINI TO JEAN AUGUSTE DOMINIQUE INGRES, ROME [Fr.]

Paris 24 December 1835.

Dear friend and illustrious colleague,

It is a long time indeed since I had the pleasure of talking with you, whom I love with all my heart, and whom I revere as a righteous man and great artist. I intended writing you several times, but some impediments, ever importunate, intervened and prevented me despite myself. I had your news indirectly, through the letters you write to the academy [1] from time to time; but they did not satisfy my desire, which was to receive [news] from you personally by eliciting it through a letter of mine which should have given you news of myself: Excuse me therefore, my very worthy friend, for having so long delayed in writing you.

I expect you have been keeping well, as has the dear and amiable Madame Ingres, to whom I beg you to present my respectful compliments. As for my health, it remains good; but I am dominated by a fundamental sadness in spite of myself, without knowing what its real cause might be: everything vexes me, but I tell this to no one, least of all to my wife, whom I fear to disturb, as the state of her health is not exempt from suffering. What helps to make me morose is perhaps my age, which weakens my organs and the springs of vitality; after all I am no longer good for much, for my compositions are showing these effects: it is time for me to shut my shop. As for you, dear friend, you are still young, and in a condition to produce things which are worthy of your fine talent. Are you doing anything with my sad face, which you had started beautifying with your brushes? Do you still intend to give a course in engraving, as you told me before you left for Rome, after your two years' Directorship, what a pleasure it would be for me, and for all your friends if such a project came true? One of your boarders, the young Elwart, has just obtained a great success with a cantata he composed in memory of Bellini.[2] They say you have evinced a good deal of interest in him; that must encourage him for it does him honor to have received your personal approbation.

Farewell my worthy friend; do not ever forget your admirer, and the sincere and unalterable attachment he has vowed you for life.

Yours devotedly L. Cherubini

Artur Holde, "A Little-Known Letter by Berlioz and Unpublished Letters by Cherubini, Leoncavallo, and Hugo Wolf," The Musical Quarterly, XXXVII (1951), 348–49.—Tr. by editor.

175   GIUSEPPE VERDI TO THE MAYOR OF BUSSETO [It.]

Busseto, the 14th day of March, 1836.

Yours esteemed of the 11th inst., No. 4266, leads me to suppose that some person, impelled by reasons unknown to me, has denounced me to the magistracy mentioned in said letter as a participant in the dissensions which arose in Busseto regarding the appointment of a *maestro di musica*. Your Lordship is surely not blind to the fact that I was an impassive spectator to this lengthy conflict.

Immersed in my beloved musical studies and all but forgetful of contentions, I expected of Justice what eventually has come about: that is, a competition desired by so many, and nothing more: I have trusted in the magistrates' wisdom, in the integrity of a judgment, and in whatever ability I might possess. Everyone knows that I did not meddle with factions, that I have never incited or thwarted any of them, that I have never been so malicious as to take pleasure in such bouts: these things I feel strongly the Government [1] should know in full, and it is for this reason that I beg you to be good enough to disabuse them on the subject; and I hope Your Lordship will do it, not because it concerns me, but rather because truth and justice require it, which virtues you have so amply shown to possess during the past dissensions. You may further assure the Government that I shall never depart from my accustomed behavior and that therefore neither my competitors nor my adversaries had or shall ever have reason to suspect that I might intrigue with or against them.

I have the honor to profess myself, with the greatest imaginable respect and esteem,

Your Lordship's

Most humble and devoted servant
Giuseppe Verdi.

Alessandro Luzio (ed.), *Carteggi verdiani*, IV (Rome: Accademia Nazionale dei Lincei, 1947), 75.—Tr. by editor.

248

176   ROBERT SCHUMANN TO HEINRICH DORN, RIGA [G.]

Leipzig, 14th Sept. 36.

My very dear Sir,

Just as I received your letter the day before yesterday and meant
to answer it, who walks in?—Chopin.[1] That was a great pleasure.
We spent a lovely day, which I still celebrated yesterday,
retrospectively. But today I firmly intend to pay my debt of
long standing, so far as it is possible within such narrow limits.
And so, 1) I think of you almost daily, often sadly, because I
studied far too untidily, always with gratitude, because I nevertheless learnt more than you think. You know, in part, how
much has happened and how many things have changed from
that day to this. The rest I'll put off till we see each other sometime, an occasion which, though it may lie in the distant future,
I am confident will present itself.

Thank you for the many tokens of your sympathy with our
endeavors.[2] Much yet remains to be done; but we are young,
and the best comes with the years. Special thanks, too, for
speaking of our newspaper and winning friends for it. I am
enclosing a few lines to Mr. Weitzmann. The *Davidsbund* [3] is
only a spiritual, romantic one, as you noticed long ago. Mozart
was just as great a confederate as Berlioz is now, or you are,
even though he wasn't exactly nominated by means of a diploma.
Florestan and Eusebius are my double nature, which, with Raro,
I should like to fuse into a Man. The rest of it is written in the
newspaper. The other concealed identities are *in part* [real]
persons; a great deal, too, regarding the life of the Davidsbündler
[is taken] from reality. I could fill whole sheets of paper.
Let this much suffice you.—In answer to your questions: 1)
(the 1 above hasn't any 2, I just noticed),—Your yearly
report begins with No. 13. I await [the report] on the music
festival with yearning. The *Iris* [4] supplement with the review
[of your conducting] is typical of *Iris;* very dull and contrived.
Why don't you send me some independent articles on music
festivals in general and on how they ought to be arranged to
educate the masses and the like, on the future of music etc.,
on present controversies etc.; do this. A comparison between
the Breitkopf paper [5] and our own would also be interesting,
but it would have to be published in another periodical

249

(*elegante Zeitung*, or *Comet*, or *Abendzeitung*). Do think about this!

2) I am looking forward to the Fantasy very much, of course. If I can be of any help to you, you need only mention it. I have met Haslinger [6] and found him very honest. I'll wait for the right moment and then write you further on the subject promptly. Besides, you may rest assured that if publishers were not afraid of the editor [in me], the world would not know me either, perhaps to the world's advantage; none the less, those black, firm, printed note-heads please one very much indeed. Let me call your attention to my Sonata in F sharp minor, and even more to a *Concert ohne Orchester* which has just been put out by Haslinger.[7] I should be glad to hear your thoughts about them.

I have a new *Ballade* of Chopin's.[8] I think it is his most genius-inspired (not most genial) work; and I told him this, that it's my favorite among all. After a long, thoughtful pause, he said with great emphasis, "That pleases me, it's my favorite too." Moreover, he played me a quantity of new Etudes, Notturnos, Masureks—all in an incomparable way. It is touching to see how he sits at the piano. You would like him a great deal. But Clara [9] is a greater *virtuoso* and gives his compos[itions] even more meaning, perhaps, than he does himself. Imagine a perfection, a mastery which appears to be unaware of itself! This winter there will be plentiful activity once more. Mendelssohn, David (brilliant mind), Lipinski, *Liszt*, Clara, two concert series, two musical papers. Twelve quartets. Good church music. Stegmayer (unhappily very lazy). Banck (good lieder composer).[10] Much besides, which I can't think of just now. In short, we lack you. Write to me soon and encouragingly, as before. I need it.   In deep friendship,

Your
RSchumann

AUTOGRAPH, Rudolf F. Kallir Collection, New York: 1 sheet, 135 × 220 mm., written on both sides. Watermark: FerdF, oak leaves.—Tr. by editor.

177   FRÉDÉRIC CHOPIN TO JULJAN FONTANA, PARIS [Pol.]

Palma, 3 December 1838.

My Juljan!

Don't release my lodgings to the landlord. I cannot send you the manuscript; it's not finished.[1] I have been as sick as a dog these last two weeks. I caught cold in spite of 18 degrees of heat, roses, orange trees, palms, fig trees. Three doctors— the most famous ones on the island—examined me. One sniffed at my spittle, the second tapped to discover where I spat it from, the third poked about and listened to how I spat it. The first one said I'd die, the second that I was dying, the 3rd that I was already dead.

Nevertheless, today I am the same as ever; only I cannot forgive Jasio [2] for not telling me what to do in case of a *bronchite aiguë* which he might have expected me to catch. I just barely managed to escape the bloodlettings, vesicatories, and packs, and today, thank goodness, I am myself again. However, my illness has affected the *Préludes,* and God knows when you will receive them. In a few days I shall be staying in the loveliest spot on earth; there I shall have sea, mountains, everything you can imagine. I shall lodge at an old monastery, huge and abandoned, whose Carthusians Mend[izabal] [3] seems to have expelled specially for me. It is near Palma and could not be lovelier. From it one sees a cloister and the most poetic graveyards—in a word, I shall be happy there.[4] But I still have no piano. I wrote to Pleyel,[5] *rue de Rochechouard.* Go and inquire about it . . . Say that I was very ill the following day and that now I am well again. For the rest, don't say too much about me or about the manuscripts. Write to me; I have not had a line from you so far. Tell Léo that I have not yet sent the *Préludes* to Albrecht.[6] Tell them that I love them very much and will write to them. Post my letter to my fam[ily] yourself at the Bourse.

Write to me. I embrace Jasio.

Ch.

Don't tell people that I've been ill, or they will gossip about it.

[= Letter 161], 186.

178A   NICOLÒ PAGANINI TO HECTOR BERLIOZ, PARIS [It.]

[Paris, 18 December 1838]

My dear friend

With Beethoven deceased, there was only Berlioz who could bring him back to life; and I, who have enjoyed your divine compositions worthy of your genius, deem it my duty to beg you kindly to accept, as a sign of my homage, twenty thousand francs which will be remitted to you by the Baron de Rothschild,[1] when you present him with the enclosed.

Believe me always

Your affectionate friend
Nicolò Paganini

Paris 18 December *1838*

178B   HECTOR BERLIOZ TO NICOLÒ PAGANINI, PARIS [Fr.]

[Paris,] 18 December 1838

O Worthy and great artist

how shall I express my gratitude to you!! I am not rich, but believe me, the Approbation of a man of Genius such as yourself touches me a thousand times more than the kingly generosity of your gift.

Words fail me, I shall rush to embrace you as soon as I can leave my bed where I am still confined today.[2]

H. Berlioz

Facsimiles of the autographs: [= Letter 138].—Tr. by editor.

179   ROBERT SCHUMANN TO SIMONIN DE SIRE, DINANT (BELGIUM) [G.]

Vienna, 15th March 1839.

I received your esteemed, long-awaited letter already a fortnight ago, my very dear Sir, and could not find a single moment in which to answer you as I should have wished. I had begun to think of our acquaintance as of a dream and thought you had quite forgotten me; but your letter tells me the contrary in a most charming manner, and I thank you warmly for the encouragement and strength your words have brought me. You will wonder at receiving my letter from here. I have been here ever since October, at first on private, then also on musical business.[1] Yet I have found few congenial persons; still, Vienna remains in many ways an exciting and enriching city for a musician, indeed I have written a good deal here, though not my best.

You ask so sympathetically about my new compositions— I have *completed* and published op. 15 *Kinderscenen* (Breitkopf & Härtel), op. 16 *Kreisleriana* (Haslinger, in Vienna), and op. 17 *Phantasie in three movements* (Breitkopf & Härtel); within four to five weeks Mechetti will publish here: op. 18 *Arabeske,* op. 19 *Blumenstück,* op. 20 *Humoreske.*—The piece [called] "Kreisleriana" is my favorite among all these things. The title can only be understood by a German. Kreisler is a figure created by E. T. A. Hoffmann, an eccentric, wild, gifted Kapellmeister.[2] You will like many things in it. The headings to all my compositions never occur to me till after I have finished a composition. The word Humoreske, too, is not comprehensible to a Frenchman. It is annoying that there are no good, accurate words in the French language for just those characteristics and conceptions which are most deeply rooted in the German nationality, such as *das Gemüthliche* (*Schwärmerische*) and *der Humor,* which is a felicitous blending of *Gemüthlich* and *Witzig.*[3] But this has to do with the whole character of the two nations. Do you know Jean Paul, our great author? I learnt more counterpoint from him than from my music master.[4] How gladly, my dear Sir, would I discuss all this with you some day, and how glad I should be to hear you [play] besides! I myself was deprived by an unhappy fate of the full use of my right hand and cannot play my things as I carry them within me. The damage to my hand consists only in this, that some of the fingers (probably through too much writing and playing in earlier times) have become quite weak, so that I can hardly use them. This has cast me down often enough; well, well, Heaven repays me now and then with a good inspiration, and so I don't think about it any more.[5]

I look forward to acquainting myself with some of your compositions; I shall have them sent to me by Schott[6] immediately. Your system of notation has only one fault, its unfamiliar appearance; people can hardly manage two staves, unfortunately. Besides, Hünten and Czerny would become despondent if it caught on, as they have barely enough ideas for *one* staff.[7] I thank you cordially for your communication; I should like to use the theme myself sometime, especially the first half, which sings beautifully.

And do not forget to publish your *letters concerning the new tendencies in pianoforte music. This would be exactly the right time;* soon other matters will come up, and then the letters would no longer be so effective. Schott would surely be happy to print the brochure, and as for a good German translation, I should attend to all that myself.—Of the older composers who have had a great influence on the new music, I give you *first of all* Franz Schubert and also Prince Louis Ferdinand of Prussia, two highly poetic natures.[8] Schubert's lieder are well-known, of course; but I value his piano compositions (especially those for four hands) *at least as highly.* Of the younger ones, I can only name Stephan Heller and Ferdinand Hiller, who follow the new ideas with talent.[9] *Eight* works by Clara Wieck, who is in Paris at the moment, have appeared so far; try to obtain them all; this is a highly remarkable artist and an even more remarkable young lady. I consider Mendelssohn *to be the first musician* of our time and take off my hat to him as to a master. He simply *plays* with everything, and particularly with orchestral masses, but how freely, how delicately, how artistically, in what a thoroughly masterful way! Bennett follows his example.[10] And *how* they both play the piano, like angels, as unpretentiously as children. Thalberg[11] is important only as a virtuoso; he has no invention, in my opinion, except in a mechanical sense. But as a virtuoso, also in the execution of compositions other than his own, he ranks among the first.

Since you, my dear friend, take such a benevolent concern in my endeavors, it may interest you to know in what order the compositions you are acquainted with were written. I was born in the y. 1810; I haven't published any of my early attempts (I began already in my 7th year); then I wrote, in the following order:

1829. Toccata begun, but not finished till 1833.—Variations on Abegg.—Papillons.—

1831. Allegro in B minor.—Etudes after Paganini.—

1832. Intermezzi. (A symphony f. orchestra that is fairly completed and a piano concerto, also not quite finished, fall in this period too [12])

1833. Impromptus.—Sonata in F-sharp minor (but finished only in 1835); sonata in G minor (soon to be published by Breitkopf).—

1834. Carnaval.—Etudes symphoniques.—

1836. Grand Phantasie (Op. 17, which is just being published by Breitkopf).—Concert sans Orchestre.—Sonata in F minor (not quite clean yet) [13]

1837. Phantasiestücke.—Davidsbündlertänze.—

1838. Novelletten. (3 large books, which will soon be issued by Härtel).—Kinderscenen.—Kreisleriana.—Arabeske.—

1839. Blumenstück.—Humoreske.—Beginning of a concerto, and a grand *romantic sonata*.[14]

I am just [working] on the last-mentioned, and I feel drawn to the piano, in order to finish it. Perhaps you too have found that my style has been getting easier and more supple. Formerly I used to ponder a long time, now I hardly strike out a note. Everything comes to me spontaneously, and sometimes it even seems to me that I could play on forever and not come to an end.

My dear Sir, you have shown such sympathy with my endeavors that I am not afraid you will accuse me of egoism. It would please me immensely if you would write *soon* again. I shall always be sure to answer you most punctually.

One of these months there will also appear a lithograph of me; [15] I shall find an opportunity of sending it to my well-wisher as soon as possible. Only [do not put it] between

Beethoven and Weber, but near them, so that I may continue to learn from them all my life.

I shall be back in Leipzig by 15th April. Please address [your letters] care of Mr. Robert Friese, bookseller, or care of Breitkopf.

I certainly hope to see you and speak with you in a few years. It is possible that I shall go to England for good, but in any case through Dinant, on the way to Paris, some day.[16]

Remember me to Mr. Antoine and do continue to favor me with your friendship.

Yours truly,
R. Schumann.

[= Letter 172], 148–51.—Tr. by editor.

180   GIUSEPPE VERDI TO GIUSEPPE DEMALDÉ, BUSSETO [It.]

[Milan, 22 April 1839]

My dear Finola

The advice you have been kind enough to give me concerning my opera[1] was very good, and as soon as I reached Milan and heard what the singers were, I disengaged myself at once, although very regretfully. Maestro [Giovanni Antonio] Speranza of Parma is composing in my stead. Poor young man! I wish him luck, but doubt very much that he will have any.

My score is still packed up, but it is not sleeping. I'll tell you this much, in strict confidence: *Perhaps it will be performed at the Teatro La Scala with Moriani, Ronconi, Mmes. Strepponi and Kemble.*[2] I cannot guarantee it, but can only hope . . . Enough—soon, perhaps even within the week, I'll write you about it.

Farewell. My wife[3] is very well and joins me in sending greetings also to yours. I embrace you fondly.

Milan, 22 April '39.

G. Verdi.

[= Letter 175], 77.—Tr. by editor.

181 HECTOR BERLIOZ TO FRÉDÉRIC CHOPIN, MARSEILLES [Fr.]

[Paris, April or May 1839]

My dear Chopin,

There are those who tell me you are well, others that you are suffering more, others finally that they have no news at all from you; to put an end to it, be so good as to drop me a few lines telling me how you are and when you will return to us.

Affectionate greetings. H. Berlioz

PS—Remember me, if you please, to madame Sand and place at her feet my most violent admiration. We have just suffered a severe opera . . . by Auber.[1]

Julien Tiersot (ed.), *Hector Berlioz: Les Années romantiques, 1819–1842* (Paris: Calmann-Lévy, Éditeurs, [1904]), 404.—Tr. by editor.

182 FRÉDÉRIC CHOPIN TO JULJAN FONTANA, PARIS [Pol.]

[Nohant, October 1839]

My Life,[1]

We start the day after tomorrow, Thursday, at 5 o'clock in the morning, and I shall be at rue Tronchet No. 5 on Friday at 3, four, or at the latest 5 o'clock. I have written to Jasio[2] today, asking him to engage that servant and to tell him to wait for me at rue Tronchet, beginning at noon. If you have time to visit me, we should be the first to embrace. You are my worthiest friend. Once more, my sincerest thanks and those of my companion for Pigal[le].[3] Now I beg you, as I no longer have any trousers, to be good enough to tell the tailor to be sure to finish the gray ones you ordered for me and to have them sent (with the waistcoat, if possible) to rue Tronchet, where Tineau will no doubt already be in attendance. (My new valet's name is in fact Tineau!!) That way I shall be able to dress as soon as I arrive.

Do the same with Dupont regarding my hat and, in return,
I engage myself to alter the *second* part of the *Polonaise* [4] for
you till I die. Perhaps yesterday's version won't please you
either, though I cudgeled my brains over it for at least 80
seconds.

My manuscripts are in order and well annotated. There are
six of them with your polonaises, not counting a 7th, an
Impromptu, which perhaps is poor.[5] I don't know yet, it's too
new (yes!). How nice if it should not turn out *à la* Orlowski
or Zimmermann or Karsko-Koń or Sowiński,[6] or a pig, or
inspired by some other animal, for, by my reckoning, it ought
to bring me at least 800 francs. Well, we shall see.

My dear, since you are so efficient, see to it that no black
thoughts and choking cough shall visit me in the new lodgings.
Attend to it! And, to make it pleasant there, erase, if you
can, several past events. It would not be amiss if I were to
find there the fruits of some years' hard work. You would place
me under an obligation if you could do that, or if you could
grow younger by the time I return; or else if you could bring
it about that we were never born.

Your
Old One

[= Letter 161], 218–19.

183   GAETANO DONIZETTI TO THE EDITOR OF THE
MONITEUR UNIVERSEL, PARIS [Fr.]

[Paris, 16 February 1840]

Sir,

An article published today in the feuilleton of your esteemed
paper concerning the [first] performance of *La Fille du
Régiment* at the Opéra-Comique [1] contains a both grave and
singular error which my honor and sense of duty require me
to point out.

The author of the feuilleton does not hesitate to allege that
my score has already been heard in Italy, at least in great part,

and that it belongs to a little opera imitated or translated after M. Adam's *Chalet*.[2]

If M. Berlioz, who rightly places conscience among an artist's chief duties, had taken the trouble of opening the score of my *Betly*,[3] whose book is indeed a translation of the *Chalet,* a score which was engraved and published by M. Launer in Paris, he might have ascertained that the two operas he cites have not a single piece in common; allow me, in turn, to state that the pieces which make up *La Fille du Régiment* have been written expressly for the Opéra-Comique, and that not one of them has ever appeared in any [other] score.

I limit myself, Sir, to pointing out this factual error, on which, besides, the whole of M. Berlioz's article rests, and I trust that your high impartiality will not refuse to admit this rectification.

G. Donizetti

16 February 1840

Guido Zavadini (ed.), *Donizetti: vita, musiche, epistolario* (Bergamo: Istituto italiano d'arti grafiche, 1948), 506–507.—Tr. by editor.

184A   FELIX MENDELSSOHN BARTHOLDY TO HIS MOTHER, BERLIN [G.]

Leipzig, 30 March
1840.

Dear mother,

My heartfelt thanks for both of your dear letters, the second of which reached me the day before yesterday. That my little 4part songs pleased you is doubly pleasing to me; how could you even question whether the Woringens were to receive the things? And why should they wish to send them back to me? In their hands they are at least as safe as in mine, and they shall receive a printed copy at Liegnitz as a matter of course; still, it will probably be quite a little while before the songs are published, even if Franz does not leave before I can send them over. We are very pleased with the news of Rebecka (to whom I am enclosing my congratulations) and with the confirmation of Albertine's. Since I am sending this letter through a favorable opportunity (Mr. Nenoch), I'm enclosing a collection of local newspaper articles, which in part attracted my own attention, in part are being forwarded expressly for you. And please have the [enclosed] letter sent to Arnold Mendelssohn, whose address I don't know.[1] Clara Wieck has arrived, but I haven't seen her yet.[2] Liszt's last concert takes place today, for the benefit of the Institute for Old and Ailing Musicians, Hiller's oratorio [3] is being performed on Thursday, and then, I hope, there will be peace and quiet at last. The helter-skelter of the last weeks has been too much. Liszt again delighted me, personally; I consider him a good, affectionate chap, when all is said, and a splendid artist. There's no question he plays more than anyone, yet Thalberg,[4] with his composure and restraint, is more accomplished, taken purely as a virtuoso, and that, after all, is the yardstick by which also Liszt must be measured, since his compositions are subordinate to his playing and are anyway designed only for virtuosity. Liszt has a certain suppleness and diversity in his fingers, and a thoroughly musical sensibility that is surely without its equal anywhere. (But I beg you, dear mother, yes, even you!—do *not* repeat these views to any stranger, whether by word of mouth or in writing; least of all to [Baroness] Pereira, who could not keep them to herself, and then I should see them in print directly. And so, to *no one*.) In a word, no musician I have seen has, like Liszt, a musical perception that runs to his very fingertips and from there pours out instantly; and with this immediacy and enormous technique and dexterity, he would leave all the others far behind, if ideas of one's own were not the most important thing in all of this, and nature seems to have denied them to him, so far at least, so that in this respect most of the other great virtuosos must be placed beside or even above him.—But there is no doubt in my mind that *only* he and Thalberg occupy the first class among the present pianoforte players, and that neither Henselt, nor Döhler,[5] nor all the others, whatever their names may be, can be assigned to it. Unfortunately, Liszt's behavior towards the public is not exactly to my liking; here, too, he has engaged in newspaper questions again, has written articles, and, in short, has taken much too much notice of a mass of petty things and neglected greater ones, for instance the arrangements for his concerts,

260

&c. &c. Whether for this or for some other reason, the fact remains that the local public liked Thalberg far better, and Liszt has made almost more enemies than friends here. Besides, the whole controversy between him and the people here is like hearing two persons perorate, both of whom are wrong, and whom one should like to interrupt constantly: the Philistines, who are mainly concerned over the expensive prices and such things, so that a decent fellow is made to feel quite uncomfortable, and who argue on that account—they may go to the devil, for all I care; and Liszt, who takes along on his travels foolish managers who infuriate everybody and then writes newspaper articles, is also not quite blameless. This evening he will play my D minor concerto, among other things; I'll write you about all this very soon, but, as I said earlier—don't repeat it to *any* stranger. Hiller's first orchestra rehearsal took place yesterday, and it sounded and went well; also this affects me as though I myself were to perform it, until we have done with it [*sic*]. During all this time, Liszt ate at our house every day, played all day long, Hiller's choir rehearsals took place, the last subscription concert is finally at hand—in short, there has been a mad to-do. There's no more room: I'll write Beckchen [6] about my fête. Goodbye, dearest mother. Write soon again

       to your
           Felix.

Photostat of the autograph, kindly supplied by the New York Public Library, Rare Book and Manuscript Collection, Music Division, its present owners. —Tr. by editor.[7]

184B   FRANZ LISZT TO MAURICE SCHLESINGER, PARIS [Fr.]

                       [London, 14 May 1840]
Sir,
     Allow me to protest against an inexact assertion in your last number but one:—
     "Messieurs Liszt and Cramer [8] *have asked for* the Legion of Honor," etc.
     I do not know if M. Cramer (who has just been nominated) has obtained the cross.

In any case I think that you, like every one else, will approve of a nomination so perfectly legitimate.

As to myself, if it be true that my name has figured in the list of candidates, this can only have occurred entirely without my knowledge.

It has always seemed to me that distinctions of this sort could only be *accepted*, but never "asked for."

I am, Sir, etc.,

F. Liszt.[9]

London, 14th May 1840.

[= Letter 159], 44–45.

185   ROBERT SCHUMANN TO HEINRICH HEINE, PARIS [G.]

Leipzig, 23 May 1840.

This letter marks the consummation of a longfelt aspiration of mine, to be permitted to enter into somewhat closer relations with you; for it is hardly to be expected that you will remember a visit in Munich many years ago, when I was still an immature youth.[1] I hope my music to your Lieder will please you. If my powers were commensurate with the fervent love with which I wrote, you might be assured of good results. Perhaps my friend Stephan Heller [2] will provide an opportunity for you to obtain a hearing of the songs.

A word from your hand, acknowledging the receipt of the above, would give me the greatest pleasure.

Your devoted

Robert Schumann.

Friedrich Schnapp, "Robert Schumann and Heinrich Heine," *The Musical Quarterly*, XI (1925), 614.

186   RICHARD WAGNER TO KING FREDERICK AUGUSTUS II OF SAXONY, DRESDEN [G.]

[Paris,] 1 December 1840

Most Serene *Lord!* Most Gracious *Lord* and King!

If, from France's capital, I dare address a submissive petition directly, and with the greatest respect, to Yr. Majesty, above all let my boldness be pardoned; for, as a Saxon and Yr. Majesty's most loyal subject, I found it impossible to let such an opportunity, of the greatest importance to me, go by without satisfying my need—ever-growing and ever more urgent,[1] in this foreign land—to express directly my deepest and most ardent veneration towards my Most Gracious *Lord* and King.

Born in Leipzig, I moved with my family, while still a child, to Yr. Majesty's capital, Dresden; here, my stepfather Ludwig Geyer, Court Actor at Yr. Majesty's Court Theater, had the inestimable good fortune to be singled out, through the magnanimous favor of the exalted Court, to such a degree that, as he was also a portraitist, he was honored with the exalted commission of portraying the Most Serene Family.

As for me, I have dedicated myself to musical composition and had already ten years ago the good fortune of seeing some of my instrumental compositions performed with success in my native city.[2] Since that time, I have held the post of Musical Director in several German cities; but I felt the urge to distinguish myself with dramatic compositions and considered the smaller German provincial theaters quite unsuitable for the establishment of the necessary reputation by dint of first performances upon their stages; and as I had not then the courage, unfortunately, to turn to Yr. Majesty in person, as I am now doing with trust and respect, I decided in the end to follow the example of so many Germans and turn to Paris for the above purpose.

Here, the outlook for the success of my plan has received a more solid foundation, chiefly through the happy circumstance that I have succeeded in winning the friendship of Mr. Meyerbeer, of glorious renown;[3] through whose active interest I have also progressed so far, that I am now engaged in the friendliest negotiations with the administration of the Académie

263

Royale de musique over an opera to be composed specially for that theater.[4]

Nevertheless, I still harbor the ardent wish of dedicating my best artistic powers to my Fatherland. Driven by this desire, I have finished here in Paris a Grand Opera entitled "Rienzi," with the specific intention of offering it to Yr. Majesty's Court Theater for its first performance; indeed for this very reason I had in mind, as some of its principal interpreters, several excellent artists whose inestimable good fortune it is to be members of Yr. Majesty's Court Theater.

This, my Most Gracious *Lord* and King, is the business which has emboldened me to seek a favorable decision through direct recourse to Yr. Majesty, magnanimous protector and patron of the Fatherland's arts. Inspired with the deep-felt and unquestioning faith in the venerated Father of his country to which every Saxon is born, I make bold to advance my submissive petition with the deepest reverence:

I petition Yr. Majesty to be graciously pleased to consent to a first performance of my opera Rienzi (the score of which I am at the same time forwarding to Yr. Majesty's Court Chamberlain and Court-Theater Intendant, His Excellency Baron von Lüttichau) in Yr. Majesty's Theater in Dresden.

If with the gracious approval of this petition I were also to experience the ineffable happiness of Yr. Majesty's deigning to permit the reverent dedication of my work to Your Magnificence, then the most brilliant public successes would appear insipid and null as against the solemn feeling of witnessing the birth of my first major production on the soil of my Fatherland, under the special, gracious protection of my most beneficent Lord and King.[5]

[= Letter 164], 147–49.—Tr. by editor.

187   RICHARD WAGNER TO ROBERT SCHUMANN, LEIPZIG [G.]

Paris, 29 December 1840

Most excellent Mr. Schumann!

I have been in Paris for almost a year and a half. I am exceedingly well, for I have not yet starved.[1] You will soon hear important news of me, because I'm on the point of becoming endlessly famous. Meanwhile—the occasion for these lines. I hear that you have composed *Heine*'s "Grenadiers" and that at the end the "Marseillaise" appears in it. Last winter I too composed it [2] and also brought in the "Marseillaise" at the end. That should be significant! I composed *my* "Grenadiers" directly to a French translation which I had ordered and which Heine approved. It has been sung here and there and has brought me the Order of the Legion of Honor and a yearly pension of 20,000 francs, which I draw straight from Louis Philippe's privy purse. Such honors don't make me immodest, and I herewith dedicate my composition to you once more, quite *privatim,* despite the fact it has already been dedicated to Heine.—You will know how to recognize this distinction and announce it in a proper manner. At the same time I declare to you that I gladly and willingly accept the private dedication of your "Grenadiers" and am awaiting the dedication copy.

Be so good as to start feeling some little affection for me, and rest assured that etc.

Your admirer Richard Wagner,
25 rue du Helder.

P.S. Don't let them tear down *Meyerbeer* so; I owe *everything* to the man, and especially my imminent celebrity.[3]

R.W.

[= Letter 164], 153–54.—Tr. by editor.

188 JOHANNES BRAHMS TO OTTO COSSEL, HAMBURG [G.]

[Hamburg, 1 January 1842]

Beloved Teacher!

Once more a year has passed, and I am reminded that during that year you have again helped me on so much with my music. How very many thanks I owe you for this! It is true I must also consider that indeed at times I have not followed your wishes, by not practicing as I ought to have. But I promise you that this year I shall fulfill your wishes through diligence and attentiveness.—

I wish you a very happy new year, and remain

Your obedient pupil

Hamburg.   J. Brahms.
1 Jan. 42.

Facsimile of the autograph: Max Kalbeck, *Johannes Brahms,* I (Vienna: Wiener Verlag, 1904), between pp. 24–25.—Tr. by editor.

189 FELIX MENDELSSOHN BARTHOLDY TO HIS MOTHER, BERLIN [G.]

Frankfurt, 19 July 1842.

My dear little mother,

Here we are again, joyful and happy after a joyful and happy voyage, and we found the dear children hale and hearty, and your dear letter tells us the same of you all, and a blue sky and warm, clear air bring one unforgettably lovely day after another—if only men knew how to show themselves grateful enough for so much happiness! And I am all too pleased to be here in Frankfurt with so many good friends and relations, in these splendid surroundings. Every morning at six I take a walk towards the Darmstadt observatory, and when I come back the children are just up, and everyone is at breakfast, and the prospect of Paul, Albertine,[1] and Switzerland is not what you'd call depressing, either. May God fulfill all

266

these happy prospects and receive joy over past and future ones as thanks! This morning Cecile[2] made up her mind to come along and to leave the children once more with her mother, who takes the greatest pleasure in them. But Cecile will repent ten times over before then; I hope nevertheless to put her in a cheerful disposition at last, and the Pauls will contribute their share in this too.—

Yesterday evening, just as I was about to drive up the Mühlberg with Veit and Bernus, we came across Hiller and his wife; on the steamer we traveled with Madame Matthieu, then with Mr. and Mrs. Rubens, in Mainz we chatted a while with the Woringens, who saw us to the train, and Prince Friedrich stopped us so long on the road that we nearly arrived too late; he had just returned from Rome; Schlemmer and his wife from Ems, Julie Schunk-Jeanrenaud (much better) from Dresden, Rosenhain from Paris, Benecke sen. from London, jun. from his property, all here at the gate, at once; that is how we live every day![3]

I must still give you some particulars about the London days, after our trip to Manchester. I couldn't make up my mind to go to Dublin, because one must spend twelve hours at sea to get there, and this thought dashed all negotiations to pieces. In Manchester we spent two quiet days with all the uncles and aunts, but when we got back to London the whirl started once more. I'll wait till I can give you an oral account of how shockingly Cecile allowed herself to be courted by Sir Edward Bulwer,[4] and of how old Rogers (Sam Rogers, do you know him?)[5] shook hands [orig.: *hands shakte*] with her and begged her to bring up her children to be as charming as herself, and to teach them to speak English as beautifully (this caused a sensation), and of how Mr. Roebuck came in (ask Dirichlet who he is)[6]—à propos, in Aachen we paid the Meyers a proper visit, but in Cologne we could barely stop for twenty minutes and so were unable to call on Louise Hensel[7]—further, of how we played at proverbs at the Beneckes' and Klingemann[8] impersonated a West Indies planter and Sir Walter Scott, and of how the Directors of the Philharmonic gave me a fish dinner at Greenwich, with whitebait and speeches, and of how my Antigone choruses were sung at the Moscheles' (I'll imitate that for you at the piano—I believe Beckchen[9] is laughing already; but why doesn't she write at all!), and of how I waited for Mr.

267

von Massow at the Brunswick Hotel and spoke with Mr. Abeken at Bunsen's, oh, and of how we dined most tediously at Mr. and Mrs. Bunsen's [10]—as I said, I'll describe all this more precisely by word of mouth. But I must write down the details of my last visit at Buckingham Palace immediately, for they'll amuse you greatly, dear mother, and me too! As Grahl put it—it's still so— Buckingham Palace is the only friendly home in England, really cozy, one feels *à son aise* in it—I know of a few others, true, but on the whole I agree with him. Joking apart, Prince Albert had had me invited to go to see him on Saturday at half past one, so that I might try his organ before my departure; I found him quite alone, and just as we were in the middle of our conversation, in came the Queen, also quite alone, in her house dress. She had to leave for Claremont in an hour, she said— "but gracious me, how very untidy it is here!" she added, noticing that the wind had knocked over all the sheets, separately, from an unbound music book onto the pedals of the organ (which forms a lovely adornment to the room) and into the corners. Saying this, she knelt down and began gathering them together, Prince Albert helped, and I wasn't idle either. Then the Prince began to elucidate the stops for me, and meanwhile she said she would put things straight herself. But then I begged that the Prince would rather play me something first—I wished to boast about it in Germany, I said, and so he played me a chorale by heart, with the pedals, so nicely and purely and faultlessly that many an organist might well have profited from it, and the Queen, who had finished her task, sat nearby and listened, very pleased. I had to play next, and struck up my chorus from St. Paul: "How lovely are the messengers." Before I had finished even the first verse, they both chimed in with the chorus in good earnest, and now Prince Albert drew the stops for me ever so skillfully during the whole piece; first he added a flute, then at the forte the full organ, at the D major the whole register, then he made such an excellent diminuendo with the stops, and so on to the end of the piece, and all of this by heart, that I was really quite delighted with it and very happy. Then the Hereditary Prince of Gotha [11] came in and there was more conversation, and the Queen said, among other things, had I composed any new songs, and she enjoys singing the printed ones very much. "You ought to sing one for him," said Prince Albert. She had to be coaxed a bit at first, then she said she'd attempt the
268

"Frühlingslied" in B flat major.[12] That is, if it was still here, because all the music had already been packed up for Claremont. Prince Albert went to look for it, but came back: it had already been packed away. "Oh, perhaps one could unpack it again," said I.—"We must send for Lady N. N.," she said (I didn't catch the name). The bell was rung, and the servants ran off, but came back embarrassed, and then the Queen went herself, and while she was out, Prince Albert said to me: "She begs you to accept this present too, as a remembrance," and gave me a little case containing a lovely ring with V. R. 1842 engraved on it, and then the Queen came back and said, "Lady . . . . has driven off and taken all my things along—I really think it is most improper!" (You cannot imagine how this amused me.) Then I said I hoped that she wouldn't make me suffer for the incident and that she would pick something else, and after a short consultation with her husband, he said, "She'll sing you something by Gluck." Meanwhile the Princess of Gotha had also come in, and so we five went through the corridors and rooms till we reached the Queen's sitting room, where a massive rocking horse was standing next to the sofa, and two large bird cages, and pictures on the walls, and beautifully bound books on the tables, and music on the piano. The Duchess of Kent came in, and while they were talking I rummaged a little among the music and found there my very first book of songs. So then I naturally asked her to choose something from that rather than the Gluck, and she did so in a very friendly way, and what did she pick? "Schöner und schöner," [13] sang it in a most charming manner, cleanly, in strict time, and with very nice expression; except that when it goes down to D after "der Prosa Lasten und Müh" and comes up chromatically, she hit D sharp both times, and since both times I gave her D, she took it right the last time, when it ought to have been D sharp, of course. But apart from this oversight it was really most charming, and I've never heard an amateur sing the last long G better, and more purely and naturally. Then I had to confess that Fanny had written the song (I found it difficult, actually, but pride must have a fall) and asked her to sing me one of my very own too. If I would help her a great deal she'd be happy to, she said, and sang "Lass Dich nur Nichts nicht dauern" really quite faultlessly and with wonderfully pleasant feeling and expression. One ought not to pay too many compliments on such an occasion, I thought

269

to myself, and merely thanked her very much indeed; but when she said, "Oh, if only I had not been so frightened; generally I have quite a long breath," I praised her thoroughly and with the best conscience in the world; for the passage with the long C, at the end, is just what she had done so well, and she had joined the next three notes to it all in one breath, as one seldom hears it done, and so I was especially amused that she herself should have begun about it. And now Prince Albert sang "Es ist ein Schnitter," and then he said I really ought to play them something else before I left and set me as themes the chorale he had played on the organ and the "Schnitter." If it had gone as usual, then I should have improvised quite dreadfully at last, for that is what nearly always happens to me when I want it to go very well; and then I should have been left with nothing but annoyance after the whole morning. But just as if I was to keep a really pleasant, happy recollection, free of any vexation, my improvisation came off exceptionally well; I was in quite a fresh mood and played long and enjoyed it myself; needless to say, besides the two themes I also took the songs the Queen had sung; but it all came so naturally that I should have liked not to stop at all, and they followed me with so much understanding and attention that I felt in better spirits there than I ever have, when improvising before an audience. Well, and then she said, "I hope you will visit us in England soon again," and then I retired and saw the lovely chaises waiting below, with the scarlet outriders, and a quarter of an hour later the palace's flag was lowered, and the newspapers said "Her Majesty left the Palace at 20 minutes past 3," and I walked to Klingemann's through the rain, and on top of all these pleasures I had the greatest one of all in telling him and Cecile everything immediately, while it was still red hot! It was a jolly morning.

I must still add that I begged for permission to dedicate the A minor symphony to the Queen, because, after all, it had been the occasion for my voyage, and because the English name looks especially well on the Scottish piece; [14] and that just as she was about to start singing, she said, "But the parrot must be taken out first, or he'll screech louder than I shall sing," whereupon Prince Albert rang and the P. of Gotha said, "I'll take him out myself!" and I said, "Allow *me* to do it!" (cf. Cousin Wolf: "Allow me, me, me!"), and that I took the huge bird cage out to the astonished servants etc. etc. Much still remains to be told by word of mouth; but if Dirichlet now takes me for a little aristocrat, because of the long description, then I swear I'm as much of a radical as ever and call to witness Grote,[15] Roebuck, and you too, my little mother, who surely are just as amused by all these details as I am.

Since I've fallen into descriptions, I must yet speak of a moment when, after a lovely crossing, we heard in the night that Ostend was only half an hour away, and I went on deck and saw a still, grey sea, and the dawn with wondrously beautiful stars, and the ship sailing point-blank towards the lighthouse (which was sending off bright, white beams), and below it a couple of red and yellow lights that showed the jetty, and England lay behind us, and the Continent, which is also lovely, before us.

Unhappily, on the Rhine we heard the ghastly news from France.[16] You were doubtless as deeply shocked as we all were, here, by the sad fate of the young man.

I didn't make the acquaintance of James (I don't like admitting my ignorance) and saw his name for the first time in your letter.

But again, a thousand, thousand thanks for that dear, beautiful letter. And I beg and pray for more and for many. I am no flatterer when I tell you what a great delight such a letter of yours is to all of us, and how earnestly we long for speedy and frequent news from you, for that's the truth; do give us this pleasure as often as you possibly can, dear mother! Many warm greetings to my sisters (I mean my sisters and brothers-in-law and nephews, all in one), and may they keep me in their affection, and write from time to time. Good-by, dear mother, till our next happy meeting!

Ever yours,

Felix.

Karl Mendelssohn-Bartholdy, "Felix Mendelssohn-Bartholdy in Buckingham-Palace," *Über Land und Meer. Allgemeine Illustrirte Zeitung*, XXV, No. 14 (1871), 6–7.—Tr. by editor.

190   GAETANO DONIZETTI TO ANTONIO VASSELLI, ROME [It.]

[Paris, 4 January 1843]

On the 31st day of last December, signor Donizetti passed, not from this life to the next, but from one bank of the Seine to the other, in order to be named a corresponding member of the French Institute.

Yesterday evening—the 3rd of the new [year] '43—the first performance of his new opera *Don Pasquale* (formerly *Marcantonio,* new libretto)[1] was given at the Italian Theater. Not a piece went without applause, the author was called out after the second act and after the third. They acted, sang magnificently. The author leaves for Vienna on the 7th.

The opera cost him infinite trouble (eleven days). Now, in Vienna, he will give *Il Duello sotto Richelieu* (eight days of travail—and not a day to spare). You are requested not to divulge my secrets, as the public won't believe them anyway, or else imagines the music was tossed off. I leave it to you whether the author would toss anything off, for Paris and Vienna!— Greet the entire household for me, and may the entire household accept my good wishes.

4. 43

[= Letter 183], 647.—Tr. by editor.

191   HECTOR BERLIOZ TO FELIX MENDELSSOHN BARTHOLDY, LEIPZIG [Fr.]

Leipzig, 2 February [1843]

To Chief Mendelssohn!

Big Chief! we promised to exchange tomahawks (savages' clubs). Here is mine, it is coarse; yours is simple!

Only Squaws (women) and Pale-faces (Europeans, whites) are fond of ornate weapons. Be my brother! And when the

272

Great Spirit will have sent us hunting in the land of the souls, may our warriors hang up our united tomahawks on the Council's door.

Hector Berlioz.

Julien Tiersot (ed.), *Hector Berlioz: Le Musicien errant, 1842–1852* (Paris: Calmann-Lévy, Éditeurs, 1927), 32–33.—Tr. by editor.

192   FRÉDÉRIC CHOPIN TO MAURICE SCHLESINGER, PARIS [Fr.]

22 July [1843], Nohant.

Dear friend, In the *Impromptu* [1] which you included with the *Gazette* of 9 July, there is a *numbered interchange* of pages which makes my music incomprehensible. Far from having the punctiliousness which our friend Moscheles [2] brings to his works—still, this time, I feel it is my duty towards your subscribers to beg you to have an *erratum* put in your next number:

page 3—read page 5

page 5—read page 3.

If you are too occupied or too lazy to write me—simply answer by means of this *erratum* in the *Gazette* and that will mean to me that you, Madame Schlesinger, and your children are in good health.

yrs. most sincerely

Chopin

Julien Tiersot, *Lettres de Musiciens écrites en français du XVe au XXe siècle*, II (Paris: Bocca Frères Éditeurs, 1936), 340–41.—Tr. by editor.

193   RICHARD WAGNER TO FELIX MENDELSSOHN BARTHOLDY, BERLIN [G.]

Berlin, 10 January 1844

My dear, dear Mendelssohn! I am so happy that you are well-disposed towards me. If I have come just a little closer to you, that is for me the most valued [event] of my entire Berlin expedition.

Farewell!
Your Richard Wagner

[= Letter 164], II, 104.—Tr. by editor.

194   GAETANO DONIZETTI TO GIUSEPPINA APPIANI, MILAN [Fr., It.]

[Vienna,] 22 [January 18]44

[Fr.:] "Here we are." "What d'you mean here we are?" "Yes, here we are. . . ." "After such a long silence?" "It is because of the long silence that I said here we are. . . ." "Brigand!" "Well well." "Lazy-bones!" "Quite so." "Ah, but tell me, don't these epithets sting you?" "Not at all, Madam, I am disposed to hear all and suffer all from a friend! . . . . ." "Quite the opposite, I am your mortal enemy . . ." I do not believe that; I have heard it said, but more politely: namely, that you breathe, and your heart throbs, only for Verdi, and even your own letter betrays you. . . .[1] but I approve of your passion; so long as you love artists of great talent, so long shall I esteem you. It cannot offend me—my turn for sympathy being over, it is necessary that another should occupy the place. The world wants new things; others, after all, have yielded the place to us, so we must yield it to others . . . Delighted to yield it to people of talent like *Verdi*. Friendship is ever apprehensive, but be well assured as to that young man's success. The Venetians will appreciate him as much as the Milanese, for hearts are everywhere the same. Talent wins appreciation everywhere etc.—In any case, if the success does not come up to his friends' hopes, that will not prevent the good Verdi from soon occupying one of the most
274

honored places in the *cohort* of composers.—[It.:] I was quite
unable to send you *D. Sebastiano*,[2] for as you know editors always
have contracts amongst themselves to publish a thing in Paris,
Vienna, Italy, England, etc. on the same day, to prevent
intrigues.—I arrived here on the last of the year—6 days later
I caught a fever. (12 days) I was obliged to stay at home.—
Today I present myself for the 1st time to *H. M.* the Empress—
La Montenegro [3] is being awaited here as a new star—I await
your letters as beneficial *dew softly* falling . . .—Embrace all
the family for me, then M. *Sandrini*, after which do not forget
dear [Miss] Bianchi . . . what about the Manzoni manuscript?—
And your dear daughters? And the painter? And the studio?
and my opinions?—and my coming to Italy?—

Facsimile of the autograph: [= Letter 183], between pp. 712–13.—Tr. by editor.

195   GIUSEPPE VERDI TO GAETANO DONIZETTI, VIENNA [It.]

[Milan, 18 May 1844]
Esteemed Maestro,
    It was a welcome surprise for me to read in your letter to
Pedroni that you are good enough to offer to attend the rehearsals
of my *Ernani*.[1]
    I have no hesitation whatever in accepting your courteous
offer, as I am certain that my music cannot fail to profit greatly
when *Donizetti* condescends to make it his concern. I may thus
hope that the musical spirit of the composition will be appreciated.
    Please be so kind as to look after the general production as
well as any necessary phrasing, especially in Feretti's part.
    To you, *Cavaliere*, I shall not proffer blandishments.—You
are one of a small number of men who possess supreme talent and
have no need of individual praise.—The favor you are conferring
on me is so outstanding that you cannot doubt my gratitude.—
With the deepest esteem
                    Your most devoted Servant
                      G. Verdi

Milan, 18 May 1844

[= Letter 183], 901.—Tr. by editor.

196   HECTOR BERLIOZ TO HIS FATHER, LA CÔTE
SAINT-ANDRÉ [Fr.]

[Paris,] 19 August 1844

Dear father,

You are probably puzzled by my silence since the big affair
of the festival . . .[1] I only wrote six lines to my uncle, while
taking a bath at the end of that battle. It was a great success
for me, of which you most likely have no inkling because of the
papers you receive—*le Siècle* and the *Revue des Deux Mondes;*
if you want to take the trouble of reading the others, those that
are not hostile, I'll send them to you. I believed I had thus done
a magnificent stroke of business, since my first day's concert had
yielded *thirty-seven thousand francs!* We were counting on the
second day's concert-dance with cheap tickets, conducted by
Strauss, to attract the crowd, the middle class, the people . . .
nothing came of it . . . I had the satisfaction (a rather disagreeable one, however) of seeing that popular music no longer
has an audience; Strauss only made two thousand six hundred
francs at the box office, and as we were partners, the expenses of
the second day had to be paid for from the receipts of the first.
Furthermore, since (*in France*) artists are veritable serfs,
assessable and liable to forced labor, the Alms administration
came and took from us a duty of *five thousand* francs; and M.
Delessert, the prefect of Police, who had sent me a veritable
army of municipal guards, police constables, etc., to keep the
peace, had me allocate the modest sum of *twelve hundred thirty-one*
francs to those gentlemen. So that, having paid this entire legion
of performers, printers, copyists, engravers, carpenters, dealers
in timber, zinc, cloth, furniture, etc., all I have left of the
gigantic proceeds is the net profit of *eight hundred and sixty*
francs . . . . The honorable members of the Cabinet were present
at the rehearsals and at the concert, they wrote charming letters
and paid for their seats like ordinary citizens; one of them paid
forty francs for four seats, the other a hundred and fifty for
fifteen. But cabinet ministers are no richer than the city of Paris,
which can't afford its policemen and imposes them on us in
exorbitant numbers.

You can therefore see whether I am wrong in saying that, in
France, artists are serfs. We pay tithe. This year, for my five
276

concerts, I have been taxed to the amount of nearly nine thousand five hundred francs. Such is the liberty we enjoy. Such is the fine reward I have reaped from the authorities for having staked my life and given Paris the greatest musical celebration which ever took place in Europe. But it was already much that they let me go ahead; I doubted it till the last. I assure you it was a curious sight, apart from the musical interest! The enthusiasm of eight thousand listeners . . . the deep silence during the pieces; the shouts, the hurrahs afterwards; all the men on their feet, waving their hats, encoring the last stanza of my Hymn to France. There was one terrible (politico-musical) moment, when the refrain from Halévy's song: "Never, in France, never shall the English rule" was struck up; it was as though a riot had broken out, it was a war-cry, it was the initial rumbling of a European revolution.

When the concert was over, I was half dead, you may be sure; they brought me linen and flannels; then, on the stage, in the middle of the orchestra, they built me a little chamber of *harps covered with their wrappers*, and I changed from head to foot before leaving. I had been copiously bled some days before, I could feel my chest starting up again!

I have been feeling a little better the last few days, but I was really exhausted and had been coughing in a horrible way. [Dr.] Amussat assures me that all I need is a complete rest . . . which, however, is no more obtainable on the market than *sleep*, *leisure*, and *oblivion*.

Nevertheless, I intend to leave for Baden in a few days,[2] where I'll try not to do anything that is fatiguing.

Adieu, dear father, my sisters will send me your news; I know that writing tires you too much and I dare not ask you for a few lines.

Your affectionate son,

H. Berlioz.

P.S.—Louis[3] sends you his love; he is growing up, he just won two prizes at his boarding school.

I am going to send you the two volumes which are about to appear; they contain [an account of] my musical journey in Germany and Italy,[4] of which you only know some fragments which were published in various periodicals and papers; now it is pretty complete.

[= Letter 191], 83–86.—Tr. by editor.

197   ROBERT SCHUMANN TO HANS CHRISTIAN ANDERSEN,
COPENHAGEN [G.]

Dresden, 14th April 1845

I am sending you this greeting through Gade; [1] if only I
myself could go to the North with him, but the homeland still
holds me fast. Since we last saw each other, my valued friend, I
have fared badly, a dreadful nervous affliction would not leave
me, and I am still not quite well. But with spring approaching,
I feel somewhat stronger and have yet greater expectations of it.

I was hardly able to work at all, nor was I allowed to do so;
but I thought a great deal, also of our *Glücksblume*.[2] You
answered me so kindly from Berlin, promised to send me the
sketch—may I remind you of it? Has it perhaps already appeared
in print? And how are you otherwise? Do you have new fairy
tales, new poems? Is *Spain* still beckoning from afar? May we
hope to welcome you in Germany soon again? A gathering like
that evening when you came to see us—poet, singer, performer
and composer, all together—will there be another one soon
again? [3] Do you know the "Schifflein" by Uhland:

—wann treffen wir
an Einem Ort uns wieder? [4]

That evening will always dwell in my memory!

My wife sends you many greetings; she gave me another little
daughter 5 weeks ago, our third. We shall spend the summer in
lovely Dresden.

Gade has written a new overture, a thoroughly inspired piece.
The Danes can be proud of this splendid musician. Also Helsted
is very talented.[5]

May I hope for an answer from you, perhaps also concerning
the Glücksblume? Then write here, to Dresden! If I can do
anything for you in Germany, appoint me to be your secretary;
it would make me happy.

With the greatest respect, your

Robert Schumann

Do you know the poems of the Baroness von *Droste-Hülshoff?* [6] They seem most extraordinary to me.

[= Letter 172], 245-46.—Tr. by editor.

198   HECTOR BERLIOZ TO GEORGE HAINL, LYONS [Fr.]

Avignon, Wednesday
2 July [1845]

My dear Mr. Hainl,

I have to come by boat up the Rhone and consequently cannot arrive in Lyons before Friday; my letter will precede me.

I should want to give a concert in Lyons only if we can do something unusual: by raising the prices, by scattering posters in neighboring towns, such as Châlons, Mâcon, Vienne, Bourgoin, Nantua, Bellay, etc., and by placarding all the steamboats on the Rhone and the Saône, we should take in nine or ten thousand francs; if this is utopian, let us forget the whole thing; it is not worth stirring up all your musical world of Lyons to obtain only average results. Besides, I am so weary of rehearsals, this drill-sergeant life has wrecked me so at Marseilles that it will require a great effort to take it up again.

For the program I should like to present I shall need:

34 violins at least;
10 violas;
11 cellos;
9 double basses;
2 flutes;
2 oboes, of whom one for the English horn;
2 clarinets;
4 bassoons;
4 horns;
2 natural trumpets;
2 cornets;
3 trombones;
1 ophicleide in C;
2 tympanists;
1 cymbal player;
1 bass drum;
1 triangle;
1 tambourine;

Plus, for a piece for 2 orchestras: [1]

4 first clarinets in B flat;
4 second clarinets in B flat;

279

1 small clarinet in *E flat;*
1 third flute;
1 piccolo in *D flat;*
2 horns;
2 trumpets;
2 ophicleides; 1 in *C*, 1 in *B flat;*
3 trombones;
2 oboes;
4 drummers.

And lastly, a chorus of 80 men (or 70) and 20 women (or 30).
A singer (*basso cantante*) and some other, a woman soloist
to complete the program, offering one or two arias of her choice.
For each performer of the large orchestra there should be one
section rehearsal and two general: for the *Military band* one
would be enough, two at the most. The choruses would have to
work in proportion to their lack of facility or the reverse.

I cannot arrange to go to Lyons in August; I must therefore
go before or during Rachel['s performances] [2] and announce
that this musical Festival will be the only one I shall give.

I am ready to accept the arrangement of sharing the receipts
after deducting five hundred francs for the expenses, but in
that case these expenses must include not only the cost of lighting
and service in the theater, the fees of the orchestra and chorus
of the theater, but also the cost of raising a 4-tier platform
covering the stage and the usual players' pit, and the cost of
the posters (double ones), which must be issued 4 different
times and printed at the rate of 60 at least per issue; 50 more
copies being set aside and sent out all around as I indicated above.
In Marseilles, the expenses charged against me were only three
hundred francs, and in Lyons we stand a much greater chance
for large returns.

Please find out, my dear Mr. Hainl, whether this is possible
and at the same time whether the poor will agree to collect only
a tenth, as they did at Marseilles and as they invariably do at
my concerts in Paris. [3]

Curiosity will no doubt be lively enough among my fellow
townsmen (as I am almost from Lyons) for a rather full house
to be plausibly counted on. Let us take advantage of this as
well as we can and give the concert soon, for my time is limited.

I shall stop at the Hôtel du Parc, next to the Place des Terreaux, and there I hope to find a word from you on arrival. My very best wishes and sincerest thanks.

Yours faithfully,

H. Berlioz

[= Letter 173], 63–67.

199   HECTOR BERLIOZ TO FELIX MENDELSSOHN BARTHOLDY, LEIPZIG [Fr.]

[Prague, 14 April 1846]

My dear Mendelssohn

I am afraid I shall not be able to come and greet you when I pass through Leipzig. This disappoints me greatly. Permit me to tell you that *in Breslau* I heard your *Midsummer-Night's Dream* and that I have never heard anything so profoundly Shakespearian as your music; on my way out of the theater I should gladly have given three years of my life for the pleasure of embracing you.

adieu   adieu

Believe me when I say that I love you as much as I admire you, and that is very much.

Yours most sincerely, both heart and soul,

Hector Berlioz

Prague 14 April 1846

P.S. Please remember me to that true artist among your friends M. David.[1]

Facsimile of the autograph: Ernst Wolff, *Felix Mendelssohn Bartholdy* (Berlin: "Harmonie," Verlagsgesellschaft für Literatur und Kunst, 1906), Appendix.—Tr. by editor.

200   FELIX MENDELSSOHN BARTHOLDY TO IGNAZ MOSCHELES, LONDON [G.]

Leipzig, 26 June 1846.

Dear friend,

The occasion of this letter is a line in a recent letter from Mr. Moore,[1] who writes me: "nearly the whole of the Philharmonic Band are engaged; a few only are left out, who made themselves unpleasant, when you were there." [2] I don't like this at all, and as I think that you in particular have such things under your control, I address my protest to you and beg you also to communicate it to Mr. Moore.

I hate nothing more than to have old, long-settled squabbles warmed up; it's bad enough that they ever existed. I have put these of the Philharmonic out of mind, and they *must have absolutely no* influence on engagements for the Birmingham Festival. If they want to discharge people because of incompetence, that is no business of mine, and I cannot object; but if *a single person* is discharged "because he made himself unpleasant when I was there," then I consider this an injustice and desire it shall *not* happen. There is certainly no cause to fear that those gentlemen will make trouble once more—I, at least, do not fear it, nor do I believe anyone over there can. Therefore I warmly beg you to let things go as they would if I had no intention of coming to England, and if they wish to show me *consideration,* the greatest favor they can do me is, precisely, *not* to show me that kind of personal consideration.

Be so good as to bring up the matter emphatically with Mr. Moore, and I hope then not to have to hear of these long-settled stories any further, that is, if my wish is carried out and *no sort of reprisal* takes place. For otherwise I'll write ten more letters of protest.

Ever

Yours

Felix.

Paul and Carl Mendelssohn Bartholdy (eds.), *Felix Mendelssohn Bartholdy: Briefe aus den Jahren 1830 bis 1847* (7th ed.; Leipzig: Hermann Mendelssohn, 1899), Part II, 307–308.—Tr. by editor.

201   FELIX MENDELSSOHN BARTHOLDY TO CÉSAR FRANCK, PARIS [Fr.]

Leipzig, 22 December 1846.

Sir,

I owe you many apologies, as I have been unable to thank you sooner for sending me your trios,[1] which I received a few months ago. But I was on a long journey at the time,[2] and, since my return, a great deal of business of all kinds has daily prevented me from writing. Be kind enough to excuse the delay, and accept my thanks which, though belated, come to you no less sincerely and gratefully.

I should very much like to talk to you in great detail on the subject of these compositions and tell you of all the things in them which please me; but I find it impossible to do so in writing, and I could not manage it even in my own language. It will have to wait, then, for the time, which I hope will soon come, when I can meet you in person, play a little music with you and chat about it, and repeat *viva voce* my thanks and the high esteem with which I have the honor to be, Sir,

Yours very truly
Felix Mendelssohn Bartholdy

[= Letter 192], 339.—Tr. by editor.

202   GIUSEPPE VERDI TO GIOVANNI RICORDI, MILAN [It.]

Milan, 29 December 1846.

My dear Ricordi,

I approve the contract you have drawn up for my new opera, *Macbeth*, which will be produced at Florence during the coming Lent, and I agree to your making use of it, but on condition that you will not allow any performances of *Macbeth* at the I[mperial] R[oyal] Theater la Scala.

I have had enough examples to convince me that here they can't or don't want to mount an opera properly, especially my

283

own. I cannot forget how very badly they staged *I Lombardi,
Ernani,* [*I*] *due Foscari* . . . etc. . . . I have another example,
Attila, before my eyes now! . . . I ask you whether this Opera
could be staged worse, in spite of a good cast? . . .

I repeat, therefore, that I cannot and will not allow any
performances of this *Macbeth* at la Scala, at least not until things
have taken a turn for the better. I feel it my duty to warn you,
for your guidance, that the condition I am now imposing for
Macbeth will henceforth be imposed for all my operas.

Farewell, Yours Affect'ly

[G. Verdi.]

Gaetano Cesari and Alessandro Luzio (eds.), *I Copialettere di Giuseppe Verdi*
(Milan: Commissione Esecutiva per le Onoranze a Giuseppe Verdi nel primo
centenario della nascita, 1913), 34–35.—Tr. by editor.[1]

203A BEDŘICH SMETANA TO FRANZ LISZT, WEIMAR [G.]

[Prague, 23 March 1848]

Dear Sir,

Fully confident of your world-renowned magnanimity and
generosity, I make bold to dedicate this product of my imagination to you.[1] True, I should have asked for permission beforehand. But unknown as I am, even in the circle of those nearest to
me, I dare take this step only on the grounds that the composition
itself will show whether it is worthy of your acceptance or not.
I take the liberty, however, of stating what decided me to make
such demands on your kindness:

From childhood I have devoted myself to literary studies,
and though I loved music I was able to practice it only for my
relaxation and pleasure. But what instruction did I have in it!
When I was 17 years of age I did not know C sharp from D
flat; the theory of harmony was a closed book to me. Though
ignorant of this I yet wrote music!

When I was 19 years old I broke the chains which bound me
to my studies and devoted myself with all diligence to music
under the guidance of a competent teacher, Joseph Proksch,[2] in
Prague. I am now 24 years old and have studied all branches

of music and produced a number of exercises so that I have achieved a certain routine. But I had to pay dearly for my instruction. Poor, helpless, without friends as I was, it was not until this year, after I had been able to secure a few lessons as a result of my public performances and some recognition of my slight talent, that I was able, after much saving, to pay back part of my debts. But when shall I be able to pay the other half?

My lessons provide me with 12 gulden a month, just enough to keep me from starving. I cannot get my compositions printed because I should have to put up money for them and am unfortunately unable to save enough. Also, I believe, I should find it hard to make a living by composing. The patrons to whom I turned promised me the moon. Up to now, however, nobody has done anything for me. Indeed I must say that I was near despair when I got the news that my parents had sunk so low as to become almost beggars. Oh Sir, what would I not have done to help them! In my distress, without prospects of help, and utterly friendless, a thought suddenly flashed through my brain: the name "Liszt" on a piece of music that lay on my table moved me to tell everything to you, an artist without equal, of whose magnanimity the whole world speaks. In order to acquaint you with my slight abilities, I composed this sketch, the first work which perhaps will introduce me to the public. I now stand before you with the request that you *kindly accept this work and have it printed.* Your name would open the doors of the musical world to my works. Your name will be the cause of my future happiness, my everlasting gratitude! May I hope as much? My impatience, my fear until your decision is made cannot be described, and I earnestly request you not to delay and not to leave me a prey to torturing doubts.

May I dare yet *one more request?* My present situation is terrible. May God preserve all artists from similar trials!—But I could very easily provide myself with a living which would make me the happiest man on earth, since I should be in a position to fulfill my one wish, namely to take care of my poor parents to the end, if I could get some support for my plan. It consists in my being able to set up a Music Institute. The one existing in Prague has about 100 pupils: one which was opened last year by a musician, and an indifferent one at that, has acquired within *one* year over eighty pupils, which means an income of about 400 gulden a month for the founders. If therefore I had

285

enough money to rent a flat and to buy at least *two* instruments, my existence would be assured, my parents would be with me, and I should be the happiest man on earth. I am both a creative artist and a pianist and I possess *no* instrument. A friend of mine allows me to practise in his flat. Truly my fate is not enviable!

I am therefore bold enough, at the risk of seeming arrogant in your eyes, to request a loan of 400 gulden, which I solemnly pledge my life to repay. I have no guarantor other than myself, and my word which is sacred to me, and therefore possibly better surety than a hundred guarantors. Please do not interpret my boldness wrongly. Not to a single living soul, yourself excepted, have I confided my distress, my wretchedness. In whom should an artist confide if not in another artist? The men of money, those aristocrats, look at the poor devil without compassion and let him starve!

In the greatest perturbation of spirit I ask you again, and I hope not in vain, not to delay your answer whatever it may mean, my happiness or my misfortune, but to deliver me from doubt, for in a few weeks Smetana may possibly no longer be. My address is 548, Old Town Square, second floor, back entrance.

I hope that you will forgive me, dear Sir, for having taken up your valuable time, but you must know the person you are asked to help.

With the greatest esteem, I remain,

Your most obedient,

Bedřich Smetana.

Prague, 23 March 1848.

203B FRANZ LISZT TO BEDŘICH SMETANA, PRAGUE [G.]

[Krzyzanowice, 30 March 1848]

Dear Sir,

The "Morceaux Caractéristiques" together with the accompanying letter were handed to me barely a quarter of an hour prior to my departure for Vienna. First of all I should like to express my warm thanks for the dedication, which I accept with all the more pleasure since the pieces are the most outstanding, finely felt, and most finished that recently have come to my

286

attention. I might perhaps permit myself one criticism, namely with regard to the title of the first one, "Gretel in the Woods." The canon seems to me too scientific a form for Gretel. The simple title "In the Woods" would, in my opinion, be preferable.

Difficult though it is today to find a good publisher for a good work unless it is signed by an already famous and current name, I nevertheless hope to be able shortly to give you news of the publication of your "Morceaux Caractéristiques," and I shall certainly do what I can to see that you get a decent fee which should encourage you to establish active contact with the publisher.[3]

Should my path lead through Prague this summer, as is probable, I shall give myself the pleasure of calling on you and thanking you personally. In the meantime allow me to assure you, dear Sir, of my feelings of esteem, and believe me to be

    Yours very truly,

            F. Liszt.

Krzyzanowice, 30 March 1848.

František Bartoš (ed.), *Bedřich Smetana: Letters and Reminiscences*, trans. Daphne Rusbridge (Prague: Artia, 1955), 24–27.

204A-B FRÉDÉRIC CHOPIN TO WOJCIECH GRZYMAŁA, PARIS [Pol.]

A

        [London,] Thursday, 11th [May 1848]

Dearest soul

I have just come back from the Italian theater. J. Lind sang for the first time this year,[1] and the Queen showed herself in public for the first time since the *Chartists*.[2] Both produced a great effect—and, on me, so did old Wellington, who sat beneath the Queen's box like an old *monarchical* dog in his kennel.—I met J. Lind, who had very graciously sent me a most excellent stall with her card. As I had a good place, I heard well. She is a typical Swede; not in an ordinary light, but in a sort of aurora

287

borealis. She is enormously effective in *Sonnambula*. She sings with assurance and purity; her piano is as continuous and even as a hair.

A stall costs 2½ guineas.

B

Edinburgh, 30 October [1848]

My dearest soul,

Have you forgotten me, that you infer from my letters, in which I wrote to you that I am getting increasingly weak, dull, hopeless, homeless—that you infer from all this that I am going to be married? On the day on which I received your dear and good letter, I put my affairs in some sort of order, in case I should give up the ghost somewhere.

I have been dragging about Scotland again, but it is too cold now and tomorrow I return to London, because lord Stuart has asked me to play on the 16th at a concert to be given for the Poles, before the opening of the ball. On the way back from Hamilton Pallace [*sic*] (60 miles from Edinburgh), where I had spent a few days with the duke and duchess of Hamilton, I caught a cold and I have not been out for five days. I am staying with Dr. Lyszcziński, who is treating me homeopathically. I don't want to pay any more visits, for the cholera is just round the corner; and because, if I collapsed, I should have to remain somewhere all winter. I had promised to return to Hamilton Pallace if the weather improved and to go from there to the island of Ayran [i.e., Arran] and stay with the proprietor of that island, the marquess of Douglas, who is the son of the duke of Hamilton and whose wife is a princess of Baden. But I shall do nothing after all. While I was at Hamilton Pallace, there were present, besides the high aristocracy of the land, the prince and princess of Parma and the prince of Lucca.

The princess is a sister of the duke of Bordeaux. She and her husband make a very gay young couple. They asked me to stay with them at Kingston. They will soon return to London, for they are settling in England, now that they have been driven out of Italy. That is all very well, but it does not attract me; and if I made haste to leave Hamilton, it was because I just cannot sit at table from 8 till half past 10 without suffering pains as I did at Gutmann's that day (do you remember?).[3] Though I
288

breakfasted in my room, came down late, and got carried on the stairs, I was still too uncomfortable. Before your letter arrived, I wrote to you from Wishaw, from lady Belhaven's, where I stayed before going to Hamilton, but it was such a bleak, irritable letter that I did well not to send it to you.

After November 16th, if matters improve over there and if the London *fogs* drive me out, I shall return to Paris, provided it is not too late to undertake the journey.

My good Scotswomen, whom I haven't seen for a while, are coming to see me today. They want me to stay longer, in order to go dragging round the Scottish palaces, here and there, wherever I am asked. They are kind, but so tedious. May the good Lord forgive them! . . . They write me every day and I never answer; but no matter where I am they arrive there at once, if they can. Perhaps this is what has given someone the notion that I am about to get married. But for that one would have to feel some physical *attrait*; now, the unmarried one resembles me too much. How could I ever kiss myself? . . . Friendship is friendship, I declared outright, and it doesn't give the right to anything more. And even if I fell in love and were loved in turn as I might wish to be, I should not get married, for we should have nothing to eat and nowhere to live. Rich women seek out rich men, and if they find poor ones they ought not to be sickly, but young and well turned out. One has the right to be poor by oneself; but when there are two, that is the greatest misfortune. I am quite willing to give up the ghost in a hospital, but I won't leave a starving wife behind me. Besides, I hardly need to write you all this, for you know my thoughts on the subject . . . [Several words crossed out.] And so, I am not in the least thinking of getting married; I am thinking of home, of my mother, my sisters. May God grant them nothing but happy thoughts. Meanwhile, what has become of my art? And my heart, where have I wasted it? [Words crossed out.] I can hardly remember how they sing at home. That world is slipping away from me, I forget, my strength fails me. [Words crossed out.] I rise a little only to fall even lower.

I am not complaining to you, but since you asked to be informed, I explain to you that I am nearer to a coffin than to a nuptial bed. My mind is fairly calm. [Words crossed out.]

Write to me. Address: Szulczewski Esq. 10 Duke Street, St. James's. Stuart's Polish literary society is there.

289

I am not sending you the fourth letter I wrote to you, but only this, which is just a fragment of another one written in a fit of impatience; so you can see that, occasionally, I am in a bad mood.

Yours till death
Ch.

[= Letter 161], 394–97.

205   RICHARD WAGNER TO HIS WIFE MINNA, CHEMNITZ [G.]

[Postmark: Weimar, 14 May 1849]

My beloved wife!

I received your letter last night when I had gone to bed late: I have got up early to answer you. All that your letter contains counts almost as nothing compared with the one fact I read in every line: the evidence of your pure and warm love, which this time you expressed to me without any torturing reproaches. Ah! In this you have done me immense good! Thank you, and preserve for me yourself and your loving heart.

The ways of fate with men are incomprehensible! The terrible catastrophe I have just experienced and the events of yesterday in Weimar have made a different person out of me and have shown me a new path. Imagine, my dear wife, how for years in my Dresden position I have nursed the deepest dejection: a new path which I entered with my art opened up for me thornily enough indeed; wherever I trod, I was hurt; with an inward fury I finally turned my back to my art, which yielded me nothing but suffering; you know that I almost begrudged the ink and the paper I needed to write a new opera. Thus, in a state of extreme discontent with my position and almost with my art, groaning under a burden which, unfortunately, you were not really willing to understand, deep in debts, so much so that my usual earnings would have satisfied my creditors only in the course of many years and under shameful deprivations, I was at variance with this world, I ceased to be an artist, I frittered away my creative powers,

290

and became a mere revolutionary (if not in deeds, at least in conviction); that is, I was seeking in a wholly transformed world the ground for some new art creations of my spirit. Now the Dresden revolution and its whole result have taught me that I am not a real revolutionary by any means, and I have seen from the evil outcome of the revolt that a real and victorious revolutionary must proceed completely without scruple—he must not think of his wife and children, nor of his house and home—his only goal is: destruction; and if the noble-minded Hübner[1] had been willing to proceed in this manner in Freiburg or Chemnitz even now, then the revolution would have remained victorious. But men of our type are not destined for this horrible task: we are revolutionaries only in order to be able to *construct* something on fresh ground; it is not *destruction* which attracts us, but the *formation of something new,* and that is why we are not the kind of men Destiny needs—these will arise from the lowest dregs of the people; we and our hearts cannot have anything in common with them. You see! *Thus* I AM PARTING *with the revolution. . . .*

I already came to terms with myself about this on my way to Weimar; and in view of a worthless future for Germany for perhaps a considerable number of years, I was only pondering how I could settle down with you somewhere, in quiet seclusion in the country, when suddenly a new way was pointed out to me in Weimar. Liszt and his friend the Princess Wittgenstein[2] are in this respect in a certain agreement with the Grand Duchess of Weimar—an agreement which has existed for some time—and together they have decided to lead me and my talent out of the miserable situation in Germany and into the world's broader path. They say that here in Germany I would perish and that my art in the end would disgust even me; this, they said, they must not allow: they must keep my creative powers fresh and joyous for the world. They are directing me to London and Paris: to London, in order to have my most recent opera *Lohengrin* translated there and to have it first performed by the English theater— *not* in Germany! That would bring me fame and especially *money.* To Paris, in order that I may write another opera for that city in the meantime. Liszt takes it upon himself to arrange everything; as he knows the present conditions, he

291

does not doubt in the least that he will bring about the Paris
commission and the London enterprise in short order. How
seriously he and my friends are interested in the matter you
can best see by the 2,000 francs I have been offered by him
for this purpose; and in general he has bound himself to provide
me fully with the money for these undertakings—and as long
as I may need it.

Ah! Dear, good wife! This has given strength to my heart,
and at one stroke I have become an entire *artist* again, I *love*
my art again, and I *hope* by means of it some day to make
my poor tried wife happy. I also hope by this remarkable means
to be able soon to satisfy *all* of my creditors. Good God!
How is it possible that even the worst has turned into the best?

I have not yet had a chance to tell Liszt about the worrisome
contents of your letter; I shall see him in an hour, and I shall
come to an understanding with him about the next steps;
you will then hear about it immediately. And now, only a few
requests, before I forget them. (1) My *Lohengrin* score is
with *Kammermusikus Uhlig* [3] in the Poliergasse; you must get
it from him. (2) Young *Ritter,* in Waisenhausstrasse next to
Semper's house, has my text of *Siegfried* and another sketch—
Die Gibelinen—which I should also like to have. [4] These things,
together with a score of *Rienzi,* one of *Holländer,* and one of
Tannhäuser, you must also send along with the other things.
I should also like to have the portfolio you had with you,
and its contents; on the big shelf at the left-hand side of the
desk there is a folder containing some compositions which I
also want to have. I should also like to have sent some copies
of the texts of *Rienzi, Holländer,* and *Tannhäuser* (at Meyer's
house). The copies of the texts of *Rienzi* and *Holländer* are
in one of the inner compartments at the right-hand side of
the desk.

I have just consulted Liszt and Professor Wolf [Wolff].
They think that I am completely safe here for the time being
and that a sudden legal action against me is in any case
impossible; the most anyone could do would be to apply to
the ministry here to arrest me; in such a case, I could depend
on the protection of the Minister Watzdorf. He is a very
liberal-minded man and a sympathizer with the German
party; in the worst case he would provide me with a passport
and send me on. I am surely safe against a surprise attack.

Now I shall tell you, my good wife, what is most on my mind: I must see *you* once again before I go to London or Paris. Listen! This coming Sunday there will be a new production of *Tannhäuser;* and my birthday is coming at about the same time; you *must* be here for that. Meanwhile, I might ramble about on foot a little in the beautiful country of Thuringia, Wartburg, etc. I also might visit Professor *Wolf* in *Jena,* who has invited me to live on a farm near Jena in complete safety and for as long as I wish, in case things should become very bad. I should then come back so as to be in Weimar and meet you there on Sunday, in order to go *with you to Tannhäuser* (which Got . . . [?] is supposed to sing very well). Perhaps we might then stay together for a few more days until my birthday, and console each other quite freely about the future. Then I should go to Paris and London; and as soon as I have signed a definite contract there, you could follow me in order that—God willing—we may never be separated again. You see! This is how it stands. Help to carry it out, and be in Weimar on Sunday! [5]

Everything for me is to be sent to Liszt's address.

I must close now; at ten o'clock there will be a rehearsal of *Tannhäuser;* the Grand Duchess wants to see me today— I shall get a dress coat from Liszt.

Now, give my most heartfelt greetings to the dear darling Wolframs! And you, my poor suffering wife! Let the ray of light which is now revealed to me enter your tortured heart too! Everything will yet turn out better than we thought. May God save you! Faithful, good Minna! Farewell! Farewell!

Your

R W

John N. Burk (ed.), *Letters of Richard Wagner: The Burrell Collection, Presented to the Curtis Institute by Its Founder, Mrs. Efrem Zimbalist* (New York: The Macmillan Company, 1950), 226–29.

206   FRÉDÉRIC CHOPIN TO MARIE DE ROZIÈRES, CHAUDFONTAINE [Fr.]

[Postmark: Paris, 14 August 1849]

My sister and Jędrz. and my niece [1] have been with me for the past 5 days. I am very tired. They too. I wish you as much happiness as I have at this moment, with a little more health, for I am weaker than ever.

Your sincere friend
Ch.

My sincere respects to M[m]e Gr. de Baulin. [2]

[= Letter 161], 416.

207   GIUSEPPE VERDI TO CARLO MARZARI, VENICE [It.]

Busseto, 14 December 1850.

[Dear Mr. Marzari,]

In order to answer yours of the 11th inst. at once, I have taken very little time to re-examine the new libretto: but I have seen enough to realize that, reduced to the present condition, it lacks character and importance; further, the dramatic moments have become very cool indeed. If it was necessary to change the name [of Francis I], then the place should have been changed too, so he could be made into a Duke or Prince of another country, for example a Pier Luigi Farnese or someone else; or the action might have been shifted back to the period before Louis XI, when France was not a united kingdom, and he could have been a Duke of Burgundy or Normandy etc. etc., in any case an absolute ruler.—In the fifth scene of Act I, all that anger vented by the courtiers against Triboletto [1] makes no sense.—The old man's malediction, so terrible and sublime in the original, becomes ridiculous here, because the motive for his malediction is not so important any more, and because this is no longer a subject speaking so boldly to his king. Without this malediction what purpose, what significance does the play have? The Duke is a nonentity:

294

the Duke must absolutely be a libertine; otherwise, Triboletto's fear that his daughter might leave her hiding place is ungrounded: and the play impossible. How does it happen that the Duke, in the last act, goes to a remote tavern all alone, without an invitation, without an appointment?—I don't understand why the sack was taken out! Of what consequence was the sack to the police? Are they afraid of its effect? Forgive me, but what makes them think they know more about the subject than I do? Who is entitled to be a Maestro? Who is entitled to say, this will be effective, that won't? A difficulty of that kind arose on account of the *horn* in Ernani: well then, did anyone laugh at the sound of that horn? Take away that sack, and it becomes improbable that Triboletto should speak to a corpse for half an hour, till a flash of lightning reveals it to be that of his daughter.—Finally, I note that they have avoided making Triboletto ugly and humpbacked!! A singing humpback? Why not! . . . Will it be effective? I don't know; but if I don't know, neither does, I repeat, the person who suggested the change. As a matter of fact, I think it is a very fine thing to depict this extremely deformed and ridiculous character who is inwardly impassioned and full of love. I chose the subject expressly because of these qualities, and if these original traits are removed, I can no longer set it to music. If I'm told that my notes will suit the present drama just as well, I answer that I have no understanding for these arguments, and I frankly state that, good or bad, I never write music at random and I always manage to give it character.

In short, what was an original, powerful play has been turned into something very common and cold. I very much regret that the Board of Directors has not answered my last letter. I can only repeat and request that what I wrote in it should be carried out, for upon my artist's conscience I cannot set this libretto to music. I have the honor to be

Yours truly,

[G. Verdi.]

[= Letter 202], 109–11.—Tr. by editor.

208   GIUSEPPE VERDI TO TITO RICORDI, MILAN [It.]

Dear Ricordi

Venice, 6 March 1853

I am sorry that I must give you sad news, but I cannot hide the truth from you. La Traviata was a failure. Let us not investigate the reasons.[1] That is what happened. Farewell farewell

G. Verdi

I shall leave the day after tomorrow: write me at Busseto—

Facsimile of the autograph: G. Morazzoni and G. M. Ciampelli, *Verdi* (Milan: A cura della rivista "La Scala e il Museo Teatrale" e della libreria editrice milanese concessionaria della vendita, 1929), 136.—Tr. by editor.

209A   ROBERT SCHUMANN TO JOHANN JACOB BRAHMS, HAMBURG [G.]

[Düsseldorf, 5 November 1853]

Sir,

Your son Johannes has become very dear to us, [and] his musical genius has afforded us hours filled with happiness. To facilitate his entry into the world, I have publicly expressed what I think of him. I send you those pages [1] and imagine that they will bring a little pleasure to a father's heart.

May you look with confidence to the future of this darling of the Muses and remain always assured of my deepest interest in his destiny!

Yours sincerely,

R. Schumann

Düsseldorf, 5 November 1853.

209B JOHANNES BRAHMS TO ROBERT SCHUMANN, DÜSSELDORF [G.]

[Hamburg, December 1853]

Honored Friend!

I take the liberty of sending you herewith your first foster children (who have you to thank for their world citizenship);[2] [and am] very anxious [to know] whether they will still enjoy the same indulgence and love on your part.

To me, in their new dress, they appear still far too proper and timid, in fact quite Philistine. I cannot yet get used to seeing these innocent children of nature in such decent clothes.

I look forward with infinite pleasure to seeing you in Hanover, so that I may tell you that my parents and I owe the happiest period of our lives to the exceeding love which you and Joachim[3] have shown us.

I was overjoyed to see my parents and my teacher once more and am spending a blissful time in their midst.

Please give your wife and children warmest greetings from your

Johannes Brahms

Berthold Litzmann (ed.), *Clara Schumann, Johannes Brahms: Briefe aus den Jahren 1853–1896* (Leipzig: Breitkopf & Härtel, 1927), I, pp. 1 & 3–4. —Tr. by editor.

210 GIOACHINO ROSSINI TO GIUSEPPE BELLENTANI, MODENA [It.]

[Florence, 28 December 1853]

The so-called Swan of Pesaro To the Eagle of Este[1] Sausage Makers.

It has been your pleasure to soar to great heights for my sake, regaling me with specially-made Zamponi and Cappelletti:[2] and it is only fitting that I, from the depths, as it were, of my Native Swamps of the ancient Padusa,[3] should raise a

297

raucous cry of particular thanks in your direction. I found the collection of your works complete in every way: and their internal mastery was savored in my company by all those whose fate it was to delight in the refinement of your notorious manipulations.

I shall not set your praises to music, for, as I told you in my other letter, 'mid such hubbub in the world of Harmony I remain an Ex-composer.[4] Well for me, and better for you. You have the skill of touching certain keys which satisfy the palate—a more dependable judge than the ear, for it bases itself on delicacy of touch at its very tip, which is where vitality begins. I shall touch but one of these keys for your gratification; the key of my deep gratitude for your many attentions: and may it serve you as a Stimulus toward loftier flights deserving of a Laurel Wreath, to crown you wherewith would be the fond wish of

Your Obliged Servant

Gioachino Rossini

Florence 28 Decem. 1853.

Facsimile of the autograph: Lodovico Settimo Silvestri, *Della vita e delle opere di Gioachino Rossini* (Milan: By the author, 1874), insert.—Tr. by editor.

211   ALBERT DIETRICH TO JOSEPH JOACHIM, HANOVER [G.]

Düsseldorf, 28 February [1854]

Dear friend,

I have terribly sad news for you and Johannes; you must let me off the minuter details for the present; I am not calm enough yet to be able to write them. In a recent letter to Brahms I hinted that Schumann's nerves were in a bad state. This has become worse from day to day; he heard music continuously, sometimes it was of the most beautiful description, but often agonizingly hideous. Later on phantom voices were added to this, which, as he thought, cried terrible and beautiful things in his ear. Last Saturday week he was seized with violent despair for the first time. From that time Schumann's mind

298

was obviously affected; the phantoms did not leave him a moment's peace. I went to see him three times a day. As a rule he was apparently calm, but sometimes he hinted at something frightful which the spirits were urging him to do— and he has attempted it—on Monday—yesterday—towards midday he managed to slip out of the house—Hasenclever,[1] I, and several others looked for him in vain until nearly half past one. About that time he was brought back by four boatmen; they had rescued him from the Rhine; he had thrown himself in from the middle of the bridge. Now, as before, he is apparently quite sensible, and yet his mind is so much affected that they do not think he will recover for some time, although the doctors have not given up hope. As you can imagine, his wife is overwhelmed by grief and despair, but they have managed to keep the worst from her; she seems to have a suspicion of it, however—but she is not to be told— she has not been allowed to go to him since, and is staying with Fräulein Leser in an agony of longing; neither I nor anybody else except the doctors and attendants may go near him—he will probably be taken to a good nursing home soon.

You can imagine what I have suffered; I was quite ill, and I am still often attacked by a kind of feverish ague. I hope I shall be able to send you better news before long. I will write to you again soon.

Schumann was not able to look at your Overture; I studied it thoroughly until Monday; I deeply admire your fine work. I should like to write a great deal about it—but it is impossible today.

Your devoted
Albert Dietrich.

Nora Bickley (ed. and trans.), *Letters from and to Joseph Joachim* (London: Macmillan and Co., Limited, 1914), 60–62.

212   RICHARD WAGNER TO FRANZ LIZST, WEIMAR [G.]

[Zurich, 16(?) December 1854]

Dear Franz,

I am beginning to find out more and more that you are in reality a great philosopher!—by comparison, I often appear to myself as a proper dunce. Apart from—slowly—progressing with my music, I have been busying myself exclusively with a man who has come like a gift from heaven—although only a literary one—into my solitude. He is *Artur Schopenhauer,* the greatest philosopher since *Kant,* whose thoughts he—as he says—is the first to have carried to their conclusion. The German professors have ignored him—wisely—for 40 years: but recently—to Germany's disgrace—he has been discovered by an English critic.[1] What charlatans all the Hegels etc. are next to him! His chief idea, the final negation of the desire to live, is terribly serious, but the only redemption. To me of course that thought was not new, and it can indeed be conceived by no one in whom it did not pre-exist. But it was awakened in me clearly for the first time by this philosopher. When I recollect the storms of my heart, the terrible spasms with which—involuntarily—it clung to the hope of life, yes, if even now the storms often swell to a hurricane—still, I have now found a sedative, which in wakeful nights helps me to sleep; it is the heartfelt and deep longing for death: absolute unconsciousness, total non-existence, absence of all dreams— the sole final redemption!—

It is strange that I have often found your thoughts in accord with mine: even if you express them differently because you are religious, I know that you mean exactly the same thing. How profound you are! In your article on the [*Fliegende*] *Holländer* you often struck me with the force of lightning. While I was reading Schopenhauer, I was with you most of the time: you just did not know it.—And so I am ripening more and more: it is only to pass the time that I play with art. In what manner I try to amuse myself you will see from the enclosed sheet.—

For the sake of the most beautiful of my life-dreams, for young Siegfried's sake, I must indeed still finish the Nibelung pieces: the Walküre has taken hold of me too strongly for

300

me to give up the enjoyment of this diversion; I have got
to the second half of the last act. The whole will not be
finished till 1856—in 1858, in the tenth year of my Hegira
I'll be able to produce it,—if it is to be.[2] But as I have never
in my life enjoyed the real bliss of love, I do still want to
erect a monument to that loveliest of dreams, in which, from
beginning to end, this love may for once be thoroughly satiated:
I have drafted a *Tristan und Isolde* in my mind, the simplest,
yet most full-blooded musical conception; with the "black
flag," which flutters at the end of it, I shall then cover myself,
in order—to die.— [3]

When you have had enough of *Rheingold*, do send it to
Fischer, the chorus-master in Dresden, perhaps instructing him
in my name to give it to the copyist *Wölfel* so that he may
finish the transcript which he has begun!—

Your encouragement concerning *Das Rheingold* was splendid:
—has it then really turned out well? I only hope there's
enough counterpoint in it to please Raff! [4] I'm terribly worried
about this.—

Marie is ill? [5]—How can I do anything to be of help to
her?—She ought to come and spend the summer on the
Seelisberg by the Lake of Lucerne: it is the most charming
discovery I have made in Switzerland; it is delightful up there,
so lovely—that I am full of longing to return up there,—to die
there!—

There we must meet next summer: I mean to write the
young Siegfried there: help me with it!! Perhaps then I will
help too!—How pure my heart is when I think of it!—Many
thanks to the Princess! at her wish, I am also enclosing the
autograph:—for the rest, no word about business! Isn't that
right? What do we care about such humbuggery?—

When shall I see your symphonic poems?—Your Faust?—
Farewell, my Franz!

Erich Kloss (ed.), *Briefwechsel zwischen Wagner und Liszt*, Vol. IX of
Richard Wagner: Briefe (Leipzig: Breitkopf & Härtel, [1910] 1912), Part
II, 42–44.—Tr. by editor.

213A JOHANNES BRAHMS TO CLARA SCHUMANN, BERLIN [G.]

Düsseldorf, 23 and 24 February 1855

My dearest friend,

I knew I should have so many wonderful things to tell you tonight that I'd never know how to begin.

I was with your beloved husband from 2 to 6 o'clock; if you could see my blissful face, you'd know more than my letter can tell you.

He received me as warmly and joyfully as the *first time*, only there did not follow the same agitation as then. Then at once he showed me your last letter and [told me] how much and how pleasantly you had surprised him. We talked at length about your travels. I told him I had seen you in Hamburg, Hanover, Lübeck and even in Rotterdam.[1] He asked particularly whether in Holland you had stayed in the *same rooms* as last winter?[2] I told him why you had mostly avoided it, which he found natural. He took great pleasure in the lovely Bach-Beethoven-Schumann programs.

Then I fetched him your picture. Oh if you had seen his deep emotion, how his eyes almost filled with tears and how he held it closer and closer and at last said: "Oh, how long have I wished for this." When he set it down, his hands were trembling very much.

He then kept looking at it and stood up often to gaze at it more closely.

The inkstand pleased him very much. Also the cigars; he maintained that he had not received any since Joachim's.

It is probable that he left some of them lying about, and (as he himself said also) he doesn't like to ask the doctors for anything. (He specifically added: "Clara certainly sent me some often, but I don't receive them.")

Then he invited me to go walking with him in the garden. What we now talked about I cannot possibly remember in its entirety! I think you'd find it hard to mention anything that did not turn up [in the conversation]. I also asked him very calmly whether he was composing anything? Then I learnt he'd written some fugues, but I was not to hear them, because they were not in order.

302

He spoke of you *much and often*. How "wonderfully" and "quite splendidly" you play, for ex. the canons, especially those in A flat and b, the Skizzen, "no one else plays *Des Abends* and *Traumeswirren* so well" etc. etc.[3] He inquired after all the children and laughed heartily over Felix's first tooth. He inquired especially after Miss Bertha, Miss Leser, Jungé and Schönerstedt, Joachim (and how!), Hasenclever etc. etc. Later he also inquired after Mayor Hammers, Nielo, Massenbach, etc., whether they are still in Düsseldorf!

He heard with great interest about Grimm's title, Becker etc.[4]

He told me a good deal concerning your travels, the Siebengebirge and Switzerland and Heidelberg, spoke also of the Countess Abegg.[5]

He looked over my C major sonata with me and pointed out several passages.

I asked him to let me have a word of greeting for you (in writing), and asked whether he wouldn't write you often?

"Oh, gladly, every day, constantly, if only I had some paper." And he really didn't have any. For he just doesn't like to ask the doctors for anything, and they of course won't give him something unless he asks for it.

And so I had some paper brought in, the large format made him very uncomfortable, and my way of reducing it didn't please him too much either. He sat down several times with the most friendly expression and tried to write. But he said he was too excited, that he'd write tomorrow.

I only hope that tomorrow won't be put off as long as usual.

Your husband marked with pencil in my notebook the things I was to get him.

A neckband; his usual one is not in good condition, and the one he was wearing "was too hospitaly for him!"

The *Signale;*[6] I'll look through this year's numbers and send them to him (selected), then [I'll] write Senff that Mr. Sch. wants to read the *Signale*.

We also spoke of the N[eue] Z[eitschrift] für Musik and what a lot of bustle and gossip it is. [We talked of his] "Gesänge der Frühe."[7]

He told me several times that Arnold ought not to wait

for his corrections, and so I told him he'd received them long ago.

But he maintained *very energetically* that Arnold couldn't have received them, for he'd given them to be sent a very long time ago, and so they [the pieces] would have been published long before now. [That] the doctors never sent anything off.

We argued back and forth for some time, I couldn't quite convince him.

Then, at my request, he wrote me the title:

Konzertstück [8] for Pianoforte and Orchestra

Op. 134

dedicated to

Johannes Brahms by

Robert.

Should I now send Senff the score etc. with the title?

He then asked me whether there were 20 volumes of his comp[ositions] high up in the cupboard; there was surely not enough room there for a 21st volume, otherwise indeed enough material: the Bach [violin] sonatas [with Schumann's accompaniments], the Cello and Violin Concertos, the Fughetten etc.

I offered to see to this, which seemed to please him very much; he refused "having it sent to him" with a smile, as though he'd enjoy it very very much anyway!

Shall we see to this when you return?

I told him you were in Berlin with J[oachim], which pleased him. He also enjoyed hearing about last Monday's B flat Symphony [performance] and about J.'s Variations. [9]

He spoke of Joachim with an enthusiasm comparable only to that which he has for you. He talked a lot about the Festival, how Joachim had already played so beautifully at the rehearsal. [10] No one had ever imagined such a tone was possible on the violin.

Then we even played a duet! He invited me to do the Caesar Overture. [11] But he didn't want to sit above, "I'm the bass." The ensemble was not very solid, but how long it is since he's played duets.

With her (you, that is) he used to play it faster, he said. He also praised the transcription very highly.

(I naturally told him nothing concerning the quintet.) [12]

304

The piano was very much out of tune, I saw to it that it would be tuned.

When I said good-bye to him, he insisted on seeing me to the station.

With the excuse that I had to fetch my coat, I asked the doctor downstairs whether he had any objection. He had none, which made me extremely happy.

(I did not speak [with the doctor] otherwise, I didn't even see him beforehand.)

The caretaker walked behind or next to us all the time. (A few steps away.)

I thought it was very nice that the heavy gate, which is always barred and locked, should have been left wide open when we left.

He made me take the programs [13] along with me, he said he knew each number, and that after all they belonged in your collection.

He wanted to give me back my Ballades [14] and was very pleased to learn they were for him.

(So many things still occur to me, I must still catch up; he was so happy that I had corrected and filled out his catalogue [of works] so painstakingly, also that I had copied "Die Glocke."

He enjoyed my Hungarian hat, just as he had the cap earlier etc.)

Imagine my bliss now, as I marched long and merrily with the dear man.

I did not look at my watch and assured him, when he asked, that I still had plenty of time, and so we walked to the Cathedral, to Beethoven's monument, and I walked him back to the highway.

He often used my spectacles, as he'd forgotten his lorgnette.

For the rest, Mr. Sch. walks at the well-known Brahmsian pace, which you so rarely can stand: very briskly!

On the way, he also asked me whether his Clara goes for a walk every day? I told him (though not quite truthfully!) that when you are with me in Düsseldorf or somewhere else, I take you for a walk every day, as you don't like to walk alone. "I can believe that, we always used to go walking together, before," your Robert said quite sadly.

We talked a great deal about his books and music, and he

was as happy as a king when he learnt I knew each single one
and its place. We teased each other a lot about this, as there
were certain books he couldn't at first remember and others
again that I could not.

I left him at the Endenich road, he embraced and kissed
me tenderly; as we parted he sent greetings only to you. He
had often done so earlier, also to Joachim, Bargiel, Miss Leser,
Bertha, Jungé, Schönerstedt. Many greetings to Dr. Hasenclever,
to everyone.

On my way I occasionally felt almost intoxicated, I was so
happy; you may well imagine how very much I wished you
were in Düsseldorf.

Your letter was a sheer joy to me, I felt as though I could
give you my hand.

I have nothing sad to write you, except that from time to
time he expressed a very urgent wish to come away, then he'd
speak more softly and less clearly, because he is afraid of the
doctors, yet he never said anything that was confused or
abstruse.

He spoke of how in March it would be a year since he
arrived at Endenich, it appeared to him that then the
countryside had already turned green, he'd had wonderful
weather, the loveliest blue sky.

Oh I can only write you quite plainly and drily what we
two talked about, the other, finer things I simply can't describe,
his wonderful quiet eyes, his warmth when he spoke of you,
his delight over the picture. Just imagine it all in the loveliest
way you can.

You will surely have no questions, after such a thorough
report? How I wish I had written more briefly, but more
beautifully.

But I wanted to write quickly and if possible everything.

Receive the heartfelt greetings of your Robert and myself,
content yourself with my good intentions, you know how gladly
I should make you happier.

With heartfelt love and devotion,

Your

Johannes.

Warmest greetings to dear Joachim.

[= Letters 209A-B], 78–85.—Tr. by editor.

213B   ROBERT SCHUMANN TO JOHANNES BRAHMS, DÜSSELDORF [G.]

Endenich, 11 March 1855

Dear friend!

I thank you for what you have sent me. The neckband fits well. And the "Signale" gave me much pleasure. I have already written to Clara and Joachim that this was all new to me. How is it that just the current volume, 1855, is so incomplete? Only Nos. 6, 8, 10, 11 and now I have received 12 in the post.

I intend writing to Dr. Härtel as soon as possible to offer him some things.[15] I don't exactly know whether the pieces for violoncello and pianoforte are called "Phantasiestücke." I am hesitant about one of them, the last, although it appears to me as the most significant; it is in D major, the first trio in A major, with wonderful basses (the violoncello sounded very well, not so the violin). I meant to ask you to have Fuchs copy the piece and to send it to me. Then I should like to approach Dr. Härtel concerning [your] Ballades [Op. 10] and tell him the plain truth, with moderation, if there is still time. The Scherzo [Brahms, Op. 4] too was a piece that had to be published, but one of your hardest as to tempo. I recently performed it to my satisfaction. And the trios![16] And the end! *Scherzo!* Isn't there any [copy of your] F-sharp minor sonata left, that is, that can be borrowed? Would you remind Clara of the Paganini Caprices,[17] that she should send them to me *soon* and, if you please, music paper (12-lined, actually 12 five-lined). I look forward to these very much. Simrock in Bonn have just put out the piano duet arrangement of the Festival Overture on the Rhine wine song [Op. 123]. My wife wrote me that she may already be able to have a new volume bound up. After Opus 123 she ought to start afresh; but on the back, the opus numbers in proper succession.

Our recent walk was not far, it ought to have been much farther. Away from here altogether! For over a year, since 4 March 1854, the very same way of life and the same view of Bonn. Away to another place! Think it over! Benrat is too near by, but perhaps Deutz, or Mühlheim.

307

Write to me soon! You say, dear Johannes, that I ought to think of you sometimes—sometimes from morning till evening. Well, good-bye until we meet soon again.   Your   R.

[= Letter 172], 406.—Tr. by editor.

214   RICHARD WAGNER TO ERNST BENEDIKT KIETZ, PARIS [G.]

Oh, Kietz!   [London, 27 April 1855]
    If I had turned back in Paris this last time, it would have been quite sensible: now I have to pay with terrible patience for the indiscretion of having let myself be tempted again. When I first arrived in London, I felt that I would have nothing to do here. My entire activity is limited to the direction of the eight concerts, the fourth of which takes place tomorrow; otherwise I haven't the least thing to occupy me. The concerts attract considerable attention, and the performances are as good as possible considering the short time for rehearsals: even my music to *Lohengrin*, of which I had to perform several excerpts in the second concert, met with success. But all this could be a true success only if I wanted to exploit it with all the means necessary here, or—to be more specific—if I could have a purpose here. But of that there can be no question whatever: to accept an engagement here as symphony and oratorio conductor and composer is far from my mind, now or at any other time. Beyond that there's nothing for me to do, and even a good German opera is quite out of the question. Thus the only thing left for me is to stick to the position—actually quite unsuitable for me—of a symphony conductor to the end. Then I'll see whether I'll have a few francs left with which to pay at least a part of the debt which originally was to have been paid off with this money; but it will turn out to be very little because of the enormously high taxes here and because I need much more than I at first believed. Besides, Mr. Albert Franck has located me here too and has reminded me in no uncertain terms to pay my debt: that's what you get out of it! Every time I earn 1 franc I must pay 10!
308

My acquaintances here are the following: 1. *Praeger,* a poor German lesson-giver! 2. *Lüders,* ditto. 3. *Sainton,* first violinist with the orchestra. 4. *Klindworth,* a pupil of Liszt who is only now looking for pupils, but cannot find any yet.[1] Otherwise I've really met no one: shall I send one of them to you to increase your fame and fortune? The press usually attacks me *à cause de* Mendelssohn and the other Jews who wish me eternal life. I'd have to do strange things in order to help you through the press here! Or through the German press? Oh, you crazy fellow! Of all people, I who *never* bother with the rabble of the press and have insulted every one of them! Be sensible and don't take me for something I'm not. It seems you have no idea of the *loneliness* in which I live!!!! Believe me that I'm sincerely happy about your successes, more than about my own: for yours can be useful to you—a thing which in my case can be true only in a very limited sense. I shall always be burdened with an extremely sad existence, I hope only for so long as my hopeless artistic productivity keeps me clinging to life again and yet again— only to torment me.

I found a true ray of light in your letter with the many good jokes about my appearance before the English: alas, how good it is to laugh again! I received your letter when I came home from the last concert with *Praeger* and *Lüders:* I read it to them immediately. That night, at the beginning of the concert, was the first time I kept my gloves on to conduct: I did that—out of malice—for a Mendelssohn symphony, a very bad symphony; but I took them off for the *Euryanthe* Overture.[2] Your advice especially made a very telling impression on us. Otherwise I am so put out of humor by my unsuitable position here that I don't even have any inclination for the work I brought along, which progresses very slowly: I am deeply disgusted with everything here, and I am more lonely than ever before. Greet Lindemann for me: tell him I'm not at all well. I only regret that his kind willingness to help me will never come to anything if we cannot live together for some time. Now I'm taking pills to counteract the English diet. Many thanks for your letter! In two months I'll see you again for a short time! Farewell and remain faithful to your London

                                        Symphony Conductor

[= Letter 205], 353–54.

215   HECTOR BERLIOZ TO THÉODORE RITTER, PARIS [Fr.]

London, Tuesday morning [3 July] 1855.

My dear Théodore,

(I detest nicknames, sobriquets, pet names, that is why I don't say: my dear Tintin.) Your letter gave me great pleasure, and if I am rather late in answering it is because, since you left, I have had a very bad time, plenty of visits, dinners and piano trios, correspondence in "The Musical World" with members of the amateur chorus as I would not let them sing in "Romeo and Juliet," luncheon at Beale's, piano rehearsals at Glover's,[1] riots in Regent's Park, a hundred arrests, workmen wanting to rescue their comrades, several hurt, my wife coming back in a fright, headache, reading Handel's "Samson," recrudescence of headache, yesterday an awful rehearsal at Exeter Hall, Glover's Cantata, style very piquant but difficult, I sweated till the gutters in the Strand overflowed, and the Finale of "Harold" and a fearsome concerto by Henselt performed by M. Klindworth [2] in a free style so that I was all on wires, for an hour on end, and Cooper, our first violin, who unable to contain himself any longer exclaimed: "Sempre tempo rubato!" and the cornets who couldn't come because of the military troupe in "l'Étoile du Nord" [3] which kept them at Covent Garden . . . you can't avoid "l'Étoile du Nord," soirée at Glover's where Meyerbeer was to come, excuses from the great man, alleging horrible colic, quotation from Heine's book, "le Marquis de la diarrée" (or "de la dyharr e") or some other spelling, (I know well enough that it is diarrhée!!!) [4] then at last Meyerbeer turning up when everybody had finished saying how sorry they were he couldn't come, congratulations on the end of his colic, wanderings in the London streets by moonlight, I go and rejoin my wife at Ernst's,[5] Mme. Ernst asks me if I like Molière, ye Gods!! and in a jiffy, well I will recite or declaim something of his: A scene from the "Misanthrope," after which the chessmen are brought up and Ernst sits down to the table with M. Louis Blanc [6] and there they are crouching over those stupid combinations till three in the morning, Ella's [7] Matinée where the said Ella presents to "his public" Meyerbeer between two Bishops, Wagner's departure, after honest Mr. Hogarth [8] had presented him in his

310

turn to M. Meyerbeer, asking the two Lions *whether they knew each other*,[9] Wagner's joy at leaving London, renewal of critics' fury against him after the last concert at Hanover Square, he conducts, of course, just as Klindworth plays the piano, in a free style, but he attracts one very much by his ideas and conversation, we go and drink punch at his place after the concert, he swears eternal friendship, he kisses me most affectionately, saying he used to be full of prejudice against me, he weeps, he prances, he is no sooner gone than "The Musical World" publishes the passage in his book in which he pulls me to pieces in the most diverting and witty fashion, frantic joy of Davison when translating same for my benefit,[10] "All the World's a stage," Shakespeare and Cervantes have said so, Ella gives me a present of a splendid book, the complete works of the said Shakespeare, "Poet," as they took the precaution to inform the visitors to the Crystal Palace.

W. SHAKESPEARE,
Poet! (very good of you to let me know)
and I shake you all by the hand, and I sign myself (as the Germans say) your very devoted

H. Berlioz, non-stop man of letters
. . . . God bless you and Farewell

A. W. Ganz, *Berlioz in London* (London: Quality Press Ltd, 1950), 203–205.

216   HECTOR BERLIOZ TO RICHARD WAGNER, ZURICH [Fr.]

[Paris,] 10 September 1855.

P.S.
And now, of course, I've had flocks of colorful thoughts which I'd like to send you. . . . I don't have time. Consider me an ass till further notice.

My dear Wagner

I enjoyed your letter tremendously. You are quite right in deploring my ignorance of German, and what you say concerning my incapacity to appreciate your works is just what I have been saying often to myself. The flower of expression nearly always fades under the weight of translation, however delicate the translation may be. There are accents, *in true music,* that want their special word, there are words that want their accent. To wrest them apart or to give them approximate equivalents is like having a goat suckle a little dog or the opposite. But there you are, I have an infernal time learning languages, it's a great deal if I can manage a few words in English and Italian. . . .

And so you are melting the glaciers, composing your Niebelungen [*sic*]! . . . It must be capital to write like that, in the presence of nature's immensity! . . . That is another joy denied me. Lovely landscapes, lofty peaks, grand vistas of the sea absorb me completely instead of provoking in me the manifestation of thought. At such times I feel and cannot express. I cannot sketch the moon except by observing its image at the bottom of a well.

I should like nothing better than to send you the scores which you ask for so kindly; unfortunately, my publishers have not given me any for a long time. But there are two and even three: The *Te Deum, L'Enfance du Christ,* and *Lélio* (*monodrame Lyrique*) which are about to appear in a few weeks, and those at least I shall be able to send you.

I received your Lohengrin; if you could have your Tanhäuser [*sic*] sent to me I should be delighted. The reunion you suggest would be a treat, but I must beware not to consider it. I have to take some displeasure trips in order to earn a living, as Paris produces nothing but ashen fruit for me.

Never mind, if we could live another hundred years or so, I believe we should get the better of many things and many people. Old Demiurge, up there, must be having many a good laugh in his sleeve at the constant success his old tricks have on us . . . . but I won't speak ill of him, he's one of your friends, and I know you protect him. I'm not pious, yet I'm full of respect for the Pius.[1] Forgive the ghastly pun with which (and with a firm handshake) I shall close. Yours ever

Hector Berlioz
19 rue de Boursault Paris

Bayreuther Blätter, XXVIII (1905), 279–80.—Tr. by editor.

217A   JOHANNES BRAHMS TO JOSEPH JOACHIM, HEIDELBERG [G.] [Telegram]

[Bonn, 28 July 1856]

IF YOU WANT TO SEE SCHUMANN ALIVE COME IMMEDIATELY.
CONSIDER YOUR HEALTH. WE ARE IN BONN DEUTSCHES HAUS.

BRAHMS

Andreas Moser (ed.), *Johannes Brahms im Briefwechsel mit Joseph Joachim*
(Berlin: Verlag der Deutschen Brahms-Gesellschaft m.b.H., 1912), I, 159.
—Tr. by editor.

217B   JOSEPH JOACHIM TO GISELA VON ARNIM, BERLIN [G.]

Bonn, Wednesday [30 July 1856]

The day before yesterday Brahms telegraphed to me that
Schumann was dangerously ill, and I came here yesterday. His
wife was here; when we got to Endenich at 4:30 in the afternoon
he had just passed away. On the last day he appears to have sunk
softly and gradually to sleep. His face was gentle and peaceful;
my last impression of the beloved master is grave but calm;
his life was pure as few others have been.

While my plans are uncertain I have ordered all letters from
Heidelberg to be sent to *Hanover*. Your letter had not yet
reached me; you will hear what I am going to do tomorrow.
There is much to see to—this is just a line.

Your mother will be shocked by the news; you will know how
to tell her.

Your friend,

J. J.

[= Letter 211], 130.

218   HECTOR BERLIOZ TO A JOURNALIST, PARIS [Fr.]

[Paris,] 24 Nov: 1857

If the *Figaro*[1] dinner could restore the body—that *rag*—I should bestride a broom without hesitation and join the witches' sabbath that you are initiating, even if my mind were to remain in the pitiable state in which it unfortunately is.

But I happen to be suffering like a demon who is compelled to take a hip bath in a stoup of holy water. There may be hardly a nosegay of *watercress* at your dinner, so I must prudently beg you to accept my regrets. Rag though it is, my rag is dear to me.[2]

Faithfully,

H. Berlioz

[= Letter 173], 191.

219   GEORGES BIZET TO HIS MOTHER, PARIS [Fr.]

Rome, 11 March 1858

Dear mamma,

You urge me not to hide from you any troubles I might have. But to whom would I tell them if not to you? Happily, I don't have any such disclosures for you, this time.

The weather is too rotten even for a dog! That is the reason for my silence concerning Rome. It is impossible to view the eternal city without sunshine: without it everything seems sad; the very masterpieces of art seem to borrow all their magnificence from it. And so, I was glad to take advantage of a few sunbeams to visit the *Foro Romano,* Nerva's Forum, Trajan's Forum, the Villa Ludovisi, Saint Peter's basilica, etc., and finally the Vatican.

The Vatican is the most beautiful and most immense museum in the world. It contains, besides the masterpieces of Raphael, of Domenichino, besides the numerous museums of antiquities, it contains its Sistine Chapel: that is where Michelangelo's admirable frescoes are, the "Last Judgment," the "Prophets" and the "Sybils," and the ceiling made up of medallions repre-

senting the Creation, the Flood, and the principal events in
Genesis, which form, not counting some hundred figures that
hold up the medallions, the immense work accomplished in three
years by the greatest artistic genius of Italy and of the whole
world. The impression I received was profound. I had seen some
splendid things in Florence, but I had expected them, while
Michelangelo! . . . To be sure, Raphael is full of gracefulness,
he is the ideal of beauty and purity, like Andrea del Sarto; but
for me, the author of the decorations in the Sistine Chapel, of
the Medici tombs in Florence, of Saint Peter's cupola, the man
who, with these three works, proved himself the greatest painter
together with Raphael, the greatest sculptor and the greatest
architect of Italy, he, I say, must rank above all the others.
He is the king of art in general.

You are right to urge me not to be lazy, but I go into society
almost every evening. At M. de Sampayo's, I made the acquaintance of M. the count de Kisseleff, the Russian ambassador.
He is a charming man. I have already dined twice at his home
and shall redine [sic] there tomorrow.

I'm sweating away at my *Te Deum* like a slave. It's devilishly
difficult and I long to be done with it, so that I can begin an
Italian opera in three acts whose book I like very much. I have
written to Ludovic Halévy and to Jules Cohen, begging them
to ask [Fromental] Halévy for fresh details on the Prix
Rodrigues, which exists [sic] and for which I am writing my
Te Deum.[1]

I don't know what is meant by the beauties of the Roman
carnival. I have told you of its gaiety, its animation, its originality: that is all one can say about it.

I became much thinner during the voyage and am not recovering; that makes me anxious. I took coffee for a week; it
reduced me to a hideous state, and I shall never again make
similar experiments. I haven't taken any for the past three weeks
and have been in excellent health. That charming fellow, Moreau,
comes to see me often, and we treat ourselves to whole scores.[2]

I shall not go to Naples till next summer, since, if I get the
Prix Rodrigues, I can make my way as far as Sicily; this summer
I shall spend a fortnight at Tivoli, as long again at Ostia, etc.,
etc. It will be delightful. And, to conclude, great news! Our
allowances are to be increased, beginning next January 1st.
What luck for me! here is a reform that has been discussed for

the past twenty years, and they decide to adopt it just when I can profit by it.

They will do well, since, for the unlucky painters and sculptors, it is untenable . . . Here is the situation. Our pension is two hundred francs a month (in Italy). We come to this:

Board	75
Wine	25
Maintenance	25
Piano	15
Washing	5
Wood (wood is extravagantly dear here), candles, postage stamps	10
Gloves, [tips] to the servant, etc.	5
Loss on the money [exchange]	5
	165

That leaves thirty-five francs, from which one must still shave off the five francs everybody pays to the fund for common expenses, cigars, gratuities to the keepers at monuments, etc., and we barely make both ends meet. For a musician who is well equipped with everything as I am, *it is quite enough and I am not complaining in the least;* but for the painters, who must pay one franc fifty an hour to the models, it is frightful: for their last-year *envoi*[3] they spend five hundred francs on models and materials. And they must also go to Paris, quite apart from their *envois*. The musician has an indemnification of fifty francs for his *envoi*, which costs him nothing, and the painters get little more. And so the increase is being awaited with impatience. It will consist of forty francs a month. We musicians shall have enough so that we can live like lords.

I shall be short of money only for the trip to Naples, but here is what I mean to do. If I don't get the Prix Rodrigues, I shall obtain an advance of two hundred francs on my maintenance. If, on the other hand, I get the prize, I'll keep all of my maintenance for two years: six hundred francs which, added to the six hundred francs' indemnification I'll receive when I go to Germany,[4] will give me twelve hundred francs beyond my pension. I will, therefore, be able to bring a thousand-franc note back to Paris; enough to supply me with linen and clothes while awaiting *my successes at the Opéra-Comique and at the Opéra.* You can see that the situation is quite favorable and that, for the moment, it would be graceless to complain.

And now a quick adieu, as I have no more space. Take both of you good care of yourselves and be assured that I am your affectionate son for life,

Georges Bizet

Louis Ganderax (ed.), *Lettres de Georges Bizet: Impressions de Rome (1857–1860), la Commune (1871)* (Paris: Calmann-Lévy, Éditeurs, 1907), 40–46. —Tr. by editor.

220   JOHANNES BRAHMS TO JOSEPH JOACHIM, HANOVER [G.]

[Leipzig,] Friday morning [28 January 1859]

Dearest friend,

Although I am still quite dazed by the sublime delights with which my eyes and ears have been assailed for the last few days through the sight and sound of the wise men of our musical town, I will force this hard and pointed steel pen of Sahr's to relate to you how it came about that here my concerto has been a brilliant and decisive—failure.

First of all, it was really done very well, I played far better than I did at Hanover, and the orchestra was excellent.

The first rehearsal excited no kind of feeling either in the performers or in the audience. No audience at all came to the 2nd, however, and not a performer moved a muscle of his face.

In the evening Cherubini's Elisa Overture was done, then an Ave Maria by him was sung languidly, so I hoped that Pfund's drums would come opportunely.[1] The first and 2nd movements were listened to without the slightest display of feeling. At the conclusion three pairs of hands were brought together very slowly, whereupon a perfectly distinct hissing from all sides forbade any such demonstration.

There is nothing more to say about this episode, for not a soul has said a word to me about the work! with the exception of David,[2] who was very friendly and took a great deal of interest in it and went to a lot of trouble about it.

Neither Rietz nor Wenzel, Senff, Dreyschock, Grützmacher, Röntgen, have made even the most casual remark. I asked Sahr a few questions this morning and was pleased at his frankness.[3]

317

This failure has made no impression whatever on me, and any feeling of depression I may have had vanished when I heard a C major symphony by Haydn and [Beethoven's] Ruins of Athens. In spite of everything the concerto will meet with approval when I have improved its bodily structure, and the next one will sound quite differently.

I believe this is the best thing that could happen to one; it forces one to concentrate one's thoughts properly and increases one's courage. After all, I am only experimenting and feeling my way as yet. But the hissing was too much of a good thing, wasn't it?

Your letter, which I received at the tavern yesterday evening, was very soothing, and I did not feel in the least annoyed with Hermann, etc., who all drank with me loyally and said not a word about the concerto etc.

Frau Schumann, I am told here, is still in Vienna; I wish she could have been here! By now you must have received an answer concerning Enzio. Regards have been and are being seen to.

The faces here looked terribly solemn when I came from Hanover, after having been used to seeing yours. I am going to Hamburg on Monday. There is to be some interesting church music here on Sunday, and in the evening a performance of Faust at Frau Frege's.[4]

Please send me Hanover newspapers at Hamburg.

I shall write again from there. My warmest greetings, dear fellow! Greet Zillinger, Emmaah etc. etc.

Your Johannes.
(In haste.)

As for the Hamburg concert, whatever you prefer!
(Hohe Fuhlentwiete 74 in Hamburg.)

[= Letter 211], 179–81, extensively revised by present editor in accordance with the original printed in Moser [= Letter 217A], 232–34.

PLATES

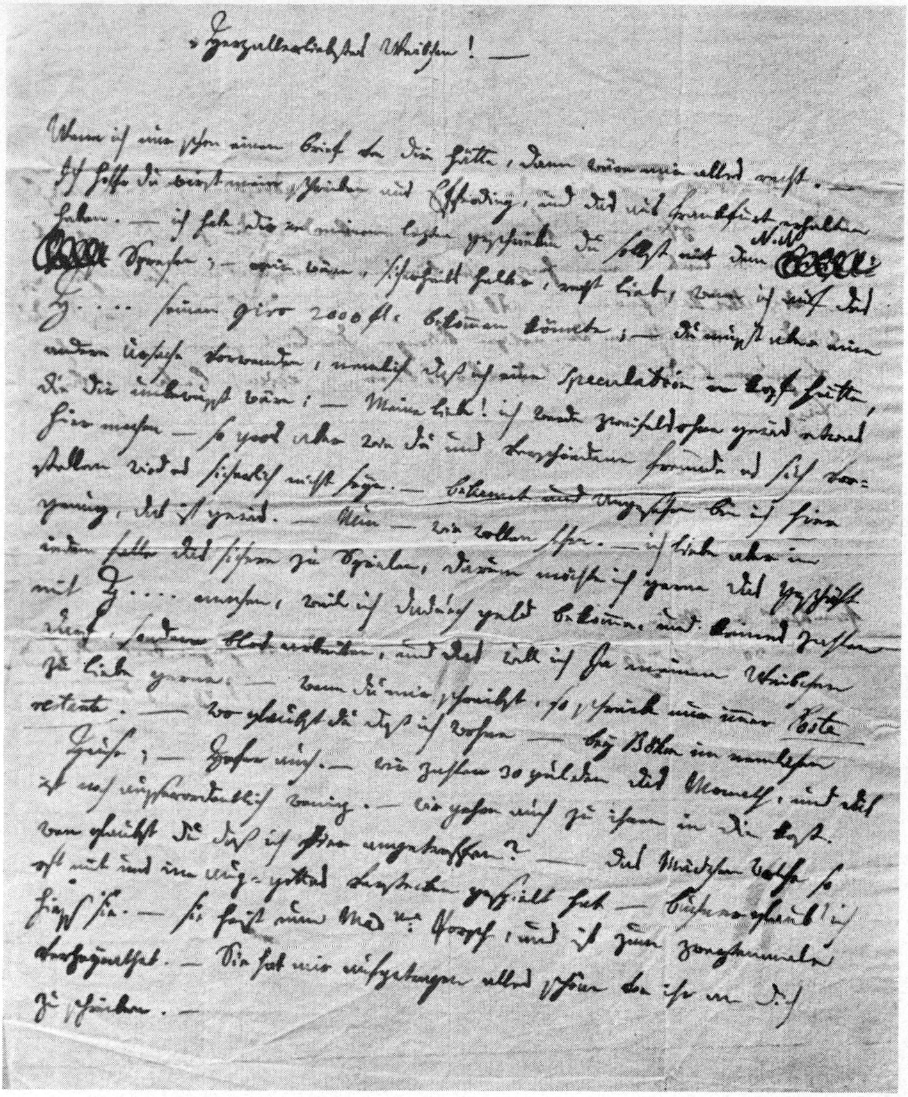

Arturo Toscanini Collection, New York

Mozart to his wife, 30 Sep. 1790 (Letter 107): recto

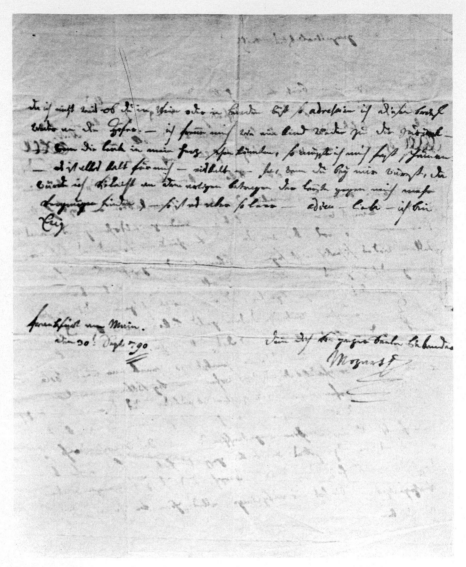

Arturo Toscanini Collection, New York

Mozart to his wife, 30 Sep. 1790 (Letter 107): verso

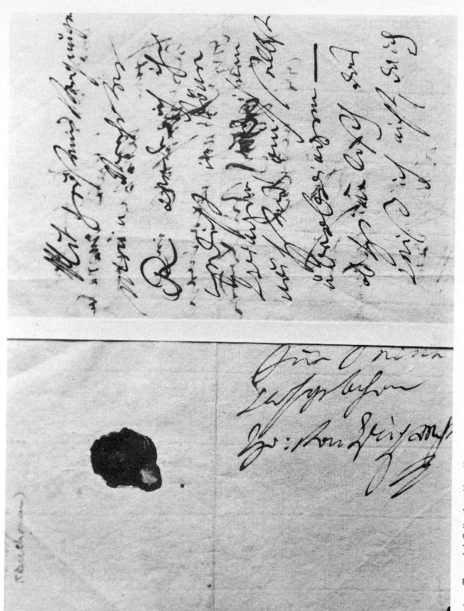

Arturo Toscanini Collection, New York

Beethoven to J. B. Rupprecht, [*c.* 22 Dec. 1814] (Letter 130) : address (with Beethoven's seal) and p. 1

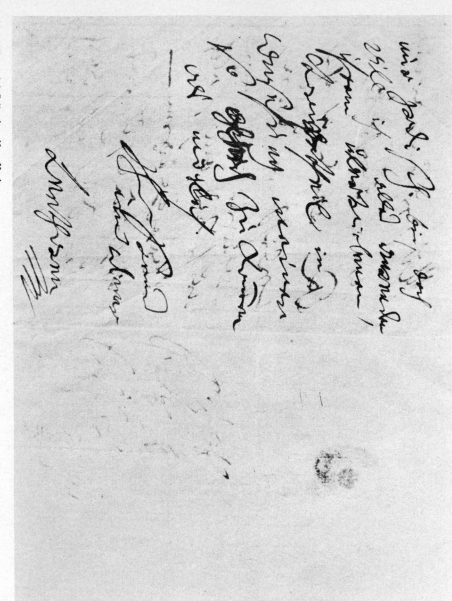

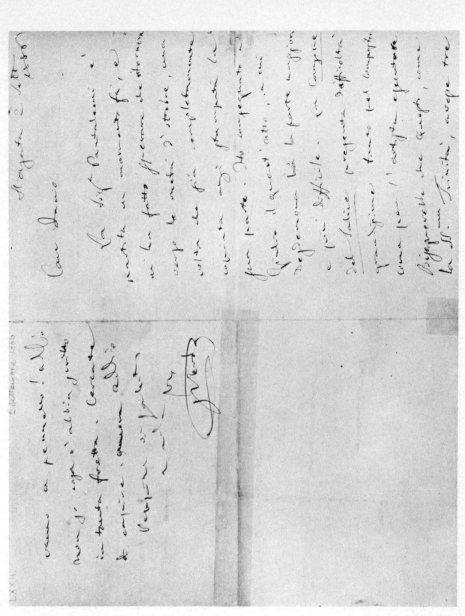

Verdi to Franco Faccio, 2 Sep. 1886 (Letter 267) : p. 1 (right), p. 4 (left)

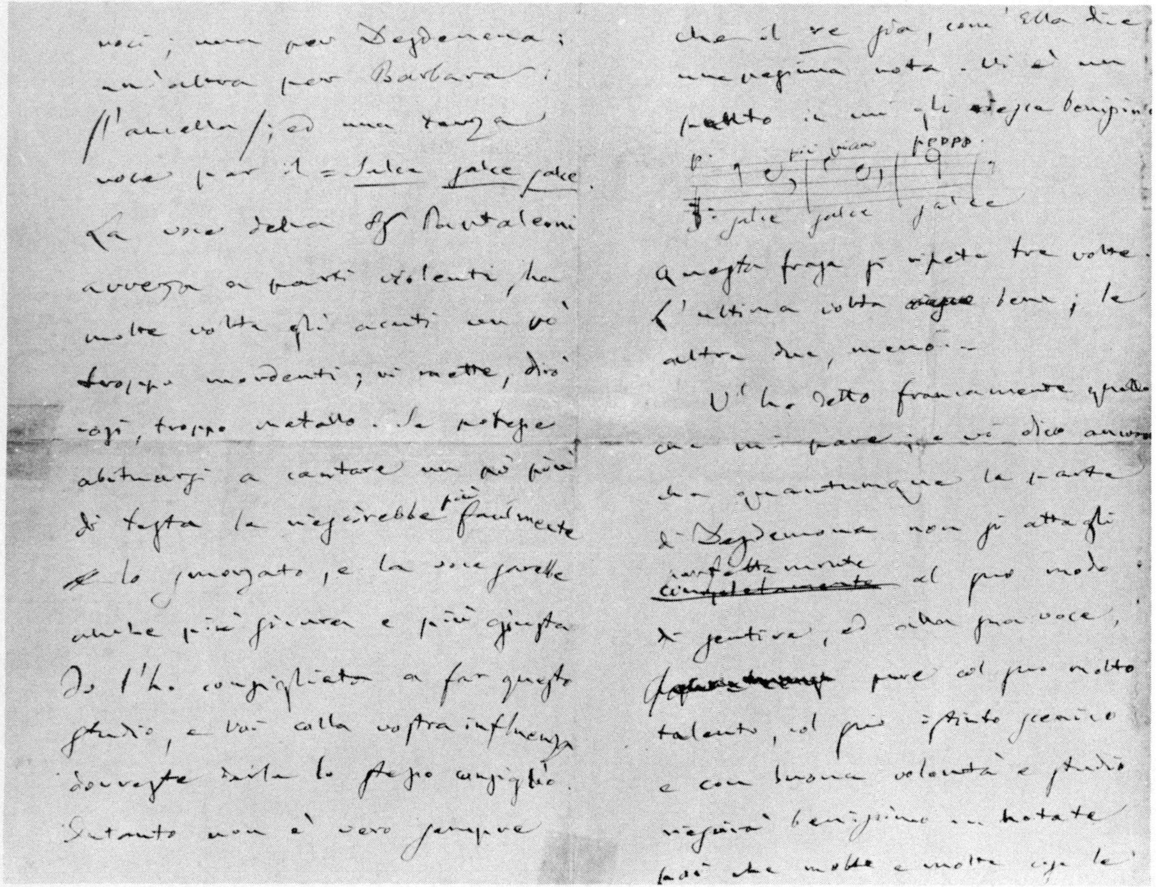

voci; una per Desdemona;
un'altra per Barbara
(l'ancella); ed una terza
voce per il = Salce salce salce.
La voce della Sig. Pantaleoni
avvezza a parti violenti, ha
molte volte gli acuti un po'
troppo mordenti; vi mette, dirò
così, troppo metallo. Se potesse
abituarsi a cantare un po' più
di testa le riescirebbe più facilmente
lo smorzato, e la voce sarebbe
anche più sicura e più giusta.
Io l'ho consigliata a far questo
studio, e voi colla vostra influenza
dovreste darle lo stesso consiglio.
Intanto non è vero sempre

che il re sia, come Ella dice,
una pessima nota. Vi è un
pezzetto in cui gli sta benissimo

Questa frase si ripete tre volte.
L'ultima volta ~~[illegible]~~ bene; le
altre due, meno.
V'ho detto francamente quello
che mi pare, e vi dico ancora
che quantunque la parte
di Desdemona non si attagli
perfettamente ~~completamente~~ al suo modo
di sentire, ed alla sua voce,
~~[illegible]~~ pure col suo molto
talento, col suo istinto scenico
e con buona volontà e studio
riescirà benissimo in notate
così che molte e molte cose le

Arturo Toscanini Collection, New York

Verdi to Franco Faccio, 2 Sep. 1886 (Letter 267): pp. 2 and 3

Berg to Paul Hohenberg, 12 Nov. 1912 (Letter 298) : p. 1 (right), p. 4 (left)

Suzanne Szekely Collection, New York

Berg to Paul Hohenberg, 12 Nov. 1912 (Letter 298): pp. 2 and 3

Mon cher ami,

J'ai appris dernièrement qu'il
s'est une «affaire Toscanini-Ravel».

Nous l'ignorions sans doute vous-même,
bien qu'on m'ait assuré que les journaux
en avaient parlé : il paraît que vous
en refusiez de me lever lorsque l'on
m'a présenté à l'Opéra, c'était pour
vous punir de n'avoir pas pris le
mouvement exact du Boléro.

J'ai toujours estimé que ai

LE BELVÉDÈRE
MONTFORT L'AMAURY (S.&O.)
9/9/30

L'auteur ne prend pas part à l'exécution
de son œuvre, il doit se dérober aux
ovations qui s'adressent ou bien à l'interprète ou à l'œuvre,
ou aux deux.

Malheureusement, j'étais mal en
plus trop loin pour que mon
abstention ne fût pas remarquée.

Pourtant, tenant à ce que mon
attitude ne devint rien à l'ironique
j'effectuai, tourné vers vous, de
vous applaudir et de vous remercier.

Mais, n'est-ce pas? de
malignité ou plutôt mieux que le

Arturo Toscanini Collection, New York

Ravel to Arturo Toscanini, 9 Sep. 1930 (Letter 312): pp. 1 and 2

Arturo Toscanini Collection, New York

Ravel to Arturo Toscanini, 9 Sep. 1930 (Letter 312): p. 3

221   GIUSEPPE VERDI TO VINCENZO JACOVACCI, ROME [It.]

Busseto, 5 June 1859.

Dear Jacovacci,

You were wrong to defend *Un Ballo in maschera* against the newspapers' attacks. You should have done as I always do: not read them, or else let them sing the tune they like best, which is another thing I've always done! Besides, this is the question: the opera is either *bad* or *good*. If it's bad, and the journalists spoke badly of it, they were right; if good, and they preferred not to appreciate it because of their own or other peoples' whims or for any other reason, it was better to let them have their say and not mind them. You must admit besides that if anyone or anything needed defending during the carnival season, it was the worthless company you made me a present of. Consult your conscience, and confess that I was a model of unusual forbearance; I might otherwise have taken my score and gone looking for singers less rotten than the ones you offered me. But *post factum,* and all that etc. . .

I'm sorry, but I can't write Ricordi[1] about lowering the rental fees, as it is not my habit to engage in this sort of business. Besides, the prices you are offering for *Aroldo,* [*Simon*] *Boccanegra* and *Ballo in maschera* seem to me (poor as those operas may be) too modest. I don't know whether Ricordi will share my view; if so, then he'll say, as I do, and as you yourself say, that *you ought to make different arrangements.* Should you, when you apply elsewhere, meet with further demands which you consider excessive, then rummage about in the old classical repertory which has fallen into the public domain, and you'll get off cheap. You need three operas? Here they are: *Nina Pazza* by Paisiello, *Armide* by Gluck, *Alceste* by Lulli. With these, apart from economic considerations, you may be sure you won't need to fight against journalists or anyone else. The music is lovely, the composers are dead, everybody has spoken well of them for the past hundred or two hundred years and will continue to speak well of them, if

319

only to speak ill of those who have not yet committed the blunder of dying.

Farewell my dear Jacovacci. Let us not think about new operas.

[= Letter 202], 575–76.—Tr. by editor.

222A　FRANZ LISZT TO RICHARD WAGNER, PARIS [G.]
[Telegram]

WEIMAR 22 MAY [1860]
CORDIAL WISHES ON YOUR BIRTHDAY FROM YOUR
FRANZ LISZT

[= Letter 212], 280.—Tr. by editor.

222B　RICHARD WAGNER TO FRANZ LISZT, WEIMAR [G.]

Paris
22 May [18]60.

My dearest Franz!

That was quite wonderful! I have just given Madame Street-Klindworth a commission which brought me very close to you. For they have taken an excellent photograph of me in Brussels, of which they sent me only one copy. The Wesendoncks [1] are in Rome now and are soon returning to Zurich: I wanted my portrait sent to them and asked Mad. Street to send one over there from Brussels. She then informed me that there was a second one at my disposal. To whom shall I send it? said I to myself. Believe it or not, I could think only of allotting it to *you*. This will tell you much about my vanity, but also how, and in what spirit, I am thinking of you!—

This is unquestionably the loveliest day we have had this year. For the first time, the sky is quite clear, a refreshing breeze is blowing from the east: everything is blooming and

turning green! As I was returning from my morning walk
with Fipps,[2] I said to myself: "It can't get lovelier than it is
now, this year! If it's as lovely everywhere else, then many
people will be thinking of you instinctively, today!" I did
not quite dare to hope as much from you; it was on my
conscience that on 22 October,[3] though I was thinking of
you, I had not written. Why? I can't remember. "Well," I
thought, "he'll at least be thinking of me! And he does have
Tristan: [4]—what more can a crazy fellow like myself expect?"
—Then I read Berlioz's latest feuilleton (today's) on Fidelio.
I haven't met Berlioz since my concert: [5] before that, it was
always I who had to look him up or invite him,—*he* never troubled
himself over me. He had made me very sad: I was not angry
with him; I merely asked myself whether the dear Lord might
not have done better to exclude women from his creation:
they are awfully seldom of any use; but mostly, as a rule, they
harm us, and in the end derive no profit for themselves. I had
again been able to study this with all but anatomic precision
in the case of Berlioz—how a wicked lady is able to ruin a
perfectly brilliant man quite to her heart's content and bring
him down to the level of the ridiculous.[6] What kind of
satisfaction can such a poor man find in it? The sad one,
perhaps, of having brought into play the sickest portion of his
essence with much flamboyance!—As I was saying, I have not
seen Berlioz since then. Then today I read his article. I was so
pleased by it, that I wrote him the following note in my
horrible French, certain that he would misunderstand me
colossally:

"Cher Maître! (for I know that my intimacy has grown
gênant to him.) [Fr.:] I have just read your article on Fidelio.
Be thanked a thousand times! It is a quite special joy for me
to hear these pure and noble accents, the expression of a soul
with an intelligence which so perfectly understands and makes
its own the most intimate secrets of another hero of the Art:
there are times when I am nearly more transported on learning
of this act of appreciation than by the appreciated work
itself, for it infallibly shows us that an uninterrupted chain of
intimate kinship ties together all great souls, which—through
this bond alone—shall never sink into incomprehension.—If
I express myself badly, I yet hope that you will understand
me not badly."—[7]

[G.:] Now God knows how he will take to this gibberish: this time, at least, if he chooses not to understand me, I'm afraid I'll have given him good grounds with my French. Nevertheless, it filled me with a special warmth to send these lines to the unfortunate man. And so I continued in this quiet contentment, all at the expense of the lovely day: life's darkest shadows resolved themselves brightly. Berlioz's article, especially, had once more clearly shown me how lonely the unfortunate man is; and that he too has such sensitive and deep feelings that the world can only hurt him and misuse his wounded irritability; that the world and the influences of his environment lead him wonderfully astray, and can so estrange him from himself that, unknowingly, he deals himself blows.[8] But exactly because of this queer phenomenon, I realized that great talents must, to be properly recognized, have only very great talents for their friends; and this afforded me the insight that, in the present period, we alone are on a par; that is—You—He—and I!—But this is the last thing one can tell him: he'll lash out, if he hears it. Poor devil: such a plagued god!—

See, dearest friend, I had come to this—: then came your dispatch with the congratulations!! Dear fellow, it is an ineffable joy to me that you not only thought of me so kindly again this time, but pleased me by communicating it to me the same day!—You dear, good, unique man! Tell me, *when* shall I see you again? Must I first express my rage to you, because you won't come?—

Now I can't write you anything else; I'm very hot and— if you like—off my rocker! The rest, after all, is of no value, and hardly worth "wagging chins" over. But I'll write soon again, if thus I can hope to entertain you. Many, many joyful thanks

from your
RW

AUTOGRAPH, Arturo Toscanini Collection, New York: 2 sheets, 254 × 202 mm., folded to form 8 pp.; last p. blank.—Tr. by editor.

222C   HECTOR BERLIOZ TO RICHARD WAGNER, PARIS [Fr.]

[Paris, 23 May 1860]

My dear Wagner

I am so pleased that you liked my articles on Fidelio. I had expended some care over them, but without the expectation that they might be the least bit useful. I have given up believing in the educability of the public by the critics; or at least I think a long time must pass before criticism bears fruit. I don't know whether you still have any illusions; as for myself, I have for some years been seeing things as they are. . . . . . You at least are full of fervor, disposed to fight; I am only disposed to sleep and to die. Nevertheless, an almost feverish joy still pervades me if, when I cry for love of the beautiful, a distant voice answers me and lets me hear an assenting, friendly salute across the vulgar din. And so, thank you for your letter; it did me good. I thought you were still in Belgium. Since we last saw each other, I have been very ill, very sad, very tormented in a thousand ways. . . . . Why, when you wrote, did you say: cher maître, like those who stand on ceremony? between us, that won't do.

So yesterday was your birthday? you Germans pay much attention to the recurrence of those days. It does give one an opportunity to manifest tender family feelings, if one has a family, and friendly feelings, if one has friends.

Well then, see what kind of a man I am; I have a family, I have splendid friends, yet if I had thirty birthdays within the year no one would dream of celebrating even one of them, so well do they know how I dislike all that . . . don't laugh; I am so ill.

Adieu, good day, be of good cheer; and don't say: cher maître any more. It sets me on edge.

Friendliest wishes, yours ever

Hector Berlioz

23 May 1860

[= Letter 216], 285–86.—Tr. by editor.

223   CHARLES GOUNOD TO RICHARD WAGNER,
PARIS [Fr.]

[Paris,] Monday 18 March [18]61.
My dear and illustrious friend.

I am both honored and touched by the gift you have so
kindly made me of your two scores, Tannhäuser and Tristan
et Yseult: I am proud that a man of your high worth should
have considered me capable of joining him in intellectual
fellowship, and I do so, let me assure you, with all the esteem
which your indefatigable courage and noble convictions
deserve.

Believe in my most sincere devotion.

Ch. Gounod.

[= Letter 216], 286.—Tr. by editor.

224   RICHARD WAGNER TO CHARLES BAUDELAIRE,
PARIS [Fr.]

Paris, 15 April 1861.
My dear Monsieur Baudelaire!

I called on you several times but never found you at home.
You can imagine how very much I want to tell you of the
immense satisfaction you gave me with your article which
does me honor and encourages me more than anything that
has ever been said before concerning my modest talent. Would
it not be possible to tell you soon, *viva voce*, how elated I
felt when I read those fine pages, which described for me,
in the manner of the best poetry—the impressions I may flatter
myself to have produced upon so superior a nature as your
own?

Be thanked a thousand times for this benefaction and believe
that I am proud indeed that I may call you a friend.

Till we meet, then? Yours most sincerely

Richard Wagner.

Wilhelm Weigand, "Eine französische Schrift über Tannhäuser," *Neue
Zeitschrift für Musik,* LXXXV (1889), 3.—Tr. by editor.

225   GIUSEPPE VERDI TO FRANCESCO MARIA PIAVE, MILAN [It.]

Dear Piave
> St. Petersburg, 7 D[ecember] 1861

I arrived here yesterday, after a very pleasant voyage. Nothing troubled us except (strangely enough) a little hot weather. De Bassini and Marini came to meet us at nine hours' distance from St. Petersburg, and when we arrived here we found Tamberlich and many artists, and many orchestral players at the station.[1] It was six o'clock in the morning, and when we got home we had a good cup of Coffee . . . and to bed.—I have a marvelous apartment, kept warm at 13 to 14 degrees,[2] an eternal springtime; [and] two excellent horses that go like lightning. Tamberlich tells me he'll write you and send you the thousand francs. *Inter nos,* he gave me to understand that you made a rather too blood-thirsty job of it.[3]

I'm waiting for those few verses . . . hurry up—

My regards to Ricordi[4] to whom I'll write later—farewell, farewell

Give me your news. .

> G. Verdi

AUTOGRAPH, Ottocaro Weiss Collection, New York: 1 sheet, 269 × 209 mm., folded to form 4 pp.; p. 3 blank; p. 4 has address.—Tr. by editor.

226   GIUSEPPE VERDI TO COUNT OPPRANDINO ARRIVABENE, TURIN [It.]

London, 2 May 1862

Dear Arrivabene,

I thought you would congratulate me because my Cantata was not performed at the Exhibition, but instead you attach more importance to this affair, in my opinion, than it deserves. I have always thought, and still do, that these occasional pieces are detestable things from the artistic viewpoint; and you may be sure that one's attention is too abstracted in these boundless halls, and nothing is, nothing can be, and—to say it outright—nothing *has* been impressive. And this is why I never wanted to write such pieces; and having this time fallen into the trap myself, when I found out upon reaching London that the Commissioners had refused the Cantata, I exclaimed: I'm safe! The day after my arrival I saw my placid [friend] Maggioni, and he told me that the *Times* was accusing me of still not having sent in my music; and so I picked up my pen as calmly as you please and wrote that letter you know of, which Maggioni translated and the *Times* kindly published! I wish I had not done it! It has been a millstone round my neck, and it brought me a hoard of letters the next day, reviling the Commission and Costa; [1] and what is more, requests for autographs from every quarter, in a most singular and wholly British manner. In other countries, those who want autographs get themselves introduced or have their *albums* presented by an acquaintance. Here, nothing of the kind: they send me letters by mail, and inside there's a stamped envelope with the address of the person for whose benefit I'm supposed to write the autograph. I don't know who the devil they may be. Add to this that all these letters are in English (always on account of that blasted letter to the *Times*) and the consequence is another millstone for Peppina [2] who must translate them for me.

And as for Italy, her music needs no performing at the Exhibition. It gets performed here every evening at two theaters, and not only here, but everywhere; for, in spite of the present decadence which the *Scholars!* have discovered, never before at any time have there been so many Italian opera houses, never have Publishers of every country printed and sold so much Italian music; and there isn't a corner of this earth where there's a theater and a couple of instruments and no Italian opera being sung. If you should ever go to the Indies or to the interior of Africa, you'll hear *Il Trovatore*.

My Cantata has been sold here to the Publisher *Cramer Beale* [Cramer, Beale & Chappell]. What he [*sic*] intends doing with it I don't know; he'll probably try to make a profit on it, and they say it will be performed at the Queen's Theater [Her Majesty's Theatre], but so far I know nothing whatever about it. [3] I'll write you if that should be the case.

I've been to the Exhibition once, but everything is too disordered for me to tell you anything on the subject.

So far, the most interesting objects are broken crates, rollers, heaps of straw, porters you have to look out for to avoid getting your ribs broken, and drops of water which fall from the glass roof to refresh the noses of the curious.

The place is absolutely dismal in all its vastness. Farewell and write to me and receive my affectionate greetings.

G. Verdi

Peppina is well and sends her best wishes.

Annibale Alberti (ed.), *Verdi intimo: carteggio di Giuseppe Verdi con il conte Opprandino Arrivabene* ([Milan:] A. Mondadori, 1931), 15–17.—Tr. by editor.

227   JOHANNES BRAHMS TO ALBERT DIETRICH, OLDENBURG [G.]

Dear Friend,   [Hamburg, before 8 September 1862]

On Monday I am going *to Vienna!* At that thought I am as happy as a child!

Of course I do not know how long I shall stay there; we shall have to dwell in uncertainty but hope that we shall still see each other sometime this winter.

The symphony in C minor is not finished, but a string quintet in F minor (2 V. Celli) is, and I should like nothing better than to send it to you and have you write me about it; still, I had better take it with me.[1]

You shall have it presently.

Enclosed are my "Handel Variations"; the Marienlieder have not yet come.[2]

The title page of your trio is still unfinished.[3]

Greet the Oldenburg friends.

I beg you not to leave me quite without letters. For the present you could write through Haslinger or Wessely & Büsing.

Meanwhile I bid you, dear Albert, and your wife, a hearty farewell.

Your Johannes.

Albert Dietrich and J. V. Widmann, *Recollections of Johannes Brahms,* trans. Dora E. Hecht (London: Seeley and Co. Limited, 1899), 51–52.

228   HECTOR BERLIOZ TO GUSTAVE FLAUBERT, PARIS [Fr.]

Paris, 4 November 1862

My dear M. Flaubert,

I wanted to hurry over to your house today but couldn't. Yet I do not want to wait any longer to tell you that your book has filled me with admiration, wonder, and even terror. . . It frightens me and I have dreamed about it these nights past. What a style! What archeological knowledge! What imagination! I say your mysterious Salammbô, with her secret, unwilling love, mixed with repulsion, for the enemy who has violated her, is a creation of highest poetry, and at the same time wholly within the bounds of veritable truth.

Allow me to shake your mighty hand and to subscribe myself your devoted admirer.

Hector Berlioz

P.S. Now let any one dare malign our language! . . .

[= Letter 173], 221–23.

229   JOHANNES BRAHMS TO HIS PARENTS, HAMBURG [G.]

[Vienna, 30 November 1862]

Dear parents,

I was very pleased yesterday, my concert went remarkably well, far better than I had hoped.

After the Quartet had been received in the friendliest way, I made an excellent impression as a pianist. Each number was roundly applauded; I believe there was real enthusiasm in the hall.

Now, of course, I could give concerts quite easily, but I don't feel like it, for it would occupy too much of my time, so that I should not have any left over for anything else.

I understand I recovered the concert's expenses; for the rest, the hall was of course filled with free tickets.

I played as freely as though I'd been sitting at home among friends, and this public is naturally much more stimulating than ours.

You ought to have seen the attentiveness, and heard and seen the applause!

I must add that Mr. Bagge was the only one who wrote so unfavorably of my Quartet [in G minor]; the other dailies praised me very much that time.

I'm very happy that I gave the concert.

By now you must be rid of your guests; perhaps you will find a minute to write?

Pass this letter on to Mr. Marxsen, and tell him also that Bösendorfer can't send any pianos away before the New Year, as they are needed too much for concerts.[1]

If he wants me to look for another one, I await instructions.

It went very badly with Grädener [2] at his concert, as far as public and critics are concerned. The papers belabored him dreadfully.

My Serenade [3] will be performed next Sunday, I think.

I wanted to have some of my songs performed at my concert yesterday; this made me run about dreadfully and caused me some unpleasantness; that is why I want to have some quiet at last.

Did you sit down to eggnog last Wednesday? Write me about it and about things generally.

The publishers here, namely Spina and Lewy, have been pressing me for compositions ever since the quartet [concert]; but I prefer many things in northern Germany, and especially the publishers, and for the time being I'll gladly do without the extra couple of Ldrs. [Louis d'or] which they might pay me here.

Does Avé visit you often, has he given you any special news of Stockhausen? [4]

What about the photograph of the Girls' Quartette, am I not going to receive it? [5]

And NB. I forget to ask, every time I write, whether Fritz [6] has completely recovered yet? And is he being industrious? He ought to study away, so he can give Trio evenings in

Hamburg next year, I'd give him a helping hand. But he must practice diligently and become familiar with music.

Write soon and love

Your

Johannes.

Warm regards to Mr. Marxsen
and don't forget about Bösendorfer.

Facsimile of the autograph: Heinrich Reimann, *Johannes Brahms* (3rd ed.; Berlin: "Harmonie," Verlagsgesellschaft für Literatur und Kunst, 1903), between pp. 22–23.—Tr. by editor.

230   HECTOR BERLIOZ TO EDWARD JEROME HOPKINS, NEW YORK [Fr.]

4 Rue de Calais, Paris
6 February 1863

Dear Sir and Colleague

I have been much moved by reading the letter you have favored me with. You say you are suffering in the cause of art; it is unhappily out of my power to offer you consolation. You doubtless have formed a very mistaken idea of the life that artists (worthy of the name) lead in Paris. If to you New Yorck [*sic*] is the purgatory of musicians, then to me, who know it well, Paris is their hell. Therefore do not be too downhearted. In the first place you are young; it is a great chance, a great advantage, a great strength, a supreme quality. I should be very glad to see you and make your acquaintance. Yet, if you came to Paris (in this hell),[1] perhaps in spite of my wish to be helpful you might find my welcome grudging, cold, the reverse of cordial. You might well find me distrait, preoccupied, tossed about by one of those storms, by some fit of violent distress of the kind I so often experience. At such times my behavior, my appearance itself, is a libel on my inner feelings and I cannot but be judged unfavorably. To be sure I should strongly regret this. Let us hope it will not turn out so. I am only afraid that you may come too late; for I wake each morning with the hope that the new day may be my last. My physical and mental sufferings leave me

330

hardly any peace; I have said goodbye to all musical illusions,
I do nothing more. I have made arrangements so that I can
at any instant say to death: Whenever you like!

If I speak about myself so much, my dear Sir, it is to make
clear a contrast between our two lives by means of which
yours may be rendered more bearable.

Music is the greatest of the arts; it is also that which in
the present state of civilization is bound to make most wretched
those who understand it at its highest, those who respect and
honor it. Nevertheless, one must continue to honor it, respect
it, love it—always. Yes, love it with that true *love* which
holds within it the essence of the noblest passions of the human
heart. One must consequently contemn the crowd and its
prejudices, put no value on success that is bought by weak
concessions, and protect oneself carefully from contact with
fools and with fanatics and with sophists who know how to
give to folly the semblance of reason.

[Eng.:] But I beg your pardon, Sir, if I give you this
counsels [*sic*; Fr.:] which you did not ask for; I close by
thanking you for the fellow feelings you have been kind
enough to express to me and by assuring you of those I feel
for you.

Let me shake you by the hand and address you in the last
words of the ghost in Hamlet:

[Eng.:] Farewell, farewell, remember me.

Hector Berlioz

[= Letter 173], 229–31.

231   GIOACHINO ROSSINI TO FERDINAND HILLER,
COLOGNE [Fr.]

[Paris, 10 August 1866]

My dear friend and Illustrious Colleague

Mr T. Mako, Publisher, was good enough to send me on your
behalf the adorable Gavotte Sarabande and Courante you
acquainted me with during your stay in Paris, which was so short.
Nothing could have been more agreeable than to receive a Souvenir

of an Artist like yourself and a friend whom I have always loved tenderly. As soon as I received the pieces I went to the Piano to read them; I realized Alas that I shall have to give up trying to perform the Sarabande, that composition being of a kind suited to Pianists of the First and not of the Fourth Class *which as you know is mine!!* this will not prevent me from playing the Gavotte and the Courante with all my might so as to bring out (if you please) all the Refinements and the masterly intentions of their *Demon* of an Author (modesty!!)

Did you have a good time at Malines, where you so worthily filled the Role of member of the jury for Germany??

Please remember me to your amiable Daughter and to Mad^e Hiller and believe me to be ever gratefully and

Affectionately yours
Rossini

P.S. Tell our dear Colleague M. Farina that every day as I Rise I rub my forehead with his eau de Cologne which is Matchlessly excellent [1]

Mad^e Rossini wishes to be remembered to you.

 Passy de Paris
  10 August 1866
Et in terra pax hominibus —— Laus Deo!!! [2]

AUTOGRAPH, Arturo Toscanini Collection, New York: 1 sheet, 340 × 217 mm., folded to form 4 pp.; pp. 3 & 4 blank.—Tr. by editor.

232   HECTOR BERLIOZ TO THE GRAND DUCHESS YELENA PAVLOVNA, ST. PETERSBURG [Fr.]

[Paris, 4 June 1868]

 I thank you, Madam, for your kindness in asking for my news. I should indeed like to come up to the opinion you have of me, but I have not yet reached that point. My strength is failing me, medical art is doing what it can, and it cannot do a great deal.

 Will you come to Paris this autumn? Shall I have the honor to see you? I am afraid you will be rather puzzled in the midst of this musical *tohu-bohu*. Today I have no ideas at all. Everything is failing me at once, I feel that I am dying; yesterday I had some musical thoughts, today they are gone. What use would they be to me?

Pardon, pardon, I am in great pain.

I must be quiet.

I shall lie down. Perhaps I shall fall asleep.

Yours, with great but useless devotion,

Hector Berlioz,
4 June 1868.

Semjon Ginsburg, "Correspondance russe inédite de Berlioz," *La Revue Musicale*, Vol. XI, Tome I (May 1930), 422.—Tr. by editor.

233   GIUSEPPE VERDI TO FILIPPO FILIPPI, MILAN [It.]

Genoa, 4 March 1869.

Dear Mr. Filippi,

I cannot resent the article in *La Perseveranza* on *La Forza del Destino,* nor have I reason to. If you were moved to raise a few objections amid your many words of praise, you were fully within your rights and did well. Besides, as you know, I don't complain of articles, even if they are hostile, just as I never express gratitude (and I may be wrong) for favorable reviews. I cherish my own independence in all things, and I wholly respect that of other people. It is for this reason that I am very grateful to you for the reserve you showed during my stay in Milan; because, as you were obliged to review my opera, it is just as well that you should not have been influenced by a handshake, or a visit paid or received. And while we are on the subject of your article, I must tell you, since you ask, that it did not and could not displease me.

I know nothing of what passed between you and Ricordi; but perhaps Giulio [1] (who, if I'm not mistaken, likes *Eleonora's cantabile* better than many other pieces) was a little puzzled when he saw it accused of being an imitation of Schubert. If this is so, then I am just as surprised as Giulio, because I, in my supreme musical ignorance, don't know how many years have

333

passed since I last heard Schubert's *Ave* [*Maria*], and it would therefore have been very difficult for me to imitate it. Don't think that when I say: *supreme musical ignorance,* I mean it as a bit of *blague.* No, it's the plain truth. There is hardly any music in my house, I have never gone to a music library, never to a publisher to examine a piece. I keep abreast of some of the better contemporary works, not by studying them but through hearing them occasionally at the theater: there is a purpose in all of this, which you will understand. I repeat, therefore, that I am the least erudite among past and present composers. But understand me right, again, to avoid all *blague*: I speak of musical *erudition,* not *knowledge* [*sapere*]. Here I should be lying, if I said that I had not pursued long and strict studies during my youth. It is because of these that I happen to have a hand that is sturdy enough to bend notes to my will and dependable enough to obtain, generally, the effects I envisage; and whenever I write something in an irregular way, it is because the strict rule will not yield what I want, and because I don't believe that all the rules which have so far been adopted are even good. The Counterpoint Treatises need to be reformed.

What a lot of words! and what's worse, so many superfluous ones. Do forgive me and accept my sincere compliments.

[G. Verdi.]

[= Letter 202], 616–17.—Tr. by editor.

234   RICHARD WAGNER TO AN UNNAMED CORRESPONDENT [G.]

Honored Sir,   [Lucerne, 12 May 1869]

The thoughts you communicate to me are the same as those which definitely determined my view of life some twenty years ago; it was they which impelled me, in a very fearless mood, to take part in the social revolution which was at that time generally feared. Since politics is not my field, they were transformed in me into artistic ideas: in two extensive essays, "Art and Revolution" (1849) and "The Art-Work of the Future" (1850), I sought to expound those ideas.

334

At that time I knew Proudhon's writings fairly well, and I was one of those who could not help believing that the success of his project for a people's bank must inevitably bring about a complete change in the material and ethical constitution of our society.

I have watched twenty years go by since then—twenty years that have not changed my views at all, but have taught me much. In so far as the world may be conceived and affected by the laws of numbers, I shall not be able—according to the laws of my own nature—to take any part in its regeneration; all that remains to me is to work upon its ethical feelings through aesthetic means. I have at last realized that in this I am expressing the true character and the peculiar gifts of the German spirit, and I am convinced that it is the function of other nations to provide the necessary detail work [*Calcul*].

As for the situation of the King of Bavaria and the dangers which threaten it, I must agree with your views. But I must point out to you that I find particular grounds for your fears in the fact that to date I have not been able to detect any sign that the King will ever be able to achieve the same insight into his own situation that he has into the state of his country and the tendency of his time.

I consider the thought of any such cooperation as you would wish to have completely futile and inadmissible.—[1]

Therewith I tell you briefly everything that has occurred to me in the serious perusal of your most valued letter, for which I thank you. Be assured of the deep respect in which I remain

Yours

very faithfully

Richard Wagner

Lucerne, 12 May 1869

Artur Holde, "Four Unknown Letters of Richard Wagner," *The Musical Quarterly*, XXVII (1941), 233.

235   GIUSEPPE VERDI TO ANTONIO GHISLANZONI, [MILAN?][It.]

St. Agata, 17 August 1870

Dear Mr. Ghislanzoni,

In the duet [1] there are excellent things at the beginning and at the end, even though it is too diffuse and long. It appears to me that the recitative might have been said in fewer lines. The stanzas are good, up to "a te in cor destò" ["Awakened in your heart"]. But after that, when the action becomes more heated, I think the *dramatic word* [*la parola scenica*] is not there. I don't know whether I explain myself when I say *dramatic word*; I mean the kind of word that carves out a situation and makes it clear and evident.

For example these lines:

> Your eyes on mine fix steadily
> And lie once more, I dare you:
> Radames lives . . . .

this is less theatric than the following (which may be ugly, if you like):

> . . . . with one word
> I'll rob you of your secret.
> Look at me, I have deceived you:
> Radames lives . . . .

Similarly, the lines:

> For Radames my heart beats
> Warmly, and you are my rival.
> —What! you love him?—I love him,
> Who am daughter of the king.

seem to me less theatric than: "You love him? but I love him also, do you hear me? The daughter of the Pharaohs is your rival!—*Aida:* My rival? So be it: I too am the daughter, etc."

I know very well that you'll say: Yes, but the verse, the rhyme, the stanza? I don't know what to tell you; but when the action demands it, I would gladly abandon rhythm, rhyme, stanza at once; I should write in free verse, in order to say clearly and lucidly all that the action demands. Unfortunately, the theater sometimes requires that both poet and composer should have enough talent not to compose poetry and music.

The duet ends with one of those usual *cabalettas*,[2] and a long one at that, for the present situation. We'll see what can be done for it musically. In any case, I don't think it's nice to have *Aida* say:

> I'll endeavor then to forget
> This love that irritates you so.

Try to send me this duet with the finale that follows as soon as possible, because I too must work if I am to finish in time.

[= Letter 202], 641–42.—Tr. by editor.

236   GIUSEPPE VERDI TO COUNT OPPRANDINO ARRIVABENE, FLORENCE [It.]

St. Agata, 13 September 1870

Dear Arrivabene,

I thank you for your letter and am happy to hear you are well. I am saddened by the events of the war and deplore France's misfortunes, and I fear that the future will be terrible for us. Ah, the North! it is a country, a people that frighten me.

I should personally have preferred a more generous policy on the part of our Government, and I should have wished that a debt of gratitude be paid . . .[1] I know very well that people will say to me: what if there is a European conflict? . . . but a European conflict will be unavoidable, and if France had been saved, we should have been saved as well.

I am writing,[2] as you know, and I would rather not write about this, but there is no help for it. I shall probably go to Parma, and I look forward to admiring your brother's pictures.

Peppina[3] sends you her best regards, and I an affectionate handshake. Give me your news and believe me

Yours affectionately
G. Verdi

[= Letter 226], 121.—Tr. by editor.

237   MODEST PETROVICH MUSSORGSKY TO VLADIMIR VASSILYEVICH STASOV, ST. PETERSBURG [Russ.]

[St. Petersburg,] 10 [1] August, '71

Centuries have passed, my dear, since I last saw you and talked things over with you; no one is to blame for this but the vicissitudes of fate. And I have a lot to tell you on our account, and for that "my own eyes" are burning to behold you and to torture your hearing "with my obscenely hoarse voice."—The criminal Tsar Boris perpetrates a certain *arioso;* in the opinion of musical sages, and above all, originating from Lodyzhky known as Fim, as well as from the knight of the marine tempests [2] so laudably transformed by you into the admiralty, this criminal *arioso* is very lovely and tickles the ear rather amusingly, and the words of this *arioso* have been cooked up by me.

Since it is disgusting and boring to watch and listen to the grinding of the criminal's teeth, the little mob of nurses breaks through after this, bawling and clamoring unintelligibly, whereupon the Tsar drives them away and sends his son to find out "why these women are howling there." . . . Whilst the son attends to this, a boyar in attendance presents himself and informs against Shuisky, and when this spy slips away the Tsarevich returns and in answer to Boris's question: "Well, what's going on there?" explains as follows:

Tsarevich

Sire, permit me to begin a true story.

Boris.

I am listening, my son.

Tsarevich

Our little *parrot* * perched in the nurses' chamber,
He chattered unceasingly, and was gay and affable.
He went up to the nurses, and begged them to scratch his poll:
He visited each one in turn, observing the proper order.

---

* *Already the seventh creature* about whom I have amiably sung: in the historical order of their appearance have jumped out (1) a *magpie,* (2) a *goat,* (3) a *beetle,* (4) a *drake,* (5) a *mosquito* with a *bedbug,* (6) a *screech-owl* with a *sparrow,* (7) this *parrot.*[3]

Nurse Nastasya did not want to scratch him;
The parrot stepped aside—he called the nurse a fool.
Nurse, much offended, seizes him by the neck.
The parrot begins to scream, and flap his wings.
Well, they coax him, they pet him, they fondle him.
Imploring him by all the clergy, they caress him, soothe him.
But no—he will have none of it:
He sits and scowls, his beak buried in his feathers,
He won't look at the nurses, he keeps on muttering something.
Suddenly he springs at a nurse.
(The one who wouldn't scratch him):
Begins to peck her—the nurse flops on the floor.
Then the nurses seemed to go mad with terror,
They began waving their arms, screaming, wanting to drive the parrot
    away,
But he was not at a loss: he marked each of them adroitly.
That, my royal father, was why they all rushed in here,
Interfering with the deliberations of thy royal thought.
Well, it seems that's all—all that took place.

With the music this fibbing turns out to be so pleasing that the above-mentioned musical sages kept their ears wide open so that by cramming them with this pleasing stuff they might please themselves sufficiently. It would be pleasant to grab you in your residence on Thursday, and if you're not terribly against it, write me, my dear, at the House of Zaremba [4] (near St. Panteleimon's) apt. No. 4.

Your

Musoryanin

Mayhap you have *anathematized* me, but the nurses prove how firmly you are seated in my brain and soul.

N.B. I seem to remember that *somebody* presented Boris with a parrot as a novelty in the Russian Kingdom—*is that so?*

Jay Leyda and Sergei Bertensson (eds. and translators), *The Musorgsky Reader: A Life of Modeste Petrovich Musorgsky in Letters and Documents* (New York: W. W. Norton & Company, Inc., 1947), 167–68.

238   MODEST PETROVICH MUSSORGSKY TO VLADIMIR VASSILYEVICH STASOV, ST. PETERSBURG [Russ.]

[St. Petersburg, 25 July 1872]

"Soon the foe will come and darkness will set in."

"Black impenetrable darkness"—thus whines the simpleton in my *Boris* and, I'm afraid, not in vain. The city of Himself-Peterbuch and its environs depict, in the two-legged department, a continuous children's camp; factory-hands wander in the streets, whistling or hoarsely singing military marches, even the women berry-vendors call and whine in a military manner, for instance:

Berries, raspberries so juicy!

and non-Russian sevenths and raspberry fanfaronade.

Innocent angels—the children, exercise with the help of carefully tooled muskets in the application of the Malthus theory and patiently wait for the commander, a more mature innocent angel who, in his turn, awaits the arch-commander, this time a young telegraph boy "carrying messages" with Zeus' thunderbolts on his shoulder straps and in his cap band, and with the face of a peasant-girl. In *Pärgala* I heard the savage war cries of those human minnows, I saw from afar the banners, badges, sabers, muskets . . . these minnows are being drilled, they say, by some hussar officer. Froggies with hanging bellies, bowed legs and also with homemade muskets can be seen marching on the *Platzparade* . . . What will come of this? Even the roosters crow marches! What is to come?

By the time you return, dear *généralissime,* all the materials for our future opera will probably be collected. I have put together a notebook and entitled it "*Khovanshchina,* a people's musical drama—materials"; on the title page I listed my sources—9—not at all bad, that: I am swamped with information, my head is like a caldron, just keep throwing stuff into it. Zhelyabuzhsky, Krekshin, Count Matveyev, Medvedev, Shchebalsky and Semevsky are already sucked dry; now I am sucking at Tikhonravov, and then comes Avvakum—for dessert. Some days ago I plunged into the very depth and found the following pearl (the dissenters' retreat in Myshetzky's narrative): "To the Germans has been sent an entire horde of demons, to cause them to be insubordinate, without unity or obedience; and to them went Teut with a regiment of demons and taught them to spread corruption; those who accepted this teaching were named Teutons and pride themselves in being sage in the accursed learning. So also to us has Lucifer dispatched his cohorts—to snare and draw us to great lust, and in particular to pride, drunkenness, *to idleness and dancing*. He also dispatched accursed women—all-knowing witches, fortune-tellers and *seers*: thus have Bacchus and Gordad with their comrades overwhelmed the entire land of the north!" (With this there is a close connection between heavenly and aerial phenomena: a thunderstorm in January and the *destruction of the sun*.) "And when they had set up their kingdom, Lucifer sent a certain man (no one knows his name): and he said to the woman in childbirth: 'I wish to kiss the great one in your womb,' and when he had kissed, he said: 'Great One! 53 sazhens in height! Thou wilt wield the great cudgel.' And then a thunderstorm broke over Moscow, it was the 6th day of January, and the sun perished. In such wise, brethren, the evil spirit led . . . from the womb, and that was the Antichrist!" [1]

On such a framework one may do much: it is pictorial, mystical, and a delightful caricature of history. There's much substance in the materials.

This epistle will not go to Moscow, but *nearer*, to [your] Melikhov house erected in Petrobourse; this occurred because of the sitting together of many people in the *izvoshchik* (namely, the drivers) and an observation of all sorts of sinful stuff among the ever criminal and lecherous Germans close to the *Stenbokovsky Passage*—they love money greatly and plunder a lot, therefore this is written: [2]

Even if the authorities do permit our opera, I shall still get a beating for my many great sins from the various Laroches, Fifs,

Tomsons etc., etc.,[3] perhaps, however, by the time everything is ready, the particle *in* may be discarded from the word *Ingermanland*,[4] and Laroche will enter the chancery of the German musical guild as a watchman (in the literal sense), Fif will become the apprentice of Bismarck's cook, and Tomson, because of his extreme and respected, although sterile, industry—will be driving away the flies from Bismarck's bald spot—and flies there will be for sure, Russian flies, no more easily driven away than the cockroaches, and in Germany there are such a lot of bedbugs that it's no wonder Shcherbina once ordered a waiter in Koenigsberg to bring a *Klopstock um Klopy zu schlagen*.[5] But however let's see who wins—we shall get a beating, and a hard one, and I am being beaten already but still who knows who will win.— (A rotten pen, but the heat is so fierce, that I'm too lazy to take another) (meaning irresponsibility or extenuating circumstances). Why, *tell me,* when I listen to the conversation of young artists—painters or sculptors, not even excepting the monumental Misha,[6] I can follow their turns of thought, their ideas, aims, and seldom do I hear anything said about technique— unless it's necessary. Why do I, *do not tell me,* when I listen to our musical brethren, seldom hear a vital idea, but mostly stuff from a school-room bench—technique and musical ABC's?

Is musical art young only because its practitioners are half-educated adolescents? How many times, unintentionally, *through absurd habit* (in a roundabout way) I would start a conversation with the brethren—and this is what happened—either I was repulsed or not given a clear answer, or, more often, was just not understood. Well, let us assume that I am unable *to present my thoughts clearly*—that is to say: to present on a tray brains with thoughts printed on them (as on a telegram). But what about themselves? Why don't they start?—evidently they don't want to? *And evidently, you, généralissime, understand me, and furthermore, you touch that very place where you should touch—with a brave, firm hand.*

Maybe I'm afraid of technique, because I'm poor at it? However, there are some who will stand up for me in art and in this respect also. I, for example, cannot bear it, when the hostess, in serving a good pie which she has prepared and we are eating, says: "A million *puds* of butter, five hundred eggs, a whole bed of cabbages, 150¼ fish . . ." You eat the pie and it tastes good, then you hear about the kitchen, and you at once can imagine the cook, always dirty, a chopped-off chicken head on a bench, gutted fish on another, and sometimes side by side, and somebody's intestines peeping out of a sieve (as though the Prussians had honored us with their presence), and more often one can visualize a greasy apron, the same apron that is used as a nose-rag, and which later will be used to wipe the edges of the pie dishes, in order to clean them . . . well, the pie grows less tasty. There is in ripe artistic productions that side of chaste purity, that when touched by dirty paws, grows loathsome.

In truth—until the artist musician rids himself of his diapers, his braces, straps, so long will the *symphonic* priests rule, setting up their Talmud "of the 1st and the 2nd editions," as the alpha and omega in the life of art. The little brains sense that their Talmud cannot be used in living art: where there are people, life—there is no place for prejudiced paragraphs and articles. And so they cry: "Drama, the stage, they cramp us—give us space!" And here they go giving free rein to their brains: "The world of sounds is unlimited!"; yes but their brains are limited; so what use is this sound of worlds, or rather world of sounds! One gets as much space when lying on "the lawn and following the flight of the heavenly clouds": there's a fleecy lamb, there's an old granddad, there's simply nothing at all, then suddenly, a Prussian soldier. I can't blame Polonius for agreeing with Hamlet about the clouds. The esteemed cloud is very changeable and in the wave of the hand may turn from a camel, to, perhaps, a Laroche.—It isn't symphonies I object to, but symphonists— incorrigible conservatives. So do not tell me, dear *généralissime,* why our musicians chatter more often about technique, than about aims and historical tasks—because, this derives *from that.*

But all the same a thought puzzles me: why do the "Ivans" (IV and III) and especially the "Yaroslav" of Antokolsky, live, why do Repin's "Volga boatmen" and even the scrofulous boy in Perov's "Birdcatcher" and the "first couple" in his "Huntsmen," and likewise the unexhibited, but seen by me "Village Religious Procession" [by Repin] live, and they so live, that when one gets to know them, one has a feeling that "you are the ones I wanted to see." And why does all that is done in the latest music, in spite of its excellent quality, not live thus, and when you hear it, it seems: "Ach, yes, I thought, that you . . ." and so on.—Explain this to me, only leave aside the boundaries of art—I believe in them only very relatively, because *boundaries*

343

of art in the religion of the artist, means *standing still.* What if someone's wonderful brains did not think and come to any conclusion; but other brains did think and did come to conclusions—where then, are the boundaries? But relatively—oh, yes! sounds cannot be chisels, brushes—well, of course, as *in each best thing there is a weakness and vice versa*—even children know this.

There's a diatribe for you to read. I saw a curious thing in *Kladderadatsch* today: the Germans ridiculed Bismarck for his desire *to be left undisturbed in Varzin.*[7] (This was declared by him in the newspapers, as is already known.) There those most respectful ones have pictured him in dressing-gown and slippers, with a dozing dog at his knee, feeding ducks and geese. As long as you are, it says, a statesman, don't dare relax. I should have said: "Feed the ducks, my dear, feed them! Only don't put the Malthus theory into practice—and even without you it will be done: people are dying off like flies." Maybe there is a hidden meaning: maybe, think the Germans, "As soon as Bismarck retires on his laurels, he will invent the destruction of man." Well, then I am in agreement with them: "Let the criminal think, but only guard us, God, lest he come to a conclusion." . . .

The epistle was intended for the ruling city of Moscow and was to have been filled with a warm thirst for a close embrace. In the hope of doing this in person (the epistle should have been received by you on May 15) I control myself and because I control myself I will have to let myself go (like a spring) and I warmly kiss you, my dear. I've taken up the cross and with lifted head, bravely and happily, I shall go forth, against *all sorts of things,* towards bright, strong, and righteous aims, towards a genuine art that loves man, lives with his joys, his grief, and his sufferings. I do not ask for your hand: you long ago extended it and I've long held it firmly, my best, my dear support.

Your
Musoryanin

13 July,[8] 1872, in Petrograd

[= Letter 237], 188–94.

239   RICHARD WAGNER TO RUDOLF FRENY,
HAMBURG [G.]

[Bayreuth, 25 October 1872]

Dear Sir,

You are proceeding quite correctly with Beckmesser. Only do
not exaggerate the foppishness; it emerges quite spontaneously:
he need not be old; many people are old already at forty. Show
great earnestness throughout: the man never jests, except when
he pretends to be gay. Huge narrow-mindedness and much bile.
Take any famous critic as your model.[1] Unbounded vehemence,
without the power to give it vent: a voice that cracks when he
becomes angry. The topmost notes are, of course, no more than
violent or ridiculous accents of speech, not song. Please pay
great attention to every written direction, and be in total accord
with the orchestra during its performance.

Yours faithfully,
Richard Wagner

Bayreuth
25 Oct. 72.

AUTOGRAPH (see Frontispiece), Jacob Lateiner Collection, New York:
1 sheet, 218 × 140 mm.; embossed crest & "RW" in upper left
corner.—Tr. by editor.

240   GEORGES BIZET TO PAUL LACOMBE,
CARCASSONNE [Fr.]

[Paris, spring 1874]

My dear friend,

Your friendly letter found me in bed, tête-à-tête with a
most acute angina.—The abscesses disappeared two hours ago—
and I'm about to get well rapidly by dint of cutlets.

I am going to leave in a few days.—I have found at Bougival
a very quiet, very agreeable little spot near the water (*1, rue de
Mesmes, Bougival, Seine-et-Oise*).

345

There I shall finish *Carmen,* which will be rehearsed in the month of August and open at the end of November or beginning of December—and begin, possibly finish, *Sainte Geneviève,* an oratorio from which I expect a great deal.[1]

Keep me informed of your work, dear friend, and for all your pampering and spoiling receive the thanks of the Bizets, father, mother, and child.

Georges Bizet.

Hugues Imbert, *Portraits et Etudes: Lettres inédites de Georges Bizet* (Paris: Librairie Fischbacher, 1894), 194–95.—Tr. by editor.

241   ANTONÍN DVOŘÁK TO THE TOWN CLERK, PRAGUE [G.?]

[Prague, 15 June 1874]

Dear Sir,

     I should be obliged if you would be good enough to furnish me with a certificate in German confirming that I am without means, as such a certificate must be enclosed with my application for the award of a State grant for artists, such application to be sent in by the 30th inst. at the latest.[1]

Prague, 15 June 1874

Ant. Dvořák m. p.[2]

Otakar Šourek (ed.), *Antonín Dvořák: Letters and Reminiscences,* trans. Roberta Finlayson Samsour (Prague: Artia, 1954), 35.

242   MODEST PETROVICH MUSSORGSKY TO VLADIMIR VASSILYEVICH STASOV, ST. PETERSBURG [Russ.]

[St. Petersburg,] Wednesday, some day or other in June '74

My dear *généralissime.*

Hartmann is boiling as *Boris* boiled—the sounds and the idea hung in the air, and now I am gulping and overeating, I can hardly manage to scribble it down on paper. Am writing 4

numbers—with good transitions (on "promenade"). I want to
do it as quickly and steadily as possible. My physiognomy can
be seen in the intermezzi.[1] I consider it successful so far. I
embrace you and I take it that you bless me—so give me your
blessing!

Musoryanin
V[otre] S[erviteur]

Curious nomination [nomenclature]: *"Promenade (in modo
russico)"*

   No. 1. *"Gnomus"*—intermezzo (there's no name for the
       intermezzo);

   No. 2. *"Il vecchio castello"*—intermezzo (also unnamed);

   No. 3. *"Tuileries (dispute d'enfants après jeux)"*;

   No. 4. Right between the eyes *"Sandomirzsko bydlo"* (*le
       télégue:* it stands to reason that *le télégue* isn't named,
       but this is between us).[2]

How well it works out!

Musoryanin

   I should like to add Vityushka's Jews.

[In the upper left-hand corner, Mussorgsky has added:] Can't
be at your place.

[= Letter 237], 271–72.

---

243   FRANZ LISZT TO HENRY WADSWORTH LONGFELLOW, CAMBRIDGE, MASSACHUSETTS [Fr.]

[Tivoli, 22 November 1874]

Illustrious Poet,

   When we met in Rome you kindly requested of Mr. Healy a
genre picture showing the two of us at the entrance to "Santa
Francesca Romana."[1] Allow me to continue this sympathetic
union by dedicating to you the musical composition of your
poem: "The Bells of Strasbourg Cathedral"—with the prelude
likewise inspired by one of your poems: "Excelsior"!—

   Excelsior! That is the motto of poetry and music. Forever

they sing the exaltation of the human soul to the ages and to
the heavens, and thus accompany the "sursum corda" daily
resounding in the churches and their *bells*.

"Vigilemus omnes"

"Laudemus Deum verum."

F. Liszt

22 November 74.
   (Villa d'Este)

Edward N. Waters, "Liszt and Longfellow," *The Musical Quarterly*, XLI
(1955), 17.

244   ANTON BRUCKNER TO MORITZ VON MAYFELD, LINZ [G.]

[Vienna, 12 January 1875]

Right Honorable Sir,

My 4th Symphony is finished. I have still improved the
Wagner Symphony (D minor) considerably. Wagner's conductor
"Hans Richter"[1] was in Vienna and told in several circles how
splendidly Wagner speaks of it. Performed it is not. Dessof[2]
held rehearsals during the holidays, had me fetched for the sake
of appearance, and later declared (breaking his word, which
he had given me still at the beginning of October) that the
program was full up.

The Philharmonic are still expecting my symphony, in part.
Brahms appears to have suppressed my C minor Symphony No. 2
in Leipzig, Richter is supposed to have expressed a wish to
perform the D minor Symphony in Pest sometime. What Hanslick has done to me can be read in the old *Presse* of 25 Dec.[3]

Even Herbeck[4] once told me I ought to find out whether I
might not get some sort of help from Wagner. I have only the
Conservatorium, on which it is impossible to live. Had to borrow
money already in September, and again later, if I did not choose
to starve. (700 fl.) No man is helping me. Stremayr[5] promises—
and does nothing. Fortunately there have come some foreigners
who are taking lessons from me—; otherwise, I should have
to go begging.

348

Hear me further: I asked all the chief piano professors for lessons; they all promised; but except for some few theory lessons, I got nothing. Your Honor sees, the thing is becoming serious. I would gladly go abroad if only I could get a sustaining position. Where shall I turn to! I should not have been brought *to Vienna* so long as I lived, had I foreseen this. It would be an easy thing for my enemies to drive me out of the Conservatorium. I am surprised this has not already happened! University students, pupils at the Conservatorium, and even the servants there are horrified at the behavior shown me. My life has lost all joy and pleasure—in vain and for nothing. How glad I should be to return to my old position! Had I only gone to England that time! [6] That is how matters stand. A handkiss to your gracious lady. Respectfully,

Your Honor's most obliged
A. Bruckner.

Vienna, 12 January 1875.
What ought I to do?

[= Letter 142], 70–71.—Tr. by editor.

245A RICHARD WAGNER TO JOHANNES BRAHMS, VIENNA [G.]

[Bayreuth, 6 June 1875]

Dear Mr. Brahms,

I beg you to let me have my manuscript of the second scene of Tannhäuser, revised by myself, which I need for the publication of the new revision of the score. It is true I have been informed that you lay claim to the manuscript as being your property, by virtue of its having been given to you by Peter Cornelius; yet I believe I need not attach any consequence to that report, as Cornelius, to whom I had only lent—and by no means given—the manuscript, could not possibly have surrendered it to a third party; indeed, he assured me solemnly that he had never done so.

It is presumably quite unnecessary for me to remind you of this circumstance, and no possible further explanation will be needed to induce you to return this manuscript gladly and amicably, as it can be of no value to you except as a curiosity, while it might remain in my son's hands as a cherished memento.

With the greatest respect yours truly

Richard Wagner.

Bayreuth, 6 June 1875.

245B JOHANNES BRAHMS TO RICHARD WAGNER, BAYREUTH [G.]

[Ziegelhausen bei Heidelberg,] June 1875.

My dear Sir,

While informing you at the very outset that I am returning you the manuscript in question "gladly and amicably," I must yet permit myself to add a few words.

Mrs. Wagner approached me years ago concerning the restitution of that manuscript; at the time, however, so many reasons were adduced to persuade me, that in the end I could sense only this: that I was being begrudged the ownership of your autograph. Unfortunately, I should have to do violence to the import of your letter if I wished to read a different meaning into it, and I should in any case have preferred, then as now, to make the sacrifice as a result of a simple request on your part.

The ownership of this Scene cannot after all be as valuable to your son—in relation to the sum total of your works—as it is to me, for although I am not actually a collector, I still like to conserve autographs which I esteem. I do not collect "curiosities."

I do not want to continue the discussion over our deceased friends and the property claim to which I believe they entitled me. They would anyway have found it better and easier simply to admit to me that they had possibly been overhasty.

I feel it almost as an obligation towards myself to answer your letter, and also Mrs. Wagner's, in greater detail—but I very much fear I should not succeed in avoiding misinterpretations, for, if you will excuse me, the saying about hard nuts to crack can hardly be used more aptly than by the likes of us with regard to you. It might possibly please you if I were no longer allowed to think I had made you a present. But in this case let me say that if you are going to rob my autograph collection of a treasure, I should be very happy if my library were to be enriched with another of your works, perhaps the Meistersinger.

I cannot hope that you will change your mind, and so I am writing to Vienna today in order to have the portfolio containing your manuscript sent to me. I urgently request you to be good enough to acknowledge receipt with a line, when it arrives.

With the greatest respect and esteem

Yours very truly
Joh. Brahms.

Ziegelhausen bei Heidelberg.

245C RICHARD WAGNER TO JOHANNES BRAHMS, ZIEGELHAUSEN [G.]

[Bayreuth, 26 June 1875]

Dear Mr. Brahms,

I thank you very much for the manuscript, which I have just received; to be sure, it does not distinguish itself by its surface charms, as it was badly mauled while being copied in Paris, but I value it—quite apart from motives of sensibility—because it is more complete than the transcript which Cornelius made at one stroke, at the time.

I am sorry that I cannot offer you anything better than a copy of the score of Das Rheingold, instead of the Meistersinger score you asked for (after repeated deliveries from Schott,[1] I have once more completely exhausted my supply); I am sending it to you today without awaiting your consent, because its distinctiveness lies in its being the de luxe copy which Schott displayed at the Vienna World Exhibition. I've been given to understand, on occasion, that my music is stage scenery: Das Rheingold will be greatly exposed to that reproach. It may nonetheless be of some interest, in following the subsequent scores of the Ring des Nibelungen, to observe that I managed to build all sorts of thematic musical matter on top of the theater wings I planted here. In this sense, perhaps Das Rheingold will be most likely to meet with your friendly consideration.

Most respectful greetings from

your truly obliged

Richard Wagner.

Bayreuth, 26 June 1875.

351

245D JOHANNES BRAHMS TO RICHARD WAGNER, BAYREUTH [G.]

[Ziegelhausen bei Heidelberg,] June 1875.

Dear Sir,

What you have sent me gives me so much pleasure, that I cannot abstain from telling you so in a few lines and [expressing] my deep gratitude for the splendid present I owe to your kindness. My best and most proper thanks, of course, I present daily to the work itself—it is not lying idle here. Perhaps this part [of the Nibelung cycle] is not so conducive at first to the thorough study which your entire great work demands; but this Rheingold has come from your own hands, and so Die Walküre may well let her beauty shine forth and try to outshine this incidental advantage. But forgive such a remark! A more cogent reason is that we find it difficult to do justice to a section which demands that we look beyond it, at the whole work. In this case, indeed, we gladly resign ourselves even more and longer.

We have, after all, the strange, if stirring, enjoyment of watching this unique work of yours raise itself gradually and come to life—much as the Romans have, when a colossal statue is being dug up. In your less pleasant occupation of witnessing our astonishment and disagreement, the only things that help, of course, are a deep feeling of conviction, and the ever-spreading, ever-growing esteem your imposing creativity calls forth.

I thank you very much again and am, with the greatest respect,

Yours
very truly
Johs. Brahms.

Max Kalbeck, *Johannes Brahms*, II, Part I (2nd ed.; Berlin: Deutsche Brahms-Gesellschaft m.b.H., 1908), 122–26.—Tr. by editor.

246 GIUSEPPE VERDI TO COUNT OPPRANDINO ARRIVABENE, ROME [It.]

St. Agata, 16 July 1875

Dear Arrivabene,

As a matter of fact, I have been at St. Agata for the past 10 or 12 days, quiet and calm, without a thought of music. I don't know whether my tour [1] was good or bad for other people, and I don't know whether enthusiasm is *contagious and stimulates* the minds of men, as you say. I would not even be able to tell you what is about to emerge from this musical ferment. Some would like to be melodists like *Bellini,* others harmonists like *Meyerbeer.* I wish for neither thing, and wish that young men just beginning to compose would never contemplate becoming melodists, or harmonists, or realists, or idealists, or futurists or the devil take whatever other pedantry. *Melody* and *harmony* ought only to be means in the hands of the artist, with which to make *Music,* and if the day should come when people give up talking of *melody* and *harmony*, of German and Italian Schools, of *past* and *future* etc. etc. etc. etc. then perhaps the kingdom of art will begin. Another affliction of our times is that all the works of these young men are the fruits of *fear.* No one writes with abandon, and when these youths start writing, their dominant preoccupation is to avoid shocking the public and to enter into the good graces of the critics! You say I owe my success to a merging of the two schools. I have never thought about it. Besides, it's an old story that has happened to others, and for quite a long time! Anyhow, my dear Arrivabene, be calm, art will not die out; and be assured that also the moderns have accomplished something . . .

I am not composing: the Emperor of Austria hasn't begged me for an opera, nor have I promised one to anybody. Peppina,[2] like myself, is in good health and delighted to breathe the fresh air (which at the moment is really fresh) at St. Agata. Write me when you have nothing better to do; greetings, also from Peppina.

Yours affectionately,
G. Verdi

[= Letter 226], 182–83.—Tr. by editor.

247   BEDŘICH SMETANA TO KAREL BENDL,
PRAGUE [Czech]

[Jabkenice, 24 July 1875]

Dear friend,

Happy as I was to see that you take such a warm interest in
my fate, I have to admit, alas, that I am unable to advise you
in any way about the rehearsals which are to take place in
Bayreuth in August.[1] Indeed it is only from your letter that I
have come to know that such big rehearsals are now to take
place. I knew nothing about it. I am now really sorry that I am
not in closer contact with Wagner. But knowing the stories about
his overbearing and rude behavior towards the musical world
with the exception of Liszt, I did not care to become acquainted
with him, indeed I avoided it on every occasion for I also am
sensitive and I cannot stand rudeness. And thus I have never
met Wagner personally.

I do know his wife personally, but I maintain that she is
too proud to put in a word for such an unimportant artist as
I doubtless am in her eyes. The only thing I would dare to
point out in this case is that the gentlemen who wish to travel
from Prague to this year's rehearsals in Bayreuth should apply
to Wagner direct with the request that he allow them to
attend the rehearsals. Of course they would have to give their
reasons and flatter him a bit. A diplomatic letter would be
needed. Whether Wagner would consent, that is the question,
indeed who knows whether he will even answer. But it is
always worth trying, there is no harm in that. If he does not
consent, then you have saved the journey and the money, for
he would not admit you on someone else's recommendation
either. I hear that Jiránek [2] also wants to go there, and, it
seems, relying upon chance. Let him make sure beforehand.
You should rather apply to Wagner jointly. Much better if
there are more of you!

As regards my illness, my opponents may be satisfied. I shall
not soon be in their way again, indeed perhaps never again.
My recovery, if indeed it is possible, will require a long time
and insofar as I know my condition, I believe that only time
will give me back my hearing, at least partially. I also went to

see Dr. Pospíšil, but he began to give me external treatment and that is quite useless. My illness is internal and it has yet to be discovered where the cause lies. That, at least, is the opinion of all the doctors I have consulted. The ear is quite healthy externally. But the inner apparatus—that admirable keyboard of our inner organ—is damaged, out of tune, the hammers have got stuck and no tuner has so far succeeded in repairing the damage. In autumn I am going to Leipzig to Hagen, who is to give me electric treatment. The last attempt! Then my fate will be sealed!

I have no great hopes and it can now be stated with certainty that my public activities are ended, for a long time at least.

Forgive me for boring you more than necessary with a description of my troubles, but your kindness caused me to do so.

With all my heart I wish that you may attain your goal and, happy and contented, attend the rehearsals in Bayreuth. They would fall on good soil. I regret sincerely that I am not able to help you in any way.

Please accept my expression of sincere friendship.

Your devoted,

Bedřich Smetana.

Jabkenice, 24 July 1875.

[= Letters 203A–B], 158–60.

248   MODEST PETROVICH MUSSORGSKY TO VLADIMIR VASSILYEVICH STASOV, ST. PETERSBURG [Russ.]

[St. Petersburg,] 23 November,[1] '75

Saint-Saëns. Aida (Verdi). Sardanapalus (Famintzin). 15, 19, and 20 *November* '75 in Petrograd.[2]

When they name the author but not his works, then (as the old nurses of art used to say) that author is a somebody—worth something. Well, let's be kind: let's not start a dispute about the opinion of the old nurses of art! Who's this M. de Saint-Saëns?—one knows of him, partly from the papers, partly from conversations. What does M. de Saint-Saëns do?—he utilizes a miniature chamber orchestra and attains with it such solidity that he shows in rich orchestral powers tiny little thoughts inspired by a tiny versifier, and calls this crumb *Danse macabre*. The trend of M. de Saint-Saëns' mind was capable of digesting such an indigestible thought (a deliberation, perhaps?) and confronts the oppressive and aching *"Dies irae—Danse macabre"* of the Abbé Liszt [3] with a sentimental miniature *"Violino solo danse macabre M. de Saint-Saëns."* This is no matter for brains. And why did these brains throw themselves into symphonic program music? One hears that the brains have brewed an opera entitled *Samson:* evidently propaganda for female labor *(coupe de cheveux)* [4]—and will have to be forbidden in Russia. I don't trust M. de Saint-Saëns' *Samson* any more than I do *his innovator's toys*. It's not merely music, words, palette, and chisel that we need—no, devil take you, you liars and dissemblers *e tutti quanti* [5]— give us living thoughts, have living talks with people, whatever *subject* you've chosen! You can't fool us with sweetish sounds: the lady luxuriously passes the box of bonbons to her *dear friend*, and that's all. You, master of orchestral powers, M. de Saint-Saëns, you—creative crumb, you are so omnivorous that you derive pleasure from various trios, quartetti, quintetti, etc., arithmetically. M. de Saint-Saëns, innovator! With every bit of brain in my skull—I deny him; with all the strength in the beating of my heart—I push him aside! A utilizer of miniatures, what business of ours is he!

But *maestro Senatòre Verdi* [6] is quite another matter! This one pushes ahead on a grand scale, this innovator doesn't feel shy. All his *Aida*—ai-da! [7]—outdistancing everything, out-distancing everyone, even himself. He has knocked over *Trovatore*, Mendelssohn, Wagner—and almost Amerigo Vespucci, too. The spectacle is wonderful, but demonstrates a fabulous impotence in personifying (with reminiscences!) the teeth-champing, hot African blood.

Sardanapalus by Famintzin: heard it twice. I beg the pardon of all *office supplies,* a substitution in our time for medieval pages and messengers, for being compelled to write about the opera *Famintzin,* composed by Sardanapalus just as Sardanapalus fell. *Total madness.*

I am very pleased by the jolt given the public by you in *"Golos"* in regard to the production of *Aida.* I am sending you,

356

my dear, an epistle for Borodin.[8] If only you could help drag out of that teacup or samovar his arrangement of the ace [second] symphony. *The dispute at Golitzin's is ripening.*[9]

I embrace you,

Musoryanin

[= Letter 237], 318–19.

249 RICHARD WAGNER TO THEODORE THOMAS, NEW YORK [G.]

Bayreuth, 8 February 1876

Dear Sir,

I seize this opportunity to express my hearty thanks for your labors in America, which have been so helpful in promoting the spirit of German music and useful to my enterprise.[1]

In respect to the affair hitherto conducted through Mr. Federlein,[2] I must first express my regret that our correspondence —rendered difficult by the great distance, and recently also by your absence from New York—has been so protracted. I wish, therefore, that this thing may be concluded, and declare myself ready to execute a composition for grand orchestra, of the caliber and character of my *Kaisermarsch,* for the celebration of the 100th anniversary of American Independence. To deliver it for shipping on March 15 to a banking house in Germany designated by you, against the payment of five thousand dollars for the receipt of the manuscript. For this sum, demanded by me, I confer upon you the entire ownership of the work in question for America, not, however, for Europe, for which I am bound by contract to B. Schott's Söhne.[3] I pledge myself, however, not to allow the German publication to be issued till six months after the American.

I do not know whether it will seem wise to you to pay the sum mentioned for the unrestricted ownership (and naturally, also the performances) of my composition, but recent experiences have determined me to ask for such an amount. I was already offered $2,250 by a Berlin publisher for a similar composition, which, by the way, would have had no connection with a national celebration. Mr. Verdi received about half a million francs from his publisher, Ricordi, for the exclusive copyright and the performances of his Requiem.[4] I may be allowed, therefore, to draw conclusions as to the value of a composition written by an author who has achieved fame. In this connection, I must pay great attention to the value of works which so far have been given away for nothing, because up to now I have not been able to save a penny from their receipts.

I therefore beg you to telegraph your acceptance of my conditions, and I authorize you to deduct the cost of the telegram from my honorarium. Or, if I do not receive the telegram at the right time, I will take it for granted that you cannot conform to my demand.[5] In either case I will always remain,

         Your very humble and obliged servant,

                         Richard Wagner.

Rose Fay Thomas, *Memoirs of Theodore Thomas* (New York: Moffat, Yard and Company, 1911), 112–13.

250   GIUSEPPE VERDI TO FERDINAND HILLER, COLOGNE [Fr.]

                           Busseto 18 April 1877

Cher Maître

Your letter was forwarded from Genoa, and I received it in Busseto; I answer it at once.

As regards lodgings, I need two bedrooms, for myself and my wife, and a sitting room: or—a large bedroom with two beds, and a sitting room. These, if possible, on the first floor, at most on the second. We shall be in Cologne not later than 14 May.

You may put the Mozart Symphony before the Requiem; and, although I generally do not like to have detached pieces performed, you may have them repeat the *agnus Dei* on the 3rd day, if it seems right to you. Still, after receiving your last letter, there occurred to me another idea, which I submit

358

to your judgment. In the place of the *agnus Dei,* why couldn't one perform the Quartet which was performed in Paris last spring? [1] As you can well imagine, I shall neither criticize nor sing the praises of this piece; but you who are a great musician, why don't you glance at it, and if you don't think it would be too much out of place in your celebrations, then each instrument ought to be doubled [*sic*] by *10* or *12,* to form an orchestra of *40* or *48* players which I myself would conduct, as I will the *Requiem.* What do you think? There would be, of course, the problem of time and rehearsals, and if you find that my idea is not good, or too hard to realize, let it stop there. [2]

Be good enough to tell me, cher Maître, whether the complete performance of the *Requiem* is still scheduled for the second day, and please address your letter to

Maestro Verdi

at

Busseto

Italy.

with kindest regards,

Yours sincerely,

G. Verdi

AUTOGRAPH, Arturo Toscanini Collection, New York: 1 sheet, 264 × 205 mm., folded to form 4 pp.; watermark: LACROIX.—Tr. by editor.

251A ANTONÍN DVOŘÁK TO JOHANNES BRAHMS, VIENNA [G.]

Prague 3. 12. 77. Žitnobranská 10. II.

Honored Sir,

I have lately received a letter from the esteemed Prof. Dr. Hanslick in which he informs me that at a recent session with His Excellency, Minister Stremayer, I was, on your kind recommendation and that of the Professor, awarded a grant for artists. [1]

At the suggestion of the esteemed Prof. Hanslick, I venture to address these few lines to you, honored Master, in order to express to you my deep-felt thanks for the kindness you have shown me.

What I count a still greater happiness, however, is the sympathy you have been good enough to accord to my modest talent and the favor with which (as Prof Hanslick tells me) you received my Czech vocal duets.[2] Prof. Hanslick now advises me to procure a German translation of these songs which you, dear Sir, would be so kind as to recommend to your publisher. It is my duty to address myself to you with one more request—that you should be good enough to be of assistance to me in this matter which, for me, is of such great importance. It would be, indeed, not only for me but also for my beloved country, of immeasurable value if you, honored Master, whose works delight in such great measure the whole musical world, would give me such an introduction.

With the earnest request that I may continue in the future to enjoy your highly valued favor, I beg your kind permission to forward to you for your inspection some of my chamber music works and compositions for orchestra.

I have the honor to be,

Your most respectful and devoted

Antonín Dvořák.

251B JOHANNES BRAHMS TO ANTONÍN DVOŘÁK, PRAGUE [G.]

[Vienna, December 1877]

Dear Sir,

Allow me quite shortly to thank you for your lines and for the great pleasure I have derived from the works you sent me. I have taken the liberty of writing about them, and especially about the "Duets," to Mr. Fritz Simrock[3] (Berlin, W. Friedrichstrasse 171).

From the title it would appear that the Duets are still your property, in which case you could sell them to Mr. Simrock. The only thing that is needed is to get a good German translation. Can you manage that? In any case I beg you not to rush the matter so that the work may not suffer in consequence. In the meantime you could perhaps send the folio to Mr. Simrock to have a look at? The rest will then follow.

Forgive my being in haste today but I should not like to have the matter delayed. Hoping to hear further from you and favorably,

I remain,

Your very respectful and entirely devoted

J. Brahms.[4]

Vienna IV, Karlgasse 9.

[= Letter 241], 38–39.

252   PYOTR ILYITCH TCHAIKOVSKY TO NADEZHDA FILARETOVNA VON MECK, MOSCOW [Russ.]

San Remo

24 December 1877 / 5 January 1878 [1]

Dear Nadezhda Filaretovna,

Yesterday I was in a state of absolute madness. Didn't I write you some foolish, indelicate thing in yesterday's letter? If so, then in the name of God pay no attention. Here's the story of my last few days. I was appointed a *delegate* to the Paris Exposition, and at the same time received a request to go there at once and stay there till the end of the Exposition. I was horrified and might have refused immediately, since I am quite free and under no obligation. Instead, I enacted a whole drama. Only today did I come to my senses and see how silly this is. I had imagined that it was my duty to go there, that I was being selfish, stupid, rude not to accept such a flattering position. I thought my brothers, and sister, and you, and all the members of the Conservatory,[2] and everyone who is well-disposed towards me must suddenly begin to hate and despise me for my laziness, cowardice, and so on. At last, after a struggle that undoubtedly cost me several days of my life, I realized it was better to refuse now than to take up my duties and then drive myself to a final collapse. Today I am calm, but I still feel unwell. I have just been to the post office and have received your letter. I cannot tell you how it has comforted me! I am in such need, just now, of warm,

361

friendly words! And there are so many in your dear letter.
I'll answer you in all detail.

All the newest Petersburg composers are very gifted persons,
but they are all infected to the marrow with the worst sort
of conceitedness and with a purely dilettantist confidence in
their superiority over all the rest of the musical world.
Rimsky-Korsakov [3] has been the recent exception. He, too, is
self-taught like the others, but a radical change has occurred
in him. He has a very serious, very honest and conscientious
nature. As a very young man he fell in with a group of
people who first assured him he was a genius, then told him
that it was not necessary to *study,* that schooling kills inspiration,
dries up creativity, and so on. At first he believed this. His
first compositions reveal a very great talent devoid of any
theoretical training. In the circle to which he belonged, everyone
was in love with himself and with one another. Each tried to
imitate this or the other of the circle's products that was
considered remarkable. As a result, the whole circle soon
lapsed into a monotony of methods, a lack of individuality,
and mannerisms. Korsakov is the only one among them to
whom it occurred, five years ago, that the ideas propagated by
the circle had really no foundation, that their contempt for
schooling, for classical music, their hatred of authorities and
standards were nothing more than ignorance. I have saved a
letter he wrote me at the time. It touched me deeply and
shook me. He was profoundly dejected when he saw that so
many years had passed profitlessly and that the path he was
pursuing led nowhere. He asked what he should do. There
was nothing for it, of course, but to study. And study he
did; but with such zeal, that school-techniques soon became
the air he breathed. In the course of one summer he wrote
an infinite quantity of counterpoint exercises, and sixty-four
fugues, ten of which he at once sent me for inspection. The
fugues proved to be faultless in their own way, but I noticed
at the time that the reaction had made too abrupt a change in
him. From contempt of schooling he had turned all at once
to the cult of musical technique. His symphony and quartet
came out soon afterwards. Both compositions are full of a
multitude of tricks but, as you quite rightly observe, they
are saturated with a quality of dry pedantry. He is evidently
undergoing a crisis now; and how this crisis will end is hard
362

to predict. Either he will become a great master or he will
founder at last in contrapuntal tricks. *Cui*[4] is a gifted
dilettante. His music is devoid of originality, but it is elegant,
graceful. It is too coquettish—sleek, so to say—and for that
reason pleases at first but quickly palls. This is because Cui is
not a musician by profession but a professor of *fortification*—
very busy, and with a great number of lectures at nearly all
the military academies in Petersburg. As he admitted to me
himself, he cannot compose otherwise than by improvising and
picking out on the piano short melodies supplied with little
chords. After happening upon some pretty little idea, he
potters about with it, trims it, decorates it, and touches it up
in every possible way. And all this takes very long; so that,
for example, he wrote at his opera *Ratcliff* for ten years! But
I repeat, there's talent in him nonetheless; at the very least,
there's taste and flair. *Borodin*[5] is a fifty-year-old professor of
chemistry at the Academy of Medicine. Again, a talent—
and even an impressive one—but lost because of a lack of
knowledge, because blind fate led him to a chair of chemistry
instead of to an active musical career. However, he has less
taste than *Cui*, and his technique is so weak he cannot write
a line without outside help. *Mussorgsky* you very rightly call
a has-been. In talent he perhaps exceeds all the others; but he
has a narrow nature and lacks the need for self-perfection,
blindly believing in the ridiculous theories of his circle and
in his own genius. Besides, there's something low about him
that loves coarseness, lack of polish, roughness. He is the direct
opposite of his friend *Cui*, who is always swimming in the
shallows, yet always seemly and graceful. This man, on the
other hand, shows off his illiteracy, is proud of his ignorance,
slops along any old way, blindly believing in the infallibility
of his own genius. But sometimes he has flashes of real talent,
not lacking, moreover, in originality. The most outstanding
person of this circle is *Balakirev*.[6] But he has grown silent
after accomplishing very little. He has enormous gifts; and
they are lost because of some fateful circumstances that have
made a saintly prig out of him, after he had long prided
himself on complete skepticism. Now he never leaves the
church, he fasts and goes to confession, bows to the relics,
and nothing more. In spite of his enormous gifts, he has done
much harm. For example, he was the ruin of Korsakov when

he assured him it was detrimental to study. In general, he is the instigator of all the theories of this strange circle, which brings together so many undeveloped, misdirected, or prematurely ruined forces.

This, then, is my honest opinion of these gentlemen. What a sad thing! With the exception of Korsakov, how many talents from whom it is hard to await anything serious! And isn't this generally the way with us in Russia? Tremendous powers fatally hindered by a sort of Plevna from taking the open field and joining battle as they should.[7] Nevertheless, these powers exist. Even a Mussorgsky, by his very lack of discipline, speaks a new language. It is ugly, but it is fresh. And that is why one may expect that Russia will one day produce a whole galaxy of great talents, who will point out new paths for art. Our ugliness is at any rate better than the sorry feebleness (disguised as serious creative work) of Brahms and the other Germans. They are hopelessly played out. We must hope that *Plevna* will yet fall to us and that the power will manifest itself; but meanwhile very little has been done. As for the French, why there, now, the forward movement is having a very strong effect. Of course, they have only now begun to play Berlioz, ten years after his death; but many new talents have appeared, many energetic foes of routine. And it is very difficult to fight *routine* in France. The French are terrible conservatives in art. They were the last to recognize *Beethoven*. As late as the forties, they still considered him no more than a wild eccentric. Fétis, the leading French critic,[8] regretted that Beethoven had made mistakes (?) in the rules of harmony and obligingly corrected those mistakes as recently as twenty years ago. My favorites among the contemporary Frenchmen are Bizet and Delibes.[9] I don't know the overture *Patrie!* of which you write, but Bizet's opera *Carmen* I know well. It is music that makes no pretensions to depth; but it is so delightful in its simplicity, so lively, so unaffected and sincere that I learnt it all practically by heart, from beginning to end. I have already written you concerning Delibes. In their aspirations towards novelty, the French are not so daring as our innovators, but on the other hand they do not pass the bounds of the possible as do Borodin and Mussorgsky.

You are nearly right about N. Rubinstein [10]—that is, in the sense that he is not at all the hero he is sometimes made out to be. He is extraordinarily gifted, intelligent (though not very educated), energetic, and clever. But his passion for adulation and a quite childish weakness for every sort of submissive and servile utterance are his undoing. His administrative skill and his ability to deal with all the powerful personages of this world are amazing. His, in any case, is no trivial nature, but it is becoming petty in consequence of the senseless, servile worship that surrounds him. Yet we must give him his due, for he is honest, in the highest sense of the word, and unselfish; that is, his work and his struggles have not been for narrow material ends, *nor for gain*. He has a passion for dispensing rewards and for upholding the infallibility of his authority in all sorts of ways. He can't bear being contradicted and immediately suspects anyone brave enough to disagree with him of being a secret enemy. He doesn't mind resorting to intrigue and injustice if only that enemy can be destroyed. All this, because he is afraid of yielding even an inch of his unapproachable position. His despotism is very often outrageous. He does not scorn to show his authority and power before poor devils who can't retort. If he meets with a rebuttal, however, he gives in at once; and then he is not beyond intriguing a little. His heart is not especially kind, though he very much likes to make a show of his fatherly kindness, and he plays the good old soul for the sake of gaining popularity. All his shortcomings stem from his mad passion for power and his unpardonable despotism. But Nadezhda Filaretovna, the services he has rendered to the cause of music! For their sake one may forgive him everything. Whatever his Conservatory may be (rather artificially implanted in Moscow soil), it nevertheless is the disseminator of sound musical ideas and taste. Twenty-five years ago, you know, Moscow was a musical wilderness. I'm often angry with Rubinstein, but whenever I remember how much his energetic activity has accomplished I am disarmed. Let us even suppose he acted chiefly to satisfy his own ambition; but then, you know, it is a good ambition. Furthermore, we mustn't forget he is a superb pianist—the best in Europe, in my opinion—and a very good conductor.

My relations with him are very odd. After he has drunk a little wine, his tenderness for me grows to the point of sickliness, and he reproaches me with lack of feeling, lack of love towards him. When he is in a normal state, he treats me very coldly. He very much likes to make me feel that *I owe him everything*. As a matter of fact, he is a bit afraid I might be a *Frondeur*. Since I am generally not too effusive, he sometimes thinks I am secretly trying to wrest his *director's* post from him!! He has tried to draw me out on this several times, and when I told him candidly that I would sooner become a beggar than a director (for nothing could be more opposed to my nature than that sort of profession), he calmed down—but not for long. In short, though he is innately very clever, he becomes blind, stupid, and naïve whenever he gets it into his head that his position as Moscow's first musician is being threatened.

If you wish, I shall tell you an incident that has caused us to be a bit *en froid* in recent years. I am very tired and will close for today. Good-by, dear, beloved Nadezhda Filaretovna. Thank you for the letter.

Your P. Tchaikovsky

I have received the books.

V. A. Zhdanov and N. T. Zhegin (eds.), *P. I. Chaikovskiĭ: Perepiska s N. F. fon-Mekk* (Moscow: Academia, 1934), I, 134–39.—Translated for this book by Vera Lateiner.

253 RICHARD WAGNER TO AN UNNAMED CORRESPONDENT [G.]

[Bayreuth, 2 February 1878]

Dearest Friend!

I think you are connected with a music lending library? Would you be so kind as to procure for me Brahms's Symphony [No. 2?] in orchestra and piano score for a short time on guarantee of the fees required? I'm not learning anything any more of what happens in the world and here you can't get such a thing. Continue being good to me and before I die you'll get from me something nice for your music publication. I now still continually need as much money as possible, for I have to cover so many expenses. The first act of *Parsifal* is composed.

Faithfully yours,

Richard Wagner

[= Letter 205], 657.

254   JOHANNES BRAHMS TO JOSEPH JOACHIM,
BERLIN [G.]

[Pörtschach, 22 June 1879]

Dear friend,

I hope very much to go over the proofs of the Concerto with
you in Salzburg, and then, to relax, we can also play a little
sonata! [1] Do let me know what the prospects are over there of
[your] coming and staying! You'll find I have taken due notice
of your hair-splitting subtleties. But I couldn't make up my mind
to change the following passage as you advised:

I shouldn't like to do without the *low* and the high first notes.
Perhaps the passage isn't strong enough for you? Can't one omit
or double some notes?

Or something of the sort? More notes, too: [2]

Now perhaps you'll take good care not to ask for a concerto
again! What excuses [me] a little is that the concerto bears your
name, and that therefore you are somewhat responsible for the
violin writing.

Warm greetings
to you and your family.

J. Br.

[= Letter 217A], II, 169–71.—Tr. by editor.

255   JOHANNES BRAHMS TO KAREL WEIS, PRAGUE [G.]

[Vienna, December 1879]

Dear Sir,

Your compositions show decided talent, and indeed much that is praiseworthy in a young man. Nevertheless, they do not seem to me to be suitable, mature enough, for publication, and I believe (as this after all is your primary concern) that you ought not to expect any advantage—pecuniary, that is—from them. As I ponder further over your letter, I cannot help wishing that you would develop your talent also in other ways, and play some instrument or other well, perhaps the piano. It will be your lot, after all, as it is with most young people, to begin by giving lessons; but in that way you will also have the happiness of standing by your father and your family usefully. It cannot prevent you from striding ahead in your own development, for when one is young, one has even too much time and energy.

Perhaps I am taking your letter too literally if I allow myself to enclose a trifle, but I *am* talking you out of a paying publisher! I expect to be in Prague for some concerts in February. Won't you look me up then? At that time, perhaps, I shall be better able to give advice than now, with these few things before me. At any rate, I shall hear your further news with sincere interest.

Yours very truly,

J. Brahms.

Max Kalbeck, *Johannes Brahms,* III, Part I (Berlin: Deutsche Brahms-Gesellschaft m.b.H., 1910), 157 n.—Tr. by editor.

256   JOHANNES BRAHMS TO GEORGE HENSCHEL, LONDON [G.]

[Vienna, Feb. 1880]

Dear H.,

Your letter reaches me just as I am happening to be at home for a few days; a very rare occurrence this winter, worse luck!

Post festum my best congratulations upon the success of your concert, which indeed must have been splendid.[1]

368

The question in your letter received today is somewhat obscure, indistinct; I hardly know what to answer: "If the indications by figures of the tempi in my Requiem should be strictly adhered to?"

Well—just as with all other music. I think here as well as with all other music the metronome is of no value. As far at least as my experience goes, everybody has, sooner or later, withdrawn his metronome marks. Those which can be found in my works—good friends have talked me into putting them there, for I myself have never believed that my blood and a mechanical instrument go well together. The so-called "elastic" tempo is moreover not a new invention. "Con discrezione" should be added to that as to many other things.

Is this an answer? I know no better one; but what I do know is that I indicate (without figures) my tempi, modestly, to be sure, but with the greatest care and clearness.

Remember me kindly to Mr. Goldschmidt, and tell him, please, that there is only one thing in the coming performance I dislike thinking of, and that is, that No. 5 will not be sung by his wife.[2] I do wish I could have heard that once from her!

In haste and with kindest greeting,

Yours,
[J. Brahms]

George Henschel, *Personal Recollections of Johannes Brahms* (Boston: Richard G. Badger, The Gorham Press, 1907), 78–79.

257   GIUSEPPE VERDI TO COUNT OPPRANDINO ARRIVABENE, ROME [It.]

Busseto, Sant'Agata 18 October 1880

Dear Arrivabene,

I thank you for the article dealing with Bellini. When all is said, I believe Florimo is doing his deceased friend an ill service.[1] Already he has provoked a letter from Romani's [2] wife, which makes Bellini look pretty small in the eyes of the public: and who knows what will emerge later. Why on earth is it necessary to go digging up a musician's letters? Letters that are always written hastily, without taking pains, without importance, since the musician knows he need not live up to a litterateur's reputation.

Isn't it enough that he should be hooted at for his notes? No sir! His letters too! Ah, fame is a great bother! These poor little famous men of stature pay heavily indeed for their popularity! Never a moment of peace for them, alive or dead!

I leave you and am going out into the fields. That is my present occupation. The weather is fine, and I stroll all day long. It's a very prosaic way of life, but it makes you feel very well.

Peppina [3] is at Cremona with her sister, and tomorrow I'll go and fetch her. Stay in good health and keep me in your affection.

G. Verdi

[= Letter 226], 260–62.—Tr. by editor.

258   RICHARD STRAUSS TO BREITKOPF & HÄRTEL, LEIPZIG [G.]

Munich, 8 February 1881

Dear Mr. Breitkopf,

Since, as a total stranger, I am about to trouble you with a request, I shall first take the liberty of introducing myself to you. My name is Richard Strauss and I was born on the eleventh of June '64, the son of Franz Strauss, chamber musician and teacher at the Music School in this city.[1] At the moment I am attending the Gymnasium, the lower sixth form to be precise, but shall wholly dedicate myself to music, in fact specifically to composition. I learnt counterpoint from Mr. Fr. W. Meyer, Court *Kapellmeister*. As for my compositions, the enclosed Festival March [2] is dedicated to my uncle, Brewery Owner Georg Pschorr, whose wish it is that the same appear from the presses of one of the top music-publishing concerns, the printing costs to be borne by him. I therefore address myself to you with the request that you will be so good as to undertake the publication of the Festival March, since your name, well-known in every respect to the musical world, is, after all, of the greatest influence in spreading the name of a young aspiring musician.—The March, as well as some other larger compositions of mine, has occasioned very favorable comments on the part of General [Music] Director Franz Lachner,[3] who has granted me gracious permission to submit to him one of my compositions from time to time. These include an unpublished symphony for full orchestra, which will shortly be rehearsed by the Ryl. Court Orchestra at the request of His Excellency General Intendant Baron von Perfall, and a string quartet, which will receive its first public performance in early March at the hands of the local quartet under the leadership of Mr. Benno Walter, *Concertmeister;* [4] I shall await the outcome of that performance and then, perhaps, take the liberty of sending you the work for your kind consideration.—Referring myself again to my earlier request, I beg you to be good enough to write me and inform me of your intentions regarding its fulfillment and the probable amount of the printing expenses.[5] I commend myself to your goodwill and remain

Yours respectfully,
Richard Strauss.

Der Bär: Jahrbuch von Breitkopf & Härtel auf das Jahr 1924, 68–70.—Tr. by editor.

259 RICHARD WAGNER TO LUDWIG STRECKER, MAINZ [G.]

Bayreuth, 30 August 1881.

Dear Sir and friend!

It seems to me that the time is ripe for arriving at a sensible agreement with the firm of *Schott's Söhne,* as personified by you.

You are acquainted with the difficulties which I opposed to the publication of my newest work, "Parsifal," as well as with my motivations for taking special precautions in that regard. It is now a question of indicating the simplest way towards an accord between us. This I shall at once expose to you, while presenting you with the following proposal.

The principal question for me is that of preventing any *theatrical* performance of "Parsifal" outside *Bayreuth.* Since *France* and *Italy* have a cartel with *Germany,* and *Belgium* and *England* are covered by your firm, my main concern is *Holland,* for there any entrepreneur could indulge in a little fun. Therefore, please try to establish my copyright regarding the sanctioning of theatrical performances, perhaps also with reference to *Denmark* and *Sweden;*—thus nothing will stand in the way of the *score's* publication, and I shall make its sale lucrative to you, for I [hereby] declare that I shall raise no objections to performances of large or small excerpts from the score at *concerts,* and shall gladly waive any royalties due me on such occasions. In this manner I would also assure you the unlimited copyright of "the tune"; and it seems to me that it would now be up to your ingenuity to protect that right, much as *Fürstner* did in Berlin: for he prosecuted the firm of *Breitkopf & Härtel* so successfully (they had published a Fantasy on the "Evening Star" from "Tannhäuser" 37 years before), that I had to come to their rescue with a declaration, in which I testified that *Liszt* had at the time been authorized to make that edition by special permission, which I—as author-publisher of "Tannhäuser"—had given him.

As for the pianoforte arrangement, the first act will be at your disposal at once, ready to be engraved; it will be quite finished by the end of the year. The full score we still need for the present, as the parts are being copied out; but by the time of the perform-ance (at the latest), the score too will be entirely at your disposal.

The price I am setting is one hundred thousand marks and the cancellation of my outstanding debts towards you. You have offered me 40,000 marks for the rights to the piano arrangement, following a three years' period during which the profits from its sale would devolve exclusively to my account. Now I desire that you pay me the 40,000 marks at this time, in conjunction with my cession of the copyright, and on the other hand am willing to receive the difference of 60,000 M. in 3 yearly install-ments beginning at the end of December 1882.

Lest you find my demands excessive, be good enough to take as an example the *English* publisher who thinks he can pay Mr. *Gounod* 100,000 Frs for an oratorio (!). I think I may favorably compare my last and—I believe—best work with that of the somewhat faded *Parisian* Maestro!—[1]

But I do not wish to close this communication without personally thanking you, dear Sir and friend, for your many tokens of willingness and kindness; this I hereby do, and at the same time send you my cordial regards.

Yours faithfully,
Richard Wagner.

Wilhelm Altmann (ed.), *Briefwechsel mit seinen Verlegern Breitkopf & Härtel, B. Schott's Söhne,* Vol. VIII of *Richard Wagner: Briefe* (Leipzig: Breitkopf & Härtel, 1911), 226–27.—Tr. by editor.

260   GIUSEPPE VERDI TO GIULIO RICORDI, MILAN [It.]

[14 February 1883]
The paper is very good, both the first and the second [kind]:
perhaps the thinner *R.B.* is better, but take care that the color
doesn't get too dark when you have it lined.

Sad Sad Sad!
Wagner is dead!
When I read the dispatch yesterday, I was simply aghast. There
is no question about it.—A great personality has passed away!
A name that leaves a most powerful imprint on the history of the
art!

[= Letter 202], 323; for the 2nd part, facsimile of the autograph, opposite
p. 322.—Tr. by editor.

261   JOHANNES BRAHMS TO EDUARD HANSLICK,
KARLSBAD [G.]

[Vienna, May 1884]
Dear friend,
You have gone away and left me a treasure, without even
looking at it. I really must write you a few words of thanks and
tell you approximately what the treasure's significance is.
There is practically no doubt that we have here the two lost
cantatas which Beethoven composed in Bonn when Joseph II died
and Leopold II ascended the throne.[1]
In other words, two major works for chorus and orchestra,
from a period in which, until now, we had not been able to place
a single composition of any importance.* If it were not for the

---

* You'll find the cantatas mentioned in Thayer I, p. 232;[2] but the auction
catalogue he speaks of (not Dubaine's [du Beine's]) is in the Vereinsarchiv.
There is no question our copies are meant; they subsequently became Hummel's
property, after his death the Leipzig dealer's, from whom finally our young
Viennese acquired them.

historical date (February 1790), one would almost certainly guess at a later period—naturally, since we knew nothing of the other!

But even if the title bore no name, one could guess at no other [composer]—it is all so thoroughly Beethoven! The fine, noble pathos, the grand inspiration and imagination, the powerful, even violent expression; and then the part-writing, the declamation, and in these all the characteristics we can possibly observe and consider in his later works.

The cantata on Joseph II's death, of course, interests us first of all.

Here no one can speak of "music made for the occasion"! If today we were to honor that unforgettable, irreplaceable man, we should be just as ardent as was Beethoven then, and everyone else.[3]

Besides, there's no such thing as "occasional music" in Beethoven, when one considers that an artist never stops creating and laboring in an artistic way, and that this is even more noticeable in a younger man than in a master.

The opening choral Lament (c minor) is immediately just like him. Every note—every word is unmistakable. An unusually lively recitative comes next (Presto, in C): "A monster called Fanaticism rose from the depths of Hell . . ." (In an aria, he is trampled down by Joseph.) I cannot help it: it is a special pleasure for me to think of those days, and of how everyone was aware of what they had lost in Joseph, as those passionate words testify; but the young Beethoven knew also what great things he had to say, and he said them loud and clear, as was fit, in a forceful prologue at the very beginning.

But now, to the words "And men ascended into the realm of light" etc., we hear the glorious F major section of the finale in Fidelio.

We have, here too, the touching, heavenly oboe melody (true, it doesn't suit the singing part, or at least it does so very awkwardly).

We have many examples of how our masters used the same idea a second time and in another place. I particularly like it here. How deeply must Beethoven have felt the melody (and so, the meaning of the words)—just as deeply and beautifully as later, when he sang out the lofty song of a woman's love—and also of a liberation!

374

After another recitative and aria, the first chorus is repeated and concludes the work; but I won't continue my description; at any rate, not of the second cantata. Besides, the interest here lies only in the music and in whatever concerns Beethoven.

But now, dear friend, I can already hear you asking: when will the cantatas be performed, printed?

And here my joy comes to an end. Printing has become so fashionable nowadays, especially of things that don't need to be **printed.**

You know my old pet wish: that the so-called complete works of our masters—even of the first-rate ones, let alone the second-raters'—might be printed a little less complete; instead they ought to be deposited, in *truly complete,* good [manuscript] copies, at the major libraries. You know how eagerly I've always tried to acquaint myself with their unpublished works. But I shouldn't want to own printed versions of everything that some of my favorite masters have written.

And I don't think it's right and good for amateurs and young artists to be led to cram their rooms and their brains with all the "Complete Works," and to have their good judgment confused.

Our Haydn has not yet had the honor of a complete edition. And a truly complete edition of his works would be impossible and unpractical; on the other hand, how easy and desirable [it would be to make] a transcript of the collected works, with several copies for the public libraries.

How little, by contrast, is being done about new editions of many works whose study and dissemination would be desirable!

For example, older vocal music of all kinds. Perhaps you will say it is not needed—but it ought to be, and it will be, more and more, beyond question. In this case sacrifices would be in order and would surely be more worthwhile in every respect.

But these are extensive themes, and I don't want to go on improvising variations on them for you; besides, they are too exclusively in the minor mode, and I know very well that also some major ones are possible and necessary.

Come soon and share the quite unique experience and pleasure of being the only person in the world, besides myself, who is acquainted with these first exploits of a hero.

Cordially yours Johannes Brahms.

Max Kalbeck, *Johannes Brahms,* III, Part II (2nd ed.; Berlin: Deutsche Brahms-Gesellschaft m.b.H., 1913), 428–31.—Tr. by editor.

262   GIUSEPPE VERDI TO COUNT OPPRANDINO ARRIVABENE, ROME [It.]

St. Agata, 10 June 1884

Dear Arrivabene,

To begin with, I'll tell you that both I and Peppina [1] are in good health, and we are glad that you also are well. And that is proved by the rather long trips you are planning to take this summer. As for us, I am not positively sure what we shall do, but there is every indication that as soon as the season settles for the better, Peppina will go to Tabiano for 10 or 12 days and I, later, to Montecatini. After that, I don't know: perhaps to Turin, perhaps even to Paris, to see whether they are still merrier than they used to be, and then, and then . . . that's all I know.

I know nothing about the poet who is Romagnosi's fellow-townsman, but I have heard the musician Puccini very well spoken of. [2] I have seen a letter that praises him very much. He follows the modern tendencies, and that is natural, but he remains attached to melody, which is neither modern nor ancient. But it appears that the symphonic element is predominant in him! No harm. Only, one ought to be cautious here. Opera is opera: symphony is symphony, and I don't believe that it is beautiful to write a symphonic fragment in an opera, simply for the pleasure of putting the orchestra through its paces. I'm only chatting away, without any consequence; I'm not sure that I have spoken correctly, in fact I am certain that what I have said is contrary to the modern tendencies. All epochs have their own imprint. History pronounces later as to which is the good epoch and which the bad. Who knows how many people in the 1600s admired that sonnet of Achillini's *Sweat, ye fires* etc. etc. more than a canto by Dante! [3]

And throughout all this, whether good or bad, keep healthy and in good spirits for some time to come.

I send you greetings from Peppina and a warm handshake from myself.

Affectionately,
G. Verdi

[= Letter 226], 311–15.—Tr. by editor.

263   GUSTAV MAHLER TO FRIEDRICH LÖHR, VIENNA [G.]

Cassel, 1 January 1885

My dear Fritz, Today, on New Year's morning, my first thoughts shall be dedicated to you. I spent this year's first minutes in a strange enough manner. Last night we sat alone at her house, and we waited almost mutely for the new year's arrival. Her thoughts were elsewhere; and when the bell tolled and tears gushed from her eyes, I felt it so dreadfully that I, I was not to dry them. She went into the next room and stood at the window silently for a while; and when she returned, quietly weeping, nameless anguish had risen between us like an eternal dividing wall, and I could only press her hand and leave. As I came out of the house, the bells were ringing and a stately chorale resounded from the steeple.

Ah, dear Fritz—it was all as though the great Stage Manager of the world had meant to make a skillful job of it. I wept in my dreams the night through.

My pathways: I have written a cycle of songs, six so far, all dedicated to her.[1] She does not know them. What could they convey to her that she doesn't already know. I am sending you the last song, though the paltry words can hardly express a particle [of it].—The songs as a whole are intended to picture a wayfaring journeyman who has suffered at the hands of destiny and now goes forth into the world, wandering without aim.

My "Trumpeter's Music" was performed at Mannheim and will shortly be performed at Wiesbaden and Karlsruhe. Without the slightest prompting on my part, of course. You know how little store I set on that piece.

Christmas Eve I spent alone, even though she had invited me to come to her.

Dear Fritz! All that you know of her is but a misunderstanding. I begged her to forgive me for everything, cast off my pride and egoism. She is worthier of love than anyone in the world. I would shed my blood for her to the last drop. Yet I know that I must leave. And I have done all that is possible to that end;

377

but the way out is still not in sight. Farewell! Now I must go to pay my New Year's visits. Write to me soon, dear Fritz. And give me news of your family!

Gustav

Alma Maria Mahler (ed.), *Gustav Mahler: Briefe, 1879–1911* (Berlin: Paul Zsolnay Verlag, 1924), 33–34.—Tr. by editor.

264   CLAUDE DEBUSSY TO EUGÈNE-HENRY VASNIER, PARIS [Fr.]

[Rome, February 1885]

Dear monsieur Vasnier,

Here I am in this abominable villa, and I assure you that my first impression is not a good one. The weather is frightful: rain, wind; you will admit that there was no need to come to Rome in order to find the same weather as in Paris, especially for someone who is filled with rancor for all things Roman.

My colleagues came to meet me at Monte-Rotondo, in a dirty little room where all six of us slept. If you knew how they have changed! Gone is the warm friendship of Paris, they are stiff, appear convinced of their importance—too much Prix de Rome, they are.

On the evening of my arrival at the villa, I played my cantata which pleased some, [but] not the musicians, for instance.

No matter. This artistic milieu the old men speak of, this fine camaraderie, seem very overrated to me. With one or two exceptions, it is difficult to talk, and I cannot help comparing these banal conversations with our good, fine conversations which helped me so much and opened my mind to a great many things, oh! yes, I miss them. Then all those people are perfectly egoistic, each one lives for himself, I've heard the musicians, Marty, Pierné, Vidal demolishing each other; Marty in the company of Pierné demolishes Vidal, Pierné in the company of Vidal demolishes Marty, and so on.[1]

Ah! when I went back to my room which is immense, where, to go from one piece of furniture to another, you have to walk a mile, how lonely I felt and how I cried!

I was too accustomed to your intelligent friendship, too

accustomed to your taking an interest in what I was doing and talking to me about it, and I will never forget, Sir, all that you have done for me, the place you were so good as to accord me in your family. I shall do all I can to prove to you that I am not ungrateful.

I shall also ask you not to forget me, and to save me the place I have in your affection, because I foresee I shall need it badly.

I have tried working, [but] I can't, and still I do whatever I can. For the rest, you know how much I love music, and you can imagine how my present state vexes me. But I cannot live this life. What brings them happiness cannot bring me any; it is not pride that makes me hate it so. No, but I cannot get used to it, I lack the special aptitudes and the indifference which would be necessary.

Yes, I repeat, I am afraid I may return to Paris sooner than you think. It might be very silly, but what then? I am also afraid of going against your wishes, of wearying your friendship, which would make me very sorry; but I assure you that if you have enough left over to pity me, you cannot accuse me of lacking courage. I am rather unwell, for the same reason, and besides, my confounded heart is averse to the air of Rome. I should so much like to work that I am dislocating my brain without finding anything except fever, which is casting me down ridiculously, leaving me without any strength.

I received your letter which made me very, very happy, and if it isn't asking too much, though I am well aware that your time is not your own, answer me [with] a long letter, to remind me of the good conversations I have mentioned.

Believe in my true friendship and affection for you.

Yours most devotedly,

Ach[ille] Debussy.

Please convey my sincere regards to Mme. Vasnier. Is Marguerite well? has she continued studying my melodies? I like Marguerite, I do indeed, I should like to make an accomplished musician of her, I think you would like that, and I should be proud of it, because I should at least have been of some use.

Kiss her for me, and also that dear little madcap, Maurice. I grasp your hand once more.

Ach.[2]

Henry Prunières, "A la Villa Médicis," *La Revue Musicale*, VII, Tome III (May 1926), 122-24.—Tr. by editor.

265   JOHANNES BRAHMS TO MARIE LIPSIUS, LEIPZIG [G.]

Vienna, 27 May 1885

Dear Madam,

I make bold to ask that you leave the letters in question unpublished. I know and admit that I always write reluctantly, hurriedly, and casually, but I am ashamed when I happen to see such an instance [of it] as yours.

It takes a certain kind of boldness to write to a cultivated, friendly gentleman, whom one does not know, as carelessly as I did in this case.

But to allow such letters to be published, to explicitly say yes—that would be more than mere boldness!

If you will permit me to state positively that I cannot think of a less welcome service than to have any of my letters published —then I shall gladly make an exception in the present case.

And you will have the better reason for including it in your book, since your readers will learn from it that I am at fault rather than you and—that I have taken care not to draw any conclusions from the intended publication of my letters as to the contents and value of your book.

There are enough people who enjoy writing letters, and who write them well, as I know not only from "Schiller and Goethe," but also from my very pleasant personal experience.

But then there are people of my sort; and their letters ought to be read and interpreted with indulgence and discretion, if the writers are worthy in other respects.

I, for example, enjoy keeping a letter of Beethoven's as a relic; but I am horrified when I think of all the things such a letter is supposed to mean and to explain!

I feel the same way concerning a musician's posthumous works.

How eagerly have I always tracked them, studied them, and copied and recopied them. How I valued these countless, superabundant tokens of the industry and genius of Haydn, for example, or Schubert.

I always wished such valuable and instructive treasures might be copied for the major libraries, to make them accessible to those who take a serious interest in them.—I shall not enlarge on my very different feelings when I see the beloved treasures in print—

380

or even supervise their publication myself to make sure that it is done properly!

In both instances, the misunderstandings and misinterpretations are quite incredible; and whether such publications are necessary and good, or superfluous and even harmful—I do not know!

At the risk of your taking the beginning of this epistle for a piece of hypocrisy,

I remain

Yours very faithfully,

J. Brahms.

[= Letter 55], II, 348–50.—Tr. by editor.

266   ANTON BRUCKNER TO BARON HANS VON WOLZOGEN [BAYREUTH?] [G.]

[Vienna, 25 March 1886]

High-born Lord!

Most Noble High Patron!

A thousand thanks for Your Lordship's gracious visit; it grieved me deeply that I did not know of it and that I could not return the visit but, especially, that I had to miss Your Lordship's excellent speech. (I have that same condition once again.)

The highly ingenious letter, so flattering to me, made me very happy! My deepfelt thanks! The poem is splendid! Unhappily, I am buried in the 8th Symphony now and have hardly any time to compose. On the 14th inst. I was in Graz, at the performance of my 7th Symph. The performance, under the ingenious Dr. Muck [1] from Würzburg, [was] excellent (14 rehearsals), the reception magnificent beyond all description. After the finale they welcomed me with trumpets and kettledrums.

On the 21st inst. the same performance [sic] in Vienna by the Philharmonic, under Richter's [2] direction, was quite excellent: the success—indescribable jubilation; 5 or 6 curtain calls, already after the first movement, and tempestuous ones at that. At the conclusion, endless enthusiasm and curtain calls; laurel wreath from the Wagner Society and banquet. The Sublime, immortal unequaled Master's picture was hung round my neck with the wreath. Very thoughtful indeed; I made it the starting point of my speech and could not help weeping bitterly; next morning too, when I received from Dresden, through my pupil Dr. Behn who is here from Germany, my dearly beloved Master's and Ideal's bust, which I smothered with kisses, weeping.

Still, the *five hostile papers* will see to the annihilation of this success with the distant public, at Hanslick's request! [3]

With gratitude and the deepest respect,

Your High-born Lordship's
most obliged
A. Bruckner.

Vienna, 25 March
    1886.

[= Letter 142], 73–74.—Tr. by editor.

267   GIUSEPPE VERDI TO FRANCO FACCIO, MILAN [It.]

St Agata 2 Sept
1886

Dear Faccio

Mme. Pantaleoni [1] left us just a moment ago, and led me to hope that she'll return towards the middle of October, once her part is entirely copied, or rather printed. I have given Giulio [2] the fourth act, in which Desdemona has the biggest and most difficult part. The *Song of the Willow* presents the greatest difficulties both to the composer and to the performing artist. The latter, like the *Holy Trinity*, should have three voices; one for Desdemona; another for Barbara (the maid); and a third voice for *"Willow willow willow."* Mme. Pantaleoni's voice, which is accustomed to violent roles, is often a little too biting in the top notes; she puts too much metal in them, so to speak. If she could get used to using her head-voice a little more, her soft notes would come to her more easily, and her voice would also be more secure and better focused. I have advised her to study in this manner, and you ought to use your influence and give her the same advice. Meanwhile, it is not true that her *d* is always a very bad note, as you say. There is a melody in which she manages it very well

This phrase is repeated three times. The last time it comes out very well; the other two times, less so.—

I have given you my candid opinion; and I add that, though the part of Desdemona is not perfectly adapted to her feeling and to her voice, yet, with her considerable talent, with her instinct for the stage, and with goodwill and much study, she will succeed very well . . . and note that there are very many things that suit her to perfection! Farewell, I don't even know what I have written you in such haste. Try to understand. Again, farewell

Peppina [3] sends her greetings
and so does
Your
GVerdi

AUTOGRAPH (see Plates V/VI), Arturo Toscanini Collection, New York: 1 sheet, 269 × 207 mm., folded to form 4 pp.—Tr. by editor.

268A   ANTONÍN DVOŘÁK TO PYOTR ILYITCH TCHAIKOVSKY, S. FROLOVSKOJE [Czech]

Prague, 14 January 1889.

Dear Friend,

When you were last here in Prague I promised to write to you about your opera "Onyegin." Now not only your request compels me to do so but my inward desire to tell you all that I felt on hearing your work. I confess with pleasure that your opera made a very deep impression upon me—an impression such as I expect from a true work of art, and I do not hesitate to say that none of your compositions has given me such pleasure as Onyegin.

It is a splendid work, full of warm feeling and poetry, and, at the same time, worked out to the last detail; in short, this

music speaks to us and penetrates so deep into our soul that
it is unforgettable. Whenever I go to the theater I feel as if I
were in another world.

I congratulate you and ourselves on this work and pray
God that you may be spared to give the world many more
such compositions.

With a warm embrace,

Your devoted

Antonín Dvořák.

268B PYOTR ILYITCH TCHAIKOVSKY TO ANTONÍN DVOŘÁK, PRAGUE [Russ.]

30/18 Jan. 1889.[1]

S. Frolovskoje

Dear, beloved, and esteemed Friend,

You cannot imagine how delighted I was with your letter.
I value your opinion of my opera very highly, not only
because you are a great artist but because you are a frank
and sincere man. I am exceedingly proud and happy that I
have been able to deserve a sincere word of commendation
from you, my dear Friend. I thank you once more from the
bottom of my heart.

Forgive me for not answering your letter immediately. In
spite of all my efforts to read your letter I could not understand
it, although I guessed that its content was agreeable. The
letter had to be sent to Moscow, to Hřímalý,[2] to be translated
and the translation reached me only today.

About ten days ago I sent a letter to A. O. Patera,[3] requesting
him to discuss with you in detail your journey to Moscow.
I have not, however, received an answer so far. I beg you,
dear Friend, give your consent and come, it is the great wish
of all of us here.[4]

My compliments to your wife and to all our common
friends: Bendl, Fibich,[5] N. P. Apraksin, Marie Federovna, etc.

With a warm embrace, dear Dvořák,

Yours,

P. Tchaikovsky.

[= Letter 241], 122–24.

384

269   GIUSEPPE VERDI TO ALFREDO SOFFREDINI,
MILAN [It.]

Genoa 11 Dec. 1890

Dear Mr Soffredini

Forgive me if I have put off answering your esteemed letter
for so long. —————

I take in the Gazzetta Musicale, and quite often read
your articles, [which are] judicious most of the time, and
always indulgent towards me. I have no cause to complain
of that indulgence; but I turn to you, and ask you whether
it makes you feel no compunction! —————

Falstaff? This is not the time to talk of it[.] I am writing
for the fun of it . . . .   with no designs . . .   no pretensions . . .   and who knows whether I'll ever finish setting it to
music[.]

I remain, dear Maestro,

Yrs. sincerely
GVerdi

AUTOGRAPH, Arturo Toscanini Collection, New York: half a sheet,
173 × 110 mm., written on both sides; watermark: [. . .]RUE & C°
[LO]NDON.—Tr. by editor.

270   GIUSEPPE VERDI TO ARRIGO BOITO, MILAN [It.]

S' Agata 12 June
1891

Dear Boito

If you've discovered a good [Mistress] *Quickly*, then I'm
the happiest man in the world. That part had me quite
preoccupied, because, apart from the dramatic interest, its
music lies very low. I could not do otherwise. Since there are
four female parts, at least one of them, after all, had to be low.

Pot-Belly [1] is on the path that leads to madness. There are
days when he won't budge, but sleeps and is ill-humored: at
other times he shouts, runs, jumps about, raises the Devil . . .

385

I'm letting him have his way for a while, but if he keeps this up I'll muzzle him and put him in a strait jacket . . .

Barberina [2] is feeling better, she gets up, and has been dining with us for the past three or four days.

Peppina [3] sends you her greetings and I an affect[ionate] handshake.

Yours

GVerdi

AUTOGRAPH, Arturo Toscanini Collection, New York: 1 sheet, 227 × 178 mm., folded to form 4 pp.; p. 4 blank; watermark: SPECIAL, figure of lion crowned with star.—Tr. by editor.

271A   HANS VON BÜLOW TO GIUSEPPE VERDI, GENOA [It.]

Hamburg, 7 April 1892

Illustre Maestro,

Deign to hear the confession of a contrite sinner!

It is eighteen years now since the undersigned made himself culpable of a great . . . great journalistic BLUNDER . . . against the last of the five Kings of Italian modern music.[1] He has rued it, he has been bitterly ashamed of it, oh how often! When he committed the aforementioned sin (perhaps your magnanimity has quite forgotten it) he was actually in a state of insanity—excuse my mentioning this (so to say) extenuating circumstance. My mind was blinded by fanaticism, by ultra-Wagnerian "Seide." [2] Seven years later, little by little, the light began to dawn. My fanaticism was purified, it became enthusiasm. Fanaticism—lamp oil; enthusiasm—electric light. In the intellectual and moral world, the light's name is: justice. There is nothing more destructive than injustice, nothing more intolerable than intolerance, as that most noble man, Giacomo Leopardi, has already said.[3]

Having at length reached "that point of insight," how I could rejoice, how much richer my life became, how vaster the field of my most treasured delights: art! I began by studying your last works: *Aida, Otello,* and the *Requiem,* of which a recent, rather weak performance moved me to tears: I have studied them not only according to the letter that kills, but

386

according to the spirit that gives life! Well, *illustre Maestro,* now I admire and adore you!

Will you forgive me, will you avail yourself of a sovereign's right to reprieve? Be that as it may, I must, since I can, confess my past fault, if only to set an example to my younger, erring brethren.

And so, faithful to Prussia's motto: *Suum cuique,*[4] I heartily exclaim: *Evviva Verdi,* the Wagner of our dear allies!

Hans von Bülow.

271B   GIUSEPPE VERDI TO HANS VON BÜLOW, HAMBURG [It.]

Genoa, 14 April 1892.

Illustre Maestro Bülow,

There is not the shadow of a sin in you!—and there is no occasion to speak of penitence and absolution!

If your former opinions were different from those you hold today, you [nevertheless] did very well to make them known; nor should I have dared complain of them. Besides, who knows . . . , perhaps you were right then.

Be that as it may, this unexpected letter of yours, written by a musician of your worth and of your importance in the artistic world, made me very happy! And not because of any personal vanity, but because I see that truly superior artists judge without preconceptions as to school, nationality, period.

If the artists of the North and the South have different tendencies, it is well that they should be *different!* Everyone ought to keep the *characteristics inherent in their nation,* as Wagner said so very aptly.

Well for you, who are still sons of Bach! And we? We too, sons of Palestrina, once had a great school . . . and our very own! Now it has become bastardized and is threatening to collapse!

If only we could start again from the beginning?!

I regret that I cannot be present at the Musical Exhibition in Vienna, for I should have had not only the good fortune of finding myself among so many illustrious Musicians, but more especially the pleasure of shaking your hand. I hope that

my advanced age will meet with the indulgence of the
Gentlemen who have so kindly invited me, and that they will
forgive my defection.

Your sincere admirer

[G. Verdi]

[= Letter 202], 375–76.—Tr. by editor.

272   GIACOMO PUCCINI TO THE EDITOR OF
IL CORRIERE DELLA SERA, MILAN [It.]

Milan, 21 March 1893

Dear Sir,

I should be grateful if you could find space for this brief
letter in your esteemed newspaper.

Maestro Leoncavallo's assertion in yesterday's *Secolo* must
have convinced the public of my good faith, for it is certain
that, had Maestro Leoncavallo, to whom I have long been tied
by bonds of close friendship, told me earlier what he suddenly
let me know the other evening, I should not have considered
[composing] Murger's *Bohème*.

Now—for reasons that can easily be understood—it is too
late for me to be as courteous as I should like to be towards
a friend and musician.

Besides, why should Maestro Leoncavallo care?

Let him set it to music, let me. The public will judge.
Precedence in art does not imply that one must interpret the
same subject using the same artistic approach. I only wish to
make known that for the last two months or so, in fact since
the first performances of *Manon Lescaut* at Turin, I have
been seriously at work on my idea and have not made it a
secret to anyone.

[Giacomo Puccini] [1]

Eugenio Gara (ed.), *Carteggi pucciniani* (Milan: Ricordi, 1958), 81–82.—
Tr. by editor.

273   CLAUDE DEBUSSY TO ERNEST CHAUSSON,
[PARIS?] [Fr.]

                              [Paris,] Thursday evening [autumn 1893]
Dear friend,
    I really have a lot of silence to be forgiven for, and you are
very kind to have half done so already; many things have happened
to me, some irksome, others pleasant, let us dwell on the
latter, as the former would hardly be news to you.
    As a result of my acquaintance with Pierre Louÿs,[1] whom
I believe you know, I took a short trip to Brussels; since that
city held no interest for me except that it contained Ysaÿe,[2]
my first visit was to him, and you will not be too astonished
when I tell you that he let out real yells of joy when he saw
me, and clasped me against his ample bosom, addressing me
with *tu* as though I were his younger brother; after which I
had to give him news of everyone, particularly yours, which,
alas, I could only speak of on the basis of letters; then,
music, frenzied music, and in one memorable evening I played
in succession the five poems [of Baudelaire], *la Damoiselle
Elue, Pelléas et Mélisande;*[3] I was as hoarse as if I'd been selling
newspapers on the boulevard. *Pelléas* had the honor of affecting
some young persons, English girls it seems; as for Ysaÿe,
it was delirium, and I really can't repeat what he said to me!
He liked your "quartet" just as much, and he is going to have
it studied.
    I have seen Maeterlinck, with whom I spent a day at Ghent;
at first, he behaved like a young girl to whom her future husband
is being introduced, then he thawed and became charming, he
talked theater with me like a really remarkable man; apropos of
Pelléas, he is giving me full authorization to make cuts and has
even shown me some very important ones, *even very useful ones!*
Now from the viewpoint of music, he says he's totally in the
dark about it, and he goes to a Beethoven symphony like a blind
man to a museum; but he's actually very nice, and speaks extraordinary things, which he discloses with an exquisite candor: at
at one point, while I was thanking him for entrusting *Pelléas*
to me, he did all he could to prove to me that it was he who was
indebted to me for having been so good as to put music under
it! Since I hold a diametrically contrary opinion, I was forced to
389

use all my diplomacy, which nature has not, after all, given me in superabundance.

Well, you can see that it was a more profitable trip than Urien's! [4]

"Correspondance inédite de Claude Debussy et Ernest Chausson," *La Revue Musicale*, VII, Tome II (Dec. 1925), 123–24.—Tr. by editor.

274   JOHANNES BRAHMS TO CLARA SCHUMANN, INTERLAKEN [G.]

[Bad Ischl, August 1894]

Dear Clara,

I hope Miss Eugenie [1] knows I should have written to her at once and comprehensively, if I'd had anything at all to say about learning to transpose. But I consider it mostly a matter of practice and habit. Anybody who has to accompany singers every day is bound to learn soon. This, in fact, is what I should recommend in the first place. Then, waltzes, easy Haydn symphonies 4-hands, and the like. The main thing, it seems to me, is to learn to handle the matter with ease and fluency. It goes without saying that here, too, a thorough knowledge of harmony is very useful.

(But how some people can keep on taking harmony lessons year in year out is more than I shall ever understand.)

That you are constantly looking over my dear songs [2] makes me very happy. . . .

Have you noticed that the last of the songs appears in my Op. 1? [3] Didn't it make you think of something too? Actually, it's meant to say something, it's meant to show the snake biting its own tail—in other words, to say symbolically: the story's ended, the circle closed.

But I know all about good resolutions, and I think them but never say them out loud to myself. At the moment, I wish I were as sensible after my 60th year as I used to be before my 20th. In those days, the Hamburg publishers, try as they might, could not tempt me to let anything be printed. Kranz offered the money in vain, which I, poor young chap, had to earn so hard elsewhere. [4] Why this was so, I can't readily or precisely say. Now, at 60, it would be high time to leave off—again, for no particular reason!!

However that may be, I'm going to do myself a favor one of these days. I'm expecting a visit from Mühlfeld, the clarinetist, and I'll rehearse 2 sonatas with him.[5] And so, it may be that we shall be celebrating (I shan't say "honoring"!) your birthday [6] with music. I wish you could be there, for he plays very well. If you were to improvise a bit in F minor and E-flat major— you'd probably happen upon the sonatas. I would send them to you—you could play them quite comfortably—only the clarinet has got to be transposed, and that would spoil all your fun! Which brings me safely back to the beginning also of this letter, and so I'll close, with warmest greetings to you all.

Yours ever,

Johannes.

[= Letters 209A–B], II, 562–63.—Tr. by editor.

275   RICHARD STRAUSS TO GIUSEPPE VERDI, GENOA [It.]

Munich, 18 January 1895
Hildegardstrasse 2.

Illustrissimo Signore!

Knowing very well from my own experience how annoying dedications are, I nevertheless dare beg that you, the true master of Italian lyric drama, will benignly accept as a sign of homage and Admiration a copy of *Guntram*, my first attempt in that genre.[1]

Not finding words to express the profound impression which the extraordinary beauty of *Falstaff* has had on me, and unable otherwise to signify to you my gratitude for this recreation of the intellect, I beg you to be good enough to at least accept the score.

I should be delighted to have the opportunity of conversing with you some day on the divine art—music, that I may thus find an incentive toward new inspiration and creation—a day which my dear patron and friend Hans von Bülow has—unfortunately —not lived to see.[2]

391

Be so good as to accept, *Illustrissimo maestro,* the assurance
of my particular respect, with which I have the honor to declare
myself

your most devoted
Richard Strauss.
Kgl. Kapellmeister.

[= Letter 175], 35.—Tr. by editor.

276   GUSTAV MAHLER TO MAX MARSCHALK, BERLIN [G.]

Hamburg, 26 III [18]96

My dear Mr. Marschalk,

Your conception of my work is so unified and so deeply felt
that I actually shouldn't wish to see it altered in any way.

If I may permit myself one observation, then it is this: I should
like to have it emphasized that the symphony begins where the
love affair leaves off; the latter is at its root—or, to put it
differently, came before in the perceptual life of the creative
artist. But the external experience became the *occasion* for the
work and not its contents; you have characterized the third and
fourth movements in a *masterly* way, and I like it especially
because it points to what is typical, universal; I shouldn't wish
the least word of it changed. This you have understood with
sympathy. The slight misgiving I have mentioned is not in the
nature of an objection, but it does confront us with the important
question of *how,* and perhaps even *why* music should be interpreted by means of words at all. I see from a remark in your
esteemed letter that we are of one mind in this and understand
each other perfectly.

Allow me to present to you my point of view in brief.—I
know, where I am concerned, that so long as I can sum up my
experience in words, I would never write any music about it.
My need to express myself musically—symphonically begins only
where the *obscure* perceptions hold sway, at the gate that leads
into the "other world"; the world in which things are no longer
separable through the agency of time and place.—

392

Just as I think it a platitude to invent music to a program, so I consider it to be unsatisfying and sterile to want to attach a program to a musical work. This is in no way altered by the fact that the *occasion* for a musical creation is doubtless to be found in an experience of the author's, and an actual one, which for that matter might be concrete enough to be clothed in words. —We stand now—of this I am certain—at the great parting of the ways, where the diverging paths of symphonic and dramatic music separate for ever, and this will soon be plainly visible to those who have a clear understanding of the essence of music.— Wagner, to be sure, made the *expressive means* of symphonic music his own, just as the symphonist, in turn, will now help himself, quite legitimately and quite consciously, to the expressive riches music has gained through Wagner's work. In this sense, all the arts, and even art and nature, are linked together. But this has not yet been given enough thought, since no *perspective* has been gained on the subject so far.—Not that I have erected this "system," as it were, and patterned my work upon it; on the contrary, I finally gained this—personal—view of things after I had written some symphonies (suffering from real labor pains in the process)—and after meeting with the same misunderstandings and questions over and over.—

And so it remains a good idea to let the listener have a few guideboards and milestones for his trip at first, while my manner still appears strange—or let us say: an astronomical chart, so he can comprehend the nocturnal sky with its sparkling worlds. —But such an explanation cannot offer *more*.—Man needs to fasten upon something *familiar*, or he is lost. That is why I should be grateful to you if you published your essay; I like it best, of all the things that have so far been said about me. Of all the interpretations that might be given, I think yours is the most appropriate, because it is the most *direct* and corresponds best with the incidental, or external, cause of the inner experience.

Having expressed myself in the above terms, you can understand that I find it a little awkward to say something to you now concerning the C minor Symphony.[1]—I have named the first movement "Totenfeier" ["Funeral Rite"], and, if you want to know, it is the hero of my D major symphony that I am burying here and whose life I am gathering in a clear mirror, from a higher point of vantage. At the same time, it is the great question: *Why have you lived?* Why have you suffered? Is all this merely

393

a great, horrible jest?—We *must* resolve these questions somehow or other, if we are to continue living—nay, even if we are only to continue dying! Once this call has resounded in anyone's life—he must give an answer; and that answer I give in the last movement.

The 2nd and 3rd movements are conceived as interludes: the 2nd movement, a *memory!* A sunny moment, clear and untroubled, in the life of that hero.

You have surely had the experience of burying a person dear to you; and then, perhaps, as you came away, suddenly the image arose of a happy hour long since vanished, which now settles in your soul like a sunbeam—nothing darkens it—you are almost able to forget what has just occurred! That is the 2nd movement!—Then, if you awaken from this sorrowful dream and have to return to chaotic life, it may well happen that this unendingly mobile, restless, unintelligible bustle of life should strike you as being *ghastly,* like the swaying of dancing figures in a brightly-lit ballroom into which you are peering from the deep night outside—from so *far away* that you *cannot* hear the *music!* Life will seem senseless to you then and a ghastly nightmare, from which you will perhaps start up with a cry of horror!—That is the *3rd movement!* What follows is perfectly clear to you anyway! — — —

And so, actually, my 2nd symphony is directly connected to my 1st! Henceforth, when I appear with a new work, please let me familiarize you with it even before it is performed. That is better than any program! You make me so happy with your understanding and "going-along"! And if you only suspected how badly I, a wayfaring journeyman,[2] have need of it, you would surely not flag in your sympathy for me and my creative work.—

Please maintain your friendly interest in me, and do not think it vain that I should require this of you. Many, many thanks! Send me your essay as soon as it is published.

Yours most sincerely,

Gustav Mahler

[= Letter 263], 186–90.—Tr. by editor.

277   HUGO WOLF TO ROSA MAYREDER, VIENNA [G.]

Stuttgart, 16 June 1896

My dearest friend,

There is so much on my mind that wants to be expressed; but where, in the turmoil that here surrounds me, am I to find the leisure to enlarge upon a thought in any way? Your first dear letter, which I should so gladly have answered at once, shamed me deeply. In it, you speak of *my* work, as if it were not our work, or rather *yours* that has given you such sheer delight. And what could I have accomplished without your collaboration? No one, of course, can so well appreciate my debt to you as I myself with my poor music, which has sucked its fill of the heart blood of its sister, poetry. There's something gruesome about the intimate fusion of poetry and music, in which, actually, the gruesome role belongs only to the latter. Music has decidedly something of the vampire about it. It claws its victim relentlessly and sucks the last drop of blood from it. Or one could also compare it to a greedy suckling, who relentlessly demands fresh nourishment and becomes plump and fat, while its mother's beauty wilts away. But this comparison is valid only with regard to the effect that music, in league with poetry, has upon the public. Unhappily, you yourself have had occasion of becoming convinced of this. I say "unhappily," because nothing has shocked me more than this groundless injustice, inherent in the preference for one art over the other. Recently, for instance, Grohe wrote me apropos of the second performance of our work that the public's attitude was rather lukewarm; that the music, indeed, did not miss having its effect, but that several defects had made themselves felt in the book. This, in my opinion, is utter nonsense, and this sort of nonsense has unfortunately become the common rule. I shall still tell you all sorts of interesting things besides, on the subject. [But] enough of this for today. Yesterday evening's song recital turned out splendidly; the big hall was filled almost to the last seat, in spite of the unbearably hot weather. The atmosphere was one of extreme liveliness. Many songs had to be repeated, and there was almost no end to the applause.

All the hubbub is over now, thank goodness. Tomorrow morning at half past 3 I go via Munich and Salzburg to Traunkirchen, where I shall stay with Köchert for a few days. On the 24th at the latest I'll be in Vienna and stay with you for a few days. Any letters that may meanwhile arrive at your home ought to be forwarded to Traunkirchen. Miss Reiss has written and asked me to convey her greetings to you and Lino. How I look forward to our meeting again! Heaps of congratulatory messages are still arriving from far and near. The devil take all celebrity.

Give my best regards to dear Lino and accept my heartfelt greetings.

Yours ever,
Hugo Wolf.

Heinrich Werner (ed.), *Hugo Wolf: Briefe an Rosa Mayreder* (Vienna: Nikola Verlag, 1921), 82–83.—Tr. by editor.

278   JOHANNES BRAHMS TO HIS STEPMOTHER, PINNEBERG [G.] [penciled postcard]

[Vienna,] 29 March 1897

D[ear] M[other] I've gone to bed awhile, for the sake of variety, and therefore can't write comfortably. But don't be afraid, nothing has changed, and all I need is patience as usual. Your affectionate Joh.

[= Letter 229], 124.—Tr. by editor.

279   GIACOMO PUCCINI TO DON PIETRO PANICHELLI, ROME [It.]

[Monsagrati,] August 1898

Dear Little Priest,

When you write to me it is always to give me news that I like. Tell our good and intelligent Vessella from me what pleasure it gave me to hear of the effect produced by his [band] arrangement of *Bohème*, and thank him very much indeed.

396

I am working at *Tosca,* and sweating with the heat and the difficulties which I encounter, but which will—I hope—be overcome. Now I should like a favor: at the end of the first act in the Church of S. Andrea della Valle there is sung a solemn *Te Deum* of rejoicing for a victory.

Here is the scene: [1] from the sacristy enter the abbot in his miter, the chapter, and all the rest, while the people watch the procession on either side. In the front of the stage one of the characters (the baritone) soliloquizes independently, or very nearly so, on what is happening in the background.

Now, for the sake of the phonic effect, I want some prayers recited during the procession of the abbot and chapter. Whether it be by the chapter or by the people, I need some murmuring of prayers in subdued and natural voices, without intoning, precisely as real prayers are said. The *Ecce Sacerdos* is too imposing to be murmured. I know that it is not usual to say or sing anything before the solemn *Te Deum,* which is sung as soon as they reach the High Altar, but I repeat (whether right or wrong) that I should like to find *something to be murmured* during the passage from the sacristy to the altar, either by the chapter or the people; preferably by the latter, because they are more numerous and therefore more effective musically.

Look for the thing I need and send it to me at once, and thus do a very kind deed to your sincere friend

[Giacomo Puccini] [2]

Giuseppe Adami (ed.), *Letters of Giacomo Puccini,* trans. Ena Makin (Philadelphia: J. B. Lippincott Company, 1931), 126–27.

280   BÉLA BARTÓK TO HIS MOTHER, BRATISLAVA
[Hung., G.]

[Hung.:]   Budapest, 22 Sept. 1899.

Dear mother,

Well, there you are: Mrs. [Rauschmann] [1] was here today at 11 o'clock, and I wasn't at home. My lesson at the academy ended at a quarter to 11, and I could have come home, of course; but I wanted to take a little walk and only got back at

397

half past 11. She probably left in such a hurry that there wasn't
any time to write [me a note?] about it. I should have liked to
speak to her, that is, to see her, to ask her how you are, etc.

Yesterday I handed in the application for exemption from
tuition.[2]

Besides, I can't understand why Mrs. [Rauschmann] didn't
make any final arrangements, since the other one was given
notice; or perhaps she didn't like the one here?

Professor Thomán[3] was interesting today. After class, at a
quarter to 11, he called me over and asked me why I had on
low shoes, since it was so chilly this morning. He thought I was
supposed to be there already at 9. But I explained that Mr.
Szabó[4] had excused me from that class (I needn't attend it for
2 weeks, as I'm already acquainted with the rudiments anyway),
still I thanked him for his admonishment, which was really kind
of him. (On Wednesdays there is score reading and on Fridays
orchestration.)

Evening.

I have just received your letter.—It would be good if you
could write him soon concerning the housekeeper, since this
one is very uneasy because of the uncertainty; if my aunt had
been at home, she would have said so.

As for harmony, the others have no more experience, but I
should like to be tops in it, of course.

At score reading, we all had to play a simple movement in 4
clefs and written in 4 parts; we'll have to practise this sort of
thing a good deal at home, and for this we need a book that
costs 1.80 forints. [In the margin:] Apart from the 10.– forints,
I haven't spent any of your money so far, but more of my own
in consequence.

I receive the milk regularly, but one or two *bájgli*[5] wouldn't
be bad. However, I can't set about writing menus now; generally, by evening I don't even know what there was for lunch;
suffice it to say that the diet is pretty varied, everything is quite
good, and I get enough.

[G.:] Now I'll write in German (for practice).

Everything would be all right, but it's sheer misery with the
piano. In the first place: the piano turns out to be worse than I
thought it was on the first day; everything buzzes and rumbles,
the pedal creaks, etc. Secondly: it's a wretched thing that I
398

should be constantly interrupted. Yesterday a captain was there, today 2 ladies; and there I am, playing my scales. And then they want me to play something; yesterday I did, but not any more today; and very soon I shall hammer away at my exercises quite freely. So far as I'm concerned, they may do whatever they please; why are they always sitting there; and I'll certainly not perform anything. But in any case, this sort of thing is fatal.

If I were to write whenever I had a free moment, I could send a card every day, and that would surely cost too much. It will be good to resolve that I'll send 2 cards every week; if there's much subject matter, then 1 card and 1 letter. You can see, after all, that when there's something to say I write gigantic letters. But when absolutely nothing occurs, I could at best fill 8 pages with nothing but menus. (Perhaps you'd find that more interesting than anything else?)

Now I shall close with many greetings and kisses. Your

Béla

Is Elsa [6] learning a lot and still *aloud?*

Prof. Koessler [7] brought some Bach examples to counterpoint, and said: *"Of course, only Bach can write such things."*

János Demény (ed.), *Bartók Béla: levelek, fényképek, kéziratok, kották* (Budapest: Magyar Művészeti Tanács, 1948), 9–11.—The Hungarian portion translated for this book by Robert Austerlitz; the German tr. by editor.

---

281   GIUSEPPE VERDI TO ARRIGO BOITO, MILAN [It.]

St. Agata, 20 October 1900

Dear Boito,

I shall be brief because writing tires me; and be it said once and for all, whenever you please and your engagements permit you to come to St. Agata, it will always be a joy to me and to us all.

I am as God wills! I'm not really ill, but my legs barely support me, and my strength diminishes from day to day. The doctor comes twice daily for the massage but I don't feel any improvement.

399

I don't know when I shall be able to come to Milan. I need
Winderling, but I don't know yet whether he is in Milan.
We agree, then. With a warm handclasp I am

Yours affectionately,
G. Verdi

Frank Walker, *The Man Verdi* (New York: Alfred A. Knopf, 1962), 508.

282   MAURICE RAVEL TO FLORENT SCHMITT, ROME [Fr.]

[Paris,] 8-4-1901

My dear Schmitt,

What shall I call my conduct towards you? I prefer leaving
that care to you, since my indulgence finds me excellent reasons
every day with which to stifle my remorse. The most important
one, though it's rather feeble, is (or is it one at all?) my in-
coercible epistolary sloth. Other reasons join it—choruses, fugues
in anticipation of the competition—among which the transcription of Debussy's admirable *Nocturnes,* with Bardac's [1]
collaboration. As I disclosed some ability in this kind of work,
I was assigned the task of transcribing the 3rd [*Nocturne*] all
by myself—*Sirènes,* perhaps the most perfectly beautiful [of
the three], certainly the most perilous [to transcribe], the more
so as it has not been heard.

How sorry I feel for you, my dear friend, that you are too
far from Paris to hear such things! This and Liszt's *Faust,* that
astonishing symphony in which the most notable themes of
[Wagner's] Tetralogy file past (in the first place precursors, and
besides so much better orchestrated).

Nevertheless, in spite of the profound pity I feel for you, I
should rather like, who knows? to be in your place.

Does Rome inspire you with savory inspirations? Is "La Peau
de chagrin" getting along well? and will it be for us your
Damoiselle Elue or, Phoebus save us from it! your *Impressions
d'Italie?* [2]

All questions which I hope you'll answer soon.

There is reason to doubt that you'll ever get a letter from

Mlle. T . . . , since a damsel must not correspond with a young man. This argument, supplied by the mother of the young person, seems specious to me, for I have always considered a woman who writes fugues as being something of a hermaphrodite.

Here these epistolary effusions must come to an end, or I shall pay by arriving late at Mme. D . . .'s dinner, where I hope to furnish some unpublished slander about you.

Looking forward to early and abundant news, I grasp your hand cordially and am your devoted

Maurice Ravel.

Marcelle Gerar and René Chalupt (eds.), *Ravel au miroir de ses lettres* (Paris: Robert Laffont, 1956), 20–21.—Tr. by editor.

283   GIACOMO PUCCINI TO GIULIO RICORDI, MILAN [It.]

Torre del Lago [summer 1902]

My dear Signor Giulio,

I have had a visit today from Mme. Ohyama, wife of the Japanese Ambassador. She told me a great many interesting things and sang some native songs to me. She has promised to send me some native Japanese music. I sketched the story of the libretto for her, and she liked it, especially as just such a story as Butterfly's is known to her as having happened in real life.

She does not approve of the name *Yamadori,* on the ground that it is feminine and otherwise not appropriate; because in Japan they are accustomed in their plays to use names that suggest, or are suitable to, the various types and characters. The uncle's name of *Yaxonpidé* is wrong too. Similarly the names *Sarundapiko, Izaghi, Sganami,* etc., are all wrong. Mme Ohyama is at Viareggio, where I shall go to see her and take notes of what she sings to me.

She is very intelligent and, although plain, is attractive.

Affectionate regards.

[= Letter 279], 146.

284   SERGEI SERGEYEVICH PROKOFIEV TO HIS FATHER,
SONTSOVKA [Russ.]

[St. Petersburg, 22 September 1904]
I have passed the examination in composition. We have just
come from there.

We arrived there at 10 a.m. and went to Kurochkin's office.
He told us to go upstairs to the third floor, but from the third
floor they sent us to the second, and from the second to the first,
and from the first back again to the third, and so on. At last
we stopped on the second floor landing to wait for Glazunov [1]
who had not turned up.

Finally at a quarter past eleven Mama went up to the third
floor to ask the assistant inspector when the examination was due
to take place. Here she met Glazunov and Rimsky-Korsakov
(I shall refer to him as R.K. for short). [2] We went downstairs
and waited for a while outside the director's private office, where
the examination was to be held. There we met Mikhail Mikhailovich. [3] Soon we were called and we went into the director's office.
It was not actually his private office but the ante-room: a long,
narrow room with one window and no furniture, but after a while
some chairs were brought in. All the examinees in special theory,
about 20 in all, were in this room. Glazunov (I shall refer to
him as G.) came out of the office. Mama and I were sitting right
next to the door. He shook hands with me and passed on with
his slow gait. He shook hands with several others, said a few
words to them and then went back to his office. After that R.K.
came out. When he saw the room full of people, he threw up
his hands:

"Have you all come to take the examination? All in special
theory?"

"Yes," everyone replied.

He went in.

After that G. came out again several times with some other
professors, talked to the examinees and went back to the office.

At last someone named Burgov or Kurdov was called, then
another two and finally I, the fourth. I took my two folios (one
contained everything I composed this year, and the other,
things composed earlier) and went into the office.

"What! Are all these your own compositions?" R.K. asked me.

"Yes," I answered.

"Do you play the piano?"

"Yes."

"That's good!" R.K. exclaimed and, pointing to the piano, he said, "Very well then, sit down and play."

There was a Mozart sonata open before me on the piano. I had played it not long ago.

"Shall I play this?"

"Yes."

I started to play.

"Good. And now play me this," he said, turning over several pages to a piece, also by Mozart, I had never seen before. I played that as well.

I forgot to tell you that besides R.K. and G. there were about ten other professors in the room. They were sitting at a table at the other end of the room, drinking tea with buns.

G. told R.K. that I was a pupil of Glière.

"What did you study with him?" R.K. asked me.

"He stayed with us last summer and the summer before and taught me music."

"What did you do in theory?"

"We went through harmony from the beginning: we did problems from the Arensky collection, but since I will be enrolling in the harmony class I didn't study harmony at all this summer."

"Yes, yes." G. confirmed. "I advised him to take a course in harmony."

"Now we must test his ear," someone said.

"Have you absolute pitch?" R.K. asked.

"Yes."

"What note is this?" he asked when I turned my back on the piano.

He played several more notes and asked me what they were. Then someone suggested trying me with a whole chord. R.K. took a chord in the bass.

"What chord is this? You needn't give me the notes, just say what chord it is."

"It is a . . . diminished seventh."

"Correct. Now listen. What have I done with it?"

"The upper D has progressed to C sharp."

"And what chord have we now?"

403

"The first inversion of a dominant seventh."

Everyone agreed that there was no need to test my ear.

"Now he ought to sing solfeggio."

"I have never sung solfeggio," I said.

"Never mind," said R.K. "Here, sing it in the bass clef."

I began to sing an octave higher, since it was too low for me, and made one mistake as a result. They said I had sung it correctly, but that I didn't know how to sing and that I ought to learn solfeggio.

"Wouldn't it be better for him to do solfeggio and harmony together? In that way he could master it in four weeks, instead of wasting a whole year."

"Yes, it could be done that way."

"Let him sing in the clefs," said the director.

"Do you know the clefs?" R.K. asked.

"Of course he does," said G., "once he writes scores."

"What! Scores too!"

"Yes, and operas as well."

"Operas!?"

They began to search for something in the alto but couldn't find anything for a long time. At last they found something.

"Oh, that's very complicated," G. remarked.

I began to sing, "O-O. . . ." Rimsky-Korsakov thought I was singing "do" and he said:

"Don't sing 'do'. . . . It isn't 'do' at all. Just sing without naming the notes."

After I had sung it they asked to see my compositions. I opened the folio with this year's compositions: *Undine, Vivo,* 2nd, 3rd, and 4th marches. *Chizhik* (variations), *Romance, Allegro, Presto.* On top was the list Mama had drawn up.

"This is the list of my compositions," I said.

"A list?" laughed R.K.

Under the list was the score of *Undine.* R.K. took it over to the director's table. Several of the examiners got up to look at it. At that moment Glazunov said to me:

"I haven't seen this one, you must have written it this summer?"

"Yes, this folio contains only this year's work. You haven't seen any of them."

R.K. came over and told me to play *Undine.*

"Let him sing it as well," someone said.

"You can't expect him to do that," said Rimsky-Korsakov.

"Oh, he sings his own things very well," said G. I had sung the *Feast During the Plague* to him last winter.

I began to play from the draft MS. R.K. stood beside me and turned the pages for me. When I had played three pages, almost up to the place where the knight first appears, he told me to stop. Then he asked me how much of the opera I had written.

"The first act."

"Why?"

"Because I didn't get the libretto of the second act."

"Who is writing the libretto for you?"

"A poetess friend of ours."

"Let him play something for the piano," one of the examiners suggested.

Under *Undine* lay *Vivo*, my best pianoforte piece, which Mikhail Mikhailovich had approved. G. took it and handed it to R.K. The latter put it on the stand in front of me and told me to play it. I did.

The examination was over. All the examiners went over to the far end of the room where the table was and started discussing how to combine the study of music and general subjects. They couldn't come to any agreement.

"Perhaps we can omit the Scripture lessons," R.K. suggested. "Does he belong to the Orthodox Church?"

I said I did.

"But perhaps he doesn't know any foreign languages," R.K. said.

G. came over to me.

"Do you know French?"

"Yes."

"Can you speak it?"

"Yes, I can."

"What about German?"

"German as well."

G. went over to R.K. "He knows both languages," he said.

After that they conversed in low voices for so long that I had time to examine the room in detail and have drawn a plan of it with explanations on the back of this sheet. At last I was allowed to go. When I went out I found Mama talking to Glazunov and R.K. Then they shook hands with us, and when R.K. had gone, Glazunov stayed with us and shook hands with us a second time. We left the Conservatoire at 12:15, and I have to be there at 10 a.m. tomorrow for study.

I kiss you

Your loving Seryozha.

I forgot to tell you about another conversation I had with R.K. He asked me where I lived.

"St. Petersburg," I told him.

"What street?"

"Sergeyevsky, near the Tavrichesky Gardens."

"Oh dear, that's very far away!"

"But we are going to move to Sadovaya soon."

"What part of Sadovaya? It's a very long street."

"Near the Pokrov Church."

"That's not very near either."

"Well, that's not so bad," someone else remarked.

S. Shlifstein (ed.), S. *Prokofiev: Autobiography, Articles, Reminiscences*, trans. Rose Prokofieva (Moscow: Foreign Languages Publishing House, n.d.), 313–16.

---

285   MAURICE RAVEL TO MAURICE DELAGE, PARIS [Fr.]

Yacht Aimée   On the Rhine, towards Düsseldorf, 5/7/05
My dear Friend,

Since yesterday we are in Germany on the German Rhine. It isn't the tragic and legendary Rhine I imagined by a long shot, for want of nixies, gnomes, and valkyries, inhabited by Burgs on steep cliffs in the midst of pine trees, Hugo, Wagner, and Gustave Doré. It's something like that a little farther, towards Cologne, it seems. Meanwhile, it's quite nice, perhaps nicer. What I saw yesterday will be impressed in the corner of my eye, together with Antwerp harbor. After a seedy day on a very wide river between hopelessly flat banks devoid of character, you come upon a city of chimneys, of domes belching flames and reddish or blue flares. This is Haum, a gigantic foundry in which 24,000 laborers work day and night. As Ruhrort is too far, we put into port here. So much the better, or we should have missed this phenomenal sight. We went all the way down to the mills

at nightfall. How can I tell you the impression these castles of
smelting make, these incandescent cathedrals, the marvelous
symphony of driving belts, of whistles, of tremendous hammer
strokes that engulf you. A red sky everywhere, somber and
flaming. Then a storm broke out. We got back horribly soused,
in varying moods, Ida [1] was terrified and felt like crying, I too,
but for happiness. How musical it all is . . . and I have every
intention of using it.

We left this morning in rainy weather. The sun was very pale,
very high. Every moment blue masses reveal themselves
through the yellow fog. Then one sees things that look like fairy
castles. They are still the monumental factories with which the
region is covered.

Now the landscapes are becoming more peaceful. The banks
are flat again, with little forests from time to time. We expect
to sleep at Düsseldorf tonight.

Write to me in Frankfurt, it will be safer. We ought to be
there in five or six days.

I shake your paws affectionately.

M. R.

We are within sight of Düsseldorf.

[= Letter 282], 38–39.—Tr. by editor.

286   CLAUDE DEBUSSY TO JACQUES DURAND, BEL-ÉBAT [Fr.]

Bellevue (Seine-et-Oise), 11 September 1905.

My dear friend,

On my way back from England [1] I spent two days in Paris,
as a perfect stranger, taking just enough time to bother Choisnel
with new corrections for "La Mer" . . . Speaking of which,
it would be very kind of you to go over them yourself: I don't
quite trust dear Gaston's eye!

Here I am, installed here, I don't know exactly for how long,
and it turns out that this place, which is perfect for quick
holidays, is at the moment quite deserted.

A few neurasthenic Americans, two or three Russians forgotten by the Japanese.

I shall finish the three "Images" for two pianos very soon, I hope . . .[2]

Colonne has written me twice on the subject of "King Lear," which I'm working on too.[3]

Madame E. Hall, the "Woman-saxophone," is politely demanding her fantasy; I should like to satisfy her, because she deserves a reward for her patience.[4]

Have you played the "Images" . . . ?[5] Without false vanity, I believe that these three pieces carry themselves well and that they will take their place in the piano literature . . . (as Chevillard[6] would say), to the left of Schumann, or to the right of Chopin . . . *as you like it* [Eng.].

(I haven't any names for the dedication.)

All my compliments for the admirable cows at the Bel-Ébat estate, and what a fine house in the background. How much more agreeable it must be to associate with all this than with musicians!

Give me your news very soon and believe in the affection of

Claude Debussy.

Jacques Durand, *Lettres de Claude Debussy à son éditeur* (Paris: A. Durand et Fils, 1927), 32–33.—Tr. by editor.

287   BÉLA BARTÓK TO HIS MOTHER, BRATISLAVA [Hung.]

Coimbra, 11 Apr. 1906.

Dear mother,

Here's the promised letter; we have happily finished the tour. Let me give you an account of this and that.

The tour itself and the performances have at any rate provided many interesting, often amusing, experiences. This musical robot-work is an ugly thing. That, at least, is what it almost turns out to be in little Vecsey's case because of the hard practicing, indeed this is the reason why he sees hardly anything of the world. He can't—because of all that practicing (since giving concerts is a serious matter, and the technical work one offers must be faultless). The public was always small; so that the Spanish impr[esario] certainly incurred a loss. For Vecsey got 1500 fr., the Paris impresario 1500 fr. also, per concert! So he had to pay 3,000 fr. per evening just in fees. But the Paris agent is an awful crook; he helps himself to 50% of the artists' fees!

The Oporto public was the most enthusiastic.

I'm having trouble with the Portuguese. The way I communicate with them is terribly funny. Even if they do understand the Spanish lingo; I barely make out their speech—and even that, rarely.

How many customs I have to get used to! For ex., hotel rooms here are left wide open, generally. In one hotel they don't shine shoes; in another they don't provide matches. Here one can have supper only at 5, there dinner only at 9. In Madrid the concert began at half past 5, in Lisbon at half past 8, and lasted till 12. In Madrid the piano stood slantwise, in Lisbon they never tuned it, in Oporto the leg of the piano chair wobbled dangerously. There are only 2 meals, but—especially at dinner—they serve an awful lot. I eat everything they serve. I couldn't possibly reckon up how many courses. At the end, pastry, cheese, coffee, nuts, apples, oranges, soft-boiled eggs, bananas: all this as a "Coda." In Oporto they prepare spinach—just think—with oil. And they piled up a mass of some unknown and incomprehensible food before me. I ate it! Might have been earthworm omelet or rat *pâté*.

I'd still like to say a few words about Vecsey.[1] He's frightfully nervous and tired of "concertizing." At any rate, this influences his actions. His views are so opposite from mine that—at least at the beginning—I repudiated his words and deeds. Even though he probably wants the very best for his son—after his fashion! But my whole nature is in direct opposition to his views.

I'm in a state of suspension now—drifting without aim or purpose. My address remains the same: Lisbon, Hotel Suisso, Rua da Princesa. My letters are being forwarded. But don't send anything important. Oh yes, please send Mrs. (Lajos) Vecsey a circular in about 2 weeks (Rákoskeresztúr, Zsófia -telep).

Now, for 1 day, I've come here to Coimbra (university, the only one here), a little town (13,000 inhabitants) with a few interesting old buildings. Beautiful location. Oporto is really quite different from Lisbon. Have you never seen the iron "Dom Luiz" bridge?

Some Portuguese peasants greeted me for the first time today. I was walking in the fields of Coimbra at dusk. They were returning from work; they took me for a priest, maybe, and said: "Bom noite." I gave them the same. In a word, I conversed in Portuguese!

K[isses] B.

[= Letter 280], 75.—Translated for this book by Robert Austerlitz.[2]

288   BÉLA BARTÓK TO STEFI GEYER [Hung.]

16 Aug. 1907.

Dialogue in Gyergyó-Kilyénfalva [Transylvania]

The Traveler: (enters) God bless you!

The Peasant Woman: Jesus keep you!

T.: Is your husband home?

P.: No, he is not at home, he took the cart to the fields this morning, to bring in the hay.

T.: Well, and how are all of you?

P.: Well, we get along somehow; we have troubles enough and as for work, there's plenty of that too.

T.: There, there! I'm sure you manage somehow.

P.: Well, and what is it the gentleman wants? (to her little daughter) Fetch a chair for the gentleman!—Here's the chair, sit down. (To her daughter) Let in the pigs!

T.: Well, you see, I've come to ask you for something you've never been asked for before, I believe.

P.: ?

T.: The neighbor's wife here said you'd know the sort of old, old songs you learnt in your youth from the old folks.

P.: Me?! old songs?! The gentleman mustn't pull my leg. Hee-hee-hee-hee-hee!

T.: But look here, this isn't a lark! I'm speaking quite seriously! I've come from far away, very far away, from Budapest, just to look for these old, old songs that are known only hereabouts!

P.: Well, and what do they do with those songs then—are they going to be put in the newspaper?

T.: Not at all! The point of this work is to preserve these songs, to put them down in writing. Because if we don't write them down, people won't know, later, what used to be sung here in our day. Because, you see, young folk know quite different songs; they don't even have any use for the old ones, they don't even learn them, though they're much lovelier than the ones made nowadays. Well, isn't that right? So, 50 years from now, no one will know that they even existed, if we don't write them down now.

P.: Is that so? (Pause) Bruhahahaha—heeheeheehee! No, I still don't believe it!

T.: (desperately) But just look at this booklet, Auntie—see, I've written down all this. (He whistles a tune) This one was sung by Mrs. András Gegő (he whistles another) and this by Mrs. Bálint Kosza. Well, you know them also, don't you?

P.: Eh, my day is over. It's not for an old woman to spend her time singing such songs; all I know now is church songs.

T.: Of course not! You're not such an old woman yet. And the others, Mrs. István Csata and Mrs. Ignác Hunyadi, they all said you know a lot.

P.: Eh, my voice isn't good any more for— — —

T.: (interrupts) You needn't have such a strong voice for this; if you just hum it softly, that will be good enough.

P.: You'd be better off going to the lads and lasses, they know so many!

T.: Not at all! All they know is new songs; I don't need those, we've got them already. There are such sad old songs here, like (he whistles):

You know it, don't you? And what are the words to it?

P.: I've heard that song sometime, but I never learnt it.

T.: Wouldn't you know another song like it, perhaps?

P.: I may know one or two; but a person can't remember them so quickly. Just when they're wanted, I can't think of one. Eh, I knew so many, once! And with all that work—the

plague take it!—you don't feel like singing any more. When
I was still a girl— — —

T.: Yes, yes. Try to think back, perhaps you'll remember some
of those old ones!

P.: (to her son) Come here! Take this over to Mrs. István
Ábrán, she's doing common work at Félice György's place.
(She ponders awhile.)—I've thought of one.

T.: (with hope rekindled) Well, let's hear it, let's hear it!

P.: Well then, how shall I say it: just speak it?

T.: Of course not! With the tune, the way people sing.

P.: (begins)

"Through this round   for - est   I   will   walk..."

(whines it to the end)
Eh, that's a very old song! [1]

T.: I know, I know, it's very lovely. But don't you know any
older ones? Think a moment.

P.: Older ones still? (She ponders)—(Suddenly, to her daughters) Damn! why did you let out the geese? When I shut
the door this morning I told you not to let them out before
the midday meal! (She ponders)—(Painful pause.)—Well,
I've thought of another.

T.: ?

P.:

In   a hedge of   roses   I   came...

T.: (interrupts) Dear me, this won't do. It isn't old, and it's a
song of the gentlefolk.

P.: Indeed it's not a song of the gentlefolk, we used to sing it
here in the village. (To her children) Well, and you try to
think, too; you also might know something, perhaps.

T.: I have no use for what the children know. Those are all
new songs! It's *oldish* old ones [I want]!

P.: Where does the gentleman hail from?

T.: I've told you already, from Budapest.

P.: God bless you! Well, and are you married?

T.: Not I!

P.: Then you are still single.

T.: Right! But try to think some more. Don't you know the

412

"Thief of Big Mountain," the song of "Kádár Kata," or "Where Are You 3 Orphans Going"?

P.: (with shattering conviction) No!!!

T.: Never heard them?

P.: (as above) No!!!!! But I'll say another one for the young gentleman.

T.: Let's hear it.

P.: The Song of Mary Magdalen— — —

T.: That's not wanted, that's a church song! (To himself, he quietly curses all the church songs in the world.)

P.: Well, have you got this one:

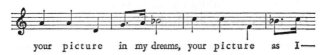

your picture in my dreams, your picture as I—

T.: (gloomily) I do![1] (Gnashing his teeth, and as affably as possible) But some sort of real country-song, the kind they don't know in Hungary?

P.: Well, would this one do, it's very old:

lit - tle muffin so round

T.: They know this too, in Hungary. We already have it.[1]

P.: But the one I'm going to tell, the young gentleman hasn't written down yet:

Through this round for—

T.: But that's the one you started with! Can't use it. (Giving up at last, he sticks notebook and pen back into his pocket.)

P.: I know a lot of church songs. The Song of Mary Magdalen— — —

T.: (Listens disdainfully.)

P.: The young gentleman won't ever hear a nicer one.

T.: Don't you know someone who knows those very old, old songs? Is your grandmother at home, perhaps?

P.: She's gone harvesting.—The young gentleman could hear a lot at christenings, or at common work. How we sing there!!

T.: Fine! But I need the songs now. Who'd know of such a singer?

413

P.: Mrs. Gyurka Sándor lives up the street at the corner, she knows *so many* that she wouldn't be done by evening.

T.: Is she home?

P.: She's home, if you please, working at her loom. Her granny is spinning, she knows many old things too.

T.: Well then, I'll go and see her.

P.: Go, young gentleman, she knows a lot, when she's had one or two drams of *pálinka*.

T.: ! Which way shall I go?

P.: Not that way, it's longer. This way is shorter.

T.: Thank you, thank you, God bless you!

P.: May the Almighty keep you.

T.: (goes away, crushed.)

Da capo al fine, from morning till night, from Monday to Sunday!

I can't stand it any longer! Impossible!

Endurance, steadfastness, patience—to hell with them—I'm going home.

This sort of comedy can't be kept up longer than 6 weeks. Even in my sleep I hear such scraps as: "Jesus keep you . . . Is he home . . . He's out, mowing . . . Church songs . . . Little forest so round, it won't go in my pocket."

Horrors! Adieu, Gyergyó plateau, I won't see you till Easter.

I shan't wear boots until Christmas, nor see any tinned food.

I received your card from Gyergyószentmiklós at Tekerőpatak. I'll look in at the Szentdomokos post office on the way back; perhaps your letter has arrived.

Best regards, still from Gyergó.

Béla Bartók

János Demény (ed.), *Bartók Béla levelei* (*az utolsó két év gyüjtése*) (Budapest: Művelt Nép Könyvkiadó, 1951), 65–70.—Translated for this book by Robert Austerlitz.

289   SERGEI SERGEYEVICH PROKOFIEV TO REINHOLD MORITSEVICH GLIÈRE, BERLIN [Russ.]

22 April [5 March] 1908 [1]
St. Petersburg

Dear Reinhold Moritsevich,

When Mama received your letter I was sure there would be a note for me. You see, I have been intending to write to you so many times that gradually I began to believe that I really had written to you, and so I have been calmly waiting for an answer and only now realize that the letter is still in my head. Do forgive me, I beg you.

This is examination time for me and there are a good many of them. Incidentally, I have already taken my pianoforte exam and it went off quite well.

Occasionally I spend an evening with the Modern Music people to whom I was introduced by Mikh. Mikh. Chernov [2] and where my music is very well received. Tomorrow I am taking them the third movement of my new sonata. [3] Most likely they will consider it a step back, but in Lyadov's opinion it is a step forward because the part-writing is clear and it has a good deal of his beloved counterpoint. . . . [4]

Are you coming back to Russia soon? I want to see you very much. We shall probably be passing through Moscow about the middle of May because Lyadov's examination will last until then.

Please convey my respects to Maria Robertovna.

Sincerely yours,
S. Prokofiev.

[= Letter 284], 156-57.

290   MAURICE RAVEL TO IDA GODEBSKA, MADRID [Fr.]

Valvins, 18/9/08

Dear Friend,

Happy journeys have no history. But they could at least have some anecdotes.

Does the heat in Spain melt pens, perhaps? If it matches that of our misty Valvins, the weather must be mild at the Puerta del Sol!

Here we hunt for shady corners; there is no fire at the Mallarmés',[1] and Ravel is working. The big flies are humming. The dragonflies have thrived. They look like winged sausages.

A wind of tragedy blew past La Grangette this afternoon. The children, who have no great liking for Miss, began showing it too openly. With the pretext that notes don't have the same names in English, Mimi disappeared at teatime.

The news, even though it was announced by Jean, that the donkey had just arrived failed to bring her from her hiding place. To obtain this result, it took nothing less than the entrance of Catherine upon the stage, a sonorous maenad chasing about the gardens. Thereupon I threatened with maternal thunderbolts that the donkey would be sent away as soon as it came within sight. Faced with the failure of these arguments, change of tactics: pathetic and penetrating picture of the poor exile, homesick in the midst of dry-hearted children who just barely stop short of biting. Mimi and Jean seemed evasive, which vexed me a great deal as you will understand, but at dinner I realized my success had been complete. Mimi was speaking pidgin French to invite conversation and Jean insisted on poking the morsels he no longer wanted onto Miss's plate. After dinner, innocent games, fisticuffs in the stomach out of sheer friendliness.

Miss obliged to go down and up the stairs twenty times, called for above and below to get kissed. Jean even more of a courtier than usual, calling her "petite miss," begging her to tell him stories, to play the piano so he could sleep, and, in the end, inviting her to go to bed with him. Provided it lasts! It would be really too fatiguing for me to be touching and sublime between every meal.

416

Just as she was about to fall asleep, Mimi confided to me
that the name *Marie* seemed black to her, while *Olga* was light.
That outdoes Rimbaud . . .[2]

Postcard from Séverac confirming that Rouart has been
informed and announcing a long letter tomorrow.

Will there be one from Madrid? I hope so, but I know
perfectly well what will come: splendid trip—take care of
the children.

Ida.

Hello to everybody.

Cipa.

Meanwhile remember me again affectionately to Cipa. Rebeso
los pies de Misia [3] and yours.

Maurice Ravel.

[= Letter 282], 73–74.—Tr. by editor.

291   GUSTAV MAHLER TO BRUNO WALTER, VIENNA [G.]

[New York, beginning of 1909]

My dear friend,

A letter from Mr. [. . .] reminded me that I still haven't
answered you, although I have been with you in spirit often
enough.—I mustn't neglect to answer one question immediately:
the [Vienna] Philharmonic did play the [3rd] Symphony
under my direction, and you had best make use of the same
parts, which should be in the possession of the *Musikverein*,
together with the score. N[. . .] will certainly place them at
your disposal.—As for myself, so much could be written that
I won't even try to begin. I have been going through such
a great deal (for the past year and a half), that I can hardly
speak about it. How could I ever describe such a monstrous
crisis? [1] I see everything in such a different light—I am so
agitated; at times I shouldn't be in the least surprised to notice
suddenly that I had on a different body. (Like Faust, in the
last scene.) I'm more eager to live than ever and find the
"habit of existence" sweeter than ever. These days of life are
just like the Sibylline Books.

417

I attach less importance to myself every day, yet I often find it incomprehensible that one keeps up the old jog-trot of daily life anyway—in all of one's "sweet habits of existence."

I very often can't help thinking of Lipiner.[2] Why don't you write me a thing about him? I'd like to know whether he still thinks of death as he used to eight years ago, when he gave me some particulars of his most extraordinary views (at my rather insistent request—I was just convalescing from my hemorrhage).

How utterly senseless it is to allow oneself to be submerged so completely by life's brutal vortex! To be false to oneself and God for even an hour, with regard to one's own self! But that is only what I write now—at the next opportunity, when I leave this room of mine, for instance, I'm sure to become as senseless again as everyone else. *What is it that thinks in us?* And what acts in us?

Strange! When I hear music—also while I am conducting— I hear quite definite answers to all my questions—and am completely clear and certain. Or rather, I feel quite distinctly that they are not questions at all.

Now don't return like for like, and write me again sometime. —The permanent orchestra here seems to be really materializing. *Would you know, in that case, of any young musician with a real talent for conducting* and other *musical experience* who would come to me as "assistent conductor" [*sic*]?

For that would have to be the stipulation, if I were to bind myself for another year. I must have someone who will prepare the ground for my rehearsals and also take over a concert now and then.

A thousand greetings, dear friend, to you and to your dear wife.

If you see Lipiner and Nanna, give them my best regards.

Your old

Mahler.

[= Letter 263], 414–16.—Tr. by editor.

292A–B RICHARD STRAUSS TO HUGO VON HOFMANNSTHAL, RODAUN [G.]

A

My dear Herr von Hofmannsthal,   Garmisch, 4th May 1909

Received the first act yesterday: I'm simply delighted. It really is charming beyond all measure: so delicate, maybe a little too delicate for the general mob, but that doesn't matter. The middle part (antechamber) not easy to put into shape, but I'll manage it all right. Anyway, I've got the whole summer in front of me.

The final scene is magnificent: I've already done a bit of experimenting with it today. I wish I'd got there already. But since, for the sake of symphonic unity, I must compose the music from the beginning to the end I'll just have to be patient.

The curtain is delightful: brief and to the point. You're a splendid fellow.[1] When do I get the rest?

All the characters are grand: drawn with clear outlines. Unfortunately I'll need very good actors again; the ordinary operatic singers won't do.

When you've finished Act II why don't you bring it here yourself and have a bit of a rest with us here? It's lovely here, you'll like it. Except that over Whitsun I shall be away at Aachen, I'm here all the time.

Once more, my very best thanks and warmest congratulations. Best regards, also from my wife, to yourself and your wife.

Yours sincerely,
Dr. Richard Strauss

B

Dear Herr von Hofmannsthal,   Mürren, 9 July 1909

Three days of snow, rain, and fog have made me come to a decision today which I don't want to keep from you any longer. Please don't get angry, but think over calmly all I'm going to say to you. Even on my first reading of Act II I felt that there was something wrong with it, that it lacked the right dramatic climaxes. Now today I know approximately what's wrong. The first act with its contemplative ending is excellent

419

as an exposition. But Act II lacks the necessary clash and climax: these can't possibly all be left to Act III. Act III must overtrump the climax of Act II, but the audience can't wait as long as that: if Act II falls flat the opera is lost. Even a good third act can't save it then.

Now let me tell you how I picture the second act. If you can think of something better still, *tant mieux*.

Well then, up to the Baron's entrance everything is fine. But from there onwards it's got to be changed.

The Baron's two scenes with Sophie are wrongly disposed. Everything of importance in these two scenes must go straight into the first scene, when the Baron must at once become so distasteful to Sophie that she resolves never to marry him. Octavian must remain a witness to the *whole* scene, quietly getting more and more furious as the Baron, not in the least embarrassed by his presence but on the contrary treating him as a young buck and bragging to him about his successes with women, performs his capers with Sophie. Then the Baron's exit, to sign the marriage contract, and his parting words to Octavian, advising him to "thaw Sophie out a bit." Then the declaration of love between Octavian and Sophie, together with the highly dramatic effect of the couple being surprised by the two Italians.

But from here onwards: Attracted by the shouting of the Italians, the Baron himself enters, and the Italians tell him everything. The Baron, at first amused rather than angry, to Octavian: "Well, my lad, it didn't take you long to learn from me." The argument between Octavian and the Baron becomes increasingly heated; they fight a duel and Octavian wounds the Baron in the arm. At the Baron's scream: "He has murdered me" everybody rushes in. Grand tableau. Scandal: "the Rose Bearer has wounded the bridegroom!" Faninal horrified. The Baron's servants bandage their master. Sophie declares she will never marry the Baron. Here Faninal's part could be a little stronger: he shows Octavian the door, informs Sophie that the marriage contract has been signed, sealed, and delivered, and that he'll send her to a convent if she won't have the Baron. Exit Octavian, furious; to the Baron: "We shall meet again." Sophie is carried off in a faint. The Baron remains alone, this time still the victor. Short monologue, partly cursing Octavian, partly bemoaning his wound, and

420

partly rejoicing in the luck of the Lerchenaus. The Italians creep in and hand him Mariandel's invitation to a *tête-à-tête*. This can be left as an effective surprise for the audience. No leading up to it. The end of the act remains as before, except that one might work in the point that the Baron does not tip them. The later scene, which you have sent me, is not necessary.

The arrangement between Octavian and the Italians can be brought up briefly at the beginning of Act III, just before Valzacchi hands the lady's maid over to the Baron. As the Baron catches sight of Mariandel he exclaims again: "The resemblance!" and this pretty theme can then recur repeatedly during the scenes between Mariandel and the Baron. The Baron in *tête-à-tête* with his right arm bandaged is also a comical situation.

What do you think of it? Don't be too anxious about motivating the Italians' change of sides. Perhaps you'll even find an opportunity to work in the little scene of Octavian outbidding the Baron with the Italians, somewhere during the confusion of the scandal ensemble with its choruses. The audience *does not need it*. They'll tumble to it all right. The more mischievous Octavian is the better. At all events the clash must come in Act II: the fade-out ending will then be most effective. At present it isn't effective because the climax preceding it is too weak. Have I made myself clear? Do please think it over. If you like I could come to Aussee to consult with you. As it now stands I can't possibly use the second act. It is not well planned and is flat. Believe me: my instinct does not deceive me. The song: "Mit dir, mit dir keine Nacht mir zu lang" can be introduced in the first, and only, scene between the Baron and Sophie. It'll then be most effective just before the curtain, as a reminiscence. I can also see a lot of comedy in the third act when the Baron, caressing Mariandel, is time and again reminded of that scoundrel of a Rose Bearer and works himself into a rage. That, as I see it, should be great fun. He thus fluctuates between amorousness and fury over the resemblance with those cursed features. A good comedy theme, I think.

Well now, I hope you won't be angry with me. But I feel that, as it now stands, I can't do anything with the second act. It's too much on one level. I must have a great dramatic construction if I want to keep myself interested for so long in a particular setting. Alternatively, Octavian might declare immediately after the duel that he too is willing to marry Sophie. Octavian could be a Baron and Lerchenau a Count; Faninal, a comical title-hunting character, wavers between the Baron and the Count, and eventually prefers the Count.

It's only an idea.

It is certainly right that in Act II Octavian should be defeated and Lerchenau, though winged, emerge victorious, until, in the third act, he is utterly and completely licked.

A possible good way of introducing the Marschallin into Act III would be if she had already, by way of gossip, learned of the events at Faninal's house. As you see, a wealth of themes: all that's wanted is the poet who could draw it all together and clothe it in graceful words, and that's you. Please don't let me down! [2]

Shall I come to Aussee? Or do you get my point? Have I expressed myself clearly enough? No ill feelings. I've started on the draft of Act II and shall compose it, for the time being, as far as Lerchenau's entrance.

With best regards, yours

Dr. Richard Strauss

A Working Friendship: The Correspondence between Richard Strauss and Hugo von Hofmannsthal, trans. Hanns Hammelmann and Ewald Osers (New York: Random House, 1961), 30–31, 36–39.

293   ARNOLD SCHOENBERG TO EMIL HERTZKA, VIENNA [G.]

Vienna, 5 January 1910

Dear Herr Direktor,

I think it would be a very good thing for me if the following were tried. Perhaps after all the two men in whose hands the Conservatory's destiny lies, the President and the Director, can be brought to realize who I am, what a teacher the Conservatory would deprive itself of, and how ungifted of them it would be to take on someone else when I am to be had for the asking. And alas I am to be had!!!

I think what I should do about it is the following. I should like some piano pieces by two of my present pupils, who constitute really extraordinary testimony to my teaching ability, to be performed at a Tk. Ver.[1] concert. If the two gentlemen responsible for the ruination of the Academy could be invited and thoroughly worked on to make them hear what more gifted and intelligent people notice for themselves—perhaps something can be done after all.

What I have achieved with these two in particular could so easily be convincing. One (Alban Berg) is an extraordinarily gifted composer.[2] But the state he was in when he came to me was such that his imagination apparently could not work on anything but *Lieder*. Even the piano accompaniments to them were song-like in style. He was absolutely incapable of writing an *instrumental movement* or inventing an *instrumental theme*. You can hardly imagine the lengths I went to in order to remove this defect in his talent. As a rule teachers are absolutely incapable of doing this, because they do not even see where the problem lies, and the result is composers who can think only in terms of a single instrument. (Robert Schumann is a typical example.) I removed this defect and am convinced that in time Berg will actually become very good at instrumentation.

But there is something else one cannot fail to observe about these two men. The fact is, their things aren't at all like "exercises" but have the maturity of "works." And these young men can, *with complete success*, tackle problems of whose existence other people have no notion or which—to say the least—they would not know how to deal with.

Yet the second (Erwin Stein) in my opinion scarcely has the makings of a real composer, he is only an imaginative, gifted musician, a conductor or something of the sort.[3] And that I could get him to write anything as good as the Rondo or the Andante that I should like to have performed is, I consider, brilliant testimony to my success as a teacher.

It doesn't take much doing to let smooth talents evolve smoothly. But when you are up against problems; to recognize them; to cope with them and—last not least—to do so successfully: that's the mark of the teacher.

Arnold Schönberg

Erwin Stein (ed.), *Arnold Schoenberg: Letters*, trans. Eithne Wilkins and Ernst Kaiser (New York: St. Martin's Press, 1965), 23–24.

294   CLAUDE DEBUSSY TO GEORGES JEAN-AUBRY, LE HAVRE [Fr.]

[Paris,] 25. III/[19]10

My dear friend,

My brother is very nice, but he's a man who is used to "Music-halls," for which I cannot really blame him! You must have upset him a little when you plunged him into music which allows itself to smile, but disdains to burst into laughter . . . Well, perhaps he (my brother) will forgive us?

What you ask regarding Mallarmé's impression of the music of the *Prélude à l'Après-Midi d'un Faune* is very far away in my memory . . .[1]

At the time,[2] I lived in a little furnished apartment in the Rue de Londres. The wallpaper represented, through a singular fancy, the portrait of Monsieur Carnot surrounded by little birds![3] Isn't it easy to imagine what the contemplation of such a thing can lead to? The need never to be at home,—among others.

Mallarmé came to see me, with a prophetic air and adorned with a Scotch plaid. Having listened, he remained silent for a long while, then said: "I had not expected something like that! This music prolongs the emotion of my poem and establishes its setting more passionately than colors."

And here are the verses Mallarmé inscribed on a copy of *L'Après-Midi d'un Faune* which he sent me after the first performance:

> Sylvain d'haleine première
> Si ta flûte a réussi,
> Ouïs toute la lumière
> Qu'y soufflera Debussy.[4]

It is, if you like, a first-class document!

At any rate, it is my best memory of that epoch, when people were not yet setting me on edge with "Debussyism."

Friendly greetings,

Claude Debussy.

Claude Debussy, *Lettres à deux amis* (Paris: Librairie José Corti, 1942), 120–21.—Tr. by editor.

295   ANTON WEBERN TO ALBAN BERG, VIENNA [G.]

Berlin-Zehlendorf. 21-XII-1911

Dear Berg,

I am sending you a little Christmas present—Kant's letters. Do not be angry with me for this, for I feel I must.

There are few things as marvelous as Christmas. You must consider: after nearly 2,000 years, the night on which a great man was born is still celebrated by nearly all men on earth as a moment in which everybody says only kind things and wishes to do good to all. That *is* wonderful.

Should not Beethoven's birthday be celebrated in the same way?

I can only agree with your decision about the brochure on Schönberg. There is only one thing, this book will not appear before the spring.

If I am to write on the *Harmonielehre*,[1] the publication will have to be postponed for a long time. I must read the book first, of course. And that will take me at least a month. I have always wished to write about it. But perhaps you or Jalowetz[2] will do it, for he too wants to write about it. I shall certainly do so too, but my essay can be published somewhere else. You already know the book so thoroughly. Our brochure could then appear sooner. Kandinsky's[3] book is excellent. I do not think I have already written to you about it; or have I? It is called *The Spiritual in Art*, published by Piper in Munich. Otherwise there is nothing new.

I am reading *Wilhelm Meister* and am deriving the greatest joy from this book. I often play the *Lied von der Erde*. It is incredibly beautiful. Beyond words.

So all good wishes for Christmas.

Your
Webern

I am giving you Kant's letters because I wish you to become acquainted soon with this splendid, remarkable mind.

I do not know very many of his works either. But I am striving towards a very exact knowledge of him.

It is remarkable that on the one hand Beethoven and Kant,

and on the other Wagner and Schopenhauer were roughly contemporaries. I always feel a spiritual affinity. The influence of Schopenhauer on Wagner was really considerable. And in the other noble pair I feel a concord of minds, although of course Kant had no influence on Beethoven such as one could speak of with the other two.

And Strindberg and Mahler?

Maeterlinck and Schönberg?

Also Strindberg and Schönberg!

Rays of God.

Die Reihe: Anton Webern (Bryn Mawr: Theodore Presser Company, 1958), 16.

296   CLAUDE DEBUSSY TO IGOR STRAVINSKY, USTILUG [Fr.]

Saturday. 13 April/1912

80, avenue du Bois de Boulogne [Paris]

Dear Friend,

Thanks to you, I have spent a lovely Easter holiday in the company of Petrouchka, the terrible Moor, and the exquisite Ballerina.[1] I imagine you must have spent some incomparable moments with these three puppets . . . and I don't know many things that measure up to what you call: "le Tour de Passe-Passe" . . . there is in it a kind of sounding magic, of mysterious transformation of mechanical souls that turn human through an incantation of which you seem to be the sole inventor up to now. Finally, there are some orchestral *certainties* the likes of which I have never seen except in Parsifal—You will understand what I mean, I'm sure!—You will go farther than Petrouchka, that is certain, but you may already be proud of what this work represents.

You must forgive me for being so late in thanking you for your friendly present, whose dedication assigns me a too splendid place in the mastery of that music which we both serve with the same zeal, with equal selflessness . . . Unhappily, I have had sick people about me recently! especially my wife, who has been unwell through several long days . . .

426

I was even obliged to be a "charman," and I may as well tell you straight off that I have no talent for that occupation.

I hope I'll soon have the pleasure of seeing you here once more, since they have the happy idea of performing you again . . .

Please do not forget the path to the house where everyone will be happy to see you once more.

Very affectionately yours
Claude Debussy

Igor Stravinsky *et al.*, *Avec Stravinsky* (Monaco: Éditions du Rocher, 1958), 199.—Tr. by editor.

297   GIACOMO PUCCINI TO GABRIELE D'ANNUNZIO, ARCACHON [It.]

Monaco, 16 June 1912

My dear Gabriele,

I am here on theater business, am leaving for our marshes tomorrow. Have you been thinking of me? I am thirsting for something of yours more than ever.

You know now what I require: love, sorrow. Great love in little souls. But do not forget the grand scene, filled with phonic power and with emotion. So write me the good word to Torre del Lago.

[= Letter 272], 399.—Tr. by editor.

298   ALBAN BERG TO PAUL HOHENBERG, [VIENNA?] [G.]

[Letterhead:]
J. BERG
VI., Linke Wienzeile 118.

Tel. $\dfrac{\text{Stelle II}}{2678}$

Vienna, ... $\dfrac{12/11}{\quad}$ 12

I haven't written to you, dear friend, in a long time. I have such an awful lot to do that I simply have no time for myself, let alone for my friends. And the present moment is the least favorable; between a lesson and a concert, I only want to send you an extract from a periodical (Physical Education, Periodical for a *Real* Life), which has just been sent to me and which is bound to stir you as deeply as me!

I didn't send you Hauptmann's book, because it *doesn't belong to me* and I had to return it. What was the other book you wanted? I can't find the postcard; I saved it too well!

On the 20th there is a concert here, in which my older lieder (Mombert) are being performed. Have you read about Schönberg's Pierrot lunaire! [1] They are the most splendid things! Melodramas with the accompaniment of piano, flute, clarinet, and strings. Fabulously beautiful!

I *must* close. I trust you are very well. And when are you coming???!!

Your Alban.

AUTOGRAPH (see Plates VII/VIII), Suzanne Szekely Collection, New York: penciled on 1 sheet, 220 × 175 mm., folded to form 4 pp.—Tr. by editor.

299 MAURICE RAVEL TO IGOR STRAVINSKY [Fr.]

[St.-Jean-de-Luz,] 26/9 14

Let me have news of you, old fellow. What's happening to you throughout all this? Édouard [1] has enlisted as an automobile driver. As for myself, I wasn't so lucky. They wouldn't take me. I'm hoping in the new exam which all those invalided out of service are going to take, and in the applications I shall make once I have the means to return to Paris.—The thought that I would leave made me do the work of 5 months in 5 weeks. My trio is finished. But I was forced to abandon the works I intended completing this winter: the *Sunken Bell*!! and a symphonic poem: *Wien*!!! Not very seasonable.[2] How is your wife, and the children? Write me very soon, old fellow. If you knew how hard it is to be so far from everything!

Affectionate remembrances to all

Maurice Ravel

No more news of the Bendis. What's become of them?

[= Letter 296], 204.—Tr. by editor.

300 ALBAN BERG TO PAUL HOHENBERG, MILITARY POST 77 [G.]

13/11 15   Bruck

My dear friend, I haven't written to you for a long time, although I have wished to do so very, very often. But I really did not have the time till now. The training at Bruck taxed me so much that in the little free time—actually there isn't any, since you are supposed to *study* then—in the little free time [available] I was always half dead. In fact, it was too much for me, also physically. After 4 weeks' training— meanwhile I had become a lance corporal—I broke down completely. After all, I had lost about 12 kg, my chest labored increasingly —— and the morale of this whole business weighed heavily upon me too. I had to go to the hospital,

429

and here I lie now with 4 others who have internal diseases, in a barrack—resting. Constantly plagued by my asthma, of course. The roentgen report has apparently turned out to be very informative for my condition, since, on the basis of the report, the local reg'l doctor is making out a med. certificate for me, in consequence of which I should be sent to Vienna for review. At any rate, I must *interrupt* the course here at the one-year volunteers' school and, should the review turn out negatively (instead of limited service, find me qualified for war service), repeat the course. That is how matters stand with me, my dear friend, and you who are an old trooper will hardly be impressed! But I can tell you with the clearest conscience that I really tried my hardest to do my bit. It does seem, however, that a sickly predisposition of some decades like my asthma, which got a little better in recent years only as a result of the uttermost care, cannot be wiped away by a complete inversion of all one's lifelong habits during 10 weeks, but, on the contrary, has to make itself felt all the more strongly.—Enough about *me! You*, dear friend, seem still to be in the midst of severe fighting, and it doesn't at all look to me as if things will change soon. On the contrary! Do let me hear from you a lot. Don't pay me back in kind for my long silence. After all, as you see, I never have very much to tell. (Naturally I'd like to tell you *a great deal* sometime concerning the past 10 weeks!)

As you probably know, Schönberg has moved back to Vienna again.[1] A splendid *Fackel*[2] has appeared: "1915." Do you have it? If not, I'll send it to you immediately (a 7-part No.). Kokoschka[3] has been lightly wounded during a cavalry patrol: silver med[al] for valor.—Webern is still in training at Leoben—artistic life in Vienna very enthusiastic, but on the lowest level.—

My people are quite well. Mama very worried about her sons. Charley[4] has difficulty marching because of extreme flat-footedness and has therefore been exempted from the 1st Marching-Comp. And Helene,[5] who sends you warm greetings, is going through a great deal with me. She's quite well, thank goodness! I hope to hear good news from you very soon.

[Right margin:] Most cordially, your Alban.

AUTOGRAPH, Suzanne Szekely Collection, New York: penciled on 1 sheet, 220 × 175 mm., folded to form 4 pp.—Tr. by editor.

301 BÉLA BARTÓK TO THE DIRECTORS OF THE BUDAPEST PHILHARMONIC SOCIETY [Hung.]

[Rákoskeresztur, 10 December 1915]

I did not wish to be a kill-joy and so did not speak up against the barbarity of your performing my 1st Suite in a mutilated way at your gala concert in Vienna. Now that this has been done once more in Budapest—as I learn from the papers—I am obliged to protest against your procedure. It is the common consensus that works of the sonata or symphony type ought not and cannot be performed with movements omitted, at serious concerts. Such a thing is acceptable at best at "zoo" concerts, or at "youth" concerts with programs of an anthological character. Not only is my present work unquestionably of the symphonic type, but what is more, the thematic interdependence of each movement is so close that there are measures in certain movements that simply cannot be understood unless they have been preceded by the earlier movements.

I must, under the circumstances, declare that I should be exceptionally grateful to you if you would never again perform any of my works. I can make this request all the more, since the regrettable state of musical affairs in Budapest has in any case forced me to withdraw completely from public participation as a composer for the past 4 years, and to refrain from producing any of the compositions I have written during that period.

Béla Bartók

Rákoskeresztur, 10 Dec. 1915.

János Demény (ed.), *Bartók Béla levelei* (Budapest: Zeneműkiadó Vállalat, 1955), 373.—Translated for this book by Robert Austerlitz.

302   CLAUDE DEBUSSY TO JACQUES DURAND, BEL-ÉBAT [Fr.]

[Paris,] 8 June 1916.

My dear Jacques,

It is "the sick man" again, who thanks you for your friendly concern . . .[1] I confess that day by day I'm losing my patience, which is being put to the test a bit too much; one may well ask whether this disease mightn't be incurable? They'd do better to let me know at once "alors! oh! alors!" (as poor Golaud says) . . .[2]

Truly, my life is too hard, and furthermore, as Claude Debussy is no longer making music, he no longer has any reason to exist. I haven't any hobbies: the only thing they taught me was music . . . This is only bearable if one writes a lot of it; but to tap on a brain that sounds hollow is not nice!

I could go on writing like this too long [even] for your benevolence . . . I had better close, remaining your devoted

Claude Debussy.

[= Letter 286], 165–66.—Tr. by editor.

303   ANTON WEBERN TO ALBAN BERG, BERGHOF AM OSSIACHER SEE [G.]

Mürzzuschlag. 1-VIII-1919.

My dear Berg,

Many thanks for your letter. I am very glad that you have already got so far with *Wozzeck*. I eagerly await its completion.[1]

I have been to Hochschwab. It was glorious: because it is not sport to me, nor amusement, but something quite different; a search for the highest, for whatever in nature corresponds to those things on which I should wish to model myself, which I would have within me. And how fruitful my trip was! The deep valleys with their mountain pines and mysterious plants— the latter have the greatest appeal for me. But not because they are so "beautiful." It is not the beautiful landscape, the beautiful

432

flowers in the usual romantic sense that move me. My object is the deep, bottomless, inexhaustible meaning in all, and especially these manifestations of nature. I love all nature, but, most of all, that which is found in the mountains.

For a start I want to progress in the purely physical knowledge of all these phenomena. That is why I always carry my lexicon of botany with me and always look for any writings that can help to explain all that. This physical reality contains all the miracles. Experimenting, observing in physical nature is the highest metaphysic, theosophy to me. I got to know a plant called "winter-green." A tiny plant, a little like a lily of the valley, homely, humble and hardly noticeable. But a scent like balsam! What a scent! For me it contains all tenderness, emotion, depth, purity.

I have written four songs to Trakl's poems. With accompaniment for E♭, B♭ and Bass clarinets, violin and cello, in varying combination: except in one song, all with three instruments. Two years ago I composed a Trakl song like this; by resuming I have completed a cycle of five Trakl songs (up to now), for this small combination.[2]

Write to me again soon. Unfortunately my holiday will soon be at an end—most of it is over now. When are you returning to Vienna? I still want to have one more biggish trip in the mountains. Perhaps to the Ennstaler Alps. Or perhaps—but it's so expensive—to the Grossglockner (with my cousin Diez). If my father cannot come here I shall certainly go to Klagenfurt. It was, of course, liberated yesterday.[3] And perhaps you will come down for a day. I shall tell you in good time.

All good wishes for your work. May I too still succeed in much and good work.

Your
Webern.

[= Letter 295], 17.

304   SERGEI SERGEYEVICH PROKOFIEV TO IGOR STRAVINSKY [Russ.]

> c/o Haensel and Jones,
> 33 West 42nd St., New York
> 10 December 1919

Dear Stravinsky,

I tell you the following with pleasure. Yesterday your *Pribaoutki*[1] were performed for the first time in America. Vera Janacopoulos sang, a very talented singer. Her approach to them was most loving, and she sang them beautifully, except perhaps for *Uncle Armand*, which is too low for her voice. The success was very great and all four songs were repeated. Lots of people in the audience laughed, but gaily, not indignantly. I sat next to Fokine[2] and we bawled "bravos" as loud as we could. The instrumentalists played well, and performed their tasks with interest. Only the viola and the bass may have been angry about it. The flutist, who had already played the *Japanese Lyrics*,[3] was so sure of himself, no difficulties could frighten him. I went to the rehearsals and tried to explain what was not clear to them. Personally I like most: 1. *Uncle Armand*. The oboe and clarinet are like the gurgle of a bottle emptying. You express drunkenness through your clarinet with the skill of a *real* drunkard; 2. The whole *Natashka,* but especially the last five bars with the delightful grumbling of the winds; 3. *The Colonel,* entirely, but especially the oboe twitters and the climax on the words "*pala propala,*" etc.; 4. Many things in the last song, but the coda above all: the clarinet's G-A-natural and the English horn's A-flat are most excellent and most insolent.

I send you my cordial greetings and best wishes. I shall be very happy to hear from you,

Yours, S. Prokofiev

Igor Stravinsky and Robert Craft, *Memories and Commentaries* (Garden City, New York: Doubleday & Company, Inc., 1960), 67–68.

305   ARNOLD SCHOENBERG TO THE *DEUTSCHE ZEITUNG BOHEMIA*, PRAGUE [G.]

---

19 November 1921

To Mr. Arnold Schoenberg

We should be extremely obliged if you would have the kindness to answer the following question, which we are submitting to the most distinguished personalities in Europe:

Which five people would you save if you were a present-day Noah and had to carry out his function on the eve of another flood?

Your answer will be published under the heading "The Choosing of the Five" in the Christmas number of "Bohemia." We shall be particularly grateful if you will let us have your answer by the 15th of December.

With most cordial thanks,

Yours very truly,

The Feature Editor's Office of the
"Deutsche Zeitung Bohemia"

[Mödling, November 1921]

Please, can't there be just a few more than five? The fact is, even I and my nearest and dearest come to more than that. And I should really like—to say nothing of the many other people I am fond of and all those I should feel sorry for—I should really like to be able to take at least my best friends with me. But it is to be hoped, surely, that the catastrophe is not imminent? What I should be very grateful for is if you would use the enclosed postcard to let me know of anyone who decides to rescue *me*, so that I can remain in his vicinity.

Arnold Schönberg

[= Letter 293], 68.

306   GIACOMO PUCCINI TO RENATO SIMONI, MILAN [It.]

1st May 22

[Letterhead:] Viareggio
Via Buonarroti

Dear Renato

Tell me the truth—you no longer have any faith in me—! Why
haven't you sent me the promised 3rd act? Have you written
it? Perhaps not—And I, down here, torment myself because
I feel I've lost your confidence—do you think I'm working for
futility[?]—perhaps so—by now the public for new music has
lost its palate—It loves or puts up with illogical music devoid
of all sense—Melody is no longer produced—or if it is it's vulgar—
People believe the symphonic element must rule, and I, instead,
believe this is the end of opera—They used to sing, in Italy—
now, no more—blows, discordant chords, false expression,
diaphanism—opalism—lymphatism—All Celtic diseases—a true
ultramontane contagion—But to return to us—just exactly how
far have you got? Why am I left alone like this, with constantly
broken promises?

Not a word from Giordani—The house of Ricordi is silent [1]—
is it under the incubus of the fox trot? I don't hear a thing
from Milan any more.

I beg you [and] Adami to tell me something; at least let me
know whether Turandot is still our Princess or whether, as a
daughter of heaven, she has got lost in the chaos—*ciao*
                     affectionately yours   GPuccini

[Marginal note, recto:] Did you get Pea's book? [2]

Facsimile of the autograph: Leopoldo Marchetti (ed.), *Puccini nelle
immagini* (Milan: Garzanti, 1949), plates 249–50.—Tr. by editor.

307   BÉLA BARTÓK TO HIS MOTHER AND AUNT,
BUDAPEST [Hung.]

Kassa [Košice], 5 Apr. 1923

Dear Mother and Aunt Irma,

Finally—after great calamities—we managed to give our concert here. We got our visas [1] only by devious means; 20 minutes before the concert some official persons showed up and wanted to ban the concert because we lacked some permit or other from the *Ministerstvo;* in the end, they mercifully granted the permission for the first and last time. The stage was so rickety that the chair, piano, and music stand started rocking at the slightest movement. The page-turner's stool had barely enough room next to the piano, so that I kept poking him in the stomach with my left elbow. There were no steps to the stage: they had been improvised out of a chair and a well-scoured kitchen stool; to everyone's jubilation, Waldbauer [2] and I swayed up and down on them. The program was printed all wrong (because a letter had been lost meanwhile); it said Brahms Sonata in D minor and, instead of Handel, the Bear Dance and the Rumanian peasant dances. The stage was badly lit, and the poor page-turner could hardly read the music; in my own sonata also Imre had to turn pages, about 4 times, which happened to the accompaniment of creaking footsteps and increased stage-tremors each time. At one point during my sonata, Imre forgot to take off his mute—the violin whined away thinly—and he didn't notice a thing, though he had a fermata midway, where he could have taken off the gadget; but he didn't take it off—and a spot marked *f*, and even *ff*, was approaching dangerously: Lord Almighty, I thought, what's going to happen! and at last had to yell to him: off with the mute! The "crowning touch" was when the page-turner knocked my music off the stand and began collecting it from the floor. At this, I very nearly burst out laughing.—I've never had such a concert.— But the hall was full; and there was plenty of applause; I netted 1400 Czech c[rowns], after expenses—and the experience wasn't very tiring, really.—I haven't the slightest idea who sent me this letter on whose blank pages I'm writing.

Well, it's time to go to bed; we start for home tomorrow at

437

12 and arrive in Budapest at 7.—As a matter of fact, they want
to arrange another concert for me here next year, a piano recital
at that.

Kisses

B.

[= Letter 280], 105–106.—Translated for this book by Robert Austerlitz.

308   ARNOLD SCHOENBERG TO JOSEF MATTHIAS HAUER, VIENNA [G.]

Mödling, 1 December 1923

Dear, esteemed Mr. Hauer,

Your letter gave me very, very great pleasure. And I can give
you proof of this. The fact is that about 1½ or 2 years ago I
saw from one of your publications that you were trying to do
something similar to me, in a similar way. After coming to terms
with the painful feeling that someone else, by also being engaged
in something I had been thinking about for pretty well 15
years, was jeopardizing my reputation for originality, which
might cause me to renounce putting my ideas into practice if I
do not want to pass for a plagiarist—a painful feeling, you will
admit—after having come to terms with this feeling and having
come to see wherein we differ from each other and that I was
in a position to prove the independence of my ideas, I resolved
to make the following suggestion to you:

> "Let us write a book together, a book in which one chap-
> ter will be written by one of us, the next by the other,
> and so on. In it let us state our ideas, exactly defining
> the distinctive elements, by means of objective (but
> courteous) argument trying to collaborate a little bit
> in spite of these differences: because of what there is in
> common a basis can surely be found on which we can
> get along smoothly with each other."

And I also meant to say: "Let us show the world that *music*,
if nothing else, would not have advanced if it had not been for
the Austrians, and that *we* know what the next step must be."

438

Then, however, I had qualms (there are always mischief-makers and gossips) lest I should be exposing myself to a refusal, and so the letter was never written. Perhaps, now, your suggestion of a school is even better. Above all, because in that way an exchange of ideas would come about spontaneously, more frequently, and without the agitatory contributions of a public maliciously looking on and provoking one to stubbornness. But the idea of the book, for the purpose of establishing the present point of view, should not be completely rejected either.

We are perhaps both in search of the same thing and have probably found related things. My point of departure was the attempt to replace the no longer applicable principle of tonality by a new principle relevant to the changed conditions: that is, in theory. I am definitely concerned with no other theories but the methods of "12-note composition," as—after many errors and deviations—I now (and I hope definitively) call it. I believe—for the first time again, after 15 years—that I have found a key. Probably the book to be entitled "The Theory of Musical Unity" ["Die Lehre vom musikalischen Zusammenhang"], originally planned about 10 years ago, often sketched out and just as often scrapped, time and again newly delimited and then again enlarged, will in the end have just the modest title: "Composition with 12 Notes." [1] This is as far as I have got in the last 2 years or so, and frankly, I have so far—for the first time—found no mistake, and the system keeps on growing of its own accord, without my doing anything about it. This I consider a good sign. In this way I find myself positively enabled to compose as freely and fantastically as one otherwise does only in one's youth and am nevertheless subject to a precisely definable aesthetic discipline. It is now more precise than it has ever been. For I can provide rules for almost everything. Admittedly I have not yet taught this method, because I must still test it in some more compositions and expand it in some directions. But in the introductory course for my pupils I have been using a great deal of it for some years, in order to define forms and formal elements, and in particular to explain musical technique.

Please do believe that my wish to reach an understanding with you springs above all from the urge to recognize achievement. This is something I have proved often enough; among other cases, also where you were concerned (I mention this in order to show you that the two occasions when you tried to

439

find an approach to me were, after all, not wasted): in my Theory of Harmony [*Harmonielehre*] I argue (on page 488 of the new edition) against the concept of "atonality" * and then continue with an appreciation of you personally: you will realize that I did that for no one's sake but my own, out of my own need to be fair: and this makes the value of my praise objectively even greater! My friends will be able to confirm, too, that although I have put my head down and charged like a bull at what I am opposed to in your ideas, in conversation I have acknowledged your achievements at least as much as I have done in my book.

It is a pleasure to be able to give you proof of all this, for your amicable advance is of a kind that should remove all misunderstandings and all grudges; and so I shall gladly contribute a share as large as yours. I should be very pleased if we could also have a personal discussion, soon, about further details. It is in particular the project of the school that I have a good deal to say about, having long been turning over the idea of starting a school for the development of style. Perhaps you will yourself name some afternoon next week when you would care to visit me (except Tuesday and Friday). Although I may be in Vienna next week, I do not know whether I shall then have time.

I am looking forward very much to the further development of our understanding [2] and remain, with kindest regards, yours sincerely,

Arnold Schönberg

NB: This letter was not dictated but written by me personally on the typewriter; thus your wish, that for the present I should not mention our discussions to any third person, has been respected.

[= Letter 293], 103–105.

---

* against the term, I mean, not against the thing itself!

309   BÉLA BARTÓK TO HIS FAMILY, BUDAPEST [Hung.]

Seattle, 18 January 1928 [1]

Dear Mother, Aunt Irma, and Elsa,

Well, I'm on my way "home," thank goodness. Meanwhile, I also played in Portland (yesterday) and so have said my farewells to the "Far West" and have started back east.

Yesterday I wrote you a card from Portland; I wonder which you'll get first: that, or this letter?

True, it's very interesting to come here once, but now I've had enough. Traveling back and forth doesn't tire me in the least; if anything, one becomes lazy doing nothing for so long. Sitting in the train for days on end, sitting in hotels, waiting to get off [trains], waiting for concerts to begin: it doesn't put you in the mood for productive work. A couple of weeks of this are no trouble at all, but after a while one has enough of it.

People are very friendly everywhere: they take me motoring and want to show me all the beautiful [sights]; if they can't, because of bad weather, they are disappointed. They show a great interest and are eager to move with the times, but they find this difficult, occasionally. These cities are so new that all cultural activity is only just beginning to take shape. This Seattle was a little place with 3000 inhabitants in 1880: now it has 400,000 inhabitants. Los Angeles' development is even more amazing: 50 years ago it had 10 or 20 thousand people, now almost 1½ million. This land spreads out so immensely—and still its arrangements are the same everywhere! I travel over distances equivalent to that between Madrid and Moscow and find exactly the same hotel accommodations, exactly the same buildings, people, and food as at the point of departure. Apropos of food! I had pork chops for lunch today (in the dining car) with some trimmings which I warmly recommend to Emil.[2] Anyhow, the pork chops were perfectly normal; then: mashed potatoes, warm beets, sliced unpeeled apple *strewn with paprika,* and a large cup of coffee with cream! I was probably expected to eat all of this at the same time, since it was brought to me all together, in fact the paprika-apple and the chops shared the same plate!

In Los Angeles I ate "avocado" (= lawyer). It's some sort of

441

fruit, the color and size of a cucumber, but its consistency is very much like butter, so that one could spread it on bread. It tastes a little like almonds, but isn't as sweet. It is usually found in the famous fruit salad (lettuce + apple + celery + pineapple + raw tomato + mayonnaise dressing).

The enclosed picture was made in Santa Monica (near Los Angeles), on the shore of the Pacific Ocean. I was only able to see Santa Caterina from a distance—as it lay, lapped by the ocean, some 30 km. off. Santa Barbara I saw from the train. I arrived in San Francisco at 8 p.m. and immediately went to the Chinese theater. It was odd to creep about in the Chinese quarter, alone and in the dark of night: lots of Chinese signs amid lots of Chinese people. I soon found the "Great China Theatre" (luckily there was also an English sign on it). This was from all points of view the most interesting thing I've seen in this country. I stayed there until midnight because I wanted at all costs to remain till the end, but it was impossible. God only knows how long a theater-performance lasts there! There wasn't a single white-skinned man in the theater besides myself and the usher. Mostly men, some women, and a bunch of children of all ages.

I'm writing this letter on the train between Portland and Denver: the trip takes 48 hours. Denver is smack in the middle of the continent.

Many kisses to all of you.
Béla

[= Letter 280], 116–17.—Translated for this book by Robert Austerlitz.

310A–C   MAURICE RAVEL TO HIS BROTHER, LEVALLOIS [Fr.]

A

Chicago   20/1/28
Mon petit Édouard,

I just telephoned the hotel office that I'm not at home: that way I'll have a few minutes of privacy. The day before yesterday, chamber music concert. Today things went well. When I returned to take a bow, all the brass served me with a fanfare.

Found springtime in Chicago; but yesterday, within 1 hour, icy cold and a ruddy wind that blows your face away, and the water and ice are scented with *eau de Javel*.[1] The city is extraordinary, much more so than New York.

Tomorrow evening 2nd symphony concert. Leaving immediately afterwards for Cleveland, where I'll arrive tomorrow morning . . .

Cleveland 26—Didn't have time to finish. The 2nd concert went well. 3,500 people on their feet. Fanfare again. Left.

B

Los Angeles   7/2/28
Mon petit Édouard,

This time it's summer: 35° [95° F.]. Brilliant sunshine; a great city covered with blossoms. Flowers which, at home, grow in hot-houses; huge palm trees that are in their own habitat . . . Walked in Hollywood, the city of the cinema. Various stars: Douglas Fairbanks who happily speaks French. The trip from San Francisco to Los Angeles very pleasant, on the rear platform almost all the time; forests of eucalyptus, huge trees you might mistake for oaks and instead they are holly trees. Diversified mountains, rocky or brilliant green. It's a bother to think that I'll return to cold weather. A packet of letters awaited me here; I have heard from everybody except you. Tomorrow evening, concert. During the afternoon, I'll go to see the factory of cinema-lions.

Love to all.   Maurice.

I was supposed to have lunch with Charlie Chaplin, but I decided it would be no more amusing for him than for me. He doesn't speak a word of French.

C

from Denver to Minneapolis   21/2/28

Denver yesterday evening. Good night. Slept 9 h. Arriving soon at Omaha to change trains. We'll leave this evening at about 10 after hearing the Omaha jazz which is famous. Denver where I spent 3 days is a city situated at an altitude of 1,600

meters (silver and gold mines). Its air is very pure. Constant
sunshine. It seems to be getting cloudy! I'm afraid of finding
cold weather next week in New York.

Love to all.

Hugs.

Maurice.

[= Letter 282], 226–27, 229.—Tr. by editor.

311A ARNOLD SCHOENBERG TO ALBAN BERG, BERGHOF AM OSSIACHER SEE [G.]

Lugano, 9 August 1930

Dear friend,

First of all, congratulations on your car and all good wishes
for much pleasure with it.—Then, many thanks for your news
about your adaptation of "Erdgeist" and "Büchse der Pan-
dora." [1] The arrangement is sure to be very good: that much one
can gather even now. I am very eager to see it as a finished
work and entirely understand your point of view in wanting
to show it only at that stage. What a third person imagines
about a house that isn't built yet is, after all, unfortunately so
irrelevant that one can't quite understand how artists of earlier
times could discuss their unbuilt houses with their friends,
though one does sometimes long to be able to do the same thing.

So I also appreciate (the hint in your last letter—it is the
second one—is evidently meant to warn me in good time) that
you are still anxious about my "Moses und Aron"; I suppose,
because you have seen some similarity to some other work treating
the same subject; something to which, as you write, "it might
have a certain external similarity." You are obviously thinking
of Strindberg. [2] A whole year ago I looked into that play for
this reason. There is in fact a certain similarity in so far as we
both make use of somewhat Biblical language and even many
outright quotations. As a matter of fact I am now, among other
revisions, removing these Biblical echoes. Not because of the
likeness to Strindberg; that wouldn't matter: But because I am
of the opinion that the language of the Bible **is** medieval German,

444

which, being obscure to us, should be used at most to give color; and that is something I don't need. I cannot suppose, considering your thoroughness and the confidence that I am sure you have in my inventive gifts, that you have found any other similarity. I don't at the moment remember what ideas Strindberg was presenting. But mine, both my main idea and the many, many subsidiary ideas literally and symbolically presented, all this is so much tied up with my own personality that it is impossible for Strindberg to have presented anything that could have even an external similarity. You would have been sure to find this on looking through the work again, all the more if—which is after all, as you know, absolutely necessary with my work— you had looked at every word and every sentence from several points of view. Really, today I can scarcely remember what belongs to me: but one thing must be granted me (I won't let myself be deprived of it): Everything I have written has a certain inner likeness to myself.

I have already finished the first scene, have sketched out a lot and hope soon to be getting up speed. I hope I'll soon be able to produce a decent definitive libretto. Then you shall have it. Meanwhile: warmest greetings to your wife and to yourself, also from my wife.

Your Arnold Schönberg

[= Letter 293], 142–44.

311B   ALBAN BERG TO ARNOLD SCHOENBERG, LUGANO [G.]

Berghof am Ossiacher See (Carinthia),
13 August 1930.

Dearest friend,

I am quite dismayed over the misunderstanding that has arisen between us because of my remark on the "external resemblance." I did not for a moment think of comparing it as to its content to any work whatsoever, let alone that I was ever worried on that account. My remark referred only to your designation "Dramatic Oratorio or something of the kind," which might give rise to the possibility of drawing a purely external comparison to stage works in which there is also an attempt to blend the characteristics of oratorio and opera; but all the latter, whether new works or old (including stage-like performances of Handel), shrink into nothingness the moment your work comes and is in process of coming into existence—and remains. Exactly as is the case with other works of yours, whose "external resemblance"—whether with regard to the choice of the symphonic-poem form ("Pelleas") or of the old suite forms, or with regard to the choice of a libretto dealing with everyday contemporary life ("Von heute auf morgen") etc. etc. . . . in other words: whose "external resemblance" will *nevertheless* allow of no comparison, excepting that all the symphonic [*two words illegible*] and all the other "suites," and all the other "topical operas" are worthless when measured against your work.

In any case, I did not make the remark in order to stress the idea of resemblance, but rather to arrive once more at the conclusion that, in spite of the possibility of such a comparison of a purely external nature, one will be an imperishable work of art, while the other is muck—and always has been.

But now you bring up still another allusion, an earlier one, with which I "doubtless meant to warn" you about "Moses und Aron." I am puzzled as to what this could be, and since I should hardly forget it, if such an outrageous thing had ever occurred to me, I am actually baffled! How can you think it possible that in such matters—relating to the thing I most highly value: your production—I should dare to "warn" you. (Just as it would never occur to me to give you advice.) I should have to be a megalomaniac, in fact: a total idiot!

At the risk of being taken for one, I am almost glad of this misunderstanding; after all, it did bring me your wonderful thoughts on those words, "external resemblance," bring your wonderful words on this concept home to me, and in addition the heart-warming, joyful news of your intense activity on "Moses und Aron" and of the progress of this work which elates me so completely, always.

Ever yours,
Alban Berg

Willi Reich, "Ein Briefwechsel über *Moses und Aron*," *Schweizerische Musikzeitung*, XCVII (1957), 260.—Tr. by editor.

446

312   MAURICE RAVEL TO ARTURO TOSCANINI, MILAN [Fr.]

MR   Le Belvédère
                    Montfort l'Amaury (S. & O.)

                                    9/9/30

My dear friend,
            I recently learnt that there was an "affaire" Toscanini-Ravel. You probably knew nothing of it yourself, though I have been assured that the papers talked about it: it would seem that I refused to stand up during the applause at the Opéra, in order to punish you for not taking the proper tempo in the *Bolero*.

I have always held that if the author does not participate in the performance of his work, he ought to evade the ovations which anyhow should be addressed exclusively to the interpreter, the work, or both.

Unfortunately, I was badly—or rather, too well situated for my abstention not to be noticed. Yet, not wishing that my attitude be left open to misinterpretation, I turned in your direction, making a show of applauding you and thanking you.

But, of course, malevolence is better suited to "sensational" news than the truth.

I hope such news has not altered your confidence in the admiration and profound friendship of your

                          Maurice Ravel

AUTOGRAPH (see Plates IX/X), Arturo Toscanini Collection, New York: 1 sheet, 272 × 180 mm., folded to form 4 pp., the last page blank.—Tr. by editor.

313   ARNOLD SCHOENBERG TO ALBAN BERG, VIENNA [G.]

[Berlin, 28 November 1930]
Dear friend,
        Your Aria[1] pleased me *very much*. A wonderfully
fine piece; excellently constructed, beautifully singable, splendid
sound—*I am very satisfied,* and if I don't say that I'm proud
of you, it is only because of the first line of the biography on
the adjoining page, which almost deprives me of the right to do
so.—I know very well that you have nothing to do with it and
that it is not your intention to disown me; and I myself know
that I teach better today than when you were my pupil. However: who wrote this? It is really strong and doesn't even have
the excuse of not wishing to damage you. For now that you
yourself are a master, nobody can reproach you with having
once been a pupil.
        This is surely comical, rather than provoking. But why
shouldn't I be allowed to adorn myself with a couple of pupils,
since ordinarily I adorn myself only with my own feathers and
never with strangers'?
        Well then, once more and in spite of it: I am very proud of
you.
                        Warmest regards
                        Arnold Schönberg
Berlin, 28.XI.1930.

Willi Reich, "Ein unbekannter Brief von Arnold Schönberg an Alban Berg,"
Österreichische Musikzeitschrift, XIV (1959), 10.—Tr. by editor.

314   BÉLA BARTÓK TO HIS MOTHER AND AUNT,
BUDAPEST [Hung.]

Mondsee, 13 July 1931.
Dear Mother and Aunt Irma,
    I won't write about Mondsee for the moment; [instead,] I'll
go back to a week ago and to the days that followed, so that I
may give you an up-to-date report of the events at Geneva.
    Well, on Monday morning I went to the Hungarian embassy

first of all; B. is on leave, so I spoke to his chief, ambassador P. (his title is actually chargé d'affaires). I asked for his opinion concerning the Toscanini motion.[1] If he hadn't been a diplomat he would have shaken his head a great deal; but as it is, he merely advised me politely not to bring this up for the time being and, first, to sound out individual members of the comité. Then we went to the League of Nations building together, so that he himself might introduce me to some of the important people there. This took place in one of the big council chambers, where everyone's seat at the large table is marked: there, in readiness, was a quantity of blank paper, League of Nations pencils, a big dossier with printed matter, and—most important of all— the mail that had arrived, which, to my great disappointment, I could not open for some time. At my right sat the famous Čapek, at my left Gilbert Murray, the English professor.[2] Many unknown faces—it took me a while to orient myself in their midst! I kept asking Čapek, Well, who is speaking now? and who now? In the middle of the room sat the translators and, along the 4 walls, all sorts of League of Nations clerks and other employee-like persons, journalists too, and later even visitors. Mr. Murray, speaking in English, opened the session. No sooner had he uttered the last word than up jumped the translator of English speeches and practically rattled off his impromptu translation. It was these translators that I admired most of all. They jot down in shorthand the speeches that are waiting to be translated and recite them in this manner, almost without faltering. Some of them, for ex. the translator of German speeches, spoke in such a manner, gesticulated with such "deep conviction," that he might have been expounding his own most sacred beliefs; sometimes he would hold forth without even glancing at his notes. The aping of these orators was really funny, especially if one of them, in his "speech," professed quite the opposite of his previous "speech": for the original of one had come from one real speaker and that of the other from the man who had tried to refute him.—On Murray's recommendation we elected Destrée, former Belgian Minister of Education, to the chair, amid general rejoicing (what if I, for ex. as a counter-proposal, had suggested our friend Čapek for this office!). Destrée called on everybody to speak in whatever language he pleased (but there would have to be a translator, of course!). After his speech, it turned out that no one wanted the French

speeches translated into English (the official languages of the
League of Nations are French *and* English; both of these
languages must be equally honored at anyone's request). So
everybody "understood French perfectly," thank God, since this
cut the length of the conferences by at least one half: with the
exception of perhaps 3 men, everyone spoke in French, excepting
those who declaimed in German. Otherwise, the German
speeches, for ex., would have had to be translated not only into
French but also into English. The translators, too, must have
been glad of this: they could chew their nails [and] read, the
whole time. At the sound of any English or German word,
however, they immediately pounced on their pencils.

I came near to bursting with attentiveness: especially in the
beginning, I found it very hard to follow some of the speakers.
They all began slowly, of course; then, as they gradually warmed
to their subject, the tempo got faster and faster. One of the
Walachians, Oprescu, I understood very well. The most talkative,
it soon developed, were this aforementioned Walachian, the
Italian Ojetti (a journalist, I think), Paul Valéry, the French
poet (60 years old), Focillon, a French art historian, and the
Swiss Reynold (don't know what he does).[3] General topics were
discussed first; motion: that a declaration be made [on] what we
think of the attitude to be adopted for the present times, what
our conception is of contemporary man, what he should be
like, etc.—After a great many *für* and *wider* [4]—and this happened
after every motion that was taken seriously—the chairman
appointed a subcommittee [consisting] of the maker of the
motion and those who had contributed the most to the discussion.
These were then to draw up a resolution between sessions which
the full assembly would either accept unchanged or modify.—
Then they established the "ordre du jour" (agenda) for the
afternoon, the following day, etc. The "ordre" was that, after
the generalities, the discussion should be according to the special
fields: literature, *music,* fine arts.—I forgot to tell you that the
chairman reported on what sort of things the predecessor of this
"comité," the defunct "sous-commission," had already accomplished (that is: the watchword was, we were not to return to
a discussion of these topics). Therefore: the matter of folk art
[and] the question of artistic translation had already been
decided (cf. the Prague Folk Art Congress in which I participated
3 years ago). But since no results could be pointed to in the field
450

of music, now therefore I—as the only musician-member—was
expected to introduce some motions, no matter what kind, just
motions, they'd accept them.

I explained that the only motions I could make would cost a
lot of money to be realized; they said that was all the same. Very
well, that evening I drafted something (concerning gramophone
recording) and read it—in German—the next day. Also Čapek
had some such proposal, and so the two were discussed together.
A subcommittee was formed; it drew up a resolution which, of
course, was quite different from the original, of no practical
use, but on the other hand costing no money. I'll show you
all this at home.

Then the following sort of things were brought up, e.g.: the
English "wreathed poet" (poeta laureatus) [5] complained that
poetry doesn't get *recited* in public enough, and, when it does,
then badly; Valéry added that it is taught all wrong in the
schools. Resolution: broadcasting companies should be requested
to have more poetry recited on their programs and to see to it
that its reciters recite well! (This, too, will have no practical
consequence!) Another resolution: cinema companies should be
requested to have an "educational" film shown as well, after
every regular film. (They won't care two hoots for us, of course,
or for the whole League of Nations; they'll go on doing whatever
is most profitable to them.) It was very funny how one speaker
affected the other. They all began with: they had heard the
previous speaker's wonderful proposals with infinite joy and
great pleasure; his ideas were excellent, only this wasn't quite so,
the other ought to be modified slightly, such and such would
be hard to realize, that was incorrect—in the end, it turned
out that nothing the previous speaker had said was any good.
Politeness, however, is what matters. Oh well, one thing is certain: this Comité won't resort to physical violence.

Thomas Mann also took the floor a couple of times, always in
German; he spoke skillfully and in a very interesting way.

At about 5 o'clock every day, the friendly rattle of plates and
cups began to be heard: League of Nations maids would place
dishes on a table and bring us tea, cakes, and other drinks from
the League of Nations' real kitchen (not its witches' kitchen),
or possibly from a neighboring restaurant. Then the chairman
would say: "Je vous donne la liberté pour dix minutes"—and
we'd have tea, free of charge.

451

One afternoon, an Italian was holding forth in earnest; suddenly, the chairman interrupted him with: Voici Madame X. (I didn't catch the name.) Then—as if by command, we all greeted (by rising) a nice-looking elderly lady, a princess or something of the sort, who floated in wearing a big hat; the chairman addressed a speech to her: we are deeply touched that you have honored us with your visit [and] are sorry indeed that your late husband cannot see us thus assembled (at this point I began to suspect something), etc. It turned out to be Mrs. Wilson (the widow of the American peace-president). She thanked us for the friendly reception with a few words in English and then sat down in the auditorium.

There was only one official luncheon and one official dinner: the luncheon was given by the secretary of the *Commission*, the dinner by its chairman. The luncheon—in a hotel—was excellent, the dinner—at the beautiful home of the chairman— not so good. Neither occasion was unpleasant for me, since I had the opportunity of talking with people I liked. During the dinner I sat next to Mrs. Thomas Mann. I also spoke a great deal with Thomas Mann. Then Nini Roll-Anker, the Norwegian authoress,[6] approached him and began to court him, telling him how wonderful this, how magnificent that book of his was. A Nini can't be expected to act differently. I was harnessed into rendering on the piano the inevitable "Evening at the Szekelers" and the "Bear Dance"; the former at the direct request of the Walachian Oprescu, who had heard me play it in Kolozsvár when he was a university professor there.

There was another luncheon, at the Hungarian ambassador's; only I and X., the (Hungarian) minister plenipotentiary, with his wife (a revolting female), were there. The ambassador's wife is American, speaks only American, but plays the Hungarian in a big way. Here there were such cleverly concocted delicacies for lunch that I can hardly remember when I ever ate the like. 5 or 6 kinds of wineglasses were lined up, all of expensive Venetian glass, dolphin-footed and other sorts. At the beginning of the luncheon they served funny-tasting *cock-tails* (= brandy), at the end of the luncheon—Tokay (it could hardly be otherwise, at the Hungarian ambassador's). Nevertheless, the luncheon was not pleasant, [even] apart from Mrs. X.'s ugly screeching; those smooth but crafty diplomats—what can I say, they're an artificial lot, not at all like the artist-tribe.

The hotel in Geneva was good, quiet, simple, family-like—a kind of *pension*, not too expensive.

Anyhow, those were the events in Geneva.

As for Mondsee: I hadn't expected too much of this American school, but it turned out to be a trained-dog show, practically.

I arrived on Friday night. The *Generalsekretär* was waiting for me, and we agreed that my pupils would be scheduled the next day at 10 a.m. How many are there? I asked. Well, 6 or so, he says (instead of 8).—The next day I show up for the scheduling, well—1 (in writing, *"one"*) pupil is present. Where are the others!? Well, 2 who have *already paid* haven't yet arrived—[they are] roaming about somewhere in Europe. As for the rest: in part [they have] canceled, in part never existed. On the other hand Mrs. P., the school's head organizer, and Mrs. C., the assistant organizer, wish to study with me—both of them old hags.—All the same to me—I said—but I must get 8 hours' worth of money, even if I teach only a single pupil.

Then, this week, more pupils began gradually to wander in—as matters now stand, I have 3 regular pupils (1 pianist, not bad; 1 composer, passable; 1 student, only for harmony, fishy; girls all 3), plus the two hags. A sixth one would have liked to study harmony with me but didn't even know the scales properly. This, I announced, was going too far!!

The Viennese Weingarten [7] went back to Vienna, because not a single pupil showed up for him.—But everybody says that this year the school is excellent and that it's just beginning to prosper now. Well, I can't imagine what it was like last year, if then it was worse than now. There's a violin teacher from Berlin; he has *one* pupil!—I devote myself much more to *each one* individually now, so that I am now teaching 8 hours a week, de facto. As for paying, they pay: today they were nice enough to send me my check for 496 Austr. shillings for this week's 8 hours.

As for everything else (bathing, walks, *Gasthof*, food), D[itta] [8] will write about all that very soon. Now let me close this little note; very sorry to have kept you waiting for it so long, but better late than never, and it would really have been difficult to put all this together any sooner, in Geneva or even here!   Many kisses,

                                               Béla.

[= Letter 280], 122–26.—Translated for this book by Robert Austerlitz.

315   ALBAN BERG TO ARNOLD SCHOENBERG, LOS
ANGELES [G.]

Alban Berg
"Waldhaus"
in Auen am
Wörthersee
Post Velden   28.8.35
Österreich

My very dear friend, has this letter arrived in time for 13
September?[1] I tried to figure it out, still it is very uncertain.
However: whether *before* or *afterwards*, ... you know
that on this day I think with especially deep feeling—of
what I wish you all the year round and in the coming
decades & always. I believe I may infer from your last letter
to Webern that you—& so, both of you—have arranged your
life for the immediate future in accordance with your intentions
— — that is, quite properly, and it would be a great relief
to us to know this. I hope you have been *all* well lately. And
since (according to reports in the W[iene]r Zeitung) "Moses
& Aron" is to be given its first performance, you must surely
have been working on it too.[2] Are you finished with it at
last? And if so: where is this work being published? Will one
be able to see it, or shall we again be obliged to yearn after it
in vain for so long, as after your last 3 works?!—

As for myself, I can inform you that the violin concerto
has been finished and ready for the past fortnight. It has
become bipartite: each section two movements: Ia) Andante
(Prelude) b.) Allegretto (Scherzo) IIa) Allegro (Cadenza)
b) Adagio (chorale elaboration [*Choralbearbeitung*]). I have
chosen a very fortunate *series* for the entire piece (since D
major & similar "violin concerto keys" are evidently out of the
question), namely:

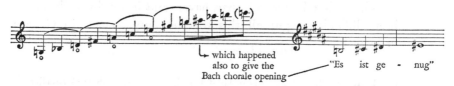

                    which happened
                    also to give the   "Es   ist   ge -   nug"
                    Bach chorale opening

After I had "finished the job," which actually nailed me
to my writing table constantly during these two or three
uniquely beautiful summer months, my hope that I might
have a good time for the rest of the summer was unfortunately
not realized. As the result of an insect bite there developed—
halfway up my spine—a hideous carbuncle, which has already
been tormenting me for a fortnight & which I shall certainly
have to put up with for just as long. So even now I cannot
go to the Prague Intern[ational] Music Festival (Karlsbad
canceled nearly at the last minute for political reasons!), and,
as a consequence, I shall again miss your work, to which I
have been looking forward so *very* much. Also Webern's &
my own. But I hope to hear it (on 2.9.) over the radio here
(mine on 6.9; Webern, since it's a chamber music concert,
won't be broadcast.)
Much illness besides, even death among close acquaintances.
To mention only the U[niversal] E[dition], where some weeks
ago Managing Director Winter's wife & Stein's father died
on the *same* day. (A short time before, Heinsheimer's father
& uncle.) And now Stein himself has been gravely ill for such
a long time. You have surely heard about this. It looked *very*
serious; the appendectomy was nearly performed too late;
hence the complications which have already lasted for 4 or
5 weeks. But now it seems the danger is over & Stein at
home.—[3]
We shall stay here for the next 2 or 3 months. I should
finally like to finish orchestrating "Lulu." And I have enough
to live on till then. What I'll undertake afterwards—must
yet occur to me. At any rate, we are afraid—even apart
from these uncertainties of existence—of the . . . . cold
weather.[4] Thank God that at least *that* will be spared you!
Our warmest greetings to both of you and, again, heartfelt
good wishes to you (also on behalf of Helene) from your Berg [5]

Facsimile of the autograph: Josef Rufer, "Dokumente einer Freundschaft,"
Melos, XX (1955), 42–44.—Tr. by editor.

316   BÉLA BARTÓK TO MRS. OSCAR MÜLLER-WIDMANN,
BASEL [G.]

Budapest, 13 April 1938

Dear Mrs. Müller,

Your sympathetic letter was immensely soothing to us! Yes, that was a dreadful time for us, too—those days when Austria was taken by surprise.[1] It's quite superfluous, I believe, to write about that catastrophe.—After all, you have put the essential into words very concisely and beautifully—exactly as we ourselves feel it. I should like to add only one thing which—for us, at least—is the most horrible at the moment. Namely, that there is the imminent danger that also Hungary will surrender to this system of robbery and murder. The only question is, when and how? How I could then continue to live or—which amounts to the same thing—to work in such a country is quite inconceivable. Actually, I'd be duty-bound to emigrate while it's still possible. But—even in the best of cases—earning my daily bread in any foreign country would cause me such colossal difficulties and mental anguish (to start again somewhere now, in my 58th year, with fruitless work such as teaching, for ex., and to depend on it entirely), that there isn't any point in even considering it. For I shouldn't accomplish a thing that way and couldn't, under such circumstances, pursue my proper and most important work anywhere else, either. And so it's all the same, whether I go or stay.—Furthermore, I have my mother here: am I to abandon her now, in her last years—no, I cannot do that! The above is in reference to Hungary, where unfortunately the "cultured" Christians are dedicated to the Nazi system, with hardly any exception: I am truly ashamed to stem from that class.

But what troubles me just as much is the thought: when (after the downfall of Czechoslovakia and Hungary) will it be Switzerland's turn, for ex. (and then Belgium's, etc.). How are things over there? But no matter how favorable the situation there might be, there is always the possibility that 1000 persons might turn up and suddenly request Germany to march in!

Now so far as my special situation is concerned, it is rather
bad at the moment, since not only have my publishers
(U[niversal] E[dition]) become Nazi publishers (the owners
and directors have simply been thrown out), but the A.K.M.[2]
(society for performance rights), to which I belong (Kodály [3]
too), is after all a Viennese society, which has now—been
"Nazified" as well. I received the infamous questionnaire only
the day before yesterday, with questions about grandparents,
etc., then: "Are you of German blood, racially related, or
non-Aryan?" Naturally, this questionnaire is not being filled
out by myself or by Kodály: our standpoint is that such
questionnairing (!) is illegal and unconstitutional. (A pity,
actually, because one could make some lovely jokes in answering,
for ex., say that we are non-Aryan—for, after all, "Aryan,"
as my dictionary tells me, means "Indo-European"; we Hungarians,
however, are Finno-Ugric, indeed perhaps even North Turkic,
racially, and so in no way Indo-European, consequently not
Aryan. Another question goes: "Where and when were you
wounded?" Answer: "On 11, 12, and 13 March in Vienna!")

But unhappily we cannot permit ourselves these little jokes,
because we must hold fast to the notion that this unconstitutional
questionnaire is of no concern to us and must therefore remain
unanswered.—The more unconstitutional acts are committed
at the A.K.M., the better for us, the more easily we can free
ourselves from its clutches (because otherwise we'd have to
remain prisoners for 10 (ten) more years, by the terms of an
unfortunate § in the statutes!). We have just heard that 2
powerful composers' societies belonging to two Western Europ.
countries would be prepared to receive us as members . . .
so now we must wait until further predictable violations of
the statutes take place, and then the necessary steps can be
taken. As for the U.E., news has just arrived during the past
few days, from a foreign but very important country, of
certain plans whose objective is our liberation. Unfortunately,
I can't give you any detailed information about this, and must
in fact ask you not to pass on even these two news items
(in the last 13 lines of this letter).[4]

Your offer of help really moved us very much! And indeed
I have 3 matters in which I should like to ask for your
assistance, provided that doesn't cause you any inconvenience.

1. I have been noticing ever since Nov. that Hungary's

politics are pursuing an increasingly crooked path: and so it
occurred to me already then that I ought to put at least the
autographs of my musical works somewhere, in a safe place.
I had actually intended to mention it already in January, but
I never had a chance to do so, because of all the confusion.
Now I am asking both of you whether you would be so kind
as to lodge these writings in your home. Of course, without
any liability whatsoever: I mean, I'd assume the entire risk
myself. These things don't occupy a great deal of space:
perhaps as much as a small trunk. I'd send a part of it over
with Mrs. Geyer, the rest I'd bring myself at the next
opportunity.

2. (This has no bearing on the crisis!) I've lost my copy of
those rough German translations of my choruses for women
and children.[5] Do you think you could ask Mr. Huber (that
is the name of your daughter's singing-teacher, isn't it?)
for his copy for a short while, and have 5 copies made of it?
I'd settle the bill through Schulthess [6] or in person (in June).

3. (This has to do with a quarrel I'm having with the
German League of Authors and Composers.) I am sending a
dossier under separate cover, registered, from which you will
learn what it is all about. I have also sent this protest to
Baden-Baden (where it has occasioned much consternation,
for which I'm truly sorry, but it is not possible to make any
exceptions). For—as you can see from the enclosed program
leaf—they wanted to perform my "5 Hungarian Folk Songs"—
another work which has been reduced to an "arrangement"
by that composers' league, the infamous Stagma.[7]—Now I
am assuming that someone, possibly Mr. Sacher,[8] is going to
that music festival: could you have him look at this piece of
writing and ask him (or the person who is going to Baden-
Baden) the following, on my behalf: a) to let me know,
after the music festival, whether the work was performed
there in spite of my protest; b) if the performance did in fact take
place, to spread the news there that I protested against it; c) if
there wasn't any performance, to let me know how its absence
was accounted for.

Did you know that in June we are going to London,
where, on the 20th(?), we shall play the 2-pf. sonata?
The Society there has engaged us for £50; prior to that, we
are playing the work over Radio-Luxembourg, on the 11th,

and so we shall still manage it, somehow, without a deficit. On our way back, we should like to go through Switzerland!

This letter has become much too long—*beg your pardon* [Eng.]! With warmest greetings to you and to Professor Müller from us both,

Yours sincerely,
Béla Bartók

P.S. Please don't show that piece about Stagma to any journalists, for the time being. (That comes later—perhaps.)

Bence Szabolcsi (ed.), *Béla Bartók: Weg und Werk, Schriften und Briefe* (Budapest: Corvina, 1957), 285–87.—Tr. by editor.

317   ANTON WEBERN TO WILLI REICH, BASEL [G.]

[Vienna,] 20 October 1939

My dear Dr. Reich,

All this time (since Sept.) I have been wanting to write to you: to ask you how you and your family are, where you are, etc. I was extraordinarily pleased, therefore, over your letter of 10 October; to hear you are well and still in Basel, and your other reassuring, good news.

Yes, I too believe that it might indeed be best for you and yours to remain where you are under the present circumstances, and that it was even lucky, perhaps, that your former plans could not be realized. And so I wish you may remain there as long as possible. But perhaps things may yet change, soon. Let us hope so, dear friend.

I was very pleased over your report of the [projected] performance of my "Passacaglia" on 7.II. under E. Schmid.[1]— I have not heard of Schmid. Is he a composer too?—In what context will the performance take place? Is it one of the orchestral concerts organized by Werner Reinhart (collegium musicum)?[2] One of the concerts with guest conductors? Does Scherchen still have the regular ones? Has there been a change in this?—It is a matter of no small moment for me to learn something about it. Perhaps you will write me soon on the subject.

If an invitation could be arranged for me, I should be very happy and should of course come *very gladly!!!*

From whom could it go out?—Perhaps from Reinhart?— After all, I used to have a *good relation* with him.—But in spite of this, he hardly took notice of me in his concert programs. I should therefore be very interested to know whether that is the case now, with the "Passacaglia"! So let me hear what the situation is!—Give my regards to Schmid!—As I say, I'd be *very glad* if I could come! If it's the above-mentioned orchestra, then it will certainly give a good performance. Under certain circumstances, my visit could even have *special consequences* for me!—Therefore, its *realization is of great concern to me!!!!*—I'm very pleased you thought of *that*. Very good, my dear Reich! I thank you very much!— Anything of the sort had already seemed quite beyond the realm of possibility for me! I see it as a good sign!

Now for the concert planned by the ISCM.[3]

Concerning myself: which lieder are being considered? How important it would be to make a good choice! For ex.: from op. 3 "Dies ist ein Lied," "Kahl reckt der Baum"; from op. 4 *"So ich traurig bin"* (this has *never* yet been sung!!) *or* "Eingang." From op. 12 "Der Tag ist vergangen" and "Gleich und Gleich." This would be a group of 5 lieder which should be done *in that order!* As for instrumental works of mine: if one could obtain a *quartet!* Which might, for instance, play at least nos. 2, 4, and 5 from it (op. 5), if not all 5 movements! That would be thoroughly feasible! And good!— Otherwise, the *violin* pieces would be more propitious than the *cello* pieces. The latter rather *not at all!* Not because I don't find them good. But they'd only be quite misunderstood. Performers and listeners would hardly know what to make of them. *Nothing experimental!!!* Create favorable conditions for the performance of the "Passacaglia"!!!

You see how it goes, all the above works are already *3 decades* old! And still I must worry! As though it were a question of "premières." Oh to be somewhat understood at last.

But that is fine, what you are doing! Now take my suggestions into consideration. And so far as your lecture is concerned: *nothing theoretical!* Rather say *how you like this music!*—This they will believe, and so a favorable effect is attained. [*Crossed out:* How happy I should have been if

460

Stein had said at least one word about my quartet in his article!] ⁴ What I've just crossed out, I'll tell you in person some day.

Just think, now I must do jobs for the U[niversal] E[dition], a fat, fat piano score. (I won't disclose more for the time being!) ⁵—Yes, in September I lost my regular position at the radio; that post has been liquidated. And there I was! So I had to seize on something, quickly!!! It's a pretty state of affairs. At the moment I have *not a single* pupil!

And so I unfortunately had to postpone work on the "Cantata" ⁶ for a while, or I should probably have finished by now. But I hope I may soon, anyway. More on this work shortly. All sorts of things could be said about it.—Well, write very soon again, and often and regularly!!! Please!— Convey my greetings *"all round"!!!* I hear no news, of course.

Write, write, my dear friend! All good wishes! To you and your dear ones! We send our warmest greetings!!!

Ever yours

W.

Except for Polnauer, I don't see anyone any more! The Humpliks of course!

This afternoon I'll at last hear the "record" of the performance of my *string trio;* Kathleen Washburne String Trio. I'm curious. "Decca" company. Perhaps you could play it sometime for a suitable circle—in case it's good. *Further particulars from Stein.*

Transcript of the autograph kindly supplied by Dr. Willi Reich, Zurich.— Tr. by editor.

318   BÉLA BARTÓK TO HIS SONS, BUDAPEST [Hung.]

110–31, 73 Road, Forest Hills, Long Island, N.Y. U.S.A. (the address thus; in 5 lines; we remain in this apartment till 7 May)

24 Dec. 1940.

Dear Béla and Péter,

I am writing to both of you, in two copies; I'm sending one copy to you, Béla, today; the other, a week from now, to you, Péter. If you, Béla, receive it, show it to Aunt Irma [1] and then send it to Péter, if you haven't yet received his copy. And you, Péter, send yours to Béla if you haven't received his yet.

It is now 1 p.m. here; you are already celebrating Christmas Eve. Our thoughts are very much with you, of course, [and we wonder] who is spending it where; we think of past Christmas Eves and—we are alone. The totally unreliable postal service is very disturbing. Up to now, *one* letter has arrived from you, Péter (the one written at the end of Oct.; by clipper, about 4 weeks ago); your card of 1 Nov. from Kolozsvár [arrived] 4 days ago, Béla, together with Elza's [2] card of the end of Oct. from Budapest (and Julis's letter of the same time).

We have written about 3 letters to you, Péter, from here; to you, Béla, about the same number. Furthermore, I cabled $250 on 27 Nov.—this is the amount, in dollars, received from the Nemzeti [National] Bank. In two of my letters I wrote on the matter of my passport, asking you to go to the [Ministry of the] Interior and speed up my passport extension; it is Number 5832, as sent there by the Hung. Consulate General here. When you have done this, then pay the costs of the cable at the Interior too, so it will cable the Consulate here that it has been done! Write us by air mail only (so long as this is possible); letters by boat take 2 months!

On 7 Dec. we moved into a furnished apartment at the above address. It is 16 km. from the center of New York, but the subway (express) station is in front of our door, so that for 5 cents we can be in the city in 20 minutes, at any time. Trains run constantly, and day and night without interruption. It's much pleasanter to live here than in the city: wide streets; you can even see fields, woods, and lakes; the motor car traffic is heavy but not noisy, the subway, however, thunders by every 5 minutes. There are shops and all conveniences nearby. The heating is so excessive that we have to turn off ¾ of the radiators; we can keep one of our bedroom windows wide open (if there's no wind). We are beginning to be Americanized, e.g. in the matter of food. In the morning, grapefruit, puffed *wheat* (!) with cream, brown bread and butter, eggs or bacon or fish. Between 2 and 4 p.m., we sometimes have coffee and bread and butter, or something else (though this is not American; because here they lunch briefly at 1); our main meal is in the evening, between 8 and 10: raw carrots, lettuce, radishes, olives, various things with bread and butter, perhaps soup; meat; sometimes cake.—Cooking takes quite a bit of time; but there are all kinds of restaurants here (these we haven't yet tried out). Some words like yeast and caraway seeds caused [us] a bit of trouble linguistically; but we are over that now. My head is filling up with all sorts of new words: subway stations, street names; railway-network plans, a mass of possibilities for changing trains: absolute necessities in order to live here, but otherwise quite barren. We live on the sixth *floor* (= 5th story), there is no story above us. The hall (called *lobby*) of the house is low, but long and wide, heated, furnished with sofas, little tables, lamps that are on all the time. Here are the tenants' mailboxes, everyone goes down for his mail himself. The superintendent: *Mr. Janosko*, alias Pan [3] Janoško, is a Slovak from the vicinity of Kassa, who still speaks Hungarian quite well (and Slovak too, of course), though he has been living here for 30 years; [he has been a] widower for 12 years, has 11 children living, all of whom by now speak only English. One of his sons-in-law— a minor employee with the electric company—took us for an outing to the seashore in his comfortable 4-passenger car. We also visited their 4-room apartment, equipped with all conveniences, and they treated us to a Janoško-made *kocsonya* [meat in aspic]. That's what a superintendent's offspring is like, here.—We've had enough trouble learning how to cope with various gadgets of the electric, gas, corkscrew, can-opener type, etc., with means of transportation, but we are managing now. Only once in a while is there any inconvenience; so, for inst., we recently wanted to take the subway to New York's southernmost part: I didn't exactly know where to change to what (the directions aren't much in evidence; in fact they are sparse and muddled), so that we jaunted around for 3 hours under the ground; finally, our time having run out, we sneaked shamefacedly home, underground of course, without having achieved our purpose.

On 25 Nov. they doctored me.[4] *That* was a ceremony. To begin with, I had to take the measurements of my head, shoulders, etc., in yards, feet, and fathoms, and send in the data. At the university, we were all arrayed in caps and gowns, then we marched in solemnly by twos, to the discreet sound of organ music. These were the precise instructions: when my name is called, I am to stand up; when the president begins to address me, I am to remove my cap; when he reaches the end of his chat, I am to start towards him so that he may hand me the diploma; meanwhile they hang on my back the pink velvet band of the Musical Order; then I may go back and sit down. And that is what happened. Luckily for us who were decorated, we didn't have to speak. A sort of dean pointed out, in his preamble, how beautiful it was that in this confused world Columbia University could thus bestow this title on a native of the Hungarian *puszta*, a son of France, an English scientist, and, well, yes, a professor of the U.S.A.

We have played in New York a couple of times; on 1 Dec. I went on tour to Cleveland and environs for 8 days; there, somewhere, I made the acquaintance of Oszkár Jászi. The Cleveland Hungarians gave a big soirée: with gypsy music and *palotás* dances(!!). Hungarians here, Hungarians there, Hungarians everywhere; but there wasn't much pleasure in it, because the 2nd generation barely manages the language in a broken way.

We often think of you and are by now very eager for news of you, Aunt Irma, Elza. Who knows how long the postal service will continue and whether something may not occur in the spring which would put an end even to this imperfect means of communication.

In compliance with the law, we reported to the—Jamaica Post Office (it's the one nearest to us, 4–5 subway stops out). They took our fingerprints in accordance with the rules and regulations (afterwards we washed with benzine, then and there) and made us take an oath; it cost us 3–4 hours, there was such a crowd there. They had counted on 3 million foreigners, but 4 million have already reported; the final number may eventually amount to 5 million.

On 9 Dec. we had a cable from Lisbon notifying us that our luggage would be shipped on the 13th, on the S.S. Excambion. This ship docked here yesterday afternoon, and we still don't know whether [the luggage] has arrived; it carried consignments for 3000 persons, so that, as of noon today, we haven't been able to track anything down. Tomorrow is a holiday, and so we shall not hear till the day after. Isn't

464

this annoying?! And we had believed we should get everything by Christmas!

One cannot write, of course, concerning the most important thing these days; but, in the long run, it doesn't really matter. Nobody, in any case, is certain of anything, and there is a lot of empty talk. It's just that the tone is quite changed, all along the line.

Many kisses to all of you.

Father

Now it is 6 p.m. Your Christmas Eve is over by now. I wonder how everything was—for everyone. We have been thinking of home continuously, practically every minute, since yesterday. I embrace you all.

Ditta

I just want to add that on the day of our arrival, on 30 Oct., we sent you, Béla, this cable:

"Arrived safely inform all."

We do not have a Christmas tree; the house has one down in the hall, with electric bulbs, as is the custom here; Pan Janoško set it up and decorated it.

Streets, squares, department stores, stations all have Christmas trees too.

[= Letter 280], 137–40.—Translated for this book by Robert Austerlitz.

319   ARNOLD SCHOENBERG TO ERWIN STEIN, LONDON [Eng.]

[Los Angeles,] November 22, 1943

Dear Erwin: first let me thank you and Rankl [1] for your cable congratulating me to my 69th birthday. I was very pleased to hear from you, because, as I had no reply to my letter from October 1942 (forty two!!!—quite a time) I was afraid you did not receive it. Have you got it? If not I will send you a copy.

I was always thinking if you would have received my letter, you would have answered, because I asked you to try whether you could not record your performance of my Pierrot Lunaire or of others of my compositions.

I teach at present my last semester at the University of California.[2] One must retire with seventy. But I have half a year of leave of absence to my credit, thus at the end of February I will teach the last time.

I think I have taught enough. It will be more than 45 years. But I intend to write now a few textbooks and finish— if possible my opera "Moses and Aaron" and the "Jakobsleiter." [3] I have begun a textbook on counterpoint. It should be in thre volumes. First: Preliminary excercises; second: Multiple counterpoint and contrapuntal compositions; third, Counterpoint in the homophonic compositions of the ninetienth century (about 1770 to the present time). This last volume, for which I have made a good outline several years ago, will be something entirely new. At least I know of no book about that.[4]

I have finished my piano concerto the last day of 1942. Since then I have written a piece: Theme and Variations for wind band and a version for symphony orchestra of the same. Besides I have worked on the counterpoint.

About my family: We are at present all well. Of course there are often flu's, as it is with children. I could be better if I would not smoke. My wife has much work to do, because we have no servant—there are practically none. I help dishwashing and preparing the breakfast.

Let me soon hear from you and your family.

Tell Rankl to write once. Do you know his adress?

Do you see Dr. Dent? [5] Give him my best greetings.

Many cordial greetings from all of us to you and your family, and I hope to hear from you now soon again.

Most cordially, yours

Arnold Schoenberg

Hans Keller, "Unpublished Schoenberg Letters: Early, Middle and Late," *Music Survey*, IV (1952), 460–61.

320   BÉLA BARTÓK TO JOSEPH SZIGETI, PALOS VERDES ESTATES, CALIFORNIA [Hung.]

Albemarle Inn,
Asheville, N.C.
30 Jan. 1944

Dear Jóska,

Don't be angry with me for not writing for such a long time. It's no use, I'm an incorrigibly bad letter-writer— and this endless hard work—urgent work, for one doesn't know how much longer one may still work. But God is my witness (if indeed he is) that I've been thinking of you a great deal, and I planned a fine, long letter to you, already at Saranac. But that's precisely the trouble: I didn't want [to write] a short one, and a great deal of determination is needed for a long one. But enough of this— — —

I'm really very sorry that it could not be you who created the violin concerto.[1] You may still remember that 3 years ago, when the piano score had not even yet appeared, I had a copy sent to you, just a photostat. No one else, at that time, had received a copy. There is still the possibility with Ormándy.[2] He wrote me on another matter and mentioned how much he regrets, etc., and would be pleased if it were still possible with you in Phil., because he listened to it over the radio and feels that such a viol. concerto hasn't been written since Beeth. Mendels. Brahms. Sic Ormándy!—The performance was really excellent.[3] What pleased me most of all was that there's no trouble with the orchestration. Nothing needs to be changed. Even though the orchestral "accompaniment" to a violin is a very delicate matter.—The critics, of course—remained true to themselves, though they wrote a shade more favorably than usual. I wouldn't even mention them, had not one of them delivered himself of the following hogwash: he didn't think this work would *displace* the Beeth. Mendel. Brahms concertos. How can anybody write such idiotic things: well, and who is that lunatic fit for an asylum who'd want to "displace" those works with his own? If he'd written that he doesn't think this concerto can be ranked with the others, or something of that sort, all right. But enough of this, too.

My health took a sudden turn for the better at the end

of Aug. At the moment, I feel quite healthy, there's no fever, my strength has come back, I can go for nice walks in the wooded mountains—yes, I'm climbing mountains (with due caution, of course). In March I weighed 87 lbs. net, now 105. I'm gaining weight. I'm getting fat. I'm expanding. You won't recognize me.—Perhaps it's because of my improved health (or vice versa) that I've been able to finish writing the work commissioned by Kusszevicki.[4] I worked on it—day and night, practically—all through September. They intend to perform it in Boston around 17–18 March, supposedly at the pair of concerts at which you'll be the soloist.[5] I should be happy if you could hear it at least in rehearsal. It's sad enough for me that I can't be present. But this [is] the situation: my doctors (would that I might never see a doctor [again]) have exiled me to this place, to convalesce and to escape the inhuman northern winter, till the end of April. Then, if there's no unforeseen trouble, they will set me free.

I've begun something very interesting (but, as usual, long-drawn) here, a type of work that I haven't done before. As a matter of fact, it's not musical work. I am organizing the texts of Walachian folksongs and making a fair copy of them. 2000 items. I think many interesting things will emerge from it, at least regarding the peasants. E.g., that it is a much greater disaster for a girl than for a young man to be jilted. We knew this before, of course, but now it can be proved, *schwarzaufweiss*,[6] by means of statistical data. Also, that girls (or women) are far more abrupt, bad-tempered: * there are many more texts of curses pronounced by girls against their faithless lads than the other way round. And these curse-texts are exceptionally odd: what a Shakespearian imagination they show, quite marvelous. I'm sorry I can't quote any of the Walachian ones, as you wouldn't understand them. But we Hungarians have a plentiful store of them, e.g.:

> "May thirteen medicine shelves
> Be emptied for your sake;
> May nine cartloads of hay and straw
> Rot in your bed.
> May your towel spit flames,
> May your washing water turn to blood."

---

* I suppose we knew this too? Or not?

Or on the other hand

"May God smite you with bread bought for money,
    With bread bought for money, and a whoring wife."

With bread bought for money—this the American city-dweller would hardly understand, for, after all, we all buy bread with money. Yes, but not the small landholding peasant: he grows the wheat himself, bakes his own bread, and, if hail beats his harvest down, then he has to buy his bread with money. Yes, but where is he going to get the money!

Just as "incomprehensible" is the Walachian girl's wish (after "A pox on you as you go to your wedding" and such charming things), "May God smite you with nine wives." Well, but that's a good wish, [and] the American would say: *varietas delectat!* [7] Yes, but the peasant has no divorce. Wife-"swapping" is only possible after a death. And a death, in turn, is a great misfortune for them: it means expenses and all sorts of troubles besides.

The "indecent" texts are quite peculiar too. They are not disgusting, townish barracks-obscenities, rather they are full of the most astonishing notions. Merriment, jovial mockery.

Well, this is how I spend my time now—and wait for my term of exile to expire.

That Vecsey–Saint-Saens [*sic*] incident arose as follows: we were in Portugal just then, in Oporto.[8] Saint-Saens was there too. Papa Vecsey wanted Frenki to meet him at all costs. I can't remember now which concerto was going to be "performed," the key, or anything else, only that the boy played the andante (2nd) movement in an impossibly slow tempo, obviously on his father's advice. The composer shows up at the hotel room and we begin to play. When we get to the 2nd movement, Saint-Saens interrupts, says "That's impossible," goes to the piano, and adjusts the tempo to a perfectly normal andante. And so this otherwise boring work (at any rate for me) became at least bearable. When Saint-Saens had left, old Vecsey burst out, "Eh, he doesn't understand a thing, after all he's not a violinist!" ** —Why are you interested in this, that is, what made you think of it?

** This took place in March 1906.

Dorothy Parrish-Domonkos [9] wrote me enthusiastically of her visit to you last summer. How did it ever happen that she played for you?

I'd be very pleased if you would write about the Boston performance.

Best wishes and cordial regards,

Béla

[= Letter 288], 183–85.—Translated for this book by Robert Austerlitz.

321   BÉLA BARTÓK TO MRS. WILHELMINE CREEL, SEATTLE [Eng.] [Written on the backs of pages from a collection of Romanian folksongs.]

Dec. 17, 1944

New York 19, N.Y.
309 West 57th St.

Dear Mrs. Creel:

Is not this a most extraordinary stationary [sic] to write on? Yet, are we not supposed to regard as our patriotic duty to save paper in this acute paper shortage, are not we? Though, of course, there still appear the advertisements of Lucky Strikes, Chesterfields etc. urging people to buy them though they have no stocks to sell. But this is a different business: nothing is allowed to interfere with the high principles of advertising business, shortage of paper or no shortage; or else the world would crumble.—So, when I got this (one sided) copies [sic] made expressly for you, and saw these nice blank pages, I could not resist to fulfil my patriotic duty—

To be so late in answering your letters is quite inexcusable. I will not even try to find and enumerate excuses, instead I will begin to give you a description of the most essential happenings of this year in my life.

You said in one of your letters that my recovering was a miracle. This is true only with some reservations: it was only a hemisemidemi-miracle. Of course, that lung-infection disappeared as mysteriously as it came—this you know from my last letter.

There are, however,—and almost continuously—some minor troubles which probably never can be completely cured and make a regular job or concertizing etc. impossible for me. So for instance, last April my spleen became rebellious. My Asheville doctor mistook it for a pleuresy [sic]. He would have me quite gallantly treated me [sic] against it, but fortunately I had to come back to New York where the mistake was at once discovered, and my spleen punished by a rude X-ray treatment. Then it appeared there is a disorder in my blood-picture, so they poisoned me with arsenic. Shall I continue? I think better not.

A few weeks ago I said "Tell me, doctor, exactly what my ailment is! Choose a nice Latin or Greek word and tell me." After a moment's hesitation he emitted: "Polycithemia." There we are again! Only, 2 years ago this meant too many red corpuscles, and now it means too many white ones.

Surely, I do not feel as agile and lively as 4 years ago, and must take great care of myself especially in unfavorable weather and so on. But I can do work, mostly "housework"; could, among others, teach. However, I have no pupils, only occasionally. So, for instance, last May, Dorothy Parrish came to New York to have a few lessons.[1] She was at that time pregnant, expected her child for December, wanted to come to New York for the winter. But I do not have news from her, except that somebody told me her husband is now overseas. At X-mas time I will have here another former pupil of mine, Agnes Butcher from Canada.

I have another new work: a sonata for violin alone, written in Asheville for Menuhin. He played it in his New York recital on Nov. 26., it was a wonderful performance. It has 4 movements, and lasts ca. 20 minutes. I was afraid it is too long; imagine: listen to a single violin during 20 minutes. But it was quite all right, at least for me.—If he ever goes to Seattle for a recital, try to induce the manager of the concert to ask for this piece. For orchestral works of mine can scarcely be performed there, anyway.

The first performance of my orchestra work,[2] written in Sept. 1943 for the Koussevitzky Foundation took place on Dec. 1. 2. in Boston. We went there for the rehearsals and performances— after having obtained the grudgingly granted permission of my doctor for this trip. It was worth wile [sic], the performance was excellent. Koussevitzky is very enthusiastic about the piece,

471

and says it is "the best orchestra piece of the last 25 years" (including the works of his idol Shostakovich!). At least, this is his personal opinion — — —. He will play it in New York in Jan. Menuhin played my concerto this year in Washington, Baltimore, Pittsburg [sic], and (in Sept.) in London (B.B.C.) twice! Next season he is going to play it in Philadelphia and probably in Boston.

I spent all my time—except those few weeks needed for the solo-violin sonata—to do some special scientific work. Perhaps you know that [I?] gave the final shape to the musical part of my Rumanian Folk Music collection during my illness. These consist of two volumes: I: instrumental, II vocal melodies. Now, this year I worked on and almost finished the III volume, comprising all the texts. This was quite an unusaul [sic] work for me. First, I had to devise a classifying system for these 1700 texts; then I studied and examined the classified material from the most various angles, and finally I made a lot of deductions on the basis of my studied [sic]. You see some of these deductions on p. L-LI; how do you like them? I had made the copy of these pages mainly to show you 3 text translations (marked with red). The first is a literal one in prose, the 2nd and 3rd I tried to translate in the original metre. In addition I am sending you another translation of — — — — now, I wonder, if you recognize it? [3]

(interruption of a few days)

In the meantime your package with the two books arrived. And I did not even yet tell you anything about last year's books! Isak Dinesen's is a wonderful one.[4] And it has a certain European flavour; I often wondered if it was originally written in English, or whether it is a translation. By the way: I never knew that Isak is a female name! Eliot [5] seems to be a remarkable poet— though, of course, I am an incompetent judge of English poetry because of language difficulties. I know some of his earlier poems from an Anthology.

And now a short account of family-life. There is a housing shortage in New York. So I stay with Ditta in a two room apartment which is, of course, too small for both of us. We very often hamper each other in our activities, but we must be glad to have got such an apartment, at least. My plan is to stay during the whole winter time in New York, and I hope the rude winter climate will not do any damage to my health.

Péter—after objection, and its revoking, joined last Febr. the Navy, had to attend there a 6 month's electric engineering course. Since Sept. he is stationed in Panama and seems to like the place.[6]

We all are very much worried about the situation in Hungary and especially in Budapest, and are cursing the Germans, but this does not give any remedy.

Are you still teaching those oriental languages? Or are your activities only in music?

Best regards and wishes from us both for X-mas and New Year.

Yours, very sincerely
Béla Bartók

[Written upside down at the top of the first page:]
Some time ago Prof. Wood [7] wrote me a letter. I will answer him soon: it is very improbable that I ever can go to Seattle!

Transcript of the autograph kindly supplied by Professor Halsey Stevens, Los Angeles.

322   ARNOLD SCHOENBERG TO HANS KELLER, LONDON [Eng.]

[Los Angeles, 10 January 1951]

Dear Mr Keller, you have my book [1] and I assume you know, what it [sic] its value—or not?

Enclosed you find a very unpleasant review, written by one of these non-musicians, who look in my music only for the twelve notes—not realizing in the least its musical contents, expression and merits. He is very stupid and insolent and would deserve a treatment like that you can give him.

I hope you are interested!

Now sharpen your pen.

Cordially yours

Arnold Schoenberg

Facsimile of the autograph: [= Letter 319], opposite p. 456.

323   ARNOLD SCHOENBERG TO KARL RANKL, LONDON [G.]

[Los Angeles,] 27 June 1951

Dear friend,

It seems likely that I must face not ever being able to finish composing "Die Jakobsleiter." Even should that be so, I still hope to be capable of composing an end to the first part.[1] But there is no chance at all of my still being able to write out the score. Now what I want to ask you is if you would, in principle, be willing to do such a score. In the manuscript there are plenty of often very full indications of my orchestral intentions. It would then be a matter of supplying, with the necessary discretion, such interpretations and elaborations as [would] make it possible to perform this part effectively.

I know Scherchen [2] could also do this, but I assume that you know "Erwartung," "Die glückliche Hand," and "Von heute auf morgen" well and are more familiar with my orchestral style than anyone else.

I should be very glad indeed if you would take this on, since alas I shall have to leave so many of my works unfinished. When am I going to get your opera?

With all very best wishes,
Arnold Schoenberg

[= Letter 293], 288.

The following abbreviations have been used in this section:

ArnM   Arnold, Denis. *Monteverdi.* "The Master Musicians." London: J. M. Dent and Sons Ltd, 1963.

Baker   *Baker's Biographical Dictionary of Musicians.* 5th ed. revised. Edited by Nicolas Slonimsky. New York: G. Schirmer, 1958.

BukMB   Bukofzer, Manfred F. *Music in the Baroque Era, from Monteverdi to Bach.* New York: W. W. Norton & Company, Inc., 1947.

GirdR   Girdlestone, Cuthbert. *Jean Philippe Rameau: His Life and Work.* London: Cassell and Company Ltd, 1957.

Grout   Grout, Donald Jay. *A Short History of Opera.* 1-vol. ed. New York: Columbia University Press, 1947.

Grove   *Grove's Dictionary of Music and Musicians.* 5th ed. revised. Edited by Eric Blom. 9 vols. London: Macmillan & Co. Ltd., 1954.

LockD   Lockspeiser, Edward. *Debussy.* "The Master Musicians." 3rd ed. revised. London: J. M. Dent and Sons Ltd, 1951.

MQ   *The Musical Quarterly,* 1915–

NOH III *Ars Nova and the Renaissance: 1300–1540.* Vol. III of *The New Oxford History of Music.* Edited by Dom Anselm Hughes and Gerald Abraham. London: Oxford University Press, 1960.

ReMMA   Reese, Gustave. *Music in the Middle Ages.* New York: W. W. Norton & Company, Inc., 1940.

ReMR   Reese, Gustave. *Music in the Renaissance.* Revised ed. New York: W. W. Norton & Company, Inc., 1959.

Strunk Strunk, Oliver. *Source Readings in Music History, from Classical Antiquity through the Romantic Era.* New York: W. W. Norton & Company, Inc., 1950.

The other references for further reading are given in full. "Source," when not followed by any other indication, refers to the source of the letter under discussion.

Letter 1

MACHAULT (or Machaut): b. in the Champagne, c. 1300; d. Reims, 1377. The most important composer of the Ars Nova in France (Mass, motets, chansons).—Peronnelle, a girl of 19, sent an admiring poem to the great man, then in his 60s; this was the beginning of a romantic relationship that forms the subject of Machault's *Voir-Dit,* a long narrative poem containing several *chansons* as well as 46 letters exchanged by the lovers. Factual details in the letters appear to bear out the title of the work: "True Tale."

[1] Ballade 33, *Nes que on porroit.* Cf. NOH III, 24–25. The meaning of *rés* is obscure.

[2] Machault seems to have been the first composer to have personally supervised the compilation of his own collected works. At least 2 of these MSS have survived (Paris, Bibliothèque Nationale).

Letter 2

See comments to Letter 1.

[1] Of Normandy; he became Charles V ("The Wise"), king of France, in 1364.

[2] *Quant Theseus, Ne quier veoir,* combined into a single 4-part composition (Ballade 34); see later in the same letter.

[3] Heroine of a 13th-century romance by that name.

Letter 3

LANDINI (or Landino, Francesco degli Organi, Francesco Cieco): b. Fiesole, 1325; d. Florence, 1397. Blinded in youth, he later became organist at San Lorenzo & the most famous composer of the later Trecento.—Sacchetti (c. 1330–c. 1400) is best known for his *Trecentonovelle,* a not wholly unworthy successor of the *Decameron.* As a poet & amateur musician, he furnished texts to the many distinguished composers among his friends. The poem he sent to Landini on this occasion was accompanied by a moody letter-sonnet deploring the decadence of their times.

Letter 4

JOHN OF ARAGON: b. Perpignan, 1351; d. forest of Foixá, 1396. As John I of Aragon (from 1387) he belongs to a venerable tradition of composer-monarchs that goes back to King David & includes, among others, such diverse figures as Nero, Henry VIII, several Habsburgs, & Frederick the Great (see Letter 69). John's court was a brilliant center of learning

& art. His compositions have not survived. Cf. ReMMA, 375–76.—Martin (1356–1410) succeeded to the throne after his brother died in a hunting accident.

Letter 5
SQUARCIALUPI: b. Florence, 1416; d. there, 1480. A famous organist, also admired as a composer (though his works are not extant), he is best known today for commissioning a lavish MS containing music by the foremost composers of the previous century (the "Squarcialupi Codex," Florence, Biblioteca Mediceo-Laurenziana).—Giovanni de' Medici (1421–63) was the younger brother of Piero (n. 1 below).
[1] Piero de' Medici (1416–69), older son of Cosimo (founder of the family's political supremacy), became the *de facto* ruler of Florence upon his father's death in 1464.

Letter 6
DUFAY: b. Hainault(?), c. 1400; d. Cambrai, 1474. The greatest master of the "first Netherlands" or "Burgundian" school, he spent his youth in Italy & continued to travel much in later years, enjoying a European reputation.—For Giovanni & Piero de' Medici, see comments to Letter 5.
[1] The fall of Constantinople to the Turks (1453) provides the most likely date for this letter. Only 1 of the 4 *Lamentations* has survived.
[2] The *fa* in *Dufay* appears in the autograph as a variant of the musical rebus given below in Letter 18, n. 2: the *f* is a C-clef, the *a* a black *longa*.

Letter 7
See comments to Letters 5 & 6.
[1] "The Magnificent"; 1449–92.
[2] Dufay's setting of this poem has not been discovered, if indeed he ever composed one.

Letter 8
MARTINI: b. Flanders(?); d. Italy, after 1492. Composer of Masses, hymns, secular music. Cf. ReMR, 220–23.—Isabella d'Este (1474–1539) had just settled in Mantua as the wife of Francesco III Gonzaga. Cf. NOH III, 391.—The opening & closing salutations are in Latin.
[1] Ercole I d'Este (1431–1505), duke of Ferrara & Isabella's father, was "one of the greatest music patrons of the Renaissance" (Reese).

Letter 9

GAFORI (or Gaffurio, etc.): b. Lodi, 1451; d. Milan, 1522. Theorist & composer, whose most important treatise, *Practica musice,* was printed in Milan in 1496.—Sforza ("Lodovico il Moro," 1451–1508), "the most perfect type of the despot of that age" (Burckhardt), was both an unscrupulous tyrant & a discriminating patron of the arts & sciences.

[1] Beneath the flattery, note the self-confidence of the Renaissance artist (cf. Shakespeare, Sonnet xviii: *So long as men can breathe, or eyes can see, / So long lives this, and this gives life to thee*).

Letter 10

HOFHAIMER: b. Radstadt (Salzburg), 1459; d. Salzburg, 1537. Perhaps the most celebrated organist of his time, he was in the service of Emperor Maximilian I from 1490 to the latter's death in 1519, then organist at Salzburg Cathedral. He wrote polyphonic lieder & organ works, & was one of the first German composers to acquire fame abroad.—Vadian (1483[4?]–1551) was a Swiss humanist.

[1] Dionisio Memmo, organist at St. Mark's, Venice; he was also active in England, where he was greatly admired by Henry VIII. The eulogy was written by Memmo's brother, Fantino.

[2] See comments to Letter 11.

[3] "That is, by accident."

Letter 11

LUTHER: b. Eisleben (Saxony), 1483; d. there, 1546. His high regard for music is amply attested by this letter & by his zeal in establishing musical norms for the Lutheran Church; not only: "he was a competent enough musician to compose melodies and at least one short motet—the four-part *Non moriar sed vivam*—and perhaps another" (ReMR, 673). —Senfl (cf. also Letter 10): b. Zurich, c. 1490; d. ?, 1556 or earlier. A pupil of Heinrich Isaac & singer at the court chapel of Maximilian I, he was the greatest German composer of Catholic church music of his time; for Senfl remained a Catholic—a fact that further illuminates Luther's love of music.

[1] Ps. iv: 9: *I will both lay me down in peace, and sleep.* It is the antiphon chanted at the beginning of Holy Saturday, in the first nocturn of matins (*Liber Usualis* [Tournai: Desclée & Co., 1961], 752).

[2] Senfl composed the piece & sent it to Luther, but it has not come down to us.

478

Letter 12
TROMBONCINO: b. ?; d. c.1530. Composer of *frottole*, secular songs to Italian texts, a type of music much in vogue at the courts of Northern Italy (especially in Mantua, where it was fostered by Isabella d'Este [cf. Letter 8]). Little is known of Tromboncino, except that he was admired by his contemporaries, who even forgave him for murdering his wife & her lover (as a later generation forgave Gesualdo, who committed the same crime).—Del Lago was a well-known music theorist.—For further information, cf. source. (The present translation incorporates Knud Jeppesen's correction of Einstein's text [*Acta Musicologica*, XXIV (1952), 154].)
[1] "Padre." Del Lago was a priest.

Letter 13
GOMBERT: b. Flanders, c. 1490; d. Tournai(?), 1556 or later. The most representative composer of the generation of Netherlanders following Josquin des Prez, whose pupil he may have been; he "formulated the final classical language and style of Franco-Flemish polyphony" (Lang).—Gonzaga (1507–57) was a soldier & statesman in the service of Charles V.

Letter 14
COCLICO: b. Flanders, c. 1500; d. Copenhagen, 1563. A theorist & rather awkward composer, Coclico claimed to be a pupil of the great Josquin, but other statements of his prove to be unfounded & cast doubts on his veracity (cf. ReMR, 512). The present letter, however, reflects the real sufferings of a composer uprooted by the violence & persecutions of the civil wars during the Reformation.
[1] John Frederick I ("The Magnanimous") had been defeated at Mühlberg & was a prisoner of Charles V.
[2] Matth. xxv: 40.
[3] *Watch therefore: for ye know not what hour your Lord doth come* (Matth. xxiv: 42). This may be no. 31 of Coclico's *Musica reservata*, though the text is not identical.

Letter 15
VIOLA: b. Ferrara, early 16th century; d. ?. Composer of madrigals & sacred music.—This letter has been included in order to introduce the name of Adrian Willaert (c. 1485–1562), the great composer of chansons, madrigals, &, notably, polychoral motets; as *maestro di cappella* at St. Mark's & teacher of de Rore, A. Gabrieli, Zarlino, Viola, & others, he had

a decisive influence on the course of Italian music in the late Renaissance & is considered the founder of the Venetian School. The volume published by Viola, *Musica nova,* is entirely devoted to madrigals by Willaert.

Letter 16
PALESTRINA: b. Palestrina, c. 1525; d. Rome, 1594.—Guglielmo Gonzaga (ruled 1550–87), besides being a successful statesman who aggrandized Mantua's territory, was a composer (see Letters 17, 20, 23).
[1] 1535–96; this important Flemish composer (madrigals, motets) spent most of his life in Mantua as *maestro di cappella* to the Duke.
[2] No. 95, *Sine nomine.*
[3] The Council of Trent had criticized the polyphonic style because it jumbled the words of the liturgy & made them unintelligible, but with the *Missa Papae Marcelli* Palestrina had shown that this need not be so. Mass no. 95 provides an even clearer setting of the text.

Letter 17
See comments to Letter 16.
[1] I.e., "scored." Polyphonic music was written down & printed in separate part-books: scores did not become common until the 17th century (cf. Letter 20, n. 2).
[2] For a discussion of the technical details in this sentence, see K. Jeppesen, *The Style of Palestrina and the Dissonance* (2nd ed.; Copenhagen: Ejnar Munksgaard, 1946), 295–301.
[3] At this period, "fugue" meant imitation of various kinds, including canon.

Letter 18
LASSUS: b. Mons, 1532; d. Munich, 1594. The free & easy tone he employs with the Duke is evidence of the status he enjoyed at the court of Bavaria. Lassus had been knighted by Emperor Maximilian II in 1570.
[1] A play on *cum gratia et privilegio,* one of the formulas used on title pages to attest that a publication had been granted official sanction.
[2] La, sol (in the soft hexachord): "Lasso." Musical rebuses have a long history; an early one is Du ♮♭ y for Dufay (see Letter 6, n. 2), while in the 19th century 2 ♯ + was a favorite signature of the painter Eugène Delacroix.

Letter 19
See comments to Letter 18.—During the Renaissance—indeed, until the end of the 18th century—musicians were eager to travel to Italy, where

they could absorb the musical atmosphere of the various cities & pick up the latest styles of composition. This explains why they were quite willing to undertake the strenuous & dangerous journey for the official purpose of hiring personnel & buying music for their princely patrons.

[1] "With all the proprieties." The recipient of the gift was, of course, Duke Guglielmo Gonzaga (cf. Letter 16).

[2] C. 1520–86; the great Venetian composer (uncle of Giovanni Gabrieli) had traveled to the North with Lassus 12 years before & had spent some time at the Bavarian court.

Letter 20
See comments to Letter 16.

[1] Composed by the Duke. 3 of his Masses survive, but it is not known whether the Mass corrected by Palestrina is one of them.

[2] I.e., "score" (cf. Letter 17, n. 1). O.E.D. gives 1701 as the date of the earliest known occurrence of "score" as a musical term.

[3] *Heaven and earth are full of thy glory* (from the Sanctus).

Letter 21
See comments to Letter 18.

[1] The Fuggers were a celebrated mercantile & banking family.

Letter 22
TALLIS: b. c.1505; d. Greenwich, 1585. BYRD: b. Lincoln(?), 1542/43; d. Stondon(?), 1623.—The letter, with the endorsement, is self-explanatory. (For information on the composers, see especially the source & Grove.)

Letter 23
GALILEI: b. Florence, c. 1520; d. there, 1591. The father of Galileo Galilei was a fiery spokesman for the Florentine "Camerata," the group of music-lovers & composers (Cavalieri, Peri, Caccini) who espoused a return to the musical recitation of the ancient Greeks & attacked the polyphonic style. Their theories did nothing for the revival of Greek music (which was unknown at the time) but did lead to the birth of opera 3 years after Galilei's death.—For Gonzaga see comments to Letter 16.—The opening & closing salutations, not printed in the source, were kindly communicated by the Archivio di Stato, Mantua, where the autograph is preserved (busta 1112).

[1] *Dialogo della musica antica e della moderna* (1581). For an English translation of parts of this important work, see Strunk, 302–22. "One of my

Dialogues" alludes to the existence of a previous dialogue, *Il Fronimo* (1568–69).

[2] These are not among Galilei's surviving compositions.

Letter 24

MONTE: b. Malines, 1521; d. Prague, 1603. Monte, with Lassus, represents the final flowering of the great Netherlandish contrapuntal art. He wrote both secular & sacred music (c. 1200 madrigals, c. 300 Masses & motets); much of his career was spent in the service of the Habsburg emperors in Vienna & Prague.—De l'Écluse (or Clusius; 1526–1609) was a distinguished botanist.

[1] Archduke Maximilian, brother of Emperor Rudolf II, had been elected King of Poland in 1586; but he was opposed by Jan Zamojski, who took him prisoner at Byczyna & caused Sigismund III to be elected instead.

[2] "10,000 Turks." The westward expansion of the Ottoman Empire had attained its peak in 1529, when the forces of Suleiman II reached the gates of Vienna; now Turkish power was on the wane.

[3] The liveliness & immediacy of this letter will, it is hoped, compensate for its lack of musical content.

Letter 25

CAVALIERI: b. c.1550; d. Rome, 1602. Director of music at the court of Ferdinand I de' Medici, he was a central figure in the monodic revolution effected by the "Camerata" (see comments to Letter 23) & one of the first composers to apply the new style to dramatic works. In fact, he himself disputed Jacopo Peri's priority as the "inventor of this way of representing in Music." His best known work is the *Rappresentatione di anima et di corpo* (Rome, 1600).—Luzzaschi (1545–1607), organist at the court of Ferrara, composed beautiful & historically important madrigals for solo voices with written-out keyboard accompaniments.

[1] I.e., Caccini. See comments to Letter 31.

[2] The celebrated three ladies of Ferrara, Tarquinia Molza, Laura Peperara, and Lucrezia Bendidio, whose voices inspired not only Luzzaschi, but Wert & even Monteverdi to write solos, duets, & trios for them.

[3] The "pure" intervals of acoustics are unmanageable in practice, & for centuries theorists attempted various ways of achieving a successful compromise by "tempering" (modifying) those intervals. Our present "equal temperament" did not emerge until the 18th century. A comma is a microtone derived from the distance between two different tunings of the same note.

[4] The *chitarrone* was a long bass lute.

Letter 26

See comments to Letter 24.—Mourentorf was the son-in-law of the publisher Christophe Plantin, who had printed Monte's first book of Masses in 1587.

[1] A reference to the continuous, devastating wars with Spain.

Letter 27

VIADANA (Lodovico Grossi): b. Viadana, near Mantua, 1564; d. Gualtieri, 1627. Composer of church music & madrigals, chiefly remembered for his *Cento concerti ecclesiastici* (Venice, 1602), which contributed to the development of thorough bass. Cf. Strunk, 419–23. Viadana had taken orders at about the time of this letter.—The mixture of 1st & 3rd persons singular occurs in the Italian original.

Letter 28

DOWLAND: b. Ireland, 1562; d. London, 1626.—Cecil (1563[?]–1612) was the son of Lord Burghley & became the 1st Earl of Salisbury under James I. At the time he was acting as secretary of state to Queen Elizabeth.—The spelling of this letter was modernized in the source.

[1] The lute.

[2] 1553–99; at the time, the great madrigalist was in the service of Cardinal Aldobrandini in Rome.

[3] Bologna.

[4] It is unlikely that all this information can have been useful to Cecil; still, Dowland seems to have returned to England by 1597. To what actions men were driven by the religious conflicts under the Tudors is demonstrated by an earlier master, John Taverner (c. 1490–1545), who was involved in the Lutheran heresy at Oxford & later worked as a regional agent for Thomas Cromwell in the suppression of the monasteries. His 3 surviving letters date from the latter period: in one he coolly reports the burning of a rood at Boston, in another he requests aid for monks whom he has dispossessed (cf. *Tudor Church Music*, I [London: Oxford University Press, 1923], liv–lvi).

Letter 29

VICTORIA: b. Ávila, 1548; d. Madrid, 1611.

[1] *Missae, Magnificat, Motecta, Psalmi* . . . (Madrid, 1600) was dedicated to King Philip III. The "Battle" Mass (*Missa pro victoria*), for 2 choirs & organ, is based on Clément Janequin's famous chanson *La Bataille de Marignan*.

483

[2] Francisco Soto de Langa (1539–1619) was a priest in the congregation of St. Philip Neri (the Oratorio) & a singer in the Papal Chapel (cf. Grove).

Letter 30

MONTEVERDI: b. Cremona, 1567; d. Venice, 1643. We are fortunate in that a great many of his letters have survived (most of them printed in the source).—Vincenzo Gonzaga (ruled 1587–1612), son of Guglielmo (see comments to Letter 16), was a man of few principles, but he inherited his father's love for music & the arts.

[1] Nothing is known of this work, which may have been a pastoral play or an intermezzo. Cf. ArnM, 16.

[2] According to information kindly supplied by the Archivio di Stato, Mantua, Monteverdi left a blank space for the date in the autograph (Autografi, busta 2).

Letter 31

CACCINI: b. Rome, c. 1546; d. Florence, 1618. One of the foremost composers of the "Camerata" (see comments to Letter 23; cf. also Letter 25) & an excellent singer. For the dedication of his *Euridice,* the earliest opera score ever published (1601), & for the important preface to *Le nuove musiche,* see Strunk, 370–72 & 377–92 respectively. Caccini's visit to the court of Henry IV of France, documented by this letter, seems to have had an important influence on the subsequent development of the *ballet de cour.* Cf. BukMB, 143.

[1] Henry IV had married Maria de' Medici, niece of Ferdinand I, in 1600; this was the occasion for which both Peri & Caccini had composed their operas to Ottavio Rinuccini's libretto, *Euridice.*

[2] Francesca Caccini (1588–c.1640) was not only a famous singer, but a composer in her own right.

Letter 32

See comments to Letter 30.

[1] As emerges from the next sentence, the contralto was a male singer. *Castrati* began to be noted in connection with the Papal Chapel as early as 1562 (cf. BukMB, 399f.); Monteverdi himself introduced their use in opera with his *Orfeo* (1607), & it is in opera that they reigned supreme for nearly 2 centuries.

[2] "Gorgia" was the general term for improvised vocal ornamentation; "trillo" (not our trill) was a specific type of "gorgia" that consisted in singing the same note many times in quick succession.

Letter 33
BULL: b. ?, c.1563; d. Antwerp, 1628. For biographical information, see especially the source.
[1] James I.
[2] Archduke Albert of Austria and his consort Isabel, eldest daughter of Philip II of Spain, had been rulers of the southern Netherlands since 1598.
[3] The immediate results of this petition are not known; but in 1617 Bull was appointed organist of Antwerp cathedral, a post he occupied until his death.

Letter 34
See comments to Letter 30.—Striggio (dates unknown) was the librettist of Monteverdi's *Orfeo* & councilor to the Duke of Mantua.
[1] The Mantuan resident in Venice.
[2] Ferdinando Gonzaga, Duke of Mantua & younger son of Vincenzo I, was to marry Caterina de' Medici, sister of the Grand Duke of Tuscany, the following Easter.
[3] In these early performances the instruments were placed behind the stage. The reference to the "lowness" of the music is not clear, & the passage has previously been rendered in various imaginative ways (here it is translated literally). A possible explanation is that such spectacles were mounted in the courtyard of the ducal palace in Mantua, where a gallery provided an upper level (cf. the courtyard settings of early English drama & the balcony of Shakespeare's stage). It may be that the instrumental music emerged more clearly from the upper than from the lower level.
[4] See Letter 25, n. 4.
[5] "The cithara must be in the city, and the aulos in the fields." Cf. *Republic* 399d.
[6] The celebrated "Lamento" is all that has survived from the opera *Arianna* (1608).
[7] *Le Nozze di Tetide*, as it turned out, was not meant to be an opera but only a set of *intermezzi*; the Duke later countermanded the work, which remained unfinished & is now lost.

Letter 35
SCHÜTZ: b. Köstritz, 1585; d. Dresden, 1672.—Moser was Secretary of the Treasury to the Elector of Saxony.
[1] *Manu propria*, "[written] in [his] own hand."

Letter 36

SCHEIDT: b. Halle, 1587; d. there, 1654.—Gueinzius was rector of the *Gymnasium* in Halle.—Cf. Letter 59.

Letter 37

See comments to Letter 30.

[1] In the *Dialogo della musica antica e della moderna*. See Letter 23, comments & n. 1.

[2] The book does not appear to have been finished, if indeed it was ever begun. The term *seconda pratica* (i.e., the "modern style" of the early Baroque as against the *prima pratica* or "ancient style" of Renaissance polyphony) first appeared in the famous foreword to Monteverdi's fifth book of madrigals (1605) & was expounded at length by his brother Giulio Cesare in a Declaration prefixed to the *Scherzi musicali* of 1607. For an English version of both texts, see Strunk, 405–12.

[3] The plague of 1630–31 (vividly described in Manzoni's *The Betrothed*) had come to northern Italy with the invading lansquenets of Emperor Ferdinand II, when he intervened in the war over the succession to the Duchy of Mantua (the main branch of the Gonzagas had died with Vincenzo II). Cf. ArnM, 42–45. By 1632 Monteverdi, long a widower, had taken holy orders, possibly in consequence of his escape from the contagion.

[4] Apparently, an actor of the *commedia dell'arte;* they often went by the names of the characters they represented on the stage.

Letter 38

See comments to Letter 30.—The Procurators were senators of the Venetian Republic charged with high administrative functions.

[1] See Letter 37, n. 3.

Letter 39

LAWES: b. Dinton, Wilts, 1596; d. London, 1662.—Milton, for whose *Comus* Lawes had written the music 4 years earlier, was about to embark on his Continental tour (1638–39). For the great poet's tribute to Lawes, see his Sonnet xiii (*Harry, whose tuneful and well-measured song . . .*), which appeared among the commendatory verses prefixed to Lawes's *Choice Psalmes* (1648).

Letter 40
(For Schütz's dates see Letter 35.)—Johann Georg I: 1585–1656.
[1] *Symphoniae sacrae*, III.
[2] 11 October; but Schütz was born on the 8th.
[3] 1572–1632; the Landgrave was a composer himself & a patron of the arts.
[4] Giovanni Gabrieli (c. 1557–1612)—Schütz calls him Johann Gabriel later in the letter—represents the high point of the Venetian School (see comments to Letter 15) & is one of the main figures in the transition from the late Renaissance to the Baroque styles in music. Like his uncle & teacher Andrea, he spent some time at the Bavarian court with Lassus (cf. Letter 19, n. 2). Schütz's apprenticeship with Giovanni was an important factor in the spread of the Baroque style to Germany.
[5] *Il primo libro de' madrigali* was published in 1611, 2 (not 3) years after Schütz's arrival in Venice.
[6] Giulio Cesare Martinengo (d. 1613), Monteverdi's predecessor in that post.
[7] On his way to Rome (1510 or 1511), though it is not known where he stopped in Venice.
[8] The Thirty Years' War had ended 3 years earlier.
[9] Giovanni Andrea Bontempi (Angelini; c. 1624–1705) did in fact succeed Schütz. He is remembered as one of the earliest composers of opera active in Germany & as the author of books on counterpoint & music history.
[10] See Letter 35, n. 1.

Letter 41
LULLY: b. Florence, 1632; d. Paris, 1687.—Colbert (1619–83) was Louis XIV's famous prime minister.—French opera was born amid intrigues & lawsuits. Its founders were the poet Pierre Perrin (c. 1625–75) & the composer Robert Cambert (c. 1628–77), whose pastoral *Pomone* was produced in 1671. Although this was a great success, Perrin, who had associated himself with crooked partners, soon found himself in prison. Lully had always maintained that French opera was an impossibility; now, however, he followed Colbert's advice & bought Perrin's royal privileges, after which he obtained orders shutting down the opera house & restricting the use of music at all other theaters, including that of his former collaborator Molière. Perrin's partners sought to contest the action in the supreme court (the Paris Parliament), but Lully, whose position was unassailable, was

already planning his 1st season as the absolute tyrant & master of French opera.

[1] The original name of the institution now known as the Opéra in Paris.

[2] Lully was unable to obtain that hall & had to be satisfied, for the time being, with a converted tennis court, where, on 15 November 1672, he began his new career with a pastoral (actually a medley of pieces from earlier works) entitled *Les Festes de l'Amour et de Bacchus*. But see Letter 42.

[3] Philippe Quinault (1635–88) was to write most of Lully's librettos.

Letter 42

See comments & notes to Letter 41.

[1] Molière died suddenly on 17 February 1673, & Lully wasted no time in taking over the theater that had housed the great dramatist's company. It was here that Lully produced all his operas. Cf. Grove, "Académie de Musique."

[2] Machines played a vital role in Baroque opera & were often the main attraction: thanks to them, audiences could enjoy storms, fires, sea battles, &, in the last act, the providential descent of a god from the sky (the *deus ex machina*).

[3] See Letter 41, n. 2.

Letter 43

LOCKE: b. Exeter, c. 1630; d. London, 1677.—Purcell: b. London, 1659; d. there, 1695. This & the next letter must make up for the absence of letters from Purcell himself. (A copy of the accounts he submitted to the Treasury in 1687 is reproduced in: Great Britain, *Calendar of Treasury Books*, Vol. VIII, Part III, pp. 1763–64; also, J. A. Westrup, *Purcell* [revised ed.; "The Master Musicians"; London: J. M. Dent and Sons Ltd, 1960], chap. v.)

Letter 44

T. PURCELL: b. ?; d. London, 1682. A composer & violinist, the elder Purcell was a Gentleman of the Chapel Royal & held various other positions at the court of Charles II. (See comments to Letter 43.)—Gostling (c. 1650–1733) was a clergyman & a famous bass singer. Cf. Grove.

[1] 1678 by the Julian, 1679 by the Gregorian calendar. Cf. Letter 51, n. 1.

[2] John Blow (1649–1708), the composer of *Venus and Adonis*, was one of Henry's teachers. William Turner (1651–1740) was a singer & composer.

[3] E & F in the hexachord system (cf. Letter 73, n. 1): a joking reference to Gostling's phenomenal vocal range.

Letter 45

CORELLI: b. Fusignano (near Ravenna), 1653; d. Rome, 1713.—Zani, a Bolognan priest, was a friend of the composer's.—Corelli's chamber sonatas op. II had appeared in Rome in July of that year & had been published in Bologna very soon afterwards; whereupon some young "virtuosi" gathered at the home of Giovanni Paolo Colonna, president of the Accademia Filarmonica, & eagerly began to play them. But when they reached the following passage, in the *allemande* of the 3rd sonata,

they stopped & looked at each other in great astonishment: Corelli had violated the sacred rule of counterpoint that forbids parallel 5ths! Colonna told them to continue, assuring them that "Arcangelo must have known what he was doing." The 5ths, however, were not so soon forgotten, & Colonna at last begged Zani to write the composer & inquire about them. The present (not wholly convincing) letter is his answer. It proved too vehement for the sensibilities of the "virtuosi," & the 5ths became a *cause célèbre*, provoking a massive exchange of letters between a number of learned authorities (cf. source for the texts in Italian).

[1] "Time is the measurement of motion with regard to the *before* and *after*."
[2] All 3 were composers of church music in the Palestrina tradition; hence they might be expected to know the "rules."
[3] Pasquini (1637–1710), organist at Santa Maria Maggiore, is especially well-known for his clavier works. Francesco Verdoni was a bass singer in the Papal Chapel. The last person could not be identified.

Letter 46

BUXTEHUDE: b. Oldesloe (Holstein), c. 1637; d. Lübeck, 1707. In the interests of intelligibility, the present translation does not do full justice to Buxtehude's prose style, though the reader can still gain some idea of its Baroque convolutions.

[1] Lübeck was famous for the *Abend-Musicken* held at St. Mary's on certain Sundays before & during Advent. These devotional concerts, which took

place in the afternoon, were given for the edification of the commercial guilds, who sponsored them. The cantata of the Prodigal Son has not survived.
[2] Cf. Letter 35, n. 1.

Letter 47
A. SCARLATTI: b. Palermo, 1660; d. Naples, 1725. At the time, he was assistant *maestro di cappella* at Santa Maria Maggiore.—Prince Ferdinand (1663–1713) was son & heir to Grand Duke Cosimo III of Tuscany (who outlived him). The Prince commissioned many operas from Scarlatti, but never employed him officially in Florence. An extensive correspondence between them (mostly unpublished) is preserved in the Medici archives.
[1] See Letter 67; Domenico was about to leave for Venice to study with Francesco Gasparini.

Letter 48
J. S. BACH: b. Eisenach, 1685; d. Leipzig, 1750. His position at Mühl-hausen, which he had obtained the previous year, was Bach's second as organist.
[1] The salutation is addressed to the Burgomaster, the Town Councilors, the school officials & other learned persons, & the ordinary burghers, re-spectively.

Letter 49
BASSANI: b. Padua, c. 1657; d. Bergamo, 1716. Bassani was a composer of operas, church & chamber music & a member of the Accademia Filar-monica in Bologna.—Perti (1661–1756), a prolific composer, was president of the Accademia Filarmonica many times & a highly respected contra-puntist. Cf. Letter 50.
[1] The scudo was the silver coin of the Pontifical States (to which Ferrara belonged since 1598), the baiocco (mentioned later) its copper fraction.

Letter 50
MARCELLO: b. Venice, 1686; d. Brescia, 1739. The witty author of *Il teatro alla moda* (excerpts in Strunk, 518–31; complete translation in MQ, XXXIV–XXXV [1948–49]) & composer of the Psalms is here sub-mitting his test piece, a 4-part Mass, for admission to the Accademia Filarmonica in Bologna; he was admitted the following year.—For Perti see comments to Letter 49.
[1] Later, "this grave style," i.e., the *stile grave* or *stile antico*, corresponding to Monteverdi's *prima pratica* (cf. Letter 37, n. 2), which was preserved

for certain types of church music—&, importantly, for the teaching of counterpoint, down to our own day.

[2] This seems to be a comment not so much on Marcello's Mass as on the "grave style" in general.

[3] "He has gained every vote who has mingled profit with pleasure" (Horace *Ars Poetica* 343).

Letter 51

HANDEL: b. Halle, 1685; d. London, 1759.—Mattheson (1681–1764), composer, diplomat, prolific & important writer on musical subjects (theory & biography), had been a close friend of Handel's during the latter's Hamburg days.

[1] Actually, 7 March. All but the last of Handel's letters are dated according to the Julian calendar, which, in England, gave way to the Gregorian in 1752. Here, the Old Style dates are retained, as they are in the earlier parts of this book (on the Continent, the Gregorian reform went into effect on 4 October 1582 in nearly all the Catholic lands, while most of the Protestant countries changed over in 1701–1702).

[2] Mattheson had evidently asked Handel (1) for his opinion on the usefulness of the rules of the *stile antico* (cf. Letter 50, n. 1) as against those of thorough bass, (2) for an autobiographical sketch, presumably for one of Mattheson's publications (it was never sent).

[3] *Das Beschützte Orchestre* . . . (1717).

Letter 52

(For Bach's dates see Letter 48.) Bach spent the years 1708–17 in Weimar, 1717–23 in Cöthen. The present document (not really a letter) shows him accepting the duties he would retain for the rest of his life.

Letter 53

(For Handel's dates see Letter 51.)

[1] Both Houses of Parliament passed the act, with Handel's name added to it, on 20 February, & George I approved it the same day.

Letter 54

RAMEAU: b. Dijon, 1683; d. Paris, 1764.—La Motte (1672–1731), librettist, poet, & critic, was an important figure in the contemporary debates on ancient *vs.* modern poetry.—It is worth noting that Rameau was 44 when he wrote this, the 1st of his letters to survive; at the time, he was chiefly known as the author of 2 theoretical treatises & composer of harpsichord music, & it was not until 6 years later that *Hippolyte et*

491

Aricie, his 1st *tragédie lyrique,* was produced at the Opéra. Cf. the last sentences in Letter 63.

[1] *Aquilon et Orithie* is the title of the published version (after 1731).

[2] The passage is described in GirdR, 67–68.

[3] All titles of compositions published in the *Pièces de Clavecin* (1724).

[4] La Motte was apparently not impressed, for he never furnished a libretto to Rameau.

Letter 55

TELEMANN: b. Magdeburg, 1681; d. Hamburg, 1767.—Walther (1684–1748), composer & organist (& a colleague of Bach's at Weimar), is especially remembered for his *Musikalisches Lexikon* (1732; facsimile ed., Kassel, 1953), the 1st such work to include biographies of composers.

[1] Walther's *Alte und neue musikalische Bibliothek* (1728) was a preliminary work that never went beyond the letter A.

Letter 56

(For Handel's dates see Letter 51.)—Colman was the English Envoy Extraordinary in Florence.

[1] Cf. Letter 51, n. 1.

[2] Antonia Margherita Merighi had been brought to London by Handel the previous year.

[3] Owen Swiney (later, MacSwiney; 1680–1754) briefly managed the Haymarket Theatre until, in 1713, he went bankrupt & made off with all the money, leaving Handel & his company high & dry; he was now living in Italy.

Letter 57

(For Bach's dates see Letter 48.)—Erdmann, an old schoolmate of Bach's, was now the Imperial Russian Resident at Danzig.

[1] From the 1st marriage: Wilhelm Friedemann (1710–84), Carl Philipp Emanuel (see Letter 80), Johann Gottfried Bernhard (1715–39), & Catharina Dorothea (1708–74); from the 2nd: Gottfried Heinrich (1724–63), Elisabeth Juliana Friderica (see Letter 66, n. 2), & Regine Johanna (1728–33). For the complicated details concerning Bach's 20 children, cf. especially the source, pp. 210–11 (with nn. 25 & 28), from which the present information is taken. See also Letter 72.

[2] *Prima, secunda:* 6th & 5th forms, respectively.

492

Letter 58

(For Bach's dates see Letter 48.)—Frederick Augustus II (1696–1763) had just succeeded to his father's titles & was elected King of Poland later that year.
[1] The Kyrie & Gloria from the B minor Mass.
[2] Bach was granted the title of Composer to the Court Chapel 3 years later.

Letter 59

(For Bach's dates see Letter 48.) This was Bach's 3rd complaint in a protracted dispute with Rector Ernesti of the Thomas-Schule over the prerogative of appointing prefects. Eventually, the king intervened in the Cantor's favor. For an identical conflict of interests 100 years earlier, cf. Letter 36.

Letter 60

VIVALDI: b. Venice, c. 1675; d. Vienna, 1741.—Bentivoglio was a wealthy patron of the arts.
[1] It is not known which of his operas Vivaldi had planned to perform in Ferrara. As for the charges against the "red priest," they are credibly disposed of in what follows. Anna Giraud (Girò) was Vivaldi's pupil & may even have lived at his house, but there is no reason to suspect their relationship.
[2] Asthma, apparently.
[3] 34 years, more exactly. The Ospedale della Pietà, like the 3 other similar institutions in Venice, was originally a foundling hospital, but by the 18th century boasted a celebrated conservatory for young ladies. Cf. Grove, "Venice."

Letter 61

(For Handel's dates see Letter 51.)—Jennens, a bachelor & gentleman of leisure, wrote the text of Il Moderato, which he added to his "improved" version of Milton's L'Allegro & Il Penseroso; these, & his word-books to Saul, Belshazzar, & Messiah, were all set to music by Handel.
[1] Messiah was given its 1st performance later that season (13 April 1742), at "the New Musick-Hall in Fishamble-Street," Dublin. See Letter 62.
[2] Matthew Dubourg (1703–67), who sat at the head of the violins also at the 1st performance of Messiah, is remembered for having improvised a long, rambling cadenza at one of these concerts; when at last he returned

493

to the tonic key, Handel is supposed to have said, "You are welcome home, Mr. Dubourg."

[3] Trinity College.

[4] I.e., the operas being given in London.

[5] "I must say, with Harlequin, that our Penelope is but a Trollop." *Penelope* was one of the 100-odd operas composed by Baldassare Galuppi (1706–85).

Letter 62

See comments to Letter 61.

[1] But Handel never returned to Dublin.

Letter 63

(For Rameau's dates see Letter 54.)—Mongeot was a young musician living in the provinces. Practically nothing is known of him (cf. GirdR, 487–88).

[1] Charles-François Panard (1674–1765) wrote vaudevilles for the Opéra-Comique; Mongeot, it would seem, planned to set to music a tragedy by that witty versifier.

Letters 64A–E

See comments to Letter 61.—These 5 letters document the creation of *Belshazzar*. Handel began to work on it on 23 August 1744 & finished it that October; the oratorio received its 1st performance at the King's Theatre on 27 March 1745.

[1] All of these singers have articles devoted to them in Grove. By far the most famous was Susanna Maria Cibber (1714–66), née Arne (she was the sister of the composer), the greatest tragic actress of her time. Her singing voice was small but extremely expressive; Handel wrote the contralto solos in *Messiah* for her. She is buried in Westminster Abbey.

[2] Only 16 of the projected 24 nights were given, because of the poor attendance.

[3] The bracketed words are unclear in the autograph. *Deborah* (composed in 1733) opened the subscription series on 3 November.

Letter 65

(For Bach's dates see Letter 48.)—Johann Elias (1705–55), Bach's 2nd cousin, had lived at the composer's house for some years while studying divinity at the University of Leipzig. At this time, he was cantor in Schweinfurt.

[1] See Letter 66.

[2] From the *Musical Offering*.

[3] Frederick the Great invaded Saxony in December 1745, during the 2nd Silesian War. C. P. E. Bach's 2 sons were Johann August (1745–89) & Johann S[ebastian?] (1748–78).

Letter 66

See comments to Letter 65.

[1] "Deferred is not canceled."

[2] Johann Christoph Altnickol (1719–59), a pupil of Bach's, married the composer's daughter Elisabeth Juliana Friderica (1720–81).

[3] Johann Abraham Birnbaum was professor of rhetoric at Leipzig. Cf. source, pp. 237f.

Letter 67

D. SCARLATTI: b. Naples, 1685; d. Madrid, 1757.—Don Fernando de Silva y Álvarez de Toledo, Duke of Huescar was King Ferdinand VI's major-domo.—This is D. Scarlatti's sole surviving letter.

[1] Scarlatti had been asked by the Duke to transcribe 2 hymns by the 16th-century composer Pierre du Hotz into modern notation (cf. source, pp. 120–21).

Letter 68

ROUSSEAU: b. Geneva, 1712; d. Ermenonville (near Paris), 1778.— Lenieps (1694–1774) was a Genevan banker who had been banned from that city in 1731 for participating in an uprising against its aristocratic government. His enemies continued to persecute him in France, & he was twice imprisoned in the Bastille through their efforts.

[1] *Le Devin du village* had received its 1st performance 4 days earlier at Fontainebleau, in the presence of the king. The next year it was produced at the Opéra, where it remained in the repertoire for 60 years.

[2] Rousseau had resorted to "copying music at so much the page" for a living. Cf. his *Confessions*, Bk. VIII, for an account of this period of his life, particularly with regard to the composition & 1st performance of *Le Devin du village*.

[3] Rousseau's was the 1st printed edition of Pergolesi's masterpiece. The Parisian performances here alluded to were to touch off the obstreperous "Querelle des Bouffons" ("War of the Buffoons"), in which Italian comic opera was (illogically) pitted against French serious opera.

Letter 69

FREDERICK THE GREAT: b. Berlin, 1712; d. Potsdam, 1786. For the musical accomplishments of the warrior king, cf. Baker, Grove.

[1] *Montezuma,* the libretto Frederick had written (in French—it was rendered into Italian verse by the court poet) for his official opera composer, Karl Heinrich Graun (1704–59). Cf. Grout, 212–14.

[2] I.e., *cavatine,* rather than the traditional "da capo" arias; the preponderance of the shorter form is of historical significance as a harbinger of the later 18th-century operatic style.

Letter 70

(For Rameau's dates see Letter 54.)—Ducharger, another unknown correspondent of Rameau's (cf. Letter 63), had written him, criticizing certain points in his music theory; Rameau sent word that the criticisms would be answered in his latest book. When Ducharger wrote again, asking when the book would appear, he received the present reply. Cf. GirdR, 493–94.

Letter 71

(For Handel's dates see Letter 51.)—For Telemann, see Letter 55.—This is Handel's last extant letter; only the signature is in his own hand, as by now he was totally blind.

Letter 72

J. C. BACH: b. Leipzig, 1735; d. London, 1782. Johann Sebastian's youngest surviving son was known as the "Milan" & later the "London" Bach, from his main centers of activity.—Martini (1706–84) was one of the most celebrated musicians of his time. Composer, teacher, theorist, & historian, he carried on a voluminous correspondence with the leading intellects & composers of the 18th century.

[1] Count Antonio Litta, Bach's patron.

[2] Bach removed to London 5 years later.

[3] Presumably Bach was working on a complete service for the dead, since the Invitatory opens matins, while the *Dies Irae* is sung at Mass. Both of these compositions survive in manuscript.

Letter 73

TARTINI: b. Pirano, 1692; d. Padua, 1770.—Lombardini (b. 1735?) studied with Tartini & became a well-known violinist; she later married another violinist, Lodovico Sirmen. Cf. Grove, "Sirmen."—This famous violin-lesson-by-correspondence was first translated by Burney (London, 1779), whose version has been reprinted numerous times. The present version, though stylistically less attractive, attempts to convey the sense of the original with greater accuracy.

[1] A in the hexachord system. The Guidonian syllables (here, la-mi-re) indicate its position in the gamut. Cf. Grove, "Hexachord."

[2] The Italian has *fughe* ("fugues"), but the ensuing quotation is from a non-fugal allegro in Corelli's op. V, no. 1.

Letter 74

BOCCHERINI: b. Lucca, 1743; d. Madrid, 1805.

[1] The petition was granted only 3 years later.

Letter 75

HAYDN: b. Rohrau, Lower Austria, 1732; d. Vienna, 1809.—Prince Nicolaus I ("The Magnificent"; ruled 1762–90) was Haydn's master for nearly 30 years; his father, Prince Paul Anton, had secured the young composer's services in 1761. In all, Haydn served 4 princes of this, the mightiest family of the Hungarian nobility; the others were Anton (ruled 1790–94) & Nicolaus II (ruled 1794–1833).—This is the earliest Haydn letter that has been preserved.

[1] The Prince was probably at this hunting lodge, on land that was shortly to be the site of the grandiose castle of Estoras (Esterház).

[2] Rahier was administrator of the Esterházy castle in Eisenstadt.

[3] Carl Friberth was a tenor in the Esterházy band.

Letter 76

(For Haydn's dates see Letter 75.)—The monastery was probably that in Zwettl, Lower Austria (cf. source, p. 11).

[1] Haydn had been commissioned to write a work to honor the abbot (on his birthday?). Here the composer indicates how he wishes the work (known as the "Applausus" Cantata) to be performed.

[2] But Haydn was right.

Letter 77

MOZART: b. Salzburg, 1756; d. Vienna, 1791.—Mozart's mother was Anna Maria (1720–78), a simple, affectionate soul (see Letter 88). His sister Marianne (1751–1829) was an excellent pianist who shared her brother's earliest triumphs when they toured as infant prodigies.—The present letter is a postscript to one written by his father, Leopold (1719–

87), who, as his mentor & general manager, accompanied him on all his early journeys. Now 14, Mozart was on his 5th musical tour, his 1st to Italy.
[1] *Recte* Nannerl, familiar form of Marianne.

Letter 78

See comments to Letter 77.—Postscript to a letter by Leopold Mozart.—This was Mozart's 2nd journey to Italy (Aug.–Dec. 1771), undertaken to compose a stage work commissioned by Empress Maria Theresa for the Milan wedding of the Archduke Ferdinand & Princess Maria Riccarda Beatrice of Modena. Mozart was handed the libretto of this *festa teatrale* (*Ascanio in Alba*, K. 111, words by Giuseppe Parini) at the end of August & finished composing all the music—overture, 33 numbers, & recitatives—by 23 September. It was performed with great success on 17 October & repeated many times. The composer was 15 years old.
[1] Mozart had apparently lost his heart to a Salzburg girl & had put Nannerl to work as his messenger.

Letter 79

GLUCK: b. Erasbach, Upper Palatinate, 1714; d. Vienna, 1787.
[1] *Iphigénie en Aulide* was the work with which Gluck proposed to conquer Paris. The libretto was by the Bailli du Roullet (see comments to Letter 84), who had fired the first shot of the campaign by writing an open letter to one of the directors of the Opéra (for a translation, cf. Strunk, 676–80). He may also have helped to draft the present letter, a highly diplomatic document that eventually led to the opera's *première* (Paris, 19 April 1774).
[2] Ranieri de' Calzabigi (1714–95), poet, librettist, & operatic theorist, wrote the words of Gluck's first "reform" operas (cf. n.3 below).
[3] *Orfeo ed Euridice* (1762), *Alceste* (1767), *Paride ed Elena* (1769), all produced in Vienna. (For the important preface to *Alceste,* cf. Strunk, 673–75.)
[4] A diplomatic bow to the adherents of Rousseau in the old "Querelle des Bouffons" (cf. Letter 68, n. 3).
[5] *Lettre sur la musique française* (1753; excerpts in Strunk, 636–54).
[6] Note how the idealization of Greek music, which was behind the 1st operatic experiments, endures as a constant element in the history of operatic theory &, especially, reform—witness Wagner, 77 years later: "We look to the splendid art of the Greeks to learn from intimate understanding of it how the art work of the future must be constituted!" (*Das Kunstwerk der Zukunft*). On the other hand, cf. Letter 84 for Gluck's more candid opinions on the "old Greeks" & "their rules."

Letter 80
C. P. E. BACH: b. Weimar, 1714; d. Hamburg, 1788.—Forkel (1749–
1818), one of the founders of modern musicology, was also the author of
the 1st full biography of J. S. Bach. Some of his most important material
was obtained from Bach's sons, as can be seen from this & the next letter.
[1] Possibly Part I of the *Versuch über die wahre Art, das Clavier zu spielen.*
[2] Lorenz Christoph Mizler (1711–78) had studied with J. S. Bach. A
theorist rather than a composer, he was also the founder of one of the
earliest musical periodicals; in its last installment (1754) there had appeared a highly informative obituary of his master (cf. source, pp. 214–
24). See also the opening lines of Letter 81.
[3] These documents have survived (cf. source, pp. 202–11).
[4] The reference is to C. P. E. Bach's oratorio *Die Israeliten in der Wüste*
("The Israelites in the Desert").

Letter 81
See comments to Letter 80.
[1] See Letter 80, n. 2.
[2] Johann Friedrich Agricola (1720–74), organist & composer, had also
studied with J. S. Bach.
[3] *Ad primum,* "to the first [item]," etc.: these are Bach's answers to a list
of questions submitted by Forkel.
[4] All organ masters (see Baker, Grove, etc.).
[5] Johann Joseph Fux (1660–1741), composer & *Kapellmeister* to the court
at Vienna, was the author of one of the most celebrated manuals of
counterpoint of all time, the *Gradus ad Parnassum* (1725), a work that
more than any other succeeded in transmitting to ensuing generations the
Baroque view of the Palestrina style—the *stile antico*—by means of rules
& exercises. Cf. Letter 50, n. 1.
[6] See Baker, etc. (For Altnickol, cf. Letter 66, n. 2.)
[7] See Baker, etc. (For Keiser, cf. Letter 99, n. 1; for Hasse, Letter 85, n. 4.)
[8] Johann Christoph Bach (1642–1703) was the cousin of J. S. Bach's
father.

Letter 82
See comments to Letter 77.—Mozart's 9th journey (Dec. 1774–Mar. 1775)
was to Munich, where he produced his opera buffa *La finta giardiniera.*
[1] "Was produced."
[2] Maximilian Joseph III (1727–77), Elector of Bavaria; he will make an
unforgettable appearance in Letter 87.

[3] Count Ferdinand Christoph Waldburg-Zeil (1719–86), Prince-Bishop of Chiemsee, was one of Mozart's patrons.
[4] A reference to the Mozarts' conflicts with their master, the Archbishop of Salzburg (cf. Letter 87, n. 10, & especially Letter 94).
[5] The Mozarts' fox terrier.

Letter 83

(For Rousseau's dates see Letter 68.)—Beloselsky (1757–1809) was for a time Catherine the Great's ambassador to the court of the Savoys in Turin.
[1] Cf. Letter 68, n. 2.
[2] Cf. Letter 98 for his dates. The opera was probably *La fausse magie*.
[3] In the original: "ces gens-là n'ont pas d'*accent* . . ." A more appropriate translation might be "cadence," the rise & fall of the voice in speaking, which, according to Rousseau (*Dictionnaire de Musique, s.v.* "Mélodie"), determines the nature of all melodies. The uninflected speech of noblemen produces melody devoid of expression, while the lively speech of peasants generates melodies that can move the heart, as in *Le Devin du village*.

Letter 84

(For Gluck's dates see Letter 79.)—François Louis Gaud Leblond du Roullet (1716–86) had been an attaché at the French embassy in Vienna when he met Gluck. For his part in introducing the composer to Paris, cf. Letter 79, n. 1. Now the Bailli (his title as Commander of the Knights of Malta) was living in Paris & adapting the libretto of *Alceste* for the French stage.
[1] Henri l'Arrivé (1733–1802), bass singer at the Opéra, was prominent in the Parisian performances of Gluck's operas.
[2] (Mis)quoted from Horace (*Epistles* I. xix. 19): O *imitatores, servum pecus* ("O imitators, you slavish herd").
[3] "Extraneous" (the literal sense!).
[4] Gluck's niece Marianne (Nanette) whom he had adopted. She died the following year at the age of 16 (on 22 April, the eve of the 1st Parisian performance of *Alceste*)—a loss keenly felt by the composer (cf. Letter 86). Burney, who heard her sing more than once, praised her great artistry.
[5] The Abbé François Arnaud (1721–84), member of the Académie des inscriptions et belles-lettres & distinguished music critic, was later to side with Gluck in the notorious squabble between Gluckists & Piccinnists (cf. Letter 89, especially n. 1).

Letter 85

(For Haydn's dates see Letter 75.)—"Mademoiselle Leonore" (maiden name unknown) later married one of Prince Esterházy's administrators. On the present occasion, she had forwarded to Haydn a publisher's request for an autobiographical sketch.

[1] *Recte*, 1732.

[2] I.e., Bruck an der Leitha.

[3] Nicola Porpora (1686–1768) was indeed a celebrated composer & teacher, & for a time a successful rival of Handel in London.

[4] Johann Adolph Hasse (1699–1783), like Porpora, was considered one of the great masters of his time.

[5] Karl Ditters von Dittersdorf (1739–99) was a prolific composer of operas & instrumental music.

[6] Baron Gottfried van Swieten (1734–1803) was to return to Vienna the following year &, as court librarian & patron of music, play a considerable role in the lives of Haydn & Mozart, especially by exposing them to the music of Bach & Handel.

[7] Cf. Letter 35, n. 1.

Letter 86

(For Gluck's dates see Letter 79.)—Wieland (1733–1813), the famous writer & earliest German translator of Shakespeare, was a great admirer of Gluck.—The main interest of this letter is that it reflects the rise of Weimar as the "German Athens." By now Goethe had settled there, at the instance of Carl August of Saxe-Weimar (1757–1828), and this was the year Herder was appointed pastor of the Stadtkirche.—After Nanette's death (cf. Letter 84, n. 4), Gluck had asked Wieland for some commemorative verses to be set to music. In his reply (cf. source, pp. 82–83), Wieland said he felt unequal to the task, but that he had passed Gluck's request on to Goethe, who had become inspired with "a great idea, which was working in his soul." Unfortunately, this did not materialize until 2 years later (as the "monodrama" *Proserpina*), & Gluck did not set it to music.

[1] Gluck had addressed a similar request to Friedrich Klopstock (1724–1803), who was a good friend of the composer's, but there is no evidence that such a poem was written.

[2] *Erwin und Elmire* (1775) had appeared as a play with songs by Johann André (1741–99).

[3] In the letter mentioned above, Wieland, a champion of German opera, had offered Gluck a libretto based on Shakespeare's play; however, he was

afraid that "this excess of love would seem too monotonous" to the Viennese. Gluck never composed a German opera.

Letter 87
See comments to Letter 77.—Mozart was traveling with his mother. Munich was the 1st stop on a journey that took them to Augsburg, Mannheim, & Paris in an attempt at bettering the 21-year-old composer's position. Unsuccessful from the very beginning, the journey came to an end with unexpected tragedy (see Letter 92).
[1] Mozart's mother had begun the letter with a few lines, ending with: ". . . we must wait and see how it will go with us; we have a great many good friends who would be happy to see us stay here." (For a complete example of a joint letter, cf. Letter 88.)
[2] Count Joseph Anton Seeau (d. 1799) was the Intendant of the newly built Residence Theater in Munich.
[3] Cf. Letter 82, n. 3.
[4] Nymphenburg, near Munich, was the magnificent country seat of the Electors. (For the Elector, cf. Letter 82, n. 2.)
[5] Franz Xaver Woschitka was 1st cellist in the Munich orchestra.
[6] Apparently an intriguer who had come between them.
[7] The owner of the Black Eagle, the inn where the Mozarts stayed when in Munich; evidently a good friend.
[8] A rich Englishwoman, mentioned by Burney as a harpsichordist possessing "uncommon rapidity and precision."
[9] There follows a chatty paragraph by Mozart's mother. The next day, Mozart continues.
[10] Count Hieronymus Colloredo (1732–1812), Prince-Archbishop of Salzburg, in whose service Leopold Mozart was to continue as Vice-*Kapellmeister* to the end of his life; the young Mozart, however, was eventually to break away (cf. Letter 94).

Letter 88
See comments to Letter 87.
[1] Cf. Letter 82, n. 1.
[2] Canon of Salzburg Cathedral.
[3] Leopold Mozart's brother Franz Alois. Leopold was a native of Augsburg.
[4] Maria Anna Thekla Mozart (1758–1841), with whom henceforward the composer was to carry on a very racy correspondence.
[5] Johann Andreas Stein (1728–92), well-known piano manufacturer. (There will be more about him & his daughter later in the same letter.)

[6] Cf. Letter 77, n. 1.

[7] Johann Baptist Vanhall (Wanhal; 1739–1813), a very prolific composer living in Vienna.

[8] The Violin Concerto in D major, K. 218 (composed in 1775).

[9] *12 Variations on a Minuet by J. C. Fischer*, K. 179 (composed in 1774).

[10] The Mozarts' tailor in Salzburg.

[11] Ignaz von Beecke (1733–1803), pianist & composer.

[12] Nanette (1769–1835) was to marry her father's successor in the manufactory, Johann Andreas Streicher (1761–1833), in 1793; they became good friends of Beethoven.

[13] K. 242 (composed in 1776).

[14] K. 284 & K. 238 (composed in 1775 & 1776 respectively).

[15] Augusta Vindelicorum is the ancient Roman name for Augsburg.—On the following day Mozart continued with what amounts to another letter, omitted here.

Letter 89

(For Gluck's dates see Letter 79.)—Anna von Fries was the wife of a Swiss financier knighted by Maria Theresa for services rendered during the 7 Years' War.

[1] By now, Nicola Piccinni (or Piccini; 1728–1800) had been summoned to Paris to write in competition with Gluck, &, while the composers remained on friendly terms, Paris split into 2 hostile camps—the Gluckists & Piccinnists. *Armide* had been produced on 23 September & was not immediately successful.—*Orphée et Eurydice* (the French version of *Orfeo*) had been Gluck's 2nd Parisian opera (2 August 1774). For *Iphigénie en Aulide* & *Alceste*, cf. Letter 79 (especially nn. 1 & 3) & Letter 84.

[2] Piccinni's *Roland* was to have a very successful 1st performance on 27 January 1778.

[3] Jean François Marmontel (1723–99), critic, dramatist, novelist, & permanent Secretary of the Académie française, was an eager partisan of Piccinni, for whom he later wrote librettos. Jean François de La Harpe (1739–1803), the famous man of letters, was also a Piccinnist.

[4] For Arnaud, cf. Letter 84, n. 5. Jean Baptiste Antoine Suard (1734–1817), critic & journalist, conducted an active campaign in behalf of Gluck.

Letter 90

See comments to Letter 87.—Continuation of a letter begun by Mozart's mother.

[1] Mozart wrote the Concerto for Flute & Harp, K. 299, for de Guines & his daughter.

[2] *Alexandre et Roxane;* the plan came to nothing.

[3] A. P. J. Vismes de Valgay (1745–1819), an ardent Gluckist, had that year become the director of the Opéra.

[4] Jean-Georges Noverre (1727–1810), the celebrated ballet dancer & choreographer, had been active in Vienna during 1767–74, & the Mozarts had met him there. He was ballet master at the Opéra from 1775 to 1780.

[5] *Les petits riens.* Mozart gave the music to Noverre as a "friendly favor." The pantomime was produced on 11 June (the composer's name was not on the program) & the score later disappeared, not to be found again until 1872, when it turned up in the Opéra's archives.

[6] See comments to Letter 92.

Letter 91

(For Gluck's dates see Letter 79.)—Guillard (1752–1814) was the librettist for *Iphigénie en Tauride,* the subject of the present letter. Gluck's last great opera (the very last, *Écho et Narcisse,* suffered from a poor libretto) was produced at the Opéra on 18 May of the following year.— Explanations of the opera's plot & of the quotations in French & Italian have been dispensed with, in order not to burden the text (& the reader) with unessential notes.

[1] "By fours."

[2] Here Gluck quotes the beginning of an aria from *La clemenza di Tito* by the famous Italian poet Pietro Metastasio (1698–1782) in order to convey an anapaestic stress pattern (French verse is measured by the number of syllables, not stresses, per line). The 3rd word in line 2 is misspelt: it should read "che."

[3] Gluck contemplated settling in Paris, but the plan did not materialize.

[4] Presumably, the Prologue in question is that to *Le feste d'Apollo* (Parma, 1769).

[5] But see the opening sentences of Letter 93.

Letter 92

See comments to Letter 87.—Bullinger was a good friend of the family & their father confessor.

Letter 93

(For Gluck's dates see Letter 79.)—For Arnaud see Letter 84, n. 5.

[1] *Iphigénie en Tauride* & *Écho et Narcisse* (see comments to Letter 91).

² Cf. Letter 90, n. 3.
³ Du Roullet (cf. comments to Letter 84).
⁴ Wife of Jean de Vaines, Administrator of the State Domains.
⁵ *Alceste* had been given there on 9 May.
⁶ "The world goes of its own accord, and does not fall, because it has nowhere to fall."
⁷ Cf. Letter 97, n. 3.

Letter 94

See comments to Letter 77.—In this, as in many other letters, Mozart uses a code devised by the family as a rather naive precaution against spies. Passages in code are here enclosed in broken brackets.
¹ Archbishop Colloredo (cf. Letter 87, n. 10).
² Cäcilia Weber was the mother of Aloisia, with whom Mozart had been in love, & of Constanze (1763–1842), whom he married shortly (& mainly as a result of the old lady's machinations). Frau Weber's late husband Fridolin was the uncle of the as yet unborn Carl Maria von Weber.
³ Mozart's salary was actually 450 gulden.
⁴ Imperial residence near Vienna.
⁵ See Letter 107, n. 4.

Letter 95

See comments to Letter 77.
¹ *Die Entführung aus dem Serail*, of which Mozart had sent his father "a little Foretaste" about a week earlier.
² Gottlieb Stephanie (1741–1800), actor, director, & playwright at the Burgtheater, fashioned the libretto of *Die Entführung* from that of *Belmonte und Constanze*, a *Singspiel* by Johann André (cf. Letter 86, n. 2) with words by C. F. Bretzner produced earlier that year in Germany. But this letter shows that Mozart had a share in the adaptation.
³ The keeper of the harem in the opera. (Comments regarding the characters & the plot will be dispensed with hereafter, since the information is readily accessible.)
⁴ Colloredo (cf. Letter 87, n. 10).
⁵ To the poet, "hui" ("im Hui" = "in a flash") seemed a stylish way of saying "schnell" ("quickly"), but to Mozart it conveyed the more usual meaning—"ugh!" as in "hui Sau" ("ugh, you pig!").
⁶ "For Messrs. the Viennese."
⁷ Josephine Auernhammer, Mozart's piano student, felt a romantic attachment for him; unfortunately, she was fat & ugly, making it "punishment enough for the rest of the day if by misfortune one's eyes happen to fall

upon her," as the composer confided to his father. Nevertheless, they performed the Double Concerto (K. 365) with great success on 23 November, at a private concert at Miss Auernhammer's home. (The other concerto referred to was a 2-piano arrangement of the Triple Concerto, K. 242.)

Letter 96
(For Gluck's dates see Letter 79.)—Valentin (given name unknown) was the Duke of Aiguillon's director of music. The substance of his letter to Gluck must be inferred from the answer.

Letter 97
(For Mozart's & his father's dates see Letter 77.)
[1] *Die Entführung aus dem Serail* had received its 1st performance on 16 July. (Cf. also Letter 95.)
[2] Through his father, Mozart had been asked to provide music for a celebration in the Haffner family of Salzburg. He wrote the "Haffner" Symphony in such haste that when he received it again from his father half a year later he commented: "The New Hafner Symphony quite astonished me—for I had not remembered a Word of it;—it should certainly be very effective."
[3] Count Stefan Zichy was the husband of one of Mozart's pupils. Prince Wenzel Anton von Kaunitz-Rietberg (1711–94), the Austrian chancellor, had befriended Mozart when the composer had first come to Vienna as a prodigy & continued to show him favor in later years.
[4] At this time, Mozart was still seeking his father's permission to wed Constanze (Leopold opposed the marriage). The consent finally arrived on 5 August—the day after the wedding.

Letter 98
GRÉTRY: b. Liège, 1741; d. Montmorency (near Paris), 1813.—Sedaine (1719–97), dramatist &, from 1786, member of the Académie française, wrote 3 libretti for Grétry, including that for *Richard Cœur de Lion*.
[1] Grétry's masterpiece had been brought out 2 days earlier.
[2] Beaumarchais' *Mariage de Figaro,* completed in 1778 but barred from the stage because of Louis XVI's personal opposition, had finally been produced with clamorous success earlier that season.

Letter 99
(For C. P. E. Bach's dates see Letter 80.)—Eschenburg (1743–1820), critic & historian, is remembered for his translations of English authors

(he edited & completed Wieland's versions of Shakespeare—cf. comments to Letter 86). His latest effort at the time was a translation of *An Account of the Musical Performances in Westminster-Abbey and the Pantheon in Commemoration of Handel* (1785) by Charles Burney; the book contained a "Sketch of the Life of Handel."

[1] Reinhard Keiser (1674–1739) was a prolific & talented composer of German operas in Hamburg (cf. Grout, 158–64). For Hasse, cf. Letter 85, n. 4; for Graun, Letter 69, n. 1.

[2] This is true; pedals began appearing in England c. 1790, though as late as 1844 Mendelssohn had to cancel a recital in the Hanover Square Rooms when he discovered the organ had no pedals.

[3] Bach's indignation must have affected his memory. The entry for 12 Oct. 1772 in Burney's *Present State of Music in Germany* . . . (1775) describes the Englishman's meeting with Bach, in the course of which the composer showed him some of his father's works (later, Burney notes, Bach sent him "several of his own and his father's most curious compositions"); what is more, the next morning "was entirely employed in visiting churches, and hearing organs, to which M. Bach was so kind as to conduct me"! Bach himself did not play, since "M. Bach has so long neglected organ-playing, that he says he has lost the use of the pedals, which are thought so essential throughout Germany, that no one can pass for a player worth hearing who is unable to use them." But in Burney's opinion, the son was learned "even beyond his father . . . and . . . far before him in variety of modulation"—an opinion obviously not shared by C. P. E. Bach himself, whose present forgetfulness must be viewed as a sign of his admiration & devotion for his father.

[4] Faustina Bordoni (c. 1700–81), famous mezzo soprano, had been brought to England by Handel in 1726; she later married Hasse. Johann Joachim Quantz (1697–1773), composer & flutist at the court of Frederick the Great (he was the monarch's flute teacher), was the author of the important *Versuch einer Anweisung, die Flöte traversiere zu spielen* (1752), a treatise on flute-playing. He, too, was in London in 1726.

[5] George III had in his youth studied with Handel & remained a staunch promoter of his music to the end.

[6] Johann Gottfried Schwanenberg (1740–1804), a composer, lived in Brunswick.

Letter 100
(For Mozart's & his father's dates see Letter 77.)

[1] Nancy Storace (1766–1817), English soprano of Italian origin, had created the part of Susanna in *Le nozze di Figaro* the previous year.

[2] The Mozarts had spent several weeks in the Bohemian capital, where *Figaro* was all the rage (in Vienna, it had been withdrawn after 9 performances). This was the visit that brought Mozart the contract for a new opera, to be performed in Prague. He must have been working on it now; *Don Giovanni* was produced on 29 October.

[3] The bass singer had created the role of Osmin in *Die Entführung* (he is discussed in Letter 95). The oboist, Johann Christian Fischer (1733–1800), had settled in London; one of his minuets had served Mozart as the theme for K. 179 (cf. Letter 88, n. 9).

[4] Mozart had become a Freemason in 1784, his father the following year.

[5] August von Hatzfeld, an excellent amateur violinist, had recently died of consumption in Bonn.

[6] Carl Thomas (1784–1858), the older of the 2 sons who survived Mozart, later became a government official in Milan, where he died a bachelor. There is a touching portrait of him in Letter 165.

[7] Letter 101 tells the rest.

Letter 101

(For Mozart's dates see Letter 77.)—Jacquin (1763–92) & his sister Franziska studied with Mozart.

[1] Presumably a copy of Tasso's pastoral poem *Aminta*.

[2] In C major, K. 521, for piano duet.

[3] Cf. Letter 35, n. 1.

[4] Leopold had died on 28 May.

Letter 102

BEETHOVEN: b. Bonn, 1770; d. Vienna, 1827.—Schaden was a lawyer Beethoven had met in Augsburg on his way home from his 1st visit to Vienna (where he had played for Mozart).—This is the earliest Beethoven letter extant.

[1] Carolins, the gold currency of Bavaria & Württemberg.

[2] "Court Organist to the Elector of Cologne," a position Beethoven held since 1784.

Letter 103

(For Haydn's dates see Letter 75.)—Carlo & Francesco Artaria had begun their music printing business in 1778; Haydn's works made them famous, & they later added such names as Mozart, Beethoven, & Schubert to their list.

[1] The proofs of op. 50 (Hoboken 44–49).

[2] *Die Sieben letzten Worte unseres Erlösers am Kreuze* ("The Seven Last

Words of Our Redeemer on the Cross"), 7 orchestral "sonatas, with an introduction and an earthquake at the end," had been published by Artaria earlier that year.

Letter 104
(For Haydn's dates see Letter 75.)—Roth was a government functionary who often held concerts at his home.—The present fragment is all that remains of the original; it first appeared in F. X. Niemetschek's biography of Mozart (Prague, 1798).

Letter 105
(For Haydn's dates see Letter 75.)—Frau von Genzinger (1750–93), the wife of a fashionable Viennese physician, was a great music lover.
[1] "The Genzingers gave soirées to which Vienna's musical élite, including Mozart, was invited" (source, pp. xxi–xxii).
[2] *Arianna a Naxos.* Peperl (Josepha) was the Genzingers' 16-year-old daughter.
[3] Franz was Peperl's brother.

Letter 106
(For Mozart's dates see Letter 77.)—Puchberg was a wealthy Viennese merchant. We have 20 letters from Mozart to this generous friend, all dating from the composer's last 3 years & nearly all requesting financial help.
[1] *Ordensbruder,* "Brother in the Order" (of Freemasons). Cf. Letter 100, n. 4.
[2] K. 589 & 590.
[3] "Emperor," i.e., Leopold II, who had succeeded to the throne at the death of his brother Joseph II earlier that year.
[4] Mozart's only title at court was that of Imperial Royal Chamber Composer, with a yearly stipend of 800 gulden, given him by Joseph II at the death of Gluck, who had held that position before him (& had received 2000 gulden yearly). Now Mozart had applied to Leopold II for the post of 2nd *Kapellmeister* (Salieri—cf. Letter 133, n. 2—was the 1st); but, notwithstanding auspicious "signs," the title went to someone else, & Mozart never improved his position.
[5] Cf. Letter 35, n. 1.

Letter 107
(For Mozart's dates see Letter 77.)—For Constanze see Letter 94, n. 2 (also Letter 97, n. 4).—Mozart had gone to Frankfurt for the coronation

of Leopold II, even though he had no official invitation (cf. Letter 106, nn. 3 & 4). He hoped that public & private performances among such a brilliant gathering might bring about a change in his fortunes; this attempt, too, was doomed to failure.

[1] Mozart's nickname for his friend Anton Stadler (1753–1812), the clarinetist for whom he wrote the trio, quintet, & concerto.

[2] Franz Anton Hoffmeister (1754–1812). A law student turned music publisher, he later became a prolific composer. He had published Mozart's Piano Quartet in G minor, K. 478, in 1785. (Cf. also Letter 117.)

[3] Franz de Paula Hofer, the husband of Constanze's oldest sister Josefa, had accompanied Mozart on this journey; he was an excellent violinist.

[4] The "Eye of God" was the name of the house where the Webers lived when Mozart moved in with them, after leaving the Archbishop's service. Cf. Letter 94.

Letter 108

See comments to Letter 105.—Haydn was on the 1st of his 2 famous visits to England.

[1] Johann Peter Salomon (1745–1815), the violinist & impresario responsible for Haydn's trip to England.

[2] It was to be *L'anima del filosofo (Orfeo ed Euridice)*.

[3] No. 91.

Letter 109

(For Mozart's dates see Letter 77.)—For Constanze see Letter 94, n. 2 (also Letter 97, n. 4). Since she was in poor health & expecting another baby, Mozart had sent her to the resort near Vienna, while he himself stayed home & worked on *Die Zauberflöte*. His health, however, was rapidly failing. In the 5 months that remained, he completed *Die Zauberflöte*, composed *La clemenza di Tito*, the Clarinet Concerto, & a couple of smaller works, & began the Requiem. At his death (5 December), "all he left was cash in the amount of about 200 gulden, miserable house furnishings, musical instruments, and a small library appraised at 23 gulden 41 kreuzer" (Einstein).

[1] This is simply a jocular allusion to his appetite; Mozart did not "starve to death."

Letter 110

(For Haydn's dates see Letter 75.)—For Puchberg see comments to Letter 106.—These fragments, first published in G. Nottebohm's *Mozartiana* (1880), are all that survives of Haydn's letter.

Letter 111

(For Grétry's dates see Letter 98.)—Rouget de Lisle (1760–1836) is best known as the author of the words & music of the *Marseillaise*, written at Strasbourg on the night of 25 April 1792, soon after France's declaration of war on Austria. The 1st part of this letter, however, deals with another work of his—the libretto for *Cécile et Ermancé, ou les Deux Couvents*, which he wrote together with Deprez-Valmont & which Grétry set to music as a *comédie mêlée d'ariettes*. At the time of the present letter, Rouget de Lisle was aide-de-camp to the commander of the army which, a few days later, would overrun Belgium.

[1] The same volunteers who had entered Paris on 30 July singing Rouget de Lisle's *War Song for the Army of the Rhine*; they were still singing it when they stormed the Tuileries on 10 August, & from that day it was known as the *Song of the Marseillais* (later, as the *Marseillaise*).

[2] Jean-Frédéric Edelmann (1749–94), pianist & composer, would later be one of the victims of the Reign of Terror (cf. MQ, L [1964], 165 ff.). Grétry himself, in his *Mémoires* (1797), was to confirm that Rouget de Lisle had also written the music of the national anthem.

Letters 112A–B

(For Haydn's & Beethoven's dates see Letters 75 & 102 respectively.)
—Maximilian Franz (1756–1801), the youngest son of Empress Maria Theresa, was the Elector of Cologne from 1784 to 1794, when he was ousted by the French invaders.—On 10 November 1792, Beethoven had returned to Vienna, which henceforward was to be his permanent home.—Only the signature of Haydn's letter is autograph.

[1] The quintet, variations, & fugue have not been identified; the partita is thought to be the Wind Octet, op. 103; the oboe concerto (in F major) is lost, but for the opening themes.

[2] 100 ducats (= 450 gulden).

[3] This letter (here, too, only the signature is autograph) was enclosed with Haydn's.

[4] In his reply to Haydn, the Elector showed himself unmoved & suggested Beethoven return to Bonn, since he was just running into debt in Vienna. Beethoven remained.

Letter 113

GOSSEC: b. Vergnies (Belgium), 1734; d. Paris, 1829. The well-known composer of symphonies & operas was a fervent champion of the

Revolution. 3 of his musical contributions to the republican cause are mentioned in this letter, a document that helped to save Pierre-Gabriel Gardel (1758–1840), the *maître de ballet* of the Opéra, from a denouncer's accusation & from the guillotine: for by now the Reign of Terror was reaching its peak, under Robespierre.—The Committee of General Security, established by the National Convention in October 1792, wielded unlimited powers in matters concerning crimes against the state & controlled the police.

[1] Marie-Joseph Blaise de Chénier (1764–1811), revolutionary dramatist & politician, was on several committees, including the Committee of General Security; he was the younger brother of André, the poet, who had just been arrested at the time of this letter & would be executed 4 months later.

[2] 6 brumaire, year II (27 Oct. 1793). Gossec did not fill in the date.

[3] Louis Michel Lepelletier, noted revolutionary who had voted in favor of Louis XVI's execution, was assassinated by a royal bodyguard on 20 Jan. 1793, the day before the king died. Jean Paul Marat was killed by Charlotte Corday on 13 July of the same year.

Letter 114
DALAYRAC: b. Muret (Haute-Garonne), 1753; d. Paris, 1809. He composed 56 operas, many of which held the stage for decades after his death, both in France & abroad.

Letter 115
(For Beethoven's dates see Letter 102.)—Simrock (1752–1833) founded the well-known music publishing firm of that name & published several of Beethoven's works.

[1] For piano duet, on a theme by Count Waldstein (WoO 67).

[2] Johann Traeg, a Viennese publisher who, beginning in 1798, brought out some of Beethoven's early works.

[3] An indication that at this time Beethoven still considered his stay in Vienna as a temporary visit.

[4] Indeed, the French armies annexed the territory west of the Rhine, & it remained a part of France until 1815.

[5] Franz Ries (1755–1846) was the Elector's music director in Bonn; he was Beethoven's friend & taught him the violin—an instrument the composer never quite mastered.

[6] Op. 103 (cf. Letter 112A, n. 1).

[7] For piano, on a theme by Dittersdorf (WoO 66); they had been published by Simrock the previous autumn.

Letter 116
See comments to Letter 75.
[1] Joseph Alois Luegmayer, house-master, was married to Haydn's niece.

Letter 117
(For Beethoven's dates see Letter 102.)—For Hoffmeister see Letter 107, n. 2.
[1] Ambros Kühnel (1770–1813) had, with Hoffmeister, recently founded the Bureau de Musique, a publishing firm that later became C. F. Peters, still active today.
[2] Beethoven's esteem for J. S. Bach dated from his youth (at 13 he could already play most of the *Well-Tempered Clavier*), & in later years he was always eager to acquire any of the rarely published works by the neglected master.
[3] The works in question are: the Septet, op. 20, the 1st Symphony, the 2nd Piano Concerto, & the Sonata in B-flat major, op. 22.
[4] The German expression is untranslatable: *Diese Sonate hat sich gewaschen, geliebtester Hr: Bruder!*

Letter 118
(For Haydn's dates see Letter 75.)—The Institut National was an amalgam of the several French academies, which had been abolished by the National Convention in 1793.—Only the signature of this letter is autograph.
[1] Cf. Letter 35, n. 1.—Haydn's international fame earned him many such honors in his later years.

Letter 119
PAISIELLO: b. Taranto, 1740; d. Naples, 1816. The noted opera composer had known fame & fortune before (he had spent 8 years in the service of Catherine the Great); now, for a season, he was *maître de chapelle* to Napoleon, who was particularly fond of his music. The following year, Paisiello went to Naples, where he continued in high positions until the last year of his life, when he was stripped of all his titles (except that of *maestro di cappella*) by Ferdinand I, King of the Two Sicilies, upon the latter's restoration to the throne.
[1] Napoleon was in fact quite busy just then, preparing to have himself elected First Consul for life.
[2] Géraud Christophe Michel Duroc (1772–1813) was Napoleon's confidant &, at the time, governor of the Tuileries.

³ Count Pierre Louis Roederer (1754–1835), a noted economist, was a personage of some influence in the Napoleonic era.

Letter 120
(For Beethoven's dates see Letter 102.)—Beethoven had 2 brothers: Caspar Anton Carl (1774–1815) was also a musician, but eventually went to work for a Viennese bank & helped the composer in many of his business transactions; Nikolaus Johann (1776–1848) followed his brothers to Vienna, became a pharmacist, acquired considerable wealth, & eventually retired on a property he bought in the country.—The famous "Heiligenstadt Testament" is not a letter. Yet, this was not deemed sufficient reason to omit such a remarkable document from the present collection. It should be noted, besides, that not one of the English translations hitherto available has rendered Beethoven's tumultuous utterance without attempting to restrain it, at least within the bounds of conventional punctuation.—The document was written at the critical turning point in Beethoven's life, when he had to face the fact that his deafness was progressive & probably incurable. The MS was discovered among his effects when he died.
¹ Here (& twice later) Beethoven left a blank space; why he omitted his younger brother's name is not clear.
² Johann Adam Schmidt (1759–1808) was a famous Viennese physician.
³ Prince Karl Lichnowsky (1756–1814) was a friend & patron to whom Beethoven dedicated his Trios, op. 1, his Second Symphony, the "Pathétique" Sonata, etc.

Letter 121
(For Beethoven's dates see Letter 102.)—Härtel (1763–1827) had joined the music publishing firm of Breitkopf in 1795, when its name was changed to its present form, Breitkopf & Härtel. The death of Christoph Gottlob Breitkopf (1800) left Härtel at the helm of the celebrated firm, which he greatly expanded.
¹ The works in question are: *Christus am Ölberge,* the "Eroica" Symphony, the Triple Concerto, & the sonatas op. 53 ("Waldstein"), op. 54, & op. 57 ("Appassionata"). By sonata "with an accompaniment," Beethoven meant one for violin (or other instrument) & piano. Only the oratorio was published by Breitkopf & Härtel, and not until 1811.
² Beethoven changed the dedication of his symphony when he learnt of Napoleon's coronation as emperor of the French.

Letter 122

(For Haydn's dates see Letter 75.)—Hummel (1778–1837), one of the most famous composers & pianists of his generation, was at this time performing the duties of music director to Prince Esterházy in lieu of the aged Haydn.

[1] *The Creation* (hardly a "little work"!).

[2] Cf. Letter 35, n. 1.

Letter 123

(For Beethoven's dates see Letter 102.)—Mayer (1773–1835) created the role of Pizarro in the 1st version of *Fidelio* (then called *Leonore*), in November 1805.—The present letter was written as a revised version of the opera was being prepared for its 2nd & last performance, after which Beethoven quarreled with the theater management & withdrew the score. *Fidelio,* in its final form, was not produced until 1814.

[1] Ignaz Xaver von Seyfried (1776–1841), a prolific composer, was the conductor at the Theater an der Wien, where the opera was being given.

Letter 124

ZELTER: b. Berlin, 1758; d. there, 1832. As a composer, he is chiefly remembered for his lieder, which are of some importance in the history of the form before Schubert. It was his lieder to texts by Goethe that first brought him to the attention of the great poet, who soon preferred Zelter's settings of his poems to all others. Through their highly interesting & voluminous correspondence, punctuated by occasional visits of Zelter to Weimar, their acquaintance ripened into a close friendship that lasted until they died (a few weeks apart). Zelter is also remembered as an early champion of Bach's music & as the teacher & proud sponsor of the young Mendelssohn, whom he presented to Goethe (cf. Letter 141).

[1] After the disastrous rout of the Prussians at the battle of Jena (14 Oct. 1806).—The abruptness of the 1st sentence & lack of an opening salutation make one suspect a cut in the published version; no other source was available, however.

[2] Zelter had been trained in his father's trade & was a qualified master builder.

[3] The central portion (containing Berlin, Potsdam, etc.) of the old margraviate of Brandenburg, whose electors had become the kings of Prussia.

[4] Possibly an allusion to Zelter's pecuniary difficulties, though the reference is unclear.

[5] By the Peace of Tilsit (7–9 July 1807) Prussia lost a considerable part of its territory & became a vassal state of France.

[6] Karl Eberwein (1786–1868), a Weimar composer & friend of Goethe, had been studying with Zelter in Berlin.

[7] In his letter of 30 October to Zelter, Goethe had deplored the lack of form & character in the works of men like Achim von Arnim (1781–1831), Clemens Brentano (1778–1842), & other members of what is known as the "second Romantic school," & had expressed horror at the productions of Jean Paul Richter (1763–1825; cf. Letter 156A, n. 1). Zelter's answer makes it clear that "Cherubini, Beethoven, and others" were, in effect, considered Romantics by their contemporaries—a classification that is justifiable on chronological grounds but not generally followed by music historians, who assign musical Romanticism to the next generation of composers.

[8] It should be pointed out, however, that Zelter had an honest affection for Beethoven (whom he knew personally) & that he often expressed admiration for his works in the later correspondence with Goethe.

[9] Suburb SW of Berlin.

[10] With his answer, Goethe enclosed "a couple of my poems" for Zelter's friend—a pretty collector's item!

Letter 125

(For Haydn's & Prince Esterházy's dates see Letter 75.)—This is Haydn's last extant letter. Only the signature is autograph.

[1] Cf. Letter 35, n. 1.

Letter 126

See comments to Letter 121.

[1] Roughly, "with due introductory salutations"—a formula used in business letters.

[2] Op. 80, the Choral Fantasy.

[3] The errata were listed (by another hand) on a separate sheet, which has been preserved.

[4] Op. 81a, known as "Les Adieux."

[5] No. 5.

Letter 127

HOFFMANN: b. Königsberg, 1776; d. Berlin, 1822. Trained as a jurist (during his last years in Berlin he was a respected official of the Court of Appeal), Hoffmann was a man of many talents. He is best known, of course, for the fantastic tales that brought him his international reputation; but he was also a gifted painter, an excellent music critic (cf. Strunk, 775–97), &, for many years, a music teacher & composer. At the time of this letter, he was music director (but also scenic designer, stage manager, etc.) of the theater in Bamberg.—Hitzig (1780–1849), a colleague in the legal profession, was one of Hoffmann's closest friends &, later, his 1st biographer.

[1] Though Goethe had revived Calderón's plays at Weimar, they made no progress elsewhere in Germany. Hoffmann succeeded in having them staged at Bamberg.

[2] Franz von Holbein, Austrian singer & actor (& an old friend of Hoffmann's), was now the director of the Bamberg theater.

[3] Goethe had prepared a "concentrated" version of the play a few months earlier.

[4] Johannes Kreisler is the partly autobiographical, partly fictional hero of a series of musical essays & sketches, later collected under the title *Phantasiestücke in Callot's Manier* (1814). Schumann's *Kreisleriana* were inspired by this droll, fantastic figure (cf. Letter 179), & Brahms, in his youth, liked to sign himself "Johannes Kreisler, Jr."

[5] A well-known tale by Baron Friedrich de la Motte Fouqué (1777–1843). Through Hitzig's intercession, the author himself prepared the libretto for what was to become Hoffmann's most successful musical work & one of the earliest German Romantic operas (cf. Grout, 363).

[6] Friedrich Ludwig Zacharias Werner (1768–1823), Romantic dramatist, was, like Hoffmann, a native of Königsberg, & the two had been acquainted since childhood.

[7] According to a characteristic medieval legend, Kunegunde, the wife of Emperor Henry III, was accused of infidelity but proved her innocence by walking barefoot (& unscathed) over a row of red-hot ploughshares.

Letter 128

See comments to Letter 121.

[1] Franzensbrunn, like Teplitz & Karlsbad (mentioned later), was a spa in Bohemia.

[2] Op. 86; Beethoven means the wording of the dedication for the title page.

[3] Baden, near Vienna, had been heavily damaged by a fire.

[4] Beethoven could not resist a pun. He is referring to the violinist Giovanni Battista Polledro (1781–1853) & at the same time calling him a coward (*poltrone* = poltroon), perhaps because of his stage fright.

[5] Prince Ferdinand Kinsky (1781–1812), one of Beethoven's patrons, died soon after the Mass was published.

[6] 3 weeks later, Goethe wrote to Zelter (cf. comments to Letter 124): "I made Beethoven's acquaintance in Töplitz. His talent astonished me; but he is, unhappily, a quite unrestrained personality who, to be sure, is not at all wrong in finding the world detestable, but who doesn't thereby make it more enjoyable for himself or for others. On the other hand, he is much to be forgiven and pitied, for he is losing his hearing, a fact that is probably less harmful to his musical than to his social side. Laconic by nature anyway, he is becoming doubly so as a result of this defect." (Source: [= Letter 124], II, 28.)

Letter 129

SCHUBERT: b. Vienna, 1797; d. there, 1828.—This earliest extant letter of the composer was most probably addressed to the 2nd of his 3 brothers, Ferdinand (1794–1859), himself a composer & school teacher, who was closest to Schubert & later inherited his MSS.

[1] Schubert was a student at the Stadtkonvikt (City Seminary). Cf. source, pp. 7f.

[2] This & the following quotation are loosely adapted from Rom. x: 11 & Luke iii: 11 respectively, & as loosely (& lightheartedly) ascribed to Matthew.

Letter 130

(For Beethoven's dates see Letter 102.)—Rupprecht (1776–1846) had written the words of *Merkenstein,* a little song for 2 voices that eventually appeared as Beethoven's op. 100 (a 1-voice setting, WoO 144, was published somewhat earlier).

Letter 131

WEBER: b. Eutin, 1786; d. London, 1826.—Wieck (1785–1873) is now chiefly remembered as one of the 19th century's important piano teachers & as the dour father of Clara (see Letter 162, n. 7), whose marriage to Schumann he opposed for so many years. He composed very little, though in younger years he seems to have had aspirations in that direction.

[1] Apparently, nothing is known about these songs (op. 7), which form the subject of the entire letter; what matters here, however, is Weber's assured & clearheaded criticism, at a time when his own songs (notably the cycle *Leyer und Schwert*) were beginning to make him famous.

[2] Parallel octaves are forbidden in strict counterpoint (cf. Letter 45 on parallel fifths) & sound awkward in free composition if used inadvertently.

Letter 132

(For Beethoven's dates see Letter 102.)—Czerny (1791–1857), whose *School of Velocity, Art of Finger Dexterity,* etc. have earned him the dislike of young piano students the world over for several generations, had studied with Beethoven (1800–1803) & was by now a well-known teacher & pianist.

[1] Spelling was not Beethoven's forte: the "Z" stands for "Zerny."

[2] Czerny had taken part in a performance of the Quintet for Piano & Winds, op. 16.

[3] In A major, op. 69; Czerny played it the following week.

Letter 133

(For Schubert's dates see Letter 129.)—"The captaincy of the Viennese Civic Guard was a kind of district office, which however subsisted only up to 1820" (source, p. 54).

[1] The vacancy (announced in the official gazette) was at the German Normal School. Laibach (today Ljubljana in Yugoslavia) was the capital of the Austrian crown land of Carniola.

[2] Antonio Salieri (1750–1825), court *Kapellmeister,* disciple of Gluck, & composer of many successful operas, was a highly respected teacher. His knowledge of the Italian vocal tradition brought him no less a pupil than Beethoven.

Letter 134

WESLEY: b. Bristol, 1766; d. London, 1837. Wesley, a nephew of the founder of Methodism, was the greatest English organist of his time & a skilled composer. In the history of music he occupies a place of honor as one of the most zealous promoters of the Bach revival.—Novello (1781–1861), founder of Novello & Co., the London music publishers, was a composer, conductor, organist, & editor, in ascending order of importance. A witty passage in *The Essays of Elia* ("A Chapter on Ears") attests to his friendship with Lamb; he was on equally friendly terms with Shelley, Keats, Hazlitt, etc.

[1] Wesley's characterizations are accurate. Edward Jones (1752–1824) was a famous performer on the Welsh harp & published several scholarly volumes on bardic music. William Ayrton (1777–1858) was one of the early directors of the Philharmonic Society, which he had helped to found in 1813, & a well-known critic.

[2] Cf. Letter 99, especially nn. 2 & 3.

[3] Cf. Letter 108, n. 1. He had died the previous December, & the reference is evidently to an auction of items from his library.

Letter 135

(For Beethoven's dates see Letter 102.)—Steiner (1773–1838) was a Viennese music publisher with whom Beethoven communicated almost exclusively by means of comical "military" dispatches: Beethoven was the Generalissimo (shades of Bonaparte!), Steiner the Lieutenant General, & Steiner's partner Tobias Haslinger (1787–1842; cf. Letter 140) the Adjutant. The firm published Beethoven's op. 90–101, 112–17, & 121a.
[1] The only new piano work Steiner published was the Sonata in A major, op. 101. Here the title appears both in German & in French: thus Beethoven's access of nationalism found an outlet, & the customers, who may never have heard of a "Hammerclavier" before (Beethoven had fabricated the word), were told that the sonata was "pour le Piano-Forte." The "Hammerclavier" Sonata, of course, is op. 106, published by Artaria & Co. in 1819. After that, Beethoven dropped the word for good.
[2] Cf. Letter 35, n. 1.

Letter 136

F. A. SCHUBERT: b. Dresden, 1768; d. there, 1827. This poor man, no doubt a worthy composer of church music, has become famous in our time on account of the present letter. He was the father of yet another Franz (or François) Schubert, whose *Abeille* ("The Bee") is still heard occasionally as an encore at violin recitals.—For Härtel, see comments to Letter 121.
[1] Cf. Letter 128, n. 4.
[2] Both F. A. Schubert & Härtel were Freemasons (cf. Letter 106, n. 1).
[3] The "real" Schubert's op. 1, composed 2 years before. It had apparently been sent to Breitkopf & Härtel by the composer or a friend, & Härtel had sent it on to the only Franz Schubert *he* knew, probably with a query as to its authenticity.
[4] In his answer, Härtel requested the return of the MS, which he then sent back to the Viennese Schubert. The firm never published any of his works during his lifetime. (*Erlkönig* was published by Cappi & Diabelli, Vienna, in 1821, 6 years after it was written.)

Letter 137

See comments to Letter 132.
[1] Karl van Beethoven (1806–58) was the son of the composer's brother Caspar Anton Carl (cf. comments to Letter 120). Upon the latter's

death in 1815, Beethoven became the boy's guardian &, filled with distrust for his sister-in-law, entered on a long & exhausting litigation to secure complete control over his ward. This he obtained in 1820, with what consequences may be seen in Letter 151. Cf. Editha & Richard Sterba, *Beethoven and His Nephew, a Psychoanalytical Study of Their Relationship* (New York: Pantheon, 1954).

[2] The German text is no clearer than the present translation—a comment that might be applied to most of the Beethoven letters in this collection. Here the composer is requesting that his nephew be taught to play such passages in a *legato* style, the notes intimately connected through the use of all five fingers, & not just in the "pearly" or slightly detached way that might result, for example, from using the same two fingers for every pair of notes. He ironically suggests that the latter kind of fingering, while it may produce a fashionably pleasing effect, ought not wholly to displace the former, which enables the pianist to play more expressively. (The point was obscured in previously published versions of this letter, because the musical examples, and sometimes the surrounding text, had been transcribed incorrectly; fortunately, the autograph proved most helpful in determining Beethoven's meaning.)

Letter 138

BERLIOZ: b. La Côte-Saint-André, 1803; d. Paris, 1869.—Pleyel (1757–1831), the founder (in 1807) of the famous Parisian piano manufactory, was an Austrian by birth; one of Haydn's favorite pupils, he composed many instrumental works & eventually settled in Paris as a music dealer & publisher.

[1] In Berlioz's *Mémoires* we read: ". . . by dint of listening to some quartets by Pleyel, played on Sundays by our amateurs, and thanks to Catel's treatise on harmony which I had succeeded in obtaining, I at last, and almost suddenly, penetrated the mystery of the formation and concatenation of chords. Immediately I wrote a sort of pot-pourri for six [instrumental] parts, on some Italian themes of which I owned a collection. Its harmony seemed tolerable." Though he later states he was 12½ years old at the time, we may safely assume that this was the same pot-pourri he sent Pleyel & that he was not much younger than 15 when he wrote it. Needless to say, Pleyel did not publish it.

Letter 139

BELLINI: b. Catania (Sicily), 1801; d. Puteaux (near Paris), 1835. At the time of this letter, he was still a student at the Conservatorio di San Sebastiano.

[1] A few sentences later, we learn she is his cousin. *Don* & *Donna* were merely the ceremonious (Spanish-inspired) forms of *Signor, Signora,* & *Signorina,* much used in southern Italy.
[2] I.e., a piano (cf. "Hammerclavier," Letter 135, n. 1), as distinguished from just a cembalo, which could still mean a harpsichord at the time.
[3] Ten ducats.

Letter 140
See comments to Letter 135.
[1] The episode occurs in the Odyssey (iv. 360ff.).
[2] Cf. a similar pun (Stein = stone) by Mozart, Letter 88 (p. 121).
[3] Werner (cf. Letter 127, n. 6) had settled in Vienna, where he became a Roman Catholic &, afterwards, a highly successful & fashionable preacher.
[4] The reading is questionable: instead of *Stund* ("hour"), Beethoven appears to have written *Mund* ("mouth," also "ward").

Letter 141
MENDELSSOHN: b. Hamburg, 1809; d. Leipzig, 1847. Zelter (cf. Letter 124) had taken the boy to Weimar the previous November, & during the 16 days they spent as guests of Goethe, Mendelssohn had thoroughly impressed the aging poet with his performances & improvisations.
[1] Zelter had assumed the direction of the well-known Berlin Singakademie (founded in 1791) in 1800. Under him it gave public performances of some of the more important sacred choral works of the 18th century &, in 1829 (with Mendelssohn conducting), the historic 1st performance of the St. Matthew Passion, which started the Bach revival in earnest.
[2] The Mendelssohns visited Weimar on their way home that summer.
[3] August von Goethe (1789–1830), the poet's son.
[4] Alexandre-Jean Boucher (1778–1861) was known not only for his playing but for his eccentric ways of attracting public notice.

Letter 142
(For Weber's dates see Letter 131.)—Weber's wife, Caroline Brandt, had been an opera singer before her marriage.—By now, Weber was famous: he held the important post of *Kapellmeister* at the Dresden opera, where his conducting marked an epoch in the history of that art; &, 2 years before, he had produced *Der Freischütz,* his most perfect opera & a great success all over Germany. He was now in Vienna to conduct the 1st per-

formance of his next opera, *Euryanthe*—a work destined to fail because of its weak libretto.

[1] Cf. Letter 140 & comments to Letter 135.

[2] Max Maria, the composer's son (& later his biographer), was just an infant at the time.

[3] *Aline, oder Wien in einem anderen Erdtheil,* a magic play by the comic actor & dramatist Ferdinand Raimund (1790–1836) with music by Wenzel Müller (1767–1835), whose song "Ich bin der Schneider Kakadu" provided Beethoven with the theme of the Variations, op. 121a. The Theater in der Leopoldstadt (today's IInd district in Vienna) specialized in such light fare.—The various performers, musical plays, etc. mentioned elsewhere in the letter are identifiable, but do not warrant special comment here.

[4] Ferdinand Piringer (1780–1829) was a Viennese official, but also a violinist, conductor, & friend of Beethoven's. Julius Benedikt (later, Sir Julius Benedict; 1804–85) had studied with Weber & accompanied him to Vienna, where, on his master's recommendation, he was appointed conductor at the Kärnthnerthor Theater. He later settled in England, where he had a very successful career.

Letter 143

(For Schubert's dates see Letter 129.)—Kupelwieser (1796–1862), a member of Schubert's intimate circle, was a fine Biedermeier painter, to whom we owe 3 of the 10 extant contemporary portraits of the composer—a full-face drawing & 2 water colors (the "Schubertians" on an excursion & playing charades).

[1] The opening lines of *Gretchen am Spinnrade* (from Goethe's *Faust*), one of Schubert's greatest lieder.

[2] Schubert had been suffering from a serious illness; he later recovered.

[3] Moritz von Schwind (1804–71), perhaps the foremost Austrian painter of his generation, was, like Kupelwieser, a member of Schubert's little circle.

[4] Maximilian Josef Leidesdorf (1787–1841), composer & pianist, was a partner in the firm of Sauer & Leidesdorf (cf. end of letter), who published some 20 works by Schubert during his lifetime.

[5] *Fierabras,* with words by Josef Kupelwieser (1791–1866), was not performed in Schubert's time.

[6] The libretto by Ignaz Franz Castelli (1781–1862) had been set to music by Schubert the previous year. The Berlin setting was by a minor composer, Georg Abraham Schneider (1770–1839).

[7] The works in question are the quartets in A minor & D minor ("Death

& the Maiden"), & the octet for string & wind instruments in F major; the 3rd of the projected set of quartets was not composed.

[8] For the Beethoven concert of 7 May 1824, see Letters 145A–E.

[9] Count Johann Karl Esterházy von Galánta (1775–1834), scion of a line collateral to that of Haydn's patrons (cf. comments to Letter 75). Schubert gave his children music lessons.

Letter 144

PAËR: b. Parma, 1771; d. Paris, 1839. A successful operatic composer in his own day, he is now considered a minor figure, representative of the period between Paisiello & Rossini. This letter has been included as a reflection of the rise of 2 new stars, Rossini & Liszt (for dates, see Letters 210 & 159 respectively). It also happens to reflect the spreading taste for autograph collecting—cf. end of Letter 124, with n. 10.

Letters 145A–E

See comments to Letter 132.—Schindler (1795–1864) was Beethoven's faithful secretary & factotum, & later his biographer. Schuppanzigh (1776–1830) was the leader of the famous ensemble that introduced so many of Beethoven's quartets to the public. Lichnowsky (1771–1837), brother of Karl (cf. Letter 120, n. 3), was a patron of the composer, who dedicated the Sonata in E minor, op. 90, to him. All 3 were intimate friends of Beethoven. For Wieck see comments to Letter 131.—The 4 curt notes from Beethoven aptly illustrate his irascible & suspicious nature (& his democratic bent—the composer of the "Ode to Joy" insults noble-man & commoner without distinction!); they were occasioned by difficulties over the impending concert of 7 May, at which a performance of the Overture in C major, op. 124 ("Consecration of the House"), was to be followed by the 1st performance in Vienna of 3 movements from the *Missa Solemnis* (the whole Mass had been heard in St. Petersburg that April) & the world *première* of the 9th Symphony. Czerny's letter is largely devoted to a description of that historic concert.

[1] Vienna had been in the throes of a violent Rossini fever, & the signatories (who included Czerny) had urged Beethoven to vindicate German music.

[2] The renovated Theater in der Josefstadt had been inaugurated on 3 Oct. 1822 with a performance of the overture, written for the occasion.

[3] Subscriptions to the forthcoming published score had come in from various German courts.

[4] Michael Umlauf (1781–1842), a regular conductor at the Imperial & Royal Theaters, had served in a similar capacity before; in fact, the per-

formers followed him exclusively. At this concert, Beethoven, now quite deaf, had to be turned around before he realized the audience was applauding. The concert at the Redoutensaal took place on Sunday, 23 May, not "next Friday" (14 May), as Czerny has it; & the program was not quite the same.

[5] Ignaz Moscheles (1794–1870) & Friedrich Wilhelm Michael Kalkbrenner (1785–1849) were 2 of the greatest pianists of the 19th century.

[6] Cf. comments to Letter 122.

[7] Carl Friedrich Peters (1779–1827) had purchased the Bureau de Musique (cf. Letter 117, n. 1) in 1814.

[8] Wilhelm Leschen & Conrad Graf were Viennese piano manufacturers (Schubert owned a Graf). Beethoven's beloved Broadwood piano, a gift from the maker, was by then about 7 years old & in need of repairs, as we learn from a letter the composer wrote on 3 Oct. (Sept.?) of that year.

[9] Cf. Letters 144 & 159.

Letter 146

(For Berlioz's dates see Letter 138.)—The composer's uncle, Victor-Abraham Berlioz (1784–c.1846), was a lawyer &, at this time, attorney general at Grenoble (cf. source).—Berlioz's escape from home, after obtaining his father's qualified permission to give up the study of medicine for that of music, is vividly described in chap. x of his *Mémoires*.

[1] Berlioz's mother, a religious fanatic, was so opposed to a musical career for her son, that his father urged him to return to Paris without seeing anyone.

[2] Jean François Lesueur (1760–1837), with whom Berlioz had been studying privately in Paris.

Letter 147

(For Schubert's dates see Letter 129.)—This was the 2nd time Goethe received some of his own poems set to music by Schubert; the 1st time (in 1816), Schubert's best friend Josef von Spaun (cf. Letter 148, n. 3) had written the covering letter. On both occasions, Goethe did not reply.

[1] *An Schwager Kronos, An Mignon,* & *Ganymed* had just been published as op. 19, with a dedication to Goethe.

Letter 148

(For Schubert's dates see Letter 129.)—Schubert's father, Franz (1763–1830), had married Anna, née Kleyenböck (1783–1860), in 1813, less than a year after the death of the composer's mother.—Schubert was on a prolonged journey in Upper Austria, trying to escape from the summer heat. His traveling companion was the baritone Johann Michael Vogl (1768–1840), who was the first to sing many of Schubert's lieder.

[1] Eduard Traweger was a merchant, Franz Ferdinand von Schiller a jurist at Gmunden.

[2] The famous *Ave Maria.*

[3] Josef von Spaun (1788–1865) was Schubert's best friend; they had met while students at the same seminary (cf. Letter 129, n. 1). Lemberg (today Lvov in the U.S.S.R.) was at the time the capital of Austrian Galicia.

[4] The 7 songs from *The Lady of the Lake,* op. 52, were in fact dedicated to Countess Sophie Gabriele Weissenwolff (1794–1847), an amateur contralto & patroness of music at Linz.

[5] All but 1 of the songs appeared with bilingual texts when they were published the following April.

[6] Pauline Anna Milder-Hauptmann (1785–1838), the famous soprano who created the role of Fidelio, had sung *Erlkönig* & *Suleika* II (its 1st performance) at her concert in Berlin on 9 June; the very favorable review she sent Schubert had evidently not been forwarded to Steyr.

[7] The compositions mentioned are: the 4-hand Variations in A-flat major (one of Schubert's greatest works), the Marches, op. 40(?), & the 2nd movement of the Sonata in A minor, op. 42.

[8] Viennese Currency (*Wiener Währung*), a paper currency adopted in 1811, when Austria had become bankrupt as a result of the Napoleonic wars.

[9] Cf. comments to Letter 129. The following sentence refers to Ferdinand's favorite tavern & to the effects of the new wine (Dornbach) served there.

[10] Schubert's brother Karl (1795–1855) was a teacher of penmanship.

[11] Ignaz (1785–1844), the composer's oldest brother, was about to marry into the Hollpein family.

[12] Schubert's sister Maria Theresia (1801–78) was married to Matthias Schneider, a schoolteacher.

[13] Schubert's stepsisters Maria & Josefine, & infant stepbrother Andreas (*Probstl,* "little provost," because he was chubby).

Letter 149

(For Beethoven's dates see Letter 102.)—Wolanek was a copyist who had been transcribing the "Dona nobis" from Beethoven's MS of the *Missa Solemnis* preparatory to publication.

526

Letter 150
(For Schubert's dates see Letter 129.)—Probst had opened a music publishing firm at Leipzig in 1823.—This & a similar letter to Breitkopf & Härtel written on the same day were apparently the beginning of a campaign by Schubert for greater recognition in Germany.

[1] Probst answered very soon, indicating that he was acquainted with Schubert's "peculiar, often ingenious, but perhaps now and then somewhat curious procedures" (source, p. 550). He asked for "agreeable and easily comprehensible" compositions, to smooth the path for more difficult ones. Schubert sent 3 works (their identity is not known), but they were turned down. The correspondence was not resumed until 1828 (cf. Letters 154 & 157).

Letter 151
(For Beethoven's dates see Letter 102.)—B. Schott's Söhne, the well-known publishing firm, was established in 1773. It published Beethoven's opus nos. 121b–128 & the Quartet in C-sharp minor, op. 131, the subject of the present letter.

[1] Franck & Co., a Viennese firm.

[2] Cf. Letter 137, n. 1. Karl had put a bullet through his head on 30 July. He recovered.

Letter 152
(For Beethoven's dates see Letter 102.)—For Moscheles, cf. Letter 145E, n. 5. He had settled permanently in London the previous year.—Beethoven dictated this & the following letter to Schindler (cf. comments to Letters 145A–E) & only signed them. He was on his deathbed.

[1] 1776–1867; an original member of the Philharmonic Society & one of its leading conductors & organizers.

[2] The German harp manufacturer Johann Andreas Stumpff (1769–1846) had moved to England in 1790.

[3] The autograph was clipped out by Moscheles & given to a friend.

[4] Moscheles replied on 1 March & enclosed £100 from the Philharmonic Society as an advance on receipts from the projected concert. See Letter 153.

Letter 153
See Letter 152, with comments & n. 4. Beethoven dictated this letter 8 days before his death.

[1] *Konventionsmünze,* or Assimilated Coinage; based on a treaty with Bavaria (1753), it continued in use along with the Viennese Currency (cf. Letter 148, n. 8), though depreciated in value.
[2] A famous passage, since it refers to a 10th Symphony; however, only the most fragmentary sketches were discovered among the composer's effects.
[3] Cf. Letter 152, nn. 1 & 2 respectively.
[4] A separate sheet in Schindler's handwriting has the set of metronome markings—one of several such sets drawn up by Beethoven for the 9th Symphony.—Rau was in the employ of Baron Eskeles, a famous Viennese banker.

Letter 154
See comments to Letter 150.
[1] In E-flat major, op. 100.
[2] Cf. Letter 153, n. 1.
[3] But cf. Letter 157.

Letter 155
PAGANINI: b. Genoa, 1782; d. Nice, 1840.—Germi, a lawyer & friend, managed the virtuoso's financial affairs in Italy.—The concerts mentioned in this letter (his 1st outside of Italy) marked the beginning of Paganini's dazzling European career. For an amusing account of the Paganini craze in Vienna, reminiscent of that over Rossini 4 years earlier (cf. Letter 145E, n. 1), see Deutsch [= Letter 129], 757; also Grove, *s.v.* "Paganini."
[1] His 1st had taken place on 29 March.
[2] Napoleon's widow was now Duchess of Parma.
[3] *Recte,* the Carinthian gate (Kärnthnerthor).
[4] Antonia Bianchi, dancer & singer, had been Paganini's mistress since 1815; it was during their stay in Vienna that the virtuoso broke with her, retaining custody of their son Achille by means of a settlement.

Letters 156A–B
SCHUMANN: b. Zwickau, 1810; d. Endenich (near Bonn), 1856.—WIEDEBEIN: b. Eilenstedt (Saxony), 1779; d. Brunswick, 1854. A slim book of lieder, published in 1826 or 1827, had brought this estimable musician & conductor some transient fame as a composer. Schumann's respect for him never waned (the *Intermezzo,* op. 4, no. 2, contains what is almost certainly a reminiscence of Wiedebein's *Gretchens Klage*), & in later years, after the two men had become acquainted personally, Schumann's wife gave piano lessons to Wiedebein's daughter (Düsseldorf,

1852).—See the present editor's article on Wiedebein in the German musical encyclopedia, *Die Musik in Geschichte und Gegenwart*.

[1] 2 of Wiedebein's lieder were set to poems by Jean Paul Richter (cf. Letter 124, n. 7), whose hypersensitive, poetic novels had a determining influence on Schumann's formative years—indeed, left a lasting imprint on his literary, & even musical style.

[2] The 11 lieder designated by Schumann as op. II. He never published these juvenilia, though he used 2 of them as the basis for the slow movements of his F-sharp minor & G minor sonatas, while a 3rd underlies the C major *Intermezzo* of op. 4. These 3 lieder were published by Brahms in 1893, in the supplementary volume of the Schumann *Gesamtausgabe*, & 6 more have appeared in the Universal Edition (ed. Karl Geiringer).

[3] 5 of the texts of op. II are poems by Justinus Andreas Christian Kerner (1786–1862).

[4] Wiedebein did not publish another book of lieder, though there had been an earlier one with which Schumann was evidently not familiar.

[5] *Studiosus juris:* Schumann had matriculated at Leipzig University as a law student.

[6] Neither the "Patriarch" (Goethe?) nor the quotation could be identified.

[7] Schumann's answer (5 Aug. 1828) reflects the enormous importance he attached to Wiedebein's letter. 10 years later, mindful of the encouragement he had received, he published it in the *Neue Zeitschrift für Musik* under the title, "Letter from an Older Master to a Young Artist."

Letter 157

See Letters 150 (with comments) & 154.

[1] The publication of the E-flat major Trio was announced in Vienna only on 11 Dec., 3 weeks after Schubert's death; it is therefore unlikely that he ever saw it in print.

[2] The 3 great posthumous sonatas were published 10 years later & dedicated to Schumann, Hummel having died in 1837.—The publication of Heine's *Buch der Lieder* in 1827 made it still possible for Schubert to set that poet's lyrics & thus become the 1st in the series of 19th-century masters whose music has become inseparable from those bittersweet paragons of Romanticism. The 6 Heine lieder appeared posthumously (in 1829) as part of the collection entitled *Schwanengesang* ("Swan Song").—The C major Quintet did not appear until 1853, & there is no evidence that Schubert ever heard it performed.

Letter 158

(For Schubert's dates see Letter 129.)—Schober (1796–1882), one of Schubert's closest friends, wrote the words for several of the composer's lieder (the most famous being *An die Musik*) & for the opera *Alfonso und Estrella*.—This is Schubert's last extant letter. He had been ailing for some time & died 7 days later, struck down by typhoid fever.

Letter 159

LISZT: b. Raiding (Hungary), 1811; d. Bayreuth, 1886.—For Czerny, see comments to Letter 132.—Cf. Letter 144 & postscript to Letter 145E.
[1] Bellini's opera *Il Pirata* (1827).
[2] Johann Peter Pixis (1788–1874), a famous pianist, made Paris his home for many years.

Letter 160

(For Berlioz's dates see Letter 138.)
[1] Berlioz had originally written *Monsieur* but apparently thought better of it & erased it.
[2] *Huit scènes de Faust,* written while Berlioz was still a student at the Conservatoire; it formed the basis for the "concert opera" *La Damnation de Faust* (1846).
[3] The following extracts from the Goethe-Zelter correspondence show how the score was received. Goethe (28 Apr. 1829): "A Frenchman has composed eight passages of my Faust and sent me the very beautifully engraved score; I should like to send it to you and receive a comment on it, if you will be so kind." Zelter (1 May): "By all means send your Frenchman's Faust along, the theme seems made for today's composers." Goethe (11 June): "I have an extra copy of Faust, therefore let this one be dedicated to you as your legitimate property and inheritance. In exchange, however, you will be so good as to send me a Zelterish word about this work and reassure me as to the odd-looking aspect of the notes." The Zelterish word (21 June): "Certain people can only express their presence of mind and their sympathy by loud coughs, snorts, croaks, and belches; Mr. Hector Berlioz appears to be one of these. The sulphurous smell of Mephisto appeals to him, therefore he must sneeze and wheeze so that all the instruments in the orchestra stir and splutter—meanwhile, not a wiggle out of Faust. But thank you for sending it anyway; the opportunity will surely arise, in the course of a lecture, to make use of an abscess, an

abortion produced by grisly incest." (Source: [= Letter 124], V, pp. 215, 218, 244, & 251.)

Letter 161

CHOPIN: b. Zelazowa Wola, 1810; d. Paris, 1849.—Nicolas Chopin (1771–1844), secondary-school teacher in Warsaw, was a native of Lorraine who settled in Poland in 1787 & never returned to France. His wife, the composer's mother, was Tekla-Justyna Krzyzanowska (1782–1861).— After graduating from the Warsaw Conservatory, Chopin visited Vienna. By this time, he had written some 30 compositions that have come down to us (mostly as posthumous juvenilia), as well as the works mentioned in this letter & parts, at least, of the Concerto in F minor.

[1] The Kärnthnerthor Theater.

[2] The old-fashioned term was borrowed from the Italian (*accademia*, "concert"), which in turn reflected the fact that learned academies had long been important musical centers.

[3] Count Wenzel Robert Gallenberg (1783–1839), ballet composer & director of the Kärnthnerthor Theater, was the husband of Giulietta Guicciardi, to whom Beethoven had dedicated the piano sonata op. 27, no. 2.

[4] I.e., the "Prometheus" Overture (Beethoven), the Variations on "Là ci darem la mano," op. 2, & the *Rondo à la Krakowiak*, op. 14 (Chopin); Charlotte Veltheim of the Saxon Court Opera sang arias by Rossini & Niccolò Vaccai (1790–1848).

[5] "Free improvisation."

[6] Wilhelm Würfel (1791–1852), pianist, composer, & an old friend of the Chopin family, was at the time assistant conductor at the Kärnthnerthor Theater.

[7] Adalbert Gyrowetz (1763–1850), a well-known composer (who, in his youth, had received encouragement from Mozart), was court *Kapellmeister*; Franz Lachner (1803–90), composer & conductor, had been an intimate friend of Schubert; Conradin Kreutzer (1780–1849) is best known for his opera *Das Nachtlager von Granada* (1834); for Seyfried, cf. Letter 123, n. 1; Joseph Mayseder (1789–1863) was a Viennese violin virtuoso & teacher.

[8] Celinski & Hube were classmates who, with 2 others, had gone to Vienna with Chopin.

[9] "A pity the lad isn't better turned out."

[10] Opera (1825) by François-Adrien Boieldieu (1775–1834).

[11] "The Rondo simply must be played here."

[12] "The Hop Plant"—title of a Polish folk song.

[13] Cf. comments to Letter 122.

[14] Cf. Letter 140 & comments to Letter 135.

[15] Count Moritz Dietrichstein (1775–1864), himself an amateur composer of lieder, waltzes, etc., was at this time director of the Court Library.

[16] Joseph Xaver Elsner (1768–1854), director of the Warsaw Conservatory, had been Chopin's composition teacher.

[17] Thomas Nidecki (1800–52), a colleague from the Warsaw Conservatory, was studying in Vienna.

[18] Cf. Letter 145E, n. 8.

[19] The translations from this, the only extensive modern source in English, are unfortunately quite unreliable. Since fresh translations from the Polish could not be commissioned in time for this edition, the editor has regretfully resorted to a second-best procedure, that of revising the translations in the light of the new French edition [= Letter 167].

Letter 162

(For Schumann's dates see Letters 156A–B.)—For Wieck see comments to Letter 131.—While ostensibly studying law in Leipzig, Schumann had begun taking piano lessons from Wieck. Then, in May 1829, he had gone to Heidelberg, where he continued his law studies as listlessly as ever.

[1] Schubert's Trio in E-flat major, op. 100. It had been published less than a year earlier (cf. Letter 157, with n. 1).

[2] Henri Herz (1803–88), the brilliant Viennese pianist; later, as a critic, Schumann showed no respect whatever for this virtuoso's salon productions, or for Czerny's. Indeed, at the end of this letter, he asks for their compositions in a bantering tone: he apparently used the music for purely mechanical finger exercises.

[3] Anton Friedrich Justus Thibaut (1774–1840), a well-known law professor at Heidelberg, was the author of *Über Reinheit der Tonkunst* (1825; trans. as *Purity in Musical Art*, 1877), a treatise that expressed his rather rarefied musical ideals; these he realized by leading a choral society in performances of sacred works by older masters, from Palestrina to Handel.

[4] Giuditta Pasta (1798–1865), the famous dramatic soprano for whom Bellini was soon to compose *La Sonnambula* & *Norma* (cf. Letter 168), & Donizetti *Anna Bolena*.

[5] Cf. Letter 156A, n. 1.

[6] The publisher of Schubert's Trio. See Letters 150 (with comments), 154, & 157.

[7] Wieck's 3 children were: Clara Josephine (1819–96), the great pianist who later became Schumann's wife (she was only 10 at this time, but had already made successful public appearances); Alwin (1821–85), who be-

came a professional violinist; & Gustav, who died in infancy. Wieck had 3
more children by his 2nd marriage (he had divorced his 1st wife).
[8] The "Trout" Quintet had been published that spring in Vienna.
[9] Dr. Ernst August Carus was professor of medicine at Leipzig University;
he & his wife Agnes, a singer, made Schumann welcome at their home.
Emilie Reichold was a talented pianist then living in Leipzig.

Letter 163

(For Schumann's dates see Letters 156A–B.)—Johanne Christiane
Schumann, née Schnabel (1771–1836), the composer's mother, had been
a widow for the past 4 years.
[1] Gisbert Rosen (1808–76), like Woldemar & Hermann von Heyden (mentioned in the next sentence), was a fellow law student.
[2] Cf. Letter 162, n. 3.
[3] For Wieck, see comments to Letters 131 & 162; for Moscheles, cf. Letter
145E, n. 5.

Letter 164

WAGNER: b. Leipzig, 1813; d. Venice, 1883. For B. Schott's Söhne, see
comments to Letter 151.
[1] Schott did not publish the arrangement.

Letter 165

(For Mendelssohn's dates see Letter 141.)—The composer's 1st visit to
England (& tour of Scotland) in 1829 was followed, late in 1830, by an
extended journey to Italy, which took him as far south as Naples. This
letter was written from one of the Borromean Islands on Lake Maggiore,
as he was about to cross the frontier into Switzerland on his way home.
[1] "Ugly Island" (Isola Bella = "Beautiful Island").
[2] Mendelssohn was an enthusiastic (& highly talented) painter—a fact that
emerges clearly enough from his vivid way of describing landscapes.
[3] Mephistopheles' words in Goethe's *Faust*, Part I (*Studierzimmer*): *Ich
bin der Geist, der stets verneint!*
[4] Mendelssohn is referring to the southern flora that manages to thrive so
far north, in the mild climate of the Italian lakes.
[5] "On the contrary."
[6] Cf. Letter 141, 3rd paragraph.
[7] "Poor chap, he's lame."
[8] The original is a pun on the word *Futter* (= "fodder" or "lining"):
. . . *weil es ihm ganz an Futter fehlt,* "for it is quite deprived of fodder/
lining."

533

[9] The episode occurs in *Titan*, a novel by Jean Paul Richter (cf. Letter 124, n. 7).

[10] In a charming letter of 14 July (source, pp. 172–77), Mendelssohn tells how he looked up an Austrian general attached to the Milan government, simply because his name (Ertmann) was the same as that of the lady to whom Beethoven had dedicated the Sonata in A major, op. 101. As it turned out, the lady was the general's wife, & Mendelssohn was cordially received at their home, where he was regaled with Beethoven stories & heard Dorothea Ertmann play the master's works.

[11] Cf. Letter 100, n. 6.

[12] Karl Ludwig Sand, a theology student, had murdered the dramatist August von Kotzebue (1761–1819), whom he considered a reactionary & a Russian spy (with some reason). Sand was executed in 1820.

[13] *A Midsummer-Night's Dream*. Mendelssohn had composed his great overture to the play when only 17.

[14] Wilhelm Hensel (1794–1861), a painter, was the husband of Mendelssohn's beloved & musically talented sister Fanny (1805–47).

[15] Joachim Murat (1767–1815), Napoleon's famous marshal (& brother-in-law), had especially distinguished himself in the Italian campaigns & was, for a time, governor of the Cisalpine Republic, later becoming King of Naples (1808).

[16] Mendelssohn's setting of *Die erste Walpurgisnacht* (Goethe) for chorus & orchestra, one of his finest works, was revised in 1842–43. Cf. comments to Letter 191.

[17] Simply a good-humored allusion to the Sunday musicales at the Mendelssohn home in Berlin.

[18] Paul Mendelssohn Bartholdy (1813–74) was the composer's brother; Karl Klingemann (1798–1862), a diplomat & amateur poet, was one of Mendelssohn's best friends.

Letter 166

See comments to Letter 163.

[1] Cf. comments to Letter 131.

[2] Hans Eggert Wilibald von der Lühe (born c. 1800) had met Schumann in Zwickau. In 1834–38 he published a "ladies' lexicon" to which the composer contributed the articles on music.

[3] A serious cholera epidemic had broken out in Germany.

[4] Cf. Letter 156A, n. 1.

[5] Schumann's handwriting was exceedingly small & hard to read.

[6] Gottlob Rudel, a Zwickau merchant, had become Schumann's guardian when the composer's father died in 1826.

Letter 167

See comments to Letter 144.—Sotte was an official of the passport bureau in Paris.

[1] Dr. Giovanni Malfatti (1775–1859) had been a friend of Beethoven's & had attended him during his last illness. (The indication that Vienna is in Austria is not as silly as it seems; Vienne, in French, could mean the town on the Rhone.)

[2] Chopin had left Warsaw (for the last time) on 2 Nov. 1830 & had arrived in Vienna on the 22nd. The revolt in Warsaw broke out on the 29th. Unable to return home, he moved on after 7 fruitless months in the Austrian capital, visiting Munich & Stuttgart, where he learnt that Warsaw had fallen to the Russians on 8 Sep. 1831. In mid-September he reached Paris, henceforward his permanent home. He only had a temporary passport, since the Russian authorities had been unwilling to let him settle in a city already full of Polish revolutionary exiles.

Letter 168

(For Bellini's dates see Letter 139.)—Perucchini (1784–1870) had befriended the composer during his stay in Venice the year before; they corresponded for a time afterwards.

[1] The date of *Norma*'s 1st performance (at La Scala, Milan).

[2] Bellini is referring to a Countess Giulia Samayloff, supposedly the mistress of Giovanni Pacini (1796–1867), a rival composer.

[3] *I Capuleti e i Montecchi* was the opera Bellini had composed in Venice (cf. comments, above).

[4] For Pasta, who sang the title role, see Letter 162, n. 4 (her "opening number," of course, was *Casta Diva*); Domenico Donzelli (1790–1873), tenor, was the Pollione; Giulia Grisi (1811–69), one of the great sopranos of the century, sang the part of Adalgisa. Note how Bellini refers to the music in terms of the singers rather than the characters—a striking reminder of the traditional method of composing operatic parts to suit specific voices.

Letter 169

(For Chopin's dates see Letter 161.)—Dziewanowski was a former schoolmate of Chopin's; the composer had summered at Szafarnia, the Dziewanowski country estate, in 1824 & 1825.

[1] Louis Philippe became "King of the French" in 1830, after the July Revolution had overthrown Charles X.

535

[2] Here the 1st edition of this letter omitted a word, which the reader may supply at will. The autograph is lost.

[3] Cf. Letter 159, n. 2.

[4] Cf. Letter 145E, n. 5.

[5] Cf. Letter 162, n. 2.

[6] John Field (1782–1837), the Irish pianist & composer (remembered chiefly for his *Nocturnes*), is one of the few figures one can point to as having influenced Chopin's highly personal style.

[7] The Carlists adhered to the deposed king, the Philippists to Louis Philippe.

Letter 170

(For Liszt's & Chopin's dates see Letters 159 & 161 respectively.) FRANCHOMME: b. Lille, 1808; d. Paris, 1884. A well-known cellist & an intimate friend of Chopin's, he composed very little, & that for his own instrument.—Hiller (1811–85) was to become one of the most distinguished musical personalities of his time. Though he failed, on the whole, as a composer, he was a respected conductor, teacher, & writer on music, & was on friendly terms with most of the great composers of the century.

[1] At Chopin's apartment.

[2] Hiller's father, Justus (original name: Isaac Hildesheim), had died on 5 April.

[3] The 12 *Grandes Études*, op. 10, had just been published.

[4] Auguste Léo, a Paris banker, was related to Hiller. What "follows" can no longer be ascertained.

[5] Cf. comments to Letters 184A–B.

[6] So far Chopin (& the others) had used the polite form "vous"; from this point he lapses into the familiar "tu."

[7] Pierre-Marie-François de Sales Baillot (1771–1842), the famous violinist, was on a concert tour (his last). "Père" was probably an affectionate title given him by the younger set.

Letter 171

(For Schumann's dates see Letters 156A–B.)—For Clara Wieck see Letter 162, n. 7. Now 13 & a well-known pianist, Clara had a special fondness for her friend, who that year honored her with a set of *Impromptus* (op. 5) based on a theme she herself had composed.

[1] Schumann was suffering from a severe chill, which, to be sure, does nothing to explain the "bandages" & "wounds"; these, however, may have been added to the description for dramatic purposes.

[2] Op. 2 (cf. Letter 161, n. 4). They had formed the subject of Schumann's 1st review (published in the *Allgemeine musikalische Zeitung* in 1831), in which he had uttered the now famous words, "Hats off, gentlemen, a genius!"

Letter 172

(For Schumann's dates see Letters 156A–B.)—Töpken (1807–80), one of Schumann's closest friends & a gifted amateur musician, had been a fellow law student at Heidelberg. He was now a lawyer but, having independent means, devoted himself to playing the piano, composing, & organizing concerts.

[1] After months of hard work, Schumann's musical periodical, the *Neue Leipziger Zeitschrift für Musik,* was about to become a reality: its 1st number appeared on 3 April, a week after this letter was written.

[2] Ferdinand Stegmayer (1804–63), conductor & composer, did not join the editorial board. The 1st issues came out under the names of Schumann, Wieck (cf. comments to Letter 131), Julius Knorr (1807–61), a well-known pianist & pedagogue, & Schunke. The latter, born in 1810, was a highly talented pianist & composer whom Schumann admired enormously; their warm friendship came to a tragic end when Schunke died that December.—By 1835, Schumann was sole editor of the periodical, which he continued to guide until June 1844.

[3] 1806–42; bass singer & composer of quartets for male voices.

[4] Op. 4, 5, 7, 8, 11, 14, & 22. But the last 3 (the sonatas) were not published until 1836 & 1838, after considerable revisions.

[5] A little joke, since Töpken was not married.

Letter 173

(For Berlioz's dates see Letter 138.)

[1] Op. 6, cantata for male voice & orchestra on the death of Napoleon.—Berlioz, having won the coveted *prix de Rome* in 1830, had spent less than 2 years (instead of the required 3) in that city. (For information on that famous award, see Grove, "Prix de Rome.")

Letter 174

CHERUBINI: b. Florence, 1760; d. Paris, 1842. The veteran composer, so admired in former days (& still admired in Germany by Mendelssohn, Schumann, & other idealists of the younger generation), was now out of fashion in France. As director of the Conservatoire, however, he managed to strike terror into the hearts of the new crop of French composers who

537

came under his salutary guidance, & one of them has left us a savage caricature of the master as a villainous old fogey (cf. Berlioz's *Mémoires*, chap. ix). The present letter should help to rectify that image.—Ingres (1780–1867), who, with his pure lines & classical restraint, might well be called the Cherubini of painters, had actually begun life as a violinist, & his lasting enthusiasm for his instrument has been immortalized in the expression "violon d'Ingres" (= a cherished avocation). At the time of this letter he was director of the École de France at the Villa Medici, official residence of the young artists & musicians who had won the *prix de Rome* (cf. comments to Letter 173; also Letters 219, 264, & 282). It was here that he completed his famous portrait of Cherubini (now in the Louvre).

[1] The Académie des beaux arts, which awarded (& still awards) the *prix de Rome*.

[2] Antoine-Aimable-Élie Elwart (1808–77) had taken the prize the year before; he later became a professor at the Conservatoire.—Bellini had died 2 months earlier, near Paris.

Letter 175

VERDI: b. Le Roncole (near Busseto), 1813; d. Milan, 1901.—When the post of church organist at Busseto fell vacant, the town split into 2 factions, one supporting the young Verdi (then in Milan studying composition), the other a certain Giovanni Ferrari. Since the latter was backed by the local clergy, the controversy soon took on a political hue, to the dismay of the authorities, who had already had a revolution on their hands in 1831. The police was alerted. Verdi insisted on a competition as the only fair solution, & when at length it was granted he won. (The clergy nevertheless appointed Ferrari to the post, but Verdi received the municipal subsidy ordinarily assigned to the organist.) In announcing the result, the mayor warned the winner not to boast of his victory lest there be more trouble. The reply, one of Verdi's earliest extant letters, is as characteristic of the man as anything he was to write or say in the long years ahead.

[1] Of the Duchy of Parma (cf. Letter 155, n. 2).

Letter 176

(For Schumann's dates see Letters 156A–B.)—Dorn (1804–92), composer, conductor, & teacher, had given some counterpoint lessons to Schumann in Leipzig. Now he was music director at St. Peter's in Riga & would later become court *Kapellmeister* at the Berlin opera.

[1] Chopin was returning from a summer visit to Marienbad, where he had

proposed to a young Polish girl, Maria Wodzińska, & been accepted. The engagement was later broken by the girl's family because of the composer's poor health.

[2] I.e., with the *Neue Zeitschrift für Musik* (cf. Letter 172).

[3] "League of David," the imaginary band of warriors invented by Schumann. He first used it in his Chopin review (cf. Letter 171, n. 2), when he introduced the characters of Florestan & Eusebius in a fictional setting & put his own thoughts in their mouths. These & other figures (e.g., Meister Raro) served him to approach his topics from varied points of view & at the same time imbued his criticism with liveliness & poetry. Their names also occur in some of his well-known piano works (*Davidsbündlertänze, Carnaval,* etc.).

[4] *Iris im Gebiet der Tonkunst,* a musical periodical directed by the poet & writer Ludwig Rellstab (1799–1860).

[5] The *Allgemeine musikalische Zeitung.*

[6] Cf. comments to Letter 135.

[7] The sonatas op. 11 & 14 (cf. Letter 172, n. 4).

[8] In G minor, op. 23; it was published that year.

[9] Cf. Letter 162, n. 7.

[10] Ferdinand David (1810–73) & Carl Lipinski (1790–1861) were well-known violinists. For Stegmayer, cf. Letter 172, n. 2. Carl Banck (1809–89) was a contributor to Schumann's journal.

Letter 177

(For Chopin's dates see Letter 161.)—Fontana (1810–69), a pianist, was one of Chopin's closest friends & a former Conservatory classmate.—Chopin's stay in Majorca & his liaison with George Sand (who went there with him & with her 2 children) have been described at length in every Chopin biography, & so need not be recounted here.

[1] The *Préludes,* op. 28, were finished in Majorca.

[2] Jan Matuszyński (1809–42), a childhood friend; he was now living in Paris & was Chopin's physician.

[3] Juan Álvarez y Mendizabal (1790–1853), Liberal prime minister, had secularized the monastic lands in Spain 3 years earlier.

[4] The monastery of Valdemosa did little for Chopin's health, which, in fact, deteriorated dangerously.

[5] Camille Pleyel (1788–1855), son of Ignace (cf. comments to Letter 138), was the present director of the firm.

[6] For Léo, cf. Letter 170, n. 4; Thomas Albrecht was a Parisian friend.

Letters 178A–B

(For Paganini's & Berlioz's dates see Letters 155 & 138 respectively.)—
For a full account of this famous episode in Berlioz's life, cf. his *Mémoires,*
chap. xlix. It led to the composition of the "dramatic symphony" *Roméo
et Juliette.*
[1] Jacob de Rothschild (1792–1868) founded the Paris branch of the
great firm. It is thought that the 20,000 francs may have come from
him & that Paganini only served as a cover.
[2] Berlioz was suffering from a severe bronchitis. 5 days later he tendered
his thanks in person.

Letter 179

(For Schumann's dates see Letters 156A–B.)—De Sire (1800?–72) was
an amateur pianist-composer & a musical enthusiast who had become
acquainted with Schumann's compositions in 1836. 2 years later he
wrote him a letter expressing his admiration. Schumann was deeply
touched at this unaccustomed sign of appreciation from abroad; as he
wrote in his answer, "mine is a quite lonely road, I know, along which
no crowds shout encouraging hurrahs" (source, pp. 109–10). After a
further exchange, Schumann showed his gratitude by dedicating the
Faschingsschwank aus Wien to de Sire.
[1] Schumann hoped to improve his circumstances in order to overcome
Wieck's objections to his marriage (cf. comments to Letter 131); the
"business" side of the venture was an attempt to move the *Neue
Zeitschrift für Musik* to Vienna if his personal plans should mature.
Nothing came of these endeavors, but it was during his stay there that
he met Schubert's brother Ferdinand (cf. comments to Letter 129) &
discovered some of the composer's greatest unpublished works.
[2] Cf. Letter 127.
[3] Nor does English have precise equivalents for these words as Schumann
understands them. Here, *gemüthlich* & *schwärmerisch* might be rendered
as "imbued with feelings awakened by the imagination"; *Humor,* then,
would be the witty (whimsical, bizarre) externalization of those feelings.
Cf. n. 4 below.
[4] Cf. Letter 156A, n. 1. *Humor,* as defined by Schumann, is one of Jean
Paul's salient features.
[5] Much has been made of the fact that, in 1832, Schumann "crippled"
the 4th (2nd?) finger of his right hand by resorting to a mechanical
device he had invented to make the finger more independent. The injury

is supposed to have been permanent & to have turned him definitively away from a virtuoso's career to one of composing. Schumann, at least, believed this, though it is difficult to understand how such an injury could have been permanent.

[6] Cf. comments to Letter 151. De Sire had evidently published some piano compositions that made use of 3 staves.

[7] Cf. Letter 162, n. 2. Franz Hünten (1793–1878) was the composer of innumerable salon pieces for the piano.

[8] Prince Louis Ferdinand (1772–1806), nephew of Frederick the Great, was a very gifted composer whose published chamber music is thought to have had some influence on Schumann. He was killed at the action of Saalfeld, before the battle of Jena (cf. Letter 124, n. 1).

[9] Heller (1813–88), a prolific composer, is still remembered for his piano études. For Hiller see comments to Letter 170.

[10] William Sterndale Bennett (1816–75) had a distinguished musical career in England, though he never fulfilled the expectations Schumann had of him as a composer.

[11] Sigismond Thalberg (1812–71), who claimed to be the natural son of Count Dietrichstein (cf. Letter 161, n. 15), was one of the most brilliant & fashionable virtuosos of the century.

[12] The youthful G minor Symphony was not published, though its 1st movement was performed at Zwickau & Leipzig in 1832–33. There exist MS fragments of 2 early piano concertos that were never finished.

[13] The *Concert sans Orchestre* (Sonata in F minor), op. 14, was already published & so is not identical with the "sonata in F minor" mentioned here, which probably remained unfinished.

[14] The "concerto" might possibly have been a sketch of what later became the 1st movement of the A minor concerto; the "romantic sonata" was probably the *Faschingsschwank* (cf. comments to this letter).

[15] By the Viennese Biedermeier painter Josef Kriehuber (1800–76).

[16] Schumann never went to England or France.

Letter 180

(For Verdi's dates see Letter 175.)—Demaldé was one of Verdi's earliest supporters & his 1st biographer. His nickname, "Finola," is a local diminutive derived from "Pino" (= "Giuseppino").

[1] *Oberto Conte di S. Bonifacio,* Verdi's 1st opera, originally intended for the Teatro Filodrammatico in Milan.

[2] *Oberto* was performed with success at La Scala on 17 November of that year, with another cast than the one mentioned here.—Giuseppina Streppони (1815–97) sang the leading feminine role in the 1st performance

of *Nabucodonosor* 3 years later; she was destined to become the composer's 2nd wife, in 1859.

[3] Margherita Barezzi; they had been married in 1836. Both their children died in infancy, & Margherita herself died soon after, in June 1840, aged 26.

Letter 181

(For Berlioz's & Chopin's dates see Letters 138 & 161 respectively.)— After leaving Majorca (cf. Letter 177), Chopin, with George Sand & her children, stopped at Barcelona, then at Marseilles. There they remained until the end of winter, since Chopin's health was so bad that they could not risk to go north at that season.

[1] *Le Lac des Fées* had been presented at the Opéra on 1 April. Daniel-François-Esprit Auber (1782–1871) is remembered for other works, e.g., *La Muette de Portici* & *Fra Diavolo*. Berlioz does not seem to have been excessively fond of his music, though his published statements are circumspect: in later years, when Berlioz was appointed librarian at the Conservatoire, Auber was his superior.

Letter 182

See comments to Letters 177 & 181.—In May, Chopin & his party left Marseilles & went to stay at George Sand's country place at Nohant. From there he made plans for his return to Paris.

[1] Many of Chopin's letters to his compatriots contain similar expressions of endearment, which were quite usual in Polish at the time.

[2] Cf. Letter 177, n. 2.

[3] George Sand had at the same time rented lodgings at 16, rue Pigalle.

[4] Fontana had asked Chopin to make some changes in the 1st of the 2 Polonaises, op. 40, which the composer was dedicating to him.

[5] In F-sharp major, op. 36.

[6] Minor composers (e.g., Zimmermann was professor of piano at the Conservatoire); Karsko-Kón = Karski-Horse, a pun that no doubt accounts for the zoological flavor of the rest of the sentence.

Letter 183

DONIZETTI: b. Bergamo, 1797; d. there, 1848.

[1] On 11 February.

[2] Adolphe-Charles Adam (1803–56) had achieved his 1st success with that 1-act *opéra comique* some 5 years earlier. Today he is best known for his music to the ballet *Giselle*.

[3] Donizetti's 54th opera, produced in Naples in 1836.

542

Letters 184A–B

(For Mendelssohn's & Liszt's dates see Letters 141 & 159 respectively.)—
Mendelssohn's mother was Lea, née Salomon (1777–1842).—Schlesinger
(c.1800–71), son of one of Beethoven's publishers, established an important branch in Paris & founded the *Gazette musicale* (to which Liszt's
letter was addressed).—Mendelssohn was now the director of the Gewandhaus concerts in Leipzig.

[1] These allusions to members of the family circle require little comment:
the Woringens were family friends; Rebecka Dirichlet (1811–58) was
Mendelssohn's younger sister; Albertine, née Hein, was his brother Paul's
wife; Arnold was his 1st cousin.

[2] By now, Clara & Schumann were deep in legal litigations with Friedrich
Wieck over their long-postponed marriage (cf. comments to Letter 131).
Liszt, who had arrived in Leipzig for a series of concerts, took Schumann's
side.

[3] *Die Zerstörung Jerusalems.* For Hiller, who was especially close to
Mendelssohn, cf. comments to Letter 170.

[4] Cf. Letter 179, n. 11.

[5] Adolph Henselt (1814–89) & Theodor Döhler (1814–56) were brilliant
pianists.

[6] I.e., Rebecka (cf. n. 1 above).

[7] The letter published under this date in Paul Mendelssohn Bartholdy's
collection (1863) & all subsequent editions is so unlike the original that
the present version must be considered its 1st edition.

[8] Johann Baptist Cramer (1771–1858), the venerable author of the
famous piano studies & of numerous sonatas.

[9] This letter has been appended to Mendelssohn's as an illustration of the
sort of behavior that disturbed him.

Letter 185

(For Schumann's dates see Letters 156A–B.)—So far, Schumann had
published only piano music. But in 1840, the year of his marriage to
Clara Wieck (12 Sep.), he composed over 120 lieder, beginning with
those of the *Liederkreis*, op. 24, to poems by Heine. These he sent to the
poet with the present letter. Heine never replied.

[1] In May 1828, on a holiday tour of Bavaria.

[2] Cf. Letter 179, n. 9. He had settled in Paris 2 years earlier.

Letter 186

(For Wagner's dates see Letter 164.)—Frederick Augustus II (1797–1854), a comparatively enlightened monarch, had ascended the throne in 1836.—Wagner & his wife Minna (née Planer; 1809–66) had been in Paris since Sept. 1839.

[1] Wagner was in disastrous financial condition, having just recently been released from debtor's prison.

[2] In 1830, a youthful Overture in B-flat major was performed by Dorn (cf. comments to Letter 176) at the Leipzig theater, but was received with derision; his C major Symphony was given at the Gewandhaus in 1833.

[3] Giacomo Meyerbeer (1791–1864), the hugely successful composer of *Robert le Diable* (1831) & *Les Huguenots* (1836), had in fact befriended Wagner & introduced him to several influential persons; he also wrote letters recommending *Rienzi* & helped to get it accepted for performance in Dresden. This did not prevent (apologists say it motivated) Wagner's attack upon Meyerbeer's compositions 10 years later, in the notorious essay on "Judaism in Music."

[4] The story, *Le Hollandais volant* ("The Flying Dutchman"), is all the Opéra bought from Wagner in the end; it was worked into a French libretto, then set to music by Philippe Dietch (1808–65). Cf. Gustave Leprince, "The Flying Dutchman in the Setting by Philippe Dietch," MQ, L (1964), 307ff.

[5] Salutation & signature are missing in the published source.—*Rienzi's* acceptance (it was performed in Dresden in 1842) represented the turning point in Wagner's early career.

Letter 187

(For Wagner's & Schumann's dates see Letters 164 & 156A–B respectively.)—Wagner & Schumann had met in Leipzig in 1831. Some years later, Wagner began contributing an occasional article to the *Neue Zeitschrift für Musik;* & after 1845, when the Schumanns moved to Dresden, they & Wagner must have seen a good deal of each other. But they never became friends. In 1846, Wagner said to Hanslick (cf. comments to Letter 261): "Schumann is a highly gifted musician, but an impossible person. When I came here from Paris I visited Schumann, told him of my Paris experiences, spoke of musical conditions in France, then of those in Germany, spoke of literature and politics—but he remained practically mute for almost an hour. Well, you can't keep talking *alone* forever. An impossible person!" Schumann had the opposite complaint: "he is a very instructed and ingenious man, but talks incessantly, and one can really not endure that in the long run." (Source: [= Letters 156A–B], 50.)

[1] Cf. Letter 186, n. 1. Needless to say, the rest of the letter is equally ironical.

[2] This is true, & Wagner's setting has been published. Schumann's, of course, is very well known (*Die beiden Grenadiere*).

[3] Cf. Letter 186, n. 3. Schumann disliked Meyerbeer's operas intensely & often expressed himself accordingly in the *Neue Zeitschrift*, though in a manner quite different from that of Wagner's later attacks.

Letter 188
BRAHMS: b. Hamburg, 1833; d. Vienna, 1897.—Cossel was Brahms's 1st piano teacher.

Letter 189
See comments to Letters 184A–B.—Mendelssohn had just returned from his 7th visit to England, where he had given the "Scotch" Symphony its 1st local performance.

[1] Cf. Letter 165, n. 18 & Letter 184A, n. 1.

[2] Cécile, née Jeanrenaud (1817–53), Mendelssohn's wife since 1837. The Mendelssohns were spending some weeks at her mother's home.

[3] Not all the persons mentioned in this paragraph could be identified. Philipp Veit (1793–1877), one of the leading painters in the Nazarene movement, was Mendelssohn's cousin. Bernus was a senator in Frankfurt. For Hiller see comments to Letter 170. "Prince Friedrich" might be Friedrich-Wilhelm-Constantin von Hohenzollern-Hechingen (1801–69), a great music lover. Julie Schenk-Jeanrenaud was Cécile's sister. Jacob Rosenhain (1813–94) was a pianist & composer. The Beneckes were relatives of Cécile; the Mendelssohns had stayed at their house while in London.

[4] 1803–73; the author of *The Last Days of Pompeii* (1834) added "Lytton" to his surname the following year.

[5] Samuel Rogers (1763–1855), the poet, banker, patron of the arts, & literary ruler of England for half a century.

[6] Gustav P. L. Dirichlet (1805–59), a well-known mathematician, was married to Mendelssohn's sister Rebecka (cf. Letter 184A, n. 1). John Arthur Roebuck (1801–79) was a radical politician. Apparently Dirichlet's —& Mendelssohn's—views were radical too (cf. later in this letter).

[7] Poetess, sister of Wilhelm Hensel (cf. Letter 165, n. 14).

[8] Cf. Letter 165, n. 18.

[9] Beckchen = Rebecka. For Moscheles see Letter 145E, n. 5 & Letters 152, 153; he was on the closest terms with Mendelssohn.—Mendelssohn had composed incidental music to Sophocles' *Antigone* the previous year.

[10] Baron Christian Karl Josias von Bunsen (1791–1860), diplomat & scholar, was the Prussian ambassador to the court of St. James's.

[11] Albert's older brother Ernest, later Duke of Saxe-Coburg-Gotha (1818–93).

[12] Op. 47, no. 3.

[13] Op. 8, no. 3. But this (& 5 other lieder in op. 8 & 9) was by Mendelssohn's sister Fanny (cf. Letter 165, n. 14). The lieder mentioned next (op. 8, nos. 5 & 4 respectively) are both by Mendelssohn.

[14] The symphony is in fact dedicated to Queen Victoria.

[15] George Grote (1794–1871), the historian, was a prominent "philosophic Radical" of the Mill-Bentham school.

[16] King Louis Philippe's son, the popular Ferdinand Philippe, Duke of Orleans (b. 1810), had been killed in a carriage accident at Neuilly on 13 July.

Letter 190

(For Donizetti's dates see Letter 183.)—Vasselli, a military surgeon, was the brother of Donizetti's wife Virginia, who had died in 1837.

[1] *Don Pasquale*'s libretto had been adapted from that of *Marcantonio*, an opera by Stefano Pavesi (1779–1850).

Letter 191

(For Berlioz's & Mendelssohn's dates see Letters 138 & 141 respectively.)— The 2 composers had last seen each other 12 years before, in Rome. Berlioz arrived in Leipzig just in time to hear Mendelssohn conduct the final rehearsal of *Die erste Walpurgisnacht* (cf. Letter 165, n. 16) in its revised version. Berlioz was so impressed that he asked to have Mendelssohn's baton as a souvenir; the latter consented, but asked to have Berlioz's baton in exchange. This inspired the Frenchman to write a letter "which *the last of the Mohicans,* I hope, would not have disavowed."

Letter 192

(For Chopin's dates see Letter 161.)—For Schlesinger see comments to Letters 184A–B.

[1] In G-flat major, op. 51.

[2] Cf. Letter 145E, n. 5.

Letter 193
(For Wagner's & Mendelssohn's dates see Letters 164 & 141 respectively.)
—Soon after the triumphant production of *Rienzi* at the Dresden opera
(cf. Letter 186, n. 5), Wagner was appointed Royal *Kapellmeister* there.
The present note was written during a short visit to Berlin, where he had
gone in order to conduct the 1st local performances of *Der fliegende
Holländer* (7 & 9 Jan.). Mendelssohn, whose official title at the Prussian
court had obliged him to move temporarily to Berlin, seems not to have
had the peace of mind or inclination to take any great interest in the
ambitious young composer on this occasion. Wagner, on the other hand,
did his best to cultivate important connections, though, after Mendelssohn's
death, he was scarcely more charitable towards him than towards Meyerbeer
(cf. Letter 186, n. 3, & the last paragraph of Letter 214).

Letter 194
(For Donizetti's dates see Letter 183.)—Giuseppina Appiani, née Strigelli,
was a celebrated Milanese beauty at whose house Donizetti was a guest in
1841–42.—From 1842, when he was in Vienna for the 1st performance
of *Linda di Chamounix*, Donizetti was in constant demand there, as both
composer & conductor.
[1] By now, Milan had heard Verdi's *Nabucco* & *I Lombardi*; at the moment,
he was composing *Ernani* for the Teatro La Fenice in Venice. Cf. Letter
195.
[2] *Dom Sébastien de Portugal* (1843), Donizetti's last opera.
[3] A soprano who had received very favorable notices in Milan; she failed
in Vienna.

Letter 195
(For Verdi's & Donizetti's dates see Letters 175 & 183 respectively.)
[1] Cf. Letter 194, n. 1. *Ernani*'s 1st performance on 9 March had been a
triumph; this was the opera that spread Verdi's fame beyond Italy.

Letter 196
(For Berlioz's dates see Letter 138.)—Louis-Joseph Berlioz (d. 1848) was
a physician, who, it will be remembered, had wished his son to follow him
in his profession (cf. comments to Letter 146).
[1] This episode is vividly described in Berlioz's *Mémoires*, chap. lii. As the

Paris industrial exhibition of 1844 was nearing its end, Berlioz happened to meet Johann Strauss, Sr. (1804–49), the "Father of the Waltz," at a café; together, they devised the plan of using the great exhibition hall, once it was emptied & before it was torn down, for a musical festival in honor of the exhibitors. They received official permission for 2 concerts, Strauss's to consist of dance music, Berlioz's of hardier fare: Overture to *La Vestale* (Spontini), Prayer from *La Muette de Portici* (Auber), Scherzo & Finale from Beethoven's 5th Symphony, Prayer from *Moïse* (Rossini), *Hymne à la France* (composed by Berlioz for the occasion), Overture to *Freischütz* (Weber), "Hymn to Bacchus" from the incidental music to *Antigone* (Mendelssohn), "Marche au supplice" from the *Symphonie fantastique* (Berlioz), "Song of the Industrialists" (written by a certain Méraux for the occasion), Chorus from *Charles VI* (Halévy), Blessing of the Daggers from *Les Huguenots* (Meyerbeer), Pleasure-Garden Scene from *Armide* (Gluck), & "Apothéose" from the *Symphonie funèbre et triomphale* (Berlioz). The orchestra & chorus personnel assembled by Berlioz totaled 1022 persons & required the services of 7 assistant conductors at the concert. 24 French horns produced "one of the greatest effects" in the slow introduction to the *Freischütz* Overture, while 80 bass singers "overwhelmed the audience" with their rendition of the Blessing of the Daggers (originally scored for 4 solo voices). Cf. Letter 198.

[2] Berlioz went to Nice instead.

[3] The composer's son (1834–67); he later pursued a career in the navy.

[4] *Voyage musical en Allemagne et Italie*, Berlioz's 1st collection of articles in book form.

Letter 197

(For Schumann's dates see Letters 156A–B.)—Andersen (1805–75) had been welcomed into the musical circles of Leipzig during his visits there.— The Schumanns had moved to Dresden the previous December; life there was quieter, & Schumann had just suffered his 1st serious nervous breakdown.

[1] Niels V. Gade (1817–90), the principal Danish composer of the 19th century, whose early works elicited Schumann's cordial support in the *Neue Zeitschrift für Musik*.

[2] An Andersen story which Schumann was considering as the subject of a fairy opera.

[3] It had taken place on 22 July 1844, in Leipzig; the performer was Clara, who played a Beethoven sonata, the singer Livia Frege (1818–91), who sang Schumann's lieder to poems by Andersen (op. 40, dedicated to

the poet). The evening was rounded off by Andersen reading some of his tales.

[4] "When shall we meet again in the selfsame place?" Schumann has altered Uhland's lines, which read: *Wann treffen wir uns, Brüder, / Auf* einem *Schifflein wieder?* ("When shall we meet again, brothers, on the selfsame boat?"). He used the poem in a setting for mixed voices, flute, & French horn (op. 146, no. 5).

[5] Carl A. Helsted (1818–1904), Danish composer.

[6] Annette von Droste-Hülshoff (1798–1848), who had published her collected poems only the year before, was soon considered the leading German poetess of her time.

Letter 198

(For Berlioz's dates see Letter 138.)—François (called "George") Hainl (1807–73) was chief conductor of the Grand Théâtre in Lyons.

[1] The "Apothéose" from the *Symphonie funèbre et triomphale.*

[2] Rachel (Élisa Félix; 1821–58), the great dramatic actress, was touring the provinces at the same time.

[3] Prof. Barzun (in the source) notes: "The usual tax on entertainments for the benefit of the poor was one-eighth of the gross receipts." See also Letter 196, p. 276.

Letter 199

(For Berlioz's & Mendelssohn's dates see Letters 138 & 141 respectively.)

[1] Cf. Letter 176, n. 10.

Letter 200

(For Mendelssohn's dates see Letter 141.)—For Moscheles see Letter 145E, n. 5 (& cf. Letter 189, n. 9).—While Mendelssohn was completing the score of *Elijah,* which was to receive its 1st performance at the Birmingham Festival 2 months later, he was being informed of the preparations taking place across the Channel.

[1] Joseph Moore (1766–1851) was the manager of the Birmingham Festivals.

[2] In 1844 Mendelssohn had conducted 5 of the Philharmonic's regular concerts. The orchestra, unaccustomed to his high standards, had had some difficulty at first, & 1 or 2 members actually were rude to him; eventually they were won over by his musicianship & skill.

Letter 201

(For Mendelssohn's dates see Letter 141.)—Franck (1822–90), by now a graduate of the Paris Conservatoire, was beginning to gain some recognition as a promising young composer.

[1] Op. 1 (3 trios) & possibly op. 2 (4th trio). Liszt, to whom they had been shown, liked them so much that he performed them & arranged for their publication in Germany.

[2] To England, for the 1st performance of *Elijah* (26 Aug.; cf. Letter 200).

Letter 202

(For Verdi's dates see Letter 175.)—Ricordi (1785–1853), founder of the famous music publishing house in Milan, had displayed remarkable foresight by acquiring the rights to Verdi's very 1st opera, *Oberto* (cf. Letter 180), thus inaugurating an enduring, & profitable, relationship between the composer & the firm.

[1] Letters from this source bear no signature, since they are reproduced from the books in which Verdi meticulously copied all the letters he wrote during extended periods of his life.

Letters 203A–B

SMETANA: b. Litomyšl, 1824; d. Prague, 1884.—For Liszt's dates see Letter 159.

[1] *Six morceaux caractéristiques*, op. 1, still in MS at the time.

[2] 1794–1864; blind pianist & pedagogue, whose music institute in Prague lasted, under the direction of his descendants, until 1933.

[3] While he did not send Smetana any money, Liszt persuaded Kistner of Leipzig to publish the pieces & became a staunch champion of the Czech composer. Cf. Letter 201, n. 1.

Letters 204A–B

(For Chopin's dates see Letter 161.)—Count Grzymała (1793–1870), formerly a career officer & deputy, had emigrated to Paris after the ill-fated Polish revolution; he now lived there, on the remnants of a considerable fortune, as a friend & patron of artists & musicians.—After the break with George Sand (1847), Chopin had been persuaded by his Scottish pupil Jane Stirling (1804–59) & her sister to visit England & Scotland, though his health was rapidly deteriorating. A factor in this decision was the February (1848) Revolution, which deprived him of several fashionable pupils, his main source of income. He arrived in London on 20 Apr. 1848; by the time he left (23 Nov.), he was a dying man.

[1] Jenny Lind (1820–87) had made her London debut at Her Majesty's Theatre the previous year, arousing the wildest enthusiasm. One of her most successful parts had been the title role in Bellini's *La Sonnambula.*

[2] The Chartist demonstration in London had taken place on 10 Apr.

[3] Adolph Gutmann (1819–82) was one of Chopin's professional pupils. The aristocratic personages mentioned earlier require no comment here (cf. *Encyclopaedia Britannica, s.v.* "Hamilton," "Charles III, duke of Parma," etc.).

Letter 205

(For Wagner's dates see Letter 164.)—For Minna Wagner see comments to Letter 186.—Royal *Kapellmeister* Wagner, chafing more at artistic than social iniquities, had embraced the popular cause during the Dresden uprising of 4 May 1849. When the revolt was suppressed by Prussian troops 2 days later, Wagner escaped to Weimar, where his friend Liszt (they had met in Paris in 1840) had recently settled down as the court *Kapellmeister;* Minna remained at Chemnitz with Wagner's sister & brother-in-law, the Wolframs.

[1] One of the leaders (together with Bakunin) of the Dresden uprising.

[2] Princess Karolyne zu Sayn-Wittgenstein (1819–87), with whom Liszt had formed a liaison in 1847, now lived with him in Weimar.

[3] *Lohengrin* had not yet been produced; Liszt performed it in Weimar the following year.—Theodor Uhlig (1822–53), composer & violinist in the Dresden orchestra, was one of Wagner's most loyal adherents.

[4] Karl Ritter was the son of Julie Ritter, an elderly widow in Dresden who, at about this time, befriended Wagner.—*Siegfrieds Tod,* finished during the previous Nov., was later to form the basis for the text of *Götterdämmerung,* whereas *Die Gibelinen* (or *Friedrich Rothbart*) never developed beyond a sketch.

[5] Minna did not come to Weimar; nor did Wagner himself attend the performance, since meanwhile a warrant was issued in Dresden for his arrest. He left that Sunday morning & eventually, after taking leave of his wife, escaped to Switzerland with a forged passport.

Letter 206

(For Chopin's dates see Letter 161.)—Mlle. de Rozières had been the piano teacher of George Sand's daughter Solange & was herself a pupil of Chopin.

551

[1] Chopin, sensing that he was about to die, had written to his sister Ludwika Jędrziejewicz in Poland, asking her to come to Paris. She arrived with her husband & daughter, & remained with the composer to the end.

[2] *Recte,* Grille de Beuzelin, a friend of Mlle. de Rozières.—Chopin died during the night of 17 Oct.

Letter 207

(For Verdi's dates see Letter 175.)—Marzari was president of La Fenice Theater in Venice, for which Verdi had been commissioned to write a new opera. The subject, taken from Hugo's play *Le Roi s'amuse,* had been renamed *La Maledizione* ("The Curse") & worked into a libretto by the composer's durable associate Francesco Maria Piave (1811–76). Verdi had begun writing the music, when the project fell foul of the Austrian censorship (Venice, at the time, was a part of the Austrian-dominated Lombard-Venetian Kingdom): the story dealt with a dissolute monarch— no matter that Francis I lived in the 16th century—& was obviously thought inflammatory, though the censor merely called it "revoltingly immoral" & "obscenely trivial." Piave hastened to make a number of changes: the king became the Duke of Vendôme, all the "immoral" situations were removed (& with them the point of the drama), & the approved "revision" was sent to Verdi, whose reaction is seen in this letter. (The opera was to undergo further transformations before it finally emerged as *Rigoletto.*)

[1] Hugo's Triboulet, later renamed Rigoletto in the opera.

Letter 208

(For Verdi's dates see Letter 175.)—Ricordi (1811–88) was the son of Giovanni (cf. comments to Letter 202), who died 9 days after the date of this letter (written immediately after the 1st performance of *Traviata* at La Fenice Theater).

[1] It is generally agreed that the singers were at fault—especially the Violetta, who was fat & therefore unable to portray the consumptive heroine very convincingly.

Letters 209A–B

(For Schumann's & Brahms's dates see Letters 156A–B & 188 respectively.) —J. J. Brahms (1806–72), the composer's father, was a proficient player on the double-bass, cello, & French horn.—On 30 Sep., young Brahms had appeared at the Schumanns' home in Düsseldorf & made a profound impression with his 1st compositions; he soon became one of the family.

[1] Schumann's famous article "Neue Bahnen" ("New Paths," in the *Neue Zeitschrift für Musik* of 23 Oct.), in which he dramatically announced the arrival of "one whose destiny should be to express the spirit of our age in the loftiest and most ideal way. . . . His name is *Johannes Brahms*."

[2] At Schumann's instance Breitkopf & Härtel had published Brahms's op. 1, 2, 3, & 4.

[3] Joseph Joachim (1831–1907), the great violinist, estimable composer, & lifelong friend of Brahms, had brought about the young composer's meeting with Schumann.

Letter 210

ROSSINI: b. Pesaro, 1792; d. Paris, 1868.—Bellentani made & sold sausages in Modena.—The "Swan of Pesaro" should have made his personal appearance in this collection long before now (cf. Letter 144 or Letter 145E, n. 1); unfortunately, however, his earlier letters are either polite & uninteresting or witty, interesting—& spurious (for example, the letter of 12 Feb. 1817 to Cicognara, most recently reprinted by G. Norman & M. L. Shrifte in *Letters of Composers* [New York, 1946], was exposed as a forgery in the 1920s). We must therefore content ourselves with this late effusion, which at least has the merit of authenticity & deals with one of the Master's weightier concerns.

[1] Modena was once ruled by the Este family.

[2] For these chopped-meat delicacies, cf. any competent Italian cookery book.

[3] Latin name for the southernmost mouth of the Po & its lagoon, N of Pesaro; it was said to abound in swans.

[4] After *Guillaume Tell* (1829), Rossini had composed no more operas, though he was at the peak of his career. His renunciation remained one of the mysteries of the age.

Letter 211

DIETRICH: b. near Meissen, 1829; d. Berlin, 1908. Though one of Schumann's best pupils, Dietrich never became an important composer.— For Joachim see Letter 209B, n. 3. Brahms was in Hanover with him, at the time.

[1] The Schumanns' physician.

Letter 212

(For Wagner's & Liszt's dates see Letters 164 & 159 respectively.)—This letter marks another important turning point in Wagner's life: his adoption of Schopenhauer's philosophy. It was to affect the composition of the rest of the *Ring* (only *Das Rheingold* had been completed by then); more importantly, it confirmed & crystallized feelings with which he was already imbued as a result of his hopeless love for Mathilde, the wife of his friend & patron Otto Wesendonk.

[1] John Oxenford (1812–77), whose "Iconoclasm in German Philosophy," an outline of Schopenhauer's system, appeared in the *Westminster Review* for Apr. 1853 & later, in German, in the *Vossische Zeitung*.

[2] The cycle was not completed till 1874 (*Tristan* & *Meistersinger* intervened).

[3] The black flag was not retained in the finished music drama.

[4] The young Swiss composer Joachim Raff (1822–82) was a member of the Liszt circle in Weimar.

[5] Princess Wittgenstein's daughter (cf. Letter 205, n. 2).

Letters 213A–B

See Letters 209A–B & 211.—For Clara Schumann's dates see Letter 162, n. 7.—After the events in Letter 211, Schumann had at his own request been taken to a private asylum at Endenich, near Bonn, where he was to live out the rest of his days. The doctors kept his wife away from him, fearing her presence might stir him too deeply; but Brahms & Joachim paid him occasional visits.

[1] Clara undertook extensive concert tours to support the family (they had 7 children).

[2] One of Schumann's last experiences before his collapse had been a tour of Holland, where his music & his wife's playing had met with unprecedented success.

[3] *Studien für den Pedal-Flügel*, op. 56, nos. 4 & 5, *Skizzen für den Pedal-Flügel*, op. 58, & nos. 1 & 7 from the famous *Fantasiestücke*, op. 12.

[4] Felix (named after Mendelssohn) had been born on 11 June 1854; he never saw his father.—No special comments need be made about the Schumanns' Düsseldorf acquaintances.—Julius Otto Grimm (1827–1903), composer & friend of Brahms & Joachim, was about to be named music director at Göttingen University; the appointment later fell through.

[5] Meta Abegg (1810–34), a beautiful woman & excellent pianist, was the "Pauline Comtesse d'Abegg" to whom Schumann dedicated his op. 1 (*Variations sur le nom Abegg*).

[6] *Signale für die musikalische Welt*, a periodical founded by the publisher

Bartholf Senff (1815–1900), who had also brought out several of Schumann's works (&, recently, Brahms's op. 5 & 6).

⁷ Schumann's last complete composition for piano (op. 133) was published that Dec. by F. W. Arnold, Elberfeld.

⁸ I.e., the *Concert-Allegro mit Introduction.*

⁹ Joachim's Variations for viola & piano, op. 10.—The Schumann works are mentioned by their usual titles & so require no further identification.

¹⁰ Schumann had renewed his acquaintance with Joachim (who had studied at Leipzig as a boy) in May 1853, when the violinist had played the Beethoven concerto at the Lower Rhine Festival in Düsseldorf.

¹¹ Schumann's overture to Shakespeare's *Julius Caesar* (op. 128).

¹² Breitkopf & Härtel had turned down Brahms's 4-hand arrangement of the Schumann Piano Quintet.

¹³ Of Clara's Berlin concert.

¹⁴ Op. 10, for piano.

¹⁵ Hermann Härtel (1803–75), son of G. C. Härtel (cf. comments to Letter 121), who, with his brother Raimund (1810–88), now headed the firm.—In the following remarks, Schumann refers alternately to his own & to Brahms's works. The cello & piano pieces are his own 5 *Romanzen,* composed in Nov. 1853 (unpublished). The other works are identified in square brackets.

¹⁶ The Brahms Scherzo contains 2 trios (interludes).

¹⁷ Not Schumann's piano transcriptions (op. 3 & 10), but the piano accompaniments he had been working on just before his illness.

Letter 214
(For Wagner's dates see Letter 164.)—Kietz (1815–92) was an unsuccessful painter Wagner had met during the impecunious Paris days (1839–42), when the 2 friends had banded together against the wolf lurking at their respective doors.—Though it meant interrupting work on *Die Walküre,* Wagner had accepted an invitation to conduct the Philharmonic Society's concerts that season: he needed the money, of course, but he also hoped to make his way in England & perhaps get the *Ring* performed there.

¹ The meeting with Karl Klindworth (1830–1916) led to a close friendship, & the pianist soon after began to prepare the vocal scores of the *Ring.*

² Cf. Letter 193. It was the "Italian" Symphony.

Letter 215

(For Berlioz's dates see Letter 138.)—Ritter (real name Bennet; 1841–86), then only a boy, was the son of one of Berlioz's friends & already a proficient pianist. A pupil of Liszt, he later composed salon music.—Berlioz was in London at the same time as Wagner (cf. Letter 214), having been called there to conduct a rival organization, the New Philharmonic Society.

[1] T. Frederick Beale (d. 1863), music publisher & one of the New Philharmonic Society's founders, befriended Berlioz in London. William Howard Glover (1819–75) was an Irish composer & the critic for the *Morning Post*.

[2] Cf. Letter 184, n. 5, & Letter 214, n. 1.

[3] The Meyerbeer *opéra comique* (1854).

[4] The present editor was unable to find this (doubtless very witty) quotation in Heine's works.

[5] Heinrich Wilhelm Ernst (1814–65), the well-known violinist, had been on close terms with Berlioz in Paris; now he was settling in London permanently.

[6] 1811–82; the French socialist leader had been living in exile since the February Revolution of 1848.

[7] John Ella (1802–88) was the director of The Musical Union, whose morning concert series was in existence from 1845 to 1880.

[8] George Hogarth (1783–1870), in addition to being a music critic, was Dickens' father-in-law.

[9] Cf. Letter 186, n. 3.

[10] In *Oper und Drama* (1852), Wagner had by turns praised & severely criticized Berlioz. James W. Davison (1813–85) was the music critic of the *Times* & one of Wagner's chief opponents in London.

Letter 216

(For Berlioz's & Wagner's dates see Letters 138 & 164 respectively.)
[1] *Je suis un impie plein de respect pour les Pies.*

Letters 217A–B

(For Brahms's & Joachim's dates see Letters 188 & 209B, n. 3, respectively.)
—Gisela von Arnim was the daughter of the authoress Bettina (1785–1859), who in turn was the sister of Clemens Brentano & wife of Achim von Arnim (cf. Letter 124, n. 7). Bettina had known both Beethoven & Goethe, & later published very untrustworthy accounts of her friend-

ship with them, together with forged letters; her literary merits must be
sought elsewhere.

Letter 218
(For Berlioz's dates see Letter 138.)—The following notes are taken from
the source.
[1] The *Figaro* (a non-political weekly) had been founded in 1854. It held
banquets "for the improvement of the French mind."
[2] The quotation is from Molière's *Femmes savantes,* Act II, scene 7, where
Chrysale says: "Indeed my body is myself and I mean to care for it /
Rag though it is," etc.

Letter 219
BIZET: b. Paris, 1838; d. Bougival (near Paris), 1875.—Bizet had been
awarded the *prix de Rome* (cf. Letters 173 & 174) the previous year &
had left for Italy on 21 Dec., arriving in Rome on 28 Jan. after much
sightseeing.—The composer's mother was Aimée Léopoldine Joséphine,
née Delsarte (1814–61).
[1] Bizet's *Te Deum* survives in MS. The Italian libretto he wished to set
to music was called *Parisina* & had already been used by Donizetti in
1833; the project did not materialize. Nor did Bizet win the *prix
Rodrigues.* L. Halévy (1834–1908) collaborated with Henri Meilhac
(1831–97) 15 years later in producing the libretto of *Carmen.* F.
Halévy (1799–1862), uncle of the above & the well-known composer
of *La Juive,* had been Bizet's teacher at the Conservatoire; Bizet married
his daughter in 1869. Cohen (1835–1901) was a minor composer.
[2] Gustave Moreau (1826–98), whose *fin de siècle* paintings later made
him famous ("Salome Dancing," shown at the Salon of 1876, impressed
Flaubert & J.-K. Huysmans), was in Rome at the time & had "a
delightful tenor voice," according to Bizet.
[3] *Prix de Rome* winners were required to send a work or works to the
Académie des beaux arts in Paris every year; these tasks were known as
envois.
[4] At this time, musicians were expected to spend their 3rd year in
Germany; but later Bizet applied for & was granted permission to spend
it in Italy.

Letter 220
(For Brahms's dates see Letter 188.)—For Joachim see Letter 209B, n. 3.
—On 22 Jan. Brahms had brought out his D minor Piano Concerto in
Hanover without success; he played it again in Leipzig 5 days later.

[1] The concerto's opening features a roll on the kettledrum. E. G. B. Pfundt (1806–71), the Gewandhaus timpanist, had elicited critical praise from Schumann in former times.
[2] Cf. Letter 176, n. 10. He was the concertmaster of the Gewandhaus orchestra.
[3] For Senff, cf. Letter 213A, n. 6. The others were distinguished Leipzig musicians.
[4] Cf. Letter 197, n. 3.

Letter 221

(For Verdi's dates see Letter 175.)—Jacovacci was the business-minded impresario of the Teatro Apollo in Rome, where *Un ballo in maschera* had had its 1st performance on 17 Feb.
[1] Cf. comments to Letter 208.

Letters 222A–C

(For Liszt's, Wagner's, & Berlioz's dates see Letters 159, 164, & 138 respectively.)—Wagner had moved to Paris in Sep. 1859, in the hope of getting some of his works produced there. Meanwhile he lived on a grand scale (though still in financial difficulties), was lionized by some of the artists & members of the beau monde, & derided by others.
[1] Cf. comments to Letter 212.—Agnes Street-Klindworth, a relation of Karl Klindworth (cf. Letter 214, n. 1), was one of Liszt's pupils & former loves.
[2] Wagner's dog.
[3] Liszt's birthday.
[4] The last act had been completed at Lucerne the previous Aug.
[5] Wagner had presented his music at 3 concerts in Jan.-Feb., after which Berlioz had published an article praising some of the pieces, severely criticizing others (notably the Prelude to *Tristan*), & concluding, with regard to the "music of the future," that he himself would never believe in it: "Non credo." Whereupon Wagner had written an explanatory letter which Berlioz had published without comment. These writings & Berlioz's *feuilletons* on *Fidelio* all appeared in the *Journal des Débats*.
[6] A reference to Marie Recio, who had lived with Berlioz after his separation from his 1st wife, the Irish actress Henrietta Smithson, in 1841 & married him when Henrietta died in 1854 (Marie herself died in 1862). The 2nd marriage was as unhappy as the 1st, & Marie, a mediocre singer, made things worse by insisting on having the leading part at performances of her husband's music.

[7] Wagner's "horrible French" has been faithfully reproduced in the translation.

[8] It is true that Berlioz—ill, overworked, & frustrated—was becoming embittered. He had completed his vast opera *Les Troyens* in March 1858 & it had been turned down at the Opéra; meanwhile he saw *Tannhäuser* accepted, largely through the intrigues of the Austrian ambassador's wife, & its failure (see comments to Letter 223) could not help but afford him grim satisfaction.

Letter 223

GOUNOD: b. Paris, 1818; d. there, 1893.—For Wagner's dates see Letter 164.—Gounod's *Faust,* produced in 1859, had made its composer famous. Wagner's *Tannhäuser,* on the other hand, fell a victim to the fierce prejudices of the Parisian audience & press when it was given at the Opéra on 13, 18, & 24 March 1861; indeed, the performances were among the most catastrophic in the history of opera.

Letter 224

See comments to Letters 222A–C & 223.—Baudelaire (1821–67), whose *Fleurs du mal* (1857) had recently brought him fame (& notoriety), was one of Wagner's great defenders in Paris. His *Richard Wagner et Tannhäuser à Paris,* 1st published in the *Revue européenne,* was later enlarged & printed separately.

Letter 225

(For Verdi's dates see Letter 175.)—For Piave see comments to Letter 207.—Verdi was in Russia to supervise the 1st performances of *La forza del destino;* its libretto was to be the last of 9 written for him by Piave. (The performances were later canceled, owing to the illness of a singer, & Verdi was obliged to return the following year.)

[1] De Bassini, Marini, & Tamberlik (not "-ich") were principal singers in the forthcoming opera.

[2] Centigrade; i.e., in the low 60s Fahrenheit.

[3] Piave had Gothic tastes, & most of his libretti are full of fate & corpses. *La forza del destino* proved too much even for Verdi, who had it revised for Milan, where it was given in its present, somewhat less bloody, form on 20 Feb. 1869.

[4] Cf. comments to Letter 208.

Letter 226

(For Verdi's dates see Letter 175.)—Arrivabene (1807–87), patriot & journalist, was among Verdi's closest friends.—Between journeys to Russia (cf. comments to Letter 225), Verdi made a trip to England. He had been asked to represent Italy at the opening of the Exhibition of 1862 with a work written for the occasion (Sterndale Bennett represented England, Meyerbeer Germany, & Auber France). He accepted the commission—possibly out of a sense of duty towards his country, since normally he refused to compose occasional works—& wrote the *Inno delle nazioni*. However, the cantata was not performed at the ceremonies, perhaps because at the end of the piece Verdi had interwoven the *Marseillaise* (which, at the time, still had a revolutionary sound to many ears) with *God Save the Queen*.

[1] (Sir) Michael Costa (1806–84; knighted in 1869), Italian-born conductor & composer.

[2] Verdi's wife (cf. Letter 180, n. 2).

[3] The *Inno delle nazioni* was given there with great success on 24 May (the *Morning Post* praised its "pompous and brilliant orchestration").

Letter 227

(For Brahms's & Dietrich's dates see Letters 188 & 211 respectively.)—This letter marks a decisive moment in the life of Brahms & the musical history of Vienna: Brahms was to settle there for the rest of his life, & Vienna, which with the death of Beethoven & Schubert had lost its musical primacy to Leipzig & Paris, was to experience a last period of glory, during which Brahms would be at the head of its list of distinguished resident composers.

[1] Brahms's 1st Symphony was not completed until 1876, & the F minor Quintet was eventually re-scored for piano & strings.

[2] I.e., from the publisher's; the *Marienlieder* (7 songs for mixed choir, op. 22) were published a little later.

[3] Presumably Dietrich's op. 9.

Letter 228

(For Berlioz's dates see Letter 138.)—Flaubert (1821–80) had just published the novel *Salammbô*.

Letter 229

(For Brahms's dates see Letter 188.)—For Brahms's father see comments to Letters 209A–B. His mother, Johanna, née Nissen (1789–1865), was 17 years older than her husband.—Brahms's Viennese debut had occurred on 16 Nov., when he had played his Piano Quartet in G minor, op. 25, at a concert of the Hellmesberger Quartet. On the 29th he gave his own concert, in the hall of the Gesellschaft der Musikfreunde; he played the Bach F major Toccata, Schumann's *Phantasie,* op. 17, his own Handel Variations, &, with the Hellmesberger Quartet, his 2nd Piano Quartet, in A major, op. 26.

[1] Eduard Marxsen (1806–87) had been Brahms's composition teacher. Ludwig Bösendorfer (1835–1919) was now the manager of the firm founded by his father; they made (& make) some of the finest pianos in the world.

[2] Karl Georg Peter Grädener (1812–83), composer & choral director, had led the Hamburg Singakademie for several years, then had preceded Brahms to Vienna, where he taught at the Konservatorium. He later returned to Hamburg.

[3] In D major, op. 11.

[4] Theodor Avé-Lallemant was a Hamburg music teacher. Julius Stockhausen (1826–1906) had recently taken up duties as orchestral & choral conductor in Stuttgart; a fine singer, he was one of the ablest interpreters of Brahms's lieder & a close friend of his.

[5] In Hamburg Brahms had organized a female vocal quartet for which he had composed & arranged various works.

[6] Friedrich (Fritz) Brahms (1835–85), known in Hamburg as "the wrong Brahms," was the composer's brother; he became a respectable pianist & teacher.

Letter 230

(For Berlioz's dates see Letter 138.)—Hopkins (1836–98) was a composer from Vermont. "He founded in New York in 1856 a music association to encourage native talent, organized free singing schools, gave lectures, edited the *New York Philharmonic Journal* (1868–85), & managed to compose some 700 works" (source).

[1] The last 3 words appear in English in the original.

Letter 231

(For Rossini's dates see Letter 210.)—For Hiller see comments to Letter 170.

[1] The firm is still active today.

[2] The 7 Weeks' War of 1866, in which Prussia & Italy attacked Austria, was practically at an end. Prussia had crushed the Austrians at Königgrätz & concluded a separate peace. The Italians, on the other hand, had suffered severe defeats at Custoza & Lissa; they signed an armistice 2 days after the date of this letter & received Venetia from the hands of Napoleon III (the Austrians having ceded the region to him rather than to Italy).

Letter 232

(For Berlioz's dates see Letter 138.)—Yelena Pavlovna (1806–73), born Princess Charlotte Marie of Württemberg, was the widow of Grand Duke Mikhail, the brother of Tsar Nikolai I. A great humanitarian, she was also a discriminating patroness of the arts. Berlioz had visited Russia for the 2nd time in 1867 at her invitation.—This is one of Berlioz's last extant letters. He died on 8 March 1869.

Letter 233

(For Verdi's dates see Letter 175.)—Filippi (1830–87) was a critic & composer.—See Letter 225, n. 3.

[1] The reference is to the son of Tito (cf. comments to Letter 208), Giulio Ricordi (1840–1912), a capable musician in his own right, who was to succeed his father many years later & reveal the traditional family flair by "discovering" Puccini.

Letter 234

(For Wagner's dates see Letter 164.)—Wagner was now living at Triebschen (on the lake of Lucerne) with Cosima, the wife of Hans von Bülow (cf. comments to Letters 271A–B) & daughter of Liszt; they would be married the following year. The composer's circumstances had taken a radical turn for the better in 1864, when young Ludwig II of Bavaria, who admired him ardently, had undertaken his support. *Tristan & Meistersinger* had been performed in Munich. Now Wagner was finishing the long-interrupted *Ring*. Soon he would turn his attention to the establishment of a festival theater designed expressly for the performance of his music dramas.

[1] It seems likely that the unknown correspondent had asked Wagner to use his influence with the king in order to better the lot of the working classes. In this sense, it is true that "politics was not his field" (cf. comments to Letter 205).

Letter 235

(For Verdi's dates see Letter 175.)—Ghislanzoni (1824–93) had recast the final scenes of *La forza del destino* for its Milan performance (cf. Letter 225, n. 3) & was now engaged in writing the libretto of *Aïda*. The present letter is one of many that passed between Verdi & his librettist during the 4 months it took the composer to write the opera.

[1] Act II, Scene i.

[2] The traditional fast-paced music that brings many 19th-century Italian arias to a rousing close. Verdi was evidently getting tired of the convention.

Letter 236

See comments to Letter 226.—The Franco-German War, begun on 19 Jul., had soon moved into its decisive phase with the French rout at Sedan & the capture of Napoleon III.

[1] For Napoleon III's intervention on the side of Italy in the war of 1859 against Austria.

[2] I.e., composing (cf. Letter 235).

[3] Cf. Letter 226, n. 2.

Letter 237

MUSSORGSKY: b. Karevo, 1839; d. St. Petersburg, 1881.—Stasov (1824–1906), critic & scholar, was the ideologist of the Russian National School.—In Feb., Mussorgsky had submitted the 1st version of *Boris Godunov* to the Committee of the Imperial Theaters, which rejected it. Now he was at work revising the opera. Here he is describing some fresh material for the scene in the Tsar's apartment.

[1] Cf. Letter 51, n. 1. Russia retained the Julian calendar until 1917.

[2] "Lodyzhky" = Nikolai Nikolayevich Lodyzhensky (1842–1916), a talented musician; by "the knight of the marine tempests" Mussorgsky means his friend Nikolai Andreyevich Rimsky-Korsakov (1844–1908), with whom he was sharing a room at about this time.

[3] 1–3 are songs, 4–7 occur in *Boris* itself.

[4] Nikolai Ivanovich Zaremba (1821–79) taught composition at the St. Petersburg Conservatory.

Letter 238

See comments to Letter 237.—While revising *Boris,* Mussorgsky projected a new opera, *Khovanshchina,* which, however, was destined to remain unfinished. In this letter he discusses these plans & draws parallels between the plight of Russia at the end of the 17th century (the period of the opera) & her present dangers, with the newly created German Empire as her neighbor.—Notes 1, 2, 4, & 6 below are quoted directly from the source.

[1] This "pearl" is from the dissenters' story "Teuton and Gordad" (actually a translation of a Polish work, "The Devil's Attack on the Race of Man"), which Mussorgsky found in Tikhonravov's *Chronicles of Russian Literature and Antiquity.* It is Peter whose legendary birth concludes the narrative,

his name being cautiously omitted in Mussorgsky's quotation. Peter returned from abroad in 1699 (the year of the *streltzi* uprising), fulfilling the dissenter prophecy of the coming of the Antichrist.

[2] This mysterious paragraph is open to a number of interpretations. The "Passage" (built by Count Steinbock-Fermor) was also used as a promenade by St. Petersburg's prostitutes.

[3] Mussorgsky had recently submitted the 2nd version of *Boris* to the Committee (see comments to Letter 237); it, too, was rejected, in Oct. of that year. Hermann Augustovich Laroche (1845–1906), Feofil Matveyevich Tolstoy ("Fif"; 1809–81), & Alexander Sergeyevich Famintzin (whose name Mussorgsky translates as "Tomson"; 1841–96) were conservative music critics.

[4] Ingermanland is the name sometimes used for the Baltic area including St. Petersburg, Novgorod, & Pskov. It was [Mili Alexeyevich] Balakirev [(1837–1910), the leader of the young National composers,] who often said that the 1st act of invading Germans would be to rename this area *Germanland*.

[5] Shcherbina, a poet, was a friend of Balakirev. The joke hinges on the fact that "klop" means bedbug in Russian: "a bedbug stick (*Klop-stock*) with which to swat bedbugs." (For the human Klopstock cf. Letter 86, n. 1.)

[6] Mikhail Osipovich Mikeshin (1836–96), a friend of Mussorgsky, is remembered for his monuments.

[7] *Kladderadatsch* was a German humorous magazine. At Varzin, in Pomerania (now Poland), Bismarck had his country estates.

[8] Cf. Letter 237, n. 1.

Letter 239

(For Wagner's dates see Letter 164.)—Freny (1825–93), a bass singer at the Hamburg opera, was about to appear as Beckmesser in the 1st local performance of *Die Meistersinger;* he had apparently consulted Wagner regarding certain aspects of the role.

[1] Originally, Beckmesser's name was to have been Hans Lick, in honor of Wagner's fiercest (or, at least, best-known) critic (cf. comments to Letter 261).

Letter 240

(For Bizet's dates see Letter 219.)—Lacombe (1837–1927) was a composer who, from 1866 until Bizet died, studied composition with him by correspondence.

[1] The production of *Carmen* was long put off & only took place on 3 March of the following year. The oratorio was probably not even begun;

soon after the staging of *Carmen*, Bizet was incapacitated by a recurrence
of the angina. He died on 3 June 1875.

Letter 241
DVOŘÁK: b. Nelahozeves (Bohemia), 1841; d. Prague, 1904.
[1] Dvořák won the annual state grant for the next 5 years; the fact that
Brahms sat on the jury was to have important consequences (cf. Letters
251A–B).
[2] Cf. Letter 35, n. 1.

Letter 242
See comments to Letter 237.—In this letter Mussorgsky announces the
completion of 4 out of the 10 numbers that were to make up the piano
suite *Pictures at an Exhibition* (a 5th one, "Two Jews, one rich and one
poor," is projected). That Jan. he had attended a memorial show of works
by his friend the artist Victor Alexandrovich Hartmann (1842–73). On
8 Feb. *Boris* was finally staged (cf. comments to Letter 237, & Letter 238,
n. 3). Soon afterwards he began working on the suite that was to be a
permanent memorial to his friend's sketches & paintings.
[1] The interludes between the characteristic pieces are all based on the
"Promenade" music & represent the composer himself walking from picture to picture.
[2] "*Bydlo* are Polish oxen. *Le télégue* is a typically Mussorgskian Frenchifica-
tion of *telega*, a Russian cart" (source).

Letter 243
(For Liszt's dates see Letter 159.)—Liszt had left Weimar in 1860 &
subsequently had settled in Rome, where he had been admitted as a tertiary
of St. Francis. He received the title of Abbé from Pius IX in 1865 &
thenceforth always wore a priest's cassock.—For a full discussion of his
meeting with Longfellow in 1868 & of the work mentioned in this letter
(*Die Glocken des Strassburger Münster*, for soloists, chorus, & orchestra),
cf. source.
[1] The picture, by the Bostonian George Peter Alexander Healy (1808–94),
actually shows Liszt alone.

Letter 244
BRUCKNER: b. Ansfelden (Upper Austria), 1824; d. Vienna, 1896.—
Mayfeld, an excellent amateur musician & one of Bruckner's patrons &
champions, was a career politician; he was now the governor of Upper
Austria.—The present letter shows Bruckner at a moment of financial

crisis, which soon passed when he was appointed to lecture at the University of Vienna that same year. The naïveté & awkwardness of his style are purposely retained in the translation.

[1] 1843–1916. (Quotation marks by Bruckner.)

[2] Felix Otto Dessoff (1835–92) conducted the Vienna Philharmonic Orchestra.

[3] For Hanslick see comments to Letter 261. The *Presse* had published an account of the deliberations by the committee charged with considering Bruckner's admission to the faculty of the University, where Hanslick was a professor. Since Bruckner was a Wagnerian, Hanslick had naturally represented the opposition.

[4] Johann von Herbeck (1831–77) conducted the orchestra of the Gesellschaft der Musikfreunde.

[5] Karl von Stremayr (1823–1904) was the Austrian Minister of Public Worship & Education.

[6] Bruckner had visited England in 1871, & his masterful organ playing had made a profound impression there.

Letters 245A–D

(For Wagner's & Brahms's dates see Letters 164 & 188 respectively.) In the 1860s, Brahms had received Wagner's autograph score of the Venusberg scene (written for the Paris production of *Tannhäuser*) from the pianist Carl Tausig (1841–71). Brahms was unaware that the score did not belong to Tausig, and when Wagner's wife & the composer Peter Cornelius (1824–74), who had given it to Tausig in the first place, wrote Brahms demanding that it be returned, he took offense & did not reply. 10 years later, Wagner at last asked for it in person. In this unique exchange between the heads of warring factions (they had met a few times in Vienna) one senses a mutual respect, in spite of the arctic temperature.

[1] Cf. comments to Letter 151.

Letter 246

See comments to Letter 226.

[1] Verdi had conducted his *Requiem* in Paris, London, & Vienna.

[2] Verdi's wife (cf. Letter 180, n. 2).

Letter 247

(For Smetana's dates see Letters 203A–B.)—Bendl (1838–97) was a prominent composer of Czech operas.—On 20 Oct. 1874, after a period of nervous tension during which he had suffered from aural hallucinations, Smetana had suddenly lost his hearing altogether; he never regained it.

[1] Rehearsals for the *Ring* were already under way at Wagner's festival theater, which was to be inaugurated 1 year later. There was an invited audience.

[2] Josef Jiránek (1855–1940), pianist & composer, was a pupil & protégé of Smetana.

Letter 248

See comments to Letter 237.

[1] Cf. Letter 237, n. 1.

[2] Camille Saint-Saëns (1835–1921) had himself conducted the 1st Russian performance of his *Danse macabre*; *Aida* had also been heard for the 1st time in Russia, while the opera by Mussorgsky's antagonist (cf. Letter 238, n. 3) had been given for the 1st time anywhere.

[3] The reference is to Liszt's *Totentanz*, for piano & orchestra. Regarding the title of "Abbé," cf. comments to Letter 243.

[4] "Hair-cutting." Saint-Saëns's most popular opera, *Samson et Dalila*, was produced 2 years later at Weimar, on Liszt's recommendation.

[5] "And all the rest of you."

[6] Verdi had just been created a senator by Victor Emmanuel II.

[7] "Ah, yes!"

[8] Alexander Porfiryevich Borodin (1833–87), Mussorgsky's celebrated colleague.

[9] In *Khovanshchina*, Act II (see comments to Letter 238).

Letter 249

(For Wagner's dates see Letter 164.)—Thomas (1835–1904), the famous conductor, though German by birth & upbringing, confined his musical activity to the United States, where he was a pioneer in the cause of good music (as his programs amply attest). He championed the music of Wagner and introduced composers like Berlioz, Liszt, & the young R. Strauss, as well as the classics, to large sections of the country. Thomas had been requested by the Woman's Department of the Philadelphia Centennial Exposition to commission a work for the occasion from Wagner.

[1] The erection of the Bayreuth festival theater was proving inordinately expensive, & fund-raising concerts had been organized in many countries.

[2] Gottlieb Heinrich Federlein (1835–1922), a New York organist & vocal teacher, published monographs on Wagner's *Ring*.

[3] Cf. comments to Letter 151.

[4] Verdi received 35,000 French francs from Ricordi, plus 50% of the receipts for the sale & rental of the score.

[5] The demand was met, but Thomas repented when he saw Wagner's new *Festmarsch,* one of the composer's weaker works. (Wagner himself was heard to remark, "The best thing about the composition was the money I got for it." This is to be understood in the light of n. 1 above.)

Letter 250
(For Verdi's dates see Letter 175.)—For Hiller see comments to Letter 170.—In the long years between *Aida* (1871) & *Otello* (1887) Verdi occasionally made public appearances conducting his *Requiem* (cf. Letter 246, n. 1). Here he is making arrangements for his participation at the forthcoming Lower Rhine Festival.
[1] Verdi's only chamber music work had been composed in 1873.
[2] The quartet was so performed at the Festival.

Letters 251A–B
(For Dvořák's & Brahms's dates see Letters 241 & 188 respectively.)
[1] This was not the 1st time: cf. Letter 241, n. 1. For Hanslick see comments to Letter 261; for Stremayr, cf. Letter 244, n. 5.
[2] The *Moravian Duets,* op. 32. They were to establish Dvořák's reputation abroad.
[3] 1838–1901; the grandson of Nikolaus (see comments to Letter 115) was now head of the firm, which meanwhile had added Brahms to its roster.
[4] As a result of Brahms's recommendation, Simrock became Dvořák's publisher. Brahms remained a loyal supporter & friend of the younger composer & later even undertook to proofread his works, which he called his "best friends."

Letter 252
TCHAIKOVSKY: b. Kamsko-Votkinsk, 1840; d. St. Petersburg, 1893.— Mme. von Meck (1831–94), the wealthy widow of a railway engineer, is remembered for her generous & tactful subvention of Tchaikovsky during the years 1877–90. Partly at her insistence they never met, but they carried on a voluminous correspondence which is now an invaluable source of information on the composer's musical views & personality. (Mme. von Meck also played an important role in the early career of Debussy, whom she employed as a house musician & tutor to her children in 1880–82, during his vacations from the Conservatoire.)—At the time of this letter, Tchaikovsky was abroad, recovering from a serious nervous breakdown occasioned by his ill-advised marriage to a former pupil (they remained

separated). He was just completing the scores of his 4th Symphony &
Eugene Onyegin.

[1] Cf. Letter 237, n. 1.

[2] Tchaikovsky had been professor of harmony at the Moscow Conservatory
since 1866; he resigned his position later that year.

[3] For his dates see Letter 237, n. 2.

[4] César Antonovich Cui (1835–1918), though a member of the "Five,"
represented their ideals in his critical essays better than in his compositions.

[5] Cf. Letter 248, n. 8.

[6] Cf. Letter 238, n. 4.

[7] Bulgarian town, whose defense by the Turks during the Russo-Turkish
War then in progress had made it world-famous. Plevna had capitulated
less than a month earlier, having deflected Russian energies from more
important tasks for 5 months.

[8] François-Joseph Fétis (1784–1871), the famous but erratic lexicographer
& theorist, was Belgian, not French.

[9] Léo Delibes (1836–91), composer of the opera *Lakmé*, the ballet
Coppélia, etc.

[10] Nikolai Grigoryevich Rubinstein (1835–81), brother of the great pianist
Anton Rubinstein (1829–94), was himself a brilliant pianist & first-rate
teacher. He was director of the Moscow Conservatory from its inception
in 1866 until his death & had personally invited Tchaikovsky to join its
faculty when the younger man was barely out of conservatory himself.

Letter 253
(For Wagner's dates see Letter 164.)

Letter 254
(For Brahms's dates see Letter 188.)—For Joachim see Letter 209B, n. 3.—
While composing his Violin Concerto, Brahms repeatedly consulted Joachim
(to whom it was to be dedicated) regarding the effectiveness & idiomatic
propriety of certain passages in the solo part.

[1] This was Brahms's way of announcing he had composed a new work: the
Violin Sonata in G major, op. 78.

[2] The passage in question (measure 338 of the 1st movement) remained
unaltered, as Brahms had it in the 1st instance.

Letter 255

(For Brahms's dates see Letter 188.)—Weis (1862–1944) was a Czech composer & conductor who later achieved considerable success with his operas, e.g., *Der polnische Jude* (1901; Metropolitan Opera House, 1921).

Letter 256

(For Brahms's dates see Letter 188.)—Henschel (1850–1934), born & educated in Germany, had an extraordinary career, both as singer & as conductor. In 1881 he became the 1st conductor of the newly formed Boston Symphony Orchestra & at various times occupied equally important positions in England (professor of singing at the Royal College of Music, etc.). He was knighted in 1914.—When Otto Goldschmidt (1829–1907), the pianist & choral conductor, was preparing for a performance of Brahms's *Deutsches Requiem* with his Bach Choir, he asked Henschel to write to Brahms & inquire concerning the interpretation of the metronome marks in the printed score.

[1] Henschel had conducted the 1st English performance of Brahms's *Triumphlied*, op. 55, on 2 Dec.

[2] Goldschmidt was married to Jenny Lind (cf. Letter 204A, n. 1). The 5th piece in the *Requiem* is the lovely soprano solo, "Ihr habt nun Traurigkeit."

Letter 257

See comments to Letter 226.

[1] Francesco Florimo (1800–88), music historian & archivist at S. Pietro a Majella (the Naples conservatory), had been Bellini's closest friend; the article in question referred to his forthcoming publication of the composer's letters. The book, *Bellini: memorie e lettere,* appeared in 1882.

[2] Felice Romani (1788–1865) had been one of the busiest librettists in the early part of the century. He wrote the books for 7 of Bellini's operas (*Norma* included), 2 of Rossini's, 4 of Donizetti's, & even 1 of Verdi's (*Un giorno di regno*—his 2nd opera).

[3] Verdi's wife (cf. Letter 180, n. 2).

Letter 258

STRAUSS: b. Munich, 1864; d. Garmisch-Partenkirchen, 1949.—The last "Mr. Breitkopf" actively associated with the publishing firm died in 1800 (cf. comments to Letter 121). A 16-year-old composer might be excused for not knowing this, however.

¹ Franz Strauss (1822–1905) was also the 1st horn player in the Munich Opera orchestra & as such had been entrusted with the important solo horn passages in *Tristan* & *Meistersinger* at their 1st performances. Wagner thought highly of him; he himself remained a violent anti-Wagnerian to the end of his days.
² Composed 4 years earlier.
³ Cf. Letter 161, n. 7.
⁴ Benno Walter (1847–1901) was a respected concert violinist; he also had his own quartet.
⁵ The work duly appeared from the presses of Breitkopf & Härtel as Strauss's op. 1.

Letter 259
(For Wagner's dates see Letter 164.)—Strecker (1853–1943) was a director of B. Schott's Söhne (cf. comments to Letter 151). The firm had published *Die Meistersinger* & *Der Ring des Nibelungen*; now it was about to publish Wagner's last music drama, *Parsifal*, which he was engaged in scoring at the time.
¹ Cf. Letter 223. Novello, Ewer & Co. had purchased the score of *The Redemption*, which would be given its 1st performance at Birmingham the following year. (For a similar remark, concerning Verdi, cf. Letter 249.)—Wagner's terms were met.

Letter 260
(For Verdi's dates see Letter 175.)—For Ricordi see Letter 233, n. 1.

Letter 261
(For Brahms's dates see Letter 188.)—Hanslick (1825–1904), professor of the aesthetics & history of music at Vienna University, wielded great power as the music critic of the *Presse* (later, *Neue freie Presse*). His reputation dated from 1854, when he published his 1st book, *Vom Musikalisch-Schönen*, which was translated into many languages. As a critic, he is remembered for his vitriolic attacks on Wagner & the "Wagnerians" (especially Bruckner—cf. Letters 244 & 266, also 239) as well as for his staunch support of Brahms, who valued his friendship without overestimating his critical acumen.—A young Viennese writer had recently purchased MS copies of 2 works that had Beethoven's name on them; he brought them to Hanslick who, being about to take a holiday, left them with Brahms. In this letter, Brahms the musicologist (he shared the task of editing the works of Couperin, Handel, Schubert, Chopin, etc.) un-

erringly identifies the pieces as 2 early Beethoven cantatas (today listed as WoO 87 & 88).

[1] There is no evidence that the works were performed at the time.

[2] Alexander Wheelock Thayer (1817–97), who from 1865 to his death was the American consul in Trieste, had published the 1st 3 volumes of his monumental Beethoven biography in a German translation. (The 4th & last volume remained unfinished; it was completed by other hands, & an English edition of the entire work appeared only in 1921.)

[3] Joseph II, an enlightened monarch, had attempted to carry out sweeping reforms in his domains.

Letter 262

See comments to Letter 226.

[1] Verdi's wife (cf. Letter 180, n. 2).

[2] For Puccini's dates see Letter 272. His 1st stage work, *Le Willis*, a 1-act opera-ballet to words by Ferdinando Fontana (1850–1919), had been successfully produced at Milan's Teatro dal Verme on 31 May. Ricordi later brought out the work in a 2-act version under the title *Le Villi*.

[3] Claudio Achillini (1574–1640) made a modest contribution to the decay of Italian poetry in the 17th century.

Letter 263

MAHLER: b. Kalište (Bohemia), 1860; d. Vienna, 1911.—Löhr was an intimate friend with whom Mahler corresponded for many years.—The composer had recently been appointed opera conductor at Kassel, where he had fallen in love with a young singer named Johanna Richter. In this letter, with its overtones of Werther & Jean Paul, he reveals the origin of his *Lieder eines fahrenden Gesellen* ("Songs of a Wayfarer"). The unhappy love affair was to leave its imprint also on his 1st & 2nd symphonies (see Letter 276).

[1] Only 4 were published.

Letter 264

DEBUSSY: b. St. Germain-en-Laye, 1862; d. Paris, 1918.—Vasnier was an architect who had been quite influential in shaping the young composer's literary & artistic tastes. See LockD, chap. ii.—Having won the *prix de Rome* (cf. Letters 173, 174, & 219) with his cantata *L'Enfant prodigue*, Debussy had discovered he was most reluctant to leave Paris. This letter was written shortly after he reached Rome.

[1] Georges-Eugène Marty (1860–1908), Gabriel Pierné (1863–1937), & Paul Vidal (1863–1931) were all to become well-known composers. Vidal was especially close to Debussy personally.

² Debussy's full Christian name was Achille-Claude (he later reversed the order).—The composer fled to Paris after a year, then returned; after another year he left Rome for good. Like Berlioz, whose *Mémoires* formed his reading just then, he cut short the required term of residence by a year; & unlike Bizet, he found Rome's artistic monuments uncongenial (he detested Michelangelo's *Last Judgment*).

Letter 265
(For Brahms's dates see Letter 188.)—Marie Lipsius ("La Mara"; 1837–1927), besides writing many valuable studies on musical subjects, edited the extensive anthology of composers' letters from which this one is taken. Having come upon certain letters by Brahms, she wrote him for permission to publish them in her book. Cf. Letter 257.

Letter 266
(For Bruckner's dates see Letter 244.)—Wolzogen (1848–1938) had been summoned to Bayreuth by Wagner himself, who had made him the editor of the newly founded *Bayreuther Blätter* in 1878. He became one of the most prolific & authoritative disseminators of the Wagnerian doctrine, remaining in Bayreuth for the rest of his long life.—Bruckner's 7th Symphony had received its 1st performance on 30 Dec. 1884 in Leipzig. Now, at last, it had also been heard in the composer's own country, where his music always met with well-organized opposition.
¹ Karl Muck (1859–1940) was the conductor at the Graz Opera at the time. Later posts during his very distinguished career included 2 terms with the Boston Symphony Orchestra (1906–08, 1912–18).
² Cf. Letter 244, n. 1.
³ At least 3 of the papers bore out Bruckner's misgivings. Hanslick called the music "unnatural, bloated, sickly, and harmful"; Max Kalbeck, Brahms's biographer, called it an "extempore comedy"; & the critic of the *Wiener Allgemeine Zeitung* declared, "Bruckner composes like a drunkard."

Letter 267
(For Verdi's dates see Letter 175.)—Faccio (1840–91) was the highly capable conductor to whom Verdi had entrusted the 1st performance of *Otello* (the event, which took place on 7 Feb. of the following year, attracted international attention).
¹ Romilda Pantaleoni (1847–1917), operatic soprano; she created the part of Desdemona.

² Ricordi (cf. Letter 233, n. 1).

³ Verdi's wife (cf. Letter 180, n. 2).

Letters 268A–B

(For Dvořák's & Tchaikovsky's dates see Letters 241 & 252 respectively.)—
In 1888 Tchaikovsky began touring Europe as a conductor of his own
works. He visited Prague in Feb. of that year, when he & Dvořák met &
became good friends; he returned there in Nov. & conducted *Eugene
Onyegin* at the National Theater.

¹ Cf. Letter 237, n. 1.

² Jan V. Hřímalý (1844–1915), a Czech violinist, taught at the Moscow
Conservatory.

³ Adolf Patera (1836–1912) was librarian of the Czech Museum in
Prague.

⁴ Dvořák accepted the invitation & went to Russia the following year,
conducting at 2 concerts organized by Tchaikovsky.

⁵ For Bendl see comments to Letter 247. Zdenko Fibich (1850–1900) was
a very prolific composer.

Letter 269

(For Verdi's dates see Letter 175.)—Soffredini (1854–1923), composer
& teacher, wrote for the *Gazzetta Musicale,* of which he later became the
editor.—Since the previous Nov. everybody knew that the veteran master
who had amazed the world with *Otello* (cf. comments to Letter 267) was
at work on *Falstaff,* a comic opera. But Verdi, now 77, steadfastly refused
to divulge any information on the progress he was making.

Letter 270

(For Verdi's dates see Letter 175.)—Boito (1842–1918), poet, composer,
& the extraordinary librettist of *Otello* & *Falstaff,* was also Verdi's chief
moral support during the composition of the latter work. Working slowly
& only when in the right mood (cf. the 2nd paragraph of the present
letter), Verdi was by now well on with the creation of his last opera; the
music was finished in another month, but the scoring took him another
year.

¹ *Pancione,* the nickname Boito & Verdi had given to their new hero.

² Strepponi (Verdi's sister-in-law).

³ Verdi's wife (cf. Letter 180, n. 2).

Letters 271A–B

BÜLOW: b. Dresden, 1830; d. Cairo, 1894. Bülow's compositions are considered negligible; his fame rests on his great artistry as a pianist & con-

ductor, his invaluable efforts in behalf of new music (especially Wagner's, but later also Brahms's), & his caustic wit.—For Verdi's dates see Letter 175.—In the past, Bülow had called Verdi "the Attila of the throat"; & in 1874 he had written a particularly virulent review of the *Requiem* (this led Brahms to obtain the score, study it, & then declare, "Bülow has made an ass of himself: Verdi's *Requiem* is a work of genius").

[1] Cherubini, Rossini, Donizetti, & Bellini were presumably the other 4.

[2] Probably a mistaken reading in the published source.

[3] "No human quality is more intolerable in ordinary life, indeed less tolerated, than intolerance" (*Pensieri*, xxxvii). A relatively unknown passage, but then Bülow was a highly educated man.

[4] "To each his own."

Letter 272

PUCCINI: b. Lucca, 1858; d. Brussels, 1924. After *Le Villi*, as it was later renamed (cf. Letter 262, n. 2), Puccini had been only moderately successful with his 2nd opera, *Edgar* (1889). It was his 3rd, *Manon Lescaut* (Turin, 1 Feb. 1893), that really launched him on his career. Even before the latter was produced, the composer had decided to base his next work on *Scènes de la vie de Bohème*, a novel by Henri Murger (1822–61). This led to a rupture with his friend Ruggiero Leoncavallo (1858–1919) who, after the brilliant success of *I Pagliacci* (1892), was himself about to write a *Bohème*.

[1] Puccini's opera was ready sooner (1 Feb. 1896), & it cast Leoncavallo's *Bohème* (6 May 1897) into the shade.

Letter 273

(For Debussy's dates see Letter 264.)—Chausson (1855–99), the well-known composer, & Debussy had recently become very good friends.— The composition of *Pelléas et Mélisande* occupied Debussy intermittently from 1892 to 1902. Cf. LockD, chap. vi. Here he describes a visit to Maurice Maeterlinck (1862–1949), the author of the original play, whose permission was needed if *Pelléas* was to be set to music.

[1] Louÿs (1870–1925) was for a time one of Debussy's most intimate friends.

[2] Eugène Ysaÿe (1858–1931), the great Belgian violinist.

[3] I.e., the fragments composed up to then.

[4] *Le Voyage d'Urien*, one of Gide's earliest works, had just been published.

Letter 274

(For Brahms's dates see Letter 188.)—For Clara Schumann see Letter 162, n. 7.

[1] Eugenie Schumann (1851–1938) was Robert's & Clara's 2nd youngest child.

[2] *49 deutsche Volkslieder,* arranged for solo voice & piano (the last 7 for solo voice & chorus).

[3] "Verstohlen geht der Mond auf," placed last in the folk song collection, is also featured in the rhapsodic slow movement of Brahms's piano sonata in C major, op. 1.

[4] And yet August Heinrich Cranz (1789–1870) is known to have published several *Phantasien* by the needy young composer, who had signed them with the pseudonym "G. W. Marks."

[5] The 2 Clarinet Sonatas, op. 120, were among the last works Brahms composed. They were only followed by the *Vier ernste Gesänge,* occasioned by Clara Schumann's last illness & death (1896), & the (posthumously published) Chorale Preludes for organ. Richard Mühlfeld (1856–1907), 1st clarinetist of the great Meiningen orchestra, also inspired Brahms to write the Clarinet Trio, op. 114, & the Clarinet Quartet, op. 115.

[6] 13 Sep.

Letter 275

(For Strauss's & Verdi's dates see Letters 258 & 175 respectively.)— Strauss's Italian is decidedly awkward, & the present translation makes no attempt to cover that fact. See also Letters 271A–B.

[1] Strauss had written his own libretto for this work (composed in 1892 & performed, unsuccessfully, in 1894).

[2] Bülow had given Strauss his start by making him his assistant conductor (later, his successor) at Meiningen & by performing his early compositions. The great pianist & conductor had gone to Egypt, hoping to recover from a lung disease, but had died soon after arriving there, in Feb. 1894.

Letter 276

(For Mahler's dates see Letter 263.)—Marschalk (1863–1940), at the time music critic of the *Vossische Zeitung,* had drafted a commentary on Mahler's Symphony no. 1, in D ("The Titan," 1st performed in 1889).

[1] No. 2, the "Resurrection" Symphony, 1st performed the previous Dec.

² Mahler identifies himself with the protagonist of his song cycle (cf. Letter 263).

Letter 277
WOLF: b. Windischgrätz, 1860; d. Vienna, 1903.—Rosa Mayreder was the librettist of Wolf's only completed opera, *Der Corregidor,* which had received its 1st performance on 7 June in Mannheim.

Letter 278
(For Brahms's dates see Letter 188.)—Caroline Luise Brahms, née Paasch (1825–1902), had become Johann Jacob Brahms's 2nd wife in 1866. The composer was always very fond of her & kept her well provided with news & other sustenance.—Brahms had been failing since the summer before (he had cancer of the liver). This is probably the last thing he wrote; he died 5 days later, at 9:30 in the morning.

Letter 279
(For Puccini's dates see Letter 272.)—Panichelli, obviously a priest & a good friend of the composer's, is not further identified in the biographies.
¹ Finale of Act I (the baritone, of course, is Scarpia).
² In the end Puccini settled upon a versicle from the Ordinary of the Mass, followed immediately by the antiphon to Ps. cxii (& the short Latin text in the published score contains 2 misprints besides).

Letter 280
BARTÓK: b. Nagyszentmiklós (Transylvania), 1881; d. New York, 1945.—Bartók's mother, Paula, née Voit (1857–1939), had been widowed in 1888.—Bartók, whose family had now settled in Pozsony (Bratislava), had just begun his studies at the Royal Academy of Music in Budapest.
¹ A friend of the family (she was the directress of a girls' school in Pozsony).
² Bartók was enrolled as a scholarship student.
³ István Thomán (1862–1941), a well-known pianist, was Bartók's piano teacher at the Academy.
⁴ Ferenc Xavér Szabó (1848–1911) taught score reading & orchestration.
⁵ Pastries filled with nuts or poppy seeds.
⁶ Bartók's sister (1885–1955).
⁷ János Koessler (1853–1926), composer & teacher of composition at the Academy.

Letter 281

See comments to Letter 270.—After *Falstaff*, Verdi still composed the beautiful *Te Deum* (1895–96) & *Stabat Mater* (1896–97) which, with 2 earlier works, were published as the *Quattro pezzi sacri*. These were his last works. During the remaining years Verdi, now a widower, gradually declined in strength. He died less than 3 months after writing this last letter to Boito.

Letter 282

RAVEL: b. Ciboure (Basses-Pyrénées), 1875; d. Paris, 1937.—Schmitt (1870–1958), the distinguished composer, was spending his 1st year at the Villa Medici, having won the previous year's *prix de Rome* (cf. Letters 173, 174, etc.).—Ravel himself was preparing to compete, & he won the 2nd prize later that year (he was never awarded the 1st, though he competed several times). By now he had written the famous *Pavane pour une Infante défunte* (whose popularity was eventually to irritate him) & this year composed his 1st significant work, *Jeux d'eau*.

[1] Raoul Bardac (d. 1950), a composer & Ravel's fellow pupil in Fauré's class at the Conservatoire. His mother was soon to become Debussy's 2nd wife.

[2] *La Damoiselle élue* had been Debussy's *envoi* (cf. Letter 219, n. 3) in 1888. *Impressions d'Italie* was sent in by a later prize-winner, Gustave Charpentier (1860–1956); the composer of the fabulously successful opera *Louise* (1900) does not seem to have inspired Ravel with reverence.

Letter 283

(For Puccini's dates see Letter 272.)—For Ricordi see Letter 233, n. 1.—From early in 1902 to the end of 1903 Puccini was engaged in composing *Madama Butterfly*.

Letter 284

PROKOFIEV: b. Sontsovka, 1891; d. Moscow, 1953.—His father, Sergei Alexeyevich (1846–1910), managed the great estate of the Sontsov family.—Prokofiev's 1st teacher had been his mother, Maria Grigoryevna, née Zhitkova (1856–1924); from 1902, he had studied with Reinhold Moritsevich Glière (1875–1956). Now the 13-year-old composer was about to enter the St. Petersburg Conservatory; in this letter he describes his entrance examination.

[1] Alexander Konstantinovich Glazunov (1865–1936) was a member of the Conservatory's faculty; the following year he became the director.

² Cf. Letter 237, n. 2. As professor of composition & orchestration, R. K. trained a host of eminent composers, from Glazunov himself to Stravinsky.
³ Chernov (b. 1879), a composer who had given Prokofiev some harmony & counterpoint lessons before he entered the Conservatory.

Letter 285
(For Ravel's dates see Letter 282.)—Delage (1879–1961) was a pupil & intimate friend of Ravel.—In the summer of 1905 Ravel was a guest aboard the luxurious yacht owned by Alfred-Charles Edwards, proprietor of *Le Matin*, the Paris daily.
¹ See comments to Letter 290.

Letter 286
(For Debussy's dates see Letter 264.)—Durand (1865–1928) & his father Marie-Auguste (1830–1909) headed the famous Parisian music publishing house.
¹ Debussy had spent the summer at Eastbourne.
² The *Images* for orchestra were originally conceived for 2 pianos.
³ Debussy never finished the incidental music to the play.—Édouard Colonne (1838–1910) was the founder & conductor of the famous Concerts Colonne.
⁴ Mrs. Richard J. Hall, a patron of the Boston Symphony Orchestra who had learned to play the saxophone for reasons of health, had commissioned Debussy to write a work for that instrument in 1895. Disliking commissions, & even more what he called "this aquatic instrument," he at last sent her an unfinished *Rapsodie* in 1911.
⁵ For piano, 1st series.
⁶ Camille Chevillard (1859–1923), conductor of the Concerts Lamoureux, gave the 1st performance of *La Mer* later that year.

Letter 287
See comments to Letter 280.—In the spring of 1906, Bartók went on a concert tour of Spain & Portugal; he shared some of the concerts with Ferenc Vecsey (1893–1935), a young violinist who at the time was being exhibited by his father as a prodigy (see also Letter 320).
¹ Lajos Vecsey, the boy's father & 1st teacher.
² Passages in this letter are missing in the source & were supplied by the present editor from the German edition [= Letter 316], pp. 228–29.

Letter 288
(For Bartók's dates see Letter 280.)—Stefi Geyer (1888–1956), then only 19, was already a well-known violinist.—This letter was written
579

during one of Bartók's numerous field trips as an ethnomusicologist; he himself is the tireless Traveler in the dialogue.
[1] It was a recent hit song.

Letter 289
See comments to Letter 284.
[1] Cf. Letter 237, n. 1.
[2] Cf. Letter 284, n. 3.
[3] In an earlier letter, Prokofiev refers to it as his 4th sonata; however, it antedates the 1st published sonata.
[4] The composer Anatol Konstantinovich Lyadov (1855–1914) taught theory & harmony at the St. Petersburg Conservatory.

Letter 290
(For Ravel's dates see Letter 282.)—Ida & Cyprien ("Cipa") Godebski were among Ravel's closest friends. Their Sunday evenings were attended by the leading artists & writers of the day, such as Toulouse-Lautrec (who painted Godebski's portrait), Cocteau, Gide, Valéry, de Falla, Stravinsky, Diaghilev, & Nijinsky. At the time of this letter, the Godebskis were taking a holiday in Spain, while Ravel stayed at La Grangette, their country home, with their 2 children—Marie ("Mimi") & Jean—& "Miss," the English governess. It was during this visit, & under the spell of his friends' children, that he composed *Ma Mère l'Oye* ("Mother Goose," 5 easy pieces for piano duet).
[1] The poet had died in 1898 & his villa, which was next door, was now occupied by his daughter & son-in-law.
[2] A reference to *Voyelles*, the sonnet in which Rimbaud ascribes a different color to each of the vowels.
[3] "I kiss Misia's feet." Misia, Cyprien's sister, was married to A.-C. Edwards (cf. comments to Letter 285).

Letter 291
(For Mahler's dates see Letter 263.)—Walter (1876–1962) had been Mahler's assistant at the Vienna Opera; he remained there until 1914.— Mahler had accepted an appointment as principal conductor of the Metropolitan Opera in 1908. The following year he also undertook to lead the New York Philharmonic Orchestra, beginning that autumn.
[1] In the summer of 1907 Mahler had been told he was suffering from heart disease.
[2] Siegfried Lipiner, dramatist & librettist, was a close friend of Mahler's.

Letters 292A–B

(For Strauss's dates see Letter 258.)—Hofmannsthal (1874–1929) & Strauss had recently completed their 1st joint effort, the opera *Elektra,* which had been produced on 25 Jan. of that year. At the beginning of Feb., Hofmannsthal drafted the scenario for a new work & Strauss accepted the idea with enthusiasm. From then until Sep. 1910 poet & musician kept up a fruitful correspondence as they worked on what became perhaps their most successful opera. *Der Rosenkavalier* was given for the 1st time on 26 Jan. 1911, in Dresden.

[1] *Sie sind ein Prachtkerl.*

[2] Act II of *Der Rosenkavalier* follows Strauss's outline quite faithfully.

Letter 293

SCHOENBERG: b. Vienna, 1874; d. Los Angeles, 1951.—Hertzka (1869–1932), the director of Universal Edition (Vienna), published the works of Schoenberg & his disciples & was one of the early champions of their music.

[1] *Wiener Tonkünstler-Verein* (Viennese Composers' Association).

[2] For Berg's dates see Letter 298.

[3] Erwin Stein (1885–1958) later became an editor for Universal Edition; after the *Anschluss* he transferred to Boosey & Hawkes in London.

Letter 294

(For Debussy's dates see Letter 264.)—Jean-Aubry (1882–1949) wrote many books & articles on musical subjects; he later settled in London, where he effectively furthered the cause of the French Impressionist composers.

[1] Debussy's famous orchestral work was based on the homonymous poem by Mallarmé.

[2] I.e., about 1892–94, the period during which Debussy was working on the piece.

[3] Marie-François-Sadi Carnot (1837–94) was President of France from 1887 to 1894. It is fairly safe to assume that the man on the wallpaper only *looked* like him.

[4] "Sylvan creature, if your flute succeeded at the first breath, listen to all the light Debussy is about to breathe into it."

Letter 295

WEBERN: b. Vienna, 1883; d. Mittersill, 1945.—For Berg's dates see Letter 298.

[1] Schoenberg's textbook had been published that year.

581

[2] Heinrich Jalowetz (b. 1882), conductor & writer, was a pupil of Schoenberg.

[3] Vassily Kandinsky (1866–1944), the nonobjective painter.

Letter 296

(For Debussy's dates see Letter 264.)—Stravinsky: b. 1882.

[1] *Petrushka*'s 1st performance had taken place on 13 Jun. 1911 in Paris.

Letter 297

(For Puccini's dates see Letter 272.)—D'Annunzio (1863–1938) & Puccini thought of collaborating on an opera more than once, but nothing ever came of it.

Letter 298

BERG: b. Vienna, 1885; d. there, 1935.—Hohenberg (1885–1956) & the composer were old schoolmates & remained intimate friends afterwards. Berg set several of Hohenberg's poems to music, though only *Sommertage* (from *7 frühe Lieder*) has so far been published.

[1] The lieder to poems by Mombert had been published in 1910 as op. 2, nos. 2–4. *Pierrot lunaire* had just been produced in Berlin (on 16 Oct.), arousing a storm of invective in the press.

Letter 299

(For Ravel's & Stravinsky's dates see Letters 282 & 296 respectively.)— When this letter was written, the 1st World War was in its 2nd month.

[1] Ravel's older brother; he was an engineer, like their father.

[2] *La Cloche engloutie* was to have been an opera based on Gerhart Hauptmann's *Die versunkene Glocke*, but the project was never realized; *Wien*, however, was resumed & completed after the war, receiving the more "seasonable" title of *La Valse*.

Letter 300

See comments to Letter 298.—Berg was now at an Austrian army training center, while Hohenberg was already at the front as a lieutenant in the infantry.

[1] Schoenberg had been teaching at the Sternsche Conservatorium in Berlin.

[2] *Die Fackel* was a Viennese literary & political periodical edited & largely written by Karl Kraus (1874–1936), a brilliant, if vitriolic, critic.

[3] The famous expressionist painter (b. 1886).

[4] Berg's brother.

[5] Mrs. Alban Berg.

582

Letter 301
(For Bartók's dates see Letter 280.)

Letter 302
See comments to Letter 286.
[1] Debussy had been operated on for cancer the year before.
[2] In *Pelléas et Mélisande*.

Letter 303
(For Webern's & Berg's dates see Letters 295 & 298 respectively.)
[1] Berg's opera was finished in 1920 & fully orchestrated in 1921; but it was not performed in its entirety until 14 Dec. 1925 (Berlin, Staatsoper).
[2] Eventually there were 6 (op. 14).
[3] The territory of Klagenfurt had been claimed by Yugoslavia after the war; a plebiscite returned it to Austria.

Letter 304
(For Prokofiev's & Stravinsky's dates see Letters 284 & 296 respectively.)
—Prokofiev had reached the U.S. by way of Siberia & Japan, playing as he went. He left for Paris in 1920, but returned to America several times in later years.
[1] Songs for voice with 8 instruments (composed in 1914).
[2] Michel Fokine (1880–1942), the great dancer & choreographer.
[3] By Stravinsky: 3 songs for soprano, 2 flutes, 2 clarinets, piano, & string quartet (composed in 1912–13).

Letter 305
(For Schoenberg's dates see Letter 293.)

Letter 306
(For Puccini's dates see Letter 272.)—Simoni (1875–1952) collaborated with Giuseppe Adami (1878–1946) in writing the libretto of *Turandot*, Puccini's last, unfinished opera.
[1] Tito Ricordi (1865–1933) was now the head of the firm.
[2] Enrico Pea (1881–1958), Italian poet.

Letter 307
See comments to Letter 280. Bartók's aunt, Irma Voit (1849–1941), lived with his mother.

583

[1] Košice (formerly Kassa in Hungary) was now in the newly created republic of Czechoslovakia.
[2] Imre Waldbauer (1892–1952) was a well-known violinist with whom Bartók often gave recitals.

Letter 308
(For Schoenberg's dates see Letter 293.)—Hauer (1883–1959), an Austrian composer, had evolved a system of "tropes" somewhat similar to Schoenberg's "composition with 12 notes."
[1] The book did not materialize.
[2] Schoenberg & Hauer did not pursue the idea any further.

Letter 309
See comments to Letters 280 & 307.—Bartók made his 1st tour of the U.S. at the end of 1927; it lasted 2 months, during which he traveled from coast to coast, presenting his own works.
[1] The letterhead has a picture of the Olympic Hotel. Bartók has drawn an arrow pointing to it & comments: "Here's where I stayed, on the 11th floor. Four elevators are in constant use. The stairs are nowhere to be seen."
[2] Emil Oláh Tóth (d. 1955), Bartók's brother-in-law.

Letters 310A–C
(For Ravel's dates see Letter 282.)—For Édouard Ravel, cf. Letter 299, n. 1.—Ravel was touring the U.S. & Canada at about the same time as Bartók (cf. Letter 309): he was in America from Jan. to Apr. 1928. This was his only visit.
[1] A redolent solution of sodium hypochlorite (used in bleaching).

Letters 311A–B
(For Schoenberg's & Berg's dates see Letters 293 & 298 respectively.)
[1] By Frank Wedekind (1864–1918). Berg was preparing the text of his opera Lulu on the basis of those plays.
[2] Moses-Socrates-Christ, fragments of an unfinished trilogy.

Letter 312
(For Ravel's dates see Letter 282.)—Toscanini: b. Parma, 1867; d. New York, 1957.—In the spring, Toscanini had taken the New York Philharmonic-Symphony Orchestra to Europe for a memorable tour. The opening concert took place at the Paris Opéra on 4 May, & one of the pieces on the program was Ravel's Boléro. The Ravel biographies go on to say that the Maestro played the work much too fast & that, when

challenged by the irate composer, he retorted that his tempo had saved the music from failure. At least 1 Toscanini biography has the story in quite a different version: the Maestro had played the piece in Ravel's own tempo, & the composer had been unable to recognize it as being correct. As usual, the angry accusations stem from the partisans, not the principals. Ravel did disagree with the tempo; "but," as he wrote to a friend on 6 May 1930, "he's a marvelous virtuoso all the same, as marvelous as his orchestra" (source: [= Letter 282], 244).

Letter 313
(For Schoenberg's & Berg's dates see Letters 293 & 298 respectively.)
[1] *Der Wein,* concert aria for soprano & orchestra.

Letter 314
See comments to Letters 280 & 307.—Bartók spent the summer of 1931 teaching at the Austro-American Conservatory at Mondsee, Upper Austria. But first he attended a folk art congress held under the auspices of the League of Nations in Geneva.
[1] On 14 May, Toscanini had been attacked by Fascist hoodlums for refusing to perform the party song at a concert in Bologna. The incident had had wide repercussions abroad, & a motion was circulated among the participants at the folk art congress to protest the brutality.
[2] Karel Čapek (1890–1938), the Czech author, & Murray (1866–1957), the classical scholar.
[3] Gheorghe Oprescu (b. 1881) is an art historian; Ugo Ojetti (1871–1946) was indeed a journalist, but also a respected author; Henri Focillon (1881–1943) was a very distinguished art historian; & Gonzague de Reynold (b. 1880) was at the time professor of French literature at Fribourg.
[4] "Pros & cons" (G.).
[5] John Masefield.
[6] 1873–1942; her psychological novels deal with the problems of middle-class women.
[7] Paul Weingarten (1886–1948), Austrian pianist.
[8] Mrs. Béla Bartók.

Letter 315
(For Berg's & Schoenberg's dates see Letters 298 & 293 respectively.)— Schoenberg had emigrated to the U.S. after the Nazis had dismissed him from his position as professor at the Prussian Academy of the Arts in Berlin. In 1935 he was professor of music at the University of Southern California.

[1] Schoenberg's birthday.
[2] The opera remained unfinished; the 1st 2 acts were presented in Zurich in 1957.
[3] For Stein, cf. Letter 293, n. 2.
[4] Probably an allusion to the growing Nazi menace in Austria.
[5] Berg died less than 4 months later as a result of the carbuncle mentioned in this letter.

Letter 316

(For Bartók's dates see Letter 280.)—Mrs. Müller-Widmann belonged to a circle of friends in Basel with whom Bartók was in frequent contact during the 1930s.
[1] Hitler had annexed Austria on 11 March.
[2] The Austrian society of authors, composers, & music publishers.
[3] Zoltán Kodály (1882–1967), Bartók's great friend & colleague.
[4] Ralph Hawkes, of Boosey & Hawkes (London), had got in touch with Bartók & Kodály, who soon afterwards made over the publishing rights to all their works to the English firm.
[5] *Twenty-seven Choruses.*
[6] Walter Schulthess (b. 1894), the Swiss conductor-composer; he was married to Stefi Geyer (cf. comments to Letter 288).
[7] The Nazi society for the protection of musical copyrights.
[8] Paul Sacher (b. 1906), the conductor of the Basler Kammerorchester.

Letter 317

(For Webern's dates see Letter 295.)—Dr. Reich (b. 1898), the well-known Viennese musicologist, had emigrated to Switzerland at the time of the *Anschluss*. A pupil of Berg & Webern, he had championed their music as editor of the periodical *23—Eine Wiener Musikzeitschrift* & is today a leading authority on the history & music of the Schoenberg school.—It must be remembered that this letter was written with the knowledge that it would probably be opened by the Nazi censor. Of special interest in it are the unmistakable signs of Webern's wish to emigrate—a wish that was not to be realized.
[1] Erich Schmid (b. 1907), Swiss composer & conductor, had studied with Schoenberg in Berlin. Webern's *Passacaglia* for orchestra, op. 1, was composed in 1908.
[2] Reinhard (1884–1951) was the director of the Musikkollegium in Winterthur, Switzerland. Under his leadership, & with Hermann Scherchen (1891–1966) as its regular conductor, the organization became famous for its performances of contemporary music.

[3] The International Society for Contemporary Music.
[4] Erwin Stein (cf. Letter 293, n. 2) had written an article on Webern in *Tempo,* the British periodical devoted to contemporary music.
[5] It was the piano score of *Das Schloss Dürande,* an opera by the Swiss composer Othmar Schoeck (1886–1957).
[6] No. 1, for soprano solo, mixed choir, & orchestra, op. 29.

Letter 318
(For Bartók's dates see Letter 280.)—As a result of his political convictions (cf. Letter 316), & at a great personal sacrifice, Bartók had left Hungary. Accompanied by his wife Ditta, he reached New York on 29 Oct. 1940. His sons remained behind (Peter Bartók was finally able to join his parents in Apr. 1942).
[1] Cf. comments to Letter 307.
[2] Cf. Letter 280, n. 6.
[3] "Mr." (in Czech & Slovak).
[4] At a special convocation, Columbia University had awarded Bartók an honorary doctorate in music. Other recipients of degrees on that occasion were Sir Cecil Thomas Carr, the English barrister, Paul Hazard of the Académie française, & Dr. Karl T. Compton, president of M.I.T.

Letter 319
(For Schoenberg's dates see Letter 293.)—For Stein see Letter 293, n. 2.—Schoenberg's English spelling has been faithfully reproduced (& the editorial *sic* dispensed with) in this letter.
[1] See comments to Letter 323.
[2] Cf. comments to Letter 315. After a year at the University of Southern California, Schoenberg had accepted a professorship at the University of California in Los Angeles.
[3] Both remained unfinished.
[4] None of these textbooks has been published.
[5] Edward J. Dent (1876–1957), the English musicologist.

Letter 320
(For Bartók's dates see Letter 280.)—Szigeti (b. 1892), the celebrated violinist, was an old friend of the composer's.—Early in 1943, Bartók's health had broken down completely; though he did not know it, he was suffering from leukemia & was to enjoy only partial remissions during the remaining 2 years of his life. Now he was spending the winter alone in North Carolina, where he had been sent under the auspices of the American Society of Composers, Authors, & Publishers.

[1] The 1st performance had taken place in Amsterdam in 1939, with the Hungarian violinist Zoltán Székely (b. 1903) as the soloist. Bartók had not been present.

[2] Eugene Ormandy (b. 1899), the conductor of the Philadelphia Orchestra.

[3] Bartók had heard the work for the 1st time the previous Oct., in New York.

[4] The work was the *Concerto for Orchestra*; it had been commissioned by Serge Koussevitzky (1874–1951) in May 1943.

[5] The 1st performance took place in Boston on 1 Dec. (cf. Letter 321).

[6] "Black on white" (G.).

[7] An American would more probably say, "Variety is the spice of life."

[8] See Letter 287.

[9] Dorothy Parrish had taken piano lessons with Bartók in Budapest.

Letter 321

(For Bartók's dates see Letter 280.)—Mrs. Creel (now Mrs. Harold Driver) is a pianist & Oriental linguist who studied with Bartók in Budapest. She taught at Washington University, Seattle, during 1940–50.

[1] Cf. Letter 320, n. 9.

[2] The *Concerto for Orchestra* (cf. Letter 320, n. 4).

[3] It was the text of the *Cantata profana*.

[4] *Winter Tales.*

[5] Bartók had received the *Four Quartets.*

[6] Cf. comments to Letter 318.

[7] Prof. Carl Paige Wood (1885–1947) was chairman of the Music Department at the University of Washington; it was at his suggestion that Bartók had been invited to Seattle in 1928 (cf. Letter 309).

Letter 322

(For Schoenberg's dates see Letter 293.)—Keller (b. 1919), a native of Vienna, emigrated to England in 1938, where he has become a leading music critic & musicologist.

[1] *Style and Idea* (New York, 1950).

Letter 323

(For Schoenberg's dates see Letter 293.)—Rankl (b. 1898), the composer & conductor, was a pupil of Schoenberg & Webern.—Schoenberg wrote this letter 16 days before he died.

[1] Schoenberg did not finish the 1st part.

[2] Cf. Letter 317, n. 2.

ALPHABETICAL LIST OF THE COMPOSERS AND THEIR LETTERS

(Note: the figures refer to letter-numbers, not pages.)

C. P. E. BACH: 80, 81, 99

J. C. BACH: 72

J. S. BACH: 48, 52, 57, 58, 59, 65, 66

BARTÓK: 280, 287, 288, 301, 307, 309, 314, 316, 318, 320, 321.

BASSANI: 49

BEETHOVEN: 102, 112B, 115, 117, 120, 121, 123, 126, 128, 130, 132, 135, 137, 140, 145A–D, 149, 151, 152, 153

BELLINI: 139, 168

BERG: 298, 300, 311B, 315

BERLIOZ: 138, 146, 160, 173, 178B, 181, 191, 196, 198, 199, 215, 216, 218, 222C, 228, 230, 232

BIZET: 219, 240

BOCCHERINI: 74

BRAHMS: 188, 209B, 213A, 217A, 220, 227, 229, 245B, 245D, 251B, 254, 255, 256, 261, 265, 274, 278

BRUCKNER: 244, 266

BÜLOW: 271A

BULL: 33

BUXTEHUDE: 46

BYRD: 22

CACCINI: 31

CAVALIERI: 25

CHERUBINI: 174

CHOPIN: 161, 169, 170, 177, 182, 192, 204A–B, 206

COCLICO: 14

CORELLI: 45

CZERNY: 145E

DALAYRAC: 114

DEBUSSY: 264, 273, 286, 294, 296, 302

DIETRICH: 211

DONIZETTI: 183, 190, 194

DOWLAND: 28

DUFAY: 6

DVOŘÁK: 241, 251A, 268A

FRANCHOMME: 170

FREDERICK THE GREAT: 69

GAFORI: 9

GALILEI: 23

GLUCK: 79, 84, 86, 89, 91, 93, 96

GOMBERT: 13

GOSSEC: 113

GOUNOD: 223

GRÉTRY: 98, 111

HANDEL: 51, 53, 56, 61, 62, 64A–E, 71

HAYDN: 75, 76, 85, 103, 104, 105, 108, 110, 112A, 116, 118, 122, 125

HOFFMANN: 127

HOFHAIMER: 10

JOACHIM: 217B

JOHN OF ARAGON: 4

LANDINI: 3

LASSUS: 18, 19, 21

H. LAWES: 39

LISZT: 159, 170, 184B, 203B, 222A, 243

LOCKE: 43

LULLY: 41, 42

LUTHER: 11

MACHAULT: 1, 2

MAHLER: 263, 276, 291

589

MARCELLO: 50
JOH. MARTINI: 8
MENDELSSOHN: 141, 165, 184A, 189, 200, 201
MONTE: 24, 26
MONTEVERDI: 30, 32, 34, 37, 38
MOZART: 77, 78, 82, 87, 88, 90, 92, 94, 95, 97, 100, 101, 106, 107, 109
MUSSORGSKY: 237, 238, 242, 248
PAËR: 144, 167
PAGANINI: 155, 178A
PAISIELLO: 119
PALESTRINA: 16, 17, 20
PROKOFIEV: 284, 289, 304
PUCCINI: 272, 279, 283, 297, 306
T. PURCELL: 44
RAMEAU: 54, 63, 70
RAVEL: 282, 285, 290, 299, 310A–C, 312
ROSSINI: 210, 231
ROUSSEAU: 68, 83
A. SCARLATTI: 47
D. SCARLATTI: 67
SCHEIDT: 36
SCHOENBERG: 293, 305, 308, 311A, 313, 319, 322, 323
F. A. SCHUBERT: 136
SCHUBERT: 129, 133, 143, 147, 148, 150, 154, 157, 158

SCHÜTZ: 35, 40
SCHUMANN: 156A, 162, 163, 166, 171, 172, 176, 179, 185, 197, 209A, 213B
SMETANA: 203A, 247
SQUARCIALUPI: 5, 7
R. STRAUSS: 258, 275, 292A–B
TALLIS: 22
TARTINI: 73
TCHAIKOVSKY: 252, 268B
TELEMANN: 55
TROMBONCINO: 12
VERDI: 175, 180, 195, 202, 207, 208, 221, 225, 226, 233, 235, 236, 246, 250, 257, 260, 262, 267, 269, 270, 271B, 281
VIADANA: 27
VICTORIA: 29
VIOLA: 15
VIVALDI: 60
WAGNER: 164, 186, 187, 193, 205, 212, 214, 222B, 224, 234, 239, 245A, 245C, 249, 253, 259
WEBER: 131, 142
WEBERN: 295, 303, 317
WESLEY: 134
WIEDEBEIN: 156B
WOLF: 277
ZELTER: 124

INDEX

CAPITALS identify the composers whose letters appear in the text and should, in each case, be taken as a cross-reference to the Alphabetical List (pp. 589–90), which is not duplicated here. Asterisks identify the recipients, and the form "X to" (e.g., "Mozart to") after their names is an abbreviation for "letter of X to" ("letter of Mozart to"). SMALL CAPITALS are used for some of the main subject headings. Page-numbers in parentheses refer to passages where the entry is discussed but not mentioned by name. Page-numbers in *italics* refer to the comments and notes. Place-names appearing in date lines and addresses are not listed unless they have topical significance or recur often in the text.

Abbreviations, list of, *475*
Accademia Filarmonica (Bologna), *489, 490;* Marcello's test piece for admission to, 61–63; Mozart, a member of, 118
Achillini, Claudio, 376, *572*
Acoustics: Cavalieri's experiments with microtones, 25; Bach's command of practical, 104–105, 107
Adam, Adolphe-Charles, 259, *542*

Le Chalet, 259

Adami, Giuseppe, 436, *583*
ADVICE: Rameau's, on writing a 1st opera, 80–81; Gluck's to a young musician, 138; Beethoven's, to Czerny, on teaching the piano, 188; Wiedebein's, to the young Schumann, 215–16; Verdi's, to an impecunious impresario, 319–20; Berlioz's, to a musician in New York, 330–31; Wagner's, on playing Beckmesser in *Die Meistersinger*, 345; Brahms's, to a young composer, 368, & to Schumann's daughter on learning to transpose, 390; *see also* Teachers, composers as
Agricola, Johann Friedrich, 106, 108, *499*
Albert, Archduke, & Isabel, (35), *485*
Albert of Saxe-Coburg-Gotha, the Prince Consort, *546;* Mendelssohn visits Queen Victoria &, 268–70.
Allgemeine musikalische Zeitung, 177, 226, (249), *537, 539*
Altnickol, Johann Christoph, 85, 108, *495, 499*
*Andersen, Hans Christian, *548–49;* Schumann to, 278
André, Johann, *501, 505*

Belmonte und Constanze, *505*
Erwin und Elmire, songs from, *501*

Andrea del Sarto, 315
*Antwerp, the mayor & aldermen of, Bull to, 35–36

*Appiani, Giuseppina, *547;* Donizetti to, 274–75
Arensky, Anton Stepanovich, 403
*Arnaud, Abbé François, (113), 123, *500, 503;* Gluck to, 131–32
Arnim, Achim von, *516;* his wife Bettina, (313), *556–57*
*Arnim, Gisela von, *556;* Joachim to, 313
Arnold, Denis, *475, 484, 486*
*Arrivabene, Count Opprandino, *559;* Verdi to, 325–27, 337, 353, 369–70, 376
*Artaria & Co., *508, 509, 520;* Haydn to, 147
"Atonality," 440
Auber, Daniel-François-Esprit, 257, *542, 560*

Le Lac des Fées, (257), *542*
La Muette de Portici, *542, 548*

Auernhammer, Josephine, 137, *505–506*
Augsburg, 146, *502, 503, 508;* Mozart in, 120–23
Austria: French Revolutionary War against, *511;* Beethoven on Austrian revolutionary impulses, 161; Schubert's summer journey in Upper, 203–205; Venice under, *552;* the war of 1866, (332), *561;* Schoenberg on Austrian musicians in the 20th century, 438; Bartók gives a summer course in, 453, *585;* the Nazi threat & the *Anschluss*, 455–61 *pass., 586; see also* individual cities
AUTOBIOGRAPHICAL SKETCHES: Coclico, 14; Dowland, 27–31; Schütz, 46–50; Telemann, 69–70; Bach, 71–73; Vivaldi, 76–77; Rameau's operatic career in brief, 81; Haydn, 113–15; Beethoven ("Heiligenstadt Testament"), 167–69; Schubert's credentials as a student, 184–85; Schumann, 253–54, 255; Wagner, 263–64; Smetana, 284–85; R. Strauss (aged 16), 370–71
Autograph collecting: Zelter asks Goethe for some poems, 174–75, & obtains them, *516;* Paër sends the latest from Paris—a Rossini

& a Liszt, 197; a missing signature, 210, 527; Wagner sends an autograph, 301; Verdi astonished at British methods of, 326; a Wagner-Brahms correspondence prompted by the latter's, 349–52; Brahms refers to his, 380
Avocado, 441–42
Ayrton, William, 186–87, 519

BACH, Carl Philipp Emanuel, (72), 492, 499, 506; his sons, (85), 495; Telemann his godfather, 108; ranks his father above Handel as an organist, 142–43; his meeting with Burney, 507

Concerto (2 claviers?) in F maj., 106
Die Israeliten in der Wüste, 106, 499
Sonatinas (2 claviers), 106
Versuch . . . (Essay . . .), 104, 499

Bach, Elisabeth Juliana Friderica, (72), 492; her marriage, 85, 495
BACH, Johann Christian, 496

Invitatory & Dies Irae (MSS), 90, 496

Bach, Johann Christoph, 108, 499
*Bach, Johann Elias, 494; J. S. Bach to, 84–85, 85–86
BACH, Johann Sebastian, 199, 243, 302, 387, 490–96 pass., 501, 515; on his own family, 72–73, 492; C. P. E. Bach's reminiscences of, 104–108, 499, & comparison of, with Handel, 142–43; Burney's opinion of, 507; his organ playing praised by Hasse & Quantz, 142; Beethoven's esteem for, 163, 513; Wesley champions, 185–86, 519; Prof. Koessler on, 399; Berg's use of Es ist genug, 454

Inventions & Sinfonie, 104
Mass in B min., B. sends the Kyrie & Gloria of, to the Elector, (73), 493
Matthäuspassion, 522
Ein musicalisches Opfer, the fugue from, 84
Preludes, 6 short, 104
Sonatas & Partitas (solo violin), 304; "nothing more perfect" than, 105
Suites (solo 'cello), 105
Toccata in F maj., played by Brahms in Vienna, 561
Das wohltemperirte Clavier, 513

Bach, Wilhelm Friedemann, (72), 492
Bagge, Selmar, 329
Baillot, Pierre-Marie-François de Sales, 243, 536
Bakunin, Mikhail Alexandrovich, 551
Balakirev, Mili Alexeyevich, 564; Tchaikovsky on, 363–64
Ballet, 81, 109, 220; Monteverdi's dances of 1604, 32; his Nozze di Tetide, 37–38; ballet de cour, 484; Mozart's Les petits riens, (126), 504; in Gluck's Alceste at

Bologna, 131–32; a maître de ballet in the shadow of the guillotine, 159, 512; Weber attends a, in Vienna, 194–95; Debussy on Petrushka, 426
Bamberg, Hoffmann in, 177–78, 517
Banck, Carl, 250, 539
Bardac, Raoul, 400, 578
*Barnim XI, duke of Pomerania-Stettin, Coclico to, 13–15
BARTÓK, Béla, 577, 579–80, 583–88 pass.

Bear Dance, 437, 452
Cantata profana, (472), 588
27 Choruses, (458), 586
Concerto (violin), 467, 472
Concerto for Orchestra, (468), 588; B. reports on the 1st performance of, 471–72
Evening at the Szekelers, 452
5 Hungarian Folk Songs, 458
Rumanian Folk Dances, 437
Sonata (2 pianos, percussion), 458
Sonata (solo violin), B. reports on the 1st performance of, 471
Suite (orchestra) no. 1, B. objects to fragmentary performances of, 431

*Bartók, Béla (Jr.) & Peter, 587; Bartók to, 461–65
Bartók, Ditta, 453, 465, 472, 587
*Bartók, Paula, (456), 577; Bartók to, 397–99, 408–10, 437–38, 448–53
*Bartók family, Bartók to, 441–42
Barzun, Jacques, 549
Basel, 459, 586
BASSANI, Giovanni Battista, 490
Bassini, De (Achille Bassi), 325, 559
*Baudelaire, Charles, 389, 559; Wagner to, 324
Bayreuth, 70; Wagner's festival theater at, 354, 355, (562), (567); his refusal to allow performances of Parsifal elsewhere, 371; Wolzogen & the Bayreuther Blätter, 573
Beale, T. Frederick, 310, 326, 556
Beaumarchais, Pierre Augustin Caron de, 506

Le Mariage de Figaro, 140, 506

Beecke, Ignaz von, 121, 122, 503
*Beethoven, Caspar Anton Carl van, 514, 520–21; Beethoven to, 167–69
Beethoven, Karl van, 188, 520–21; his attempt at suicide, (209), 527
BEETHOVEN, Ludwig van, 233, 256, 302, 305, 380, 389, 467, 503, 508, 511–28 pass., 534, 535, 543, 548, 556, 560, 571–72; Haydn intervenes in behalf of, 157–58; on Bach, 163; on having to be a businessman, 164; the "Heiligenstadt Testament," 167–69, 514; Zelter on, 174, 516; Goethe on, 518, & B. on Goethe, 179; on teaching the piano, 188; Boucher's meeting with, 193; Weber's meeting with, 194; Czerny on the

concert given by, in 1824, 199–200; a fit of temper, 206–207; Berlioz a worthy successor of, 252; Tchaikovsky on, in France, 364; Webern on Kant &, 425–26

Canon on "Tobias Haslinger," WoO 182, 191

Cantatas, WoO 87 & 88, Brahms identifies & describes, 373–75, 571–72

Christus am Ölberge, B. offers, to Härtel, (170), 514

Concerto (piano) no. 2, 163, 513; "not one of my best," 164

Concerto (piano) no. 5, 176, 516

Concerto (violin), 467; Joachim's performance of, praised by Schumann, (304), 555

Concerto (violin, 'cello, piano), offered by B. to Härtel, 170–71, 514

Fantasie (piano, chorus, orchestra), 176, 516

Fidelio, 515, 526; B.'s exasperation over the performance of, in the 2nd version, 172; Wagner's reaction to Berlioz's article on, 321–22, 323, 558; Brahms discovers the archetype of a section in the Finale of, 374

Juvenilia, various, sent by Haydn to the Elector of Cologne, 157, 511

Mass in C maj., 178, 179, 517

Merkenstein, (180), 518

Missa Solemnis, (206), 526; 3 movements from, at their 1st Viennese performance, 196, 199, 524

Overture ("Consecration of the House"), at B.'s 1824 concert, 196, 199, 524

Overture to *Egmont*, 176

Overture to *Prometheus*, (220), 531

Partita (Wind Octet, op. 103?), 157, 162, 511

Quartet, op. 131, 527; not a compilation, 208

Quintet (piano, winds), (184), 519

Die Ruinen von Athen, 318

Septet, 163, 164, 513

Sonata (piano), op. 22, B. pleased with, 163, 513

Sonata (piano), op. 27, no. 2, 531

Sonatas (piano), op. 53, 54, 57, offered by B. to Härtel, 170–71, 514

Sonata (piano), op. 81a, 176, 516

Sonata (piano), op. 90, 524

Sonata (piano), op. 101, 520; brings Mendelssohn & the Ertmanns together, 534

Sonata (piano), op. 106, 520

Sonata ('cello, piano), op. 69, 184, 519

Symphony no. 1, 163, 164, 513

Symphony no. 3, offered by B. to Härtel, 170–71, 514

Symphony no. 5, 548

Symphony no. 9: 1st performance of, 196,

199–200, 524; Wagner offers to make a piano arrangement of, 229–30

Variations (piano), WoO 66, 162, 512

Variations (piano 4-hands), WoO 67, 161, 512

Variations (violin, 'cello, piano), 523

*Beethoven, Nikolaus Johann van, 514; Beethoven to, 167–69

Belgium, 323, 456; about to be invaded during the French Revolution, 156, 511; Debussy in, 389–90; *see also* individual cities

*Bellentani, Giuseppe, 553; Rossini to, 297–98

BELLINI, Vincenzo, 353, 521, 530, 532, 535, 575; his death, 247, 538; Verdi on the publication of his letters, 369–70, 570

  I Capuleti e i Montecchi, 239, 535

  Norma, 532, 535, 570; B. reports on the 1st performances of, 239–40

  Il Pirata, 218, 530

  La Sonnambula, 532; Chopin hears Jenny Lind in, 288, 551

*Beloselsky, Prince Alexander, 500; Rousseau to, 110–11

Benda, Franz, 108

*Bendl, Karel, 384, 566; Smetana to, 354–55

Benedict, Sir Julius, 194, 523

Bennett, William Sterndale, 254, 541, 560

*Bentivoglio d'Aragona, Marquis Guido, 493; Vivaldi to, 76–77

*BERG, Alban, 582, 584–86 pass.; Webern to, 425–26, 432–33; Schoenberg to, 444–45, 448; Schoenberg on the progress made by, as his student, 423

  Concerto (violin), B. describes, to Schoenberg, 454

  7 frühe Lieder, 582

  Lulu: B. preparing the text of, (444), 584; hopes to finish scoring, 455

  Vier Lieder, op. 2, 428, 582

  Der Wein, 585; Schoenberg on, (448)

  Wozzeck, 432, (583)

Berg, Helene, 430, 455

Berlin, 85, 106, 108, 196, 213, 234, 235, 278, 304, 372, 453, 515, 516, 523, 526, 534, 555, 582, 583, 586; Bach in, 104–105, 107; Haydn's music criticized in, 114–15; Napoleon's occupation of, 172–73; the Singakademie, 192, 522; Mendelssohn & Wagner in, 274, 547; Schoenberg dismissed by the Nazis in, 585

*BERLIOZ, Hector, 364, 521, 530, 537, 538, 540, 542, 547–49 pass., 556–62 pass., 567, 573; Paganini to, 252; decides to be a composer, 202, 525; Chopin transmits greetings from, 243; a *Davidsbündler*, 249; his charge of plagiarism refuted by Donizetti, 258–59; Mendelssohn &, 546; Wagner on,

& his letter to, 321–22; on music "in the present state of civilization," 331
Le Cinq Mai, (537); how B. found a melody for, 246
La Damnation de Faust, 530
L'Enfance du Christ, 312
Harold en Italie, 310
Huit scènes de Faust, sent to Goethe, 219, & explicated by Zelter, 530–31
Hymne à la France, 548; the public's reaction to, 277
Lélio, 312
Roméo et Juliette, 310, 540
Symphonie fantastique, 548
Symphonie funèbre et triomphale, (279), 548, 549
Te Deum, 312
Les Troyens, 559
Mémoires, 521, 525, 538, 540, 547–48; Debussy reads, 573
Voyage musical en Allemagne et Italie, 277, 548

*Berlioz, Louis-Joseph, (202), (525), 547; Berlioz to, 276–77
Berlioz, Marie. See Recio
*Berlioz, Victor-Abraham, 525; Berlioz to, 202
Bianchi, Antonia, 213, 528
Bimberl, 109
Birmingham, 571; preparations for the 1st performance of Elijah in, 282, 549
Birnbaum, Johann Abraham, 86, 495
Bismarck, Prince Otto von, 564; miscellaneous thoughts on, by Mussorgsky, 342, 344
*Bizet, Aimée Léopoldine Joséphine, 557; Bizet to, 314–17
BIZET, Georges, 557, 564–65, 573

Carmen, 557, 564–65; B. at work on, 345–46; Tchaikovsky praises, 364
Patrie, 364
Te Deum (MS), 315, 557

Blanc, Louis, 310, (556)
Blom, Eric, 475
Blow, John, 55, 488
BOCCHERINI, Luigi, 497
Böhm, Georg, 107
Bösendorfer, Ludwig, 329, 330, 561
Boieldieu, François-Adrien, 531

La Dame blanche, Chopin's improvisation on a theme from, 221

*Boito, Arrigo, 574, 578; Verdi to, 385–86, 399–400
Bologna, 30, 212, 489; Gluck's Alceste in, 131–32; the Toscanini incident in, 585; see also Accademia Filarmonica
Bonaparte. See Napoleon I
Bonn, 161, 508, 511, 512; Beethoven in,

145–46, 373; Schumann at Endenich near, 302–308, 554; his death there, 313
Bontempi, Giovanni Andrea, 51, 487
Boosey & Hawkes, 581, 586
Bordoni, Faustina, 142, 507
Borodin, Alexander Porfiryevich, 357, 567; Tchaikovsky on, 363, 364
Boston, 468, 470, 471, 472, 570, 573, 579, 588
Boucher, Alexandre-Jean, 522; his meeting with Beethoven, 193
*Brahms, Caroline Luise, 577; Brahms to, 396
Brahms, Friedrich, 329–30, 561
*Brahms, Johann Jacob, 552, 577; Schumann to, 296; Brahms to, 328–30
*Brahms, Johanna, 560; Brahms to, 328–30
*BRAHMS, Johannes, 298, 467, 517, 529, 545, 552–61 pass., 565–77 pass.; Schumann to, 307–308; Wagner to, 349–50, 351; Dvořák to, 359–60; Schumann's article on, 296, 553; at Schumann's deathbed, 313; Bruckner suspects, of conspiring against him, 348; Tchaikovsky on, 364; Wagner sends for a symphony by, 366

Balladen, op. 10, 305, 307
Concerto (piano) no. 1, 557, 558; B. plays, in Leipzig, 317–18
Concerto (violin), 467; B. seeks Joachim's advice while writing, 367, 569
49 deutsche Volkslieder, a link between, & B.'s op. 1, 390, 576
Ein deutsches Requiem, 570; B. on the metronome indications in, 369
Lieder (Sechs Gesänge), op. 3, (297), 553
Lieder (Sechs Gesänge), op. 6, 555
Marienlieder, 327, 560
Quartet (piano, strings), op. 25, performed by B. at his Vienna debut, 329, 560
Quartet (piano, strings), op. 26, performed by B. at his own recital in Vienna, 328, 561
Quintet (piano, strings), in the version for strings, 327, 560
Scherzo, op. 4, (297), 553, 555; praised by Schumann, 307
Serenade, op. 11, 329
Sonata (piano), op. 1, (297), 303, 553; a retrospective view of, 390, 576
Sonata (piano), op. 2, (297), 307, 553
Sonata (piano), op. 5, 555
Sonata (violin, piano), op. 78, B. announces the completion of, (367), 569
Sonata (violin, piano), op. 108, 437
Sonatas (clarinet, piano), 576; B.'s offhanded account of, 391
Symphony no. 1, 327, 560
Symphony no. 2, 366(?)
Triumphlied, 570

BRAHMS, Johannes (cont.)
Variations (piano), op. 24, 327; performed by B. at his own recital in Vienna, 561
See also 576
*Breitkopf & Härtel, 249, 253, 255, 256, 514, 520, 527, 553, 555, 570–71; R. Strauss to, 370–71; Wagner to the rescue of, 372; see also Härtel
Brentano, Clemens, 516, 556
Broadwood & Sons, Beethoven's piano from, (201), 525
BRUCKNER, Anton, 565–66, 571, 573
Symphony no. 2, B. suspects Brahms of "suppressing," 348
Symphony no. 3, praised by Wagner, 348
Symphony no. 4, 348
Symphony no. 7, introduced to Austria, 381–82, & reviewed in Vienna, 573
Symphony no. 8, B. at work on, 381
Bruhns, Nicolaus, 107
Brunswick, 507; Dowland at the court of Duke Henry Julius of, 28; the fair at, 143
Brussels, 320; Debussy visits Ysaÿe in, 389
Budapest, 348, 438, 473, 588; Bartók as a student in, 397–99; his dissatisfaction with musical conditions in, 431; see also Hungary
*Budapest Philharmonic Society, Bartók to the directors of, 431
*BÜLOW, Hans von, 391, 562, 574–75, 576; Verdi to, 387–88
Bukofzer, Manfred F., 475, 484
BULL, John, 485
*Bullinger, Abbé Joseph, 126, 504; Mozart to, 130–31
Bulwer, Sir Edward (later Bulwer-Lytton), 267, 545
Burckhardt, Jacob, 478
Burney, Charles, 142, 497, 500, 502; on J. S. & C. P. E. Bach, 507
An Account of the ... Commemoration of Handel, criticized by C. P. E. Bach, (142–43), 507
The Present State of Music in Germany ..., quoted, 507
*Busseto, the mayor of, 538; Verdi to, 248
BUXTEHUDE, Dietrich, 107, 489
BYRD, William, 481

Caccini, Francesca (la Cecchina), 33–34, 484
CACCINI, Giulio (24–25), 481, 482, 484
Euridice, 484
Le nuove musiche, 484
Caldara, Antonio, 108
Calderón de la Barca, Pedro, Hoffmann on the plays of, 177, 517
Calendars, Julian & Gregorian, 488, 491, 563

California: Bartók in, 441–42; Ravel in, 443
Calzabigi, Ranieri de', 102, 498
Cambert, Robert, 487
Camerata (Florence), 481, 482, 484
Canon, 480; by Purcell, 54; Marcello's use of, 62; Beethoven's Haslinger, 190–91; by Smetana, 287; Schumann's Studien für den Pedal-Flügel, (303), 554
Čapek, Karel, 449, 451, 585
Carl August, grand duke of Saxe-Weimar, (116), 501
Carnot, Marie-François-Sadi, on Debussy's wallpaper, 424, 581
Carr, Sir Cecil Thomas, (464), 587
Castelli, Ignaz Franz, 196, 523
Castrati, 484; Monteverdi auditions a contralto, 34–35; Bontempi, 51
CAVALIERI, Emilio de', 481, 482
*Cecil, Sir Robert, 483; Dowland to, 27–31
'Cellists. See Violoncellists
Cervantes Saavedra, Miguel de, 311
Chaplin, Charles, 443
Charles V, Emperor, 479
Charles V, king of France, as duke of Normandy, (2), 476
Charles X, king of France, (242), 535, 536
Charpentier, Gustave, 578
Impressions d'Italie, 400, 578
*Chausson, Ernest, 575; Debussy to, 389–90
Chénier, Marie-Joseph Blaise de, 159, 512
Chernov, Mikhail Mikhailovich, 402, 405, 415, 579
CHERUBINI, Luigi, 317, 537–38, 575; Zelter on, 174, 516
Chevillard, Camille, 408, 579
Chicago, Ravel in, 442–43
Chiemsee. See Zeil
Chitarrone, 25, 37, 482
*CHOPIN, Frédéric, 408, 531–32, 535–39 pass., 542, 546, 550–52 pass., 571; Berlioz to, 257; recommended to the authorities by Paër, 238; spends a day with Schumann, 249, 250; "black thoughts," 258, 289
Ballade in G min., C.'s & Schumann's favorite, 250, (539)
Concerto no. 2, 531
Études, op. 10, 536; played by Liszt while C. tries to write a letter, 242, 243
Impromptu in F-sharp maj., 258
Impromptu in G-flat maj., 273
Polonaise, op. 40, no. 1, 258, 542
Préludes, op. 28, 539; their completion delayed, 251
Rondo à la Krakowiak, 220, 221, 531
Variations, op. 2, 220, 221, 531; reviewed by Schumann, 537; a "sympathetic proposal," 244
*Chopin, Nicolas & Tekla-Justyna, 531; Chopin to, 220–22

Chorus. *See* Opera, Oratorio, Sacred music, Singers & singing

Church music. *See* Sacred music

Cibber, Susanna Maria, 81–82, 84, *494*

Cithern, 37; an Arab, 43–44

Clarinet, 139, 428, 433; Stravinsky's alcoholic, 434; *see also* Stadler, Mühlfeld

Clavichord, Mozart at the, 121

Clement XI, Pope, 61

Cleveland: Ravel in, 443; Bartók in, 464

Clusius. *See* L'Écluse

Cobham, Sir Henry, 27

COCLICO, Adriaen Petit, *479*

Vigilate, quia nescitis ..., 14

Cocteau, Jean, *580*

Cohen, Jules, 315, *557*

*Colbert, Jean Baptiste, *487;* Lully to, 52–53, 53–54

Collected or complete works: Machault's, *476;* Schütz wishes to publish his, 50; C. P. E. Bach on preserving juvenilia, 142–43; an unusual set of, 298; Brahms's attitude on, 375, 380–81

Colloredo, Count Hieronymus, prince-archbishop of Salzburg, (118), 135, *500, 502, 505, 510;* Mozart's break with, 132–34

*Colman, Francis, *492;* Handel to, 70–71

Cologne, 267, 406; Verdi prepares to conduct in, 358–59

Colonna, Giovanni Paolo, *489*

Colonne, Édouard, 408, *579*

Columbia University, Bartók honored by, 463–64, *587*

Commissioned works: Palestrina's Mass no. 95, 16; Monteverdi's *entrate* & *balletti* of 1604, 32; his *Nozze di Tetide,* 36–38; Bassani's problem with, 60–61; Haydn's "Applausus" Cantata, 98–100; Mozart's *Ascanio in Alba,* (101), *498;* his "Haffner" Symphony, 140, *506;* Verdi's *Inno delle nazioni,* 325–27, *560;* Wagner's American *Festmarsch,* 357–58

*Committee of General Security, *512;* Gossec to, 159

COMPOSING, THE ACT OF: Monteverdi writes incidental music, 32; Handel at work on *Belshazzar,* 81–84; Bach, 107; Mozart inspired, 101; Gluck preparing the Paris version of *Alceste,* 111–12, & revising the libretto of *Iphigénie en Tauride,* (127–29); Mozart at work on *Die Entführung,* (135–37), (139); London too noisy for Haydn, 154; Beethoven's dream-voyage generates a canon, 190–91; Schubert's devotional music, 204; Paganini composing for the G string, 213; Wiedebein advises the young Schumann, 215–16; *Faust* & Berlioz, 219; Schumann, 236; Berlioz comes out with a melody, 246; Schumann at the piano, 255; Donizetti not a dawdler, 272; Berlioz &

Nature, 312; Verdi at work on *Aida,* 336–37; Mussorgsky revising *Boris,* 338–39, sketching *Khovanshchina,* 340–41, composing *Pictures at an Exhibition,* 346–47; Brahms consults Joachim, 367; Verdi at work on *Falstaff,* 385–86; Puccini composing *Tosca,* 397; Strauss & Hofmannsthal collaborate on *Der Rosenkavalier,* 419–22; Schoenberg develops "composition with 12 notes," 439

Compton, Karl T., (464), *587*

Concerts. *See* Performances, specific

CONDUCTING & CONDUCTORS: an incompetent, 75; Haydn must forgo conducting *The Creation,* 171; Beethoven asks another to take his place, 172; Weber, *522;* Beethoven & Umlauf, 200, *524–25;* Berlioz & Mendelssohn exchange batons, 272–73, *546;* Berlioz's unusual arrangements at the 1844 exhibition, *548;* Mendelssohn reacts to an insult, 282, *549;* Wagner a guest of the Philharmonic Society, 308–309, 311, Berlioz of a rival organization in London, 310–11; Bruckner put off by some eminent conductors, 348; Theodore Thomas, *567;* Verdi prepares to conduct in Germany, 358–59; Bruckner's 7th Symphony under Muck & Richter, 381; Tchaikovsky, *574;* Mahler in New York, 417–18; Toscanini, Ravel, & the *Boléro,* 447, *584–85;* Koussevitzky conducts Bartók's *Concerto for Orchestra,* 471–72.

Cooper, James Fenimore, Schubert on his deathbed reads, 217

The Last of the Mohicans, 546

CORELLI, Arcangelo, 92, *489*

Sonata, op. II, no. 3, (55–56), *489*
Sonata, op. V, no. 1, 92–93, *497*

Cornelius, Peter, 349, 351, *566*

Cornett, 18, 37

Corriere della sera, Il, Puccini to, 388

*Cossel, Otto, *545;* Brahms to, 266

Costa, Sir Michael, 326, *560*

Council of Trent, *480*

Couperin, François, *571*

Cramer, Johann Baptist, 261, *543*

Cranz, Heinrich August, 390, *576*

*Creel, Wilhelmine, *588;* Bartók to, 470–73

CRITICISM & REVIEWS: Corelli's parallel 5ths, 55–56, *489;* Rameau addresses a young critic, 89, *496;* Haydn's music attacked in Berlin, 114–15; Gluckists & Piccinnists, 123–24, (131), *503;* Beethoven on the Leipzig reviewers, 164; Hoffmann, *517;* Schubert on the value of, 204; Zelter explains Berlioz to Goethe, *530–31;* Chopin waits for his Viennese reviews, 221, 222; *Norma* castigated by the press, 239, 240; Schumann's article on Chopin's op. 2, *537;*

he founds the *Neue Zeitschrift für Musik*, 245, 537, & discusses it, (249); Donizetti parries an attack from Berlioz, 258–59; Meyerbeer's music criticized by Wagner, 544, & by Schumann, 545; Wagner reacts to bad reviews, 309; Verdi reacts to bad reviews, 319; Berlioz & the "music of the future," 558; he despairs of educating the public, 323; Baudelaire & *Tannhäuser*, (324), 559; Brahms's notices after his Viennese debut, 329; Verdi responds to a critic, 333–34; Mussorgsky on his critics, 341–42; Tchaikovsky discusses the Russian National School, 362–64; some Viennese opinions on Bruckner's 7th Symphony, 573; Bülow & Verdi, 386–87, 575; Bartók on a review of his Violin Concerto, 467; Schoenberg prompts a rebuttal, 473

Cui, César Antonovich, 569; Tchaikovsky on, 363

*CZERNY, Carl, 226, 229, 519, 524, 525, 530, 532; Beethoven to, 184, 188; Liszt to, 217–18; his imagination impugned by Schumann, 254

   La leggerezza, 201
   Variations on *Il Pirata*, 218

DALAYRAC, Nicolas, 512
*D'Annunzio, Gabriele, 582; Puccini to, 427
Dante, 376
David, Ferdinand, 250, 281, 317, 539
Davison, James W., 311, 556
DEBUSSY, Claude, 568, 575, 579, 581, 583
   Cinq Poèmes de Baudelaire, D. plays, for Ysaÿe, 389
   La Damoiselle élue, 400, 578; D. plays, for Ysaÿe, 389
   L'Enfant prodigue, 572; D. plays, for his fellow students, (378)
   Images (orchestra), D. working on, in the original 2-piano version, 408, 579
   Images (piano), 1st series, "to the left of Schumann...," 408
   La Mer, 407, 579
   Nocturnes, Ravel transcribes, 400
   Pelléas et Mélisande, (432), 575, 583; D. plays parts of, for Ysaÿe, then obtains Maeterlinck's approval, 389–90
   Prélude à l'Après-Midi d'un Faune, Mallarmé hears Debussy play, 424
   Rapsodie (saxophone), (408), 579

Delacroix, Eugène, the musical signature of, 480
*Delage, Maurice, 579; Ravel to, 406–07
Delibes, Léo, 569; Tchaikovsky's esteem for, 364
*Del Lago, Giovanni, 479; Tromboncino to, 12
*Della Rovere, Francesco Maria II, Victoria to, 31

*Demaldé, Giuseppe, 541; Verdi to, 256
Dent, Edward J., 466, 587
Denver, 442, 443–44
Des Prez, Josquin, 479
Dessoff, Felix Otto, 348, 566
Deutsch, Otto Erich, 528
Deutsche Zeitung Bohemia, Schoenberg to, 435
Devil, music's effect on, 11
Diaghilev, Sergei Pavlovich, 580
Dietch, Philippe, 544
*DIETRICH, Albert, 553, 560; Brahms to, 327
Dietrichstein, Count Moritz von, 221, 532, 541
Dinesen, Isak, 472
Dirichlet, Gustav P. L., 267, 271, 545
Dirichlet, Rebecka (née Mendelssohn), 259, 261, 267, 543, 545, 546
Dittersdorf, Karl Ditters von, 115, 501, 512
Döhler, Theodor, 260, 543
Domenichino, 314
*DONIZETTI, Gaetano, 532, 542, 546, 547, 557, 570, 575; Verdi to, 275; on Verdi, 274–75

   Anna Bolena, 532
   Betly, 259
   Dom Sébastien de Portugal, 275, 547
   Don Pasquale, the 1st performance of, 272, 546
   La Fille du Régiment, attacked by Berlioz, is defended by D., 258–59
   Linda di Chamounix, 547
   Maria di Rohan (*Il Duello*...), composed for Vienna, 272

Donzelli, Domenico, 239, 535
Doré, Gustave, 406
*Dorn, Heinrich, 538, 544; Schumann to, 249–50
Double bass, 100, 434, 552
DOWLAND, John, 483
Dresden, 108, 192, 213, 267, 382, 544, 581; Schütz's examination & installation at, 48–49; Bach honored in, 107, 142; Weber in, 522; Wagner asks to have *Rienzi* produced in, 263–64; his position in, 547; Schumann in, 278, 548; Wagner & the 1849 uprising in, 290–93, 551
Dreyschock, Raimund, 317
Droste-Hülshoff, Annette von, 278, 549
Dublin: Handel in, 78–80, 493–94; Mendelssohn forgoes visiting, 267
Dubourg, Matthew, 78, 493–94
*Ducharger, Monsieur, 496; Rameau to, 89
Düsseldorf, 303–306 *pass.*, 407, 528, 554, 555; Brahms meets the Schumanns in, 552; Schumann's attempt at suicide, 298–99
*DUFAY, Guillaume, 477; Squarcialupi to, 7–8; the signature of, 477, 480

   Lamentations, 6, 477

Du Hotz, Pierre, (86), *495*
*Durand, Jacques, *579;* Debussy to, 407–408, 432
Duroc, General G. C. M., 166, *513*
*Du Roullet, the Bailli, (102), 131, *498, 500, 505;* Gluck to, 111–13
*DVOŘÁK, Antonín, *565, 568, 574;* Brahms to, 360–61; Tchaikovsky to, 384

  Moravian Duets, op. 32, recommended by Brahms to Simrock, 360–61, *568*

Dynamics: Tartini on, 92; Haydn demands strict observance of his, 98; Mozart's, in *Die Entführung,* 136; Beethoven exasperated at the neglect of his, 172; he corrects, in the proofs of his 5th piano concerto, 176; Schubert on, in his Trio, op. 100, 212
*Dziewanowski, Dominik, *535;* Chopin to, 240–42

Eberwein, Karl, 173–74, 175, *516*
Edelmann, Jean-Frédéric, 156, *511*
Education of composers. *See* Musical education of composers
Edwards, Alfred-Charles, *579, 580*
Einstein, Alfred, quoted, *510*
Eliot, T. S., 472
*Elizabeth, queen of England, 27–30 *pass.,* 483;* Tallis & Byrd to, 21–22; her opinion of Dowland, 29
Ella, John, 310, 311, *556*
Elsner, Joseph Xaver, 222, *532*
Elwart, Antoine-Aimable-Élie, 247, *538*
England: Dowland in exile from, 27–31; persecutions under the Tudors, *483;* Bull's flight from, 35; Handel naturalized, 66; organs in, 142, *507;* Haydn's 1st trip to, 152–55, 155–56; Wesley's advocacy of Bach in, 185–86, *519;* Schubert hopes to become known in, 204; Beethoven's gratitude towards, 211; Mendelssohn's 7th trip to, 267–70; Chopin in Scotland &, 287–90, *550–51;* Bruckner in, (349), *566;* Debussy back from, 407, *579; see also* individual cities
*Erdmann, Georg, *492;* Bach to, 71–73
Ernst, Heinrich Wilhelm, 310, *556*
Ertmann, General Stephan & his wife Dorothea von, 233; Mendelssohn's acquaintance with, *534*
*Eschenburg, Johann Joachim, *506–507;* C. P. E. Bach to, 142–43
Essex, Robert Devereux, earl of, 28
Este, Ercole I d', duke of Ferrara, (8), 9, *477*
*Este, Isabella d', *477, 479;* Joh. Martini to, 8–9
Esterházy, Prince Anton, *497*
*Esterházy, Prince Nicolaus I, 114, (162), *497;* Haydn to, 96–97
*Esterházy, Prince Nicolaus II, *497,* (*515*); Haydn to, 175; to his administrator, 162–63

Esterházy, Prince Paul Anton, *497*
Esterházy von Galánta, Count Johann Karl, 197, *524*
Euclid, 56
Examination: Schütz's, in Dresden, 49; Marcello's test composition, 61–63; Bach's, in Leipzig, 72; Mozart's, in Bologna, 118; Prokofiev's, at the St. Petersburg Conservatory, 402–406

*Faccio, Franco, *573;* Verdi to, 381–82
Fairbanks, Douglas, 443
Falla, Manuel de, *580*
Famintzin, Alexander Sergeyevich, (342), 355, 356, *564*
Federlein, Gottlieb Heinrich, 357, *567*
Ferrara, *482;* the singing ladies at, 24–25; Bassani's duties at the Cathedral, 60–61; Vivaldi forbidden to visit, 76–77
Fétis, François-Joseph, 364, *569*
Fibich, Zdenko, 384, *574*
*Filippi, Filippo, 562; Verdi to, 333–34
Fipps, 321
Fischer, Johann Caspar Ferdinand, 106
Fischer, Johann Christian, 121, *503, 508;* Mozart on, 143–44
*Flaubert, Gustave, *557, 560;* Berlioz to, 328

  Salammbô, 328, *560*

Flood, Schoenberg & the, 435
Florence, 18, 25, 33, 283, 315, *476, 477, 490, 492;* Dufay sends cantors to, 7; Dowland in, 28–30; *see also* Camerata
Flute, 136, 139, 434, *549;* a flutist in trouble, 96; the Duc de Guines, 125; Quantz, *507*
Focillon, Henri, 450, *585*
Foggia, Francesco, 56
Fokine, Michel, *583;* Prokofiev attends a New York concert with, 434
Fontana, Ferdinando, *572*
*Fontana, Juljan, *539, 542;* Chopin to, 251, 257–58
Food: Haydn on his, 149; Rossini's panegyric on sausages, 297–98; Mussorgsky illustrates a point with an analogy about, 342–43; Bartók's culinary reports from Budapest, 398, Portugal, 409, the West Coast, 441–42, & New York, 462–63
*Forkel, Johann Nicolaus, *499;* C. P. E. Bach to, 104–106, 106–108
Fouqué, Baron Friedrich de la Motte, *517*

  Undine, 177–78

Fox trot, 436
France: origins of French opera, (52–54), *487–88;* "French style," 70; Rousseau, *La serva padrona,* & the "War of the Buffoons," 87–88, *495;* Gluck offers to bring his reform to, 102–103; the Revolution, 156, 159–60, *511–12;* Haydn honored by, 165; occupation of Prussia, 172–73; Che-

rubini at the Conservatoire, 537–38; "artists are serfs" in, 276–77; Verdi on the Franco-German War, 337; Tchaikovsky on music in, 364; see also individual cities
FRANCHOMME, Auguste-Joseph, 536
Francis I, emperor of Austria, (194), (238)
*Franck, César, 550; Mendelssohn to, 283

Trios, op. 1 (& op. 2?), 283, 550

Frankfurt on the Main, 23, 70, 213, 243, 407; Mozart in, 151–52, 509–10; Mendelssohn in, 266–67
Frankfurt on the Oder, 14, 192
FREDERICK THE GREAT, 476, 495, 496, 507, 541

Montezuma (libretto), (88), 496

*Frederick Augustus II, elector of Saxony, 493; Bach to, 73–74
*Frederick Augustus II, king of Saxony, 544; Wagner to, 263–64
Frege, Livia, (278), 318, 548
Freemasons: Mozart & his father, (144), (150), 508, 509; F. A. Schubert & G. C. Härtel, 187, 520
French horn, 171, 549, 552; 24 horns produce an effect, 548; Franz Strauss, 571
*Freny, Rudolf, 564; Wagner to, 345
Frescobaldi, Girolamo, 106
*Fries, Baroness Anna von, 503; Gluck to, 123–24
Froberger, Johann Jacob, 106
Fugger, Hans Jacob, 20
Fugue: Palestrina's use of the term, 17, 480; Bach's canonic, from the Musical Offering, 84; Tartini's use of the term, 497; Bach's grasp of a subject's potential, 105; his study & teaching of, 107; C. P. E. Bach on his father's organ fugues, 142; Mozart improvises fugues privately, 121, & in public, 123; an unidentified, by Beethoven, 157; the "Consecration of the House" Overture & the Credo in the Missa Solemnis, 199; Schumann writes fugues at Endenich, 302; Rimsky-Korsakov's 64 fugues, 362; Ravel's fugues, 400, & his opinion of women who write them, 401
Funerals, a lean year for, 72
Fux, Johann Joseph, 107, 108, 499

Gabrieli, Andrea, 18, 479, 481, 487
Gabrieli, Giovanni, 481, 487; Schütz's studies with, 47–48
Gade, Niels V., 278, 548
GAFORI, Franchino, 478
GALILEI, Vincenzo, 42, 481–82

Dialogo . . . , 22, 481, 486; Monteverdi on, (42)
Il Fronimo, 482

Gallenberg, Count Wenzel Robert, 220, 531
Galuppi, Baldassare, 494

Penelope, 79, 494

Gardel, Pierre-Gabriel, 159, 512
Gasparini, Francesco, 490
Gazette musicale, La Revue et. See Schlesinger, Maurice
Gazzetta Musicale, 385, 574
Geiringer, Karl, 529
Geneva, 103, 231, 243, 495; Rousseau on, 110; Bartók in 448–53, 585
*Genzinger, Maria Anna von, 509; Haydn to, 148–50, 152–55
George I, king of Gt. Britain, (66), 491
George II, king of Gt. Britain, (78)
George III, king of Gt. Britain, (142), 507
Germany: Dowland in, 28, 31; the early Baroque in, 487; the "German Athens," 501; organs in, (142), 507; German music vindicated by Beethoven, 199–200, 524; Schubert anxious to become better-known in, 208, 527; Schumann on certain aspects of the national character, 253; Wagner on, after the Dresden uprising, 291; prix de Rome winners in, 557; Wagner on the role of, in the process of regeneration, 335; Verdi on, in 1870, 337; Mussorgsky's fear of, 340–44 pass., 563, 564; Tchaikovsky on contemporary composers in, 364; Verdi on Italian & German music, 387; Ravel visits the Ruhr, 406–407; the Nazi era, 454–61 pass., 586–87; see also individual cities
*Germi, Luigi Guglielmo, 528; Paganini to, 212–13
Gesualdo, Carlo. See Uxoricides
Geyer, Ludwig, 263
*Geyer, Stefi, 458, 579, 586; Bartók to, 410–14
*Ghislanzoni, Antonio, 562; Verdi to, 336–37
Gide, André, 575, 580

Le Voyage d'Urien, 390, 575

Giraud (Girò), Anna, 76–77, 493
Girdlestone, Cuthbert, 475, 492, 494, 496
Glazunov, Alexander Konstantinovich, 578, 579; at Prokofiev's examination, 402–405
*Glière, Reinhold Moritsevich, 403, 578; Prokofiev to, 415
Glover, William Howard, 310, 556
GLUCK, Christoph Willibald, 269, 498, 500–506 pass., 509, 519; his artistic principles, 138

Alceste, 102, 123, 498, 503; adapted for Paris, 111–12, 500
Armide, 548; produced in Paris, 123–24, 503; recommended by Verdi, 319
Écho et Narcisse, (131), 504
Le feste d'Apollo, (128?), 504

INDEX

GLUCK, Christoph Willibald (cont.)

Iphigénie en Aulide, 111, 123, *503;* offered to the Opéra, 102–103, *498*
Iphigénie en Tauride, (131) ; Gluck revises the libretto of, 127–29, *504*
Orfeo ed Euridice, 102, *498;* the Paris version of, 123, *503*
Paride ed Elena, 102, *498*

Gluck, Marianne (Nanette), (113), (115–16), *500, 501*
God Save the Queen, 560
*Godebska, Ida, 407, *580;* Ravel to, 416–17
Goethe, August von, (193), *522*
*Goethe, Johann Wolfgang von, 177, 187, 214, 380, *515–17 pass., 522–25 pass.,* 529, 533, 534, 556, (572);* Zelter to, 172–75; Mendelssohn to, 192–93; Schubert to, 203; Berlioz to, 219; in Weimar, *501;* Gluck on, 116; Beethoven on, 179, & G. on Beethoven, *518*

An Mignon, An Schwager Kronos, (203), *525*
Erlkönig, 187, *520*
Die erste Walpurgisnacht, 235, *534; 546*
Erwin und Elmire, 116, *501*
Faust, (196), (230), 301, 318, 400, 417, *523, 533, 559;* Berlioz sends his *Huit scènes* to G., 219, & Zelter is asked for an opinion, *530–31*
Ganymed, (203), *525*
Proserpina, 501
Wilhelm Meister, 425

Goldberg, Johann Gottlieb, 108
Goldschmidt, Otto, 369, *570*
GOMBERT, Nicolas, *479*
Gonzaga, Ferdinando, duke of Mantua, (36–38 pass.), *485*
*Gonzaga, Ferrante, *479;* Gombert to, 13
*Gonzaga, Guglielmo, duke of Mantua, *480, 481, 484;* Palestrina to, 16, 16–17, 19; Galilei to, 22–23
*Gonzaga, Vincenzo I, duke of Mantua, *484, 485;* Monteverdi to, 32–33, 34–35
Gonzaga, Vincenzo II, duke of Mantua, *486*
Gorgia, 35, *484*
GOSSEC, François Joseph, *511–12*
*Gostling, John, *488;* Thos. Purcell to, 55
GOUNOD, Charles, *559*

Faust, 559
La Rédemption, 571; Wagner on the composer of, 372

Grädener, Karl Georg Peter, 329, *561*
Graf, Conrad, 201, 222, *525*
Graun, Johann Gottlieb, 108
Graun, Karl Heinrich, 108, 142, 496, 507

Montezuma, (88), *496*

Greek music, ancient: Galilei on, 22; the Camerata &, *481;* Monteverdi on, 42; ideal-

600

ization of, in the history of opera, *498;* Gluck on the "rules" of Greek dramaturgy, 111
GRÉTRY, André Ernest Modeste, 110, 160, *506, 511*

Cécile et Ermancé, ou les Deux Couvents, 156, *511*
La fausse magie, (110), *500*
Richard Cœur de Lion, G. proposes alterations in, 140–41, *506*

Grimaldi, Nicolò (il Nicolino), 58
Grimm, Julius Otto, 303, *554*
Grisi, Giulia, 239, *535*
Grote, George, 271, *546*
Grout, Donald Jay, 475, 496, 507
Grützmacher, Friedrich (Sr.), 317
*Grzymała, Wojciech, *550;* Chopin to, 287–88, 288–90
*Gueinzius, Christian, *486;* Scheidt to, 40–41
*Guillard, Nicolas François, *504;* Gluck to, 127–29
Guines, the Duc de, 125, & his daughter, 125–26, *504*
Gutmann, Adolph, 288, *551*
Gyrowetz, Adalbert, 220, *531*

Habsburgs, *476, 482; see also* given names
*Härtel, Gottfried Christoph, *514, 520, 555;* Beethoven to, 170–71, 176, 178–79; F. A. Schubert to, 187; his sons, 307, *555*
*Hainl, François ("George"), *549;* Berlioz to, 279–81
Halévy, J.-F.-Fromental-É., 315, *557*

*Charles VI, *548;* a chorus from, & a "politico-musical" moment, 277
La Juive, 557

Halévy, Ludovic, 315, *557*
Halle, the chapel in, under Scheidt, 40–41
Hamburg, 70, 302, 318, 330, *491, 507, 561, 564;* Brahms on his youth in, 390
Hammerclavier, 186–87, *520, 522*
HANDEL, George Frideric, 199, 226, 437, 446, *491–96 pass., 501, 507, 532, 571;* esteemed by Bach, 108; C. P. E. Bach's comparison of his own father &, as organists, 142–43

*L'Allegro . . . , *493;* performed in Dublin, 78–79
*Belshazzar, *494;* H. at work on, 81–84
Deborah, 84, *494*
*Messiah, *494;* its composition & 1st performance, 78, 79–80, *493;* H. makes alterations in, 82
Samson, 310

Hanover, 297, 302, 313; Brahms's 1st piano concerto at, 317, 318, *557*
*Hanslick, Eduard, 359, 360, *544, 564, 568,*

571; Brahms to, 373–75; Bruckner &, 348, 382, 566, 573

Vom Musikalisch-Schönen, 571

Hapsburgs, 476, 482; *see also* given names
Harp, 37, 113, 123, 527; the Duc de Guines' daughter, 125–26; Edward Jones, 185–86, 519; unprecedented use of, by Berlioz, 277
Harpsichord, 37, (68), (69–70), 98, 105, 491, 522; Haydn's early studies, 113
Hartmann, Victor Alexandrovich, 346, 565
*Haslinger, Tobias, 193, 194, 221, 250, 253, 520; Beethoven to, 190–92
Hasse, Johann Adolph, 142, 499, 501, 507; esteemed by Bach, 108; his testimonial for Haydn, 114
*Hauer, Josef Matthias, 584; Schoenberg to, 438–40
Hauptmann, Gerhart, 428

Die versunkene Glocke, Ravel's projected opera based on, 429, 582

HAYDN, Joseph, 206, 207, 318, 380, 390, 497, 501, 508–11 *pass.*, 513, 515, 521, 524; on Mozart, 148; on Mozart's death, 155–56; intervenes in Beethoven's behalf, 157–58; on being a "servant," 162–63; Brahms on the complete works of, 375

L'anima del filosofo, (154), 510
"Applausus" Cantata, 98–100, 497
Arianna a Naxos, (149), 509
Quartets, op. 50, 147, 508
Die Schöpfung (*The Creation*), (171), 515
Die Sieben letzten Worte . . ., 147, 508–509
Symphony no. 91, 154
See also 114

Hazard, Paul, (464), 587
Healy, G. P. A., 347, 565
Hegel, Georg Wilhelm Friedrich, 300
Heidelberg, 303, 313; Schumann at the University of, 222–29, 532, 537
*Heine, Heinrich, 216, 265, 310, 529, 543, 556; Schumann to, 262; greetings from, 243

Die beiden Grenadiere, 265, 545
Buch der Lieder, 529

Heinsheimer, Hans, 455
Heller, Stephen, 254, 262, 541, (543)
Hellmesberger Quartet, 560–61
Helsted, Carl A., 278, 549
Henry VIII, king of England, 476, 478
Henry IV, king of France, (33–34), 484
*Henschel, Sir George, 570; Brahms to, 368–69
Hensel, Fanny (née Mendelssohn), 269, 534, 546

Italien ("Schöner und schöner . . ."), Queen Victoria sings, 269

Hensel, Wilhelm, 234, 534, 545
Henselt, Adolph, 260, 310, 543
Herbeck, Johann von, 348, 566
Herder, Johann Gottfried von, 501
*Hertzka, Emil, 581; Schoenberg to, 422–23
Herz, Henri, 223, 226, 241, 532
*Hiller, Ferdinand, 254, 260, 261, 267, 536, 541, 543, 545; Liszt, Chopin, & Franchomme to, 242–43; Rossini to, 331–32; Verdi to, 358–59

Gavotte, Sarabande, Courante, Rossini on, 331–32
Die Zerstörung Jerusalems, Mendelssohn involved in producing, (260), (261), 543

*Hitzig, Eduard, 517; Hoffmann to, 177–78
Hofer, Franz de Paula, 152, 510
HOFFMANN, Ernst Theodor Amadeus, 253, 516–17; on Johannes Kreisler, 177; Schumann on the same subject, 253

Undine, 177–78

*Hoffmeister, Franz Anton, (152), (153), 510; Beethoven to, 163–64
HOFHAIMER, Paul, 478
*Hofmannsthal, Hugo von, 581; R. Strauss to, 419, 419–22
Hogarth, George, 310, 556
*Hohenberg, Paul, 582; Berg to, 428, 429–30
Holbein, Franz von, 177, 517
Holland, 143, 371; the Schumanns in, 302, 554
*Hopkins, Edward Jerome, 561; Berlioz to, 330–31
Horace, (62), (111), 491, 500
Horn. *See* French horn
Horse, 20
*House of Lords, Handel to, 66
Hünten, Franz, 254, 541
*Huescar, the Duke of, 495; D. Scarlatti to, 86–87
Hugo, Victor, 406

Le Roi s'amuse, 552

*Hummel, Johann Nepomuk, 200, 221, 373n., 515; Haydn to, 171; Schubert's intended dedication to, 216, 529

Concerto (piano) in A min., Schumann plays, 222, 223
Concerto (piano) in B min., 226
Grande Fantaisie in E-flat maj., 200
Sonata (piano) in F-sharp min., Schumann on, 223

Hungary, 23, 24, 148, 197, 473, 497; Bartók in Transylvania, 410–14; his misgivings over Nazism in, 456–58; he leaves, 587; *see also* Budapest

Improvisation: Mr. Dubourg's long journey, 493–94; in Bach's clavier works, 107; Mozart astonishes, 121, 123; the young Men-

delssohn, *522;* Moscheles, 201; Chopin, 220, 221; Schumann, 223; Mendelssohn at Buckingham Palace, 270
In pace in id ipsum, antiphon, 11
*Ingres, Jean Auguste Dominique, *538;* Cherubini to, 246–47
*Institut National (Paris), *513;* Haydn to, 166
Instruments: Machault on using, with a vocal composition, 2; Schütz orders strings for, 39–40; Monteverdi on some exotic, 43–44; Berlioz's requirements for an average concert, 279–80; *see also* individual instruments, Orchestration
Iris im Gebiet der Tonkunst, 249, *539*
Isaac, Heinrich, 478
Italy: Dufay in, 7, *477;* Hofhaimer values his fame in, 10; Lassus in, 18–19, *480–81;* Dowland in, 29–31; "Italian style," 70; Italian *intermezzi* at the Opéra & the "War of the Buffoons," 87–88, *495;* Mozart in, 100–101, *498;* Gluck on Italian opera, 102; Mozart on the importance of Italian credentials in Germany, 117, & on the Elector's indifference to his, 118–19; he writes an *aria di bravura,* 136; Wiedebein's metaphor on music in, 215; Schumann on hearing Italian music in, 224; Mendelssohn in, 230–35, *533;* Bizet in, 314–17; Verdi in London finds Italian music needs no representation, 326; the war of 1866, (332), *561;* Verdi on Italian & German music, 387; Puccini on the death of song in, 436; *see also* individual cities

*Jacovacci, Vincenzo, *558;* Verdi to, 319–20
*Jacquin, Baron Gottfried von, *508;* Mozart to, 145
Jalowetz, Heinrich, 425, *582*
James I, king of Gt. Britain, (35), *483, 485*
Janequin, Clément, *483*

La Bataille de Marignan, 483

Jazz, 443
*Jean-Aubry, Georges, *581;* Debussy to, 424
Jean Paul. *See* Richter, Jean Paul
Jena, 192, 293; battle of, *515, 541*
*Jennens, Charles, *493;* Handel to, 78–79, 79–80, 81–82, 82, 82–83, 83, 83–84
Jeppesen, Knud, *479, 480*
Jiránek, Josef, 354, *567*
*JOACHIM, Joseph, 297, 302–307 *pass.,* 553–55 *pass., 557, 569;* Dietrich to, 298–99; Brahms to, 313, 317–18, 367; Schumann on, 304

Variations (viola, piano), 304

*Johann Georg I, elector of Saxony, (39), *487;* Schütz to, 46–52
JOHN I, king of Aragon, as heir apparent, 476–77

John Frederick I, elector of Saxony, (14), *479*
Johnson, John, 28
Jones, Edward, 185–86, *519*
Joseph II, Emperor, (134), *509, 572;* Brahms on, 373–74
Josquin des Prez, *479*

Kalkbrenner, Friedrich Wilhelm Michael, *525;* Czerny on his playing, 200, 201; Chopin honored by, 241
Kandinsky, Vassily, 425, *582*
Kant, Immanuel, 300; Webern on Beethoven &, 425–26
Karlsbad, 179, 221, 455, *517*
Kassel: Schütz in, 47; Mahler in, 377–78, *572*
Kaunitz-Rietberg, Prince Wenzel Anton von, 132, 140, *506*
Keiser, Reinhard, 108, 142, *507*
*Keller, Hans, *588;* Schoenberg to, 473
Kerl, Johann Caspar, 106
Kerner, Justinus A. C., 214, *529*
*Kietz, Ernst Benedikt, *555;* Wagner to, 308–309
Kings, musical. *See* Rulers, musical
Kinsky, Prince Ferdinand, 179, *517*
Kirnberger, Johann Philipp, 108
Klindworth, Karl, 309, *555, 558;* Berlioz on his playing, 310, 311
Klingemann, Karl, 235, 267, 270, *534*
Klopstock, Friedrich, 115, 116, *501;* a bilingual pun on, 342, *564*
Kodály, Zoltán, 457, *586*
Koessler, János, 399, *577*
Kokoschka, Oskar, Berg gives news of, 430
Kotzebue, August von, *534*
Koussevitzky, Serge, 468, 471–72, *588*
Kraus, Karl, *582*
Krebs, Johann Ludwig, 108
Kreutzer, Conradin, 220, *531*
Kriehuber, Josef, (255), *541*
Kühnel, Ambros, 163, *513*
*Kupelwieser, Leopold, *523;* Schubert to, 195–97

Lachner, Franz, 220, 370, *531*
*Lacombe, Paul, *564;* Bizet to, 345–46
La Harpe, Jean François de, 123, *503*
Lamb, Charles, *519*
*La Motte, Antoine Houdar de, *491, 492;* Rameau to, 66–68
La Motte Fouqué. *See* Fouqué
LANDINI, Francesco, 476
Lang, Paul H., *479*
L'Arrivé, Henri, 111, *500*
LASSUS, Roland de, *480, 481, 482, 487*
Lassus, Rudolf de, 18
LAWES, Henry, *486*
League of Nations, Bartók at, 449–52, *585*
*L'Écluse, Charles de, *482;* Monte to, 23–24

Leidesdorf, Maximilian Josef, 196, 197, *523*
Leipzig, 47, 69, 70, 176, 181, 187, 222–28
pass., 256, 263, 281, 348, 355, 373n., *494,
495, 527, 529, 532, 533, 538, 541, 543,
544, 550, 555, 560, 573;* Bach's dissatisfaction with, 71–72; Beethoven on the reviewers in, 164; Paganini in, 226; the
1836–37 season in, 250; Liszt visits, 260–
61; Berlioz in, *546;* Andersen at the
Schumanns' in, (278), *548–49;* Brahms on
the reception given his 1st piano concerto
in, 317–18, *557–58*
*Leipzig, the Town Council of, Bach to,
64–66, 74–75
*Lenieps, Toussaint-Pierre, *495;* Rousseau to,
87–88
Leoncavallo, Ruggiero, Puccini's rupture with,
388, *575*
*Leonore, Mademoiselle, *501;* Haydn to,
113–15
Leopardi, Giacomo, 386, (*575*)
Leopold II, Emperor, (151), 373, *509, 510*
Lepelletier, Louis Michel, 159, 160, *512*
Leprince, Gustave, *544*
Leschen, Wilhelm, 201, *525*
Lesueur, Jean François, (202), *525*
Liberati, Antimo, 56
Librettists, librettos. *See* Words & music
Lichnowsky, Prince Karl, 168, *514, 524*
*Lichnowsky, Count Moritz, *524;* Beethoven
to, 198
LIEDER: Zelter, *515;* Beethoven's *Merkenstein*,
(180), *518;* Weber comments on Wieck's,
181–83, *518;* Schubert's *Erlkönig* in the
wrong hands, 187, *520;* he quotes
Gretchen, 196; he sends 3 Goethe settings
to the poet, 203; his Walter Scott settings,
203, 204; Schumann, impressed with Wiedebein's works, sends him his own early
efforts, 214–16, *528–29;* Schubert's Heine
settings, 216, *529;* Schumann sends Heine
the *Liederkreis,* op. 24, 262, *543;* Queen
Victoria & Prince Albert sing Mendelssohn,
268–70; an evening at the Schumanns',
278, *548–49;* genesis of Mahler's *Lieder
eines Jahrenden Gesellen,* 377–78, *572;*
Wolf gives a concert, 395; Berg pre-
disposed to, 423
Lind, Jenny, (369), *570;* Chopin hears, 287–
88, *551*
Lipiner, Siegfried, 418, *580*
Lipinski, Carl, 250, *539*
*Lipsius, Marie, *573;* Brahms to, 380–81
*LISZT, Franz, 250, 309, 356, *524, 530, 536,
543, 553, 554, 556. 558, 562, 565, 567;*
Smetana, to, 284–86; Wagner to, 300–301,
320–22; youthful successes in Paris, 197,
201, 218; appraised by Mendelssohn, 260–
61; helps César Franck, *550,* Smetana, 287,

550, & Saint-Saëns, *567;* receives Wagner
in Weimar after the Dresden uprising,
290–93, *551;* a transcription by, & a law-
suit, 372
Eine Faust-Symphonie, 301; Ravel's admi-
ration for, 400
Die Glocken des Strassburger Münster, sent
to Longfellow by L., 347, *565*
Totentanz, (356), *567*
Litta, Count Antonio, (90), *496*
Liturgical music. *See* Sacred music
LOCKE, Matthew, *488*
Lockspeiser, Edward, 475, *572, 575*
Lodovico il Moro. *See* Sforza
Lodyzhensky, Nikolai Nikolayevich, 338, *563*
*Löhr, Friedrich, *572;* Mahler to, 377–78
*Lombardini, Maddalena, *496–97;* Tartini to,
91–95
London, 143, 213, 291, 292, 293, 458, 472,
496, 501, 507, 508, 566, 581;* a laughable
opera season in, 79, & another in the mak-
ing, 80; Handel plans an oratorio season
in, 81–82, 84; Haydn in, 152–55, 155–56;
Mendelssohn in, 267–70, *545–46;* Chopin
in, 287–89 *pass., 550–51;* Wagner in,
308–309, 310–11, *555;* Berlioz in, 310–11,
556; Verdi in, 325–27, *559–60; see also*
Philharmonic Society
*Longfellow, Henry Wadsworth, *565;* Liszt
to, 347–48
Los Angeles, 441, 442; Ravel in, 443; Schoen-
berg in, 454, 465–66, *585, 587*
Louis XIV, king of France, (52–54 *pass.*),
487
Louis XV, king of France, (87), (*495*)
Louis XVI, king of France: suppressed Beau-
marchais' *Figaro, 506;* his execution, (159),
512
Louis Ferdinand of Prussia, Prince, *541;*
Schumann on, 254
Louis Philippe, king of the French, (238),
241, (242), 265, *535, 536, 546*
Louÿs, Pierre, 389, *575*
*Lucca, the Government of, Boccherini to, 95
Ludwig II, king of Bavaria, 335, *562*
*Lübeck, the commercial guilds of, *489–90;*
Buxtehude to, 57
LULLY, Jean Baptiste, 103, *487–88*
Alceste, Verdi recommends, 319
Armide, 103
Les Festes de l'Amour et de Bacchus, 488
Lute, 12, 18, *482;* Dowland performs, 28;
see also Chitarrone
LUTHER, Martin, 48, *478, 483*
Luzzaschi, Luzzasco, *482;* Cavalieri to, 24–25
Lyadov, Anatol Konstantinovich, 415, *580*
Lyons, 88; Berlioz arranges a concert in, 279–
81, *549*

INDEX

MACHAULT, Guillaume de, *476*

La Fontaine amoureuse (Morpheus), 1
Ne quier veoir, (3), *476*
Nes que on porroit, (1–2), *476*
Quant Theseus, (3), *476*
Le Livre du Voir-Dit, *476*

MacSwiney. *See* Swiney
Maeterlinck, Maurice, 426; Debussy visits, apropos of *Pelléas et Mélisande*, 389–90, *575*
MAHLER, Gustav, 426, *572, 576–77, 580*

Das Lied von der Erde, Webern on, 425
Lieder eines fahrenden Gesellen, (*394*), (*577*); their origin, 377–78, *572*
Symphony no. 1, *572, 576;* M. on, 392–94 *pass.*
Symphony no. 2, *572, 576;* described by M., 393–94
Symphony no. 3, 417

Malfatti, Dr. Giovanni, 238, *535*
Mallarmé, Stéphane, (*580*), *581*

Prélude à l'Après-Midi d'un Faune, M. hears Debussy's musical version of, 424

Mann, Thomas, Bartók hears, 451, & meets, 452
Mantua, 26, 43, 77, *477, 479–81 pass., 484– 86 pass.;* Lassus in, 18
Manzoni, Alessandro, 275

I promessi sposi (The Betrothed), 486

Marat, Jean Paul, 159, *512*
Marenzio, Luca, 28
Maria Theresa, Empress, 114, (131), *498, 503, 511*
Marini, Ignazio, 325, *559*
Marmontel, Jean François, 123, *503*
*Marschalk, Max, *576;* Mahler to, 392–94
Marseillaise, La. See Rouget de Lisle
Marseilles, 279, 280, *542*
*Martin of Aragon, *477;* John of Aragon to, 5
Martinengo, Giulio Cesare, (48), *487*
*Martini, Giambattista, *496;* J. C. Bach to, 90–91
MARTINI, Johannes, *477*
Marty, Georges-Eugène, 378, *572*
Marxsen, Eduard, (297), 329, 330, *561*
Mary Tudor, queen of England, 21
*Marzari, Carlo, *552;* Verdi to, 294–95
Masefield, John, (451), *585*
Mass. *See* Sacred music
*Mattheson, Johann, *491;* Handel to, 63–64

Das Beschützte Orchestre . . ., (63), *491*

Matuszyński, Jan, (251), (257), *539*
Maximilian, Archduke (16th cent.), 23, *482*
Maximilian I, Emperor, *478*
*Maximilian Franz, elector of Cologne, *508,

511; Haydn to, 157–58; Beethoven to, 158
Maximilian Joseph III, elector of Bavaria, *499;* "very gracious" to Mozart, (109.); refuses to employ him, (117), (118–19)
*Mayer, Friedrich Sebastian, *515;* Beethoven to, 172
*Mayfeld, Moritz von, *565;* Bruckner to, 348– 49
*Mayreder, Rosa, *577;* Wolf to, 395–96
Mayseder, Joseph, 220, *531*
Mechetti, Pietro, 253
*Meck, Nadezhda Filaretovna von, *568;* Tchaikovsky to, 361–66
*Medici, Duke Cosimo I de', Viola to, 15
*Medici, Grand Duke Ferdinand I de', (24), *482, 484;* Viadana to, 26–27; Caccini to 33–34; Dowland plays for, (28)
*Medici, Prince Ferdinand de', *490;* A. Scarlatti to, 58
*Medici, Giovanni de', *477;* Squarcialupi to, 5–6; Dufay to, 6–7
Medici, Lorenzo de', honors Dufay & sends him verses for music, 7–8
Medici, Maria de', queen of France, (33–34), *484*
*Medici, Piero de', 6, *477;* Dufay to, 6–7; praises Dufay, 7
Meilhac, Henri, 557
Memmo, Dionisio, (10), *478*
Mendelssohn Bartholdy, Cécile, 267, 270, *545*
Mendelssohn Bartholdy, Fanny. *See* Hensel, Fanny
MENDELSSOHN BARTHOLDY, Felix, 250, 356, 467, 507, 515, 522, 533–34, 537, 543–46 pass., 549, 550, 554; Berlioz to, 272–73, 281; Wagner to, 274; Schumann on, 254; on Liszt, 260–61; visits Buckingham Palace, 268–70; Berlioz &, *546;* Wagner &, 309, *547*

Antigone, incidental music to, 267, *546, 548*
Concerto (piano) no. 2, 261
Concerto (violin), 467
Elijah, 549, 550
Erndtelied ("Es ist ein Schnitter..."), Prince Albert sings, then M. improvises on, 270
Die erste Walpurgisnacht, 235, *534;* Berlioz impressed with, *546*
Frühlingslied, op. 47, no. 3, 269
A Midsummer-Night's Dream, incidental music to, Berlioz on, 281
Overture to *A Midsummer-Night's Dream*, (234), *534*
Pilgerspruch ("Lass dich nur nichts..."), sung by Queen Victoria, 269
St. Paul, Victoria & Albert join M. in a chorus from, 268
Symphony no. 3, 270, *545, 546*

604

MENDELSSOHN BARTHOLDY, Felix (cont.)

Symphony no. 4, conducted by Wagner with his gloves on, 309, *555*

*Mendelssohn Bartholdy, Lea, *543;* Mendelssohn to, 259–61, 266–71

Mendelssohn Bartholdy, Paul, 235, 266, 267, *534, 543*

*Mendelssohn Bartholdy family, Mendelssohn to, 230–35

Menuhin, Yehudi, plays Bartók's sonata for solo violin, 471, & his concerto, 472

*Mercure de France, Gluck to, 102–103

Merighi, Antonia Margherita, 70, *492*

Metastasio, Pietro, *504*

La clemenza di Tito: quoted by Gluck, 128; Mozart version, *510*

Metronome indications: for Beethoven's op. 131, promised by him with an imprecation, 208–209; he sends, for the 9th Symphony, 211, *528;* Brahms on, 369

Meyerbeer, Giacomo, 353, *547, 556, 560;* Wagner's relations with, 263, 265, *544;* Schumann's opinion of, *545;* in London with Berlioz, 310, & Wagner, 310–11

L'Étoile du Nord, 310
Les Huguenots, *544, 548*
Robert le Diable, *544*

Michelangelo: Bizet on, 314–15; Debussy &, *573*

Milan, 131, 230, 231, 235, 256, 333, 400, 436, *478, 496, 508, 538, 541, 547, 559;* J. C. Bach in, 90; Mozart in, 101, *498;* Schumann in, 224; Mendelssohn in, 233, *534;* Bellini in, for the production of Norma, 239–40, *535;* Verdi withdraws his operas from La Scala, 283–84; Puccini's Le Villi produced in, *572*

Milder-Hauptmann, Pauline Anna, 204, *526*

*Milton, John, *486, 493;* H. Lawes to, 46

L'Allegro & Il Penseroso, 78, *493*
Comus & Sonnet xiii, *486*

Mizler, Lorenz Christoph, 104, 106, *499*

Molière, 310, *487, 488*

Les Femmes savantes, quoted, 314, *557*
Le Misanthrope, 310

Mombert, Alfred, 428, *582*

MONEY MATTERS: Lassus on, 20; Bassani on the going rates for Masses, 60–61; Bach's income & expenses, 72; Vivaldi's financial involvement in an operatic production, 76–77; Bach gets an expensive present, 85–86; Mr. Albert's plan for Mozart, 117–18; Gluck's Armide a box office success, 124; Mozart on living in Paris, 126; his salary in Salzburg, 133, *505;* box office receipts for Die Entführung, 139; young Beethoven

in financial straits, 146; Mozart destitute, 150–51; his stipend in Vienna, *509;* his Frankfurt venture, 151–52, *509–10;* Haydn on London prices, 154; Mozart sends money to his wife, 155; his estate, *510;* Haydn intervenes in Beethoven's behalf, 157–58; Haydn refuses to obey, 162–63; Beethoven prices some of his works, 163–64, 170–71; young Schubert tries to widen his resources, 179–80; Beethoven aided by the Philharmonic Society during his last illness, 210–11, *527;* Schubert accepts a low fee for his E-flat maj. Trio, 211; Paganini puts money in the bank, 213; Chopin teaching much, earning little, 242; Berlioz's windfall, 252; his monster concert of 1844 unprofitable, 276; his negotiations with Lyons, 279, 280; Smetana hopes to improve his desperate situation, 285–86, *550;* Liszt comes to Wagner's aid, 292; Wagner's London venture unremunerative, 308; Bizet on the cost of winning the prix de Rome, 315–16; Verdi's advice to an impresario, 319–20; Dvořák without means of support, 346; Bruckner ditto, 348–49; Wagner honors American independence for a price, 357–58; Brahms sends a "trifle" to a young composer, 368; Wagner sets conditions for Parsifal, 372; a crooked impresario, 409

*Mongeot, Monsieur, *494;* Rameau to, 80–81

*Moniteur Universel, Le, Donizetti to, 258–59

MONTE, Philippe de, *482*

MONTEVERDI, Claudio, *482, 484–87 pass.;* on the human element in dramatic music, 37–38; on the prima & seconda pratica, 42

Arianna, 37–38, *485*
Madrigals, Bk. V, *486*
Le nozze di Tetide, (36–38), *485*
Orfeo, 37–38, *484, 485*
Scherzi musicali, *486*

Monteverdi, Giulio Cesare, *486*

Moore, Joseph, 282, *549*

Moreau, Gustave, 315, *557*

Moritz, landgrave of Hesse-Kassel, *487;* a patron of Dowland, 28, & of Schütz, 47, 48

*Moscheles, Ignaz, 241, 267, 273, *525, 527, 546, 549;* Beethoven to, 209–10, 210–11; Mendelssohn to, 282; Czerny on his playing, 200, 201; Schumann hopes to study with, 228

Concerto (piano) in G min., 226

Moscow, 341, 344, 415, *574;* Tchaikovsky & N. Rubinstein at the Conservatory in, 364–66, *569;* the former invites Dvořák to, 384

*Moser, Wilhelm Ludwig, *485;* Schütz to, 39–40

*Mourentorf, Jean, *483;* Monte to, 26

*Mozart, Anna Maria, (101), *497, 502, 503;*

Mozart to, 100–101, 109; writes in her son's letter, 120; her death, 130–31

Mozart, Carl Thomas, 145, *508;* Mendelssohn meets, 233, 235

*Mozart, Constanze, 140, (145), *505, 506, 509, 510;* Mozart to, 151–52, 155; Haydn in touch with, after Mozart's death, 155–56

*Mozart, Leopold, (100–101), (109), (130–31), *497–98, 502, (505), 506, 508;* Mozart to, 117–19, 120–23, 125–26, 132–34, 135–37, 139–40, 143–45; his last illness, 144–45, & death, 145

Mozart, Maria Anna Thekla, (120), *502*

*Mozart, Marianne (Nannerl), 120, (126), (130–40 *pass.*), *497, 498;* Mozart to, 77–78, 78, 119

MOZART, Wolfgang Amadeus, 199, 206, 207, 358, 403, *497–511 pass., 531;* on playing the piano, 121–22; on the limits of musical expression, 135; on death, 144; Haydn on, 148, & on his death, 155–56; Mendelssohn on the letters of, 233; a *Davidsbündler,* 249

Ascanio in Alba, (101), *498*

La clemenza di Tito, 510

Concerto (clarinet), *510*

Concerto (2 claviers), 137, *506*

Concerto (3 claviers), (137), *506;* M. performs, 122

Concerto (flute, harp), *504*

Concerto (piano), K. 238, performed by M., 122–23

Concerto (violin), K. 218, performed by M., (121), *503*

Don Giovanni, 508; Mendelssohn plays the overture for M.'s son, 233

Die Entführung aus dem Serail, 508; its composition, (135–37), *505,* & production, (139), *506*

La finta giardiniera, the 1st performance of, (109), *499*

Le nozze di Figaro, 507, 508; Haydn dreams of, 149

Les petits riens, (126), *504*

Quartet (piano, strings) in G min., *510*

Quartets (strings), K. 589 & 590, 150, 151

Requiem, 510

Sonata (piano), K. 284, performed by M., 122

Sonata (piano 4-hands) in C maj., 145, *508*

Symphony no. 35, commissioned, 140, & written, *506*

Variations (piano), K. 179, *503, 508;* performed by M., 121

Die Zauberflöte, 199, *510;* Mendelssohn plays the overture for M.'s son, 233

Muck, Karl, 381, *573*

Mühlfeld, Richard, Brahms &, 391, *576*

*Mühlhausen, the parishioners of, Bach to, 59–60

Müller, Wenzel, *523*

*Müller-Widmann, Mrs. Oscar, *586;* Bartók to, 456–59

Müthel, Johann Gottfried, 108

Munich, 17, 20, 213, 395, 425, *535, 562, 571;* Mozart in, (in 1775), 109, *499;* (in 1777), 117–19, *502;* Schumann in, 262

Murat, Joachim, *534;* Mendelssohn hears recollections of, 234–35

Murger, Henri, 388, *575*

Murray, Gilbert, 449, *585*

MUSIC PRINTING & PUBLISHING: an early publication (*Musica nova*), 15; Tallis's & Byrd's losses from, 21; difficulties of, in the Low Countries in wartime, 26; Viadana has his own works printed, 27; Victoria *ditto,* 31; Schütz intends doing so, 50; Bach's edition of the *Musical Offering,* 84; Rousseau publishes Pergolesi's *La serva padrona,* 87–88; a case of piracy, 147; Dalayrac's troubles during the Reign of Terror, 160; Donizetti explains international arrangements for, 275; Wagner specifies how *Parsifal* is to appear, 371–72; Brahms on the excesses of, 375; *see also* Publishers, composers &

MUSICAL EDUCATION OF COMPOSERS: Schütz, 46–49; Telemann, 69–70; Bach, 106–107; Haydn, 113–14; he reports on his pupil Beethoven, 157; Schubert, 184–85; Schumann as a piano student, 222–29 *pass.,* 237, *532;* his counterpoint studies, 249, *538;* Brahms, aged 8, 266; Smetana, 284–85; Verdi, 334; Bartók's studies in Budapest, 397–99; Prokofiev's entrance examination in St. Petersburg, 402–406; his activities as a student there, 415; Berg, 423; *see also* Teachers, composers as

MUSSORGSKY, Modest Petrovich, 563–67 *pass.;* Tchaikovsky on, 363, 364

Boris Godunov, 346; M. revises, 338–39, *563;* the 2nd version rejected, *564;* he quotes from, 340; its 1st performance, 565

Khovanshchina, 567; M. sketching, 340–41, 563–64

Pictures at an Exhibition, M. working on, 346–47, 565

Naldi, Antonio, 25

Naples, 6, 88, 240, 315, 316, *513, 533, 534, 542;* Squarcialupi back from, 5; not suited to D. Scarlatti's talent, 58; Gluck's operas in demand there, 132

*Napoleon I, 170, 234, *513, 514, 520, 528, 534;* Paisiello to, 165–66; occupies Berlin, 172–73

Napoleon III, *561, 563*

INDEX

Neue Zeitschrift für Musik, 303, *529, 539, 540, 544, 545, 548;* founded by Schumann, 245, *537;* he discusses it with Dorn, (249); his Brahms article in, (296), *553*
New York, 357, 443, 444, 471, *561, 567;* Berlioz's advice to a musician living in, 330–31; Mahler in, 417–18, *580;* Prokofiev attends a concert in, 434; the Philharmonic-Symphony Orchestra in Europe with Toscanini, (447), *584–85;* Bartók in, 462–65, 472–73
Nicolino (Nicolò Grimaldi), 58
Nidecki, Thomas, 222, *532*
Nijinsky, Waslaw, *580*
Noah, 435
*Novello, Vincent, *519;* Wesley to, 185–86
Noverre, Jean-Georges, 126, *504*
Nuremberg, 75; Schütz orders strings from, 39–40

Oboe, 157, 374, 434, *511;* an inspiring hautboyist, 101; J. C. Fischer, 143–44, *508*
Ojetti, Ugo, 450, *585*
Omaha, jazz in, 443
OPERA: origins, *481, 482, 484;* Monteverdi on his *Orfeo* & *Arianna,* 37–38; Bontempi in Dresden, *487;* the birth of French, (52–54), *487–88;* machines in, 53, *488;* Rameau on his qualifications for, 66–68, *491–92;* "opera style," 65, 70; Handel engages singers, 70–71; Vivaldi barred from producing his, 76–77; a laughable season in London, 79, & another in the making, 80; Rameau on writing one's 1st, 80–81; 1st performance of Rousseau's *Le Devin du village,* 87, *495;* Pergolesi's *La serva padrona* & other *intermezzi* at the Opéra, 87–88; the "War of the Buffoons," *495;* Frederick the Great's libretto for Graun, 88, *496;* Mozart's *Ascanio in Alba,* (101), *498;* Gluck offers his reform to France, 102–103; 1st performance of Mozart's *La finta giardiniera,* (109); Rousseau on aristocratic characters in, 110, *500;* Haydn lists 3 early works, 114; Gluck prefers choruses to confidants, 116; Gluckists & Piccinnists, 123–24; Gluck revises the libretto of *Iphigénie en Tauride,* (127–29), not without trouble, 131, & tells of a Bologna performance of *Alceste,* 131–32; Mozart at work on *Die Entführung,* (135–37); he reports on its 2nd performance, (139); Grétry makes alterations in *Richard Cœur de Lion,* 140–41; Haydn on his own operas & on Mozart's, 147–48; Grétry's *Le deux Couvents* shortened & rebaptized, 156; Dalayrac's works threatened by the Reign of

Terror, 160; *Fidelio* (2nd version) mauled by the orchestra, (172), *515;* Hoffmann seeks a librettist for *Undine,* 177–78, (*517*); rehearsals for the 1st performance of *Euryanthe,* 193–95; 2 unperformed operas by Schubert, 196; Bellini reports on the 1st performances of *Norma,* 239–40; Verdi's *Oberto,* (256), *541;* Auber, 257; *La Fille du Régiment,* attacked by Berlioz, is defended by Donizetti, 258–59; Wagner asks to have *Rienzi* produced at Dresden, 263–64; Donizetti turns out *Don Pasquale* & *Maria de Rohan (Il Duello...)* expeditiously, 272; Verdi's *Ernani* in Venice, (274), *547,* & Vienna, 275; he forbids future productions at La Scala, 283–84; *Rigoletto* bowdlerized by the censor, (294–95), *552; Traviata* falls through, 296; Rossini's retirement, 298, *553;* Wagner at work on *Die Walküre* & planning *Tristan,* 300–301; Verdi's advice to the impresario after the failure of *Un ballo in maschera,* 319–20; the Paris production of *Tannhäuser,* 324, *559; La Forza del destino* in St. Petersburg, (325), *559;* Verdi on the universal appeal of Italian, 326; criticism of *La forza del destino* prompts him to speak of his art, 333–34; Mussorgsky at work revising *Boris Godunov,* 338–39, & planning *Khovanshchina,* 340–41; Wagner on how to play Beckmesser in *Die Meistersinger,* 345; *Carmen,* 345–46, *564–65;* Wagner on *Das Rheingold,* 351, Brahms on *Das Rheingold* & *Die Walküre,* 352; Mussorgsky on *Aida,* 356; Tchaikovsky on *Carmen,* 364; Wagner's arrangements for the publication of *Parsifal,* 371–72; Puccini's *Le Villi,* *572;* Verdi hears of Puccini, 376; Verdi auditions the 1st Desdemona, 382–83; Dvořák on *Eugene Onyegin,* 383–84; Verdi at work on *Falstaff,* 385–86; Puccini's rupture with Leoncavallo over *La Bohème,* 388, *575;* R. Strauss sends Verdi his 1st opera, 391; Mahler on the parting of the ways between symphony &, 393; Wolf's *Corregidor,* (395), *577;* Puccini does research for *Tosca,* 397, & *Madama Butterfly,* 401; Strauss, Hofmannsthal, & *Der Rosenkavalier,* 419–22; Puccini gives D'Annunzio his requirements for a libretto, 427; he is kept waiting for *Turandot* & laments the demise of opera, 436
Oprescu, Gheorghe, 450, 452, *585*
Oratorio, 114, 308, 346, 372, 445–46, *484;* C. P. E. Bach's *Die Israeliten...,* 106, *499;* he praises Handel's oratorios, 142; Beethoven offers *Christus am Ölberge* to Härtel, (170), *514;* Haydn must forgo conducting *The Creation,* (171); Hiller's *Die Zerstörung Jerusalems,* (260), (261),

543; Victoria & Albert sing *St. Paul,* 268; preparations for the 1st performance of *Elijah,* (282), *549; see also* Handel (works)
Orchestration: Monteverdi's, for a ballet, 32; his ideas on, for maritime subjects, 37; Haydn on problems of balance, 100; details of, in *Die Entführung* described by Mozart, 136, 139; the Berlioz orchestra, 279–80; Prokofiev on Stravinsky's, 434
Organ, 2, 34, 59, 144, (185), *576;* a 15th-century, 5–6; Cavalieri's experimental, 25; English & German organs, 142, *507;* Prince Albert's, 268
Organists: Bach, 59, 104, 107; masters studied by him, 106–107; his pupils, 108; Telemann, 70; Handel, 78; Bach & Handel compared by C. P. E. Bach, 142; the latter's neglect of the organ, *507;* Mozart, 121; he is offered a position, 126; Beethoven, 146, *508;* Schubert, 185; a loud organist, 232; Verdi competes for a position, *538;* Prince Albert & Mendelssohn, 268; Bruckner, *566; see also* Landini, Squarcialupi, Hofhaimer, Memmo, Luzzaschi, Bull, Wesley
Ormandy, Eugene, 467, *588*
Otto, Franz, 245, (*537*)

Pachelbel, Johann, 106
Pacini, Giovanni, *535*
PAËR, Ferdinando, *524*
*PAGANINI, Nicolò, 255, 307, *528, 540;* Berlioz to, 252; Schumann disconsolate at missing, 226

   Concerto no. 3, 213
   La tempesta, 213

PAISIELLO, Giovanni, *513, 524*

   Nina, recommended by Verdi, 319

PALESTRINA, Giovanni Pierluigi da, 387, *480, 481, 489, 499, 532;* on the intelligibility of words set to music, 16, 17

   Missa Papae Marcelli, 480
   Missa sine nomine (no. 95), 16

Panard, Charles-François, 81, *494*
*Panichelli, Don Pietro, *577;* Puccini to, 396–97
Pantaleoni, Romilda, *573;* Verdi describes her voice, 382–83
Parini, Giuseppe, *498*
Paris, 110, 116, 213, 235, 242, 254, 256, 267, 275, 280, 291, 292, 293, 308, 316, 331, 332, 351, 359, 376, 409, 429, 476, *502, 521, 525, 539, 540, 543, 551, 552, 555, 556, 557, 560, 566, 572, 573, 579, 583;* Dowland in, 27–28; Caccini in, 33–34; founding of the Opéra, (52–54), *487–88; La serva padrona* & other *intermezzi* at the Opéra, 87–88; the "War of the Buffoons," *495;* Gluck offers *Iphigénie en Aulide* to the Opéra, 102–103; he prepares *Alceste* for, 111–12; Gluckists & Piccinnists, 123–24, *500, 503;* Mozart in, 125–26, 130–31; Gluck proposes to settle in, (128), *504,* prepares to go there, 131; Grétry's *Richard* & Beaumarchais' *Figaro* the hits of the season, 140; the *Marseillaise* becomes the rage in, 156; republican spectacles in, during the Revolution, 159; Paisiello's troubles in, 165–66; the Rossini vogue in, 197; young Liszt astonishes, 197, 201, 218; Chopin settles in, 238, *535,* & reports on his progress there, 241–42; his return from Majorca, 257–58, *542; La Fille du Régiment* attacked by Berlioz, defended by Donizetti, 258–59; Wagner's 1st stay in, 263–65, *544; Don Pasquale's première,* 272; the 1844 exhibition in, enhanced by the efforts of Johann Strauss Sr. & Berlioz, 276–77, *547–48;* Chopin leaves, in the wake of the February Revolution, 289, *550–51;* Berlioz must seek a living elsewhere, 312; Wagner returns to, 320–23, *558;* his *Tannhäuser* produced in, 324, *559;* Berlioz's uncomplimentary epithet for, 330; Tchaikovsky just escapes being sent to, 361; Debussy likes Rome less well than, 378–79; Mallarmé visits him in the Rue de Londres, 424; an "affaire" Toscanini-Ravel, 447, *584–85*
Parma, 18, 128, 131, 256, 288, 337, *504, 528, 538, 551*
Parrish, Dorothy, 470, 471, *588*
Parrot, 270, 338–39
Pasquini, Bernardo, 57, *489*
Pasta, Giuditta, 239, *532, 535;* Schumann on hearing, 224
Pavesi, Stefano, (272), *546*
Pea, Enrico, 436, *583*
PERFORMANCE PRACTICE: Machault on performing a *ballade,* 2; Tromboncino on performing a *frottola,* 12; Galilei's monodic style, 22; Cavalieri on singing to a novel tuning, 25; Monteverdi's suggestions for a ballet, 32; his concern over the balance between voices & instruments, 37; Handel's forces in action, 78; Haydn on the correct preparation of a cantata, 98–100; Mozart arranges *Die Entführung* for wind band, 139–40; audience reaction & conducting arrangements at Beethoven's 1824 concert, 200, *524–25;* the program at Chopin's Viennese debut, 220; Berlioz employs 1,022 performers at a concert, 276–77, *547–48;* his arrangements for a normal concert, 279–80
PERFORMANCES, SPECIFIC: Handel's *L'Allegro ... in Dublin,* 78; the 1st performance of Rousseau's *Le Devin du village,* 87, *495,* & of Mozart's *La finta giardiniera,* 109; Mozart plays privately at Heiligkreuz, 121, pub-

licly in Augsburg, 122–23; Gluck's *Alceste* in Bologna, 131–32; the 2nd performance of *Die Entführung,* 139; Haydn attends a concert in London, 154; Beethoven gives a benefit concert, 179; his 1824 concert in Vienna (1st performance of the 9th Symphony, etc.), 196, 198–200, *524–25;* Chopin's Viennese debut, 220–22; Bellini on the 1st performances of *Norma,* 239–40; *Don Pasquale*'s *première,* 272; "the greatest musical celebration which ever took place in Europe," 276–77, *547–48; Traviata* a failure, 296; 1st Leipzig performance of Brahms's Piano Concerto no. 1, 317–18; 1st performance of *Un ballo in maschera,* 319, *558; Tannhäuser* in Paris, (324), *559;* Brahms introduces himself to Vienna, 328–29, *560–61;* Bruckner's 7th Symphony in Graz & Vienna, 381; Prokofiev attends a Stravinsky *première* in New York, 434; Bartók & Waldbauer give a joint recital, 437; Toscanini conducts Ravel's *Boléro* at the Opéra, 447, *584–85;* Menuhin plays Bartók's solo sonata, 471; Koussevitzky conducts Bartók's *Concerto for Orchestra,* 471–72

PERFORMER, COMPOSER &: Machault on not taking liberties with his music, 2; Handel & Dubourg, *493–94;* Haydn gives instructions for a performance he cannot attend, 98–100; Beethoven exasperated with his orchestra for disregarding dynamics, 172, & with Czerny for not playing a sonata "as it was written," 184; Schubert on how to perform his E-flat maj. Trio, 211–12; Wagner cautions a singer to adhere to the score, 345; Bartók objects to cuts in his work, 431; Ravel & Toscanini, 447, *584–85;* Papa Vecsey & Saint-Saëns, 469

Pergolesi, Giovanni Battista, *495*

La serva padrona, Paris performances & Rousseau's edition of, 87–88, *495*

Peri, Jacopo, *481, 482, 484*

Euridice, 484

Peronelle d'Unchair, 476; Machault to, 1–2, 2–4

Perrin, Pierre, 52, *487*

Perti, Jacopo Antonio, 490; Bassani to, 60–61; Marcello to, 61–63

Perucchini, Giovanni Battista, 535; Bellini to, 239–40

Peter the Great, a dissenter legend about, (341), *563–64*

Peters, Carl Friedrich, 201, *513, 525*

PETITIONS: Gafori applies for a clerkship, 9; Coclico offers to teach in Stettin, 13–15; Tallis & Byrd ask Queen Elizabeth to compensate their losses, 21–22; Viadana asks for charity, 26–27; Victoria requests lar-

gesse, 31; Monteverdi begs not to be worked to death, 32–33; Bull applies for a position, 35–36; Monteverdi demands redress for an insult, 44–45; Schütz asks to be pensioned, 46–52; Lully requests structural changes for his opera house, 53–54; Buxtehude asks for continued subvention, 57; Bach requests his release from Mühlhausen, 59–60; Handel applies for British citizenship, 66; Bach wishes to move to Danzig, 71–73; he asks for a title, 73–74; he denounces an incompetent student, 74–75; Boccherini applies for a position, 95; Haydn writes the Elector in Beethoven's behalf, 157–58, & Beethoven adds his own plea, 158; Paisiello asks Napoleon to settle a difficulty, 165–66; Schubert applies for a position in Carniola, 184–85; Beethoven on his deathbed appeals to the Philharmonic Society, 209–10; Wagner begs to have *Rienzi* produced in Dresden, 263–64; Smetana turns to Liszt in his distress, 284–86; Dvořák asks Brahms for a recommendation, 359–60

Pfundt, E. G. B., 317, *558*

Philadelphia, 467, 472, *588;* Wagner's *Festmarsch* for the Centennial Exposition in, 357–58, *567–68*

Philharmonic Society (London), 185, *519;* Beethoven appeals to, 209–10, & expresses gratitude for their help, 210–11; Mendelssohn fêted by, 267; his reaction to an incident during rehearsal, 282, *549;* Wagner a guest of, 308–309, 311, *555*

Philip II, king of Spain, 30, 31, *485*

Philip III, king of Spain, (31), *483*

Pianists: Mozart describes Nanette Stein's playing & his own, 121–22; Czerny rebuked by Beethoven, 184; young Liszt in Paris, 197, 201, 217–18; Moscheles & Kalkbrenner appraised by Czerny, 200; Schubert, 204–205; Viennese reactions to Chopin, 220–22; Schumann as a student, 223; his plans for a career, 228; he compares Chopin with Clara Wieck, 250; he tells of the accident to his hand & evaluates some contemporaries, including Mendelssohn, 253–55; Mendelssohn evaluates Liszt & compares him with Thalberg, 260–61; Brahms (aged 8), 266; Smetana too poor to own a piano, 286; Brahms introduces his 1st Concerto to Leipzig, 317–18, & himself to the Viennese public, 328–30, *560–61;* Rossini's position in the history of piano playing, 332; Prokofiev examined, 403; Bartók in the Iberian peninsula, 408–10, & in Czechoslovakia, 437; *see also* Pixis, Würfel, Herz, Henselt, Döhler, Klindworth, Rubinstein (N.), *et al.*

Pianoforte, 122, 157, 305, *502*, *518*, *521;* Haydn's disobedient, 149; the advantages of transcriptions for, 163; rebaptized by Beethoven, 186–87, *520;* his advice to Czerny on teaching, 188, *521;* Bellini unable to obtain a, 189; some Viennese makes & Beethoven's Broadwood, 201, *525;* Chopin uses a Graf, 222; Wagner begins a transcription of Beethoven's 9th Symphony, 229–30; Chopin orders a Pleyel, 251; Schumann composes at the, 255; Bösendorfer, 329, *561;* Brahms advises a young composer to study the, 368; Bartók's, highly unsatisfactory in the early days, 398–99, & sometimes later, 409

*Piave, Francesco Maria, *552, 559;* Verdi to, 325

Piccinni, Nicola, 123, *503*

Roland, (123), *503*

Pierné, Gabriel, 378, *572*

Piracy, 147

Piringer, Ferdinand, 194, *523*

Pixis, Johann Peter, 218, 241, *530*

Plantin, Christophe, *483*

Plato, quoted, 37, *485*

Plevna, 364, *569*

Pleyel, Camille, 251, *539*

*Pleyel, Ignace, *521;* Berlioz to, 189

Poland, *493, 563, 565;* the war of succession in (16th cent.), 23, *482;* "Polish style," 70; the Warsaw revolution of 1830, 238, *535; see also* Chopin

Polledro, Giovanni Battista, 179, 187, *517*

Porpora, Nicola, taught Haydn, 114, *501*

Portugal, Bartók in, 408–10, *469*

Prague, 143, 147–48, 181, 213, 284, 287, 354, 368, 450, 455, *482, 550;* celebrates a victory over the Turks, 24; Mozart in, *508;* Smetana hopes to open a music school in, 285–86; Tchaikovsky in, 383, *574*

Prima pratica, 42, *486, 490–91; see also Stile antico*

Prix de Rome, 538; Berlioz a recipient of, *537;* Bizet in Rome after winning, 314–17, *557;* Debussy *ditto,* 378–79, *572–73;* Schmitt *ditto* but not Ravel, 400–401, *578*

*Probst, Heinrich Albert, 225, 226, *527;* Schubert to, 208, 211–12, 216

*Procurators of St. Mark, *486;* Monteverdi to, 44–45

*Prokofiev, Sergei Alexeyevich, *578;* Prokofiev to, 402–406

PROKOFIEV, Sergei Sergeyevich, *578–79, 583*

Juvenilia, 404–405, 410

Proksch, Joseph, 284, (*550*)

Proudhon, Pierre Joseph, Wagner on, 335

Publicity: Hofhaimer directs his own, 10; Gluck introduces himself to Paris, 102–103; London hears of Haydn's arrival, 153;

Beethoven entreated to give a concert, 199, *524;* Liszt writes to the newspapers, 260, 261–62; Berlioz saturates the Lyons area, 279, 280

PUBLISHERS, COMPOSERS &: Monte to his publisher in time of war, 26; Haydn, his music pirated, finds Artaria negligent, 147; Beethoven sends Simrock the latest news from Vienna, 161–62; he offers 4 works to Hoffmeister, 163–64; he offers Härtel the "Eroica," "Appassionata," etc., 170–71, scolds at misprints, 176, plans a title page & discusses Goethe, 178–79; he orders Steiner to rebaptize the pianoforte, 186–87, & sets Tobias Haslinger to music, 190–92; Berlioz tries his luck, 189; Schubert contacts publishers in Germany, 208, *527;* Beethoven reassures Schott he was only joking—op. 131 is *not* a compilation, 208; Schubert sends Probst his E-flat maj. Trio, 211–12, & offers him his last works, 216; Wagner suggests Schott publish his piano arrangement of Beethoven's 9th Symphony, 229–30; Chopin rectifies an *erratum,* 273; Verdi informs Ricordi *Traviata* has failed, 296; Brahms, approached by Viennese publishers, declines, 329; Wagner emulates Verdi in the matter of fees, 357–58; Dvořák recommended to Simrock by Brahms, 360–61; R. Strauss sends his op. 1 to "Mr. Breitkopf," 370–71; Wagner sets his terms for *Parsifal,* 371–72; Puccini informs Ricordi of his work on *Madama Butterfly,* 401; Debussy tells Durand about his latest works, 407–408; Schoenberg enlists Hertzka's help to obtain a position, 422–23; *see also* Music printing & publishing

PUCCINI, Giacomo, *562, 572, 575, 577, 578, 582, 583;* Verdi hears of, & expresses his opinion, 376; "great love in little souls," 427

La Bohème, 396; P.'s rupture with Leoncavallo over, 388, *575*

Edgar, 575

Madama Butterfly, P. at work on, 401, *578*

Manon Lescaut, 388, *575*

Tosca, P. at work on, 397

Turandot, P. kept waiting by the librettists, 436, *583*

Le Villi, 572, *575*

*Puchberg, Johann Michael, *509, 510;* Mozart to, 150–51; Haydn to, 155–56

*Purcell, Henry, 55, *488;* Locke to, 54

PURCELL, Thomas, *488*

Quantz, Johann Joachim, *507;* praised Bach's organ playing, 142

Versuch einer Anweisung . . ., 142, *507*

Quinault, Philippe, 53, *488*

Rachel (Élisa Félix), 280, 549
Racine, Jean Baptiste, 111
Raff, Joachim, 301, 554
Raimund, Ferdinand, 194, 523
RAMEAU, Jean-Philippe, 491, 492, 496; on taste & science, 66–68

Aquilon et Orithie, (68), 492
Pièces de Clavecin (1724), (68), 492
Thétis, 68
Observations sur notre instinct . . . , 89

*Rankl, Karl, 465, 466, 588; Schoenberg to, 474
Raphael, Bizet on Michelangelo &, 314–15
*Ravel, Édouard, 429, (582); Ravel to, 442–43, 443, 443–44
RAVEL, Maurice, 578–82 pass., 584–85

Boléro, the cause of an "affaire" Toscanini-Ravel, 447, 584–85
Jeux d'eau, 578
Ma Mère l'Oye, 580
Pavane, 578
Trio, 429
La Valse, originally Wien, left unfinished for obvious reasons, 429, 582

Rebuses, musical, 18, 477, 480
Recio, Marie, (310), 558; causes Wagner to ponder, (321)
Recitals. See Performances, specific
Reese, Gustave, 475, 477, 479
*Reich, Willi, 586; Webern to, 459–61
Reinhard, Werner, 459, 460, 586
Reinken, Jan Adams, 107
Rellstab, Ludwig, 539
Reutter, J. A. K. G. von, Jr., 113
*Revolutionary Committee, Dalayrac to a, 160
Revolutions. See Wars
Richter, Hans, 348; conducts Bruckner's 7th Symphony in Vienna, 381
Richter, Jean Paul, (232), 234, 237, 534, 540 572; Goethe on, 516; Schumann &, 214, 224, 253, 529
*Ricordi, Giovanni, 550, 552; Verdi to, 283–84
*Ricordi, Giulio, 333, 382, 562, 572; Verdi to, 373; Puccini to, 401
*Ricordi, Tito (I), 319, 325, 333, 358, 552, 562, 567; Verdi to, 296
Ricordi, Tito (II), 583
Ries, Franz, 161, 512
Rietz, Julius, 317
Rimbaud, Arthur, 417, 580
Rimsky-Korsakov, Nikolai Andreyevich, (338), 563; Tchaikovsky on, 362–63, 364; examines Prokofiev, 402–406
Rinuccini, Ottavio, 484
*Ritter, Théodore, 556; Berlioz to, 310–11
Roebuck, John Arthur, 267, 271, 545
Roederer, Count Pierre Louis, 166, 514
Röntgen, Engelbert, 317

Rogers, Samuel, 267, 545
Roll-Anker, Nini, 452, (585)
Romani, Felice, 369, 570
Rome, 18, 20, 43, 56, 77, 95, 228, 247, 267, 546; Dufay in, 6; Dowland's intelligence from, 28–30; music a beggar in, 58; Mozart in, 100–101; Berlioz dips into liquid history, 246; Un ballo in maschera produced in, 319, 558; Liszt in, 347, 565; See also Prix de Rome
Rore, Cipriano de, 479
Rosenhain, Jacob, 267, 545
ROSSINI, Gioachino, 531, 553, 561, 570, 575; his vogue in Paris, 197, & Vienna, (199), 200, 524; his music heard by Schumann in Milan, 224; his retirement, 298, 553; spurious letters ascribed to him, 553

Guillaume Tell, 553
Moïse, 548

*Roth, Franz, 509; Haydn to, 147–48
Rothschild, Baron Jacob de, 252, 540
*Rouget de Lisle, Claude Joseph, 511; Grétry to, 156

La Marseillaise, 265, 560; its creation, 156, 511

ROUSSEAU, Jean-Jacques, 495, 498; Gluck's tribute to, 103

Le Devin du village, the 1st performance of, (87), 495, 500
Confessions, 495
Lettre sur la musique française, (103), 498

*Rozières, Marie de, 551, 552; Chopin to, 294
Rubinstein, Nikolai Grigoryevich, 569; Tchaikovsky on, 364–66
Rulers, musical, 476; see also Este (Isabella d'), Gonzaga (Guglielmo), Moritz of Hesse-Kassel, Albert (the Prince Consort), Victoria (Queen)
*Rupprecht, Johann Baptist, 518; Beethoven to, 180
Russia, 315, 339, 534, 563, 564, 567; the Warsaw revolution crushed by, 535; the Russo-Turkish War, 569; Tchaikovsky on Russian music, 364; see also Moscow, St. Petersburg
Russian National School, 563, 564; Tchaikovsky on, 362–64

*Sacchetti, Franco, 476; Landini to, 4
Sacher, Paul, 458, 586
SACRED MUSIC: Luther on music & theology, 11; a motet by Coclico, 14; Palestrina sends a Mass to the Duke of Mantua, 16, corrects one by the Duke, 19; Galilei's responsories & Lamentations, 22; Monte's Masses remain unpublished in time of war, 26; some liturgical works by Viadana, 27; Vic-

INDEX

toria's "Battle" Mass, 31, *483;* Scheidt's difficulties in the administration of his duties, 40–41; Monteverdi at St. Mark's, 42; Buxtehude & the *Abend-Musicken* at Lübeck, 57, *489–90;* Bach unable to have a "well-regulated church music," 59; Bassani perplexed over the secular aspect of his duties, 60–61; Marcello submits a Mass to the Accademia Filarmonica, 61–63; Bach's duties in Leipzig, 64–66, 74–75; "church style," 70; Bach's B minor Mass, (73), *493;* his troubles with an incompetent choir leader, 74–75; J. C. Bach's service for the dead, 91, *496;* C. P. E. Bach on his father's church music, 104; Beethoven's C major Mass, 178, 179; the Berlin Singakademie, *522;* 1st Viennese performance of parts of Beethoven's *Missa Solemnis,* 199; Thibaut at Heidelberg, *532;* Verdi about to conduct the *Requiem,* 358–59; *see also* Oratorio

Sahr, Henrich von, 317, 318

St. Petersburg, *524, 563, 564;* Verdi in, 325; Mussorgsky on militarism in, 340; Saint-Saëns in, 355–56; Prokofiev at the Conservatory, 402–406, 415, *578–79, 580; see also* Russian National School

Saint-Saëns, Camille, *567;* Mussorgsky's opinion of, 355–56; Papa Vecsey &, 469

Sainton, Prosper, 309

Salieri, Antonio, 184, *509, 519*

Salomon, Johann Peter, 153, 185–86, *510, (520)*

Salzburg, 122, 205, 367, 395, *478, 498;* Mozart's dissatisfaction with, (109); he attempts to leave, 117–19, *502;* he resigns his post at, 132–34

San Francisco, 443; Bartók in, 442

Sand, George, 257, *539, 542, 551*

Sand, Karl Ludwig, 233, *534*

Saxophone, Debussy & the, 408, *579*

SCARLATTI, Alessandro, *490*

SCARLATTI, Domenico, *490, 495;* his father writes in his behalf, 58

*Schaden, Joseph Wilhelm von, *508;* Beethoven to, 145–46

SCHEIDT, Samuel, *486*

Scherchen, Hermann, 459, 474, *586*

Schiller, Friedrich von, 200, 380

*Schindler, Anton, 209, *524, 527, 528;* Beethoven to, 198

*Schlesinger, Maurice, 243, *543, 546;* Liszt to, 261–62; Chopin to, 273

Schmid, Erich, 459, 460, *586*

Schmidt, Johann Adam, 168, *514*

*Schmitt, Florent, *578;* Ravel to, 400–401

Schneider, Georg Abraham, (196), *523*

*Schober, Franz von, *530;* Schubert to, 217

Schoeck, Othmar, *587*

*SCHOENBERG, Arnold, 425, 426, 430, *581,*

582, 584, 586–88 pass.; Berg to, 445–46, 454–55

Concerto (piano), 466

Erwartung, 474

Die glückliche Hand, 474

Die Jakobsleiter, 466, 474

Moses und Aron, 454, 466, (586); gives rise to a misunderstanding between S. & Berg, 444–46

Pelleas und Melisande, 446

Pierrot lunaire, 466, *582;* Berg on, 428

Theme & variations, op. 43, 466

Von heute auf morgen, 446, 474

Harmonielehre, 425, 440, (581)

Style and Idea, (473), *588*

Schopenhauer, Arthur: Wagner &, 300, *553–54;* Webern on Wagner &, 426

*B. Schott's Söhne, 254, 351, 357, *527, 533;* Beethoven to, 208–209; Wagner to, 229–30; he sets conditions for the publication of *Parsifal,* 371–72, *571*

Schubart, Johann Martin, 108

*Schubert, Ferdinand, 205, (217), *518, 526;* Schubert to (?), 179–80

SCHUBERT, Franz Anton, *520*

SCHUBERT, Franz (Peter), 333, 334, 380, *508, 515, 518, 519, 520, 523–32 pass.,* *560, 571;* his brothers & sisters, 205–206, *526;* Schumann on, 223, 224–25, 226, 254

Alfonso und Estrella, 530

An die Musik, 530

An Mignon, An Schwager Kronos, (203), *525*

Ave Maria (Ellen's Gesang III), (203–204), *526;* Verdi's *Pace, mio Dio* suspected of being an imitation of, 333–34

Erlkönig, 526; falls into the wrong hands, 187, *520*

Fierabras, (196), *523*

Ganymed, (203), *525*

Gretchen am Spinnrade, (196), *523*

The Lady of the Lake, 7 lieder from, 203, 204, *526*

Marches (piano 4-hands), op. 40(?), 204, *526*

Octet, 196, 208, *524*

Quartets in A & D min., 196, *523*

Quintet (piano, strings), 226, *533*

Quintet (strings), *529;* offered to Probst by S., 216

Rondo (piano 4-hands) in A maj., Schumann on, 224–25

Schwanengesang, 529

Sonata (piano), op. 42, 205–206, *520*

3 Sonatas (piano), posthumous, *529;* offered to Probst by S., 216

Suleika II, 204, *526*

Trio, op. 100, *528, 529, 532;* S. sends it to Probst with performance instructions,

211–12, inquires when it will appear, 216; Schumann on, 223

Variations (piano 4-hands) in A-flat maj., 204, *526*

Die Verschworenen, 196, *523*

Waltzes (piano), 223, 226

*Schubert, Franz (Sr.) & Anna, *525;* Schubert to, 203–206

SCHÜTZ, Heinrich, 485, 487

Il primo libro de' madrigali, (48), 487

Symphoniae sacrae, III, (46), 487

Schulthess, Walter, 458, *586*

*Schumann, Clara (née Wieck), 226, 260, (278), (297), (299), 307, 318, *518, 528, 532, 536, 543, 548, 554–55, 576;* Schumann to, 244; Brahms to, 302–306, 390–91; Schumann on the artistry of, 250, 254, 303; at Schumann's deathbed, 313

*Schumann, Johanne Christiane, *533;* Schumann to, 227–29, 235–37

*SCHUMANN, Robert, 408, *517, 518, 528– 29, 532–45 pass., 548–49, 552–55 pass., 558, 576;* Wiedebein to, 215–16; Wagner to, 265; Brahms to, 297; "the most important letter I've ever written," 227–29; spends a day with Chopin, 249, 250; the *Davidsbund*, 249, *539;* discusses his own works, those of leading contemporaries, & his career, 253–56; Wagner &, *544–45;* his attempt at suicide, 298–99; is visited by Brahms at the Endenich asylum, 302–306; his death, 313; an observation by Schoenberg on, 423

"Abegg" Variations, 255; "Countess Abegg," 303, *554*

Allegro, op. 8, 245, 255

Arabeske, 253, 255

Die beiden Grenadiere, Wagner writes S. apropos of, 265, *545*

Blumenstück, 253, 255

Carnaval, 255, *539*

Concert-Allegro mit Introduction, dedicated to Brahms, (304), *555*

Concerto (piano), *541*

Davidsbündlertänze, 255, *539*

Fantasie, 253, 255; played by Brahms in Vienna, *561*

Fantasiestücke (piano), 255, (303), *554*

Faschingsschwank aus Wien, 540, *541;* Schumann at work on (?), 255

Gesänge der Frühe, 303–304, *555*

Humoreske, 255; its title explained by S., 253

Impromptus, 245, 255, *536*

Intermezzi, 245, 255, 528, 529

Kinderscenen, 253, 255

Kreisleriana, 255, *517;* one of S.'s favorites, 253

Lieder, op. II, *529;* S. sends them to Wiedebein, 214–15, who comments on them, 215–16

Lieder, op. 40, (278), *548–49*

Liederkreis, op. 24, sent to Heine by S., 262, *543*

Das Schifflein, 549

Skizzen für den Pedal-Flügel, 303, *554*

Sonata in F min. (*Concert sans Orchestre*), 245, 250, 255, *537, 541*

Sonata (piano) in F-sharp min., 245, 250, 255, *529, 537*

Sonata (piano) in G min., 245, 255, *529, 537*

Studien für den Pedal-Flügel, (303), *554*

Toccata, 245, 255

"Neue Bahnen," (296), *553*

See also 255, 304, 307

Schunke, Ludwig, 245, *537*

*Schuppanzigh, Ignaz, *524;* Beethoven to, 198

Schwanenberg, Johann Gottfried, 143, *507*

Schwind, Moritz von, 196, *523*

Scott, Sir Walter, 203, 204, 267

The Lady of the Lake, 203, *526*

Seattle, 471, 473; Bartók in, 441, *584*

Seconda pratica, 42, *486*

*Sedaine, Michel Jean, *506;* Grétry to, 140–41

Seeau, Count Joseph Anton, 117, 118, *502*

Senff, Bartholf, 303, 304, 317, *555*

*Senfl, Ludwig, *478;* Luther to, 11–12; suffers an accident, 10

Seyfried, Ignaz Xaver von, 172, 220, *515, 531*

*Sforza, Lodovico Maria, *478;* Gafori to, 9

Shakespeare, William, 177, 233–34, 281, 468, 485, 501, 507; Berlioz is given the complete works of, 311

Antony and Cleopatra, 116

Hamlet: Berlioz quotes, 331; Mussorgsky sympathizes with Polonius, 343

Julius Caesar, 304, *555*

King Lear, 408

A Midsummer-Night's Dream, 281; Mendelssohn advised not to read, 234, *534*

Romeo and Juliet, 177, 310, (517), *540*

Sonnet xviii, quoted, 478

See also Verdi (*Macbeth, Otello, Falstaff*)

Shostakovich, Dmitri Dmitrievich, 472

Signale für die musikalische Welt, 303, 307, *554–55*

Simonelli, Matteo, 56

*Simoni, Renato, *583;* Puccini to, 436

Simrock, Fritz August, Brahms recommends Dvořák to, 360–61, *568*

*Simrock, Nikolaus, *512, 568;* Beethoven to, 161–62

Simrock, Peter Joseph, 307

SINGERS & SINGING: cantors sent to Florence by Dufay, 7; Isabella d'Este a prospective pupil, 8–9; the ladies of Ferrara, 24–25;

Caccini & his daughter sing for the French court, 33–34; Monteverdi auditions a male contralto, 34–35; Scheidt's students, 40–41; Monteverdi insulted by a chorister, 44–45; Schütz as a choirboy, 47; Gostling, 55; Handel engages singers for the coming season, 70–71; Bach's wife & daughter enhance the family ensemble, 73; his choirs in Leipzig, 74–75; his singing voice, 105; Vivaldi & Anna Giraud, 76–77, 493; Handel's singers in Dublin, 78, & in London, 81–82, 84; Haydn requests a clear enunciation, 99, 149; a Milanese singing master, 101; Haydn as a choirboy, 113–14; Mozart fashions vocal parts to suit his singers' capacities, 135–36; they have an accident, 139; F. S. Mayer, 172, 515; Schubert's training at school, 184, 185; the original cast of Euryanthe rehearses, 193–95 pass.; Czerny on Beethoven's vocal music, 200; Vogl & Schubert, 203–204; Schumann on hearing Giuditta Pasta, 224; the original cast of Norma, 239, 535; Queen Victoria & Prince Albert give a private performance, 268–70; a politico-musical moment at the Paris exhibition, 277, & a quartet sung by 80 basses, 548; Berlioz engages singers for an average concert, 280; Chopin describes the art of Jenny Lind, 287–88; Berlioz's second wife, 558; the original cast of La forza del destino welcome Verdi to Russia, 325; Wagner on how to play Beckmesser in Die Meistersinger, 345; Verdi reports on the soprano who is to create the part of Desdemona in Otello, 382–83; he seeks a Mistress Quickly for the 1st performance of Falstaff, 385; see also Lieder, Opera, individual singers
*Sire, Simonin de, 540; Schumann to, 253–56
Sirmen, Ludovico, 497
Slonimsky, Nicolas, 475
Smart, Sir George, 209, 210, 211, (527)
*SMETANA, Bedřich, 550, 566, 567; Liszt to, 286–87
Smithson, Henrietta, 558
*Soffredini, Alfredo, 574; Verdi to, 385
Soto de Langa, Francisco, 31, 484
*Sotte, C. P., 535; Paër to, 238
Spain, 278, 416, 580; Chopin in, 251, 539, 542; Bartók in, 409, 579; see also John I, Philip II, Victoria (Tomas L. de)
Spaun, Josef von, 204, 525, 526
Spontini, Gasparo, 548
SQUARCIALUPI, Antonio, 477; Dufay sends greetings to, 6
Stadler, Anton (Gooseberry-Face), 151, 510
Stage fright: Polledro's, at a concert with Beethoven, 179; Chopin nearly overcomes his, 220–21; Queen Victoria confesses to, 270

*Stasov, Vladimir Vassilyevich, 563; Mussorgsky to, 338–39, 340–44, 346–47, 355–57
Stegmayer, Ferdinand, 245, 250, 537, 539
*Stein, Erwin, 423, 455, 461, 581; Schoenberg to, 465–66
Stein, Johann Andreas, 120–23 pass., 502
Stein, Nanette, 503; Mozart describes her piano playing, (121–22)
*Steiner, Sigmund Anton, 191, 520; Beethoven to, 186–87
Stephanie, Gottlieb, 135–37 pass., 505
Sterba, Editha & Richard, 521
Stile antico (grave): Marcello on, 62, 490–91; Handel on, (63–64), 491; D. Scarlatti on, (86); Fux's Gradus ad Parnassum, 499
Stirling, Jane, (289), 550
Stockhausen, Julius, 329, 561
Storace, Nancy, 143, 144, 507
Strauss, Franz, 370, 571
Strauss, Johann Sr., & Berlioz go into partnership, 276, 547–48
STRAUSS, Richard, 567, 570–71, 576, 581

  Elektra, 581
  Festmarsch, op. 1, sent to "Mr. Breitkopf" by S., 370–71
  Guntram, sent to Verdi by S., 391
  Der Rosenkavalier, S. & Hofmannsthal collaborate on, 419–22, 581

*Stravinsky, Igor, 579–83 pass.; Debussy to, 426–27; Ravel to, 429; Prokofiev to, 434

  Petrushka, 582; Debussy on, 426
  3 Poems from the Japanese, 434, 583
  Pribautki, Prokofiev reports on the 1st American performance of, 434

*Strecker, Ludwig, 571; Wagner to, 371–72
Stremayr, Karl von, 348, 359, 566
Strepponi, Giuseppina, 256, 326, 327, 353, 370, 376, 383, 386, 541–42
*Striggio, Alessandro, 485; Monteverdi to, 36–38
Strindberg, August, 426, 444–45
Strungk, Nicolaus Adam, 107
Strunk, Oliver, 475, 481, 483, 486, 490, 498, 517
Stumpff, Johann Andreas, 209, 211, 527
Suard, Jean Baptiste Antoine, 123, 503
Swieten, Baron Gottfried van, 115, 501
Swiney, Owen, 70, 492
Switzerland, 192, 266, 301, 303, 456, 459, 586; Schumann back from, 224; Mendelssohn on his way to, 231, 533; Wagner escapes to, after the Dresden uprising, 551; Wagner at Triebschen, 562; see also Basel, Geneva
*Szigeti, Joseph, 587; Bartók to, 467–70

TALLIS, Thomas, 481
Tamberlik, Enrico, 325, 559

INDEX

TARTINI, Giuseppe, *496*
Tausig, Carl, *566*
Taverner, John, *483*
*TCHAIKOVSKY, Pyotr Ilyitch, *568–69, 574;* Dvořák to, *383–84*

Eugene Onyegin, 569, 574; Dvořák on, *383–84*
Symphony no. 4, *569*

TEACHERS, COMPOSERS AS: Dufay's singing pupils, 7; Joh. Martini prepares to teach Isabella d'Este, 8–9; Coclico at German universities, 14; Palestrina corrects Guglielmo Gonzaga's compositions, 16–17, 19; Lassus trains choristers, 20; Byrd's duties prevent him from teaching, 21; Scheidt's difficulties in Halle, 40–41; Bach's duties in Leipzig, 64–66; his troubles with a student, 74–75; his teaching methods, 107–108; Tartini gives a lesson by correspondence, 91–95; Haydn's early days as a teacher, 114; Mozart teaches composition to an uninspired pupil, 125–26; he seeks pupils, 151; Haydn & his student Beethoven, 157–58; Zelter on learning the basic skills, 174; Weber comments on some songs by Wieck, 181–83; Schubert applies for a position, 184–85; Beethoven on teaching the piano, 188; Schumann gives piano lessons while studying law, 223, 226; Chopin much in demand, 241; Cherubini, *537–38;* Smetana hopes to better his situation by opening a school, 285–86; Bruckner hunts for students, 348–49; Debussy as tutor, *568;* Schoenberg describes his pupils & methods, 422–23; he takes pride in being Berg's teacher, 448; Bartók gives a summer course, 453; Webern has no pupils after the *Anschluss,* 461; Schoenberg must retire from his university position, 466; Bartók has no pupils in New York, 471; *see also* Musical education of composers
*TELEMANN, Georg Philipp, *492, 496;* Handel to, 89–90; Bach &, 108
Texts. *See* Words & music
Thalberg, Sigismond, *541;* Schumann on, 254–55; Mendelssohn compares Liszt with, 260–61
Thayer, Alexander Wheelock, 373n., *572*
THEORY, MUSICAL: Palestrina corrects Guglielmo Gonzaga's compositions, 16–17; Scheidt's teaching of, 41; Monteverdi on the *prima & seconda pratica,* 42; Corelli's parallel 5ths, 55–56, *489;* Handel on the modal *vs.* the contemporary approach, 63–64; Rameau on the role of, in composition, 66–68; Mozart explains why he chose a certain key, 135–36; Weber finds faulty modulations & parallel octaves in songs submitted to him by Wieck, 181–83 *pass.;*

Schumann on, 223; Verdi on the "rules," 334; Mussorgsky dislikes talk of, 342–43; the "Petersburg composers" &, 362; Brahms on learning to transpose & on taking harmony lessons, 390; Bartók's program of studies at the Academy in Budapest, 397–99 *pass.;* Prokofiev's examination in, 402–406; Schoenberg on the development of his "composition with 12 notes," 439; *see also Stile antico*
Thibaut, Anton Friedrich Justus, *532;* Schumann on, 223–24, 226; encourages Schumann to follow his vocation, 228
Thomán, István, 398, *577*
*Thomas, Theodore, *567, 568;* Wagner to, 357–58
Thorough bass, 69, *483, 491;* Bach's skill in realizing a, 105; his instruction in, 107
*Töpken, Theodor, *537;* Schumann to, 245
*Toscanini, Arturo, 449, *584–85;* Ravel to, 447; attacked by the Fascists, *585*
Toulouse-Lautrec, Henri de, *580*
Traeg, Johann, 161, *512*
Trakl, Georg, 433
Transylvania, Bartók looks for authentic folk songs in, 410–14
Trieste, *572*
Trillo, 34, *484*
TROMBONCINO, Bartolomeo, 479

Se la mia morte brami, 12

Turin, 376, 388, *575*
Turkey, 11, 43, *482;* capture of Constantinople, (6), *477;* a Turkish rout, 23–24; "Turkish music," 135–37 *pass.,* 139; the Russo-Turkish War, *569*
Turner, William, 55, *488*

Uhland, Ludwig, 278, *549*
Uhlig, Theodor, 292, *551*
Umlauf, Michael, 200, *524–25*
United States: Theodore Thomas's activity in, 357, *567;* Prokofiev in, 434, *583;* Bartók's 1st visit to, 441–42, *584;* Ravel in, 442–44, *584;* Schoenberg an immigrant, *585; see also* individual cities
Universal Edition, 455, *529, 581;* taken over by the Nazis, 457; Webern does "jobs" for, 461
Uxoricides. *See* Tromboncino

Vaccai, Niccolò, *531*
*Vadian, Joachim, *478;* Hofhaimer to, 10
*Valentin, Monsieur, *506;* Gluck to, 137–38
Valéry, Paul, 450, 451, *580*
Vanhall, Johann Baptist, *503*

Concerto (violin) in B-flat maj., played by Mozart, 121

*Vasnier, Eugène-Henry, *572;* Debussy to, 378–79

615

*Vasselli, Antonio, 546; Donizetti to, 272
Vecsey, Ferenc, 579; Bartók's tour with, 408–409, 469
Veit, Philipp, 267, 545
Veltheim, Charlotte, 220, 531
Venice, 10, 12, 51, 239, 478, 485, 535; the Venetian School (late Renaiss.), 479–80, 487; Dowland in, 28, 30, 31; Monteverdi's duties in, 42; the plague in, 43, 486; Monteverdi publicly insulted in, 44–45; Schütz in, 47–48; D. Scarlatti leaves for, 58, 490; Vivaldi at the Pietà, 77, 493; Ernani in, (274), 547; Rigoletto bowdlerized by the censor in, 294–95, 552; Traviata a failure in, 296, 552
*VERDI, Giuseppe, 538, 541–42, 547, 550, 552, 559–63 pass., 566, 567, 573, 574–75, 578; Bülow to, 386–87; R. Strauss to, 391–92; Donizetti &, 274–75; "my supreme musical ignorance," 333–34; on contemporary music, 353; Wagner takes note of, 358, 567; on opera & symphony, 376

Aida, 355, 386, 562, 567; Verdi alters the libretto of, 336–37; Mussorgsky on, 356
Aroldo, 319
Attila, 284
Un ballo in maschera, 1st performance of, 319, 558
I due Foscari, 284
Ernani, 284, 295; about to be produced in Venice, (274); its triumph there, 547; Donizetti supervises its production in Vienna, 275
Falstaff, 578; V. at work on, 385–86, 574; R. Strauss expresses his admiration for, 391
La forza del destino, 562; V. in St. Petersburg to supervise its production, (325), 559; Pace, mio Dio suspected of being an imitation of Schubert's Ave Maria, 333–34
Un giorno di regno, 570
Inno delle nazioni, V. in London in connection with, (325–27), 559–60
I Lombardi alla prima Crociata, 284, 547
Macbeth, V. will not let La Scala produce, 283–84
Nabucodonosor, 542, 547
Oberto Conte di S. Bonifacio, (256), 541, 550
Otello, 386, 573, 574; V. reports on the soprano who is to create the part of Desdemona, 382–83
Quartet (strings), (568); V. suggests a string orchestra performance of his, 359
Quattro pezzi sacri, 578
Requiem, 566; Wagner on supposed arrangements for its publication, 358; V. prepares to conduct it in Germany, 358–

59; Bülow & Brahms on, 575, & Bülow's retraction, 386–87
Rigoletto, bowdlerized by the Austrian censor, (294–95), 552
Simon Boccanegra, 319
La Traviata, a failure at its 1st performance, 296, 552
Il Trovatore, 356; heard in the Indies & in Africa, 326

Verdi, Giuseppina. See Strepponi
Verdi, Margherita, (256), 542
Verdoni, Francesco, 57, 489
Verstigan, Richard, 28
VIADANA, Lodovico, 483
Victoria, Queen, 546; sings for Mendelssohn, 268–70; is seen by Chopin at the opera, 287
VICTORIA, Tomas Luiz de, 483
  "Battle" Mass, 31, 483
  Missae, Magnificat, ..., (31), 483
Vidal, Paul, 378, 572
Vienna, 10, 77, 95, 115, 131, 147, 152, 154, 170, 190, 196, 205, 218, 286, 318, 351, 387, 396, 431, 433, 440, 453, 482, 498, 500, 504, 508, 509, 510, 512, 514, 522, 524, 580, 581; Haydn's early years in, 113–14; no German opera in, 116; Mozart settles in, 134; he caters to the Viennese taste, 136, 137; Die Entführung produced in, 139; Haydn on Viennese food & hospitality, 149; Beethoven moves to, 511; ice is scarce but a revolution unlikely in, 161; Boucher meets Beethoven in, 193; Weber in, 193–95, 522–23; Rossini fever in, 524, & a Beethoven antidote, 199–200; Moscheles & Kalkbrenner come to, 200–201; Paganini fever in, 212–13, 528; Chopin makes his Viennese debut, 220–22, 531–32; Schumann plans to study in, 228; Chopin returns, 535, then leaves for Paris, 238; Schumann in, 253, 540; Donizetti composes for, 272; his popularity there, 547; Brahms about to move to, 327; a musical center once more, 560; Brahms presents himself to the Viennese public, 328–30, 560–61; Bruckner's difficulties in, 348–49, 565–66; Hanslick, 571; Bruckner's 7th Symphony introduced to, 381–82, & reviewed, 573; Schoenberg attempts to improve his situation in, 422–23; Berg reports on activities in, during the 1st World War, 430; Bartók "wounded" in, 457
Vienna Philharmonic Society, 348, 381, 417, 566
*Viennese Civic Guard, the captaincy of, 519; Schubert to, 184–85
Viola: Bach's predilection for, 105; Haydn's use of, 99
VIOLA, Francesco, 479, 480

Violinists: Tartini's lesson, 91–95; two inspiring, 101; Bach, 105; Haydn's early studies, 113–14; Mozart, 121; Beethoven, 512; Schubert, 185; Paganini, 212–13; Ingres, 538; Schumann praises Joachim, 304; Brahms consults Joachim, 367; Debussy plays for Ysaÿe, 389; Vecsey plays for Saint-Saëns, 469; see also Dubourg, Lombardini, Hofer, Polledro, Boucher, Schuppanzigh, Mayseder, Baillot, David, Lipinski, Sainton, Ernst, Waldbauer, Szigeti, Menuhin, et al.
Violoncellists. See Boccherini, Woschitka, Franchomme, Grützmacher
Vismes de Valgay, A. P. J., 126, 131, 504
VIVALDI, Antonio, 493
Vogl, Johann Michael, 203, 526
Vogler, Johann Caspar, 108
*Voit, Irma, 462, 464, 583; Bartók to, 437–38, 448–53
Voltaire, 111

Wagner, Cosima, 350, 562, 566; Smetana's opinion of, 354
*Wagner, Minna, 544; Wagner to, 290–93
*WAGNER, Richard, 356, 386, 387, 406, 498, 533, 544, 551, 555–59 pass., 562, 564, 566–68 pass., 571, 573, 575; Berlioz to, 311–12, 323; Liszt to, 320; Gounod to, 324; Brahms to, 350–51, 352; his relations with Meyerbeer, 310–11, 544, Schumann, 544–45, & Mendelssohn, 547; discovers Schopenhauer, 300, 553–54; Berlioz describes meeting him in London, 310–11; Berlioz's "Non credo," 558; political activity renounced by, 334–35; Bruckner's 3rd Symphony praised by, 348; Smetana unwilling to meet, 354; Verdi on the death of, 373; Bruckner honored by the Wagner Society, 381–82; Mahler on the symphonic element in the works of, 393; Webern on Schopenhauer &, 426

Les deux grenadiers, W. writes Schumann about, 265
Festmarsch, W. agrees to write, for the Philadelphia Centennial Exposition, 357–58, 567–68
Der fliegende Holländer, (263–64), 292, 300, 544, 547
Juvenilia, 263, 544
Kaisermarsch, 357
Lohengrin, 291, 292, 312, 551; W. conducts excerpts from, in London, 308
Die Meistersinger von Nürnberg, 351, 554, 562, 571; W. interprets the role of Beckmesser for a singer, 345, 564
Parsifal: W. reports finishing Act I of, 366; his terms for its publication, 371–72, 571; Debussy mentions, in connection with Petrushka, 426

WAGNER, Richard (cont.)
Rienzi, 292, 547; W. asks to have it produced in Dresden, 263–64, 544
Der Ring des Nibelungen, 312, 351, 554, 555, 562, 567; W. hopes to finish it by 1856, 300–301; Ravel prefers Liszt's "Faust" Symphony to, (400)
Das Rheingold, 554; Liszt's encouragement, 301; W. characterizes it for Brahms, 351, who expresses a preference for Die Walküre, 352
Die Walküre, 555; W. at work on, 300–301; Brahms's esteem for, 352
Siegfried, W. plans to compose, 301
Die Götterdämmerung, 551
Tannhäuser, 292, 293, 312; the Paris performances of, enlist Gounod's sympathy & Baudelaire's support, 324, 559; W.'s MS of a scene from, prompts a correspondence with Brahms, 349–52, 566; Liszt's transcription of the Evening Star precipitates a lawsuit, 372
Tristan und Isolde, 321, 324, 554, 562, 571; drafted by W., 301; the Prelude criticized by Berlioz, 558
Die Gibelinen, 292, 551
Das Judenthum in der Musik, 544
Die Kunst und die Revolution, 334
Das Kunstwerk der Zukunft, 334; quoted, 498
Oper und Drama, (311), 556
Siegfrieds Tod, 292, 551
Waldbauer, Imre, 584; gives a joint recital with Bartók, 437
Waldstein, Count Ferdinand von, 512, 514
Walter, Benno, 371, 571
*Walter, Bruno, 580; Mahler to, 417–18
*Walther, Johann Gottfried, 492; Telemann to, 69–70
"War of the Buffoons," 495, 498
WARS, REVOLUTIONS, POLITICAL UNREST: Machault cannot travel because of hostile troops, 1, 2; Dufay writes music on the fall of Constantinople, 6; Coclico persecuted for his faith, 13–14; Monte reports on a battle, 23–24; difficulties of publishing during the Low Countries' wars with Spain, 26; Dowland in exile for his Catholic leanings, 27–31; Bull must flee for the same reason, 35; invaders bring the plague to Italy, (43), 486; the Prussian invasion of Saxony, 85, 495; French Revolutionary War, 156, 511, & the Reign of Terror, 159–60, 511–12; Beethoven remarks on the repercussions in Vienna, 161; Napoleon occupies Prussia, 172–73; the July Revolution, 241, 535; the Warsaw revolution of 1830, 238, 535, 550; the February Revolution prompts Chopin's decision to go to England & Scotland, 550–51; the Chartist

demonstration, 287, *551;* Wagner & the Dresden uprising, 90–93, *551;* Rossini comments on the end of the 7 Weeks' War, 332, *561;* the Franco-German War, *563,* & a prophecy by Verdi, 337; Tchaikovsky draws an analogy from the Russo-Turkish War, 364, *569;* the 1st World War finds Ravel unable to join the army, 429, & Berg in a military hospital, 429–30; Toscanini attacked by Fascists, (449), *585;* the Nazis expel Schoenberg, *586;* Austria menaced, (455), *586,* & overrun, 456–59; Webern in Vienna under the Nazis, 459–61; Bartók separated from his sons by the 2nd World War, 461–65

Weber, Cäcilia, 133, *505,* (*510*)

WEBER, Carl Maria von, 256, *518;* a cousin of Mozart's wife, *505;* meets Beethoven, 194

    Euryanthe: rehearsals for the 1st performance of, 193–95, *522–23;* Wagner conducts the overture with his gloves off, 309

    Der Freischütz, *522;* Berlioz conducts the overture with great effect, *548*

    Leyer und Schwert, *518*

*Weber, Caroline, *522;* Weber to, 193–95

Weber, Max Maria von, (194), 195, *523*

WEBERN, Anton, 430, 454, 455, *581,* *586–87*

    Cantata, op. 29, 461, *587*

    Passacaglia, op. 1, 459–60, *586*

    Sechs Lieder, op. 14, 433, *583*

    Trio (strings), 461

    See also 460

Wedekind, Frank, (444), *584*

Weimar, 192, *515–17 pass.,* *522,* *566,* *567;* Bach in, 59, 72, 107, *491,* *492;* Gluck on the authors living in, 116; the "German Athens," *501;* Wagner in, after the Dresden uprising, 290–93, *551*

Weingarten, Paul, 453, *585*

*Weis, Karel, *570;* Brahms to, 368

Wellington, the Duke of, Chopin sees, 287

Wenzel, Ernst Ferdinand, 317

Werner, Friedrich Ludwig Zacharias, 178, 192, *517,* *522*

Wert, Giaches de, 16, *480,* *482*

Wesendonk, Mathilde & Otto, 320, *554*

WESLEY, Samuel, *519*

Westrup, J. A., *488*

Wieck, Clara. *See* Schumann, Clara

*Wieck, Friedrich, 245, *518,* *524,* *537,* *540,* *543;* Weber to, 181–83; Czerny to, 199–201; Schumann to, 222–26; his children, *532–33;* Schumann studies with, 222–29 *pass.,* 237, *532*

*WIEDEBEIN, Gottlob, *528–29;* Schumann to, 214–15

*Wieland, Christoph Martin, *501,507;* Gluck to, 115–16

*Wilhelmine, margravin of Bayreuth, Frederick the Great to, 88–89

Willaert, Adrian, 15, *479–80*

*William V, duke of Bavaria, Lassus to, 17–18, 18–19, 20

Wilson, Mrs. Woodrow, 452

Winter, Hugo, 455

Wittgenstein, Princess Karolyne zu Sayn-, 291, (301), *551,* *554*

*Wolanek, Ferdinand, *526;* Beethoven to, 207

WOLF, Hugo, *577*

    Der Corregidor, (*395*), *577*

*Wolzogen, Baron Hans von, *573;* Bruckner to, 381–82

WORDS & MUSIC: Landini returns a poem he has set to music, 4; John of Aragon asks for texts he can set, 5; Lorenzo the Magnificent sends Dufay some verses for music, 7–8; Palestrina on the intelligibility of words in vocal music, 16, 17; Monteverdi on the same, 35; he criticizes a libretto, 36–38; Handel & his librettist work on *Belshazzar,* 81–84; Frederick the Great writes a libretto, 88; Haydn on correct enunciation in recitatives, 98, 99; Gluck on the ideal libretto, 102–103; C. P. E. Bach on his father's settings of sacred texts, 104; Rousseau on speech as the source of melody, (110), *500;* Gluck distinguishes between a play & a libretto, 111, & criticizes the French adaptation of *Alceste,* 112; he requests commemorative verses from Klopstock, Wieland, & Goethe, 115–16, & discusses a German opera based on *Antony and Cleopatra,* 116; he revises the libretto of *Iphigénie en Tauride,* 127–29; Mozart revises the libretto of *Die Entführung,* 135–37; Grétry suggests changes in *Richard Cœur de Lion,* 140–41; Hoffmann, unable to versify, seeks a librettist for *Undine,* 177–78; Weber stresses the relationship of lieder to their texts, 181–83 *pass.;* Schubert dedicates Goethe settings to the poet, 203; young Schumann on Jean Paul's & Kerner's poems as lieder texts, 214; Berlioz inspired by *Faust,* 219; his whimsical muse, 246; Schumann on the titles of his piano pieces & on learning counterpoint from Jean Paul, 253; Verdi on a mutilated libretto, 294–95; Berlioz on translating texts that have been set to music, 311–12; Verdi makes clear his dramatic requirements to the librettist of *Aida,* 336–37; Mussorgsky "cooks up" some words for *Boris Godunov,* 338–39; Liszt & Longfellow, 347–48; Debussy & Maeterlinck, 389–90; Mahler on the relationship between words & music, 392–93; Wolf's gruesome similes on the subject, 395; Strauss & Hofmannsthal, 419–22; Debussy & Mallarmé, 424; Puccini & D'Annunzio, 427

Woschitka, Franz Xaver, 117–19 *pass., 502*

Würfel, Wilhelm, 220, *531*

Xanthippe. *See* Recio

*Yelena Pavlovna, Grand Duchess, *562;* Berlioz to, 332–33

Ysaÿe, Eugène, *575;* Debussy's visit to, 389

*Zani, Matteo, *489;* Corelli to, 55–57

Zaremba, Nikolai Ivanovich, 339, *563*

Zarlino, Gioseffo, *479*

Zeil, Count, prince-bishop of Chiemsee, 109, 117, *500*

Zelenka, Jan Dismas, 108

ZELTER, Carl Friedrich, 192, *515, 516, 518, 522;* on Cherubini & Beethoven, 174; on Berlioz, *530–31*

PIERO WEISS

Piero Weiss, the compiler of *Letters of Composers Through Six Centuries*, is a native of Trieste. He and his family left Italy in 1938, going first to Switzerland, then to England, and finally to the United States, where they settled in New York. There the young Weiss attended the Horace Mann School for Boys and Columbia College, at the same time pursuing his piano studies with Isabelle Vengerova, composition with Karl Weigl, and conducting with Rudolph Thomas and, at Tanglewood, Leonard Bernstein.

His debut as a concert pianist occurred in New York in 1949, and during the next twelve years he performed extensively in the United States and in Europe, both in recital and as a soloist with orchestras. At the end of that period Mr. Weiss, who had always felt a keen interest in the history of music and whose knowledge of languages enabled him to read widely on the subject, returned to Columbia as a graduate student in musicology.

Mr. Weiss has been a piano teacher since the age of nineteen. Now, as a faculty member of Columbia University, he also teaches the history of music. He considers his concert career "suspended, not ended." This hiatus has enabled him to complete the present collection of letters and to work on an extensive study of Goldoni and eighteenth-century comic opera in Italy. Mr. Weiss, his wife, and their son, Antonio Francesco, live in New York.